CW01024052

The Cyril Scott Companion

Jane Emmet von Glehn
March 1907.

The Cyril Scott Companion

Unity in Diversity

Edited by

Desmond Scott, Lewis Foreman

and Leslie De'Ath

THE BOYDELL PRESS

First published 2018
The Boydell Press, Woodbridge

ISBN 978 1 78327 286 0

The Boydell Press is an imprint of Boydell & Brewer Ltd
PO Box 9, Woodbridge, Suffolk IP12 3DF, UK
and of Boydell & Brewer Inc.
668 Mt Hope Avenue, Rochester, NY 14620–2731, USA
website: www.boydellandbrewer.com

A CIP catalogue record for this book is available
from the British Library

This publication is printed on acid-free paper

Typeset in Adobe Arno Pro by
Sparks Publishing Services Ltd—www.sparkspublishing.com

Printed and bound in Great Britain by
TJ International Ltd, Padstow, Cornwall

Frontispiece: Cyril Scott, March 1907. Pencil drawing by Jane Emmet de Glehn (1873–1961)

DEDICATION BY DESMOND SCOTT

To Corinne,
my most ardent advocate and sternest critic,
who put aside her own important literary work
to ensure that my contributions to this book
were the best they could be.

To Amanta,
because without the website of her grandfather Cyril Scott
that she began in the year 2000, this Companion book would not exist.

To Dominic,
whose gentle encouragement and tact
helped solve any problem that arose.

Contents

APPENDICES

CATALOGUES, DISCOGRAPHY AND BIBLIOGRAPHY

Illustrations

PLATES

Plates I–XVII appear between pages 322 and 323
Plates XVIII–XXXI appear between pages 386 and 387

FIGURES

Unless otherwise indicated, all illustrations are supplied by the Scott Family Archive and are reproduced by permission.

Tables

Contributors

Peter Atkinson
Peter Atkinson recently obtained a doctorate from the University of Birmingham, where he also worked as a Teaching Associate. His PhD thesis was titled 'Regeneration and Re-Enchantment: British Music and Wagnerism, 1880–1920'. He has presented his work on British music at conferences across the UK and Ireland, and his research has also been published in *Music & Letters* and *Notes*, including his extended study 'An Ireland Built Anew: Bax's Tintagel and the Easter Rising' (*Music & Letters* 97/1 [Feb. 2016])

Martyn Brabbins
Conductor Martyn Brabbins emerged on the international musical stage after winning the Leeds conducting competition in 1988. The Musical Director of English National Opera, he is remarkable for the breadth of his sympathies, which range from the latest new music, such as Birtwistle's *The Mask of Orpheus*, through Havergal Brian's *Gothic Symphony* at the Proms, and on to David Matthews's symphonies and Dutton's recording of orchestral songs by Sibelius's teacher, Toivo Kuula. His Brian series with the Royal Scottish National Orchestra (and as we write with ENO) for Dutton is definitive, as is his pioneering four-volume CD survey of Cyril Scott's orchestral music on Chandos. His catalogue of premieres encompasses an international repertoire. He has long-standing relationships with many orchestras, and was Artistic Director of the Cheltenham Festival 2005–2007.

Leslie De'Ath
Leslie De'Ath is a Canadian pianist, conductor, vocal coach, author and pedagogue who teaches at Wilfrid Laurier University, Waterloo, Ontario. He has recorded extensively as a soloist and chamber musician, particularly British and French piano literature – including Algernon Ashton, Billy Mayerl, Florent Schmitt and the complete piano works of Cyril Scott. His involvement in the recording medium has yielded an *Editor's Choice* designation in *Gramophone* magazine and a Grammy nomination. He is an authority on lyric diction and edits a standing column in that field in the *Journal of Singing*. His conducting has concentrated on opera, including several Canadian premieres.

Peter Dickinson
Peter Dickinson was born in Lytham St Annes, Lancashire; went to Cambridge as Organ Scholar of Queens' College; then spent three formative years in New York. There are four full CDs of his music on Albany; three on Naxos; and six on Heritage of his performances or music. As a pianist Dickinson enjoyed a twenty-five-year partnership with his sister, mezzo Meriel Dickinson. His books include studies of Lennox Berkeley (two), Billy Mayerl, Aaron Copland, John Cage, Lord Berners and Samuel Barber. He is an Emeritus Professor of the Universities of Keele and London and chair of the Bernarr Rainbow Trust. *Peter Dickinson: Words and Music* was published by the Boydell Press in 2016.

Lewis Foreman

In the 1970s and 1980s Lewis Foreman researched repertoire for the Kensington Symphony Orchestra, Opera Viva and other groups for the London fringe, planning many concerts. Since taking early retirement as a librarian in 1997, he has been a freelance writer, specialising in obituaries and British music. He has written more than two-dozen books, including *Bax: A Composer and his Times*, now in its third edition. With his wife he wrote the widely admired *London: A Musical Gazetteer* for Yale University Press (2005). He has advised various record companies on unrecorded repertoire, in recent years for Dutton Epoch, and his hundreds of CD booklet notes and session photographs are well known. A study of British symphonies, commissioned by the Boydell Press, is in progress.

Katherine Hudson

Katherine Hudson is the daughter of the biographer Derek Hudson, and the granddaughter of composer Norman O'Neill. Trained at the London Academy of Music and Dramatic Art, she worked for a number of years in the theatre. First published by the Oxford University Press in Edward Blishen's *Miscellany* series, she subsequently wrote two books for children: *The Story of the Elizabethan Boy-Actors* and *The Story of Geoffrey Chaucer*. Her *A Royal Conflict: Sir John Conroy and the Young Victoria* was published by Hodder & Stoughton in 1994, and she has written for *The Times*, *The Daily Telegraph* and various specialist journals, co-editing with Stephen Lloyd a republication of her father's biography, *Norman O'Neill: A Life of Music*, for Em Publishing in 2015.

Valerie Langfield

Valerie Langfield is an independent scholar and freelance musician, based in south Manchester. A contributor to several major dictionaries, her main research centres on twentieth-century English song, especially that of Roger Quilter and Cyril Scott, and on nineteenth-century British opera. She is a founder-member of Retrospect Opera and has produced editions of a number of British operas for recording and performance, particularly the operas of Balfe, Loder, Macfarren and Smyth. She is currently editing the diaries of Edward Dent and also a collection of his letters to John B. Gordon, staff producer at Sadler's Wells in the 1930s.

Kurt Leland

Kurt Leland received his Bachelor of Music degree in clarinet performance and music composition from Ohio Wesleyan University, and his Master of Music degree in composition from the University of Illinois at Champaign-Urbana, where he studied with Herbert Brün. His choral works have won several prizes and have been performed and recorded by Harold Rosenbaum's New York Virtuoso Singers. Leland is also an award-winning poet, and author/editor of eight non-fiction books, including *Music and the Soul: A Listener's Guide to Achieving Transcendent Musical Experiences* (2004, dealing extensively with Cyril Scott's occult writings on music). He is a national lecturer for the Theosophical Society in America.

Stephen Lloyd

Stephen Lloyd has had a life-long interest in British music. For sixteen years he was editor of *The Delius Society Journal*, and his books include a biography of H. Balfour Gardiner, a collection of Eric Fenby's writings on Delius, *Sir Dan Godfrey: Champion of British Composers*, *William Walton: Muse of Fire* (Boydell Press, 2001) and *Constant Lambert: Beyond The Rio Grande* (Boydell Press, 2014). In addition to record sleeve notes, programme notes, reviews and articles, he has contributed to the first *Percy Grainger Companion*, the *John Ireland Companion*, the *Studies in Music* Grainger Centennial Volume, *An Elgar Companion*, *Information Sources in Music* and volumes on Delius, Walton and Bliss. More recently, with Katherine Hudson, he prepared the revised version of Derek Hudson's *Norman O'Neill: A Life of Music*; he is currently editing, with Diana and Brian Sparkes, *Music in their Time*, the memoirs of Dora and Hubert Foss.

Steven Martin

Steven Martin is an Anglican priest. Before ordination training at St Stephen's House, Oxford, Steven read music at the University of Exeter and completed his PhD at the University of Bristol. The subject of his thesis was the history of opera in Britain *c.* 1875 to 1939. In 2010 he was awarded the McCann Research Scholarship at the Royal Academy of Music, which enabled him to look more closely at the history of the travelling opera in Britain during the early twentieth century. Steven has served on the board of trustees of the Carl Rosa Trust Ltd since 2014.

Rohinten Mazda

Born to Zoroastrian parents Daddy and Mehroo Mazda in Poona, India, on 17 April 1946, Rohinten Mazda came to England in June 1956 and later attended Milton Abbey School in Dorset before settling in London. He subsequently qualified as a barrister as a member of the Inner Temple and worked for a short spell at the Bar before pursuing a career as a Legal Adviser in the Inner London Courts' Service. Rohinten married the late Parsi concert pianist Hilla Khursedji in 1976 in India. Now retired, he makes frequent visits to India to visit family and devotes his time to his interests in music, poetry and natural history. As detailed in his 'Reminiscences' (below), he was adopted by Cyril Scott as his godson.

Richard Price

Richard Price is Professor of the History of Christianity at Heythrop College, University of London. He has published largely in the field of Early Church History but has a special interest in drama, poetry and music of the period between 1890 and 1920. Apart from the music of Cyril Scott, he has made a special study of the works of Scriabin, Rubbra and Sviridov.

Edmund Rubbra

Composer and pianist Edmund Rubbra started his working life as a railway clerk in Northampton. He became a pupil of Cyril Scott when, as a teenager, he promoted a local concert of Scott's music, which the composer heard about. Scott offered free lessons, which Rubbra could accept because, as a railway employee, he enjoyed subsidised travel. Later a student of Gustav Holst, he established a freelance musical career as concert pianist and composer, later broadcaster and teacher of composition at Oxford and London. His Second Violin Sonata attracted a wide audience, while his orchestral and choral music signalled him as a significant new talent. Active as a composer for more than fifty years, he produced a significant and distinctive body of work in most forms.

Desmond Scott

Desmond Scott is the son of Cyril Scott. He emigrated to Canada from the United Kingdom in 1957 and has spent his life in the Arts as a theatre director, actor and sculptor. Scott taught at the National Theatre School, and directed the first professional Canadian production of Samuel Beckett's *Waiting for Godot*, for the Manitoba Theatre Centre, Winnipeg, in 1961. His exhibition of bronze sculptures in 1990 was inspired by the play, and he served as President of the Sculptors Society of Canada from 1995 to 1997. Scott contributed an article on his father's and Percy Grainger's enduring friendship for Penelope Thwaites' *New Grainger Companion* (Boydell Press, 2010). He was awarded the Queen's Diamond Jubilee medal in 2012 in recognition of his recording books for the Canadian National Institute for the Blind for the past forty years.

Martin Yates

Conductor Martin Yates's pioneering recordings for Dutton Epoch – now more than fifty discs – mainly with the Royal Scottish National Orchestra and the BBC Concert Orchestra include the symphonies of his teacher, Richard Arnell, a variety of Vaughan Williams discoveries, and Widor's orchestral music. Yates's remarkable orchestrations and realisations of unfinished works includes music by Ireland, Elgar, Mendelssohn, Arnell, Moeran (Second Symphony), Bax (Symphony in F) and Cyril Scott. His ongoing forensic examination of Vaughan Williams's manuscripts has already yielded recordings of *Fat Knight* and the complete extant music for the film *Scott of the Antarctic*, much not used in the film. His orchestrations of the ballets *Manon* (MacMillan), *Don Quixote* (Acosta) and *Carmen* (Scarlett) have been widely danced at Covent Garden and abroad.

Foreword

MARTYN BRABBINS

DURING the course of the past twenty-five years it has been my privilege and pleasure to play a part in bringing before the curious listening public the music of many previously neglected composers. This process has involved many live public performances and the recording of dozens of CDs. Composers explored include Havergal Brian, Cecil Coles, Sir Alexander Mackenzie, Frederic Lamond, York Bowen, William Wallace, Friedrich Kiel, Robert Fuchs, Sergei Bortkiewicz, Sigismund Stojowksi, da Motta, Coke, Alkan, Adolf von Henselt, Samuel Coleridge-Taylor, David, Goedicke, Hubay, Mortelmans, Edward MacDowell – well, the list could go on, but the idea is clear. There is so much fine music awaiting discovery and rediscovery, and deserving of an audience.

As a conductor with training as a composer, composers and their music are at the heart of my performing passion. I have a strong desire faithfully to serve the composers' wishes, and, above and beyond that, to discover new music both by living composers and by those unfortunate composers whose music has undeservedly fallen out of fashion. Musical fashion being quite fickle, it has been very, very easy for a less well-known or an under-supported composer to fall by the wayside.

It was my good fortune in 2003 to be approached by Chandos Records about recording a number of Scott's orchestral works with the BBC Philharmonic Orchestra in Manchester. By focusing the remarkable sound of that ensemble on this revival – four CDs of orchestral recordings – we were able to showcase some dozen worthwhile scores which were very favourably received by the CD-reviewing journals and the public, reminding us that Eugene Goossens described Cyril Scott as the 'father of modern British music'. A bold epithet indeed!

Scott was certainly a remarkably creative figure. A friend of Stravinsky, Richard Strauss and Percy Grainger, and a fine pianist, he was a composer with a large and varied output, ranging from works for solo guitar and harp through his vast output of solo piano music, chamber music, choral works, concerti (for piano, harpsichord, violin, cello and oboe), ballets, operas and symphonies. This in itself would be a quite impressive legacy, and worthy of celebration. But that is far from the whole story. Scott was a published poet, author and philosopher – writing on subjects ranging from natural medicine to the occult, Christianity to sleeplessness, health food and, my personal favourite, cider vinegar! I find myself in awe of the intellect and imagination of a man who was able not only to create new worlds of sound, but also to articulate ideas and concepts on such a wide range of very forward-looking topics.

Neptune, the tone poem of 1935, is perhaps my favourite of Scott's orchestral works, and one which I recorded in April 2003. Originally it was entitled *Disaster at Sea* – depicting the sinking of the *Titanic.* The revised score is full of captivating and original ideas. There can be few more striking openings in all British orchestral music: celli, divided in three parts, play pizzicato a chord of D-flat major then glissando up to a chord of F major; they play it three times. It is quite unparalleled in the orchestral literature in my experience, and a perfect piece of musical 'scene-setting'.

Unsurprisingly, *Neptune* contains some powerfully original storm sequences, with Scott displaying a very fine mastery of orchestral colour and a compelling sense of dramatic pacing. There may be hints of his friends Strauss (*Zarathustra*) and Stravinsky (*Firebird*) in Scott's work, but it is none the worse for that! And melodic and harmonic unity are never sacrificed for mere effect. *Neptune* really is a score that should be heard in the concert halls of the UK on a regular basis, sitting comfortably alongside other familiar oceanic depictions by Britten, Bridge and Bax.

My enthusiasm for the music of Cyril Scott, and for the man himself – I am sure he would have been a fascinating companion – has been rekindled in writing this foreword a decade and more after the recordings made in Manchester. Scott is certainly at the top, in terms of originality and quality, of the list of neglected composers I referred to earlier. One has to hope that the music of Scott, one of Britain's most original twentieth-century composers, will enjoy a growing renaissance, and that readers of this volume will spread the word, increasing the appreciation and exposure of the music of this wonderfully gifted creative mind.

Preface

DESMOND SCOTT

THIS book is divided into chapters. Chapters 1–7 give some background to the work of my father, Cyril Scott; Chapters 8–16 are concerned with his music in its entirety; Chapters 17–23 deal with his writings; and Chapters 24–6 are reminiscences from those who knew him personally. To put the rest in context, this brief biography outlines the more significant events in his long life.

Scott's story as a composer is not unfamiliar. He achieved early fame as a modernist, acclaimed both in Britain and abroad, then mainstream music went in another direction until by the end he had been almost completely passed over. Thirty years after his death in 1970, however, a revival and re-appraisal of the music began that is still continuing today. Yet music was only the foremost of many other activities. He also wrote two autobiographies, *My Years of Indiscretion*[1] in 1924 and *Bone of Contention*[2] in 1969. An extraordinarily versatile man, he believed that the more subjects he became interested in, the less chance there was of being unhappy.[3] Those subjects included poetry, philosophy, playwriting, painting and health.

Scott was born on 27 September 1879 to middle-class parents in Oxton, a suburb of Birkenhead, a ferry-ride across the Mersey to Liverpool. His mother was very conventional and a devout Church of England churchgoer. As Scott relates in his early autobiography, she entered a theatre only twice in her life and both times felt most uncomfortable doing so.[4] His father was more open-minded. Professionally he worked in the shipping industry, Liverpool at that time being one of the busiest ports in England, but his real interest was in the study of ancient Greek. As Scott remarked, 'he spent too much time studying the Greek Bible to accept the narrow interpretation of any one Church or clergyman.'

As a boy, Cyril showed a precocious talent for music and was fortunate in having a family that not only encouraged him but was wealthy enough to send him to the Hoch Conservatory in Frankfurt, a young institution that had begun taking students in 1878, just a year before Scott's birth. He first went to study piano in 1891, stayed there for eighteen months, then returned to England and began teaching and performing. He then decided he was more interested in composition than in being a pianist, and at the age of sixteen went back to the Conservatory for a further three years.

Those Conservatory years were among the most significant of his life. He abandoned the Christianity of his parents and became for ten years a committed agnostic. At this point, too, he met both the poet Stefan George and his fellow-student and lifelong friend Percy Grainger; he kept photographs of those two very different men in his study wherever he lived. George instilled in him a love of poetry, and

[1] *My Years of Indiscretion* (Mills & Boon, 1924).

[2] *Bone of Contention* (Aquarian Press, 1969).

[3] Ibid., p. 11.

[4] *My Years of Indiscretion*, p. 130.

Scott adopted George's ideas about 'art for art's sake', dressing the part with flamboyant clothes and wearing his hair unfashionably long. In 1899 he dedicated his first symphony to George, who was instrumental in getting it performed a year later in Darmstadt. It was entirely due to Grainger that it could be played at all, because, as Scott relates in *Bone of Contention* (p. 84), his copyist had let him down and the two of them were forced to spend the whole night frantically writing out the parts. Without Grainger very many of Scott's works, including this symphony, would have been lost, for he kept withdrawing them and they survive solely because of Grainger and his Melbourne museum.

This first symphony had to wait over a hundred years for its second performance, when it and a number of major Scott compositions were brilliantly played by the BBC Philharmonic under Martyn Brabbins on Chandos CDs. Listening to them I was able to hear and appreciate much of my father's music for the very first time.

In 1901 Scott's first publisher was Arthur Boosey, who paid him a retainer to produce a specified number of songs and short piano pieces yearly. They were highly popular and provided a welcome steady income, but subsequently he felt they detracted from his more serious compositions. Later he met William Elkin, and then William's son Robert, and they became his publishers and friends for many years thereafter.

Also in 1901 Scott's *Heroic Suite* was performed in Manchester, with Hans Richter the famous Wagner conductor at the podium; but the work that catapulted him to the public's attention was the London performance in 1903 of his Piano Quartet, in which Scott had persuaded Fritz Kreisler to take the violin part. As he wrote years later in *Bone of Contention* (p. 88), it 'brought my name before the public in a manner which, short of murder, nothing else could have done. Reviews ... appeared in all the papers, including *The Church Times* – and thus before my mid-twenties I had been launched on the uncertain waters of my career!'

Scott's second symphony was premiered in London in 1903, but that one, too, he rejected as immature. He did, however, salvage three movements and style them as *Three Symphonic Dances*. In 1920 he and Grainger made a two-piano arrangement of the first dance, and their enjoyment in playing it is delightfully obvious from the Klavier Records LP of 1973.

Sometime in 1904 or early 1905 Scott ceased being an agnostic and became interested first in Vedanta, then in theosophy, and finally in occultism, eventually writing nine books on the subject. 1905 also saw the publication of his first volume of poetry, and over the next ten years he produced five books of his own verse and translations of Stefan George and Charles Baudelaire.

The Piano Sonata, Op. 66, the best known of his four piano sonatas, premiered in 1909; Grainger played it throughout the USA and Canada for more than thirty years. I have a letter from him to Cyril written from Moose Jaw, Canada, in January 1952:

> Darling Cyril [which is how he addressed all his missives to Scott], I have now played yr Sonata in 4 places (one in USA, 3 in Canada) and am amazed to find how much response there is to it. It gets just as much applause as my Chopin group, or my Bach, which I think is remarkable, seeing that I am playing every-

> where in small country towns ... It is 35 degrees below zero here just now but the strange thing is, it doesn't *feel* cold at all. I am wearing my summer trousers, no overcoat or hat, yet there is no sting of cold at all.

Only Percy Grainger could possibly have written that!

Gustav Mahler's widow, Alma Mahler, a musician herself, invited Scott to Vienna in 1911, having been impressed by his Violin Sonata No. 1. The visit was highly successful and led to concerts of Scott's work in both Frankfurt and Cologne.

An extensive tour of his Piano Concerto with him as soloist, a tour that would have included Vienna, was planned for 1914, but World War 1 intervened and he did not perform it there until four years after the Armistice, in 1922, this time accompanied by his novelist wife, Rose (herself Viennese-born), whom he had married in the previous year.

The 1920s saw Scott's reputation at its highest. His music was thought innovative, and his harmonies daring, providing a complete break from the academic writing of such men as Hubert Parry and Charles Villiers Stanford. Stanford called some of Scott's songs 'blasphemous', which, of course, delighted Cyril. Major works in this decade included the *Karma Suite* (1924), a Concerto for violin and cello (1926), *The Melodist and the Nightingales* (1929), *Festival Overture* (1929), plus numerous songs and works for solo piano.

As well as contributing frequently to a number of music journals, Scott had been writing books on a wide variety of subjects, and publishing many of them anonymously. The first was *The Real Tolerance* in 1913.[5] In it he outlined the philosophy that became his 'Unity in Diversity' credo, asking for unlimited tolerance, with differences to be acknowledged and respected, not condemned. In 1920 he published *The Adept of Galilee*[6] and the first book of the *Initiate* trilogy.[7] The second *Initiate* book followed in 1927.[8] In 1921 *The Autobiography of a Child* appeared.[9] Also published anonymously, this described the childhood traumas of an unnamed character and was, as Scott explained right at the beginning of the book and just below the title, 'written from the psycho-sexual analytical standpoint: for doctors, parents, teachers and psychologists'. Though written during World War 1, it was not published until 1921, when one might have expected a loosening of strictures concerning matters of sex. That, however, was not the case; the attitude, according to Scott, remained one of 'hypocritical intolerance'.[10] The notorious Lord Alfred Douglas brought an action against the publishers, the book was banned, and all copies ordered to be burned.

Scott was fortunate during the war years. Considered unfit for active service, he spent much of this period giving charity concerts. Wartime travel was possible, too,

[5] *The Real Tolerance* (A. C. Fifield, 1913).

[6] *The Adept of Galilee* (George Routledge & Sons, 1920).

[7] *The Initiate, by his Pupil* (Routledge & Kegan Paul, 1920).

[8] *The Initiate in the New World* (New York: E. P. Dutton, 1927).

[9] *The Autobiography of a Child* (Kegan Paul, Trench, Trubner, 1921).

[10] *Bone of Contention*, p. 34. [Editor's note: The book he describes here is unnamed but it is, in fact, *The Autobiography of a Child.*]

Figure 0.1 Photo of Granville Bantock, Cyril Scott and Joseph Holbrooke at Harlech in August 1917

so at the invitation of friends he went to Florence – Italy being on the side of the Allies in that war – and was delighted to find himself a celebrity. There was a concert of his works, and he was awarded a medal by the Leonardo da Vinci Society. Near the end of the war Scott went on holiday to Harlech, North Wales, with a friend – the American-born photographer and student of the occult Alvin Coburn. With Harlech Castle as a backdrop Coburn took a photo of the three composers who all happened to be there at the same time: Granville Bantock, Cyril Scott and Joseph Holbrooke (Fig. 0.1).

In her biography of her father, Myrrah Bantock wrote her impressions of Cyril Scott:

> As a young man Cyril Scott was quite incredibly handsome. He was slim, always elegant, very intense and very much aware of the impression he strove to create. I never remember seeing him move quickly. He drifted, walking and sitting with the studied grace of a Beau Brummel. He wore the most expensive tie-pins, watch-chains and rings. During the day he was seldom seen. He worked on his music and read books on reincarnation and strange cults. In the afternoons he slept, and on his door would be pinned a notice:
>
> DO NOT DISTURB. I AM IN AN ASTRAL SLUMBER.
>
> We all thought highly of Scott's music. It was exotic, poetic, beautiful and full of fantasy with a characteristic sense of refinement. It was Scott's harmonic idiom that captivated us in those days.[11]

World War 2, by contrast, was a difficult time for Scott. By then it was rare for a major orchestral work of his to be performed, and one or two songs and a few short piano pieces were all that was heard. It had been thought that as soon as war was declared London would be heavily bombed. People were desperate to go anywhere, as long as it was out of the city, and the family split up. Father took us children down to his sister Mabel's house in Somerset, and Mother went to her friend Melanie Mills, in Sussex.

Once I was back at school and Vivien had gone to join the WAAF, Father left our aunt's home and spent the war years going from one guest-house to another throughout Somerset and Devon. He was sixty, in poor health, short of money, and believed he would not live to see seventy. Without a piano to help him compose, he began in 1942 writing a lengthy memoir with the revealing title *Near the End of Life*. In addition, he revised all his earlier poetry, added new poems, and called the volume *The Poems of a Musician*. During this period he also wrote six full-length plays and a sixty-page document entirely in doggerel, complete with proposed illustrations, that he called *The Rhymed Reflections of a Ruthless Rhymer*.

In a guest-house in Devon in 1943, Scott met Marjorie Hartston, who was recuperating from a disastrous early marriage. They became friends, and he was delighted to discover that she was clairvoyant. By the time the war ended they had decided to stay together. Through her he was able to re-establish pyschic contact with his spiritual guru (with whom there had been no communication for some time), while she discovered her purpose in life. Scott wrote about this new friendship to Percy Grainger, who, with extraordinary generosity, had already decreed that his English royalties were to go to Scott, since money could not be taken out of Britain during wartime. Grainger now suggested that Scott should borrow, rent-free, a small bungalow he and Ella owned in Pevensey Bay, near Eastbourne, until the pair found something more permanent. Eventually Cyril and Marjorie bought a house together in Eastbourne, at 53 Pashley Road. Though they never married, Cyril at first claiming Marjorie as his 'ward', he later had her change her name officially to Marjorie Hartston-Scott. Still, my parents did not divorce. Though separated, they remained friendly, writing to each other regularly and commiserating with each other over publishers and financial problems.

[11] Myrrha Bantock, *Granville Bantock – A Personal Portrait* (J. M. Dent, 1972), p. 134.

Figure 0.2 The church in Pevensey where Scott is buried

Scott's final decades were as productive as his early ones. Fully aware that he would hear almost none of it, music still poured out of him. He produced a symphony which he designated the second, but was in fact his fourth (1951/2); a full-length opera, *Maureen O'Mara* (1946); and the hour-long *Hymn of Unity* (1947). There were also three string quartets, two string quintets, a Sinfonietta for organ, harp and strings, a cello sonata, a piano sonata and three violin sonatas. He also continued to write prose, the most important works of this period being *Die Tragödie Stefan Georges*,[12] *The Boy Who Saw True*[13] and *Man the Unruly Child*. There were

[12] *Die Tragödie Stefan Georges: ein Erinnerungsbild und ein Gang durch sein Werk* (Eltville am Rhein: L. Hempe, 1952).

[13] *The Boy Who Saw True* (Neville Spearman, 1952).

Figure 0.3 Scott's gravestone, bearing his motto, 'Unity in Diversity'

two books on health – *Simpler and Safer Remedies for Grievous Ills*[14] and *Medicine, Rational and Irrational*[15] – plus pamphlets on cider vinegar, black molasses, sleeplessness and constipation.

In 1964 the Cyril Scott Society was formed, with Sir Thomas Armstrong as President, 'to promote performances and recordings of Scott's music'. Sadly, the Society was short-lived.

Though the lack of interest in his music pained my father, it never made him bitter. Perhaps his deep belief in occultism sustained him, for he continued composing and revising until three weeks before his death at ninety-one. He was an unusually accepting man and, as he said to me, 'If my music is worth anything, sooner or later it will be played. If it is not, better it not be heard.'

On the last day of 1970 he died; he was buried in the churchyard at Pevensey Bay (Fig. 0.2). The simple tombstone (Fig. 0.3) reads:

HERE LIE THE ASHES OF

CYRIL SCOTT

MUSICAL COMPOSER, POET & AUTHOR

27 SEPT. 1879 – 31 DEC. 1970

UNITY IN DIVERSITY

[14] *Simpler and Safer Remedies for Grievous Ills* (Athene Publishing, 1953).

[15] *Medicine, Rational and Irrational* (True Health Publishing, 1946).

Acknowledgements

In bringing to completion a huge project such as this book, which has matured over many years, there are numerous people we, the editors, would like to thank. We begin with Laurie J. Sampsel, whose *Cyril Scott: A Bio-Bibliography* in 2000 spearheaded the revival of interest in the music of Cyril Scott that resulted years later in the completion of this *Companion*. Next, Corinne Langston Scott, whose tireless assistance and support, dedication and attention to detail, has enabled this book to see the light of day. We would like to thank all our contributors who gave so freely (in both senses) of their time and expertise, including Peter Atkinson, Martyn Brabbins, Peter Dickinson, Katherine Hudson, Valerie Langfield, Kurt Leland, Stephen Lloyd, Steven Martin, Rohinten Mazda, Richard Price and Martin Yates, not forgetting Finley Eversole, David Harvey and Andrew Plant who did not in the end become part of the *Companion*, but whose hard work is very much appreciated. Graham De'Ath, for his work in setting many of the musical examples; Maja Fuchs, for her research into Rose Allatini's family background; and Imogen Gassert for her invaluable work on the history of the banning of Rose's book *Despised and Rejected* during the First World War, and Nicola Bauman of Persephone Books for its elegant reissue in 2018.

Thanks also to Serena and Michael Gilbert for Scott family photos and Gordon McElroy for photographing some of the scores. Most photographs and illustrations are from the Scott family archive, but BBC Concert Orchestra and Dutton session photographs are by Lewis Foreman and are his copyright. The jacket painting of Cyril Scott by George Hall-Neale is reproduced by courtesy of the National Portrait Gallery, London, and by permission of the copyright holder, the Cyril Scott Estate. The frontispiece drawing of Scott by Jane de Glehn from the Scott collection is reproduced courtesy of David Messum for the Estate of Jane Emmet de Glehn. Thanks to Katherine Hudson, for information on Miss Remington, and to Rohinten Mazda, for supplying the score to Scott's two-piano transcription of Bach's Concerto in C. Special thanks to Amanta Scott whose brilliant and comprehensive website at www.cyrilscott.net has done so much in making Scott better known to the general public. Thanks to Adrian Yardley for permission to reprint his father's (the composer Edmund Rubbra) material originally written for *The Daily Telegraph* and the BBC.

Deep gratitude to the late Bernard Benoliel and to Bruce Roberts, formerly with the RVW Trust, whose phone call finally announced the recording of four CDs of Scott's major orchestral music. Subvented by the Vaughan Williams Trust and recorded by Chandos Records, this completely changed assessment of Scott's music by a wider musical and critical constituency. Equal thanks too to Michael J. Dutton of the Dutton Epoch CD label for exploring Scott's chamber music and taking on the release of Leslie De'Ath's complete recording project of all the solo piano music and Martin Yates's editions of the early concertos. Conductors Martyn Brabbins and Martin Yates have played a significant rôle directing pioneering orchestral recordings, Brabbins directing the Chandos series, and Yates reconstructing, editing and providing performing editions from incomplete manuscripts, and subsequently recording them with the BBC Concert Orchestra for Dutton Epoch.

We are particularly grateful to all the staff of the Grainger Museum in Melbourne where so much Scott material is preserved, with special thanks to Astrid Krautschneider, who is no longer with the Museum, and Carl Temple and Lauren Davis. Peter Horton and Michael Mullen at the Royal College of Music, David Candlin at the Harrison Sisters Trust, Dorothy Motoi of the University of Canterbury, New Zealand and Em Marshall-Luck at the English Music Festival. Paul Pulford and Christopher Sharpe, for their advice on Scott's editing of the Schumann Cello Concerto.

Libraries and Archives consulted include the Central Music Library collection at the Buckingham Palace Road Library, Westminster; Westminster Central Reference Library; The London Library; the BBC Written Archives Centre at Caversham; the British Library and the library of the Faculty of Music at the University of Toronto, together with the Scott Collection and the personal collections of the editors and contributors. Thanks also to Richard Horrocks of the Liverpool Central Library for research into Scott's early Quartet, Op 12, which is held by that library, and to Oliver Lomax for a Keith Prowse catalogue. Quotations sourced from files at the BBC Written Archive Centre at Caversham remain BBC copyright and are reproduced with thanks for research assistance and with acknowledgements to the BBC.

Short quotations and references from the literature are footnoted throughout and are used with due acknowledgement to the publishers. Criticism is quoted from a wide variety of sources including *The Manchester Guardian, Daily Telegraph, The Times, Sunday Times,* the *Musical Standard, Liverpool Mercury, Gramophone, Musical News, Musical Opinion,* the *Musical Times, Tempo,* the *BBC Music Magazine* and from *MusicWeb International.* Wherever possible texts quoted have been taken or checked from the printed hardcopy original sources and all images have been taken from originals held in contributors' collections and from the Scott collection, with thanks to a variety of dealers at ephemera fairs.

Musical examples from unassigned works are reproduced by permission of the Cyril Scott Estate, and of published scores by permission of their publishers which are formally listed and acknowledged on pp. 633–39. To all our thanks.

Every effort has been made to trace copyright holders; apologies are offered for any omissions, and the publisher will be pleased to add any necessary acknowledgements in future editions.

Stephen Lloyd, Graham Parlett and Jeffrey Wall acted as independent proof readers and we are most grateful for their time and expertise without which various infelicities would have slipped through. For any that remains the editors take full responsibility.

Finally, we would like to thank our team at Boydell: our editor Michel Middeke, our copy editor Dr Marianne Fisher and our long-suffering Production Manager, Rohais Haughton, for their expertise and patience, which has finally delivered the finished project so expertly.

Editors' Note

CYRIL Scott's many and varied interests afford a perfect example of his motto, Unity in Diversity. The intent of this book is to give in one volume a broad picture of his entire output – musical, literary, dramatic and philosophical. The volume therefore includes discussion of works hitherto completely unknown. We hope it will lead readers – who may be acquainted with only one aspect of Scott's œuvre, be it musical, literary or the immensely popular health books – to look further and discover just how much more there is to learn about this remarkable man. The varying approaches of the different contributors can, in our opinion, only enhance the material discussed. Readers interested in another approach are further directed to *The Aesthetic Life of Cyril Scott*, by Sarah Collins, published by the Boydell Press in 2013.

This is not intended primarily as an academic textbook, being as much for the general reader as for the scholar. But those interested in performing the music, from beginning students to amateur musicians and dedicated professionals, will find the listing of Scott's work, divided into separate categories, an indispensable reference work for years to come.

Inevitably there is a measure of repetition from chapter to chapter, but this has been deliberately retained in the interest of the integrity of each account.

I

SCOTT IN CONTEXT

1

From Frankfurt with Love: Friendships Observed through Correspondence and Reminiscence*

STEPHEN LLOYD

On 17 February 1947, in a 'Round Letter to Friends', Percy Grainger wrote in his characteristic if quirky 'Blue-eyed (Nordic) English':

> All men ... are trained to think of themselves as ONE-BODIES ((persons)) & LONE-HANDERS ((individuals)), when, in real-hood ((reality)), we are merely pack-beasts (like the poor wolves). The 5 limbs of the 'Frankfurt Group' (Scott, Quilter, Gardiner, Sandby, Grainger) think of themselves as 5 OTHERY ((different)) tone-wrights. In real-hood we are just one 5-fold man, struggling to voice the heart-stirs of Blue-eyed Man at the turn of the hundred-year-stretch ((Century)). Today we may think we see other-hoods of mood, style & taste between Scott & Sandby, Roger & Gardiner. But in 200 years time all our toneries will seem heart-breakingly alike. (Our business is to strive that it will SEEM AT ALL.) All this MEUM-&-TEUM is flounderingness.

Cyril Scott, Percy Grainger and their friends and contemporaries have often been classified as the 'Frankfurt Group', a term chiefly of convenience with which to denote the coterie of expatriate composers who, by studying abroad, stood apart in outlook and education from the mainstream of the conservative British musical establishment at the turn of the century.[1] This term does not apply to the pianists Frederic Lamond and Leonard Borwick, who preceded Scott & Co.; to fellow English students Herbert Golden[2] and Thomas Holland-Smith, who studied at the same time as Scott; or to others such as the Australian composer and pianist F. S. Kelly, who followed afterwards. Nevertheless, there may be some confusion as to the actual composition of the Group, since Grainger admits the Danish cellist Herman Sandby[3] to his list, while noticeably absent is the name of Norman O'Neill, who had died tragically in 1934 as the result of a road accident. Grainger may well

* This article is an expansion of 'Grainger and the Frankfurt Group', my contribution to the Percy Grainger Centennial volume of *Studies in Music* (no. 16, 1982), pp. 111–18. I would like to acknowledge Laurie Sampsel's *Cyril Scott – A Bio-Bibliography* (Greenwood Press, 2000), which has been an invaluable source in the writing of this article.

[1] Grainger warned Sir Thomas Armstrong against regarding the Group as a body of conformists; they were, he insisted, 'united only by their hatred of Beethoven'. Armstrong, 'The Frankfurt Group', *Proceedings of the Royal Musical Association*, 17 November 1958, p. 2.

[2] Scott dedicated his *Three Frivolous Pieces* for piano (Forsyth, 1903) to Herbert Golden.

[3] (Peter) Herman Sandby (1881–1965), Danish cellist and composer.

have been thinking of the 'living limbs' of the Group, but even though Scott properly numbers O'Neill among this gathering and writes warmly about him in his later autobiography[4] (his *Danse nègre* of 1908 is dedicated to Norman and Adine O'Neill), his name is omitted from the title page of Scott's first autobiography, *My Years of Indiscretion* (1924), which is dedicated to Grainger, Quilter and Gardiner as 'the friends of my student-days',[5] a dedication that may itself appear odd because Scott's and Gardiner's periods of study at Frankfurt did not officially overlap.

Much of this confusion arises through the varying ages of the members of the Group. These spanned some seven years, as a result of which at no time were they all studying together at Frankfurt. By the end of 1896 Grainger was fourteen, Sandby was fifteen, Scott was seventeen (Fig. 1.1), Quilter and Gardiner nineteen, and O'Neill twenty-one. When Scott arrived in October 1896, Gardiner had left to enter Oxford. A year later, as Quilter and Sandby were near completing their first calendar year of study, O'Neill too had left. Sandby was to remain more a close acquaintance of Grainger's; O'Neill (whom Grainger referred to in a 1955 letter to Scott as 'a tame cat') was on much friendlier terms with Balfour Gardiner, who became his close neighbour in London – they lived almost opposite each other in Pembroke Villas.

Table 1.1 may help clarify the matter of attendance at the renowned Hoch Conservatoire.[6] The numbers represent the semesters each member attended, as officially recorded by the Conservatoire (two a year, commencing in September and April), but this takes no account of periods of private study or extended stay. Blank, unshaded sections denote periods when they were in Frankfurt for 'unofficial' private reasons. As this table shows, Scott was the first of the Group to study at Frankfurt and, unlike any of the others, had two distinct periods during which he was enrolled at the Conservatoire.

Quilter's biographer, Valerie Langfield, has written that he spent four and a half years at Frankfurt but adds that the precise period is 'debatable'.[7] Scott wrote to Grainger on 8 October 1899 urging him to prevent Quilter from returning to England; according to Scott, Quilter was still in Frankfurt in January 1900, when his First Symphony was performed in Darmstadt. There is some uncertainty too about Grainger's actual period of study. At one point he broke off study with Iwan Knorr, his appointed professor of composition, in favour of Karl Klimsch, an amateur musician. But, as Grainger's biographer, John Bird, has stated, it is not possible to ascertain for certain how long he studied with Knorr. In the spring and summer of 1900 Grainger took an extended holiday in Italy, France, Holland, England and Scotland with his mother, Rose, who was recovering from a nervous breakdown. In the autumn he resumed his piano studies (with James Kwast) and his private lessons with Klimsch. However, a further breakdown necessitated that he become

[4] *Bone of Contention* (Aquarian Press, 1969).

[5] In *My Years of Indiscretion* (Mills & Boon, 1924), O'Neill receives only a single mention – that he 'left fairly soon after my arrival' (at Frankfurt). Scott's study of humour, *The Ghost of a Smile* (Andrew Dakers, 1939), dedicated to Grainger, Quilter and Gardiner as 'my three oldest friends', was published after O'Neill's death.

[6] This table is adapted, with acknowledgement, from the one in Peter Cahn's article 'Percy Grainger's Frankfurt Years', *Studies in Music* 12 (1978), p. 110.

[7] Valerie Langfield, *Roger Quilter: His Life and Music* (Boydell, 2002).

Figure 1.1 Scott the young dandy at seventeen, in Frankfurt

Table 1.1 The number of Conservatoire semesters per academic year attended by members of the Frankfurt Group (and fellow students)

	1891–1892	1892–1893	1893–1894	1894–1895	1895–1896	1896–1897	1897–1898	1898–1899	1899–1900	1900–1901	1901–1902
Scott	2	2				2	2	2			
O'Neill		1	2	2	2	2					
Gardiner				2	2						
Grainger					2	2	1	2	1		
Quilter						1	2	1	?		
Sandby						1	2	2	2	1	
Franckenstein						2	1				

the family bread-winner and earn his living as a pianist, by performing and teaching. Mother and son left for England in the summer of 1901. Balfour Gardiner's stay in Frankfurt was considerably extended by private study, then in 1900 he went on to another conservatoire in Germany to study conducting. Even so, while the table should be treated with a degree of caution, at least it gives a general picture of the period of study enjoyed by the five normally regarded as constituting the Frankfurt Group, with the addition of two fellow students.

Born on 27 September 1879 in Oxton, a few miles from Birkenhead on the Wirral Peninsula, Cyril was the third and last child in the Scott family, with an elder sister, another boy having died in infancy. His father worked in shipping but his chief claim to fame was as an authority on biblical Greek. It was his mother who showed the musical instinct; she was a reasonably competent pianist. Apparently Cyril could play the piano before he could talk: 'I was always clamouring to be lifted on to the piano stool, after which I would play by ear till exhausted.'[8] Consequently, when only twelve years of age, 'one winter's morning in 1891' he was taken by his mother to Frankfurt, principally to study the piano, together with his sister, for whom a place was found 'in a school in a near-lying Spa'. As Cyril's mother spoke no German, they were accompanied by a German spinster returning home via Frankfurt, who kindly helped them in the snow to find a suitable pension for Cyril. Over a meal at the chosen guest-house, some fellow occupants recommended that, before returning, Mrs Scott take her son to hear *Lohengrin* at the city's opera house, and Cyril was duly introduced to Wagner.

Although in his earlier autobiography, *My Years of Indiscretion* (1924), Scott chose to bypass his childhood years and hardly mentions this first visit to Frankfurt, he gives a detailed account in his much later 'life story and confessions', *Bone of Contention* (1969). There he writes of the rather unnerving experience of being auditioned by the austere and 'awe-inspiring' principal, Dr Bernard Scholz, a 'frightening apparition' in front of whom he was first required to play on the platform of the Conservatoire's empty concert-hall before being subjected to an aural test. All of this was then repeated after one of the professors had been summoned and, although he was officially too young for the Conservatoire (thirteen being the minimum age), because of 'the young Herr's unusual talent' an exception was made in his case and he was accepted. His piano professor was the Italian Lazzaro Uzielli (who became a naturalised German); fellow pupil Thomas Holland-Smith, some fourteen years Scott's senior (who became a life-long friend), acted as interpreter as Uzielli spoke no English. For theory he had the 'painfully ugly' Engelbert Humperdinck (who left in 1897), and for his general education Conrad Schmidt, presumably at the preparatory school that was associated with the Conservatoire.

Mrs Scott clearly had sufficient belief in her son's musical ability to make the journey to Germany without any certainty of his being admitted to the Conservatoire, but it is all the more surprising that a boy of such a tender age should be uprooted from his home background, taken to a foreign country and left in the care of strangers when as a child he suffered – through no fault of his 'wise and understanding parents' – an 'unhappy existence' because of 'very poor health and inner sensitivity'. He was subject to 'countless fears ... of being scolded ... of the dark, of thunder,

[8] *Bone of Contention*, p. 19.

of accidents', and had frequent fits of melancholy. These 'painful idiosyncrasies' he only revealed in old age in *Bone of Contention*.[9] Yet music 'never ceased to be the one absorbing interest', and his first stay in Germany, which lasted eighteen months, 'during which time I did not return to England even in the long summer holidays', seems to have passed without anxiety. For the first of his vacations, at Easter, he was invited to visit his sister at her girls' school, where 'she was enjoying a more or less happy existence'.

Once he was back home after his first Frankfurt stay, teachers for harmony and counterpoint and for the piano were found for him, as well as a private tutor for this 'freak of a son who was too sensitive to be sent to school'.[10] As this tutor lived some distance away Cyril had a lengthy daily walk.[11] However, one day on this walk he was noticed by Hans Lüthy, a middle-aged Swiss gentleman who introduced himself at a musical soirée and in due course became his mentor and one of a number of people who were to have a strong influence on him. Cyril dedicated the song *The Time I've Lost in Wooing*, composed in July 1893, to Hans Lüthy and his wife, Carrie. Lüthy was a pronounced agnostic and before long Cyril adopted a similar outlook.

Until he was sixteen Scott had, in his own words:

> serious intentions of becoming a pianist, and of going to Leschetizky in Vienna for 'a few finishing touches'; but towards my seventeenth year I entirely altered my views and preferred a composer's career instead. For that reason I decided to go to Iwan Knorr at Frankfurt, and seriously to take up the study of composition.[12]

At the same time, he realised that he was quite unread, 'so during the next three years Mr Lüthy posted to Frankfurt such books as he deemed essential "for the good of my soul"'.[13] Lüthy retired to Vevey in Switzerland, on the northern shore of Lake Geneva, and Cyril visited him there. It was a friendship that lasted some twelve years, only ending when Cyril showed too serious an interest in one of Lüthy's daughters.

Scott commenced his second period of study at Frankfurt in the autumn of 1896, his principal professors being Uzielli once again and Iwan Knorr.[14] It was then that he was to form important friendships that would last a life-time. Nearly sixty years later, in January 1956, he gave a twenty-minute talk for the BBC on those friends – the members of the 'Frankfurt Group'.[15] He began:

[9] Ibid., pp. 24–5. Grainger, who was thirteen when he arrived at Frankfurt, had of course his mother in attendance.

[10] *Bone of Contention*, p. 57.

[11] He and his father walked the two and a half miles to the Birkenhead Ferry, after which Cyril craftily pocketed the bus fare he was given for the remainder of the journey.

[12] *My Years of Indiscretion*, p. 12.

[13] *Bone of Contention*, p. 61.

[14] In 1925 Uzielli made the journey to Essen for the premiere of Scott's opera *The Alchemist*.

[15] 'The Frankfurt Group: Talk by Cyril Scott', 5 January 1956, BBC Home Service, 19:50–20:05. Annotated typed script given to me by Sir Thomas Armstrong, 24 April 1992.

> The 'Frankfurt Group' consisted of Roger Quilter, Balfour Gardiner, Norman O'Neill, Percy Grainger and myself. It was in Frankfurt that we all met for the first time, as students, and formed friendships that lasted throughout our lives – that is, until death brought some of them to a close; for only two of the group now remain, Percy Grainger and myself. In those days – around the eighteen-nineties – the Frankfurt Conservatoire had already become famous for its excellence.

He went on to describe his composition teacher, Iwan Knorr, for whom he had much admiration and who had been his main reason for making his second visit to Frankfurt:[16]

> He was really a German, though he had lived many years in Russia, and looked rather like a Russian. He was in his early forties, and incidentally had known Tchaikovsky who had influenced his entirely unacademic outlook. In fact he was noted for his broadmindedness ... He had always told us that although we must learn the rules, it was not to stick to them for ever but to know how to break them with discretion and taste. This 'doctrine' I followed later on with less restraint and discretion than did Quilter, O'Neill and Gardiner ... Knorr was a splendid teacher in every way; he seldom lost his temper but administered all reproofs by witty sarcasms – much to the discomfort of some of the female pupils in the classes. Where actual composition was concerned, if we were disgruntled at having to change some of our most cherished bits, he would often say: 'Write what you like for your own enjoyment. But, as what you bring to the lesson is for learning-purposes only, do not write it with your heart's blood.'

Next Scott discussed the individual members of the Group:

> **Roger Quilter** was one of the most original and entertaining characters I have ever met. What with his gestures and his humour, if he had not been a musician he would have made an excellent comedian, for he had a type of wit entirely his own. Moreover he exuded refinement and charm. In spite of this, being essentially tender-hearted, he was always getting into trouble with his successive landladies because he would insist on feeding the birds. For unfortunately the birds were not content just to feed off his crumbs but would leave on the window-sill certain indications of their visits, which so enraged the landlady that one day she stormed into his room and said (in German): 'This is not to be tolerated. Very unrefined!' After that Quilter looked out for other apartments. 'Really!' he said. 'Such hard-heartedness. The poor little birds.' His next landlady, a snobbish Frau Doktor Somebody or other, he contrived to offend in a different way. There was at that time a new and rather expensive metal called Kaiser Zinn, out of which various elegant ornaments and vessels were made. Thinking to please the Frau Doktor, the generous Quilter gave her some of those ornaments for Christmas. But instead of being pleased she was insulted because, she said, it wasn't real silver.

[16] Scott's *Trio in E moll*, Op. 3 (1900), bore the dedication 'To Prof Iwan Knorr in profoundest gratitude and affection'.

Of Quilter's talents, Iwan Knorr remarked: 'He will never be a great composer. But his compositions will be as charming as he is himself.'

Balfour Gardiner was a very different type, yet just as individual in his own way. In contrast to the tall, pale-faced Quilter, Gardiner was a rosy-complexioned young man who spoke with an Oxford accent and amused us all with what might be described as his good-natured cantankerousness. He appeared to be in a constant state of dissatisfaction with everything, especially with his own compositions. In fact this hyper-critical attitude was in a sense to prove his undoing, for in the end he largely gave up composing and took to forestry instead. And yet Iwan Knorr said he was one of the most intelligent pupils he ever taught …

After Gardiner left Frankfurt, he thought that 'just for fun', as he said, he would go in for a music exam at Oxford. 'I was hopelessly ploughed', he afterwards told us. 'They put me such silly questions. One was "Why was Schumann a great composer?" As I don't agree that Schumann was a great composer, what could I say?' And that was that. Gardiner's likes and dislikes were never the conventional ones.

About **Norman O'Neill** I have to be somewhat brief, for in our student days I saw far less of him than I did in after life. Although we were both pupils of Iwan Knorr's, we did not attend the same classes, and for another thing he was a man who seemed to take everything and everybody, including myself, as a huge joke, which made it difficult to discuss with him anything at all serious – and in those days I took life very seriously. Not that his chronic mirthfulness was the sign of a frivolous nature; far from it, for he had a very good brain. And certainly he had the Irishman's genius for witty metaphor. I remember him saying of a certain gross-looking music critic (long since deceased): 'He has a face like a bad smell.' He himself, I may add, was blest with the most striking good-looks and great personal charm. After O'Neill's talents had matured, he developed an especial flair for writing music for the theatre. This was both fortunate and unfortunate in one sense; for the trouble with theatre music is that when the plays are no longer put on the music is apt to be forgotten. In consequence the name Norman O'Neill is nowadays not so very often seen on concert programmes. He died, as the result of an accident, in his fifty-ninth year.

We now come to the still-living **Percy Grainger**, who is and was even in our student days as different in character from all the rest of us as it is possible to imagine. There was hardly a single subject on which we could agree with him. Though he and I did share the same enthusiasm for certain great composers, especially Bach and Wagner. To begin with, there was our teacher. Whereas the rest of us loved and admired Iwan Knorr, Grainger disliked him and declared he had learned nothing from him at all. But what amused us most of all about the young Grainger was his fantastic ideas. Indeed, so extravagant did they seem that we could not take them seriously but regarded them as the vapourings of youth, to vanish with maturity. And yet we were quite wrong: he has retained them throughout his life. For instance, he maintains that no democrat should ever write a concerto, because that entails giving a more important part to one player than to the rest. (As I have been guilty of writing several concertos, needless to say I don't agree with him.)

> Another of his strange ideas concerns the English language; he wants to abolish all French and Latin words and return to what he calls Nordic English. Thus, he thinks that instruments should be called 'tone-tools' – a chorus 'singer-host' – chamber music 'room-music' – a museum a 'hoard-house', and so on. As for Italian expression marks, he thinks that 'molto crescendo' should be 'louden lots', and in choruses 'tenuto al fine' 'hold till blown'. When we have pointed out that such directions are not only inartistic but rather vulgar, he retorts: 'I like them to be inartistic and vulgar.' ...
>
> And with that I must end these very inadequate thumbnail sketches of my fellow-students. And if I have said somewhat little about my unillustrious self, it is because egotism is not an attribute I could ever bring myself to admire.

* * * * *

For his second period of study in Frankfurt Scott lodged with a succession of landladies, but towards the end of his stay, in the spring of 1899, having arranged for his lessons to be confined to only two days in the week, he moved to the beautiful village of Cronberg, which lies in the foothills of the Taunus mountains, about forty-five minutes distant from Frankfurt by rail. Grainger cycled to visit him once or twice a week, and Scott would show him his latest work or they would go out for walks. Quilter was also an occasional visitor.[17]

Norman O'Neill was probably the first of the Frankfurt Group with whom Cyril became acquainted. O'Neill also studied with Knorr and Uzielli, and although his time at Frankfurt overlapped both of Scott's periods of study, it was only near the end of his stay that he came across Cyril. While at Frankfurt O'Neill met his future wife, a young French girl, Adine Rückert, who was studying the piano privately with Clara Schumann.[18] In June 1896, after Clara's death, she had to return to Paris but the two kept in touch, through a lengthy correspondence and with frequent meetings in Paris or London. They were later married, in France, in July 1899. On 1 October 1896 O'Neill wrote to Adine about a 'little English boy' in his class, 'only about 16, but a really great talent for composition'. He invited Scott to tea four days later, feeling it, as he explained, 'a duty "to be kind" to him as he knows a great friend of mine (with whom I lived here) who looks after him!'[19] Afterwards, he repeated to Adine, 'He has a very great talent for composition, and such good fingers! It was rather nice to see a regular English school-boy again, & to hear all those

[17] Quilter dedicated an early song, *Mond, du bist glücklicher als ich* (n.d.), 'To Cyril Meir Scott from the composer', and *Four Songs of Mirza Schaffy*, Op. 2 (1903), 'In remembrance of Frankfort days'.

[18] Clara Schumann was head of the Conservatoire's pianoforte department from 1878 until 1892, when illness and increasing deafness forced her to resign. She continued to teach the piano privately.

[19] Letter, 3 October 1896, from the correspondence between Norman O'Neill and Adine Rückert, London, BL, 71456–71472. The 'great friend' was probably Thomas Holland-Smith, with whom O'Neill shared lodgings in Frankfurt for a while.

old school expressions again!' Later that month they played together a Schumann piece for two pianos.

At an impressionable age Scott came into contact with a number of strong personalities whose influences were to mould his thinking and behaviour. Through fellow student Clemens von Franckenstein[20] he met the German poet Stefan George, eleven years his senior,[21] who instilled in Scott a love of poetry and introduced him to the verses of Ernest Dowson, many of which he was later to set.[22] (His own poem, or ballad, *The Soul of Cynara* shows his admiration for Dowson's art.)[23] George also imbued him with several artistic doctrines, two of which were to stand him in good stead in later years when his music was little appreciated: first, that 'no artist worthy of the name ever writes for the public, but solely for art itself'; and second, that 'every artist should be pleased when he receives adverse criticism, for to be easily understood shows one not to be worth understanding'. After the first performance of his Violin Sonata No. 1, no doubt with the latter principle in mind, Scott wrote to Roger Quilter: 'My concert I think was certainly an artistic success especially so as all the notices were bad almost.'[24]

A rather different outcome from this friendship was the way in which Scott modelled his appearance on George and took on the poet's air of arrogance and show of personality. (He even imitated George's scripted handwriting.) George invited Scott and Franckenstein to visit him at his home in Bingen, on the Rhine, and as O'Neill was a great friend of Franckenstein's, he came too, the three of them cycling the not insignificant distance of forty miles from Frankfurt. However, although O'Neill showed due respect to his host while in his presence, he treated him 'as a subject for mirth' in his absence (somewhat to Cyril's surprise and dismay), and O'Neill and George never met again.[25] Cyril, the youngest of the three:

[20] Baron Clemens von Franckenstein (1875–1942), German operatic composer and conductor, of the Moody-Manners Opera Company in England from 1902 to 1907, before taking up posts at Wiesbaden and Berlin. His brother Sir George Franckenstein became Austrian ambassador to England during the Nazi annexation.

[21] Stefan George (1868–1933), symbolist poet and leader of a group that revolted against materialism. While in Paris in his youth he came into contact with Mallarmé and Verlaine. When he later became acclaimed by the Nazis he went into voluntary exile in Switzerland, where he died. In 1898 Scott set six of his verses as *Sänge eines fahrenden Spielmanns*, Op 1. Schönberg also set several of George's verses, most notably in the song-cycle *Das Buch der Hängenden Gärten* (1908), and Webern set verses from his *Der siebente Ring* (1907–8). In 1910 a translation by Scott of a number of George's poems was published.

[22] Scott did not, as has been erroneously stated, meet Ernest Dowson, who died in 1900. No such meeting is recorded in either of his autobiographies.

[23] *The Soul of Cynara*, from a volume of Scott's poems, *The Vales of Unity*, published in 1912.

[24] Letter from Scott to Quilter, 7 April 1908. He added: 'The violin sonata is by far the best thing I have done.' The sonata was premiered at the Bechstein Hall on 24 March 1908.

[25] *Bone of Contention*, p. 103.

> was the only one to arouse George's special interest. Several times he came to see me in my modest rooms in Frankfurt, several times he invited me to Bingen and when, during the last months of my student days I had moved with my effects to Cronberg ... he came to visit me and stayed a few days each time.

Although Scott did not respond to George's homosexual advances (about which Franckenstein had warned him), despite his admiration for the poet he began to feel ill at ease in his presence. In a moment of confession George had earlier suggested that their friendship would be much easier when Scott had passed the age of twenty-three and had 'shed those idealising elements' that George found attractive in a youth. But things came to an abrupt end one day when George told him 'never to cross his path again'. This friendship was, however, later renewed 'on a much more comfortable and secure footing', and they met at intervals in the years before World War 1.

* * * * *

In September 1897 O'Neill was back home with his parents, starting to make his living as a composer in anticipation of his marriage. A year later, after a holiday in the Tyrol with Clemens von Franckenstein, he paid a return visit to Frankfurt, and on 6 September 1898 he wrote to Adine: 'I saw some nice work of Scott's after dinner today – when I went back to his rooms. His imitation in every kind of way of S George is too comic!'

On 6 December Adine was visiting Frankfurt and she wrote to Norman, who was then in England:

> I walked then with Scott who talked the whole time about himself & Stefan George. The boy is simply killing. I will tell you about it; he makes himself perfectly ridiculous as really one could think anything of that friendship. He is coming here tomorrow a'noon to play me his latest things. I ask him, knowing he hates women for the present. He said to Fis[c]her,[26] 'Does women make any effect on you?'!

Norman replied the next day:

> I wonder what Scott will turn out when he is through all these poses. He ought to find some girl who will really get him under her influence, the best thing that could happen to him!

Ten days later Adine gave a fascinating account of the regard in which many of Cyril's compositions were held and how, to her ears, they compared with Grainger's:

[26] Carlo Fischer (1872–1954), American cellist who studied at the Hoch Conservatoire 1894–9 and was a friend of O'Neill and the Graingers. He performed O'Neill's Cello Sonata with the composer.

> Today the little Scott came.[27] He played me an amount of work – not all Knorr says that the quantity of things he had done since the summer is quite wonderful. A trio, a string quartett, a sonata piano & violin, a sonata piano & also etc. he played me préludes for the piano. Some of them are nice, some other I did not care. Then the Trio is awfully nice but the string quartette is really the best and must sound so well, so full of go, character and so clever too. I know you would like it. He gets so excited at the performance of his works. After we went together to the Graingers & we made Percy play some of his own compositions. It's awful & sounds so queer. The themes are nice but spoiled by awful discordings harmonies, the littler chap enjoys that! I played them your variations and your slow C mi piece. We had tea & Scott went to the piano and for an whole hour played Tristan & Isolde but perfectly wonderful the way he did it & he got more & more excited, got quite mad and we really were obliged to stop him otherwise we would still be there.[28]

The humorous tenor of the correspondence, together with the difference between Cyril and Norman's ages, perhaps suggests why theirs was not to be such an intimate relationship, unlike that Scott enjoyed with Grainger and Gardiner.

Nevertheless, Cyril was a fairly frequent visitor to the O'Neills in London at 4 Pembroke Villas, and much later their daughter Yvonne was to enjoy a warm friendship with him. She came to know him when she was about sixteen, and towards the end of her life remembered him as 'an enormous influence on my life – my greatest friend of all'.[29] He would occasionally visit her at her boarding school and take her out – to the delight or envy of her school friends, who were fascinated by this person in black hat and cape. Then, while she was sixteen and seriously ill, confined to bed for many weeks with heart trouble, Cyril came nearly every Monday with Lily of the Valley (its smell apparently being good for the heart), two books and some sweets, and, in keeping with the various health cures that he was interested in, he would recommend homeopathy to her. He was a frequent correspondent. She often went to tea with him and his wife, Rose, when they lived in London at Ladbroke Grove, and when she was having boyfriend problems he would give her advice on such topics as jealousy and envy.

The interior of Scott's house was something no visitor could forget. The first feature to be encountered was a sculpture in plaster of himself by Derwent Wood,[30] then there were the stained-glass windows and his uncomfortable Gothic furniture, both of which he designed and had made in imitation of the German artist Melchior Lechter; his own murals adorned the walls, there was a green grand piano with gold designs, and a talking parrot that he kept for many years, which would surprise

[27] A curious adjective to use, as Scott was then nineteen.

[28] 17 December 1898. Some small corrections to Adine's punctuation have been made for ease of reading; otherwise her idiosyncratic English has been left unchanged.

[29] Yvonne Hudson (*née* O'Neill, 1916–1996), in conversation with me at her home in Guildford, 8 September 1991.

[30] Francis Derwent Wood (1871–1926). The original bronze was first exhibited in the Fourth Exhibition of the International Society of Sculptors, Painters and Gravers (London) in 1904.

the visitor with sudden and rather rude interjections. Scott dedicated a humorous piano piece, the scherzo *Miss Remington* (1934), to Yvonne, its title referring to the then familiar advertisement depicting a secretary named after the typewriter manufacturer; earlier her mother, Adine, had been the dedicatee of the piano piece *Intermezzo* (Elkin, 1910).

In 1903 Adine O'Neill was appointed head music mistress of St Paul's Girls' School, with which she was associated for thirty-four years. (Norman O'Neill wrote the music for the school song.) The *Saint Pauls Girls School Book, 1904–1925* records that in 1908 Mrs O'Neill 'gave the first audition at which her pupils played selections from the works of Cyril Scott and Norman O'Neill'. But it seems that a few years later the suitability for young girls of Cyril's popular piano pieces was being challenged. It may have been after a school concert that Thomas Dunhill wrote to Adine on 28 August 1915:

> I feel it is a little difficult to answer your question without seeming to say something which might be construed into a very small & merely personal prejudice – & I am especially diffident when the composer is a brother Englishman! But you ask me frankly & I feel I must answer frankly – & I hope you will believe that I am a person without any jealousy of any kind – which is the sober truth. But I do think those little pieces of Cyril Scott which so many of the girls played are very unhealthy & of no particular educational value. They are of course very clever – but I somehow feel that to give such music so extensively in a school is a little analogous to dosing the girls with literature such as, say, Oscar Wilde. This being my opinion I did not feel I could give an honest report without expressing it.

The outcome of this exchange is not known.

* * * * *

The member of the Group with whom Scott was to have the closest and longest-lasting friendship was Percy Grainger. They met at the home of Grainger's teacher, Karl Klimsch, to whom Percy had turned after falling out with Iwan Knorr. The Klimsch family had 'raved about the sweet & gifted little boy [Cyril] had been on his first stay', and Klimsch's daughter Pauline was keen to bring them together.[31] In an eightieth-birthday broadcast tribute to Cyril, Percy remembered the occasion: 'When we met the person who introduced [us] said, "Percy's writing a concerto." And Cyril Scott said to me, "Do you know anything about musical form?" and I said, "No." He said, "Well, you can't call it a concerto." And that was the beginning of our friendship!'[32] In that eightieth-birthday tribute Grainger went on to refer to Scott as a 'man

[31] 'My First Meeting with Cyril Scott', in *Self-Portrait of Percy Grainger*, ed.by Malcolm Gillies, David Pear and Mark Carroll (Oxford University Press, 2006), p. 87.

[32] WQXR (New York) broadcast, 1959. The 'person who introduced us' was Pauline Klimsch, daughter of Karl Klimsch (*Self-Portrait of Percy Grainger*, p. 87). As regards the piece, a piano-concerto movement in C minor (1896) by Grainger, edited by John Lavender and orchestrated by Benjamin Woodgates, received its first

I have admired all my life and a man who really made me a composer'. He spoke warmly of the 'great deal of compassion in his music', and how he was 'benevolent, kindly and helpful to other people'.

Scott and Grainger were the original thinkers of the Group, and acted in many ways as sounding-boards for each other's creativity. Sir Thomas Armstrong has written that 'there is no doubt that Cyril Scott was a musician of truly original mind',[33] and the conductor Basil Cameron, who had a close association with the Group, said in a BBC broadcast that 'there is no doubt that Cyril Scott's flamboyant originality in his music and his enthusiasm for experiment spurred Grainger on to carry into effect a whole train of innovations in musical composition that were already stirring in his mind.'[34] Even Scott's professor of composition, Iwan Knorr, remembered him as 'brilliant, revolutionary', and elsewhere Grainger generously acknowledged his debt to Scott:

> It seems to be as if I might never have been a modernist composer but for my contact with Cyril Scott. When he found me ... I was writing in the style of Handel & seemed to know nothing of modern music. 'Aren't you interested in writing modern music?' he said to me. 'What do you mean by modern music?' I answered. He played me Grieg's Ballade & Tchaikovsky's Theme and Vars (both quite new to me). Then, his own modernist music was a fiery awakener of my own modernistic powers. It is true that, as a boy of 11 or 12, in Australia, I had heard in my head my Free Music, made up of beatless lilts, gliding interval-less tones & non-harmonic voice-leadings. But this early tone-vision had no connection with the conservative composing I was doing in Frankfurt in the pre-Scott days. So ... one may say that I never would have become a modernist composer without Cyril Scott's influence. But my influence upon him, in a modernising sense, was soon to become equally great. My discordant diatonic harmonies ... were an influence. Still more so my irregularly-barred music ... which, after a few years, led Scott to ask my permission to take up this aspect into his own music, with results seen in his Piano Sonata op 66 & numberless other works. His extremely discordant harmonic style ... was, I think, evolved without influence from me. It, in turn ... influenced my discordance in 'The Warriors' & the Pastoral in the Suite 'In a Nutshell' [inscribed 'For my dear comrade in art and thought Cyril Scott'].[35]

It was a two-way traffic of influence and admiration. Grainger could write of Scott's 'amazing genius' during the Frankfurt days and how he 'outsoared all others in composition';[36] Scott in turn wrote to Grainger in 1911: 'Saturday was a gorgeous

performance by Penelope Thwaites and ensemble at Kings Place, London, on 8 October 2014.

33 Armstrong, 'The Frankfurt Group', p. 3.

34 'Percy Grainger (born July 8, 1882)', broadcast talk by Basil Cameron, *BBC Music Magazine*, 6 July 1952. Extract rebroadcast 30 June 1968.

35 'English-Speaking Leadership in Tone-Art', in Thomas Slattery, *Percy Grainger: The Inveterate Innovator* (Instrumentalist Co., 1974), pp. 270–1.

36 John Bird, *Percy Grainger* (Elek, 1976), p. 29; reprinted edn (Oxford University Press, 1999), p. 33.

time for me – for Heaven's sake let's repeat it often – it is more help to me, hearing your work, than anything on earth.'[37] And in 1936 he acknowledged that 'Grainger influenced me, not so much by the colour and texture of his music as by his ideas. To him I certainly owed the idea of writing in irregular rhythm.'[38]

Another aspect of Scott's broadening of the Group's vision was touched on by Grainger in his letter to Sir Thomas Armstrong: 'When Cyril returned to F[rankfurt]. in 1896 the books & pictorial art we got to know thru him were the plays of Maeterlinck … the poems of Stefan George & Ernest Dowson, Walt Whitman, Aubrey Beardsley.'[39] How far Scott's absorption in the artistic ferment of the 1890s affected the others in the Group is not easy to assess. Suffice it to say that on his return to Germany he brought with him an awareness of the literary movements and cross-currents both at home and on the Continent. Scott became engrossed in many *fin-de-siècle* figures. His fascination for the Pre-Raphaelites and the Symbolists inevitably led him to Maeterlinck, whose works inspired three early orchestral pieces: the *Pelleas and Melisanda* overture, Op. 5;[40] the *Princess Maleine* overture, Op. 18;[41] and the *Aglavaine et Sélysette* overture, Op. 21.[42] (It was probably mere coincidence that, as a composer of theatre music, in 1909 O'Neill wrote incidental music for the first English production of Maeterlinck's *The Blue Bird*.)

* * * * *

Friendship was very much the Group's unifying element, though not so much from their activities while studying at Frankfurt as from their prolonged companionships

[37] Letter from Scott to Grainger, 27 February 1911, quoted in Eileen Dorum, *Percy Grainger: The Man behind the Music* (IC and EE Dorum, 1986), p. 66.

[38] 'Grainger and Frankfurt', in *The Percy Grainger Companion*, ed. Lewis Foreman (Thames Publishing, 1981) p. 54. The use of irregular rhythms nearly became a contentious issue, as Grainger wrote to Karen Holten, 23 May 1907: 'Cyril has done me the compliment of telling me that he also is going to write "irregular music"; music with irregular bars. I don't like it; I prefer to do my own experiments myself … I am very jealous on these matters. I so long for the world to have to say "such & such was an Australian's discovery".' See *The Farthest North of Humanness: Letters of Percy Grainger, 1901–14*, ed. Kay Dreyfus (Macmillan, 1985), p. 111.

[39] Letter from Grainger to Sir Thomas Armstrong, 1958, quoted in the latter's article 'Delius Today' in the 1962 Bradford Delius Centenary Festival programme book, p. 18. How much this was due to the influence of Hans Lüthy is uncertain.

[40] The Overture to *Pelleas and Melisanda*, Op. 5, was dedicated 'To Herrn Willem de Haan – in grateful remembrance of January 8th 1900' (when Scott's First Symphony was performed). A copy was inscribed to 'H. Balfour Gardiner wishing him the highest and greatest inspirations: – from his sincere C. S.'

[41] Performed 22 August 1907 (Proms, cond. Henry Wood); revised with chorus and performed in Vienna, May 1912, conductor Franz Schrecker; and reworked as the *Daily Telegraph* prize-winning *Festival Overture* (1929–33) for orchestra, organ and chorus or orchestra alone (Queen's Hall, 9 May 1934, cond. Adrian Boult). It was dedicated to Grainger, who experimented with various orchestrations and conducted the work himself in America.

[42] Composed *c.* August 1901. (Letter to Gardiner, 28 August 1901.) Unperformed.

that remained for the rest of their lives, strengthened by correspondence and occasional meetings, even though they were each to pursue different courses. There was no rivalry, no competitiveness, but instead a readiness to bring support and encouragement to each other, with a genuine interest in each other's success. This unity was something that Grainger particularly strove to preserve, not just during his lifetime, but also for posterity in the Grainger Museum on the campus of Melbourne University. Theirs was a brotherhood, a fellowship, and the many mutual dedications and their extensive surviving correspondence testify to this. Grainger's 1947 round-letter (or 'send-writ' as he would term it) is like a rallying call from a general responsible for the morale of his troops, with a distinct element of 'the old school tie' about it.

In that same letter to Sir Thomas Armstrong, Grainger tried hard to define other, stronger, musical bonds between the members of the Group.

> As I think of the other ones (Scott, Quilter, Gardiner & myself) & seek to find a characteristic that marks our group off from other British composers it seems to me that an excessive emotionality (& particularly a tragic or sentimental or wistful or pathetic emotionality) is the hallmark of our group ... All we 4 composers spoke German as fluently as English – tho not necessarily grammatically. I think it might be true that the exaggerated tenor of German emotionality had some influence on us all 4. The influence, if any, lay in the willingness to take such emotional views of things. The feelings themselves were typically English in their wistfulness and patheticness. Perhaps it might be true to say that we were all of us PRERAFAELITE composers ... Under 'prerafaelite' I understand art which takes a conscious charm from what is archaic, an art in which KNIGHTS or heros are always present. And what musical medium could provide the agonized emotionality needed? ... I think the answer is 'the CHORD'. The chord has a heartrending power we musical prerafaelites needed. Based on Bach, Wagner, Skriabine, Grieg & Cesar Franck Cyril, Balfour & I became chord-masters indeed ... If the chord gave us human unity, irregular rhythms gave us the tally of English energy – that is, in fast tempos (at slow tempos irregular rhythms are, of course, hardly distinguishable from regular ones).

As Sir Thomas (who knew Grainger, Quilter, Scott and especially Gardiner) has shown, the 'chord' (which he defined as a version of a chromatic chord on the major sixth of the scale with its ninth and appoggiaturas)[43] was neither invented by the Group nor became their exclusive property – one only has to look, for example, to the music of Delius. Yet their thinking was essentially chordal, especially Scott's, who, as his harmonic language crystallised, made increasing use of the 1-4-7 chord (which is, in fact, the 'upper half' of Scriabin's 'mystic' *Prometheus* chord), notably to much effect in the Third Piano Sonata (1956).

At Frankfurt, as Scott explained in his first autobiography:

> my ideal was to invent a species of Pre-Raphaelite music, to consist mostly of common chords placed in such a way as to savour of very primitive church

[43] Armstrong, 'Delius Today', p. 19.

> music, thereby, as I thought, reminding its listeners of old pictures. I even wrote a Symphony and a pretentious Magnificat along these lines, and was rewarded by exciting the admiration of both Quilter and Grainger.[44]

Scott's admiration for Stefan George led him to compose six songs with piano to texts by George, the *Spielmannslieder*.[45] These bear the lengthy dedication 'These few songs may the names of dearest friends adorn: Hans Lüthy, Clemens Franckenstein, H. Balfour Gardiner, T. Holland Smith [and] In remembrance of hard striving colleagueship to Roger C. Quilter one of the best & dearest friends of his sincere Cyrillus'. It was Holland-Smith who had impressed on the young Scott the need for any composer of merit to have a style of his own, and during his Frankfurt years and those immediately following Scott was very much a composer in search of a style.

A small number of Scott's works were performed while he was at Frankfurt. He played his *Variations on an Original Theme*, for piano, in an examination concert in the spring of 1898, and in June 1899 an early piano trio was performed at a Conservatoire concert with Sandby and Grainger as two of the three players. But his first orchestral venture had to wait until after he had left Frankfurt, when his first symphony, completed April 1899, was given at Darmstadt on 8 January 1900. This performance came about through the influence of Stefan George, who was the son-in-law of Willem de Haan (1849–1935), conductor at the Darmstadt opera house. Scott repaid this kindness by dedicating the symphony 'In the truest friendship + admiration to the Poet Stefan George to whose art I am indebted for many of my best and most religious ideas'. When Scott played the work on the piano to de Haan the latter confessed that some of it was rather too modern for his taste, but he nevertheless agreed to its being performed the next season. Early in 1899 Scott wrote to Gardiner about the progress he was making with the symphony:

> My dear Balfour
> I was indeed glad to get your letter & to hear such good news of Percy. It is well you get on together & I am in expectation of your own new work … Of the Symphony I am doing three movements at once. 1st Andante & Finale. The Final[e] is very strong & ugly, modulates a lot & is very extravagant. I have done most of the Andante. On Friday I sent Percy a cantilene for Cello, something for Sandby. I certainly put all my lifeblood into it & it seems very good[.] If you visit him you will see it. Otherwise nothing new.[46]

On 26 June, from Brussels, he wrote excitedly to Percy that de Haan admired both the symphony and the *Spielmannslieder*. On 29 August, from Oxton, he wrote that de Haan wanted him to conduct the work himself at Darmstadt. Another letter, dated 2 October, concerned 'instructions for copying symphony wanted urgently by de Haan', to be followed on the 8th and 11th by two more relating to 'copying

[44] *My Years of Indiscretion*, pp. 25–6.

[45] *Sänge eines fahrenden Spielmanns von Stefan George* (August, 1899).

[46] Written in Stefan George's printed style, possibly April 1899.

instructions'.[47] Cyril returned to Germany the day before the first rehearsal of the symphony, only to be met with problems. First, it turned out that the copyist had failed to complete his task, and consequently Cyril and Percy had to sit up all night preparing the parts before taking a very early train to Darmstadt the next day. The plan had been for de Haan to conduct the first rehearsal and for Scott to take over the second rehearsal the following day and the performance. But it soon became clear that Scott did not yet have the necessary experience, and de Haan conducted in his place. Quilter was still in Frankfurt, as were Grainger and his mother, and they came to the concert together with Gardiner, Iwan Knorr, Stefan George and Hans Lüthy, who had travelled from Liverpool especially for the occasion. By all accounts the work had a mixed reception, with some hissing mingled among the applause. 'One ought to play that to the Boers,' Gardiner overheard someone say, 'then they'd run as far as the Equator.'[48]

Fortunately, the existence in the Grainger Museum of the manuscripts of some of Cyril's early works has enabled them to be resurrected and recorded, and the Chandos CD of the First Symphony has shown it to be a most approachable and delightful work, with an especially expressive pastoral second movement *andante*.[49] The last movement, with a slight Lisztian ring dominated by a brass chorale-like figure, was presumably what would have sent the Boers running! Although in no way representative of his later music, it was nonetheless a considerable achievement for the twenty-year-old Scott, demonstrating a gift for melody and a fine command of orchestration.

There were hopes that the symphony would receive a second performance at Frankfurt, and Scott consequently prolonged his stay in Germany, spending 'three stimulating weeks with Grainger and his mother – who treated me almost as a son – stimulating because his own compositions were beginning to excite my admiration as they have done ever since'.[50] Grainger showed him his *English Dance* for orchestra, 'which gave me the most pronounced musical thrills' (Percy dedicated the work to Cyril),[51] and in exchange Scott showed him his recently completed overture to *Pelleas and Melisanda*. 'The *Magnificat* was also brought out from the depths of my trunk, and at Grainger's request played on the piano – with an obligato of whistling, humming, etc. – to various musical friends who turned up for tea or supper at the Pension where we were staying.' One such person was Percy's father on a rare visit. 'Very reverent!' was his comment when Cyril had finished,[52] at which both Cyril and Percy burst into laughter. With Cyril now a confirmed

[47] From a summary of the correspondence between Scott and Grainger, 1899–1960, Grainger's copies held in the Grainger Museum. This is an extensive correspondence, comprising several hundred letters and postcards.

[48] *My Years of Indiscretion*, p. 38.

[49] CHAN 10452, BBC Philharmonic, Martyn Brabbins. Recorded October 2007. The start of the third movement, of which two pages were missing, was reconstructed by Leslie De'Ath.

[50] *My Years of Indiscretion*, p. 39.

[51] Gardiner also composed an *English Dance*, which he dedicated 'To Percy Grainger who first taught me "The English Dance"'.

[52] *Self-Portrait of Percy Grainger*, p. 22.

agnostic, reverence certainly had not been the intention.[53] Both works, he added, were eventually consigned to the crematorium as 'the best and safest place for them'.[54] As it turned out, instead of the hoped-for second performance of the symphony, the overture to *Pelleas and Melisanda* was given at Frankfurt on 1 February, conducted by Max Kämpfert.[55]

Illness delayed Cyril's return home, and Stefan George invited him to Berlin where he received an entrée into George's circle of friends. He stayed with Balfour Gardiner's brother, the eminent Egyptologist Alan Gardiner, and his wife,[56] and while in Berlin he visited the artist Melchior Lechter, whom he had first met through George in Frankfurt and whose flat of stained-glass windows and Gothic furniture was strongly to influence him. Indeed, as he wrote, his own house was to bear 'as close a resemblance to Lechter's in atmosphere as it has been possible for me to reproduce'.[57] Describing Scott's Liverpool house, Grainger wrote to his mother: 'Cyril's place here is 1st class, style perfect, & furniture that he has designed is simple & strong. Nice Lechter & other pics, of course the whole thing wld give me the Fantods to live in, but I appreciate it as an excellent realisation of *his* ideals.'[58] Lechter's work was much influenced by the pre-Raphaelites and by Stefan George, several of whose anthologies he illustrated. He had an interest in music and was also an occultist. It is not surprising that a friendship ensued that lasted for several years.[59]

* * * * *

Back home again with his Frankfurt studies completed, Scott divided his time between composing and practising the piano, with the intention of launching himself with a recital in Liverpool and gaining pupils to provide an income. He gave his first public recital on 18 October 1900 in St George's Hall, Liverpool. Through the University College he struck up a close friendship with Charles Bonnier, professor

53 The *Magnificat* of 1899 bears the multiple dedications: 'To those friends without whose admiration and influence this work could never have been written: Percy, Roger, Eric, Agnes, Hans, Carry in all affection and gratitude'. Despite his agnosticism, in 1935 Scott composed an Evening Service consisting of a *Magnificat* and *Nunc Dimittis*, and a *Jubilate*.

54 The holograph full score of the (First) Symphony has in fact survived in the Grainger Museum at Melbourne (together with another copy of the full score in a copyist's hand), as well as a piano score, in Grainger's hand, of the *Magnificat*. See Phil Clifford, *Grainger's Collection of Music by other Composers* (University of Melbourne, 1983).

55 Recorded on Dutton CDLX7302 by Martin Yates and the BBC Concert Orchestra, the overture to *Pelleas and Melisanda* is a most impressive and atmospheric work.

56 Scott dedicated the song *A Gift of Silence* (Elkin, 1905) 'to Heddie and Alan Gardiner'.

57 *My Years of Indiscretion*, p. 42.

58 24 October 1902, from 129 Canning Street, Liverpool; see *The Farthest North of Humanness*, p. 18.

59 To Melchior Lechter (1865–1937) Scott dedicated both the song *Sorrow* (a setting of Dowson; Elkin, 1904), and his *English Suite* (Suite No. 1 for Orchestra), Op. 6, completed March 1900 with the inscription 'To Meister Melchior Lechter affectionately dedicated in profoundest admiration of himself and his art'.

of French literature, from whom he learned the art of writing verse. They shared a house in Canning Street, Liverpool, to which another close friend, the singer and composer Frederic Austin, was a frequent visitor.

Scott made many visits to Germany, and to Frankfurt in particular. (In Frankfurt he was a welcome guest of Uzielli's first wife, and at Cologne of Uzielli and his second wife.) It was probably during these return visits to Frankfurt that he got to know Balfour Gardiner. After two years at Frankfurt, Gardiner had returned home to enter New College, Oxford, in October 1896, at the same time that Scott renewed his Frankfurt studies. But he returned to Frankfurt in between the Oxford terms and he was back in Germany in the summer of 1900 for private study with Knorr. As a token of this new friendship Cyril inscribed to Gardiner a printed copy of an early song, *April Love*, 'To Henry Balfour Gardiner as a small return for the sympathy without which one could never work – May 1900', and on another song, *Ad domnulam suam*, 'In remembrance of Frankfurt – Xmas 1900.'

In January Gardiner went on to Sondershausen, some fifty miles west of Leipzig, where he studied conducting and had his first two orchestral performances, a symphony and an overture, neither now extant. Even when separated the Group's camaraderie, enthusiasm, mutual interest and support remained strong. Perhaps in the days of their youth their judgements not unexpectedly gave rise to some over-assessment of themselves and each other, but the strength of their friendships is particularly evident from their many mutual dedications, borrowing of ideas and themes, and from their surviving correspondence, which also provides an insight into the works in progress. They were ever keen to hear each other's works and to offer advice or criticism. Balfour Gardiner, who came from a wealthy background, was much loved and respected by the others of the Frankfurt Group, as much for his warmth and generosity as for his musicianship. Unfortunately his highly self-critical nature made him give up music in later life and not live up to the high hopes that his friends had of him as a composer. Scott in particular had great respect for him, as the following mainly undated letters indicate. They also show Scott's musical fertility and his youthful energy and excitement:

> I was so glad to have seen you again & hear all your new work. Your melodies are still ringing in my ears & I am so glad to have them. This is a splendid place & I am with charming people. The weather is mending too & it promises well. But I am not inclined to write yet. No doubt you are writing a grand first movement. I wish you luck. Do write me often from Sondershausen & tell me what [you are] doing, and ever so many thanks for all your kindnesses. From your affectionate & admiring friend.[60]
>
> Percy wrote me such good news – namely that you had been doing such fine work, original & glorious, and such a change to what I heard. Well done! My dear friend – there is nobody more convinced of your genius than I was if it would only come out – and now it is doing so.[61]

[60] Undated letter from Ward Hill, Farnham.

[61] Letter from Scott to Gardiner, [April 1901], from 64 Canning Street, Liverpool.

> My dear Balfour,
> Did I not tell you all along how good you were & now at last you come to believe it. It delighted me beyond words to get your letter & hear good news. There is but one pity, that is my not hearing it. Well some day no doubt I shall. I expect to come back from Switzerland about Sept. 15th. There is nothing I should like better than a day or two with you. If your Vtet is not Vtmäsig then start again, the one idea being to make it so. I destroyed my Quartett on that account & the new movement is another thing altogether both in technique & idea. Every part has equally something to do. I just finished it yesterday. I shall see Percy on the 16th. He had a great success & is getting on well. Do write to me in Switzerland .... Keep me posted as to all your doings. That is all I have to say so farewell. Work on hard for one who thirsts for your beauties & genius with feverish haste.[62]

In July 1901 there was encouragement from Grainger, writing to Gardiner:

> Your lovely E♭ mel. is a fine invigorator of dull moments, it takes its place among the very lovely. I had a joke with Scott about it. He says he does not like it as well as most of your other things, but when I played it among other things, he started up with 'What is that lovely thing?' etc. So you see how much one may rely on a person's opinion. I am longing to hear more of yours.

That summer, before going abroad, Scott called on Grainger and his mother, Rose, who were then living in London in Kensington. Cyril was particularly struck by one piece that Percy played to him. From Vevey, where he was staying with Lüthy, he wrote to Gardiner on 13 August 1901:

> Your remarks are quite right as they always are. But, when one is in the 'erste leidenschaft' everything is harmony. You will notice it by all, Grainger, yourself etc. When that craze is over one gets into more important things as well, makes use of the harmonic experiments in a less crude manner & later on one invents harmony again which would never be as striking though. But at any rate you will see a harmonic change in me when we meet.
>
> Since I am here I did the Prelude to Aglavaine & Salysette, one movement of a Piano Quartett & a Pianoforte Sonata,[63] the latter being the strongest if not even the best thing I have done for a long time – but I will not say much as I have lost a lot of confidence of late & tomorrow I may dislike it. After hearing Grainger's Cello piece all my work seems insipid. The boy is a genius of the first water – possessor of a strength and originality, pathos & beauty which baffles all description. And as to you well I am very anxious to hear your new work. Your idyllic phrase has been a source of great pleasure to me and many others. May there be many more like it. Write to me whenever you can & describe your work a bit, even if it be only on a postcard. I should love to see Knorr again, he always sets me straight. I am all for the Heroic at present – the p. Quartett & Piano Sonata are tremendously

[62] Letter from Scott to Gardiner, 9 July [1901], from 129 Canning Street, Liverpool.

[63] Introduced by Grainger on 29 November 1901.

> so – perhaps the landscape causes it. Well I shall be charmed to receive you to my house.

In *My Years of Indiscretion* Scott wrote of the cello piece (*A Lot of Rot* for cello and piano, composed March 1901, and later renamed *Youthful Rapture*):

> it absolutely transported me. There was a painted, powdered pathos about it, to use my own words at the time, which haunted me with its beauty for weeks afterwards. Grainger had caught something of the sad, sentimental vulgarity of the music-hall … And even months later it was still the memory of this music-poem which prompted me to write my 'Two Pierrot Pieces',[64] with their atmosphere of the variety stage.[65]

Either that work or Grainger's similarly themed *Love Verses from 'The Song of Solomon'* must have been very much in Scott's mind when he was engaged on his early Piano Concerto in D (referred to in the next letter), as the main theme in the dreamy middle movement of this recently resurrected concerto is based on an idea that owes much to Grainger.[66] There are similarities with his *Youthful Rapture* and the *Love Verses*, too, though one must bear in mind that Percy himself has written that 'many elements in [my] early style (such compositions as *Love Verses from the Song of Solomon* & *The Inuit*) were strongly influenced by Scott's then style'.[67]

From Vevey again, on 28 August 1901, Scott gave Gardiner a progress report:

> The Piano Quartett is done all but a little Intermezzo which I want to place between the last two movements. Formal[ly] is it different to anything I have done. The movements are Prelude, Scherzo, Andante (Intermezzo not done) and Finale – Lento. Sonata form has arrived at the time of further development. Old methods do not satisfy me any longer. The Prelude is one great Cantilene from beginning to end, the theme coming in in different ways & different keys from time to time. It gives a tremendously bedeutend [distinguished] ring to the work. You must broaden your mind for it and not think me chaotic or formal[ly] bad for branching off in a new direction. Imagine the beginning of the Mathäus Passion in a modern style with a broad sweeping theme, then you have a vague idea of it. The 2nd & third section of the Piano Sonata do not come up to the first section so I am changing them. If it is I that bring you ideas which is doubtful there is plenty [to]

[64] *Pierrot triste*, dedicated to Ernest Thesiger, and *Pierrot gai*, dedicated to T. Holland-Smith (Boosey, 1904).

[65] *My Years of Indiscretion*, p. 61.

[66] Concerto in D for piano and orchestra, Op. 10, realised and completed by Martin Yates. Recorded November 2012 by Peter Donohoe, BBC Concert Orchestra, cond. Martin Yates. Dutton CDLX7302.

[67] 'An Untamed Buffalo', in *The All-Round Man: Selected Letters of Percy Grainger, 1914–1961*, ed. Malcolm Gillies and David Pear (Clarendon Press, 1994), p. 121. Scott has described the *Song of Solomon* as 'a choral composition replete with melodic beauty of a touching and appealing type'. See 'Grainger and Frankfurt', in *The Percy Grainger Companion*, p. 54.

> show – 2 movements[68] of Piano Concerto (of which you only heard snatches & never saw) Symphonic Fantasia, 1 movement of String Quartett, Ballade of Dark Rosaleen, Prelude to Aglavaine & Selysette, Piano Sonata & Pianoforte Quartett.

* * * * *

As Scott freely admitted in *Bone of Contention*, at Frankfurt 'I had developed some extremely unpleasant characteristics which were to cause much pain to my parents … By the time I was nineteen I had become a most unbearable and arrogant young man', sporting long hair and curious ties that he felt befitted an artist and a musician.[69] However, it seems that much of this arrogance had rubbed off by 1901, as Grainger wrote a little later to Herman Sandby about a visit by Scott:

> There is Scott, from whom I have just had a delightful visit, who is absolutely incapable of jealousy for *anybody*, & who would do anything for poor little ME …
>
> Scott has grown *so very* much nicer again than he was in Frankfurt last Xmas, he is quite his dear affectionate old self once more, & charming hours we have enjoyed together. He simply *raves* about Cello-piece & is going to copy it & get it done in Liverpool privately … He has completely changed his style once more, & now it is far greater, larger, & still finer in form. He has certainly been influenced (as regards form) by my work, & himself asserts that his present period is entirely the outcome of the Cello piece. His last things are most original, chiefly of great unbroken flow, & he has whole movements that are 'aus einem Guss' [a perfect whole] like 1st chorus Matthäus Passion. He has written a piano sonata for me which I consider the *only* successful modern Klavier sonata … Then there is the Piano-quartette, simply gigantic in impression, *all* flow. The 1st movement (every instrument playing solo expresivo) rises & falls like a great SONG, the 2nd (a scherzo) is lively & beautiful & breaks out into a huge Dance-like climax at the end, melodic and rich. The slow movement I admire less, the flow is good but it is not strong inventively to my mind. 4th movement (Intermezzo) is splendid, delicate & pastoral & flowing & *ECHT* Scott.
>
> The Finale I consider bad in form, it being Flowing yet *very* much broken-up, however there are glorious melodic bits in it. The *whole* work is nothing less than gigantic, & would sound better than *any* previous chamber music work … Besides these is a 'Study for an English Requiem' merely a sketch for a big choral work he is about to begin. The sketch is unceasing melodic continuance. There is also a Cello piece that he calls privately 'Fürchterliche Eier für Cello & Klavier' [Frightful Eggs for Cello and Piano], it is inspired (title & music) by 'A Lot of Rot' & is a development of my piece in that the Cello never ceases for one moment from beginning

[68] This may relate to two items in the Grainger Museum catalogue: Study for a slow movement – No. 1 Andante; Study for a slow movement – No. 2 Largo, both on Lausanne-Vevey manuscript paper.

[69] *Bone of Contention*, p. 74.

to end, & that the flow is better & the form more consistent, but it is not perhaps so bedeutend [important].[70]

Hans Lüthy was one of two friends able to pull a few strings and arrange for Scott to meet Hans Richter, conductor of the Hallé Orchestra. Cyril played through his *Heroic Suite* on the piano to this 'very elusive gentleman', who consequently conducted the first English performance of any orchestral work of his, at Manchester in December 1901, and at Liverpool a month later. (O'Neill had met Richter in October 1897 and described him to Adine as 'quite charming – a nice fat simple old German!')[71] Cyril mentioned his own meeting with Richter in a letter to Balfour in November:

> My dear Balfour
> Thank you so much for sending me Palestrina. You do not know how stimmungsvell it made me – fancy your not appreciating him. He gives me ideas like anything. Let me know when you want it back I hope not soon though … Percy is getting on grandly I am so glad. He is playing my Sonata on the 25th at a Song Festival & then later on again. I have done no work at all hardly – I don't know what has come over me. I am usually so prolific. I am too well.
>
> I dined with Richter on Wednesday. He is a delightful old chap & very amusing indeed, awfully well disposed towards me. In L'pool he is going to move the Berlioz & put me in at the 2nd concert. So that is all in order. He talks of doing the work in Bradford & Leeds too.[72]

Just over a month later he wrote again:

> Thank you for your letter. You do not seem to be very bright & I can sympathise. For the last week I have been in the most awful Stimmung possible – if one's life was always this way it would hardly be worth living. As to the Suite,[73] well, that is not till tomorrow week. It might do you good to hear it. In fact I believe it would & by that time you will have got over your travels & feel on the go again most likely. However I am not going to persuade you. All I know that in my present Stimmung I am glad to see any dear friend & if you find after trying to work some time that you get no further then you had better come! I am going to London about the 27th. I shall take a room near Percy for a week so I hope to see you. I have written a jolly good Waltz [*An English Waltz*] suitable for P. & another song.[74]

[70] Letter from Grainger to Sandby, from 31 Gordon Place, Kensington, 27 September 1901. *The Farthest North of Humanness*, pp. 3–4.

[71] Letter from Norman to Adine Rückert, 27 October 1897, in Derek Hudson, *Norman O'Neill: A Life of Music* (Quality Press, 1945; rev. ed. Em Publishing, 2015), p. 27 (p. 30 rev. ed.). Seven years later Richter was to conduct the first performance of Elgar's First Symphony.

[72] Letter from Scott to Gardiner, 2 November 1901, from 27 Albert Road, Southport.

[73] *Heroic Suite* (Orchestral Suite No. 2), Op. 7, performed at Manchester on 12 December 1901 and at Liverpool on 14 January 1902. Scott himself conducted the first and last movements at Bournemouth on 19 November 1903, together with the Pastorale and March from his *English Suite*, Op. 6.

[74] 4 December 1901.

Gardiner did go to hear the suite, and Scott tried to persuade him to stay for its second performance, in Liverpool, two days later:

> Splendid that you come after all. But cannot I induce you to spend Friday with me in Liverpool. I could then show you my work & Bonnier goes to Paris that day & I am not off till Saturday. You would favour me greatly by doing that for then I shall not be alone. Why should you go to an hotel? ... Next year I contemplate a Symphony & am summoning all my energies for that ... Did you see the bad notice of Sonata in 'Times'. I am glad.[75]

The most important work to occupy Scott's attention in 1902 was his Second Symphony, which Henry Wood had programmed for the next season's Proms. He wrote to Gardiner:

> From what you say I am convinced that your Vtett[76] must be good. If you get doubtful about it send it here to me. For my own part my score of the Symphony [No. 2] is such a laborious one that it gets on but slowly. The slow movement is the one I am working on at present, the first movement not being composed yet although the ideas are more or less thought out. You will regard this certainly as the 'voluptuousness of purity' & as to polyphony it oversteps everything. The first cantilene is 56 bars in length. I hardly expect to have the whole Symphony done before the summer but I will try & get one movement done by Easter at least. I suppose you will go & hear my IVtett on Thursday next at Leighton House. It would be kind of you to write & let me know how it went.[77]

The following year the Sextet for piano and strings, Op. 26, was the work with which he seemed most satisfied. With the symphony nearing completion, he was calling on Gardiner, with his sharp critical musical brain that would spot anything amiss, to give the manuscript a thorough check before the orchestral parts were made:

> I am coming to London on the 11th & hope to see you about that time there & to hear anything you have done. The 6tet is by far the best chamber music I have done & harmonically is a great advance – only in 3 movements but I may add [another] for the next season Broadwood concert. In the mean time I want to begin the Requiem.[78] Forsyths are publishing the 6 pieces[79] & the 3 frivolous pieces & I expect them to be out soon. The [English] Waltz[80] appeared last Wednesday &

[75] 9 December [1901].

[76] Gardiner's String Quintet in C mi, first performed November 1903. Now lost/ destroyed, though the last movement was reworked *c.* 1936 by Grainger as *Movement for Strings* (Schott, 1949).

[77] Undated letter, from 129 Canning Street, Liverpool.

[78] Grainger had much earlier written to Sandby, on 27 September 1901: '"Study for an ENGLISH REQUIEM" merely a sketch for a big choral work he is about to begin'.

[79] Scott's *Six Pieces* for piano, Op. 4 (Forsyth, 1903), were 'dedicated to Professors Iwan Knorr and Lazzaro Uzielli in grateful remembrance of my student days'.

[80] *An English Waltz*, Op. 15 (Novello, 1903), was dedicated to Grainger. Adine O'Neill performed it in her second Promenade appearance, on 28 September 1906.

> the songs will be shortly. If you can perhaps correct the last two movements of the Symph. I should be glad before sending them to the copyist. The 1st are done & gone. Let me hear from you very shortly.

Grainger had taken up the rather flashy *English Waltz* the previous year when touring with Adelina Patti, playing it in many towns and bringing Scott's name before the public. 'Great enthusiasm after the Waltz – well-earned encore', Percy wrote to his mother after playing it in Newcastle-upon-Tyne.[81] Cyril followed it with a number of piano 'trifles' that became popular and, as he later wrote, 'did me both good and harm, in that on the one hand they made my reputation and on the other hand they killed my reputation as a composer of larger and more serious works'.[82] He was to some extent himself responsible, as he became very popular as a pianist at society functions. Eugene Goossens described him 'wearing a cravat which made him look like a good-looking reincarnation of Chopin, [an] exotic personality and lovable but aloof man [who] played his delicate piano works as no one else since has been able to play them'.[83] Scott was later to consider that none of his early orchestral works was satisfactory until the *Two Passacaglias on Irish Themes*, first performed in 1914.[84]

Balfour Gardiner, in contrast, was not someone who found composition easy, his self-critical nature always having the upper hand, and Scott suggested that they went away to the country, to the Cheshire village of Helsby, where between them they could thrash out these problems, with Cyril offering Balfour ideas when he was at a standstill. Cyril tentatively put the idea to his friend in his next letter:

> My dear old Balfour
> I had not a moment to write before – so busy have only just returned from London these last days – since then very hard work. Of London this: Wood will do Symphony in the Autumn – Booseys are printing the IVtet & two songs. Dairy & Yvonne of Brittany.[85] Richter (I hear from Forsyth) will do some recent work of mine at his concerts in London next season (Autumn). The [English] Waltz will appear in a fortnight. For it I get a royalty of 2d for 1st 300 then 4d. On the songs 3d which is very good as royalties go. I also saw Stanford who spoke of you & wants to do my Heroic Suite at the Royal College. Apart from that various singers are singing [my] songs & pianists are playing [my] piano pieces.
>
> Now as to work, dear old boy. I have used up your glorious Steigerung in the finale of a Piano Sextett which I am writing (I begun with the Finale). I have also written two good songs quite different from any I have done before & harmonically really good. I am working from morning till night till May & then return to London again.

[81] Letter from Percy to Rose Grainger, 9 October 1902, *The Farthest North of Humanness*, p. 11.

[82] *Bone of Contention*, p. 91.

[83] Eugene Goossens, *Overture and Beginners: A Musical Autobiography* (Methuen, 1951), pp. 94–5.

[84] *Bone of Contention*, p. 92.

[85] Piano Quartet, Op. 16 (Boosey, 1903); *Dairy Song* (dedicated to Quilter); and *Yvonne of Brittany* (Dowson), Op. 5 (Boosey 1903).

> I heard of some delightfully cheap farm houses in Helsby. Do let us live in the summer at two separate farm houses. It would be simply ripping & we could work like hell. Write & tell me about your new work etc. as soon as you can.[86]

He elaborated on his suggestion in his next letter, as Balfour, typically, was already showing some doubts as to the plan's worth:

> My dear Balfour,
> I was so pleased to get your letter – how delightful it will be in Helsby. But I want you to put yourself entirely in my hands. In the first place 6 weeks is not long enough. I want you to keep yourself absolutely free till Xmas. You must really do that. Your music is your first consideration & until you can get your ideas to go as they ought all else must be put aside. Why the distractions (non-musical alas) of Oxford? … Helsby is a lovely place. In your first letter you said 6 months with me would do you good. Now it has dwindled down to 6 weeks. You seem such a mixture of weakness & strength, one day great prospects, the next day chaos, lack of enthusiasm – logical thinking out (dangerous game) do take the bull by the horns & don't complain until you have done that, do place yourself in my hands. Study as it were with me & at any rate we will get your technique in order, I will give you ideas how to go on when you get stuck to the best of my ability & even if your inspiration is not as happy as it might be you will find very soon on these lines it will pick up. Do consider this prospect very carefully or if meditating upon it has the usual disastrous effect, then don't think about it but plunge into the water head first. We will take a week's holiday in September & go to London to hear the Symphony[87] & you to see your father & then you must come back either to rooms nearer Liverpool or again Helsby. With your life & your means it is utterly ridiculous that anything should prevent you.[88]

Things seemed more promising from the tone of Scott's next letter:

> Thank you for your letter & suggestions. I got those delightful cans alright & will return the hamper. Yes, the rooms are taken from June 15th … I am half way through a Finale for a string quartet – the waltz is selling well & I have another publisher on my track. The Sonata I hear & see was a great success played by Miss [Evelyn] Suart. The 9 pieces Forsyths are doing ought to be out soon …[89]

In May the sextet was performed at the Chelsea home of Mrs Lowrey, a society hostess well known to the Frankfurt Group. Indeed, in the early years of the century an *ad hoc* chorus that might consist of Scott, Quilter, Grainger, Gardiner, Sandby, Franckenstein, Frederic Austin, Gervase Elwes, and the painter and actor Ernest

[86] Undated letter, from 64 Canning Street, Liverpool.

[87] Symphony No. 2, Promenade concert on 25 August 1903, Queen's Hall Orchestra, cond. Henry Wood.

[88] 20 April 1903.

[89] 6 May 1903.

Thesiger[90] would meet at her house to try out Grainger's part-songs. From Chelsea Scott wrote to Gardiner:

> My dear old chap
> When are you coming up to town? I am simply longing to see you & I have all sorts of news to tell you. Everybody is mad about my new work & your glorious steigerung finds great favour. Miss Suart the little pianist who you saw & liked at the Broadwood Concert is awfully keen & wants to meet you. They are charming people. Dear old Francky is back in town & the Sextett is on the 26th here ... Metzlers want to take over & publish <u>all my works</u>. Sandby is back playing better than ever. I wrote a movement of a string IVtet did I tell you. My new work is as different to the last as you could wish. I saw Richter who is going to do my things next season because he will then have room for novelties. In ten minutes we have a rehearsal of 6tet. You ought to hear one you know before the performance. Now do come up, or at any rate write.[91]

The sextet[92] quite likely went through several revisions until it emerged as the Piano Quintet, because much later in life Scott wrote about that borrowed idea:

> There was a theme in a Piano Trio[93] of [Gardiner's] which I especially liked. 'Aw,' he said distainfully [*sic*], 'I hate the thing. I'll give it to you if you can make anything of it.' The theme is now incorporated in the Piano Quintet for which I was many years ago awarded the Carnegie Prize. Perhaps save for that theme I would never have received the award![94]

Thematic borrowings and mutual influences were quite common among the Group. Gardiner's *A Sailors' Piece* for piano (dedicated to Quilter) leans heavily on Grainger's *Gumsucker's March*. A tune 'cribbed' from Scott's early unperformed *Magnificat* was given a new lease of life in Grainger's *Mock Morris*.[95] Scott's *Victorian*

[90] Ernest Thesiger (1879–1961) met Scott at Mrs Lowrey's, and his music 'was a revelation to me, and I knew at once that I had found what I had been searching for in the way of music. Till then I had thought Wagner the last word in music, but now the possibility of a new language was hinted at.' See Thesiger, *Practically True* (Heinemann, 1927), reprinted in *Portrait of Percy Grainger*, p. 39.

[91] Undated letter (May 1903), from Queen's House, Cheyne Walk, Chelsea, home of Mrs Lowrey, a devoted admirer of Grainger, who, at her urging, had his first sexual experience with her (*Self-Portrait of Percy Grainger*, pp. 95–6).

[92] Performed 28 May 1903 in London with Grainger and Sandby among the performers. The violinist, Alice Liebmann, and Grainger were at Scott's house in Liverpool in October 1902.

[93] Surviving sketch, Frankfurt, August 1898. Like many of Gardiner's early works it was later lost/destroyed.

[94] 'The Late Balfour Gardiner and our Student Days: Some Reminiscences by Cyril Scott', *The Music Teacher*, September 1950. The award-winning work was the Piano Quintet No. 1, first performed in June 1920 and published in 1925.

[95] Bars 9–12. Lewis Foreman, 'Miscellaneous Works', in *The Percy Grainger Companion*, p. 138.

Waltz was built on a fragment by fellow student Thomas Holland-Smith. Grainger devoted considerable time to the 'free treatment' or revision of works by his colleagues. Scott's early piano sonata of 1901, dedicated 'to Percy Grainger as a token of intense admiration and love and in remembrance of the days of our youthful inspiration', in Percy's editorial hands became the shorter *Handelian Rhapsody*. Scott was often affected by Grainger's melodies, one example being the delicate *My Robin is to the Greenwood Gone*, whose principal tune emerges slightly transformed in the slow section of the first movement of Scott's Piano Concerto No. 1. (Scott follows Grainger's alteration to the very start of the 'Old English' tune so that the first two notes read G – G instead of the original E – G.)

It was the form of Scott's works that received the severest critical attack. In reviewing the first performance of the Piano Quintet, Edwin Evans commented on 'some lovely moments' but had some serious doubts about the structure:

> It is cast in one movement, which was rather unwise of Mr Scott. To unify a work that runs on continuously for over half an hour, to distribute points of emphasis and of repose so that the hearer's attention shall never flag, to show one mood growing logically out of another, and to make the last few pages seem not a mere finish but a conclusion – not a dismissal but an exit – all this demands organic architectural power, and it is precisely this power that Mr Scott most conspicuously lacks.[96]

The matter of structure and flow had come to a head with Scott's second symphony, which received its only performance under Henry Wood at the Proms on 25 August 1903. Scott's declared intention was 'to secure continuous flow, without a cadence from beginning to end of the movement', but, as *The Times* critic pointed out, he had set himself a difficult task, not merely 'of avoiding the cadence, but of making the avoidance necessary'. Robin Legge, music critic of *The Daily Telegraph* and an acquaintance of the Frankfurt Group, had some interesting observations to make on Scott in a letter to Roger Quilter on 31 August 1903:

> I don't agree that C. S.'s symph. is great & you know I'm level minded enough in these things. I am quite sure he will have to modify his idea of flow for flow's sake in instrumental music. That there is much that is astonishingly brilliantly good & beautiful of course I grant you, but the music does not seem to me to be abstract music – but to be, roughly speaking, a concourse of lovely, sweet & remarkably voluptuous – almost sensuous – sound. It is decadent rather than strong – exotic if you like, & magnificent, but 'great' is a very large expression. Every man may be & no doubt is influenced by Wagner – but C S adopts – half assimilates almost the actual texture of *Siegfried*, & there is a suspicion of mannerism in much of his harmony. After all, endless melody is a mannerism, an artificiality. Mind you, & believe me, I recognise as well as you all the good things C S says & I would not want published what I say here. I am sure C S himself, no fool, will see some of it himself as he grows in age and wisdom – if he can be kept away from petticoat influence. If not, then he'll be useless to the world & to himself, for he is not the

96 *The Sunday Times*, 13 June 1920. Aeolian Hall, London String Quartet and Evlyn Howard-Jones.

> strong man that Percy is though he is in a sense more purely musical. C S must develop his mental strength: he must live & live in this world, not in the fetid atmosphere of a crowd of mutual admirers & quasi courtiers. If he will, then he will by God's grace develop into the biggest – greatest – thing we have produced. There's my sentiments for your private delectation.

Unless Legge's comments were directed mainly towards the symphony's first movement, *Andante*, which is no longer extant, his concern with flow seems less important today with regard to the other three movements, which Scott revised as *Three Symphonic Dances*.[97] But one can agree with his description of 'voluptuous – almost sensuous – sound' in the luscious slow movement, a richness which was much later to find its counterpart in Grainger's Pastoral from his suite *In a Nutshell* (1915–17). Grainger was sufficiently impressed by the three dances to arrange them for two pianos in 1922 and to record the first for a Duo-Art piano roll with Cyril while he was in America.

* * * * *

With his more refined life style, Roger Quilter was probably the member of the Group with whom Scott had the least contact. But that is not to mean that there was any lack of friendship, as a letter of April 1908 shows:

> My dear old Roger
> I was so glad to get your sweet letter, & to hear you will soon be back again in town. I am longing to see something of you once more like in old times.
>
> My concert I think was certainly an artistic success especially so as all the notices were bad almost. The violin sonata is by far the best thing I have done.
>
> ... You asked me about Fauré. I love a lot of his things & met him personally in Paris two years ago.
>
> Do let me know when you return & we will have a 'vortrags abend['] of new works. I suppose you knew that Knorr is made Director now in place of old Schulz.
> Best love
> Ever yrs.[98]

More than mere friendship, there was a remarkable collective generosity among the Group. In July 1910 Grainger wrote to his Danish girlfriend, Karen Holten, a friend of Herman Sandby:

[97] Recorded on Chandos CHAN 10407, with Martyn Brabbins conducting the BBC Philharmonic. In the absence of the symphony's manuscript, it is difficult to determine the extent of Scott's revisions of the three movements, two of which he conducted himself at Birmingham in June 1907. If there were any, they may have been just a few judicious cuts. One similarly wonders whether his revision of *Disaster at Sea* (first performed 1933) as *Neptune* amounted to anything more than a change of title, since the *Titanic* programme is still very evident, even to the extent of a liner-motif, imitation fog-horn, Morse Code signals and clear statements of 'Nearer, my God, to Thee'.

[98] Letter from Scott to Quilter, 7 April 1908, from 274 Kings Road.

> Last night I met Cyril. He looks so notably younger and fresher again, and it was a pleasure to see him like that, and the firm Schott Söhne Mainz have made an excellent contract and are going to print his orchestral and instrumental works ... Only yesterday morning I was planning that if I make a lot of money this winter that I would give the money for publishing an orchestral work of Cyril's.[99]

Some of Grainger's works were also to be published by Schotts, and in February 1911 he was playing several pieces to Willy Strecker, the firm's representative. Cyril was present, and Percy wrote to Karen:

> The evening of the day before was so delightful ... We were all rarely [*sic*] happy. Cyril was so enthusiastic for me and of course infected Strecker by it, Cyril without a *spark* of jealousy, doesn't know it, completely abstractly enthused and delighted that I will be published by the same publisher as him ... Cyril looked splendid and is happy and fresh again.[100]

Grainger only found out later, as he told Sandby: 'Dear old Roger has been a friend indeed. It was he who fixed up Schotts for me, & he wants to pay for the expense of printing a few of my bigger scores'.[101] Quilter, in fact, offered to pay for the publication of Grainger's *Father and Daughter*. Percy himself was also generous, in directing some of his royalties towards Cyril when he was in more difficult financial circumstances.[102]

* * * * *

The music of the Frankfurt Group had its finest representation in the two series of concerts organised, financed and in part conducted by Balfour Gardiner in London's Queen's Hall in 1912 and 1913. Consisting almost exclusively of British music – with the exception of Borodin and Tchaikovsky's Piano Concerto No. 1, in which Grainger was the soloist – and with a good number of premieres and first London performances of works by Holst and Vaughan Williams, it was an excellent showcase for Grainger, whose works appeared in seven of the eight concerts. Each of the other members of the Group was represented, and Scott had his *English Dance* and *Fair Helen of Kirkconnel* (soloist Frederic Austin) performed in the first series.[103] These works came under Gardiner's close scrutiny – he was to conduct them. He wrote to Grainger on 3 May 1911: 'I looked at Cyril's *Scherzo* going home in

[99] Letter from Grainger to Karen Holten, 15 July 1910, *The Farthest North of Humanness*, p. 375.

[100] Letter from Grainger to Karen Holten, 27 February 1911, ibid., pp. 405–6.

[101] Letter from Grainger to Herman Sandby, 10 August 1911, ibid., p. 419.

[102] Eileen Dorum, *Percy Grainer: The Man behind the Music*, p. 62.

[103] The first London performance of *The Ballad of Fair Helen of Kirkconnel* (dedicated to Frederic Austin) was given at the Bechstein Hall on 5 June 1905, with Austin the soloist and a young Thomas Beecham conducting. The *English Dance* was the third of *Three Dances*, Op. 20.

the train last night. Even that – every note of it will have to be rescored.' As for *Helen of Kirkconnel*, three days later he was writing: 'Austin is staying with me; & we have been rescoring Cyril's "Helen". I have never come across a work with such possibilities of instrumentation. Needless to say Cyril has missed them all.' The planning of these concerts was undoubtedly a most exciting time for the Group, often meeting at Balfour's house with such others as Austin, Bax, and Holst also present. At the time of the first series Scott was, in Grainger's words, 'a sea of enthusiasm and fire'.[104]

Also well represented in the series was Frederick Delius, around whom all the members of the Frankfurt Group, with the exception of Scott, were to gravitate. In March 1907, possibly at the request of Henry Wood, Scott had written to Delius[105] suggesting some accommodation in Chelsea for when he visited England the next month from his home in France. In April Delius wrote home to his wife, Jelka, 'Cyril Scott I have also seen & he is really very nice.'[106] Three days later he wrote of meeting Grainger, whom he considered 'more gifted than Scott & less affected'.[107] On 23 July the critic Robin Legge wrote to Delius:

> Balfour Gardiner tells me he is going over to see you – also Cyril Scott. The latter is devoted now only to 'occultism' – & is seen everywhere with a black Yogi who is supposed to hold in his head all the Secrets of the Universe. Scott is a whole-hogger in the matter.[108]

Scott attended Fritz Cassirer's performance of Delius's *Appalachia* in Queen's Hall in November and afterwards wrote a letter of self-centred appreciation that was hardly likely to endear him to Delius, saying that 'although my own productions may not be over sympathetic to you – yet I hope that will not lead you to think I can not rise to the beauties of yours!' He added, with reference to an earlier concert when Delius's Piano Concerto had been given, 'I could not help feeling [it] was not an adequate expression of yourself.' Unlike the remainder of the Group, he was not to make trips to visit Delius in France.

The outbreak of World War 1 terminated plans for further Balfour Gardiner concerts, and Grainger's departure to America, where he was essentially to remain for the rest of his life, might have put a seal on the activities of the Frankfurt Group. But they continued after the war, if on a less frequent basis. In 1920 and 1921 Scott made his only visit to America and Canada, performing his piano concerto in Philadelphia on 5 November 1920 with Stokowski conducting (a fact he omits from both autobiographies).[109] In New York he met the Graingers, and Percy and Cyril seized the

[104] Letter from Grainger to Karen Holten, 15 March 1912, *The Farthest North of Humanness*, p. 451.

[105] Delius came to England in April 1907 to make arrangements for the performance of his Piano Concerto in October at the Promenade Concerts under Henry Wood.

[106] Lionel Carley, *Delius: A Life in Letters*, vol. 1 (Scolar Press, 1983), p. 285 n. 3.

[107] Ibid., p. 287.

[108] Ibid., p. 295.

[109] He played the concerto in Vienna in 1922.

opportunity to record for the Duo-Art system a piano roll of Scott's *Symphonic Dance No. 1* arranged by Grainger for four hands.

Tragedy was soon to strike, with Rose Grainger's death by suicide in New York in April 1922. 'Mother always loved Cyril & Roger', Percy had written, and during Cyril's Frankfurt days Rose had quite likely filled the role of surrogate mother while he was abroad. Indeed, he wrote in his second autobiography that he would always remember her with great affection, and that 'she treated me almost like a second son until her tragic death'. On her death it was even reported in the papers that her will stipulated that on Percy's death the estate was to be divided between Cyril and her sister, Clara Aldridge.[110] Percy had been away when the tragedy occurred; while returning by train to New York on 3 May he wrote to Balfour Gardiner as 'the only reliable one I can turn to for so many different things involved', giving him clear instructions regarding his unpublished works 'should my body break under this strain'.[111] Over a month later he made a new will, leaving a sum to his aunt Clara and the residue of the estate to Gardiner, adding that should Balfour predecease him the estate would pass to Cyril.[112] Irresponsible and possibly inaccurate reporting in the press at the time of his mother's death had greatly disturbed Grainger, but as a consequence of this tragedy something else threatened to break up his friendship with Cyril. With his interest in spiritualism Cyril had suggested to Percy the possibility of making contact with his mother through a medium. Grainger's reply was unequivocal:

> It has made me very wretched that you have tried to deliver this 'message' to me in spite of what I wrote you of not wishing to receive any such messages thru a 3rd person, because of my instinctive feelings about such things & my lack of belief in spirit messages. It is not that I prize my disbelief higher than yr belief. On the contrary, I admire you deeply & yr religious nature & for the time you have devoted to these theories – yr beliefs being what they are. But I do not share yr beliefs & I cannot & will not have these things forced upon me. To receive a message that purports to come from my adored mother, of the genuineness of which you are convinced but of the genuineness of which I am not convinced, is the greatest possible agony to me … This matter will break up our old & lovely friendship if you do not exercise tolerance with my disbelief just as I exercise tolerance with yr belief.[113]

Fortunately their friendship was too deeply rooted; Scott meant much to Grainger, as it seems he had to his mother. Percy has written: 'Mother sometimes said to me, "If you should die, I would try not to be too desperate. I should devote myself to the career of some other great composer, such as Cyril."'[114]

In August 1922 Grainger made a visit to the Continent, with some folk-song collecting in Denmark. By chance he bumped into Gardiner, who had been staying

[110] *The Daily Telegraph*, 24 May 1922, as quoted in Dorum, *Percy Grainger: The Man behind the Music*, p. 132.

[111] *The All-Round Man*, pp. 55–60.

[112] Ibid., p. 56 n. 1.

[113] 21 October 1922, ibid., p. 62.

[114] *Self-Portrait of Percy Grainger*, p. 50.

with Delius, and together they travelled through Norway. It was their first meeting for eight years, with Grainger later declaring that Balfour had been the only one of his friends willing to go anywhere with him after his mother's death. In December Gardiner, Grainger and Quilter met in London to hear the first performance of Bax's First Symphony.

The Group's last collective flowering came in July 1929, when a festival of British music was held at Harrogate. Planned by Basil Cameron, conductor of the Harrogate Municipal Orchestra, with assistance from Grainger, this time it was far from representative of British music in general, with the notable absence of works by Elgar and Vaughan Williams. It was in fact a blatant showcase for the Frankfurt Group, all of whom performed except for one absentee: Balfour Gardiner was then becoming disillusioned as a composer and let it be known that he would not attend, writing to Grainger on 26 May: 'I have been now telling you for years that I dislike music, & that it worries me & depresses me & I cannot understand why you do not believe me.' Sixteen days later he added a sad coda: 'Music has been the best thing I have known in life. Like youth, it has left me.'

The programme for the festival is worth listing.

July 24
O'Neill: Festal Prelude *The White Rock*, conducted by O'Neill
Delius: *A Song before Sunrise*, conducted by Cameron
Scott: Piano Concerto (No. 1), soloist Scott, conducted by Cameron
Quilter: *I arise from dreams of thee*, f.p. soloist Mark Raphael, conducted by Quilter
O'Neill: *Alice in Wonderland* – ballet music, conducted by O'Neill
Grainger: *Jutish Medley*, conducted by Cameron
Scott: piano solos *Pierrot triste, Water-Wagtail, Pastorals No. 3, Souvenir de Vienne, An English Waltz*, soloist Scott
Quilter: songs *The Jealous Lover, It was a lover and his lass, Weep you no more, To Althea from Prison*, soloist Mark Raphael
Gardiner: *Shepherd Fennel's Dance*, conducted by Cameron

July 25
Arne: Overture in B♭
Delius: *On Hearing the First Cuckoo in Spring, Summer Night on the River*
Quilter: *A Children's Overture*, conducted by Quilter
Scott: Scena for soprano and orchestra, *Rima's Call to the Birds*, f.p. (orchestral version)[115] soloist Gertrude Johnson, conducted by Cameron
Bax: *Romantic Overture*
Grainger: *Hill Song No. 2*, conducted by Cameron, *Spoon River*
Herbert Bedford: tone poem *Hamadryad*
Quilter: *Three English Dances*, conducted by Quilter
Scott: Songs, soloist Gertrude Johnson
Warlock: *Capriol Suite*

[115] *Rima's Call to the Birds* was first heard at the Wigmore Hall, 4 May 1927, with Gertrude Johnson and the Brosa String Quartet.

July 26
Purcell arr. Hurlstone: Suite for Strings in C
Holbrooke: *The Birds of Rhiannon*
Unspecified aria sung by Frank Phillips
Scott: 'Dance of the Citizens' from the ballet *The Short-Sighted Apothecary*, conducted by Scott
Leslie Heward: *Nocturne* for small orchestra
Grainger: *Youthful Rapture*, soloist Beatrice Harrison, conducted by Cameron
[Gibbons arr. Fellowes: *Fantasia*, planned but not played]
[Byrd arr. Terry: *The leaves be green*, planned but not played]
Frederic Austin: Suite *The Insect Play*, conducted by Austin
Cecil Milner: Tone poem *In a Pine Forest*
German: 'Bourrée and Gigue' from *Much Ado about Nothing*

From now on meetings of members of the Group were to be much less frequent. The ever generous Gardiner took O'Neill and Frederic Austin to Italy and Yugoslavia in April 1931, meeting Franckenstein in Munich. In July 1936 Grainger, now married, went with his wife, Ella, and Roger Quilter to the Dolmetsch concerts at Haslemere. In September, Percy and Ella, Cyril and Balfour went on holiday together in France, meeting again in October at Balfour's Dorset house at Fontmell Hill, when Cyril's *Festival Overture* was down for performance at Bournemouth with Balfour's *Shepherd Fennel's Dance*. Cyril's and Grainger's scores had been 'the profoundest influences at the most impressionable period' of his life, Balfour confessed in a letter to Percy. That year Grainger wrote to Quilter enquiring whether he would go with him to hear Scott's *Ode to Great Men* at Norwich in September.[116] He urged: 'It seems to me so important for composers of the same generation to boast each other, appear in togetherness & hear each other's works together.' In November, from Sweden, Percy was asking Quilter for tickets for two nights of his opera *Julia*, which was to be presented in December at Covent Garden.[117] 'I am asking Cyril to come with us one night', he added. Scott went and thought it a 'winner'.[118]

After World War 2 for about two and a half years Ella Grainger gave Cyril the use of a cottage in Pevensey Bay, in Sussex, and in October 1946 Gardiner saw him there for the last time. He wrote to Percy: 'I enjoyed seeing Cyril at Pevensey. I took a friend with me, and Cyril gave him some pills & five-finger exercises. He recommended me to take molasses out of a Silo.'[119] In his last years Grainger devoted much energy towards his Museum, in which he amassed a treasure trove of exhibits principally of the Frankfurt Group – their correspondence, their music and even such things as samples of their clothing, pressing all his friends for contributions

[116] 24 September 1936, Basil Maine, London Philharmonic Orchestra, Heathcote Statham conducting.

[117] British Music Drama Opera Co. Ltd, London Symphony Orchestra, conducted by Albert Coates.

[118] Letter from Scott to Quilter, 4 December 1936, quoted in Langfield, *Roger Quilter: His Life and Music*, p. 91.

[119] Letter from Gardiner to Grainger, 27 December 1946. Gardiner–Grainger correspondence in the Grainger Museum.

to his 'hoard-house'. To meet one particular request, Cyril even had a suit specially made to match an old photo for a display in the Museum.[120] As one last act of kindness, Ella Grainger wrote out Cyril's Second String Quartet, which was published by Elkin in 1957, in her own neat manuscript, a task that took three months. 'There I was', she wrote to Scott from New York in October 1957:

> unskilled, pushing an unwilling steel nib onto a glazed paper, the India ink drying on the nib before it reached the paper ... But I was glad to sit at it as much as I could, away from the hurly burly of too much housekeeping and such. Now it is over I miss it. There were some beautiful passages in it, too, that from time to time Percy played on the piano in order to find out if we were Oright about some of the chords. And the swirl of melody in the last movement was enchanting.

The quartet was 'Dedicated to Percy and Ella Grainger'. Writing to Scott in August 1954, Grainger had described it as 'a stunning work'.

O'Neill was the first of the Group to die, on 3 March 1934, aged fifty-eight. Gardiner was next, on 28 June 1950, aged seventy-two. Quilter, suffering at the end from mental illness, died on 21 September 1953 at seventy-five. Percy and Cyril, each with their own individual approaches to health, whether it be vigorous exercise or health cures, outlived the others, with Percy dying from cancer on 20 February 1961 aged seventy-eight, and Cyril living to the fine age of ninety-one, dying on 31 December 1970.

It was once a commonplace for people to say that the days of their youth or their school days were the happiest of their lives; for Cyril Scott this may well have been true of his time at Frankfurt. The love he showed for 'this beautiful city' and the pleasure he had in revisiting it; the deep affection he had for two of his professors, which had showed in the sorrow of their parting;[121] the excitement of recognition as a composer which came his way in those early years; and, perhaps above all, the strong lasting friendships that began at this time – all these brought a happiness that he was probably never to find again. No doubt with much feeling and Presidential pride – and no little humour – he might have claimed: 'Ich bin ein Frankfurter.'

[120] See illustrations in my *H. Balfour Gardiner* (Cambridge University Press, 1984), p. 215.

[121] 'There were tears in [Knorr's] eyes when he bade me farewell'; and, 'I suffered acutely when I came to take leave of Herr Uzielli'. Both *Bone of Contention*, p. 67.

2

Cyril Scott, Debussy and Stravinsky

RICHARD PRICE

SCOTT'S REPUTATION

DURING the heyday of his fame, between 1905 and 1925, Cyril Scott enjoyed an international reputation as a musical modernist, to a greater extent than any of his English contemporaries. Throughout his lifetime he was probably better known, and certainly more highly esteemed, abroad, particularly in France and Germany, than in his own country. This situation arose in the first place from personal contacts. His composition teacher at Frankfurt, Iwan Knorr, was greatly respected, and continued to speak with admiration and affection for his one-time student.[1] Scott also enjoyed the friendship and patronage of the poet Stefan George, a major figure in German literature, and to whose influence was due the premiere of Scott's First Symphony, at Darmstadt in 1900. Meanwhile, in Austria he benefited from the admiration of Alma Mahler (the wife, then widow, of the great composer), who greatly admired the Violin Sonata of 1908 and secured performances of some of his orchestral works in Vienna.[2] Of Scott's friendship with his French contemporaries Debussy and Ravel I shall speak below.

In England, in contrast, his major works were largely forgotten after their not very frequent premieres. But this was balanced by the popularity of his short piano pieces among those who took an interest in the latest musical developments.[3] These pieces had the great advantage that most of them were easy to play, while the piano pieces being written at this time by Debussy and Ravel were too difficult for amateur pianists.[4] Scott's piano music is likely to have played a major role in popularising the 'new harmony' that (with the political help of World War 1) brought to an end the dominance of English musical life by nineteenth-century German Romanticism. But though this emphasis on Scott the modernist stimulated interest in his music while he was still a member of the *avant-garde*, it did his standing no good when, from the

[1] It was due to the influence partly of Knorr and partly of his fellow student Percy Grainger that Scott was so early put on the path of musical innovation. In contrast, his London contemporaries Vaughan Williams and John Ireland developed their distinctive idioms more slowly, since they were held back by their teacher, Charles Villiers Stanford, who thought that the language of music had reached its final perfection with Brahms.

[2] See Scott, *Bone of Contention* (Aquarian Press, 1969), pp. 76 and 136–7.

[3] Gerald Cumberland, a noted journalist of the period and a keen champion of musical modernism, tells in his *Set Down in Malice* (Grant Richards, 1919), p. 262: 'In pre-war days I very rarely let a week go by without playing something of his.'

[4] Note a remark made to Scott by the wife of George Bernard Shaw: 'G. B. S. spends most of his free evenings playing your things. He *can* play them!' – as narrated in Cyril Scott, *My Years of Indiscretion* (Mills & Boon, 1924), p. 232.

mid-1920s, musical fashions changed drastically. Scott's music now sounded dated. Those with an interest in modern music turned their gaze elsewhere, to newer gods.

Particularly damaging to Scott's reputation was the sobriquet he had acquired of the 'English Debussy'. For one thing, Debussy's standing was not at all as high a century ago as it is today. He was looked upon as an eccentric with an exquisite but limited personal style, whose work lay outside the main tradition of European music, of which Richard Strauss was seen as the leading living representative. Debussy, moreover, died in 1918, and his later works were generally regarded as evidence of decline – a view that Scott himself shared and which has only been rejected under the influence of Messiaen, Boulez and others since World War 2. If the title the 'English Debussy' was originally no more than a piece of pigeon-holing by people who knew little about Debussy and still less about Scott, it came to typify Scott as a marginal figure, belonging to a now-closed chapter in the history of music, and more of an imitator than an innovator. The relation of Scott to Debussy, both the man and the music, requires our close attention.

SCOTT AND DEBUSSY

We know from Scott's autobiographical writings (*My Years of Indiscretion* and *Bone of Contention*) that he and Debussy were acquaintances throughout the decade preceding World War 1. In this period Scott spent much of the year touring abroad, and when in Paris he was regularly Debussy's guest. Debussy was shy and taciturn, and Scott was careful what he said to him, and which of his own works he played to him – notably (as he tells us) the Violin Sonata, the (First) Piano Sonata, and the *Deuxième suite*, which, indeed, he dedicated to the older man. Debussy was impressed by the free-flowing arabesques and interweaving lines so typical of Scott's music, and agreed to write some words of judicious praise for the use of Scott's publishers. These run as follows:[5]

> Cyril Scott is one of the rarest artists of the present generation. His rhythmical experiments, his technique, even his style of writing, may at first sight appear strange and disconcerting. Inflexible severity, however, compels him to carry out to the full his particular system of esthetics, and his only.
>
> The music unfolds itself somewhat after the manner of those Javanese rhapsodies which, instead of being confined within traditional forms, are the outcome of imagination displaying itself in innumerable arabesques. And the incessantly changing aspects of the inner melody are an intoxication for the ear – are, in fact, irresistible. All these qualities are more than sufficient to justify confidence in this musician, so exceptionally equipped, although quite young.

Debussy's insistence that Scott's 'system of esthetics' was 'his only' is important evidence that the great man himself did not consider Scott his disciple.[6] Indeed, the

[5] I take them from the cover of *Handelian Rhapsody*, published in 1909.

[6] See too *My Years of Indiscretion*, p. 103: Debussy told Scott (in the early 1910s) that their styles were quite different.

degree of his influence on Scott has often been exaggerated.[7] It is clear from what Scott wrote about Debussy in his autobiographical writings, and also in his *Music: Its Secret Influence throughout the Ages*, that he respected, but did not worship, the older man, whose music he found delicate and refined to excess.[8] And like other English composers of his generation, such as John Ireland, he was unaffected by what seem to us now to be the most significant aspects of Debussy's style: his eschewing of romantic rhetoric, his intricate counterpoint (even when writing for the piano) and his innovations in musical structure. What impressed everyone at the time, and what influenced so many younger composers, was Debussy's harmony, partly its seductive and exotic atmosphere, but still more its 'non-functional' character – its use of modulations to create atmosphere, as local points of colour, rather than to serve musical structure (or so it was perceived at the time).

Two forms of non-traditional modulation were particularly noted in Debussy's music and adopted by his imitators. One was the prominence in many of his works of chromatic modulation, where adjacent chords or bars are in unrelated keys and movement from one to another depends on semitonal shifts with a single note or two remaining unchanged as an anchor. Frequent use of this device within the same piece or movement serves to destroy the sense of a home key to which return can be expected. Ex. 2.1 provides an example from Debussy's *Cloches à travers les feuilles* (*Images* for Piano II. 1, of 1907). Scott used this same device with his typical verve and lack of restraint in his early maturity. The effect in his First Piano Sonata (1909) is of excessive restlessness. But in the works that followed, he often swings backwards and forwards between two or three unrelated harmonies, creating a mesmeric effect of near-stasis. One example comes in *The Garden of Soul-Sympathy* (*Poems* for piano, 2), where there is alternation between three harmonies, with B as the note that links them (Ex. 2.2). This is the classic manner of the works that won Scott renown as a leading modernist in the 1910s. At the same time, the rhythm of Scott's music was equally innovative. There are many pages of Scott where every bar has a different length, and there is no sense of a constant rhythmic pulse. This combination of fluid harmony and fluid rhythm produces music that surges and ebbs in a continuous flow, typically reserving cadential resolution to the very end of a work or movement.[9]

A different form of modulation, though similar in its disruptive effect on the sense of a key, is the shifting of every note of a complex chord up or down the same interval. This was already familiar from the use of pure whole-tone harmony, as in Dargomyzhsky's *The Stone Guest* of 1872; indeed, in whole-tone harmony no other form of modulation is possible. The effect is monotonous, and it requires subtle and varying textures to preserve musical interest (as is achieved in Debussy's *Preludes* I. 2, *Voiles*). It is when the harmony is more complex that this device becomes truly

[7] For instance, by Cecil Gray in his *A Survey of Contemporary Music* (Humphrey Milford, 1924), p. 251: 'Cyril Scott provides us with imitation Debussy.' Yet Gray was one of the most perceptive critics of his day.

[8] See *My Years of Indiscretion*, p. 105; *Bone of Contention*, pp. 127–8; and *Music: Its Secret Influence throughout the Ages*, expanded edition (Rider & Co., 1950), pp. 78–82.

[9] For perceptive comment on this aspect of Scott's music see Sarah Collins, *The Aesthetic Life of Cyril Scott* (Boydell Press, 2013), pp. 183–91.

Ex. 2.1 Debussy, *Cloches à travers les feuilles*, bars 14–19

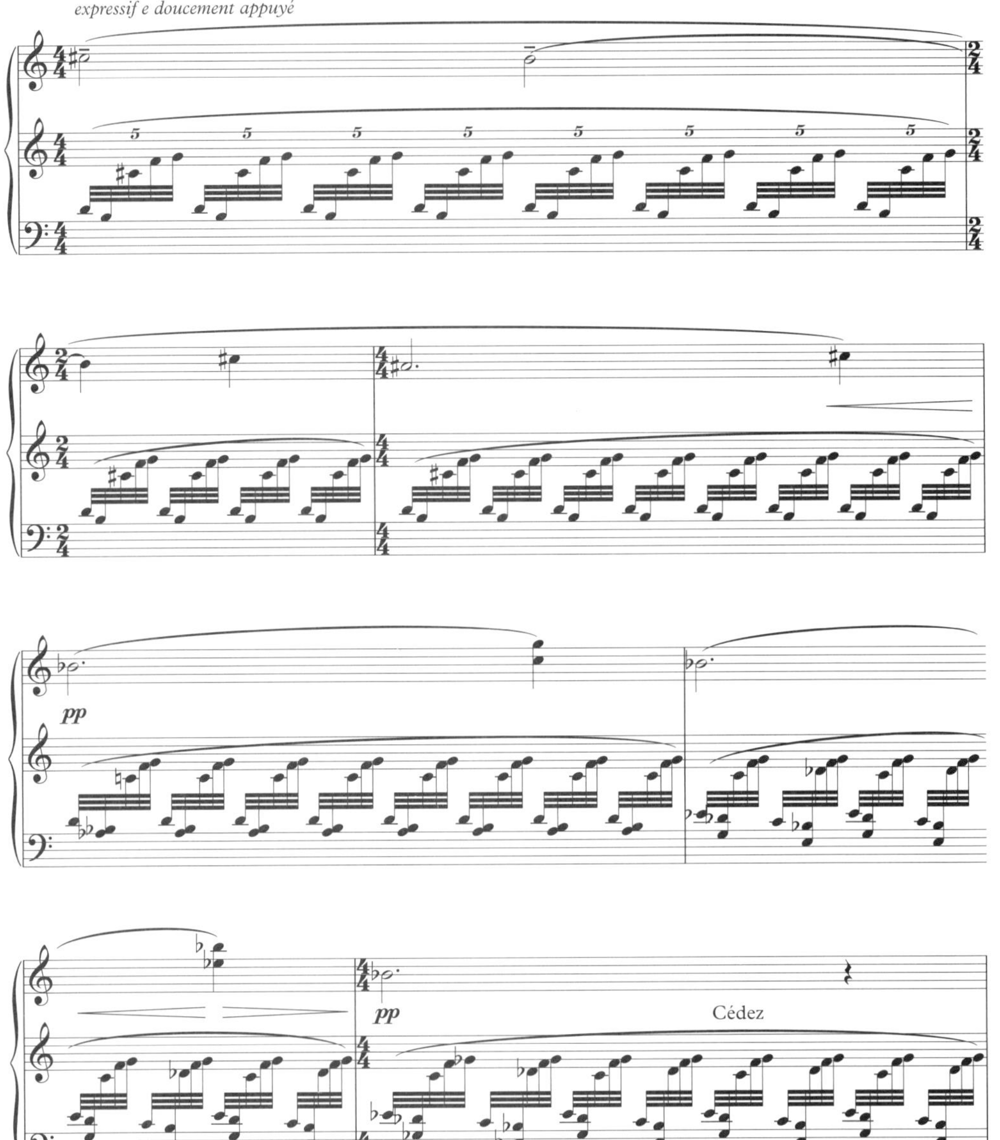

Ex. 2.2 Scott, *Poems*, p. 10 last two bars, and p. 11 first line

effective. There are some examples in late Liszt, as also in Mussorgsky, but it was Debussy who made the most effective use of this device, as in the opening bars of *Et la lune descend sur le temple qui fut* (*Images* II. 2) (Ex. 2.3). Distinctive of Debussy's creation of such sequences is the subtlety and restraint he exhibits, in contrast (for example) with the crudity of the comparable passages in the contemporary Russian composer Vladimir Rebikov. This subtlety was not lost on Scott, whose use of this device is manifestly indebted to Debussy, as in the bars given below of *By the Waters of the Nile* (No. 2 of *Egypt*, 1913) (Ex. 2.4).[10]

It was the frequency of harmony reminiscent of Debussy in Scott's music, and this alone, that led him to be called the English Debussy. But it does not follow automatically that he was a mere imitator of the older man, and the extent of his debt needs careful investigation. As noted above, Scott's appreciation of Debussy was limited, and this must have restricted the amount he could learn from him. As for the development of his own harmonic style, the breakthrough occurred in 1902, notably in his *Two Poems* for voice and piano, Op. 24.[11] Typical is the sequence for piano alone that opens the first of them (*Voices of Vision*), with its rapid and continuous chromatic modulations (Ex. 2.5).

Now, it happens that it was around this time, as Scott narrates in *My Years of Indiscretion*, that he made his very first acquaintance with the music of Debussy, when he spent an evening perusing the vocal score of *Pelléas et Mélisande*.[12] This

[10] My copy of this work was printed in Kiev, together with most of Scott's suites for piano, in 1930 – interesting evidence of his continuing fame in eastern Europe.

[11] These are the songs, dedicated to Mr and Mrs Robin Legge and published in 1903, that Scott mentions in *My Years of Indiscretion* (p. 92) as having been written soon after the premiere of *Heroic Suite* in December 1901. Contrast to them the major piano work of 1901, the Sonata in D (of which an abridged version was published as *Handelian Rhapsody* in 1909), which is firmly diatonic, with only incidental chromaticisms.

[12] *My Years of Indiscretion*, pp. 65–6 (from which the quotation below is taken). Scott does not provide a date, but from the context this appears to be 1902, as stated by

Ex. 2.3 Debussy,(3) *Et la lune descend sur le temple qui fut*, first three bars

Ex. 2.4 Scott, *Egypt*, p. 5, third line, first four bars

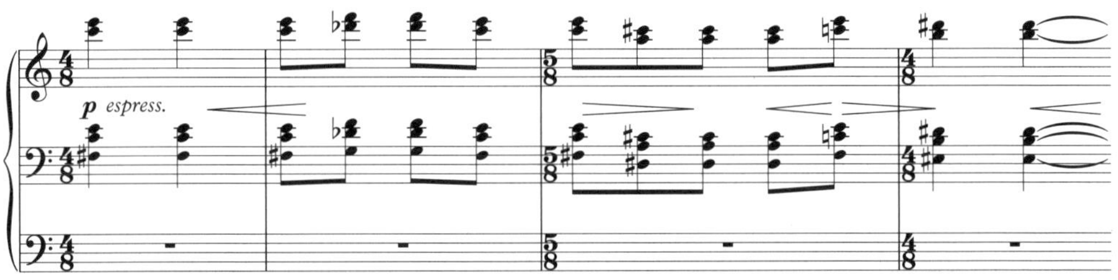

work is saturated with chromatic modulations and non-functional harmony. But before we identify it as the catalyst that transformed Scott's style, three facts must be taken into account. First, these songs (as Ex. 2.5 illustrates) do not sound in the least like *Pelléas*. Second, it is quite possible that they were composed before Scott's discovery of Debussy. And third, what impressed Scott in the Debussy work was not its particular vein of chromaticism (which he found more curious than satisfying), but its modal harmony. To quote his own words:

> Here was the very Pre-Raphaelite atmosphere I had dreamed of, and to a certain extent already created in my own compositions. True, there was to me a flavour of something exotic, which I naturally did not feel in my own music, and which struck me more by its strangeness than by its absolute beauty.

Scott then narrates how, when he heard the opera on a visit to Paris 'a year or two later' (probably in 1904), he found it mannered and monotonous. He concludes, 'I like it on the whole the least of all his compositions.' None of this suggests that his first (and very brief) acquaintance with Debussy's music in 1902 was a transformative experience. It may well be that he followed it up by exploring his piano music, but none of the piano music that Debussy had published by this date was as advanced in idiom as *Pelléas*. We may conclude that the characteristic harmony of Scott's early maturity, with its reliance on constant chromatic modulation, was his own invention. Once he had embarked on this path, Debussy was an encourage-

Collins, *The Aesthetic Life*, p. 83. Scott's first acquaintance with the music of Ravel, which may have influenced him more, occurred only later.

Ex. 2.5 Scott, *Two Poems* for voice and piano, Op. 24, p. 3, first line

ment and an example, as were other contemporaries, such as Ravel, but of none of these was Scott a mere imitator.

This is not just a matter of chronology. The fact is that Scott's music only rarely sounds like Debussy's.[13] The diaphanous sound of Debussy, and the evocation of the external world – the world of nature but also the worlds of ethnic music and the music hall – are very different from the mood and affinities of Scott, with its saturated harmony and esoteric atmosphere, its suggestion of joss-sticks and oriental meditation. Characteristic of Scott's music, amid all the surge and afflatus deriving from late Romanticism, is an inner detachment, attributable partly to the oriental influences he sought out, and partly to a certain aloofness or dispassion in his temperament, going together with his intense intellectual curiosity. His music reveals a spiritual aristocrat, akin to Stefan George, the German aesthete and sage who made so strong an impression on him during his adolescence.[14]

SCOTT AND STRAVINSKY

While the similarities between Scott and Debussy have always been noted, and indeed exaggerated, Scott's music has never been thought of as remotely akin to that of Igor Stravinsky. The influence of *The Rite of Spring* on the 'Barbaric Dance' with which Scott's ballet *Karma* of 1924 opens is obvious, but this was only a fleeting imitation, arising from the scenario at this particular point in the ballet. Indeed, most people would think of Scott and Stravinsky as polar opposites. For Scott's music as I described it above – floating and curving, to the extent of seeming invertebrate to those who dislike it – does not at first glance have anything in common with the sharp, abrupt rhythms of *Petrushka* or *The Rite of Spring*. Percy Grainger used to claim that Scott's rhythmical experiments had influenced Stravinsky, but this claim has been ignored or dismissed.[15] Yet there is a kinship between them, and there is evidence that at a crucial stage of his development Stravinsky knew and admired the music of Scott.

The key evidence is to be found in Scott's volume of memoirs *My Years of Indiscretion*, where he describes a visit he paid to Stravinsky at his home in Clarens

[13] An example is the orchestral *Aubade*, Op. 77 (1911).

[14] See Collins, *The Aesthetic Life*, pp. 52–67, and the relevant chapters in Scott's autobiographies.

[15] See John Bird, *Percy Grainger* (Oxford University Press, 1999), p. 67. Bird himself is sceptical of Grainger's claim.

Ex. 2.6 Stravinsky, *Rite of Spring*, first nine bars, bassoon line

in Switzerland. He does not provide a date, but he does relate that Stravinsky was at the time working on *Le Rossignol*, which places the visit in late 1913 or early 1914; a precise date of 23 October 1913 is suggested by an extant piano score of *The Rite of Spring* given to Scott and signed by Stravinsky on this day. To quote Scott's own words (pp. 204–5):

> It was while staying with the Darvell family at Clarens that I made the acquaintance of Stravinsky, and spent a long evening with him at his apartment. His reception of me was most cordial, and his appreciation of such works of mine as he knew exceedingly generous. It was not long before he took out the Piano Sonata and played me what he considered to be the best passages. 'This is all very kind of you' I said at length, 'but I would much rather hear something of yours.' He then showed me part of the 'Rossignol' on which he was at work; also portions of the 'Sacre du Printemps'.

This is significant in that it makes it highly probable that Stravinsky was a keen admirer of Scott's Piano Sonata (published in 1909) at the very time, from 1911 to 1913, when he was composing *The Rite of Spring*. The two works share a sense of adventure, of exhilaration, and also (it could be said) a certain inner coldness. Their musical language, in both harmony and accentuation, is utterly different; and yet there is a common element. *The Rite* begins with a celebrated bassoon solo, one of the great defining moments in twentieth-century music (Ex. 2.6).

This sequence is built up by the free growth and diminution of its motif, generating an irregular rhythm (and irregular barring) as it proceeds on its way. This is precisely the way in which rhythmic irregularity occurs in Scott's Piano Sonata – not rhythmic innovation as an end in itself, but the generation of rhythmic irregularity through the freedom with which melodic motifs expand and contract. Compare to the opening of *The Rite* a melodic line from one of the pages of the Scott Sonata (Ex. 2.7).

It was this liberation of motivic development from the straightjacket of a regular rhythmic pulse, even more than his harmony, that was Scott's great contribution to the language of music; it was in its time truly revolutionary. To say that Scott anticipated Stravinsky is not to say that Stravinsky 'imitated' Scott. Great composers do not operate in this way. Scott himself was a modest man, and is unlikely ever to have made any such claim, or to have believed that such a claim could be made. But

Ex. 2.7 Scott, Piano Sonata, p. 10, bars 2–15, melodic line only

what, surely, we are permitted to surmise is that Stravinsky, at the time when he was embarking on his own epoch-making rhythmic experiments, found encouragement, and a forerunner, in the cardinal feature of Scott's most innovative work.

The notion that a minor composer could have exerted any degree of influence on one of the most original works in the history of music will appear to some to be impudent and absurd. But one must distinguish two different ways in which the history of music can be analysed and narrated. An historian of music may restrict himself to a limited repertoire of great works that have never ceased to be models and inspirations. Or he can hunt out developments and influences wherever they are to be found, often in works that are quite forgotten (and sometimes deservedly forgotten). What one must not do is treat the acknowledged masterpieces as if they exist on some exalted height, untouched by all the eddies and crosscurrents going on below. Innovators like Erik Satie and Charles Ives have their place in the history of music, and Cyril Scott is be counted among their number.

3

Cyril Scott and the BBC

LEWIS FOREMAN

FROM the beginning the BBC operated a civil-service-style records and filing system, which particularly in the early decades maintained a rigorous permanent record of activities. Furthermore, decisions and arrangements across the BBC were based on the circulation of paper minutes, which were extensively annotated by participants in any particular project, leaving a vivid paper-trail of how things were done and what those involved really thought. To examine these archives we need to refer to the BBC Written Archives Centre at Caversham, where there are files on Cyril Scott as a composer, and contracts for him as a contributor, both as pianist and (very occasional) speaker.

While Cyril Scott was widely respected in his lifetime, not only as a composer but also as a pianist, that regard was based on an enduring established reputation, particularly for his light music and especially piano pieces, rather than constant performances of his latest and more elaborate compositions. His chamber music and songs tended to be heard more than his more ambitious orchestral works.

Championed by Sir Henry Wood, Scott was heard on various occasions during the first thirty years of the Queen's Hall Promenade Concerts, and he enjoyed a number of performances in the early days after the BBC took over in 1927. The Queen's Hall Promenade Concerts (which moved to the Royal Albert Hall after the Queen's Hall was bombed in 1941) are a good measure of the BBC's interest. Between 1927 and 1954 Scott enjoyed nine orchestral billings (though only eight actually took place, because of a wartime cancellation) and seven solo songs with piano. Scott's last orchestral performance at the Proms was in 1954, since when nothing by him has been heard at these concerts. For the record, this is Scott's representation from 1927:

Orchestral

1931 (15 September): Piano Concerto No. 1
1932 (20 September): Overture *Noël*
1934 (30 August): *Festival Overture*
1939 (22 September): *Two Passacaglias on Irish Themes* [cancelled]
1940 (5 October): *Ode to Great Men* [not organised by the BBC and cancelled owing to an air raid]
1944 (21 July): *Festival Overture*
1947 (20 August): *Festival Overture*
1948 (13 September): Oboe Concerto
1954 (27 July): *Two Passacaglias on Irish Themes*

Songs

1927 (31 August) *Osme's Song* (Gwladys Naish with piano)
1928 (11 August) *Blackbird's Song* (Doris Vane with piano)
1928 (29 August) *In the Silent Moonbeams* (Astra Desmond with piano)

1928 (13 September) *The Unforseen* (Trefor Jones with piano)
1929 (16 September): *Blackbird's Song* (Doris Vane with piano)
1930 (19 September): *Blackbird's Song* – Northern Proms
1932 (15 August): *A Song of London* (Horace Stevens with piano)

Scott only appeared once as a pianist – on 15 September 1931 – when he played his own First Piano Concerto, a work he had performed across Europe and America. In pre-BBC days he had twice conducted his own *Two Passacaglias on Irish Themes* (Proms 1921, 1924).

In addition, Rose and Cyril Scott were credited as joint translators of Gottfried Benn's German words when Hindemith's oratorio *Das Unaufhörliche* ('The Perpetual') was performed by BBC forces at Queen's Hall on 7 May 1934.

The files in the Written Archives Centre reveal the general view in the BBC Music Department of the 1930s and 1940s as having been that Scott's light music and earlier orchestral scores were popular repertoire material, while his later scores, in which he embraced a more advanced and personal language, were problematic. These works were not well received by BBC music staff, most of whom were trained at the Royal College of Music and held the (untested) belief that such music would not suit a wider audience; the works therefore gradually vanished from view. Scott's contemporaries Frank Bridge and John Foulds found themselves in a similar position.

Scott's English champions included Henry Wood at Queen's Hall and Dan Godfrey at Bournemouth. There was also his Liverpool contemporary Thomas Beecham, who presented Scott's *The Ballad of Fair Helen of Kirkconnel* in 1905 at one of his very earliest London concerts. Wood conducted Scott's Second Symphony at a Promenade Concert in August 1903, and a Rhapsody (called No. 1) during the Proms the following year. In 1907 the play *Princess Maleine* by the then fashionable Belgian poet and playwright Maurice Maeterlinck inspired Scott to compose a concert overture of the same name. At the Proms in 1913 Henry Wood programmed his *Two Poems for Orchestra*. There were also such orchestral works as *Aubade*, the *Christmas Overture*, and the still unperformed hour-long *Nativity Hymn*, setting an elaborate text by Richard Crashaw, which achieved publication in the post-war Carnegie competitions. Here the adjudicators reported it to be: 'A work of strong individuality and great musical interest, laid out on a large scale and showing deep insight into the meaning of Crashaw's poem. The music is wholly modern in style and idiom, and requires an exceptional orchestra.'[1]

Scott's international standing briefly survived World War 1, and Scott carried off a successful tour of the USA and Canada, but a generation of new composers soon established themselves, and their reputations inexorably eclipsed Scott's.

Cyril Scott survived longest in his chamber-music repertoire, writing more than two dozen substantial scores together with a huge number of piano pieces including not only popular encores, many of them published in albums and sets, but also four piano sonatas (only three of them numbered). Scott's piano music in Dutton Epoch's recording with pianist Leslie De'Ath fills nine CDs. Like the piano sonatas,

[1] Percy A. Scholes, *New Works by Modern British Composers*, 2nd series (Stainer & Bell [for Carnegie UK Trust], 1924).

the six sonatas for violin and piano span his whole career, four of them numbered, two with evocative titles. The first dates from 1908, but the others were written in the 1950s when he enjoyed a late burst of composition. The *Sonata lirica* appeared in 1937 and a *Sonata melodica* in 1950.

Scott's five piano quintets exemplify his extensive surviving chamber music. An early piano quintet was performed in Liverpool in 1901 with Scott at the piano, but then was repudiated in favour of a second quintet written in 1907 and first heard in March that year at London's Bechstein (later named 'Wigmore') Hall, again with Scott at the piano. In April 1914 he appeared at the same hall in another quintet, in fact a revision of a sextet he had first played in London in 1903. After World War 1 Scott repudiated many of these early chamber works and produced a fourth piano quintet, which appeared as No. 1. First performed at London's Aeolian Hall in 1920, he successfully submitted it to the Carnegie music publishing competition, and, winning a Carnegie Award, it was published in 1925. Commenting on the Viola Sonata in March 1939 one BBC official noted: 'This seems to be quite good C. S. and to have more to it than a good many of his productions.' The numbered Second Quintet did not appear until 1952, and remained almost unknown. A similar pattern obtained with his seven string quartets (eight if you count the 'Divertimento' of 1920) – three delightful early scores giving way to a numbered series of four, the first dating from 1919, the others from the late 1950s or sixties. There were other chamber works including the popular early piano quartet and quintets. There were also sonatas for viola, cello and flute.

So what was the BBC's attitude to this music when it came on the scene in the 1920s, and more especially in the 1930s and beyond? One of the earliest assessments came of the then new Violin Concerto in the late 1920s. Aylmer Buesst wrote to Percy Pitt about it:

> Concerto for Violin & Orchestra. It is a pity that the great natural gifts, the knowledge, & the technical attainment which go to the making of this work should not have been used to better purpose. For to me it is all but so much wasted effort. Great as is the demand for a violin concerto I cannot see this ever appealing to either player or public. It is diffuse, derivative, & in general, tedious. Yet there are passages of great beauty in it, but unfortunately they do not get anywhere.
>
> I fear that insincerity of purpose is largely responsible – the craving to appear 'modern' at all costs. Hence the total lack of character. It is with regret that I judge it thus, & I trust that others will be given a chance to prove me quite wrong.
>
> The composer would have been well advised to submit a clear & better written score.

The striking comparison in idiom is surely with the Delius string concerti, and the clue that this may not be a reliable assessment for us nearly ninety years on is Buesst's citing the work's modernity as his objection. Certainly, as presented on the Chandos recording at the beginning of the twenty-first century, we come to a somewhat different conclusion.

April 1940 was not an opportune moment to start a campaign for recognition by the BBC, but Scott's 1927 setting of words by W. H. Hudson, which he called *Rima's Call to the Birds* (published by Elkin in vocal score in 1933), came before the BBC panel that month. The work had originally been conceived for soprano and string quartet and was thus performed at London's Wigmore Hall in May 1927. Later, orchestrated, it was heard at the Harrogate Festival in the summer of 1929. However, later, the BBC's panel – which consisted of the conductor (and composer) Reginald Redman; Julian Herbage, BBC programme planner; and Clarence Raybould, conductor – appear to be coming fresh to it. Their comments were:

> This is the sort of score that seems to convey little to the eye. It might produce an exotic effect to the ear but is not I imagine for general consumption.
>
> (Redman)

> A certain 'theatrical' effect would possibly be achieved in performance, but I cannot help feeling that the musical idiom is in reality completely tawdry.
>
> (Herbage)

Raybould was inclined to be more pragmatic – 'I don't feel that this calls for an official criticism. If a singer wished to include it in a programme, it could then be considered.' The German offensive in France ending with Dunkirk followed soon after, and the issue of Scott's music was for the time being forgotten in the face of more serious and immediate issues.

The BBC's view of Cyril Scott was at its lowest point during World War 2 and the early 1950s. Then both the composer and his champion, the music publisher Robert Elkin, submitted a wide range of his music to a largely unsympathetic constituency of BBC music staff and their moderately celebrated advisers. As a fascinating study in changing aesthetic values and sympathies, it has been interesting to view these assessments from fifty and sixty years on, as the very works with which they were unhappy have more recently been recorded and given a very positive critical reception. This change in our view of Scott might be accounted for by very real changes in the artistic and musical climate. Also one wonders whether it is significant that most of these assessments were made from scores, and in the absence of any performance. As we have subsequently seen (or rather heard), the sound of Scott's music can have a significant role in shaping our appreciation.

Perhaps we should start with the most intemperate and bad-tempered rejection of a Scott work, which for me seems to have been that accorded Scott's *Irish Serenade* for string orchestra, when it was read by Eric Warr in 1951:

> This music is spineless, unhealthy and pathetically ineffectual. It contains hardly any passages that could not be assembled by an ill-taught student after a few weeks fumbling at the piano. I would oppose any suggestion of broadcasting it.[2]

Among BBC music staff in the 1940s, Herbert Murrill, himself a composer, was perhaps the most conscientious in trying to come to an assessment of several composers who were out of favour at the time – including George Lloyd, Havergal Brian and Cyril Scott. Murrill was Director of Music from 1947 to 1952. He rejected all these composers, but only after thoroughly reading scores and seeing the compos-

[2] Score reading report, 23 February 1951.

ers personally. In truth, the music found no sympathy with the prevailing aesthetic of the times. Writing in November 1942 about the Concertino for two pianos of 1933, Murrill had written:

> Like all Scott's work in larger forms, the music is vague and esoteric and, in my opinion, scarcely maintains interest. But this work certainly requires less in the way of orchestral resources than is usually the case, & thus would be more easily placed in programmes. I am inclined to say – give it a trial run.[3]

In March 1948 Cyril Scott made a great effort to approach the BBC with a selection of his music, and Murrill spent the weekend with him reviewing scores. Scott was hoping for a Promenade Concert performance. Murrill reports at length:

> Cyril Scott always asserts that we do not know his more recent compositions and has been keen for somebody to look at them with regard to possible performances and with a view to next season's Promenade Concerts.
>
> I spent the weekend with him and went through a large mass of his recent work. He most strongly urges a large piece for chorus and orchestra with two soloists called, HYMN OF UNITY. This probably takes considerably over an hour in performance and is a deeply felt and sincere piece of anti-war propaganda. Unfortunately, the composer has written his own text and, although its sincerity cannot be doubted, its literary quality and suitability for musical setting are open to question. It lacks poetic presentation of its facts and has some of the literary flavour of a Times leader. I do not consider it suitable material for setting and it comes off particularly badly in Scott's latest manner, which is a rich and, at times, rather formless harmonic texture. The composer is right to have avoided contrapuntal devices since he wishes the words of the text to be clearly heard. On the other hand, an hour of very cloying and static harmony seems to me quite unacceptable, and I cannot recommend the work for broadcast purposes.
>
> He has written also an opera on a much lighter text (again his own words), but I did not hear much of the music and what I did hear was in the same style as the Hymn. I feel this would be no more acceptable than the larger work.
>
> There are two TRIOS FOR STRINGS, the second just completed. The first is now in the proof stage and I could not get much idea of it as, by mischance, the score had not been returned with the parts. The little I could judge from an examination of the separate parts seemed quite acceptable. The second trio is still in Manuscript and I quite liked the look of it. Scott admits that he wrote it 'as a discipline', and it is obvious that, in a work cast for three solo strings, harmonic extravagance is less likely. It seemed clean and acceptable writing and I have asked the composer to let me have score and parts as soon as the latter are available. I believe it could well be included in programmes if we can get a string trio interested in it.
>
> I should like to suggest for serious Prom. consideration another work just completed, CONCERTO FOR OBOE AND STRINGS. Some of the composer's harmonic mannerisms are certainly present, but without these the work would

[3] Score reading report, 23 November 1942.

> hardly be by Cyril Scott and I found them in such a small work not displeasing. The composer has shown the work to Leon Goossens, who has expressed his interest. I imagine it would play about twenty minutes. Scott is at present making the piano arrangement from the score so that Goossens can begin rehearsals. I have asked him to let me have the score when it is available.
>
> Finally, I saw two movements of his latest work, a SONATA FOR 'CELLO AND PIANO. My impression here is that the piano has again led the composer into some harmonic extravagances and we may find the complete work discursive and rather formless. It is unfair, however, to judge on two movements only, and I expect we shall see the complete work in due course.

In December 1948 Herbert Murrill minuted J. S. Lowe in response to his reading report of 18 December on six works submitted by Cyril Scott.

> I feel as you do about the Sonata and the Two Piano Variations, which I have heard. [Lowe found them 'turgid and over-full of notes'.] I think the Harpsichord Concerto might be done if a modern work for this instrument is required. It makes nice noises! BUT – I'd rather place the Oboe Concerto (last season's Proms) and wish you would discuss this with Eric Warr. String Quartet is a bit over-written. But the Scherzo is a breathing-place melodically at all events! Idyll and Idyllic Fantasy should, I think, be done in a suitable programme – either Home or Third. Do please consider, therefore, these two, the Quartet and the Oboe Concerto.

In fact, the Oboe Concerto had been performed by Leon Goossens in a Promenade Concert in September 1948, but failed to find a subsequent regular slot in the repertoire and was then forgotten until recorded by Jonathan Small with the Royal Liverpool Philharmonic Orchestra conducted by Martin Yates in 2010 for Dutton Epoch.

It was probably a younger generation of composers at that time employed as BBC readers who responded least sympathetically to Scott's music. Perhaps the least diplomatic was Arthur Benjamin. In 1953 and 1954 he examined what was then known as Symphony No. 2 – now known as No. 4 (we have since revisited the withdrawn Symphonies Nos. 1 and 2) – and the late Clarinet Quintet. In October 1953 Benjamin wrote about the symphony: 'Let's face the fact that Cyril Scott is one of the tragedies of British Music. With the best will in the world, the BBC could not perform this sort of amorphous piffle.'[4] A year later came the Clarinet Quintet, and Benjamin despaired at coming to a view, writing: 'I am out of sympathy with this style, so improvisatory, so "atmospherical", so devoid of interesting counterpoint; but in view of the composer's "past" I simply don't know what to say??'

Interestingly, the panel on which Benjamin served (there were usually three readers) also included the Hungarian emigré Mátyás Seiber, and Julius Harrison, composer and conductor. Seiber, in particular, came to the panel without any historical baggage as Scott's music was unfamiliar to him. Commenting on the symphony he wrote:

> This is not really symphonic material. Consequently first and last movements are rather weak, whilst the slow movement and scherzo are much more acceptable.

[4] Report 27 October 1953.

> He seems to be best at a lyrical movement like the slow movement of this symphony. (This is the first large work of Scott's I have seen.) I don't think one can sustain interest for such a long time with one type of parallel harmony only and with hardly any contrapuntal interest. If one could take out the two middle movements, I should say yes, but as a whole I am rather doubtful.[5]

Julius Harrison, as a conductor of many years standing, must have been fully aware of Scott, his style and his reputation. His report, while negative, was more conciliatory:

> The first movement is too rhapsodic both in the music and the orchestration to be accounted symphonic. It needs stronger contrapuntal treatment than has been accorded it. The second movement, not too strong in thematic interest, yet has some touches of that individual style C. S. has made for himself. The Scherzo is the best movement and full of whimsies. By the time the finale is reached the absence of contrapuntal treatment is felt. The ever-changing time-signatures belong more to the spirit of Rhapsody than the Symphony. I do not feel that a performance is possible, viewing the work as a whole.[6]

When it came to the Clarinet Quintet, which they examined in October 1953, Julius Harrison wrote (26 October):

> Very regretfully I must admit that this Quintet contains many a muddle of sounds that seem to have no sense of direction. C. S. seems to be trying to write in the up-to-date dissonant idiom, dragging in (on strings) so many technical devices – tremolos, trills, etc. etc. – that in the sum total of the music due confusion exists. Much of the clarinet writing is in the weak register of the instrument just below the break, and so is ineffective. Not once has C. S. given the clarinet its 'head' in the highest register. No.

Mátyás Seiber was also unimpressed:

> I have many objections to this work. Formally it seems to fall to pieces; it is much too episodic; its style is turgid and rather outmoded; it is not real chamber music, but makes the impression of some orchestral music reduced. The clarinet is hardly ever treated individually; it mostly merges into the 'mass'. Altogether rather unsatisfactory.

In November 1953 the producer Leonard Isaacs was asked to look at the printed vocal score of the choral work *La belle dame sans merci*, a poem previously set by many British composers. Isaacs, the son of the celebrated blind Manchester concert pianist Edward Isaacs, would soon leave the BBC for a leading academic appointment in Canada, but with a history as a concert pianist himself he played through the vocal score at the piano. He was not impressed with what he found:

[5] Matyas Seiber, 23 October 1953.

[6] Julius Harrison, 26 October 1953

> I … must say that I completely agree with A. H. M. P. (s) that it is a messy and unworthy piece of music. Its first impact is one of 'atmosphere' but after 10 pages one realises that one is getting absolutely nowhere. The melody has no shape, there is a total absence of contrapuntal interest, the monotonous metre of the words is faithfully reproduced in the music, in one place I suspect him of having changed the text (bottom of page 21 of the piano score: 'so kissed to sleep' surely is in the original 'with kisses four'), the parallel motion becomes nauseating after a time and the long successions of passages in 3rds and 6ths bespeak piano music and not orchestral music; worst of all in their aimlessness are the masses of added 6ths and dominant 7ths. I have never come across a more unfulfilled piece of music. A page full of unresolved dominant 7ths is like eating a tin of golden syrup. I cannot honestly believe that a performance of this work in 1953 would bring anything but discredit upon the composer and I cannot with anything like a clear conscience recommend it for performance in Third Programme.

Isaacs is certainly a musician whose views one has to respect, but a quarter of a century on we find the climate was beginning to change, and the BBC did eventually broadcast *La belle dame,* when in 1979 it was sung by the baritone Michael George with the BBC Singers and the BBC Concert Orchestra conducted by Ashley Lawrence. This attracted some enthusiasm from listeners. More recently Stephen Lloyd has found it a 'fine setting of Keats'.

The symphony *The Muses* is dedicated to Beecham, perhaps in gratitude for his conducting the first performance of *La belle dame sans merci* at the 1934 Leeds Festival. While not a steady champion of Scott's works, Beecham had earlier been responsible for a number of first or early performances, among them *Helen of Kirkconnel* for baritone and orchestra, the *Aubade, Two Passacaglias on Irish Themes,* Piano Concerto No. 1, and the substantial single movement *The Melodist and the Nightingales* for cello and small orchestra.

September 1942 was perhaps not an auspicious time for Scott to seek a BBC performance. Herbert Murrill wrote on 22 September 42 about *The Muses*:

> I honestly don't see the placing of this and similar works of Cyril Scott. They require vast resources, much programme space, and lots of rehearsal. In return for this one would expect music playable in the finest concerts at peak listening times. Instead, we get rather flimsy, esoteric works that could only appeal to a minority of even the musically inclined. I would turn this down on the sheer basis of impracticability.

In January 1943 the conductor Clarence Raybould writes:

> I feel we have already wasted too much of our Music programme time & our orchestral resources on Scott's effusions. This present work, despite its high-flown sub-titles is no whit better than anything else I've seen of his for some years: it is a dreary waste of meandering harmonies & I cannot see any possible justification for its broadcast.

Now that the symphony has been recorded it is apparent that earlier assessments were wide of the mark, for what is revealed on hearing the work is a powerful aural imagination – though possibly one exhibiting an aesthetic which could not have found any sympathy in Scott's lifetime. Reviewing the Chandos recording, Stephen Lloyd wrote:

> At many places in this symphony one is pleasantly surprised at Scott's feeling for momentum; there is nothing here of the languid want of direction one has felt in lesser works. This is altogether an impressively engineered disc with very persuasive performances from the BBC Philharmonic under Martyn Brabbins that hopefully will encourage a fresh assessment of Scott, one that is not based on second- and third-hand opinions.[7]

What earlier commentators seem to have missed is that, without the benefit of a quality performance, Scott's ability to create mood or atmosphere is not always apparent. As Lloyd continued in his review:

> The opening pages could grace many a Hammer Horror film, tragedy being very much the key word, and its textures and mood in some respects resemble the opening of Bax's Second Symphony in its powerful build-up. Even a wind machine adds to the bleak picture. At 9' 11" epic poetry is surely represented by a wonderfully Ravellian passage that is heavily indebted to *Daphnis and Chloe*. It is not until the quiet characteristic rising and falling phrase at 11' 40" that we can feel with certainty the unmistakable stamp of Scott. The second movement is a scherzo of tremendous energy and spirit. This is not merely light comedy for the merriment is impish, Puckish, with tricks that the Gods play. Scott's brilliant scoring may surprise many listeners. The slow movement is a lush *L'après-midi* but with an uneasy and uncertain resolution. The last movement opens with timpani and wind machine, and immediately a steady rhythmic pulse – a sort of moto perpetuo – drives the wordless chorus (with a nod again to *Daphnis*) to its climax with organ.

Peter Dickinson, writing in *Gramophone* about that same recording, headed his review 'the warmest of welcomes for a remarkable discovery in 20th-century British music', and Calum MacDonald in the *BBC Music Magazine* praised the extraordinarily imaginative orchestration and described the CD as 'an important act of restitution' and 'an eloquent case for fine music, unnecessarily consigned to oblivion without the courtesy of a hearing'.[8]

In 1946 Scott submitted his 'Christmas Overture' *Noël*. This work had already been heard at a Promenade Concert in 1932, though the panel appears not to have acknowledged this. On this occasion the panel consisted of Lennox Berkeley, composer; Mosco Carner, music critic; and Herbert Howells, composer. They met on 10 December 1946. Their comments are worth reading at length:

> I can't frankly find sufficient real musical value here to justify reviving this work. Apart from the fact that its idiom is very much dated, it seems to me to lack real thought and power of construction. There is a lot of very pleasant orchestral sound, but the tunes which the composer uses seem to lose rather than to gain by his treatment of them. Thus the lovely 'In Dulce Jubilo' is to my mind ruined by

[7] Stephen Lloyd review of Chandos CHAN10211 on MusicWeb-International, May 2004, available through www.musicweb-international.com.

[8] Peter Dickinson in *Gramophone*, June 2004, p. 51; Calum MacDonald in *BBC Music Magazine*, available online through www.classical-music.com.

> the weak chromatic harmonies that accompany it on page 45. It is a pity that such elaborate treatment should not yield a better aesthetic result.
>
> (Lennox Berkeley)

> In addition to the fact that the music, as my colleague points out, bears too conspicuously the stamp of its time as to be acceptable nowadays, the work breaks down on account of its diffuse, rather incoherent and repetitive treatment. There are some lovely sounds in it, it is true, but such pointillist as shown here – and unoriginal for that matter – creates a watery, monotonous effect. Not recommended.
>
> (Mosco Carner)

> This must decide itself on a purely musical question: 'Is this the way to do a Fantasy on Christmas Tunes?'. I for one, think it an impossible proceeding to link these well-known and highly-traditionalized tunes to this particularly unsuitable harmonic idiom. Moreover, the work grows too scrappily on the broken ground of 'The Twelve Days'. The climax, when it comes, is more one of volume of sound than of an inescapable conclusion following upon a reasoned argument. I wish I c^{d} recommend it. I can't.
>
> (Herbert Howells)

While researching this chapter, the full historical file of *Radio Times*, the BBC weekly listing of the next week's broadcasting, has been digitised and become available and searchable online. Consequently it is possible to search the appearance of Scott in the programme schedules. This reveals a rather different assessment of him as a composer, though the programmes themselves tend to reinforce the image of him as essentially a composer of songs and popular piano music. A 'standard' statement about Scott appears in several issues of *Radio Times* during the 1920s, of which the following is a typical example (with the billing for the programme from 5XX Daventry for 31 August 1929):

> CYRIL SCOTT is one of those versatile people who win distinction in more than one field. He is a composer, a poet, and an author of note on philosophic subjects. Born in Cheshire in 1879, he was a student at Frankfurt, where more than one other young Englishman who has since stepped into the front rank of composers, was with him. At the end of his student career he lived for a time in Liverpool, teaching and playing, and his first important orchestral piece, the Heroic Suite, was played there as well as at Manchester with Richter conducting. Soon afterwards [actually *before*] his *Pelleas and Melisande* was given in Frankfurt. Other works of his have figured at Sir Henry Wood's concerts and elsewhere; Sir Thomas Beecham has interested himself in more than one of them, and as far afield as Vienna his music has been played. Best known by his songs and smaller pieces, he deserves a more important position than his native country accords him for his bigger and more serious works. We are given too few opportunities of hearing them. In some ways less definitely English than his contemporaries, his music is in every way original, and modern without any of the more startling dissonant effects in which the present-day composer inclines to express himself.

While the repertoire heard on the BBC is circumscribed, between the wars he was certainly taken seriously, to the extent that the BBC commissioned a short operetta from him, *Janet and Felix* or 'Singing Sickness', heard in November 1931.[9] Unfortunately even the overture of this apparently approachable confection is lost, and so we only have the billing in the *Radio Times* to remind us that it ever took place. It received two performances, first on the Regional Programme on Thursday 26 November at 21:15, with a second performance on the National Programme on Friday 27 November at 20:00. *Radio Times* prints the story (Fig. 3.1):

> THE overture of this whimsical operetta, whose text and music are both Cyril Scott's, with its distant fairy voices, and its hints of the uncanny, prepares us at once for the mood in which to listen, and then, in the first scene, we are introduced to the heroine practising her singing. The unlucky hero appears later. In the second scene his mother is consulting a Harley Street specialist about her son's sad case; this is dialogue until near the end, when music leads into the third scene - a school of singing. There, everything, even conversation, must be sung, and the music is typical of Cyril Scott's whimsical fun, including a rehearsal by male voice chorus with flute accompaniment - in which he makes merry over his own 'Ratcatcher' – and a brilliantly comic burlesque of an operatic duet by Sauerbier, sung by the heroine, and the maestro of the school. Scene IV is the garden of the school, where no better fortune attends a second proposal by the hero, and the fifth is the cave of the sprite, who was the innocent cause of all the trouble. What befell there and afterwards must be left to unfold itself, as it does unmistakably. And all through the piece, the laughter of the unfeeling sprite can be heard breaking in and fading away again.

C.W.H.

'JANET and FELIX'
or 'Singing Sickness'
An Operetta
by CYRIL SCOTT

Characters in the order of their appearance:
Janet Suckling .... TESSA DEAN
Felix Fairchild .... JOHN ARMSTRONG
Mrs. Fairchild (*his mother*) ANN STEPHENSON
Dr. Kurtz (*the nose and throat specialist*) J. HUBERT LESLIE
Students at Signor Pindello's Academy THE WIRELESS CHORUS
Signor Pindello (*The maestro*) BERTRAM BINYON
John McKay (*coach and accompanist*) J. HUBERT LESLIE
Kiddle (*a student*) .... STANLEY RILEY
The Sprite (*cause of all the trouble*) WYNNE AJELLO

Scene I.—The Drawing-room of Janet Suckling's Flat.
Scene II.—Dr. Kurtz's Consulting Room
Scene III.—Signor Pindello's Operatic Academy—the Practice Room
Scene IV—Pindello's Academy—the Garden
Scene V.—The Wishing Seat in a Cave on the Yorkshire Moors
Scene VI.—Pindello's Academy—the Practice Room

Adapted and Produced by
GORDON McCONNEL
At the piano: Alan Paul
The Wireless Chorus and The B.B.C. Theatre Orchestra
Conducted by Leslie Woodgate
TONIGHT AT 8.0

Figure 3.1 Advertisement for *Janet and Felix* in the *Radio Times*, November 1931 (see also p. 227)

[9] For *Janet and Felix*, see also Chapter 14, below.

Cyril Scott's BBC status between the wars did not survive World War 2, and although there was a limited appreciation of his music in the 1930s, after 1945 the mood of the times was against him. In 1934 his pupil Edmund Rubbra opened his article about Scott as follows (for the complete text see Chapter 4):

> In England the chief propaganda for Cyril Scott's art has too often been made by the insistent but small pipings of blackbirds and water-wagtails, and it is doubtful if a reputation can be upheld by such feathery means. For a juster estimate of his worth Mr. Scott has had to go to the Continent, where for thirty years his large orchestral and chamber works have been known and appreciated.
>
> The reasons for the neglect or dismissal of Mr. Scott's major works in England are not far to seek. In the first place, he studied in Germany and made strong contacts there; in the second, his musical thought runs instinctively counter, not only to the accepted traditions of English music from Purcell to Elgar and Elgar to Walton, but to all the many and varied pre- and post-war experiments represented by Schönberg's atonal 'Pierrot Lunaire', Copland's jazz concerto and Stravinsky's neo-classic 'Duo Concertant'. In other words, his style, although simplified in the more recent works such as the 'Mystic Ode' for chorus and orchestra and the orchestral 'Noël', has remained remarkably consistent and uninfluenced by contemporary guests.
>
> This consistency has, however, seemed to some critics a proof that Mr. Scott was caught in the fine-spun web of his own thought; but such an assumption rests on an apprehension of the music as a vertical instead of a linear or horizontal structure. Cyril Scott, like all romantics, is essentially a melodist, and really to get within the skin of any work of his it is necessary to view the chords, not as static chunks, agreeable or disagreeable in themselves, but as collections of simultaneously sounded melodic units.

In the December 1963 issue of the *Musical Times* Elkin organised Schott and Boosey & Hawkes to support them in jointly taking a whole-page advertisement to advertise Scott's music that was available from them, though it seems to have had little effect at the time.

Academic assessment of Scott's music remained unfavourable, Frank Howes writing in 1966 that 'by the time he was seventy his idiom had come to sound old-fashioned and indeed ineffective'.[10] Stephen Banfield, in his magisterial study of English song, writes 'Scott's problem was the gulf between his aesthetic aims and his creative execution … many of Scott's involvements and aspirations now seem glib and facile.'[11] John Caldwell, in the second volume of his major two-volume history of British music, published in 1999, contented himself with saying, 'Scott wrote in all the major forms, but he was probably most successful as a miniaturist: even so, his chromatic excesses are apt to conceal a poverty of substance.'[12] Nevertheless, all these

[10] Frank Howes, *The English Musical Renaissance* (Secker & Warburg, 1966), p. 193.

[11] Stephen Banfield, *Sensibility and English Song*, vol. 1 (Cambridge University Press, 1985), p. 91.

[12] John Caldwell, *The Oxford History of English Music*, vol. 2 (Oxford University Press, 1999), p. 389.

CYRIL SCOTT

In this announcement the publishers named below have combined to draw attention to some of the major works of Mr Cyril Scott, now in his 85th year but still composing vigorously and still developing his own very individual style. Because of the popularity of certain songs and short piano pieces, Mr Scott has come to be regarded in his own country (though not abroad) solely as a miniaturist; it is to correct this impression that his publishers invite consideration of the works here listed.

SYMPHONIC WORKS

Symphony 'The Muses' (E)

Symphony No 2 (E)

Festival Overture (E)

Ode to Great Men (E) (tenor or orator, contralto chorus and orchestra)

Aubade (S)

Two Passacaglias (S)

Noel, a Christmas Overture (S)

Early one morning (B)

Neapolitan Rhapsody (B)

SMALL ORCHESTRA

Suite Fantastique (S)

STRING ORCHESTRA

Irish Serenade (E) (commissioned for the Festival of Britain)

First Suite for strings (B)

CONCERTOS

Harpsichord and chamber orchestra (E)

Two violins and orchestra (E)

Concertino for two pianos and orchestra (E)

Oboe and string orchestra (E)

Pianoforte and orchestra (S)

Violin and orchestra (S)

CHORAL WORKS

La Belle Dame sans Merci (E) (bar solo, chorus and orchestra)

Mystic Ode (E) (male voice chorus and orchestra)

Mirabelle ('A Quaint Cantata') (B)

CHAMBER WORKS

String Quartets Nos 1, 2 and 3 (E)

String Quintet (E)

Divertimento for string quartet (E)

Quartet for violin, viola, cello and piano (B)

Sonata Melodica, violin & piano (E)

Sonata for flute and piano (E)

Key to publishers:

E—ELKIN & CO LTD 160 Wardour Street W1

S—SCHOTT & CO LTD 48 Great Marlborough Street W1

B—BOOSEY & HAWKES LTD 295 Regent Street W1

910

Figure 3.2 Advertisement by Elkin, Schott and Boosey & Hawkes in the *Musical Times*, December 1963

assessments pre-date the extensive recording of Scott's orchestral music, including those works that had eluded commentators by being preserved in the Grainger Museum in Melbourne, Australia. An adequate assessment of Scott's music, in the round, has proved to be something that could never be adequately achieved without a tradition of performance, and performance by top-line performers.

In 1979, the Scott centenary year, the BBC broadcast a wide range of Scott's orchestral and chamber music, clearly part of an initiative to survey Scott's music in performance. In addition to a broad selection of piano solos and solo songs, the orchestral items and chamber music heard over the years (in chronological order) have been:

25 April 1977: *Summer Gardens* (suite for orchestra)
7 September 1979: *La belle dame sans merci* (baritone, chorus & orchestra)
25 September 1979: *Aubade*
25 September 1979: Piano Concerto No. 1
15 October 1979: *Three Dances* for orchestra, Op. 22
23 December 1979: String Quartet No. 4
23 December 1979: Piano Quartet, Op. 16
12 December 1982: Clarinet Trio (1953)
19 December 1982 Clarinet Quintet
8 July 1986: String Quartet No. 4
7 August 1995: *The Alchemist* [extended extracts from the opera]
21 November 1999: *Aubade*
21 November 1999: Piano Concerto No. 1

In addition to this, the growing range of recordings means that more and more of the music is now being heard. However, although Lyrita had established the precedent when recording the two piano concertos with John Ogdon, the LPO and Bernard Herrmann, it was only when a large tranche of the major orchestral works was recorded by Martyn Brabbins with the BBC Philharmonic Orchestra for Chandos, in remarkable performances and recorded sound, that Scott's true achievement was suddenly revealed to a wide audience.

These were performances given by BBC forces, in this case the BBC Philharmonic Orchestra in Manchester, yet they were not performances promoted as the result of a corporate assessment and decision by the BBC Music Department. Rather, they were the outcome of an initiative by a record company, in this case Chandos, working in a contractual climate whereby the orchestra (for the BBC) and the record company had a shared contract, while the orchestra's management were effectively the brokers agreeing the arrangements and 'selling' the recordings to Radio 3 as they were made. Four CDs were made over a period of four years.

1. 15–17 April 2003 (Symphony No. 3, *The Muses*; *Neptune*; Piano Concerto No. 2)
2. 8 and 9 September 2005 (Symphony No. 4; Piano Concerto No. 1)
3. 16 and 17 March 2006 (*Three Symphonic Dances* [Symphony No. 2]; Violin Concerto)
4. 17 and 18 October 2007 (Symphony No. 1; [2nd] Cello Concerto (1937))

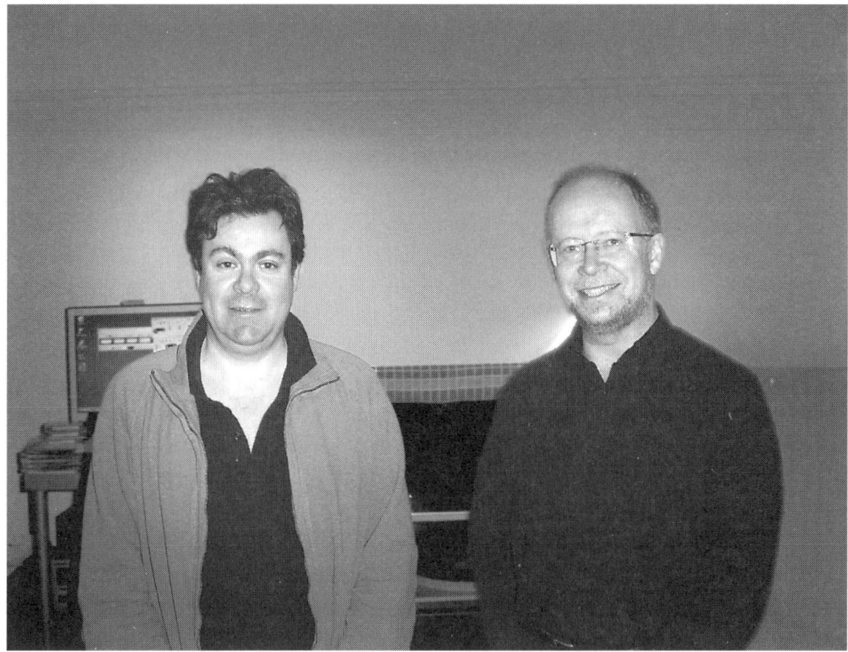

Figure 3.3 Michael Dutton and Leslie De'Ath in Dutton's editing studio at Watford, 27 February 2007

The orchestral recordings were preceded by a number of surveys of different aspects of Scott's chamber music that were, in fact, initiatives spearheaded by the artists concerned. Issued by Dutton Epoch, these started with the London Piano Quartet playing the Piano Quartet, Op. 16, and the 1926 Quintet, issued in 2002. Recorded in August 2003 the Archæus Quartet's programme of String Quartets 1, 2 and 4 proved an award-winning disc, the *Gramophone* reviewer writing, 'This is fascinating music and very persuasively played.'[13] Later there was violinist Clare Howick accompanied by Sophia Rahman in the *Sonata lirica* and a wide range of violin miniatures and encores.

The idea of producing a complete recording of all the works for solo piano, and including works for two pianos, was a striking one, and once conceived it was remarkably quickly completed on nine Dutton Epoch CDs issued as five volumes, some consisting of two CDs. A typical initiative of one artist with a sympathetic record company, this was a scheme of Leslie De'Ath's, who was the pianist throughout (Fig. 3.3). Having the support of an academic institution was vital in this success, the piano music recorded in the Maureen Forrester Recital Hall at the Faculty of Music at Wilfrid Laurier University, Waterloo, Ontario. Having all the music in one specific genre available so conveniently, especially in such sympathetic performances, has led to a positive reception. When the final volume appeared Peter Dickinson wrote in *Gramophone* that there was here 'such a quantity of immediately

[13] Ivan March in *Gramophone* Awards issue 2004 (vol. 82 no. 985) p. 85.

attractive piano music that you'd expect to hear something on Classic FM every week'.[14]

The re-evaluation of the choral works in performance must wait on funding being made available to record them, but the availability[15] of the BBC's broadcast of extended extracts from the opera *The Alchemist* shows how effective a work such as this can be on CD even when it really needs stage action to make its full impact.

The composer Josef Holbrooke died in 1958, and Cyril Scott published a tribute in which he associated himself with 'a handful of young composers ... who refused to toe the academic line and who shocked the professors and the staider section of the public by choosing to go their own rebellious way regardless of the consequences'.[16] We might well think that he is writing autobiographically when he complains: 'A creative artist may have something of value to give to the world, but if the cost of getting it over to the public be heavy, then not lack of merit but lack of money may prove the obstacle to a deserved fame.' Scott's closing words in this obituary seems to be looking forward to his own eventual acceptance by the wider public:

> This is not to say that the actual appreciation of the beautiful does not fluctuate, but Beauty ever remains, and to it man always returns. And so, when composers of genius eventually emerge with the inspiration to create the concordant and the beautiful in a new form, then once again will music enter a new phase. And what may well happen is that some of these composers now alleged to be behind the times, may actually be in advance of the times, because they will be more in tune with the future than with at any rate the extremist phase of the present.

[14] Peter Dickinson in *Gramophone*, September 2009, pp. 73, 75.

[15] The broadcast of excerpts from *The Alchemist* has been issued on CD by the Oriel Music Trust (OMT 362; opera@orielmusic.org).

[16] Cyril Scott, 'A Tribute to Josef Holbrooke', *Musical Times*, August 1958, pp. 425–6.

4

A Contemporary Composer's View of Cyril Scott's Music: 'The Subtle Composer of the Prize-Winning Overture'[1]

EDMUND RUBBRA

THE awarding of the first prize in THE DAILY TELEGRAPH Overture Competition[2] to Cyril Scott will focus attention again upon a musician whose intensely personal output we have perhaps too readily thrust aside in favour of newer excitements.

In England the chief propaganda for Cyril Scott's art has too often been made by the insistent but small pipings of blackbirds and water-wagtails, and it is doubtful if a reputation can be upheld by such feathery means. For a juster estimate of his worth Mr. Scott has had to go to the Continent, where for thirty years his large orchestral and chamber works have been known and appreciated.

The reasons for the neglect or dismissal of Mr. Scott's major works in England are not far to seek. In the first place, he studied in Germany and made strong contacts there; in the second, his musical thought runs instinctively counter, not only to the traditions of English music from Purcell to Elgar and Elgar to Walton, but to all the many and varied pre- and post-war experiments represented by Schönberg's atonal 'Pierrot Lunaire', Copland's jazz concerto and Stravinsky's neo-classic 'Duo Concertant'. In other words, his style, although simplified in the more recent works such as the 'Mystic Ode' for chorus and orchestra and the orchestral 'Noël', has remained remarkably consistent and uninfluenced by contemporary guests.

This consistency has, however, seemed to some critics a proof that Mr. Scott was caught in the fine-spun web of his own thought; but such an assumption rests largely on an apprehension of the music as a vertical instead of a linear or horizontal structure. Cyril Scott, like all romantics, is essentially a melodist, and really to get within the skin of any work of his it is necessary to view the chords, not as static chunks, agreeable or disagreeable in themselves, but as collections of simultaneously-sounded melodic units.

Much might be written on the influence of the printed score on musical criticism. Certain it is that clever counterpoints, intellectually exciting on paper, may be valueless as music, while dull-looking blocks of chords, dismissed with a mental shrug, may prove of vital worth if aurally apprehended in the right way.

It is difficult for us to realise, so familiar are we with the latest products of musical 'syntheticism' (to use Constant Lambert's expressive word), that Mr. Scott was at one time a revolutionary figure in modern English music. Probably the aspect in his

[1] Cutting from Edmund Rubbra's scrap-book, *Daily Telegraph*, 5 May 1934. Reprinted by kind permission of Adrian Yardley and the Edmund Rubbra Estate.

[2] The prize-winning composers in 1934 were: First prize – Cyril Scott; Second prize – Frank Tapp (overture *Metropolis*); Third prize – Arnold Cooke (*Concert Overture*).

music that was felt as particularly strange and disturbing was the length and rhythmic freedom of his melodic line. This, coupled with an elusive tonality, was sufficient to label him as an off-shoot of French Impressionism, even as an 'English Debussy'.

Debussy certainly admired Scott's work; but the outlook and methods of the two composers are vastly dissimilar. Debussy was essentially a harmonist, for his melodic span, although rhythmically freer, was even more closely punctuated than the classical phrase: but Cyril Scott's music is freely end expansively lyrical, therein betraying, in spite of exotic titles and strange scales, its thoroughly English origin.

It has little of the attenuated finesse of the Frenchman's work; by comparison it is even hearty, and, in spite of appearances to the contrary, Scott has not departed far from the diatonic bases of such a work as his early 'English Waltz'. Often an impression of chromaticism is given by the similar motion of a diatonic tune at several pitches. The following example from his opera, 'The Alchemist',

should not be viewed as a series of sevenths, but as a coloured web made up of a diatonic tune played in five simultaneous minor keys, D, G, F, A, and B. (The slight alteration in the last chord is characteristic of the composer's frequent avoidance of what might degenerate into a mannerism.) This procedure is of course not new, as it is but an extension of the medieval 'organum' when one tune was sung at different pitches to accommodate the naturally varied vocal registers.

Even the relationship between the following seemingly irreconcilable chords (from the piano 'Pastorale') is made by the vocal movement of the right-hand inner E, F, and F-sharp, and the left F-sharp, G and G-sharp. To play these chords as aggregates of equally dense molecules would be to destroy the harmonic relationships.

The above two examples sufficiently show the type of chord most favoured by Scott. Extensions of the chord of the seventh, a Wagnerian inheritance, abound in his work. Even the simpler chords of his later manner are the result of subtracting certain elements from the earlier exuberant chord clusters. The subtraction of the two upper notes of the following chord

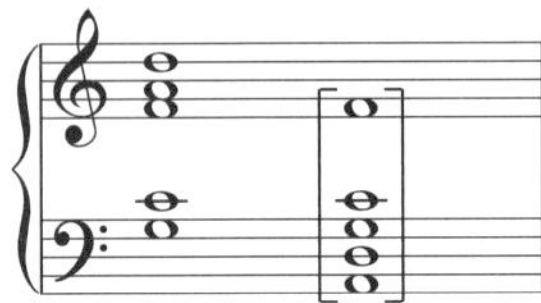

leaves a chord built up of fourths. Or if, instead of subtracting, we place the two upper notes below the root, we get a five-note chord built of fourths.

In this way the composer has linked up his later chords with an early fondness for fourths as melodic leaps (see the 'Chinese Serenade' for piano). This chord, built of superposed fourths, has for Scott a mystical significance, and its extensive use in the later works brings a welcome austerity after the kaleidoscopic pattern-making of much of his earlier manner.

* * * * *

In viewing Mr. Scott's work as a whole, or in listening to any particular work, we should never lose sight of the fact that he revels in the almost physical lusciousness of certain combinations of sounds. Something of the pleasant feeling that we obtain in touching a ripe peach can be got from taking many of Scott's chords from their context and rolling them, so to say, round our emotional tongues.

The trouble with this procedure, as in Stravinsky's pre-occupation with sheer physical rhythm, is that the sounds begin to cloy with use. But Scott is a craftsman as well as a colourist, and the constant flow of the melodic parts in any succession of chords is sufficient to keep the mind alert. Colour, then, becomes incidental to the lyrical outpouring.

Cyril Scott's best work is certainly contained in his large-scale orchestral, choral and chamber music. As it is precisely these works that are the least known in this country, it will not be out of place to enumerate here the most important as a reminder that performances would be welcome. There are two operas, *The Shrine* and *The Alchemist*[3] (the latter performed in Essen in 1925), a *Nativity Hymn* (Crashaw) and *Mystic Ode* for chorus and orchestra, *Rima's Call to the Birds*, a scena for soprano and orchestra, *Two Passacaglias* and *Noël* for orchestra, a string trio, a string quartet and a piano quintet. Lastly there is a fascinating violin concerto, performed in Bournemouth but unknown in London. All these works, being the mature expression of a richly-endowed musical nature, merit a wider acknowledgment from the composer's countrymen.

[3] See pp. 206–17 for a full account.

5

'Music for the Martians': Scott's Reception and Reputation at Home and Abroad

PETER ATKINSON

The more philosophical composer adopts an attitude rather of pleasure than contempt when his works are condemned, because he realises there is a certain grave disappointment in being immediately understood; in knowing that a work of art, which has taken him months of thoughtful labour to accomplish, should be comprehended in a few moments by a man who is probably incapable of writing a note of music himself.[1]

ALTHOUGH Scott later dismissed these comments – along with the rest of his attack on music critics which appeared in his book *The Philosophy of Modernism* (1917) – as a 'youthful indiscretion',[2] his relationship with the press remained predominantly one of mutual hostility for the rest of his life. Apart from a very brief period near the start of the twentieth century when he was hailed as one of the 'coming men' of British music, Scott endured a lifetime of largely negative criticism. By surveying the reception of his music in the press, we can see how critical attitudes towards him developed both during and after his lifetime. This chapter shows how early views of Scott as a promising but immature composer were followed by his rise to fame in 1903 and then by his acquiring a reputation as Britain's foremost 'ultra-modern' composer. Scott's reception in America and on the Continent is also considered, before tracing the fading of his stardom in the 1930s, his obscurity after World War 2, and ultimately the revival of interest that has taken place since the new millennium.[3]

The earliest public performances of Scott's works took place in Germany: his First Symphony was performed in Darmstadt in January 1900, and his overture to *Pelleas and Melisanda* was heard in Frankfurt two months later.[4] The mixed reaction that greeted the symphony was, in some respects, a sign of things to come. Scott later recalled of the occasion that 'half the audience applauded and half hissed', and while two of the German newspapers 'loaded [his] work with abuse', another 'praised it

[1] Cyril Scott, *The Philosophy of Modernism: In its Connection with Music* (Kegan Paul, 1917), p. 84.

[2] Cyril Scott, 'What I Mean By "Critics"', *Chesterian* 1/5 (February 1920), pp. 142–6.

[3] The list of reviews of Scott's works that appears in Laurie Sampsel's *Bio-Bibliography* has served as an excellent starting point for this study, but I have intentionally tried to add to her list by citing further reviews and other sources that are not included in her book. Laurie J. Sampsel, *Cyril Scott: A Bio-Bibliography* (Greenwood Press, 2000).

[4] The performance of the symphony was conducted by Willem de Haan on 8 January 1900 at the Royal Court Theatre. The overture was conducted by Max Kämpfert at the Frankfurt Palmengarten on 13 March 1900.

out of all proportion to its merits', describing Scott as England's 'musical Messiah'.[5] One critic particularly disliked the 'illogical peculiarities' of the fourth movement, which he felt betrayed 'a very distinctive, but underdeveloped artistic taste'.[6] The performance of *Pelleas* seems to have caused less controversy.[7] The review of the concert which appeared in the *Musical News* may constitute the first ever mention of Scott in the British musical press. According to the reviewer, *Pelleas* was 'original from beginning to end', the performance was a 'great success' and Scott's works would 'have to be reckoned with in the near future'.[8]

As Table 5.1 demonstrates, the majority of the early English performances of Scott's compositions before the London premiere of his Piano Quartet in E, Op. 16, were in Liverpool, with a few other performances occurring in London, Manchester and Bath. Scott's piano recital at St George's Hall, Liverpool, in October 1900 was the first of these performances to receive widespread press coverage. As Scott performed just one of his own works at the concert – the Piano Sonata in D, Op. 17 – critics focused largely on his pianistic, rather than compositional, abilities.[9] The *Musical News*'s critic, however, complained that the sonata had no 'definite plan' and that 'the first of the two movements ... resembled an extension of the extemporaneous interludes' Scott played between his pieces. Nonetheless, the reviewer wrote of Scott's 'present power and future promise'.[10] When Percy Grainger played the sonata in London a year later, it attracted similar criticism from *The Times*, whose critic thought it to be 'incoherent'.[11]

These reviews of the sonata touch on a couple of themes that appeared repeatedly in the criticism of Scott's works in the early years of the century: first, that Scott showed great 'promise' but his works had yet to emerge from an immature stage of development;[12] and second, frequent accusations of incoherence or 'a want of

[5] Cyril Scott, 'Early Memories', *British Musician & Musical News* 5 (February 1929), p. 43; Scott, *My Years of Indiscretion* (Mills & Boon, 1924), p. 38.

[6] A. Wadsack, 'Correspondenzen: Darmstadt. Um 8. Januar', *Neue Zeitschrift für Musik* 96 (July 1900), pp. 356–7.

[7] 'This time there were no hisses', Scott later recalled. Scott, *My Years of Indiscretion*, p. 39.

[8] L. F. B., 'Foreign Intelligence: Frankfort-am-Maine', *Musical News* 28 (March 1900), p. 280.

[9] Remarks on Scott's piano-playing were unanimously positive. See, for example, 'Music in Liverpool and District', *Musical Times* 41 (November 1900), p. 752; W. J. Bowden, 'Music in the Provinces', *Musical Standard* 14 (27 October 1900), p. 265; and 'Mr. Meir Scott's Pianoforte Recital', *Liverpool Mercury*, 19 October 1900, p. 8.

[10] W. A. R., 'Provincial: Liverpool', *Musical News* 19 (October 1900), p. 360. The version of the sonata which survives today is in one movement, suggesting that Scott revised the work between the time of the Liverpool performance and the date on the extant manuscript (11 September 1901).

[11] 'Mme. [Julia] Rudge's Concert', *The Times*, 2 December 1901, p. 13.

[12] One critic thought Scott might become 'one of the greatest composers that the world has yet seen': see 'Final Promenade Chamber Concert', *Bath Chronicle and Weekly Gazette*, 8 May 1902, p. 8. See also reviews of Scott's Piano Trio in E minor, Op. 3: 'Mrs Norman O'Neill's Concerts', *Musical Times* 42 (January 1901), p. 31;

Table 5.1 Early public performances of Scott's works in England

Work	*Date*	*Venue*
Dairy Song and *Little Lady of My Heart* (songs)	9 July 1900	Liverpool, Liverpool College of Music
Piano Sonata in D, Op. 17	18 Oct 1900	Liverpool, St George's Hall
	29 Nov 1901	London, Steinway Hall
Piano Trio in E, Op. 3	6 Dec 1900	London, Steinway Hall
Piano Quintet (1900)	26 Nov 1900	Liverpool, Woolton Hall
	9 Feb 1901	Liverpool, Ernst Schiever Classical Chamber Concert
	6 May 1902	Bath, Promenade Chamber Concert
'Pastorale' from *Idyllic Suite*	12 Dec 1900	London, Westminster Town Hall
Idyllic Suite (all four movements)	8 May 1902	Bath, Promenade Symphony Concert
Heroic Suite	12 Dec 1901	Manchester, Free Trade Hall
	14 Jan 1902	Liverpool, Philharmonic Hall
Ballad of Fair Helen of Kirkconnel	Jan or Feb 1902	Liverpool
	12 Mar 1902	London, Bechstein Hall
	19 Mar 1902	Liverpool, Birkenhead Music Hall
An English Waltz	12 Mar 1902	London, Bechstein Hall
	19 Apr 1902	Liverpool, Ernst Schiever Classical Chamber Concert
	6 May 1902	Bath, Promenade Chamber Concert
	24 Oct 1902	Liverpool, Harrison Concert
Piano Quartet in E, Op. 16	19 Apr 1902	Liverpool, Ernst Schiever Classical Chamber Concert
	12 Feb 1903	London, St James's Hall

unity',[13] usually linked to the fragmentary and improvisatory nature of his music, the lack of 'fundamental themes', or the over-repetition of short phrases.

All of these criticisms appeared in Arthur Johnstone's review of the 1901 performance of Scott's *Heroic Suite* in Manchester. Johnstone's final piece of advice for Scott was to 'remember that instrumental colouring never was or could be anything but quite a secondary matter in composition'.[14] This was another common criticism of modern music at the time, frequently employed by a certain group of 'liberal

of his Piano Quintet (*c.* 1900): W. J. Bowden, 'Music in the Provinces', *Musical Standard* 15 (February 1901), p. 111; and of his *Heroic Suite*: 'Music in Liverpool and District', *Musical Times* 43 (February 1902), p. 121; W. J. Bowden, 'Music in the Provinces', *Musical Standard* 17 (January 1902), p. 62.

[13] 'The Hallé Concerts', *Manchester Evening News*, 13 December 1901, p. 4.

[14] 'The Hallé Concerts', *Manchester Guardian*, 13 December 1901, p. 5. As was usually the case in newspaper criticism at the time, the review is not signed, but it is almost certainly by Johnstone, who was then the *Guardian*'s chief music critic. (The Wagner worship in the paragraph below the review of Scott's concert also suggests it was him.)

critics' who, Matthew Riley writes, were 'open-minded' to musical 'progress' but had 'limits to their tolerance, stemming from their commitment to "beauty", their insistence on incremental change in music history, and their idealist aesthetics'.[15] For these critics, colour was a kind of beauty which 'appeal[ed] to the senses and the nerves rather than the mind', and was thus not an important factor in judging the true worth of a composition.[16]

The performances of Scott's *Heroic Suite*, though reported in the national press, did little to boost his profile outside of the north of England. It was the London premieres of his Piano Quartet in E, Op. 16, and Second Symphony that earned him widespread recognition for the first time.[17] On the whole, both works were received warmly by audiences and critics alike. The quartet's premiere (on 12 February 1903) was reported in newspapers across the country. The *Sheffield Daily Telegraph*, for example, noted that 'The work was so favourably received that [Scott] was obliged over and over again to bow his acknowledgements.'[18] Even J. A. Fuller Maitland, the chief music critic of *The Times*, who would later become one of Scott's harshest detractors, wrote that the quartet was 'unquestionably successful'.[19] Charles Villiers Stanford was one of a minority who did not look upon the quartet so favourably, owing, according to Scott's later account, to 'the divergence of [their] musical outlook' and Scott's 'ideas on continual musical flow'.[20] After the success of his Piano Quartet, there was a tangible feeling of excitement and anticipation leading up to the premiere of his Second Symphony at the Proms on 25 August 1903. In the programme notes accompanying the performance, Edgar F. Jacques wrote that 'Discerning minds have for some time past regarded the composer of this symphony as one of the "coming men" amongst British creative musicians.'[21] As with the reception of the quartet, most of the reviews of the symphony were positive, and applause from the audience apparently 'burst forth' at the end of the performance, causing Scott to be 'twice called to the platform'.[22]

[15] Matthew Riley, 'Liberal Critics and Modern Music in the Post-Victorian Age', in *British Music and Modernism, 1895–1960*, ed. Matthew Riley (Ashgate, 2010), p. 13.

[16] Ibid., 22. It is interesting to note the similarity between Johnstone's advice to Scott and William Henry Hadow's assessment of Debussy's music in 1906, in which he wrote that 'there is nothing to replace tonality except colour, and man cannot live by colour alone'. Quoted in ibid., p. 18.

[17] Scott later wrote that the performance of his Piano Quartet had put his 'name before the public in a manner which, short of murder, nothing else could have done'. Scott, *Bone of Contention: Life Story and Confessions* (Aquarian Press, 1969), p. 88.

[18] 'London Correspondence', *Sheffield Daily Telegraph*, 13 February 1903, p. 4.

[19] 'Concerts', *The Times*, 13 February 1903, p. 9. 'Although music reviews in *The Times* were unsigned', writes Meirion Hughes, 'on stylistic grounds it is most probable that Maitland undertook most of the reviewing, leaving minor musical occasions (and the uncongenial ones) to his assistants.' Meirion Hughes, *The English Musical Renaissance and the Press, 1850–1914: Watchmen of Music* (Ashgate, 2002), p. 31.

[20] Scott, *My Years of Indiscretion*, p. 72. For a detailed discussion of Scott's concept of 'musical flow', see Sarah Collins, *The Aesthetic Life of Cyril Scott* (Boydell, 2013), pp. 183–90.

[21] Programmes for Promenade Concerts, 25 August 1903, British Library, h.5470.

[22] 'Music and Musicians', *Sunday Times*, 30 August 1903, p. 6.

As a result of his newfound fame, Edwin Evans – a critic and prominent advocate of modern music in the early twentieth century – wrote a lengthy article on the young composer for the *Musical Standard*. The article was part of a series he wrote for the journal on the subject of 'Modern British Composers', and in it Evans credited Scott with ushering in a 'new phase of English music'.[23] Similarly, in 1905, Constance Smedley wrote that Scott 'headed' a new 'iconoclastic' 'brotherhood of [British] composers' that included Delius and the other members of the 'Frankfurt Group'.[24] Both Evans and Smedley remarked on the 'modern' characteristics of Scott's music: its uninterrupted 'flow' and the absence of stable tonality – both essentially Wagnerian techniques pushed to a new extreme.

In the first decade of the century Scott was initially considered by critics such as Fuller Maitland to be the 'English counterpart' of the 'ultra-modern' Debussy and Ravel. The three composers were united, according to Maitland, by their 'persistent avoidance of anything that can be mistaken for a connected melody or pleasing harmony'.[25] From 1904 onwards, however, more and more critics began to feel that Scott's experiments went beyond those of Debussy, Ravel and the other representative modern composer of the time, Richard Strauss. An anonymous critic for the *Musical Standard*, reviewing the 1904 premiere of Scott's orchestral *Rhapsody*, Op. 32, wrote that the work was 'out-Straussing Strauss; absurd in so young a composer. The whole system of music cannot be turned upside down like this at the whim of a youngster'.[26] Three years later, reviewing a concert at the Bechstein Hall, the *Manchester Guardian*'s critic wrote that 'one can say without hesitation that Strauss is not at all modern in comparison with Mr. Scott'.[27]

With the first performances of Scott's most 'modern' works yet – his Violin Sonata, Op. 59, and Piano Sonata, Op. 66 – in 1908 and 1909, his music went well beyond the acceptable limits of incremental change in music history advocated by the 'liberal critics'. Many of the reviews of these works expressed outrage, confusion or disgust. The *Manchester Guardian* wrote that Scott's Violin Sonata produced in

[23] Edwin Evans, 'Modern British Composers: IX', *Musical Standard* 20 (September 1903), pp. 162–3. Evans later wrote another series of articles, under the same heading, for the *Musical Times* between 1919 and 1920.

[24] Constance Smedley, 'A Renaissance in British Music', *Musical Opinion and Music Trade Review* 29 (October 1905), p. 29. Smedley was an author, illustrator and regular contributor to newspapers and journals.

[25] 'Concerts', *The Times*, 3 May 1904, p. 10. When Maitland wrote the entry on Scott (probably in about 1907) for the second edition of *Grove*, his opinion had not changed: 'Finding himself hampered by the limitations of musical conventions, he threw himself into the ultra-modern school of composition ... Mr. Scott may be best described as the English counterpart to Debussy'. 'Scott, Cyril Meir', in vol. 4 of *Grove's Dictionary of Music and Musicians*, 2nd edn, ed. J. A. Fuller Maitland (London: Macmillan, 1911), p. 390. See also Maitland's review of Scott's Piano Sextet (premiered 1906): 'Concerts', *The Times*, 23 March 1906, p. 10.

[26] 'Cyril Scott's Rhapsody, No. 1', *Musical Standard* 22 (September 1904), p. 176.

[27] 'Music in London', *Manchester Guardian*, 13 March 1907, p. 7. This concert included performances of Scott's Piano Sextet and a new Piano Quintet.

listeners 'a feeling of irritation and impatience',[28] while the *Musical Times* surmised that Scott's objective was to 'express torturing and unpleasant thoughts, and moreover to express them in an unpleasant manner'.[29] One German critic was equally appalled, writing that Scott's attempt to 'outdo' Reger, Strauss and Debussy resulted in a work that 'barely still contains music'; it was 'just torture'.[30] The Piano Sonata fared no better. George Lowe, critic for *Musical Opinion*, wrote that the sonata produced in him 'a feeling of utter bewilderment' and compared the publishing of such a work with 'the throwing down of the glove as an act of challenge'.[31] The 'ultra-advanced sonata'[32] was also the subject of an article in the *Musical News* titled 'The Acme of Ugliness',[33] and in a later review from 1912 the composer Edgar Bainton linked the work to a '"futurist" school'.[34]

Before World War 1, the words 'futurist' and 'futurism' were associated above all, in the British musical press at least, with the music of Schönberg rather than the Italian movement. It is interesting to note that the language used in the reviews of Scott's sonatas is strikingly similar to that used by English music critics when they first encountered Schönberg's *Five Orchestral Pieces* in 1912.[35] But while some British critics positioned Scott at the forefront of modernism, alongside Schönberg, the latter's disciple, Alban Berg, wrote following the performance of Scott's *Princess Maleine* overture in Vienna in 1912 that Scott's music did not 'have the least resemblance to [Schönberg's]'. Berg conceded the work was 'no doubt modern' but felt that it was 'never-ending mush'.[36]

As Scott's 'serious works' began to receive more negative reactions from the press, Scott was also becoming increasingly known as a composer of miniature

28 'Music in London: Mr. Cyril Scott's New Works', *Manchester Guardian*, 26 March 1908, p. 7.

29 'Concerts of British Music', *Musical Times* 49 (May 1908), p. 323.

30 Wilhelm Altmann, 'Besprechungen: Musikalien', *Die Musik* 10/24 (1910–11), p. 375.

31 George Lowe, 'Three Modern Pianoforte Sonatas', *Musical Opinion and Music Trade Review* 33 (November 1909), pp. 115–16.

32 As it was described by the *Manchester Courier*: 'New Music: Songs and Instrumental Pieces', *Manchester Courier and Lancashire General Advertiser*, 18 December 1909, p. 11.

33 I have been unable to locate the original article, but extracts from it were printed in Walter Bernhard, 'Out and About', *Musical Opinion and Music Trade Review* 33 (February 1910), p. 341.

34 Edgar Bainton, 'Some British Composers: No. 1. Cyril Scott', *Musical Opinion and Music Trade Review* 35 (June 1912), p. 621.

35 The *Globe*, for example, described Schönberg's work as resembling 'the dismal wailings of a tortured soul'; like Scott, Schönberg was frequently accused of 'incoherence'. See Deborah Heckert, 'Schönberg, Roger Fry and the Emergence of a Critical Language for the Reception of Musical Modernism in Britain, 1912–1914', in *British Music and Modernism*, ed. Riley, p. 52. The *Manchester Guardian*'s description of Schönberg's attempt to express 'agonising emotions' is also similar to the *Musical Times*'s critique of Scott's Violin Sonata. See Alfred Kalisch, 'A Futurist Composer', *Manchester Guardian*, 4 September 1912, p. 6.

36 *The Berg-Schönberg Correspondence*, ed. Juliane Brand, Christopher Hailey and Donal Harris (W. W. Norton & Company, 1987), pp. 89, 87.

piano pieces and short songs that appealed to popular taste. Scott would later claim that these 'potboilers' had 'deflected attention from [his] more serious works', and earned him an 'undesired reputation'.[37] Nonetheless, he seems to have had no qualms about these pieces earlier in the century, telling his friend, the Australian-born composer F. S. Kelly, that 'he considered nothing' in his concert (consisting largely of 'potboilers') at the Bechstein Hall in April 1913 'as at all pandering to popular taste'.[38] Scott held a number of annual concerts dedicated to his own works at the Bechstein Hall before World War 1 (in 1906–9, 1911 and 1913–14). The popularity of these concerts – the newspapers reported 'large', 'enthusiastic' and 'fashionable' audiences – was largely due to the potboilers which dominated their programmes.[39] One critic remarked in 1911 that Scott's 'songs and pianoforte pieces are constantly to be seen on concert programmes', and a year earlier the *Monthly Musical Record* reported that German and French translations of Scott's most popular songs were in preparation, demonstrating the extent of the fame that these works afforded him.[40] Like the public, the critics usually preferred Scott's smaller works to his 'serious' compositions. Of the 1907 Bechstein concert, *The Times* reported that 'In shorter forms ... Mr. Scott's music possesses far more shapeliness and purpose',[41] and of the 1906 concert the *Athenæum* wrote that 'In compositions of short compass the avoidance of a cadence proved far less harmful.'[42] Though these pieces may have shaped negative perceptions of his music in later years, in the earlier part of the century they actually sustained Scott's popularity in bourgeois circles of London Society at a time when his serious works began seriously to fall out of favour.

The most significant performance of Scott's music during the years of World War 1 was the premiere of his Piano Concerto No. 1 in London in May 1915.[43] The reac-

[37] Scott, *Bone of Contention*, p. 94.

[38] *Race Against Time: The Diaries of F. S. Kelly*, ed. Thérèse Radic (National Library of Australia, 2004), pp. 293–4. Collins has also pointed that many of these works are 'dedicated to [Scott's] closest and most valued friends and mentors', suggesting 'that their conception and composition was not always as flippant as he later implied'. Collins, *The Aesthetic Life of Cyril Scott*, p. 84.

[39] See, for example 'Music: This Week', *The Athenæum* 4412 (16 March 1907), p. 330; and 'Concerts', *The Times*, 23 March 1906, p. 10. Of the 1913 concert one critic wrote that 'The large appreciative audience clearly showed that Mr. Scott's popularity is an established thing.' 'Cyril Scott's Recital at Bechstein Hall', *Monthly Musical Record* 43 (May 1913), p. 121.

[40] 'Our Pictorial Supplement', *Monthly Musical Record* 41 (February 1911), p. 34; John S. Shedlock, 'Cyril Scott and his Art Work', *Monthly Musical Record* 40 (November 1910), p. 242.

[41] 'Bechstein Hall', *The Times*, 13 March 1907, p. 12.

[42] 'Music: This Week', *The Athenæum* 4092 (31 March 1906), p. 406.

[43] The premiere seems to have initially been scheduled for a concert at the Proms on 3 September 1914, but this never came to fruition. Scott's *Aubade* for orchestra, Op. 77, was also due to be played during the same Proms season, on 22 October, but this performance never occurred either. Notices for these performances appeared in numerous newspapers and journals. See, for example, 'Promenade Concerts, 1914. New British Compositions', *Sunday Times*, 12 July 1914, p. 7; 'Drama and Music', *Manchester Guardian*, 11 July 1914, p. 6; 'Occasional Notes: The Promenade Concerts', *Musical Times* 55 (August 1914), p. 513.

tion in the press was largely negative.[44] The *Manchester Courier* linked the work to a 'Futurist' movement,[45] and the *Newcastle Daily Journal*'s critic thought that the work was interesting only as an 'experiment': 'it was valuable as showing that a British composer can write even stranger music than has been composed by any foreigner'.[46] The *Observer*'s critic compared the concerto unfavourably with Ravel, writing that while 'the French composer suggests that he knows very well what he is doing ... the English composer ... suggests entirely the opposite'.[47] For some critics Scott's music was already beginning to seem old fashioned. Ernest Newman's prediction, in 1915, that Scott would soon cease to be thought an *enfant terrible* proved to be prescient:

> Cyril Scott has paid the penalty of specializing in the newest freak-fashions of his own artistic generation by becoming the most outmoded English composer of the next generation. The bulk of his published music is almost as old-fashioned as the hobble skirt; in another ten years it will be as old-fashioned as the crinoline.[48]

In the winter of 1920–1 Scott's publisher, Elkin, arranged for him to tour North America as a composer, pianist, conductor and lecturer. According to Scott's own account, the tour was artistically and financially 'a gratifying success'.[49] Scott was already well known to the American public by 1920. Positive assessments of the composer had appeared in American and Canadian journals in the years preceding the tour,[50] and the Russian-American composer, pianist and champion of modern music Leo Ornstein performed Scott's Piano Sonata No. 1, Op. 66, along with a number of his smaller piano pieces, in various American cities during the war years.[51]

[44] The enthusiastic review that appeared in *The Times* proved a surprising exception. See 'Festival of British Music', *The Times*, 17 May 1915, p. 5. The composer Kaikhosru Sorabji also wrote positively about the concerto, referring to it as 'the only important contribution of any British composer to the literature of the piano'. Kaikhosru Sorabji, 'Modern Piano Technique', *Sackbut* 1 (July 1920), pp. 116–20, at p. 119.

[45] 'Festival of British Music', *Manchester Courier and Lancashire General Advertiser*, 17 May 1915, p. 4.

[46] Counterpoint, 'Music and Musicians: The British Composers' Innings', *Newcastle Daily Journal*, 21 May 1915, p. 3.

[47] 'Festival of British Music: Mr. Cyril Scott's Piano Concerto', *Observer*, 16 May 1915, p. 14.

[48] Ernest Newman, 'English Music, Present and Future: II. – The Men', *The Nation* 17 (3 April 1915), p. 16.

[49] Scott, *Bone of Contention*, pp. 163, 165; Scott, *My Years of Indiscretion*, p. 251.

[50] See, for example, Arnold S. Potter, 'Cyril Scott: The Man and his Works', *Harvard Musical Review* 4 (February 1916), pp. 6–8; and W. O. Forsyth, 'Cyril Scott', *Canadian Journal of Music* 2 (March 1916), p. 196.

[51] Ornstein played the sonata in December 1915 in a New York recital described by the press as comprising 'ultra modern and futurist music'. See 'Notes on the Coming Concerts', *New York Tribune*, 28 November 1915, p. 7. Ornstein also performed Scott's *Danse nègre, Irish Reel* and *Impressions from the Jungle Book*. See 'Mr Ornstein's Recital', *Boston Daily Globe*, 12 January 1916, p. 11; and Richard L. Stokes, 'Symphony Opens with Admirable Program', *St. Louis Post-Dispatch*, 23 November 1918, p. 12.

Scott's reputation rested, above all, on the piano miniatures, as evidenced by an article on the composer in an Atlanta newspaper:

> Practically all musicians of attainment and many piano students already play some of Mr. Scott's shorter works. In fact, one or two of his compositions are amongst the most popular which are now being played. However, the number of people in this city who have heard his entire and more involved works for the piano are very few.[52]

Nonetheless, the same newspaper reported that Scott was 'probably the most talked of figure in the musical life in America this season'.[53] Tickets for his recitals sold out in New York, Boston and Atlanta,[54] and many of the critics, though unconvinced by the Piano Sonata, reported a positive reaction from the audience. There were 'several encores' in Boston, and in Chicago 'Scott was received ... with great enthusiasm'.[55]

The biggest event of the tour was the performances of Scott's Piano Concerto No. 1 and his *Two Passacaglias on Irish Themes* by the Philadelphia Orchestra, conducted by Leopold Stokowski at the Academy of Music, Philadelphia on 5 and 6 November and at Carnegie Hall on 9 November. Reviewing the concert, Henry Edward Krehbiel of the *New York Tribune* suggested Scott's music was 'like a poison or a noxious and baneful gas',[56] and claimed that members of the audience left the hall after hearing it:

> There were ... a considerable number who walked out of the room after the first movement of the pianoforte concerto, a large number after the conclusion of that work, and a still larger number after the performance of the first of Mr. Scott's Passacaglias.[57]

[52] 'Cyril Scott to Appear in December', *Atlanta Constitution*, 5 December 1920, p. 3. Richard Aldrich of the *New York Times* remarked that 'Mr. Scott is by no means unknown to this public by name and through some of his music though it has hitherto been mostly music in the smaller forms'. Aldrich, 'Music: The Philadelphia Orchestra', *New York Times*, 10 November 1920, p. 23.

[53] Louise Dooly, 'Recital by Cyril Scott Proves Intellectual Treat', *Atlanta Constitution*, 18 December 1920, p. 10.

[54] See 'Cyril Scott has a Bright Recital', *Boston Daily Globe*, 23 November 1920, p. 5; 'Cyril Scott, Famous Pianist, Here Today', *Atlanta Constitution*, 17 December 1920, p. 8; Scott, *My Years of Indiscretion*, p. 257.

[55] 'Cyril Scott has a Bright Recital', *Boston Daily Globe*, 23 November 1920, p. 5; 'Cyril Scott', *Chicago Daily Tribune*, 24 December 1920, p. 11.

[56] H. E. Krehbiel, 'Philadelphia Orchestra at Carnegie Hall', *New York Tribune*, 10 November 1920, p. 8. Fellow New York music critic Richard Aldrich wrote that Krehbiel 'was never an ardent admirer of Debussy, of the later Strauss, and still less of those who have troubled the surface of the musical waters since'. See Barbara Mueser, 'The Criticism of New Music in New York: 1919–1929' (PhD diss., City University of New York, 1975), p. 60.

[57] H. E. Krehbiel, 'The Critic of the Present and Composer of the Future', *New York Tribune*, 21 November 1920, p. 5.

Richard Aldrich's review of the Carnegie Hall concert for the *New York Times* made no mention of walk-outs, but noted that Scott's music – only 'politely applauded' – was 'an acquired taste and that more time is necessary for acquiring it'.[58]

Elsewhere, the reception of the Piano Concerto and the *Irish Passacaglias* was mixed. Frederick Stock, conductor of the Chicago Symphony Orchestra, remarked that these works 'were interesting but added nothing to the world's collection of bizarre music'.[59] James Huneker of the *New York Evening World* attended a performance of the *Passacaglias* in Boston, and wrote that Scott's 'music [was] for the Martians of the fantastic H. G. Wells'.[60] Although Scott's reputation as an iconoclast was beginning to wane by this time – in England at least – during his American tour the press often used words such as 'modern', 'modernist', 'ultra modern', 'radical' and 'radicalism' when discussing his music,[61] and the alignment with Wells's science-fiction served to reinforce the modernist association.[62]

In terms of English premieres of his larger works, the 1920s were less eventful for Scott than the two preceding decades. Nonetheless, it was often reported in the press during this period that Scott was one of the best-known English composers on the Continent. Edward Dent wrote in 1920 that 'Cyril Scott and Elgar are ... regarded in Germany as the representative English composers'.[63] In 1922 a Danish critic, Fritz Crome, wrote that Scott was considered the English representative of an 'experimental "modernist" movement', aligning him with Francesco Pratella and Schönberg.[64] A Dutch book published in 1925 referred to Scott as '*the* great [musical]

58 Richard Aldrich, 'Music: The Philadelphia Orchestra', *New York Times*, 10 November 1920, p. 23.

59 Ruth Miller, 'Resume of the Symphony Season Just Finished', *Chicago Daily Tribune*, 24 April 1921, p. 4.

60 James Huneker, *New York Evening World*, 6 February 1921. Quoted in Mueser, 'The Criticism of New Music in New York', pp. 52–3.

61 See, for example, 'Concert by Cyril Scott, Pianist and Composer', *Boston Daily Globe*, 1 February 1921, p. 8; 'Mr. Cyril Scott in Philadelphia', *Christian Science Monitor*, 13 November 1920, p. 12; Richard Aldrich, 'Music: The Philadelphia Orchestra', *New York Times*, 10 November 1920, p. 23; Louise Dooly, 'Recital by Cyril Scott Proves Intellectual Treat', *Atlanta Constitution*, 18 December 1920, p. 10.

62 Matthew Riley notes that although Wells 'was hardly a literary Modernist ... by choosing to focus his writing on science rather than human relationships he had inverted traditional literary canons with almost as much force as his modernist successors'. Matthew Riley, 'Music for the Machines of the Future: H. G. Wells, Arthur Bliss and *Things to Come* (1936)', in *British Music and Modernism*, ed. Riley, pp. 249–68, at p. 250. Incidentally, Scott knew Wells personally. See Scott, *My Years of Indiscretion*, pp. 161–2; and *Bone of Contention*, p. 151.

63 Edward J. Dent, 'Foreign Literature: Letters from Germany, I. – First Impressions', *Athenæum* 4723 (5 November 1920), p. 628. Edwin Evans remarked in 1923 that until the end of World War 1 'only two English composers were known ['over a good section of the Continent'], Elgar and Cyril Scott'. Edwin Evans, 'Introductions: VII. Cyril Scott', *British Music Society Bulletin* 5 (July 1923), pp. 208–11.

64 'Music in the Foreign Press: Denmark and Schönberg', *Musical Times* 63 (May 1922), p. 328.

figure in England'.[65] Even as late as 1935 it was reported that Scott was 'known and honoured widely in Germany ... he and Arnold Bax lead the field in popularity'.[66]

In February 1922 Scott's Piano Concerto No. 1 was 'successfully' performed in Vienna, as were a number of his smaller piano pieces and songs at subsequent concerts.[67] Perhaps most significantly, Scott's one-act opera *The Alchemist* was performed in Essen (on more than one occasion) in 1925. *The Daily Telegraph*'s review of the premiere was reprinted in the *New York Times*:

> The cordiality of the reception accorded to this work by a foreign composer was as remarkable as it was gratifying. ... The attention of the packed house was held from start to finish by the arresting and unconventional qualities of the work.[68]

The *Musical Times* quoted the *Essener Allgemeiner Zeitung*, which reported that the 'applause was very enthusiastic'.[69] In 1928 Scott's ballet *Karma* was 'produced with great success' in Vienna,[70] and in 1930 the *Musical Mirror* reported that Scott was again 'meeting with great success in Germany':

> His mime-ballet, *The Short-sighted Apothecary*, will be produced in Berlin next spring, while his overture, *Noel*, was performed for the first time last month. Mr. Scott has also been invited to give several performances of his Piano Concerto.[71]

Back in Britain, there was no such success. Scott tried his hand at theatre music for a production of *Othello* in 1920. Much of the music, however, including the prelude, was drowned out by noise from the audience. *The Times*'s critic, probably H. C. Colles – for whom Scott's music held little more appeal than it did for his predecessor, Fuller Maitland – wrote that 'Mr. Scott's theatre music is bad because he cannot forget the concert room'.[72] Performances of new works by Scott now received far less attention in the British press than they used to. The premiere of his *Suite fantastique* by the London Chamber Orchestra in 1926 was scarcely noticed. Where it was reviewed, it received the same criticism as his *Heroic Suite* had a quarter of a century earlier: Scott was advised against putting 'orchestral effect [i.e. colour] first and

[65] Rient Van Santen, *De Piano en hare Componisten* (Kruseman, 1925). Quoted in Herbert Antcliffe, 'View-Points in Musical History', *Sackbut* 6 (May 1926), pp. 279–82 at p. 281.

[66] Keith Barry, 'In Search of Music', *Musical Times* 76 (August 1935), pp. 698–701.

[67] 'English Music in Vienna', *Observer*, 19 March 1922, p. 8. See also Paul Bechert, 'British Music at Vienna', *Musical Times* 63 (June 1922), pp. 395–6; 'More English Music in Vienna', *Observer*, 16 April 1922, p. 8; [Untitled], *Musical Times* 63 (April 1922), p. 271.

[68] 'Cyril Scott's "Alchemist"', *New York Times*, 5 July 1925, p. 5.

[69] 'Occasional Notes', *Musical Times* 66 (July 1925), p. 623.

[70] 'Occasional Notes', *Musical Times* 69 (March 1928), p. 247.

[71] [Untitled], *Musical Mirror*, 10 January 1930, p. 6.

[72] 'Music in the Theatre: The Case of "Othello"', *The Times*, 21 February 1920, p. 12. See also M. 'Drama: "Othello" at the New Theatre', *Athenæum* 4687 (27 February 1920), pp. 284–5.

foremost, and to consider that the thematic means whereby that effect is created is a secondary matter'.[73] By 1928 and the premiere of Scott's Violin Concerto, there was a sense that the critics felt they had heard it all before: '[the concerto] adds nothing to the range of the composer's style', wrote a critic for the *Musical Times*, 'The idiom is familiar.'[74]

The Piano Concerto was by far Scott's most popular orchestral work in the inter-war period, receiving after its premiere at least four further English performances by 1930. However, the critics' reviews were, by and large, negative. After a performance at a British Music Society concert on 14 June 1921, Edward Dent contrasted the 'supposed Celestial candies' of Scott's music with the sublime 'realities' and 'infinites' of Holst's *The Planets*.[75] This is typical of the criticism levelled at Scott during this time, criticism that considered his music to be too trivial, too affected and too feminine. Percy Scholes, music critic at the *Observer*, held just such an opinion of Scott: 'If he is to justify one-time British hopes, and the current Continental beliefs, he will have to stir himself, cast off this cloak of dilettante grace, and show us a man beneath it'.[76] By the end of World War 1 the decadence, aestheticism and the associated 'feminine' qualities that Scott (and his music) had absorbed from Stefan George in the 1890s had become distinctly unfashionable. Moreover, the perceived popularity of Scott's miniature piano pieces and songs was now increasingly viewed with contempt by many critics.

Despite his fading stardom, the 1930s saw the premieres of a number of Scott's larger-scale works, including his cantata *La belle dame sans merci*, which 'pleased the audience' at the 1934 Leeds Festival,[77] and his *Festival Overture*, which was performed by the BBC Symphony Orchestra in the same year. The American premiere of the latter work, three years later, was heard by an audience of over 2,000 in New York,[78] but the *New York Herald* reported that the music – 'up to date but not rad-

[73] 'Recitals of the Week: American Women's Club', *The Times*, 26 November 1926, p. 12. This work was performed again in 1928 at a British Music Society concert in Bournemouth. *The Times* liked the work no better on this second hearing, writing that it failed to produce a 'genuinely mystical character'. 'Opera in England: British Music Society at Bournemouth', *The Times*, 4 May 1928, p. 14.

[74] 'Music in the Provinces', *Musical Times* 69 (March 1928), p. 260.

[75] Edward J. Dent, 'The World of Music: A Festival of British Music', *Illustrated London News*, 25 June 1921, p. 870. See also P[ercy] A[lfred] S[choles] 'Music of the Week: The British Music Society', *Observer*, 19 June 1921, p. 10. Other performances of the Piano Concerto include those in Bournemouth (1917), Harrogate (1929) and Hastings (1930). See 'Music in the Provinces: Bournemouth', *Musical Times* 58 (May 1917), p. 227; 'Festival of British Music: First Concert at Harrogate', *The Times*, 25 July 1929, p. 12; 'Hastings Musical Festival: Mr. Scott's Concerto', *The Times*, 28 February 1930, p. 12; 'Brahms and Cyril Scott', *Hastings and St. Leonards Observer*, 1 March 1930, p. 5.

[76] P[ercy] A[lfred] S[choles], 'Music of the Week: Cyril Scott', *Observer*, 1 June 1924, p. 10.

[77] 'Leeds Musical Festival: New Choral Work by Cyril Scott', *The Times*, 4 October 1934, p. 10.

[78] 'Westchester Fete Attended by 2,600', *New York Times*, 23 May 1937, p. 45.

ical' – 'seemed somewhat disappointing' and proved 'rather ineffective'.[79] Scott, along with some of his supporters, wrote bitterly about the BBC's treatment of him towards the end of his life,[80] and Diana Swann has suggested that he was shunned by the BBC for failing to conform to its 'hidden set of criteria'.[81] However, in addition to the *Festival Overture* performance, the BBC's various ensembles did perform and broadcast the premieres of a number of Scott's other 'serious' works in the 1930s. This included a performance by the BBC Symphony Orchestra of Scott's tone poem *Early One Morning* in 1931, the BBC Wireless Chorus's premiere of the cantata *Mirabelle* in 1933,[82] and the composer's own performance of his Piano Sonata No. 2 in 1934.[83] On 26 and 27 November 1931 there were broadcasts of Scott's operetta *Janet and Felix*, a work 'specifically written for the microphone', performed by the BBC Theatre Orchestra.[84] None of these broadcasts received a great deal of attention from the press, though the *Manchester Guardian* passed a positive judgement on the operetta:

> Mr. Scott throughout combines his more profound qualities as a musician and poet with a light and whimsical touch and a capacity for dialogue as delightful as any that may be heard in modern entertainment.[85]

Later in the decade came the premiere of Scott's Harpsichord Concerto, received favourably by the *Musical Times*,[86] and a performance at the Wigmore Hall – attended by 'a large audience' – of his String Trio No. 1 and Sonata for viola and piano. Neville Cardus's review of the Wigmore Hall concert confirmed the accuracy of Ernest Newman's predictions of twenty-four years earlier:

> to hear [the two works] was as though we had been taken back over the years in some sort of time machine ... as far as the music heard at this concert revealed, the contemporary linear composers may never have lived. ... It was strange in

79 'Final Concert in Westchester Festival is Held', *New York Herald Tribune*, 23 May 1937, p. 28.

80 Scott, *Bone of Contention*, pp. 223–4. Clinton Gray-Fisk, for example, asked in 1957 what was 'behind the B.B.C.'s senseless and ruthless ostracism of Cyril Scott'. Clinton Gray-Fisk, 'Letters to the Editor: Cyril Scott', *Musical Opinion* 80 (February 1957), p. 271.

81 Diana Swann, 'Cyril Scott (1879–1970)', *British Music Society News* 71 (September 1996), pp. 254–6.

82 'Wireless Notes: A Cyril Scott Cantata', *Manchester Guardian*, 13 April 1933, p. 12.

83 'Wireless Notes and Programmes', *Manchester Guardian*, 10 January 1931, p. 12; 'Wireless Notes', *Manchester Guardian*, 23 February 1934, p. 10.

84 'The Programmes: An Operetta', *The Times*, 27 November 1931, p. 6. See p. 59.

85 N. E., 'Yesterday's Broadcast: Cyril Scott's Operetta', *Manchester Guardian*, 27 November 1931, p. 10. See also 'Wireless Notes', *Manchester Guardian*, 26 November 1931, p. 10.

86 'The Concerto ... is one of the works that arrive at long intervals to reassure us as to Mr. Cyril Scott's essential musicianship and creative gift'. [William] McN[aught, junior], 'London Concerts: The Angel Grande Orchestra', *Musical Times* 79 (May 1938), p. 383.

> these hard-bitten percussive times to hear the old echoes of a departed sensibility. There is no future for it, and perhaps it will soon evaporate altogether.[87]

Many other critics remarked on the old-fashioned nature of Scott's 'vertically' conceived music during the 1930s and after World War 2.[88] A 1954 review of his *Sonata melodica* for violin and piano, for example, stated that the 'inherent characteristics' of Scott's music 'strike one as vertical and not horizontal. Posterity will have little difficulty in placing this work in its period of harmonic experimentation. It is of considerable *historic* interest.'[89]

It was also in the 1930s that reviews of Scott's music began more frequently to be shaped by the growing awareness in musical circles of the composer's interest in occultism and theosophy. This was undoubtedly in part due to the publication of Scott's book *The Influence of Music on History and Morals: A Vindication of Plato* in 1928, and the revised and extended version of this, *Music: Its Secret Influence Throughout the Ages*, published five years later.[90] One critic wrote in 1935 that Scott's devotion to 'the study of the mystical' had made music 'secondary with him, so that his pen has gone musically weary'.[91] The belief that Scott's extramusical interests distracted him from music and ultimately hindered his compositional abilities was a criticism made frequently both during and after his lifetime. For some commentators, Scott's beliefs were something to be mocked and could be used to further condemn his music, as demonstrated by *The Times*'s sneering review of the 1947 Proms performance of the *Festival Overture*:

> It does quite clearly depict a great gathering of initiates ... Just as one begins to be caught up in the communal spirit of festivity one finds one's mind vaguely saying 'But why are all these vegetarians wearing academic robes?'[92]

87 N[eville] C[ardus], 'Music in London: Cyril Scott', *Manchester Guardian*, 22 March 1939, p. 13.

88 Percy Grainger wrote that what united the music of the 'Frankfurt Gang' was their use of 'the CHORD'. Quoted in Stephen Banfield, *Sensibility and English Song: Critical Studies of the Early 20th Century*, vol. 1 (Cambridge University Press, 1985), 106.

89 My emphasis. B. W. G. R., 'Reviews of Music', *Music & Letters* 35 (April 1954), p. 172.

90 Cyril Scott, *The Influence of Music on History and Morals: A Vindication of Plato* (The Theosophical Publishing House, 1928); *Music: Its Secret Influence Throughout the Ages* (Rider & Co., 1933).

91 Sonya Michell, 'Moments Musical: Cyril Scott', *Christian Science Monitor*, 23 January 1935, p. 15.

92 'Promenade Concerts', *The Times*, 22 August 1947, p. 6. There were critics who saw Scott's mysticism in a positive light, but they were in the minority. A. E. Keeton, for instance, praised the 'healing therapeutic strain' in the music of Scott, Delius and Holst, which she thought was due to 'an underlying spiritual occultic vein in their make-up'. A. E. Keeton, 'A Cyril Scott Two-Piano Work', *Musical Opinion* 71 (July 1948), p. 426. This was a review of Scott's *Theme and Variations* for two pianos, first performed in 1931. See 'Music of the Week: Federation of Music Clubs', *Observer*, 18 January 1931, p. 19; and 'Federation of Music Clubs', *The Times*, 16 January 1931, p. 10.

Between World War 2 and Scott's death, premiere performances of his works were largely confined to chamber music. One of his larger works, an Oboe Concerto, was performed at the Proms in 1948, but it did nothing to contribute to a revival of interest in his music. *The Times* noted that it 'did not amount to much', and another critic wrote that it was merely a 'stylistic curiosity'.[93] On the whole, reviews of Scott's late chamber works were negative, or neutral at best. Perhaps the most recurrent theme was that his music was 'unfashionable'. The *Musical Times*'s review of his Piano Sonata No. 3 remarked that the work was 'unfashionably lush and romantic in idiom'. More damning was Peter J. Pirie's remarks on the work in *Music & Letters*:

> The whole style is wrong, and the methods cannot stand lengthy exposition. This Sonata might well serve several young contemporaries as a lesson in what happens to a composer who overworks a fashionable idiom in his youth.[94]

The establishment of a Cyril Scott Society in 1962 aimed at 'stimulating the performance and recording of his works'.[95] The Society did not achieve a great deal of success, though it did organise a concert dedicated to Scott's works at the Royal Academy of Music in 1964. Following the concert, Robert Henderson of the *Musical Times* remarked that the chamber works performed 'all had a rather nostalgic, retrospective flavour',[96] and he noted that 'Apart from some piano pieces and songs, few of us now know anything of the music of Cyril Scott.'[97]

The last performance during Scott's own lifetime that attracted significant press attention was that of his Piano Concerto No. 1 to celebrate the composer's ninetieth birthday. Though the audience were apparently enthusiastic, the critics were not overly impressed. Ronald Crichton of the *Financial Times* wrote that it was 'a ragbag of a score, with good ideas jostling commonplace ones', and thought it was 'unlikely to start off a full-scale revaluation of Scott's music'.[98] A couple of other reviews made reference to Scott's interest in mysticism and the occult, serving to reinforce the image of the composer as a reclusive eccentric of a bygone age, an image that was often then projected, explicitly or otherwise, onto his music.[99]

In 1963 Scott's one-time student Edmund Rubbra reflected on the English musical scene before World War 2, writing that there was an:

[93] 'Promenade Concerts', *The Times*, 16 September 1948, p. 7; Warren Stannard, 'Oboe Music', *Notes* 7 (December 1949), p. 137.

[94] Peter J. Pirie, 'Reviews of Music', *Music & Letters* 37 (July 1956), p. 312.

[95] 'A Cyril Scott Society', *Musical Times* 103 (April 1962), p. 250.

[96] Robert Henderson, 'London Music: Cyril Scott', *Musical Times* 105 (1964), p. 444.

[97] Ibid.

[98] Ronald Crichton, 'Elizabeth Hall: Cyril Scott', *Financial Times*, 1 November 1969, p. 5.

[99] See J. O. C., 'Birthday Present', *The Times*, 1 November 1969, p. 3; Geoffrey Crankshaw, 'Concerts: South Bank: 90th Birthday', *Music and Musicians*, 18 December 1969, p. 52.

> opposition for a dozen or so years after the end of the first World War between the Holst–Vaughan Williams *ethos* and that summarised by the music of such composers as Scott, Delius, Ireland and Bax.[100]

Rubbra goes on to write that the latter 'school' had come to be seen as a 'local phenomenon' which seemed in the 1960s to be of less importance than the 'far stronger musical personalities of Holst and Vaughan Williams'. This was a common view in the years after 1945, and it was around this time that narratives of the 'English Musical Renaissance' which placed Parry and Vaughan Williams at the centre began to develop, pushing such composers as Scott to the fringes.[101]

That Scott had become an obscure and almost forgotten figure by the time of his death in 1970 is demonstrated by the brevity of the obituaries he received in the *Musical Times* and the *Guardian*, the latter offering up a mere thirty-two words.[102] *The Times* provided a much lengthier obituary but ultimately concluded that Scott failed as a composer 'due to lack of concentration and self-criticism' and because his interests in mysticism and theosophy 'were allowed to compete with his music'.[103] Writing eight years later, on the occasion of the centenary of Scott's birth, Christopher Palmer opined that, in addition to Scott's 'extra-musical interests', it was his eclecticism – 'he could not be pigeonholed as a folklorist, neo-classicist, nature-mysticist or romantic-decadent' – that 'rendered him suspect' and contributed to the decline in his reputation.[104]

There were very few performances of Scott's larger works between 1970 and the end of the century. The performance of his *Hourglass Suite* for chamber orchestra a few months after his death was criticised in *The Times* for 'doodl[ing] along rather aimlessly',[105] while the *Financial Times* noted that the work was 'unlikely to do much to rescue his reputation'.[106] Significant recordings were also few and far between during this period. Most notable were John Ogdon's recordings, with the London

[100] E[dmund] R[ubbra], 'Reviews of Books: *Vaughan Williams*. By A. E. F. Dickinson', *Music & Letters*, 44 (July 1963), pp. 283–4.

[101] In Frank Howes's 1966 book on the English Musical Renaissance, Scott receives only two pages in a chapter tellingly named 'Tributaries from Frankfurt, Birmingham and Elsewhere'. Frank Howes, *The English Musical Renaissance* (Secker & Warburg, 1966), pp. 192–4. Scott fared no better in three subsequent books on the same topic. See Peter J. Pirie, *The English Musical Renaissance* (Victor Gollancz, 1979); Michael Trend, *The Music Makers: Heirs and Rebels of the English Musical Renaissance* (Weidenfeld & Nicolson, 1985); and Meirion Hughes and Robert Stradling, *The English Musical Renaissance, 1840–1940: Constructing a National Music*, 2nd edn (Manchester University Press, 2001).

[102] 'Obituary: Cyril Scott', *Musical Times* 112 (February 1971), p. 172; 'Cyril Scott Dies at 91', *Guardian*, 1 January 1971, p. 20.

[103] 'Obituary: Mr Cyril Scott, Prolific English Composer', *The Times*, 1 January 1971, p. 12.

[104] Christopher Palmer, 'Cyril Scott: Centenary Reflections', *Musical Times* 120 (September 1979), pp. 738–41.

[105] Alan Blythe, 'Polyphonia Orchestra, Elizabeth Hall', *The Times*, 22 May 1971, p. 19.

[106] Ronald Crichton, 'Practical Cats', *Financial Times*, 22 May 1971, p. 10.

Philharmonic Orchestra, of Scott's two piano concertos (1975 and 1977),[107] and the Marco Polo CD containing five of Scott's orchestral works (1994).[108] While the recording of the First Piano Concerto was, for one *Gramophone* critic, 'evidence that [Scott] has been most unjustly treated',[109] the second concerto was accused in the same publication of utilising 'thoughtlessly applied mannerisms' that were acceptable only in his 'short piano pieces and songs' (strikingly similar criticism to that which Scott received seventy years earlier).[110] The 1994 recording of orchestral works was greeted with no great fanfare: 'The music lacks any great variety of mood, and generally Scott's material seems less striking than that of Joseph Holbrooke.'[111]

Since the year 2000 there has been a flurry of premiere recordings of Scott's works. The 2004 Chandos recording of his Symphony No. 3, Piano Concerto No. 2 and the tone poem *Neptune* were described by Peter Dickinson as 'a remarkable discovery in 20th-century British music'.[112] David Babcock's review of the same CD in *Tempo* was equally enthusiastic, concluding that:

> Scott has much to recommend him as a composer whose music rewards repeated hearings. There are melodic ideas of distinction, memorable yet never banal. His forms are new and original, spontaneous without sacrificing solidity. The orchestration is striking and personal. Above all, he has an individual voice transcending all influences.[113]

The 2004 CD ushered in a series of further recordings of Scott's orchestral works (many of which had not been heard for decades, if ever before), and these have been received positively for the most part. The Cello Concerto on the 2008 Chandos recording – composed in 1937 but never performed during Scott's lifetime – was described as a 'remarkable piece' by Andrew Clements, 'quite unlike anything else being composed in Britain in the 1930s'.[114] Similarly, Geoffrey Norris has written

[107] The second recording also included Scott's *Early One Morning* for piano and orchestra.

[108] The works included on the CD were Scott's *Aubade*, Op. 77, *Neapolitan Rhapsody*, *Suite fantastique*, *Two Passacaglias on Irish Themes* and *Three Symphonic Dances*.

[109] T[revor] H[arvey], 'Reviews: Orchestral: Scott', *Gramophone* 53 (September 1975), p. 471.

[110] M[ax] H[arrison], 'Reviews: Orchestral: Scott', *Gramophone* 54 (April 1977), p. 1556.

[111] A[ndrew] M. L[amb], 'Reviews: Orchestral: C. Scott Orchestral Works', *Gramophone* 72 (July 1994), p. 56.

[112] Peter Dickinson, 'The warmest of welcomes for a remarkable discovery in 20th-century British music', *Gramophone* 82 (June 2004), p. 53.

[113] David Babcock, '[Review of] Cyril Scott: Symphony No. 3 *The Muses*; Piano Concerto No. 2; *Neptune*. Howard Shelley (pno), Huddersfield Choral Society, BBC Philharmonic, c. Martyn Brabbins. Chandos CHAN 10211', *Tempo* 59 (July 2005), pp. 78–9.

[114] Andrew Clements, 'Scott: Symphony No 1; Cello Concerto, Paul Watkins / BBCPO / Brabbins', *Guardian*, 15 February 2008 <http://www.theguardian.com/music/2008/feb/15/classicalmusicandopera.shopping3> (accessed 3 April 2015).

that the 2006 recording of Scott's Fourth Symphony enhances Scott's 'credentials as an individualist in English music'.[115]

Robert Muuse's recordings (2011) of thirteen of Scott's songs represent another invaluable contribution to the Scott discography, as do Leslie De'Ath's complete recordings of the piano music. In stark contrast to the criticisms of a hundred years earlier, it is Scott's larger-scale piano works, in particular the four sonatas, rather than the piano miniatures, that have been most warmly received by twenty-first-century critics. Calum MacDonald, reviewing De'Ath's and Michael Schäfer's recordings of Scott's piano music, has written that '[t]he music ranges from the frankly trivial or salony ... to the imposing (the Sonatas, or the huge fugue that concludes the *Deuxième Suite*) and the powerfully evocative'. MacDonald concluded after the release of the fifth and final volume of De'Ath's series that Scott 'wrote far too many pot-boiling miniatures that one would gladly trade in for a few more pieces of sustained hard thinking like the Second Sonata'.[116] A significant number of Scott's chamber works have also been put on disc over the last decade. These have been received less enthusiastically than the orchestral works, though still much more favourably than they were in Scott's own lifetime. Andrew Clements, for example, has remarked that the 'harmonic approach' of some of Scott's later chamber works – recorded by the Gould Piano Trio in 2010 – 'produces the sensation of wading through aural treacle' (echoing earlier twentieth-century criticisms).[117] By contrast, Clare Howick and Sophia Rahman's recordings of Scott's Violin Sonatas Nos. 1 and 3, and his *Sonata melodica*, were described by John France as 'important and rewarding pieces that deserve to be in the repertoire'.[118]

The flood of recordings has resulted in more concert performances of Scott's works. These include the first public performances in over a hundred years of Scott's

[115] Geoffrey Norris, 'Scott: Piano Concerto No 1; Symphony No 4; Early One Morning', *Telegraph*, 22 April 2006 <http://www.telegraph.co.uk/culture/music/classicalmusic/3651741/Classical-CDs-of-the-week-Shostakovich-Mozarts-Requiem-and-more.html> (accessed 3 April 2015).

[116] Calum MacDonald, [Review of Chandos CHAN 10376; Dutton Epoch CDLX 7150; and Dutton Epoch CDLX 7155], *Tempo* 60 (October 2006), pp. 49–50; MacDonald, 'Scott: Piano Music', *Website of the BBC Music Magazine*, 20 January 2012, <http://www.classical-music.com/review/scott-piano-music> (accessed 3 April 2015). For similar remarks on the superiority of the 'serious' piano works over the miniatures, see Peter Dickinson's reviews of the second and fourth volumes of De'Ath's recordings in *Gramophone* (December 2005), p. 99; and (August 2007), p. 73.

[117] Andrew Clements, 'Plant/Cooper/Adams/Gould Piano Trio/Scott: Piano Trios Nos. 1 & 2; Clarinet Quintet; Clarinet Trio etc.', *Guardian*, 5 February 2010 <http://www.theguardian.com/music/2010/feb/05/scott-plant-cooper-adams> (accessed 3 April 2015). Similarly, Stephen Johnson had mixed feelings about the Piano Quartet and Piano Quintet released on CD by Dutton: 'Almost any passage taken at random will reveal Scott's flair for voluptuous harmony, his rhythmic and melodic freedom, but it's difficult to find a sense of shape in his extravagant, improvisatory wanderings'. Stephen Johnson, 'Scott: Piano Quartet, Op. 16; Piano Quintet', *Website of the BBC Music Magazine*, 20 January 2012 <http://www.classical-music.com/review/scott> (accessed 3 April 2015).

[118] John France, [Review of Cyril Scott CD NAXOS 8.572290], September 2010, <http://www.musicweb-international.com/classrev/2010/Sept10/Scott_8572290.htm> (accessed 3 April 2015).

overture to *Pelleas and Melisanda* in Cambridge and London in March 2013, and a performance of the original version of the Violin Sonata, Op. 59, at the University of Birmingham in the same month.[119] The interest in Scott shows no signs of abating, as previously unperformed and unknown works continue to be discovered and recorded. In January 2015 a Cello Sonata (composed in 1958) was performed for the first time at Keele University, and the work has been released on CD by EM Records.[120] Alongside the performances and recordings, the new millennium has seen an increased scholarly interest in Scott. The most significant publication since Laurie Sampsel's pioneering *Bio-Bibliography* (2000) has been Sarah Collins's *The Aesthetic Life of Cyril Scott* (2013),[121] but there have also been valuable additions to the literature by Bob van der Linden, Lisa Hardy, Leslie De'Ath and Nalini Ghuman, among others.[122]

The revival of Scott's music in recent years is, of course, part of a wider trend that has seen the resurrection of a number of British composers born during the Victorian era. How Scott's reputation will ultimately fare in comparison with the likes of Joseph Holbrooke, Granville Bantock, John Ireland, Arnold Bax, Rutland Boughton and others remains to be seen. One would imagine that Scott has a better claim than most to being an early British 'modernist' composer, but despite the surge of scholarly interest in British music and modernism during the last decade, Scott has so far been overlooked.[123] Understandably, work in this area has tended to focus on composers whose reputations are already well established, such as Elgar and Vaughan Williams, but whose music from before World War 1 was not perceived at the time to be 'modern' to the same extent, or in the same way, as Scott's was. (A comparison of Scott's Piano Sonata No. 1, Op. 66, Elgar's First Symphony,

[119] Both performances of the overture were by the Cambridge University Symphony Orchestra, conducted by Martin Yates. The Cambridge performance took place at West Road Concert Hall on 9 March, and the London performance at the Cadogan Hall on 15 March. The Violin Sonata was performed by Andrew Kirkman (violin) and Clipper Erickson (piano) on 18 March.

[120] The performance on 28 January 2015 was by Richard Jenkinson (cello) and Benjamin Frith (piano). See Discography p. 585.

[121] See also an article by Collins in which Scott features prominently: 'Practices of Aesthetic Self-Cultivation: British Composer-Critics of the "Doomed Generation"', *Journal of the Royal Musical Association* 138/1 (2013), pp. 85–128.

[122] Bob van der Linden, 'Music, Theosophical Spirituality, and Empire: The British Modernist Composers Cyril Scott and John Foulds', *Journal of Global History* 3 (2008), pp. 163–82; Linden, *Music and Empire in Britain and India: Identity, Internationalism, and Cross-Cultural Communication* (Palgrave Macmillan, 2013), pp. 33–54; Lisa Hardy, *The British Piano Sonata, 1870–1945* (Boydell, 2001), pp. 53–68; Leslie De'Ath, 'Cyril Scott as Composer-Pianist and Author', *British Music Society News* 106 (June 2005), p. 304; De'Ath, liner notes for *Cyril Scott: Complete Piano Music*, vols 1–5 (2005–9), Dutton; Nalini Ghuman, *Resonances of the Raj: India in the English Musical Imagination, 1897–1947* (Oxford University Press, 2014).

[123] See, for instance, *British Music and Modernism, 1895–1960*, ed. Riley; the special issue on the subject of British music and modernism in the *Musical Quarterly* 91/1–2 (Spring–Summer 2008), pp. 1–150; J. P. E. Harper-Scott, *Edward Elgar, Modernist* (Cambridge University Press, 2006); Harper-Scott, *The Quilting Points of Musical Modernism: Revolution, Reaction, and William Walton* (Cambridge University Press, 2012).

and Vaughan Williams's *Sea Symphony* – all completed around 1908 – should make this quite clear.)

Whatever one thinks of Scott's modernist credentials, it can hardly be denied that he occupied an important position in British music, particularly in the years *c.* 1904–15. As this study has shown, Scott had the rare distinction of being a British composer who was widely known and (in some circles at least) held in high regard on the Continent and in America.[124] And how many other British composers were writing music before 1910 (and even as early as 1904) that was considered more extreme, more 'modern', than that of Strauss and Debussy? Christopher Palmer's prediction in 1979 that 'Allotting [Scott] his proper place in the history of the English Revival' would be a 'long and laborious process' has proved true, and it is evident that work still needs to be done before his real significance is established. Since the start of the new millennium, however, this process has come some way, and now that so much of Scott's music can be heard for the first time, it seems set to continue.[125]

[124] An interesting question – one rarely considered in relation to British composers – is to what extent Scott's music may have had an influence on foreign composers. Percy Grainger's bold claim that Scott's adaption of his (Grainger's) 'irregular rhythms' directly influenced Stravinsky's own use of rhythm in the *Rite of Spring* cannot be dismissed offhand if we are to believe Scott's account of his meeting with Stravinsky in the early part of the century: 'His reception of me was most cordial, and his appreciation of such works of mine as he knew exceedingly generous. It was not long before he took out the Piano Sonata [op. 66] and played me what he considered to be the best passages … He then showed me part of the "Rossignol" on which he was at work; also portions of the "Sacré du Printemps".' *A Musical Genius from Australia: Selected Writings by and About Percy Grainger*, ed. Teresa Balough (University of Western Australia, 1982), p. 141; Scott, *My Years of Indiscretion*, pp. 204–5. In America, too, Scott's influence was not negligible: a young Aaron Copland heard Scott play his Op. 66 Sonata in New York during his American tour, and was apparently 'so impressed with the sound of the *Sonata* that he went at once to a music store and purchased a copy of the work'. Julia Smith, *Aaron Copland: His Work and Contribution to American Music* (Dutton, 1955), p. 34.

[125] Palmer, 'Cyril Scott: Centenary Reflections', p. 741.

6

Rose Allatini: Theme and Variations

DESMOND SCOTT

IN 1921, when Rose Allatini married Cyril Scott, she was awaiting publication of her sixth novel, *When I was a Queen in Babylon* and he had just returned from a successful tour of the US and Canada.

A very talented woman in her own right, Rose produced forty novels, publishing the last one at age eighty-eight and jotting down notes for yet another, before dying two months short of her ninety-first birthday.

Rose Laure Allatini was born on 23 January 1890 in Vienna, at number 8 Plösselgasse, to a wealthy, cultured Jewish family. Her father, Roberto Allatini, was Italian-Greek, born and raised in Salonika. Her mother, Bronislava (Bronia) Rapoport von Porada, was Austro-Polish, the family originally coming from Warsaw.

In 1895, when Roberto Allatini was posted to the Italian embassy in London, the family found a house at 18 Holland Park, an elegant and secluded street. This was a world away from the busy thoroughfare of Holland Park Avenue, where Rose was to live later, after her marriage to Cyril broke up at the beginning of World War 2.

Her happiest times as a young girl were visits to her glamorous, sophisticated relatives in Vienna, and her memories of that romantic city before 1914 remained embedded deep in her consciousness, and featured in several of her novels.

Love and romance are important in her work, but to consider her merely as a romantic novelist is seriously to misread her writings. Though the tone is often comic, Rose had a serious purpose. Unusually among fiction writers, the spiritual was as important to her as the temporal. Her skill as a writer of fiction enabled her to engage readers with an engrossing tale while also discussing, questioning and illustrating what mattered to her in ways a formal essay never could.

Reincarnation, including karma, was central to her beliefs and a major factor in bringing her together with Cyril Scott. It would be interesting to know what led her in that direction – certainly it was not her very conventional parents. Whatever the reason, from her second novel on reincarnation became a dominant theme in very many of her books, especially as it related to the problem of healing. She was plagued with ill health all her life, so it was of more than academic interest for her. Another theme was music, which is seen in her writing as an adjunct to healing. Most of her lead characters engage in some kind of musical activity. A third theme, one that produced some of her most engaging books, was the family. Brought up in England from the age of five and never having experienced virulent anti-Semitism herself, she delighted in her Jewish heritage and mixed parentage. She gives many of her heroes and heroines the same attributes, as if the mixed ethnicity somehow bestowed on them a quality not possessed by others.

Rose left her parents' palatial, comfortable home as soon as she was twenty-one and found lodgings in Fitzroy Street, Soho, having discovered, as Virginia Woolf was to do some twenty years later, that in order to become a writer, she had to have a place of her own, free of parental interference. After several rejects writing as

R. Allatini (female novelists still not being accepted as readily as male ones), *Happy Ever After* was accepted by Mills & Boon and published a few months before the outbreak of World War 1, on 14 March 1914.

Most novelists begin by writing from their own experience, and Rose was no exception. Her novel concerns a large cosmopolitan family living in London, and the heroine is a writer of mixed parentage. The book is written with great humour, but the title is ironic: the heroine settles for security rather than love. Reviews were good, and encouraged her to continue writing. Her second novel, *Payment*, is interesting historically for its description of life in London during the first weeks of the war. *Root and Branch*, her third novel, appeared in 1917; the publisher was the greatly respected George Allen & Unwin.

Not one to shy away from controversy, Rose chose euthanasia as her subject, and the question whether under extreme circumstances a mercy killing was permissible in order to free someone from unbearable agony. Rose thought not. She suggested that if the bad karma caused by some situation in the past was not worked through in this life, it would remain having to be dealt with in future ones. Reviews were excellent, but praise of the critics notwithstanding, sales of *Root and Branch* were poor and produced nowhere near enough to support her financially. Rose had to return home for a few months. She also wanted to be home for the wedding of her younger sister Flora that summer.

Allen & Unwin's contract with Rose gave them an option on her next novel. They were looking forward to a long and profitable association with her, even though one of the directors, Cecil A. Reynolds, warned her that they were coming to the conclusion her work was too intellectual for the ordinary run of novel readers.[1] Imogen Gassert, who wrote on Allatini in her DPhil thesis, takes up the story:

> What the publisher received, was not at all what they were expecting. They were shocked to discover that the subjects of *Ishmaelites*, as *Despised and Rejected* was first called, were homosexuality and pacificism, and were immediately aware that publishing it could bring police action ... Of the two, pacifism in the middle of a terrible, long drawn-out war that showed no sign of ending, was the more inflammatory.[2]

Here are examples of the sort of passage that caused concern:

> 'There can be no doubt that every Englishman knows what he's fighting for,' declared Mr Blackwood. 'Yes, he's told that he's fighting for honour and glory and freedom, and to defend his home and country from a dastardly enemy. And the German boy is told exactly the same. And they both believe it, bless them. When they're both out there, dying a foul death side by side, perhaps they may wonder

[1] Imogen Gassert, 'Collaborators and Dissidents: Aspects of British Literary Publishing in the First World War, 1914–1919' (DPhil thesis, University of Oxford, 2001). For all the material on the publishing of *Despised and Rejected*, the Allen & Unwin correspondence, and the subsequent trial of C. W. Daniel I am deeply indebted to Dr Imogen Gassert.

[2] Ibid.

> if it was true, and if it was worth while, and why they let themselves be driven out to kill and kill and be killed by each other.'[3]

> It's no use pretending that 'this is a war to end war'. I don't believe it. Do you believe that the British are fighting for disarmament, for democracy, for world-peace, any more than the Germans are? The governments of all big nations organise warfare with the same ends in view – extension of power; consolidation of empire; commercial and political advantages.[4]

Not surprisingly, this caused a major disruption in the Allatini household. Rose wrote to Stanley Unwin:

> I have had a terrific upheaval with my very military and narrow-minded family; as the result of it, shall be compelled to publish 'Ishmaelites' under a pseudonym. As I am unfortunately economically dependent on my family I can't go against them in this + it would be an awful thing for them + injurious to my father's diplomatic position – they say – if such a book as mine were to appear under their name.[5]

The Allatinis were recent Jewish immigrants, anxious to assimilate and to be accepted into British society. A pacifist, homosexual book with the Allatini name on it would have been absolutely disastrous to their position. Not only that, Rose's sister Flora was about to be married to an officer from Britain's most elite regiment, the Dragoon Guards. Captain Matthew Talbot Baines had been seconded to the Royal Flying Corps from the Guards and was, moreover, recuperating from a war-wound. The marriage would be the best sign of acceptance they could wish for. Conceding the need for a pseudonym, the first of many Rose used during her long career, she cheekily chose A. T. Fitzroy, after the Soho Square she had lived in when she first left home. Allen & Unwin, though fully recognising the book's literary merit, were not prepared to take the risk and suggested another publisher, C. W. Daniel.

Daniel, a pacifist himself, ran a small press and had already been in trouble over a pacifist pamphlet. Nevertheless, he decided to publish *Ishmaelites*, renaming it *Despised and Rejected* (Fig. 6.1). Issued on 22 May 1918, with a heroine who, if not lesbian, was certainly bisexual, plus a hero not only homosexual but also pacifist, it is not surprising that reviews were mixed. Several praised the skill of writer A. T. Fitzroy, whom they correctly deduced was a woman. *The Times Literary Supplement* (June 6) thought the book well written and ended by remarking that 'as a frank and sympathetic study of certain types of mind and character it is of interest but it is not to be recommended for general reading'. The *Manchester Guardian* (June 16) headed its review 'A Propagandist Astray'. One review that was particularly scathing was written by James Douglas. It appeared in the *London Opinion* on 24 August.

[3] A. T. Fitzroy [Rose Allatini], *Despised and Rejected*, quoted in Gassert, 'Collaborators and Dissidents', p. 193.

[4] Fitzroy, *Despised and Rejected*, quoted in Gassert, 'Collaborators and Dissidents', p. 196.

[5] Ibid.

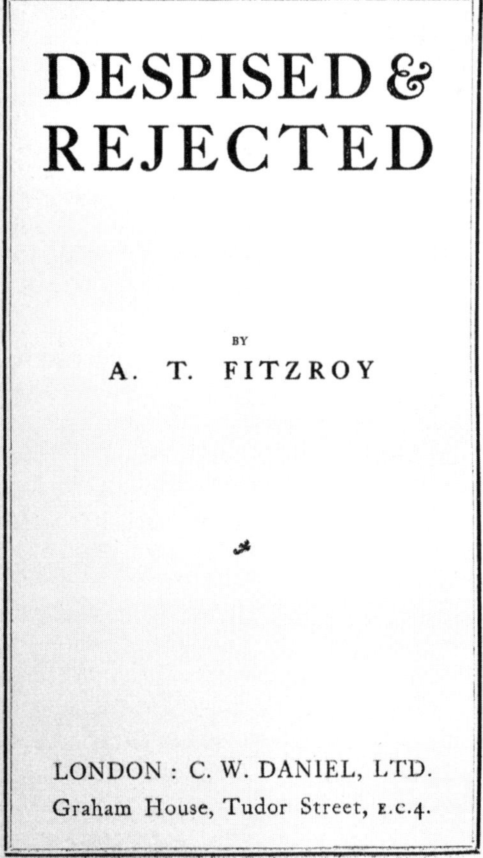
DESPISED & REJECTED

BY

A. T. FITZROY

LONDON : C. W. DANIEL, LTD.
Graham House, Tudor Street, E.C.4.

Figure 6.1 Title page of *Despised and Rejected*

For its virulence, and as an indication of the temper of the times, it deserves to be quoted in full:

> A thoroughly poisonous book, every copy of which ought to be put on the fire forthwith ... Of its hideous immoralities, the less said the better; but of its sympathetic presentation, in the mouths of its 'hero' and of other characters, of pacifism and conscientious objection, and of sneering at the English as compared with the Hun, this needs to be asked:
>
> What is the use of our spending hundreds of thousands of pounds on propaganda, and tens of thousands more on Censorship, while pestiferous filth of this kind remains unsuppressed. The book is published by C. W. Daniel Ltd ... and I imagine it will not be long, after the authorities have examined this literary fungus before he is a Daniel brought to judgement.

Little more than a month later, on 27 September, Daniel was indeed brought before the courts, pleading not guilty to a charge of 'making statements in a printed book likely to prejudice recruiting and training of persons serving in the armed forces'.

Not obscenity, you notice. Judgement was given on 10 October. Rose was fined £110, Daniel £350 and all unsold copies of the book were seized.

Had she waited even a year or two after the war ended, the pacifism would not have been a legal issue, and the fact of *Despised and Rejected* being the first overtly homosexual novel ever published might well have given it the *succès de scandale* that Radclyffe Hall's *The Well of Loneliness* enjoyed a decade later. As it was, it disappeared completely from the literary scene. This must have been a huge disappointment for Rose, but it did not stop her, and she began almost immediately on her fifth novel.

Despised and Rejected was not, however, to be consigned to oblivion. Of the forty novels she wrote it is the only one to be reprinted for today's readers, not once but three times. The first was in 1988, in a paperback edition by the Gay Men's Press, GMP Publishers, London, with an introduction by Jonathan Cutbill. Twenty-two years later, in 2010, the second version appeared, this time a scholarly annotated edition from the University of Rhode Island. Edited by Brett Rutherford, it was illustrated with posters and cartoons from the period and footnotes explaining things unfamiliar to American readers. In addition to those two very different reprints there is yet a third planned for 2018. On 15 May 2017 Amanta Scott, who created and maintains the Cyril Scott website, received an email from Nicola Bauman, publisher of Persephone Books, London, asking permission to produce a special edition of *Despised and Rejected* to celebrate its centenary in 2018. How amused Rose would have been to learn that her prohibited book would be still in print 100 years later.

Her fifth novel, *Requiem*, was published in 1919 under her own name with yet another publisher, Martin Secker. It is a largely comic book, despite the unexpected tragic ending that gives it its title. It allowed Rose's sardonic wit full play and dealt with the vibrant, precarious life of actors, artists and musicians eking out an existence in and around Soho. Of one artist's bad imitation Rubens she remarked it was 'less like the *Birth of Venus* and more like the birth of Rugby football'. On a more serious note, the novel could also be read as a version of the story of the Wandering Jew, in this case Louis, a man of mixed parentage and considerable talent ceaselessly searching for a meaning to life. There is no rest for him in death or even the grave. He is killed by a shell exploding in the trenches, leaving only unburied fragments behind. The book also contains a discussion of reincarnation, with arguments put both for and against (pp. 189–91). Reviews on the whole were good, particularly one from the *Aberdeen Free Press* of 10 January 1920 that ended: 'It is a keen pleasure to read a book which is written in faultless English, a pleasure too seldom enjoyed to be left without remark.' For a Viennese-born Austro-Polish Greek-Italian woman, that must have been high praise indeed.

It is not known exactly where or when Rose and Cyril Scott first met, but it was possibly at The Firs, a rest home run by Alec Chaplin and his wife Nelsa, sometime between 1917 and 1920. Scott describes The Firs in *Bone of Contention* as a:

> rather dilapidated guest house into which drifted human wreckage of all descriptions, derelicts broken and battered in body and mind – derelicts certain not only of welcome, but in most cases of healing for their particular ill.[6]

[6] Cyril Scott, *Bone of Contention* (Aquarian Press, 1969), pp. 158 *et seq.*

The Chaplins, particularly Nelsa, played a significant part in both the Scotts' lives. She was an extremely gifted psychic, clairvoyant and healer, and not only gave Rose relief both from physical pain and mental stress but also provided her with material for five of her novels: *Root and Branch, When I was a Queen in Babylon, Waters Meet, For Benefits Received* and *Oracle*, which has as its dedication: 'For The Little One' (Mrs Chaplin). The novel concerns a rest home like The Firs and healing work akin to that of the Chaplins. Writing of Mrs Chaplin, Rose said: 'If you asked her, I think she would only tell you that she doesn't claim to be anything but a channel – a dedicated channel – through which Divine healing power can be directed wherever it is needed.'

In 1921, Rose was thirty-one and Cyril forty-two. She was a beautiful woman, and he a handsome man, but, clearly, physical attraction was not the primary reason for their coming together. Scott's attitude to marriage was most unusual. In *Bone of Contention* he remarked that he did not consider being in love a basis for matrimony, 'seeing that that state is full of illusions; no one really knows a person with whom he (or she) is in love, he merely imagines he does. As for marrying for the sake of having children, I had no such desire.' He insisted that it was his spiritual guru, K. H., who suggested he get married, since living alone tended to make a man selfish and an introvert. It was, therefore, an arranged match – as Rose's parents' marriage had been – but arranged by a higher power in whom both Rose and Cyril had complete faith.

An important factor was that K. H. was also Rose's master and had already, so Scott wrote, discussed the marriage with her; she had agreed to it, 'albeit at some sacrifice to herself'.[7] But the most compelling reason (which, surprisingly, he does not mention) was surely that Rose was also clairvoyant, and could therefore contact K. H. directly and relay his messages to Scott, who was not.

Cyril returned from his concert tour in April 1921 and the pair were married a month later, on 8 May. The Allatini family would have been happy to give their elder daughter a fashionable wedding in St George's, Hanover Square, as they had done for Flora, but the couple wanted none of that. They chose a registry office in the Harrow Road, a civil ceremony and no publicity. There were no guests. Rose's parents attended; Eugene Goossens and Constance Holme were the witnesses.

On 29 July 1921, two months after her marriage, Rose's sixth novel, *When I was a Queen in Babylon*, was released, with Rose returning to her first publisher, Mills & Boon. There is romance and much humour in *When I was a Queen in Babylon*, masking, as often happens in Rose's books, the serious purpose underlying it. Reincarnation, the working out of bad karma, and the understanding of it feature prominently. Mills & Boon today are known largely as publishers of light-weight romance novels such as *Harlequin*, but in the 1920s they also produced more serious work, including biography. In 1924, for example, they published Cyril's first autobiography, *My Years of Indiscretion*. As soon as her book came out Rose and Cyril left for Vienna and Germany, where they remained for several months visiting friends and relatives.[8] Cyril knew and was happy in Rose's favourite city, having

[7] Ibid., p. 177.

[8] Ibid., pp. 136 and 179.

first gone there in 1911. He spoke fluent German, though not as well as Rose, whose competence was a great help when they later collaborated on an English libretto of Paul Hindemith's *Das Unaufhörliche* ('The Perpetual'; 1931).[9] Back in London, they moved into Cyril's small house at 24 Newton Road, Bayswater.

Rose took her marriage very seriously. For the first six years she devoted herself entirely to Cyril and wrote nothing of her own. She not only proofread all his literary manuscripts but, being very knowledgeable about music, also helped correct his scores, even copying one, *Bumble-Bees*; her distinctive handwriting can be found on many of them, including one for the ballet suite *Karma* (1924). In 1922, expecting the arrival of their first child, the couple moved to a larger house in St John's Wood, at 33 Hamilton Terrace. On 17 January 1923 a daughter, Vivien Mary, was born; she was followed three years later, on 10 December 1926, by myself, Desmond Cyril. Between the births of her first and second child, however, Rose became seriously ill and as a result lost her clairvoyant ability. In 1927 her father died, and it was not until 1929 that she returned to writing. Now calling herself R. L. Scott, she wrote a play with her old friend George Owen, which he also produced, entitled *The Golden Key*. It was put on at the Q Theatre, Kew, which was then recognised as a major try-out venue. The play is a light comedy for the first two acts, but Rose's message in the last act – that the key to happiness lies in giving happiness to others – was considered by the critics to be out of keeping with the rest of the play, and it did not transfer to the West End.

During this period three people entered Rose's life, the most important being H. K. Challoner (Janet Melanie Ailsa Mills). Melanie Mills was interested in psychic phenomena and healing. A healer herself, she wrote several books describing her psychic experiences and became Rose's closest friend. The other two arrivals were Melanie's cousin, Aline Nielson, and David Anrias (Brian Ross). Ross, as Anrias, is featured in *The Initiate in the Dark Cycle*, and Cyril also writes of him at length in *Bone of Contention* (pp. 198–201). In 1932 and 1933 the Scotts rented places for the summer, close to Rye, where Melanie, Ross and Aline visited them. Ross's *Through the Eyes of the Masters,* published by Routledge, Kegan & Paul in 1932, is dedicated 'with affection to Rose and Cyril Scott in memory of the time spent at Rye during 1932'. Nielson and Ross were both professional astrologers, and it is reasonable to assume that is was as a result of meeting them that Rose wrote a story about two astrologers, 'Galileo', and included it in a volume of short stories called *White Fire*.[10] This book is unique in Rose's output for being published under the name Mrs Cyril Scott. Around this time, while on holiday in Yorkshire, Rose, Cyril, Ross and Mills collaborated on a musical show called *Forwards and Backwards*. Judging from Rose's handwriting on it, she was in charge of the overall script, while Cyril wrote the music, the lyrics and most of the individual scenes, the other three contributing two scenes each.

Two years later, Rose changed her name yet again. In 1935, as Lucian Wainwright, but with the same publisher, Martin Secker, she produced *Girl of Good Family*. This is a delightful, funny and largely autobiographical book. Her style, self-mocking and

[9] Schott Music, Mainz.

[10] Martin Secker, 1933.

always acutely aware of the absurdity of the situation, is assured. Sasha, the *Girl* of the title, like Rose, is an author and comes from a wealthy multi-national Jewish family. She feels she is an old maid after her younger sister's fashionable wedding, and laments that her books do not even justify themselves by being successful. The novel parallels the period of Rose's own life up to 1935, and some of it takes place during World War 1.

Rose's own mother, Bronia, was a sweet-natured but very timid woman. Rose was no doubt thinking of her when she wrote sympathetically of the mother in her book that:

> Only the fact of her marriage to a 'neutral' redeemed her from being technically, as well as actually, an 'enemy alien', and she grew morbidly apprehensive lest this be discovered in quarters where such discovery might lead to possible unpleasantness. She, who had always been such a lover of social gaiety, had begun to shun the most casual encounters, fearing the questions that might be asked about those relatives of hers who were on the wrong side of the fighting-line.
>
> (p. 186)

Oracle, published in 1937, Rose's last novel as Lucian Wainwright, was the only one published by Methuen. It seems that everyone to whom she submitted a manuscript recognised her ability, was intrigued by the combination of a good story with an unusual philosophy behind it, and felt it well worth publishing; but when sales failed to meet expectations, they sooner or later declined to venture further. The search for a publisher after Methuen continued.

We now reach 1 September 1939. War was imminent. London, it was thought, would be the immediate target of the Nazi bombs, and those who could were scrambling to leave the city.

Cyril's sister, Mabel Lee, and her husband, Edwin, had a small house in Somerset, but it could accommodate only three. It was decided that Cyril would take the children now aged seventeen and thirteen, until school term began two weeks later; Rose, meanwhile, chose to go and stay temporarily with Aline Nielson in Winchelsea, hardly the safest place to be, but for the moment getting out of London was all that mattered. She stayed with Nielson for three weeks, during which time Melanie Mills, also in flight from London, rented a small house in Beckley, a little village some miles from the coast, five miles from Rye, and moved there with her elderly mother, Mrs Mills. Rose joined them and this became her second home for the duration of the war.

In 1941 she found Andrew Dakers to replace Methuen, and he published *Family from Vienna*, the first novel of a family trilogy, and also Rose's first as Eunice Buckley, the name she was to use thereafter. Books two and three followed in quick succession: *Destination Unknown* in 1942, and *Blue Danube* in 1943. The complete family trilogy received excellent notices, and for the first time in her forty years of writing her sales warranted reprinting; but it was her misfortune, or perhaps she would say her karma, that wartime paper restrictions prevented this from happening. By the time the war was over her publisher was engaged in other projects.

By 1944 the Scotts had decided not to live together again when the war ended. They had always led a very amicable but largely separate existence, and Rose was now an established author with more than twelve books to her name, the last three of which had proved very successful. She wanted to return to London, partly to be near her publishers, but chiefly to be near the many health practitioners, both orthodox and unorthodox, whom her continuing poor health required. For Cyril, in contrast, bomb-scarred London had no appeal. It was crowded, dirty and too expensive. Also, in 1943 he had met Marjorie Hartston at a guest house near Barnstaple. A young woman in her thirties, she was open to learning about Cyril's occult beliefs. He, at a low point in his life, was happy to have a responsive listener. She also turned out to be psychic, and was instrumental in restoring communications between him and his spiritual guru, K. H. The Scotts remained friends after Cyril had moved to Sussex, writing to each other frequently and offering mutual support and encouragement. After meeting Hartston for the first time Rose wrote:

> What a sweet creature Marjorie is and how lucky you are – or rather what good karma you must have made to draw to yourself such a companion.
> Much love, dear[11]

In early 1946 Rose rented a flat at 159 Holland Park Avenue, where she stayed until a few months before her death thirty-five years later. Though she came from a family of wealth, most of it was lost in the two world wars. The income from her books was minimal, and her lifestyle was far from lavish. The flat was rent controlled and, in the post-war years, cheap. It also meant the landlord did the absolute minimum. She had to walk up three flights of stairs to reach it, and there was no lift. Both the kitchen and bathroom were antiquated, but Rose was not concerned with renovations. All that mattered to her was her writing. She lived frugally, saving her money for the six-week trip she took to Switzerland every year with Melanie Mills, a practice that lasted for over thirty years. But these trips were no extravagant indulgence. Rose went not only for her health, always feeling better in the mountain air, but also because it was where she found ideas for her books. She liked to find a quiet spot, if possible close to a little waterfall or a running stream, and there she would write in longhand the first draft, which she would read to Melanie after dinner, attentive to her comments, and respectful of her critical acumen. When she returned to London, she would revise and type it out on her aged Remington typewriter, ready to submit to the publisher.

Publishers continued to be the problem. In the late 1960s her current one, Robert Hale, who had published seven of her books, told her he could not renew the contract. Rose was in despair, but then thought she had found a solution. The Theosophical Society was contemplating going into fiction, and her new novel, *Diamonds in the Family*, with its occult overtones, would be an excellent choice for them. The story concerns rivalries and jealousies persisting through three generations of a cosmopolitan family based in Vienna, and the situations arising from a necklace of beautiful diamonds that result in hatred and even murder. It was and is one of her best. Rose assumed that she would keep her small but loyal group of followers, and that they would be augmented by readers in the Theosophical Society, a

[11] Letter in my possession.

large international organisation with branches all over the world. Sadly, that did not happen. Writing to Cyril, she lamented:

> It has been a dead flop. The TS have boycotted it because it is a novel – and the ordinary libraries ditto because it bears the TS imprint. I was their Experimental Rabbit in the field of fiction which they haven't any idea or the organisation to handle, and it looks as if the Rabbit may well have died under the experiment … It looks like the end of the road for me as a writer, and you of all people, my dear, will realise what such a prospect means to me. I only live by the creative fire in me – just as you do.

Fortunately, it was not the end. Robert Hale reconsidered, accepted her next book (*The Flaming Sword*) and remained her publisher for her final ten books. 'Acquiring merit', as Rose remarked to Scott, telling him Hale made little or no money from her.

Among Rose's many novels two in particular stand out: *For Benefits Received* (1960) and its sequel, *Fiorina* (1961). Both explore a subject she wrote about more often than any other, that of healing. In the first book a miracle cure occurs in an orthodox medical family to a child of Italian and English parents, creating ironical situations when unwelcome publicity is focused upon it. The cure, however, is not permanent and the young woman, Fiorina, is again left paralysed. The story – dramatic, moving and full of both tension and humour – is of her spiritual journey, ending when she echoes in gratitude the title of the book, giving thanks for benefits received. The sequel follows Fiorina some years later, now living in her parents' old villa on Lake Maggiore. She has become a spiritual focus, and people from very different backgrounds come to her for help. Many questions about miraculous healing are raised, including the problem of why one person is cured and another not. Fiorina's death at the end is seen not as a tragedy but as the fulfilment of a life, and Rose's ability to tell a good story and to create unusual but entirely believable characters is such that the philosophy never overwhelms the narrative, but rather becomes an integral part of it.

Rose was above all a storyteller, and her books can be read simply for the tales, the characters and dilemmas, and the light humorous touch she gives them. They can be read, too, for the constant thread that runs through them all. This begins as early as 1919, in *Requiem*, where the heroine says:

> I believe that we go on – that there is no real extinction. From the first beginnings and glimmerings of consciousness, the spirit in us, that is just a spark of the universal God-spirit, struggles upwards, through a thousand lives, through a thousand changes, till it's fit to rule the stars. Death is just the transit from one form of life to another.

And concludes with this final passage from her last book, *Work of Art* (1978):

> I'd like to tell those poor devils who are going through their different kinds of hell that there's a purpose in it all, purpose that can lead them from terrifying darkness to light and joy they've never dreamt of … I'd try and make them feel

> that the whole living, throbbing cosmos with all the beings in it, all its wonderful, intricate mechanism of circling planets and stars and inter-related star-systems is alive with creative love and joy, the joy of perpetual self-revelation, self-giving to and through every star and atom – and that they can come to share in it and there can be a sort of joy even in suffering if you look upon it differently, feel that it's clearing away some of the muck we human beings have made of the divine powers relegated to us.
>
> (p. 162)

In the summer of 1980 Rose moved to a retirement home in the country, close to her friend Melanie. On 22 November 1980, she died; she was buried in Hastings.

7

Memories of the Man I Barely Knew

DESMOND SCOTT

It might seem strange to begin a memoir on one's father by saying one hardly knew him, but my sister Vivien and I were not at the centre of our parents' universe. In the London house where I was born they had many other things to occupy them besides us. We lived in the nursery, looked after by nannies.

In those early years I saw my mother for an hour a day, around four o'clock (teatime), and my father even less, but this is not to suggest they were unloving or uncaring parents. Both of them would always come and kiss us goodnight.

As a small child I used to have bad earaches and one of the strongest memories I have of my father is of him coming up to the nursery and, on this occasion, instead of the nanny putting drops in my ears, Father put his hands to my head, close but not touching. I could feel the warmth of them. He shut his eyes and concentrated, willing the pain to leave me and enter him. After a while he shook his wrists as if he were shaking down an old fashioned thermometer. That was my earache, which he had absorbed, now leaving him. After I fell asleep and woke up next morning, the earache was gone. Whether his method simply caused me to relax, or whether his hands did have healing power, I have no idea, but I basked in his love and attention. Laying his hands on me was an example of 'therapeutic touch', something my daughter, Amanta, has inherited. It is now quite widely practised, but in 1930 was considered quackery, at least in orthodox medical circles.

In my sixth year the family moved to another part of London, to a large house near Holland Park where my maternal grandmother lived. Father worked on the main floor, composing and writing, Mother wrote her novels on the second floor, and my sister and I lived on the third. The downside for us was not being allowed to be too boisterous or noisy in case it distracted our parents. Fortunately, there was the square, available to those of us who lived in the houses surrounding it, where we could be as loud as we wanted.

Vivien went off to boarding school, and in due course I followed. This meant being absent from our parents for at least eight months of the year. (I should point out that this was typical of middle-class families of my generation, as was having not only a nanny, but also a cook/housekeeper and two housemaids. We were not rich, but domestic help was cheap at the time.) In the 1920s and 1930s my father was a prominent figure, and on that account received bursaries for the expensive schools we children were then able to attend. At my first school we wore knitted jerseys with blue and grey school colours, sold to the parents at a very high price. My mother, to save money, asked for the pattern and decided to knit one for me, but the result was not quite the same as those the school provided. The other boys immediately seized on this, to my great shame and embarrassment.

Young children accept their surroundings as normal, whether in a castle or a cottage, and it is only in retrospect that I realise how unusual the furniture in our house was. In the entrance hall there was a most curious piece that looked as if it should

Figure 7.1 The hall stand in the house at Ladbroke Grove

belong in a church. It was quite high, about 6' tall and 2' deep, made of wood and painted green. It had two seats, covered in a dull green and gold fabric, and separated by a slender pillar that divided above head height into two gothic arches. Above the arches the top and sides were crenellated. One could hang a coat in it, or sit down and change one's shoes (Fig. 7.1). Also in the hall, at the foot of the staircase, was the bust of my father aged twenty-two, by Derwent Wood (Fig. 7.2).

Figure 7.2 Bust of Scott by the sculptor Derwent Wood

Figure 7.3 The dining-room table and chairs moved from the London house

There were three rooms on the main floor. Going from back to front, there was first the dining room, with a long refectory table of light oak and eight heavy, high-backed, throne-like chairs, also oak and not very comfortable (Fig. 7.3). Father had either designed them, or bought them from church furnishers in Liverpool. He kept them when he moved to Eastbourne after the war, and, because the table was too big to fit in the smaller house and he was a very practical man, he chopped a few

Figure 7.4 Melchior Lechter, whose aesthetic style Scott admired

feet off and had them made into coffee tables. At one end of the London dining room was a sideboard, also oak, and at the other a large birdcage that housed Charlot, a bad-tempered grey parrot who responded only to father and who, unless approached very gently and carefully, tended to nip everyone else. He was named after André Charlot, for whom Scott had written the *Karma Suite* and the *Masque of the Red Death* for two of his *Revues*.

Next to this room was father's study, where, once again showing his practicality, he had had a special upright piano made. Closed, it looked like an ordinary piano, but he had had the lid removed and replaced with a wide board which, when opened, became a place for his manuscript paper, still leaving space underneath for him to play whatever he was composing. I did not go in there often, not simply because he was always working, but because it was a small room and seemed gloomy to me as a little boy.

The drawing room was large and sunny with big windows looking onto the square. The furniture was all green and gold-trimmed, the same green as the hall-stand. Father had designed most of the pieces, modelled closely after those of his friend Melchior Lechter (Fig. 7.4). In *Bone of Contention* he wrote: 'Lechter lived

Figure 7.5 Skeleton clock and cabinet set on trestles in the house at Ladbroke Grove; these were stolen from the house in Eastbourne, along with many other items, after Cyril's death

in a top flat that he had furnished almost exactly like a chapel. The furniture, of his own design was ecclesiastical in every detail, and even his bedroom was arranged to look like a mediaeval picture.' Our drawing room was not quite that extreme, but it was unusual enough for both Yvonne Hudson (composer Norman O'Neill's daughter) and the composer Edmund Rubbra to take note of it when they came to visit. There was a gold skeleton clock in which one could see the works, set in a green frame shaped like a church door, standing on a green chest (Fig. 7.5). There was also a tall chest of drawers full of music, which I much later discovered was called a Wellington. Practical and very useful, the drawers were hinged so they fell flat when opened, allowing one to pull out manuscripts without bending them (Fig. 7.6). These pieces all went to Eastbourne with my father after the war. On the walls Father had painted imaginary Italianate landscapes with tall dark cypress

Figure 7.6 Chest of drawers known as a 'Wellington' in the house at Ladbroke Grove

Figure 7.7 Stained-glass windows by Edward Burne-Jones in Scott's drawing room

trees and deep ochre sunsets. There were reproductions of Florentine sculptures on pedestals around the room, and two gorgeous stained-glass windows, about 7' high and 2' 6" wide: *Angel with Lute* and *Angel with Instrument*, designed by Sir Edward Burne-Jones and given to Father by an admirer (Fig. 7.7).[1]

The Broadwood grand piano, also green and gold, stood in a corner by the drawing-room windows. Round it Father had stencilled, in big gold letters copied from a script of Lechter's, 'Melody is the cry of Man to God'. It was not until many years later I discovered that round the other side was written, 'Harmony is the answer of God to Man'. Sometimes Father would play for me – *Water-Wagtail, Rainbow-Trout* or a few pieces from *Zoo*, a collection of piano pieces he had written for children and dedicated to Vivien and me (Fig. 7.8). The piano eventually wore out; there were plans to ship it to Melbourne, as Grainger very much hoped to have it for his Museum, but no one had the funds for its passage.[2] The works were beyond repair,

[1] These were originally installed in Heweis Chapel, St James's Church, Marylebone, London, which was demolished in 1914. They were then given by Cyril Scott to Methodist Chapel, Exford, Devon, in 1947. The chapel closed in 1979 and the windows are now in a permanent collection at the Whitworth Gallery, University of Manchester. They were displayed in an exhibition of Pre-Raphaelite work at Tate Britain in 2012.

[2] Letter written to Percy Grainger, 18 July 1919, now in the Grainger Museum, Melbourne.

ZOO
Als Herr Elefant, der vom Land ist, im Zoo ankam, war er doch erstaunt über den Luxus.
When Mr. Elephant arrived at the Zoo, he brought a large trunk, but no other baggage.

Figure 7.8 Page from *Zoo, Animals for Piano*, written for Vivien Mary and Desmond Cyril Scott, with illustrations by Willy Harania; text in both English and German by Cyril Scott

but the case, along with the hall-stand, is now in the Wirral museum, close to Scott's birthplace in Cheshire.

Rubbra, in his ninetieth-birthday tribute to Scott, refers to a writing pad on the desk with a quotation from the Indian Celestial Song: 'To work thou hast the right, but not to the fruits thereof.' I have no personal memory of it, but I repeat the quotation because its austerity is a sharp reminder that the excessive romanticism of the room was only a part of Cyril Scott, and not the whole.

I enjoyed going into the drawing room because I liked the smell of incense my father often burned. He said it helped him when composing. And I specially liked it when he smoked his pipe. No ordinary briar, it had a long mouthpiece to which was fastened a length of rubber tubing; this was fixed to one end of a glass container, manufactured specially for him, half-filled with water. The bowl of the pipe, filled originally with Three Nuns tobacco, and later with herbal mixture, was stuck into an opening at the top. The whole contraption hung down to his waist from a length of black ribbon round his neck, so the smoke would not get in his eyes when he was working. It was a portable hubble-bubble. Passing the smoke over water was supposed to lessen the effect of the nicotine, and it made a cheerful bubbling sound that I loved (see Plate XXV). I also remember fondly the green eyeshade he wore, making him look like an old-fashioned newspaper editor. It was in that room too, some years later, that I played chess with him after learning how to play it at my prep school. There was one memorable evening when I actually beat him. I rushed off to tell everyone my triumph, though even then I had a suspicion that he let me beat him on purpose, for he was a kind and gentle man.

Later, when World War 2 broke out, the family split up. Father spent the war years in a variety of lodgings in Somerset and Devon, and I joined him for two weeks of the year at most during my summer holidays – not the best way to get to know him! I remember long silent walks with him through country lanes, wondering what he was thinking but too shy to ask, imagining that, perhaps, being almost half a century older than me, he didn't know what to say to an adolescent. I never knew until quite recently what a very low period in his life this was. To his credit, he never burdened me with his problems, but remained his usual cheerful self. We stopped sometimes to pick stinging nettles to take home. He said they were good for you; boiled with dinner, they tasted like spinach. The nettles were all part of his interest in natural foods and homeopathy. In this, as with much else, he was far ahead of his time. Now one can buy nettles, dandelions and a host of other once-ignored greens in the supermarket, or expensively packaged in pill form. Sixty years ago, that was unheard of.

Sometimes his interest in natural treatments got him into hot water, literally. He told me ruefully that pine oil was good for the skin, so he thought it would make good bath oil. Not having any on hand, he tried mineral turpentine, primarily a paint solvent, and proceeded to pour a generous measure into his bath. For a few minutes he said it was fine, but then it began to burn and he went nearly frantic trying to wash it off. Make sure you know exactly what you are using before you start experimenting with anything, was his advice. No more turpentine in the bath! Another disaster was the time he attempted to brew herbal beer that, much to my childish glee, exploded all over the kitchen floor.

In one of the guest houses where he spent World War 2, my father met Marjorie Hartston. They became friends and, by the time the war ended, they had decided to stay together. They settled in Eastbourne on the Sussex coast. When I turned eighteen, with the war still on, I joined the Royal Navy and was overseas for three years, returning to London in 1948.

In Eastbourne, Father had become a familiar figure, walking through the town with his broad-brimmed hat on, looking a little like Ezra Pound, for by then he had grown a beard. He would wave his walking stick in cheerful greeting to his many friends, or stop to chat with the local vet and try to resist when told a hard-luck story about a cat needing a home. He loved all animals, particularly cats, especially Siamese, and often had three or four in the house. Sometimes when I went to visit, I would find a new one. He would look at me sheepishly, spread his hands and say, 'What could we do, no one else would take it.'

I enjoyed seeing Father on my occasional Eastbourne visits. I think the advantage of not being close to him as a child was that I could appreciate him as an individual, not simply as a parent. He appeared to feel the same about me, telling me he approved of me as a person, not merely because I was his son. I liked that.

On these visits my cue to get up for breakfast was always the noise coming from the room where Cyril did his exercises. He had a small motor, fixed to a table and bolted to the floor; this had a belt about 2" wide and 3' or 4' long fastened to one end.

He would stand, put the belt round his waist, and buckle the other end to the motor. When he turned it on it would vibrate and he could massage his whole body with it, back and front. I imagine it helped keep him healthy, as did the walks he continued to take daily, and the cold baths he took until he was eighty. From his bedroom balcony there was a splendid uninterrupted view of the Downs and, in the far distance, the sea. He would do deep-breathing exercises there, then cuddle one of the cats that had, in theory, been forbidden to come into his room, and then go down for breakfast. He was a methodical, hardworking man and his routine seldom varied from day to day. Two or three hours in the morning, followed by a walk before lunch at one, would be spent answering letters. After lunch he would work again, either writing or composing until about five, with a break for a cup of tea, followed by a nap before dinner. Then he would work for another two or three hours afterwards. He always read two or three newspapers and, if I were there, he would find a joke or interesting item to read me.

Mail was delivered by nine, and every day there would be letters requiring answers on occult questions, others on health matters, resulting from his books on alternative medicine – books such as *Doctors, Disease and Health*[3] or *Victory over Cancer*[4] – and from the little pamphlets on cider vinegar and black molasses. There were very few on music, because by then he had been bypassed almost totally. I remember one letter he read me in which someone in Australia wanted his advice on building a colour organ. Since I did not know what that was, he explained that for each note of music there is a colour equivalent, and if you could make an instrument that produced the colours on a screen as well as sounding the notes, you would create an entirely new sensory experience. What Father was interested in, though, was not so much the aesthetics, as using it for curative purposes. He felt that certain harmonies, certain chord combinations and sequences in conjunction with their colours, properly used, could be a very potent source of healing on the subconscious level, particularly in cases of mental illness.

He was always happy to explain things if asked, but volunteered very little information on his own. At that stage in my life, preoccupied with my own career, and not interested enough to read any of his books, I did not ask. Now, of course, I deeply regret it. Those long walks in the country during the war would have been a great opportunity for him to have introduced his beliefs and discussed some of those books with me, but that was not his way.

Both my parents deliberately left me to discover for myself the paths I would take, spiritual and otherwise. For that I am grateful. I am grateful too that, highly unconventional themselves, they gave me a standard, conventional, middle-class upbringing and educated me at a minor public school, Eastbourne College. Growing up, though I was in no way religious, I enjoyed singing hymns in the school chapel and was eventually confirmed Church of England (Anglican), because that was the accepted thing to do. Now I am inclined towards my parents' belief in karma and reincarnation. It seems to make greater sense to me than mainstream Christianity.

[3] Methuen & Co., 1938.

[4] Methuen & Co., 1939.

Clairvoyance, Father felt, was a talent that some were born with, like singing or being brilliant at maths. He also believed it needed to be developed, or it would wither. He told me that he never possessed it himself, and my mother lost the facility due to poor health (before I was born). Lacking that talent, he was unable to contact his guru directly, but always needed an intermediary. He describes the process in his best-known book on music and occultism, *Music: Its Secret Influence throughout the Ages.*[5]

After I emigrated to Canada in 1957 I saw my father only three more times: the first on our honeymoon when I brought my wife, Corinne, to meet him in Eastbourne; the second when we brought our children, Amanta and Dominic, for a visit; and the last on 20 July 1969, arriving late at night after a business meeting in London. The following evening he, Marjorie and I sat in front of the television set and watched a man land on the moon. Born when the horse and carriage still ruled the streets and 'digital' pertained to fingers or numbers, not computers, it must have been an almost unbelievable sight for him, like something out of a novel by Jules Verne.[6] Though I was as excited as anyone seeing the images beamed back from the moon, the memory that will remain with me always is of entering my father's room, expecting him to be asleep at one in the morning, but finding him, a normally undemonstrative man, sitting up in bed with shining eyes and a broad grin on his face, flinging his arms wide open to welcome me.

EPILOGUE

Nearly thirty years later, after Marjorie's death in 1987, I discovered all my father's papers had been left to me. The family, knowing the house and contents had initially been left to Marjorie, assumed she had allocated everything down to the last crotchet and comma to the university or college of her choice. That turned out not to be the case. Nothing had been arranged, and she had died intestate. My sister Vivien lived in England but was neither able nor willing to deal with the situation on her own, so Corinne and I went back and forth from Canada for several months, sorting things out, staying for two-week sessions, aided occasionally during that time by Vivien, and also by our daughter Amanta, who accompanied us for a full session.

The small house was filled to overflowing. Along with Cyril's many music files in cabinets throughout the house, Marjorie, meticulous about saving everything of Cyril's, had called in early manuscripts from publishers that were piled high on every chair and table. The box room contained countless bags of Christmas, birthday and greeting cards, as well as filing cabinets full of correspondence on health and the occult.

One afternoon, just as we were packing up to return to Canada the phone rang. It was the Ralph Vaughan Williams Trust asking if they could come and look at

[5] Rider & Co., 1933. New (American) edition with introduction by Desmond Scott published by Inner Traditions, 2013.

[6] Jules Verne, 1828–1905: prolific novelist, poet and playwright, most famous for *Around the World in Eighty Days, Twenty Thousand Leagues under the Sea, Journey to the Centre of the Earth* and *From the Earth to the Moon.*

Scott's manuscripts with a view to recording some of them. At a time when almost nothing had been recorded, this was most exciting. Half an hour later and we would have missed their call! We arranged for a visit when next we were over, and Trustees Bernard Benoliel and Bruce Roberts came down and spent an afternoon poring over manuscripts. This resulted in the Trust sponsoring four CDs of orchestral music. They were recorded by the BBC Philharmonic with Martyn Brabbins conducting, and undoubtedly sparked the current revival of interest in the music of Cyril Scott, almost all of which is now available.

II

THE MUSIC

8

Discovering, Editing and Recording Cyril Scott

MARTIN YATES

CYRIL Scott was a composer I had known about since I was a student in the early 1980s. My composition teacher, Richard Arnell, had been a great friend of the film composer and conductor Bernard Herrmann, and it was Bernard Herrmann who had steered the great John Ogdon through the first recording of Scott's Piano Concertos for Richard Itter's Lyrita label. Herrmann, I was told by Arnell, was a lover of British music of the twentieth century: more specifically, a type of British music that was less about Edwardian splendour and more about a new and progressive practice; not overtly contemporary, still based in melody, but with a sound that was highly stylised and particular to its composer.

Arnell himself was lucky enough to have had several of his works conducted by Herrmann, including his First Symphony; Piano Concerto, Op. 44; and the world premiere of his cantata *The War God*, first performed to mark the original gathering of the United Nations in San Francisco. Herrmann took on the music of Arthur Bliss, too. For Herrmann to discover the music of Bliss and Arnell is fairly understandable. Bliss was an important figure in the British music establishment: he was the music director of the BBC and would later become Master of the Queen's Music. He also had an American wife, and was well represented at the New York World's Fair by his barnstorming Piano Concerto, played at its New York premiere by Solomon. Arnell, meanwhile, was an up-and-coming member of the artistic Greenwich Village set, with several important New York commissions and premiers behind him.

How Hermann came to know the music of Cyril Scott is not known to me; when he did, he found in it something that totally fitted with his quest for progressive music that was underpinned with recognisable motifs. Anyone who knows Bernard Hermann's own music will be unsurprised by this affinity, as his music is motif-based in the same way. Melodies emerge from these melodic motifs, but they are not necessarily the *raison d'être* of the work.

Scott was a maverick and a polymath, the type of person rather mistrusted these days because of our latent fear of anyone being that clever and knowledgeable. He was a composer, a poet, a painter, a writer on the occult and also a very early proponent of alternative medicine and the importance of dietary healing. All of this is background to my wanting to know more about this remarkable man, firing my interest to such a degree that I searched for two unfinished works and then attempted to complete and record them.

In the early 1980s Richard Arnell gave me two LPs. He had asked me to help him move some boxes around in his flat in Belsize Park, which in the event proved to be the orchestral parts for most of his prodigious output (his publisher had decided to terminate their publishing agreement and had thrown out the orchestral material). During this significant effort I saw some LPs and Arnell said I could take what I wanted. I selected a few, and when I was leaving he held out two more and told me that they would be of more interest than any of the others I had under my arm.

They were the piano concertos of Cyril Scott.[1] As soon as I heard the opening of the first one I was hooked. The style was so unusual, colourful and bold; here was a composer clearly with an ear for a wonderful tune and also an ear for orchestration, and refusing to pander to any style other than his own. His piano writing left me in no doubt that he must have been a very impressive pianist, and the way he used the piano and the orchestra together and apart showed a remarkable understanding of what we now call the Romantic piano concerto. These concertos are gladiatorial in their truest sense, with a nod in the direction of Rachmaninov (who hasn't looked in that direction?), yet with a harmonic complexity and understanding of Ravel and, more noticeably, Debussy. I lived with these recordings until I finally succumbed and upgraded my record collection to a CD collection.

Fast forward to 2010, when I was in Melbourne conducting. I was interested in seeing the sketches of E. J. Moeran's unfinished Second Symphony and I had arranged to see the curator at the University Library, where I had been told they had the manuscript of the short score. (In due course I was able to produce a performing edition of this symphony and record it with the Royal Scottish National Orchestra; happily for me, it was quite well received.)[2] While I was there one of the assistant librarians came in and she mentioned that it was a shame that the Percy Grainger Museum was closed for renovation, as I would have had a field day in there.

I knew there was a museum of Grainger's music and instruments, but I was surprised to hear that there was a collection of manuscripts of other composers that Grainger had collected over the years. I was told that he had a habit of asking his composer friends and, indeed, any composer he met, if they would like to donate any manuscripts, short scores or notebooks to his collection. The upshot of this is that a variety of works survive in the Grainger Museum which would otherwise have been lost. The assistant librarian mentioned a few illustrious composers who had donated to the collection, and at the end, as an afterthought, added: 'Oh, there are a few by Cyril Scott.' I went back to the UK and found that the catalogue of the Grainger collection was online,[3] and while looking through page after page I found that there was a short score of an incomplete early Piano Concerto and also an early Cello Concerto. Both of these pre-dated the published First Piano Concerto and the known Cello Concerto.

I immediately emailed the Grainger collection to see if I could have copies, and I was told that it was possible, but that I had to seek permission from the composer's estate, namely Cyril Scott's son, Desmond, who lived in Toronto. I wrote to him and explained that if I could attempt to finish them, and if I made a half decent job of them, I would like to record them for Dutton Epoch, the label with which I have a longstanding relationship. Very quickly I received a response. Desmond pointed out that the Piano Concerto had been looked at by various musicians and judged to

[1] Lyrita SRCS 81 and 82.

[2] Dutton Epoch CDLXD 7281.

[3] [Editor's note: It had earlier been published in hard copy – Phil Clifford, *Grainger's Collection of Music by Other Composers*, Percy Grainger Music Collection 1 (Grainger Museum, University of Melbourne, 1983).]

be not in any fit state to be completed, but that the Cello Concerto[4] appeared not only to have been completed, but was also extant in full score. He said that I was welcome to have copies of both works and, once I had looked at them, and if my report was favourable to the possibility of completing them, then I could attempt to do so. But quite understandably he wanted me to look at them first so as to be certain about them before he finally gave permission.

When the parcel of music photocopies arrived I could not open it quickly enough and was very soon immersed in the Cello Concerto. I could see straight away that this was fairly complete, and even though some pages were not scored there was a piano score on some of the lower staves showing what the intended accompaniment could be. The cello writing was assured, as was the orchestration; the work is in four sections, including a cadenza, and plays continuously in one movement. The rhapsodic nature of the music was immediately evident and, although in four sections, the melodic material from one is adapted or reworked from an earlier movement each time. Sitting down at the piano I stopped short when I played the second subject (Ex. 8.1). This melody is wonderful, so transparent to start with and then building in intensity and passion, while retaining its beautiful simplicity. As I played it, it went straight into that category of melodies that I knew I would not forget; it felt as if I had known it forever, it was that good.

To discover that this Cello Concerto had the opus number 19 made clear that it was far from the work of a beginner, though why it had never been played has remained a mystery. The only assumption one can make is that at the time he felt it not to be 'modern' enough, when he had already started exploring a more advanced harmony. It was clearly rescue-able and should surely find an audience. Its quality was confirmed by the cellist Raphael Wallfisch, who edited the virtuoso cello part to make it playable as a concert work.

Subsequently I started going through the many pages of the Piano Concerto, which date from 1900, a time when Scott seemed to complete and then withdraw several substantial scores. The first movement, Adagio maestoso, had a solo part entirely written and there were some early pages of full score, all neatly written out. This could not be the sheet music of a first draft. The handwriting was so neat, an effort had been made to be clear. Many dynamics, phrasing and articulation marks were there, and there were even some suggested bowings marked in. There were rehearsal numbers too. This may seem a minor point, but rehearsal numbers are almost always a very late addition to a score; composers either leave them to an editor or copyist to add in, or when they do mark them in themselves this is done generally to go with the phrases, an impossibility if I had been dealing with a first-draft sketch. The fact that it must have once been near performance was reinforced for me when I realised that it had the opus number 10.

The second movement is styled an Intermezzo and includes the cadenza. Here the opening was scored and written in the same manner as the first movement, but the manuscript was much less well ordered. Pages were not connected; there were phrases that had no ends, and then the next page would start with something

[4] Phil Clifford's catalogue lists it (p. 239) as: MG C2/SCO-44 Concerto for cello and orchestra, op. 19/ by Cyril Scott. – 1 full score ([83]p. on folded double leaves 28 stave B.& H. Nr. 20. C ms. paper) in cardboard cover; 36cm. – Holograph (ink).

Ex. 8.1 Scott, [Early] Concerto for cello & orchestra, Op. 19 (1902), second subject

Ex. 8.1 continued

different. There were a few pages on which there were notes and ideas, and it was on those pages I could see the thread the movement was intended to take. The finale started with several pages scored out. The handwriting was not as clear here and the piano part would often continue without accompaniment for some while; then the orchestra would come back in, not in a deliberate fashion, but more as if the movement was being worked out. The pages after a while were not connected from one to another and I could not make head nor tail of what should happen.

I decide to lay out the pages on my living-room floor in a random order, and try to pick them up based on how the last bars of one page linked to the first bars on another page. After an hour or so I had what turned out to be half of the last movement in the correct order. The pencilled page numbering bore no relationship to this, but it was obvious that it worked musically. Later I was told that the page numbers were added once the manuscript was in the possession of the Grainger museum. I could see in the Piano Concerto ideas of such boldness and originality, as well as a pathway through the work. Thus I had the manuscript of an almost complete first movement; a second movement with two of the three projected sections complete, and a Finale that was incomplete. It was all so convincing that I wrote to Desmond and told him that in my opinion it could be done, and that I really wanted to work on both these works. He agreed, and I at once called Dutton Epoch and told them of the project. Within days the recording project was up and running, with the BBC Concert Orchestra enthusiastically agreeing to become involved.

I finished the rough draft of the Piano Concerto within a month and then put it aside to work on the Cello Concerto. That task only took me about two weeks because, as I have said, the manuscript of this work was in a much more completed state. I spent some time revising the Piano Concerto, especially the ending. The piano part was so virtuosic right from the start that for some time I was unable to find anything that could be realised out of Scott's ideas and would also give a real show-off end to the concerto. It had to feel like it was as close to what the composer at least intended in its style. The notes of course are based on material from the movement. Eventually I was as happy with it as I could be, and set about creating a piano reduction of both concertos so that they could be rehearsed without the orchestra.

It seems clear that this Piano Concerto must be the concerto by Cyril Scott that Paderewski seemed set to perform in 1901, though there is no trace of such a performance having taken place. After the later Piano Concerto No. 1 appeared during World War 1, Scott dismissed talk of this earlier concerto by saying it was a bad work and that he had destroyed it (although he used the principal theme from the slow movement for his song *Evening Hymn*, published by Boosey in 1904). This must explain why no final fair-copy full score survives, and we must be grateful to Percy Grainger that he should have preserved what we have of the work; maybe Grainger valued it more highly than his friend Scott did in earlier years. So striking a score was clearly a significant achievement for its young composer, and if only Paderewski had taken it up it would surely have gone round the world.

Choosing the soloists was simple, and both of them were excited by the project. Within a matter of weeks scores were in the post to two of Britain's greatest soloists: the pianist Peter Donohoe and cellist Raphael Wallfisch. Peter and I spoke at length on the telephone before the recording sessions and sorted out issues of tempi and general interpretation, while Raphael and I got together when he played the entire concerto as I accompanied on the piano. Even though I knew that these works were both very special, it only became obvious how special as the three days of rehearsals and recording started.[5]

The recording sessions took place at the Watford Colosseum (Fig. 8.1).[6] It proved the most perfect acoustic for this music. The BBC Concert Orchestra were playing for the recording, and Mike Dutton, the owner of Dutton Epoch and essentially the man who gave us the financial green light, was also there. First on was the Cello Concerto, and although I had been working on the music for many weeks, it proved to be a true revelation hearing it. Raphael Wallfisch had edited the solo cello part, so that it really showed both the material and the instrument off to its maximum potential, while allowing those passages that were at first impossible to play to become playable. This may sound as if I am saying that Raphael re-wrote the solo part in places, which up to a point I am, but I should make it clear that from concertos by Beethoven, Brahms and Schumann right though Tchaikovsky and up to the present day, composers have been guided by soloists on what is playable and what is not. The fact that this took place in the composer's absence was simply because the work had not been played when the composer was alive to work on this aspect. The glorious second subject melted everyone's hearts, and as the first day progressed it was obvious that this work just had to be heard. It was with some sadness that we finished the Cello Concerto because it had made such an impression on all of us involved in the project.

Next we worked on the overture *Pelleas and Melisanda*, another score from the Grainger Museum; this turned out to be a highly descriptive tone poem evoking

[5] 26–28 November 2012.

[6] The celebrated recording venue formerly known as Watford Town Hall.

Figure 8.1 Desmond Scott addressing the BBC Concert Orchestra during the Watford recording sessions, November 2012

Maurice Maeterlinck's doomed lovers of the title. At the time Cyril Scott's overture was one of many orchestral works on this theme, pre-dating Debussy's opera. Melody after melody poured out of this piece with climaxes of Wagnerian proportions. (My mentioning Richard Wagner is no accident, as the music in *Pelleas* is clearly influenced by Wagner and his school of thought.)

It is strange, when one thinks about Debussy's ambivalence to Wagner, that Wagner and Debussy are bound together in Scott's brilliant take on this subject. Relistening to the recording where Scott is at his Wagnerian best, one notices that he uses a very simple, almost jaunty, melody from just after letter L to lead us into a seriously opulent climax at Letter M that really does takes the material much further than one suspected was possible (Ex. 8.2). I am not denigrating when I suggest that Wagner was also a master of this in his operas. In fact, this kind of writing is indeed operatic, and leaves me wanting to know what the Operatic Scott sounds like!

Pelleas & Melisanda had received a first performance in Frankfurt in 1900, but the orchestral material had long since disappeared. Why it was not played again is just inexplicable. Of course there are lots of overtures of tone-poem proportions, and also many tone poems, but for music of this quality to languish forgotten is surprising. I say it is surprising, but of course there are literally thousands of symphonies,

Ex. 8.2 Scott, *Pelleas and Melisanda* overture, Op. 5 (1900); piano reduction edited from the manuscript by Martin Yates

operas, concertos and all manner of chamber music waiting to be rediscovered, and in some cases heard for the first time!

Finally Peter Donohoe arrived, and we began the Piano Concerto. Like Raphael he had totally immersed himself in the soundworld of the young Cyril Scott, and he played the work as if he had known it all his life. Peter likes to play through the entire score of whatever it is he is going to record, and this works especially well when we are all (soloist, orchestra and conductor) on a voyage of discovery. We went from the heroism of the towering first movement (Ex. 8.3) into the chilly first subject of the second, and we knew that this was again something special. The chill of the first part of the slow movement gradually gave way to a sunnier melody before we hit the high jinks of the finale: this was, of course, the least complete movement in the manuscript, but I like to feel that we arrived at a performing version that convinces.

By the time the three days were up everyone involved was excited and moved in equal measure. Excited by the sheer exuberance and ability of this young composer, and moved because he never heard the two concertos. What led him simply to abandon two such well-crafted and well-structured works? There may be no reason other than his putting them aside to work on something else, giving them to Percy Grainger, and forgetting all about them. It does seem most cavalier when viewed from the early part of the twenty-first century, but then again, as his later works show, Cyril Scott was a perfectionist. Although both these concertos are full of glorious melodies and great ideas, perhaps he knew later on that they were written in a style that was not his later voice. Both works are very much in debt to the general Romantic style of the time, and we know from his mature music that this style is not where Scott the composer ends; it is very much where he starts.

The music of Scott that I have encountered as a conductor is progressive melodically as well as harmonically, at least for its time. In my opinion Scott did not write a melody simply to lead the listener through a work; he appears to have demanded that his melodies rather decorate his harmonic structure, because it is his harmony that leads the way. He was unashamed of writing outside of the rules; indeed there are moments where he appears deliberately to break the rules. One such moment appears in the Cello Concerto where the harmony goes chordally: E major – D Minor – G (with a B in the bass). It cannot even be said that this works like a folk-song, a mode popular at this time with many a composer. If this kind of harmonic progression owes anything to anyone it is to Richard Strauss, himself very well versed in the art of unrelated chord progressions. In many ways it is the harmonic structure of both *Pelleas* and the Cello Concerto that marks the soundworld of Scott as unique. It is less noticeable in the Piano Concerto, as that owes so much more to the large Romantic piano concertos of the era, but when you compare this style to Scott's later music, such as the Double Violin Concerto (existing only in piano score – see note, p. 458), you can see that eventually he was led to simplify the texture, while yet retaining his very special soundworld.

In the later works, even *The Melodist and the Nightingales* for cello and orchestra (which I have also had the pleasure of recording),[7] you can see a thinning out of

[7] Dutton Epoch CDLX 7326.

Ex. 8.3 Scott, Concerto in D for piano & orchestra, Op. 10 (1900), first movement; completed and edited from the manuscript by Martin Yates

Ex. 8.3 continued

the textures, where the harmonies are somehow more implied than obvious. Even this was bold and adventurous in Cyril Scott's time, and I venture to opine that we were to wait for the likes of Steve Reich and Philip Glass (and the minimalists) to take this idea to its eventual emasculated conclusion. I use the word emasculated on purpose, because the implication of melody and harmony in the minimalists does, in my opinion, take away some of the angst and ardour that music is capable of; maybe that is deliberate, but what Scott achieves by his implied harmony and melody retains – no, *celebrates* – the arguments and richness of music with the human spirit at its core.

I have made a multitude of recordings and to me all of them are special, but if I had to single one out as being an all-round favourite, from the musical point of view, to the people who came together to realise this extraordinary project, I would have to pick out this recording of early Cyril Scott.

9

'Years of Indiscretion': The Early Piano Works, 1898–1909

LESLIE DE'ATH

SCOTT'S musical output is substantial, and allows for a diachronic study of his musical style to be undertaken through his output in at least four media: piano music, chamber works, orchestral works and songs. Of these, he had the most abiding interest in writing for the piano, and for a variety of chamber combinations. These media represent all periods of his creative life, and provide the best glimpse of his stylistic attributes as they transformed from period to period. Accordingly, here we shall survey Scott's piano output in a roughly chronological order.

As with many other long-lived composers of the earlier twentieth century, Scott's music exhibits a wide variety of compositional approaches, and the internal evidence of the music itself is often a fair guide as to when a composition might have been written.[1] One is perhaps initially struck by how different the works preceding

[1] One thinks of composers as varied as Stravinsky, Schönberg, and Florent Schmitt in this light. The last of these was in fact an acquaintance of Scott's, with an even greater propensity to compose in widely differing styles of the day – and masterfully in each. In his young adulthood Scott was given to visiting the Continent for about four months of every year, and became acquainted with many renowned composers of the day besides Debussy, with whom he has long been too closely compared. I am in possession of a letter from Schmitt to Scott, dated only 19 April but, to judge from its content, written about 1949:

> Cher Monsieur,
> Peut-être vous souvenez-vous encore, après trente-cinq ans, d'une matinée chez vous, à Londres, avec Ravel et Maurice Delage, vous, au piano, sifflant et jouant votre sonate de violon. Depuis j'ai eu le plaisir de dîner avec vous, à Paris, chez Mme de Chaumont-Guitry. Et nos relations, je le regrette, en sont restées là, bien que j'ai cherché plusieurs fois à vous revoir lors de voyages rapides à Londres.
>
> Voici une occasion de raviver de vieux souvenirs: je me permets de vous adresser M. François d'Albert, l'excellent violiniste hongrois, en vous demandant d'avoir la bonté de vouloir bien l'aider dans ses démarches pour se faire connaître en Angleterre.
>
> Merci de ce que vous pourriez faire pour lui. Et, en ne renonçant pas à l'espoir de vous retrouver un jour, je vous envoie mes voeux très amicaux.
>
> Florent Schmitt / 37 r. Calvaire St. Cloud S.O. [Seine-et-Oise]

Scott speaks of this letter in his *Bone of Contention: Life Story and Confessions* (Aquarian Press, 1969), p. 225:

> Meanwhile, from the Continent had come a letter from the eminent French composer, Florent Schmitt, its object being to effect a meeting between the Hungarian violinist, Dr. Francois D'Albert and myself. This meeting produced unforeseeable results; for apart from being a musician with outstanding gifts, D'Albert turned out to be such an ardent admirer of my works that he organised an entire concert of them in Dublin, where he lived for a time after choosing to leave Hungary for political reasons.

World War 1 are from those of the inter-war years, and from those of his later life. The stylistic changes, however, do not equate simply to the passing of time; indeed, some aspects of Scott's musical style remained with him for life, largely unaltered by external forces. Foremost among these is his sense of lyricism, instilled in him by his musical training in youth. This aspect of his writing remains Romantic at its core, in much the same sense as it does with the Second Viennese School, even as his harmonic language transformed radically over the years.

Scott's earliest systematic training at the piano was with the Italian pianist Lazzaro Uzielli at the Hoch'sche Conservatorium in Frankfurt (1891–3), and upon his return to Liverpool with Herman Steudner-Welsing, a Viennese musician living there at the time.

> He [Steudner-Welsing] had two deplorable habits; he jammed down the pedal and would often forget to release it, and further he snorted violently all the time he performed ... One was not always quite sure of getting one's lesson, for the poor little man suffered from an inordinate craving for spirits ... Fortunately for me he taught me none of his bad habits but only some useful ones.[2]

Scott's early studies in theory, during the first Frankfurt period and with no less a figure than Humperdinck, were sadly unstimulating ('Of how to teach he had no conception at all").[3] Although Scott dabbled in composing as a child from the age of seven, his serious training as a composer had to wait until his second Frankfurt sojourn (1895–8). His lessons with Iwan Knorr during those years set the pattern, and his early piano works naturally bear the hallmarks of dutiful apprenticeship on the one hand, and, on the other, of Knorr's encouragement to explore the compositional styles and techniques of a remarkably wide range of composers and periods. We have no way of knowing how many of Scott's early compositions, whether for piano or for more ambitious combinations, were destroyed, but we do know that many of them found their way to the fireplace by his own self-criticism. Even fewer would have survived had it not been for the efforts of his curatorially minded friend, Percy Grainger.

It is difficult to ascertain a precise chronology for the compositions of Scott's student years, as one is aided only by the completion dates Scott often appended to his manuscripts. It seems that the earliest piano pieces to have survived (with or without Scott's blessing) are the *Erste Ballade* in D minor, and two *Studies for a Slow Movement*, the holographs of which are preserved in the Grainger Museum in Melbourne. It is tempting to speculate on Scott's intention with the two studies. Were they simply student exercises that might possibly be used at a later point in a multi-movement piano or chamber work? Are they all that now exists of a work that was abandoned or

The letter is revealing on another count: it is the only evidence we have that Scott's ongoing interchange with French composers happened in Britain as well as in France, at least on one occasion. D'Albert settled in Dublin, where he arranged for a few concerts of Scott's music. Afterwards he moved to North America, living in Montreal for several years, then accepting a teaching position at the Chicago Conservatory of Music, where he arranged for Scott to receive an Hon. Mus. Doc.

[2] *Bone of Contention*, p. 58.

[3] *Bone of Contention*, pp. 50–1.

destroyed? If so, they were likely 'either/or's, since they are both in the same key, albeit quite different in tempo and mood. Are they piano works, or short scores of something more ambitious? One early production of Scott's student days was the *Variations on an Original Theme,* which was performed at an examination concert in 1898, but is now lost. Presumably Knorr assigned the budding teenage composer an exercise in variation technique as a traditional means of exploring compositional creativity.

Soon after graduating from the Conservatorium, Scott turned his attention to composing on an ambitious scale. A *Magnificat* for chorus and orchestra, his first two symphonies and other smaller orchestral works, a piano concerto, a cello concerto and a few chamber works date from the turn of the century. His earliest published piano works are perhaps student essays, of which only a few survived his own severe self-criticism through to publication. The first piano works to possess opus numbers are the *Three Frivolous Pieces,* Op. 2, followed by the *Six Pieces,* Op. 4, all of which were published in 1903 by Forsyth, though written before the turn of the century. Grainger, who harboured a lingering sense throughout his life that he and Scott had done their finest composing in their earlier years, stated in a letter to Scott fifty years later:

> You started right off [composing] with full-fledged charm, which the 3 Frivolous Pieces & the early Album pieces published by Forsyth (which would make a delightful small orchestral suite, by the way) have as truly as the top-rung of your piano pieces.[4]

The *Three Little Waltzes,* Op. 58, apparently date from the same years, the late opus number no doubt explicable by their delayed publication by Elkin in 1906. The *Six Pieces* are miniatures dedicated 'To Professors Iwan Knorr and Lazzaro Uzielli in grateful remembrance of my student days.' On a somewhat larger scale are the *Three Frivolous Pieces,* Op. 2, of which the third, *Valse scherzando,* is the most compelling. Scott felt kindly enough towards it to record it himself in 1929, by which time he had conferred upon it a 20-bar postlude. This revision is not found in any published form, perhaps due to the change of publisher that transpired the following year. Scott evidently felt that his creations remained malleable in form and content, and that a published score can at best reflect only one moment in an ongoing creative continuum. This philosophy of music's inherent mutability was shared by Scott and Grainger, both of whom were known to perform their works (and those of others) quite differently in their details from one occasion to the next, as the spirit dictated. In Scott's case, this was intimately bound up with his developing conception of the occult role of music in all planes of existence, visible and invisible. There are several instances of his revising earlier works after varying lapses of time. Four of his piano works were republished in revised form around 1929, twenty or more years after being composed.[5]

Scott's first major works for piano are *An English Waltz,* Op. 15, and the Sonata in D, Op. 17. In between the two, he composed his first concertante work, the Piano Concerto in D of 1900. Scott had the pleasure of meeting Paderewski in person at a Liverpool concert given by the Polish pianist. Paderewski asked to have the

[4] Grainger Museum, 12 August 1949 [02.0078].

[5] *An English Waltz* (1903/1929); Piano Sonata No. 1, Op. 66 (1909/c1929/c1935); *Pierrot gai* (1904/1929); *Impromptu (A Mountain Brook)* (1904/1929).

Ex. 9.1 Scott, Sonata in D, Op. 17, theme 'i'

Ex. 9.2 Scott, Sonata in D, Op. 17, theme 'ii'

concerto sent over to his hotel room so he could peruse the score, but Scott relates that 'he never played it, and I am glad he did *not* – for it was a bad work'.[6]

Although the manuscript of the Op. 17 Sonata in D was completed on 11 September 1901, a performance by the composer of a two-movement version had taken place in Liverpool on 18 October 1900. It is tempting to wonder if either the *Andante* (S 161) or *Largo* (S 162) – the two manuscript studies mentioned above – was the additional movement on that occasion. Their tonality (B-flat major) is not an inconceivable key relationship to the D major of Op. 17. Perhaps all three extant works are the remnants of an earlier plan to compose a three- or four-movement sonata, which plan was abandoned by the autumn of 1901.

The original Op. 17 is an intriguing experiment – Scott's first attempt at a large-scale form for keyboard. One feels the thrill not only of the Victorian pomp of its opening bars, but also of a composer in the full flight of youthful discovery and empirical experimentation. It demonstrates honest élan, albeit arguably turgid in its end result. Its structure can be related to standard first-movement sonata form (see Table 9.1): there is a recognisable recapitulation (bar 201), though the middle section (bars 111–200), where one might expect developmental material, introduces

[6] Scott, *My Years of Indiscretion* (Mills & Boon, 1924), p. 84. Some of Scott's denunciations of his own early efforts seem unduly harsh. This work has since been revived and recorded, and stands on its own merit (see pp. 120–6).

Ex. 9.3 Scott, Sonata in D, Op. 17, theme 'iii'

Ex. 9.4 Scott, Sonata in D, Op. 17, theme 'iv'

Ex. 9.5 Scott, Sonata in D, Op. 17, theme 'v'

a new idea, *Andante doloroso* (iv), as if to function as a surrogate slow 'second movement' within a continuous sonata-fantasia structure. As the material of the middle section unfolds, two further ideas are presented, followed by two unusual structural features: a tonal recapitulation to D major (bar 156), but employing the *Andante* theme (iv); and a false recapitulation (bar 167) of the opening theme (i), immediately breaking off into distant keys and exploring repeated figurations. This double red-herring serves to heighten the effect of the true recapitulation, which unfolds predictably until the *Andante* theme returns (bar 274), now in the home key, as a prelude to a *fugato* coda (bar 293) based on (iv) that builds to a climactic ending. The five main thematic ideas of the sonata (Exx. 9.1–9.5 / bars 1, 33, 74, 111, 137 and 145) are sufficiently similar in character and shape to be considered variants of an overarching lyrical plan – a fact which serves to blur the work's structure while unifying its content.

Grainger was the dedicatee of Op. 17, as well as of *An English Waltz*, and performed the premiere of the single-movement original in November of 1901. He considered it:

> the *only* successful modern Klavier sonata. He has completely changed his style once more, & now it is far greater, larger, & still finer in form. He has certainly been influenced by my work ... The 1st theme ... is simply perfect, with changing meters, clangey, like bells, & most Scotty, & heroic.[7]

But by 1909 he was to write to his mother from Hobart: 'I will have much pleasure in playing this piece. It contains so many good things, only it was all too long before. (It wants the knife!)'[8]

This revision found its way to print in 1909, with the singular title *Handelian Rhapsody*. Grainger is credited merely as 'editor' in the publication, even though the alterations and truncations are drastic. Grainger's revisions tighten the work formally, and reduce its length by more than half (342 bars become 164). A comparison of the two versions (Table 9.1) provides detail, and reflects the differing compositional aesthetic of the two composers.

In several spots of the original Scott extends transitional passages, latching onto a figuration and repeating it through a series of extensions. These episodic sections can be disarmingly lengthy, and tend to lose themselves in their own inventiveness. This hallmark of Scott's writing established itself in this work, and figures prominently in the works of the ensuing years, culminating in the *Deuxième suite*. Grainger's 'knife' boldly slashed most of these passages (the square brackets in Table 9.1), along with the brief *fugato* passage toward the end of the original, and transposed themes (v) and (vi) up a whole tone. The preparation for the return of D major (bars 172–91) on the dominant chord was fully excised, as was the extended chromatic chordal passage (bars 192–200) that serves as one final bump on the road to the recapitulation. This passage merits quoting (Ex. 9.6) as illustrating one of Scott's favourite compositional techniques – that of writing a fast-paced succession of chromatically enriched harmonies that threaten to digress wildly into other keys, without actually abandoning the home-key destination. Grainger's removal of this is perhaps unfortunate, if only because it is so exemplary of Scott's free-ranging harmonic style. He evidently also felt that the original grandiose tonic-chord ending overstays its welcome, and would benefit from some harmonic elaboration of his own (bars 337–42 = *HR*, bars 159–64).

The Op. 17 manuscript reveals a further under-recognised influence in Scott's early works: that of Wagner. Scott shared with Debussy and many others a tendency to worship at the Wagnerian shrine in the years of young adulthood. Scott, however, retained a life-long admiration for Wagner's noble, if flawed attempt, as he saw it, to effect 'the formation of a great brotherhood of art'.[9] Wagner's technique of

[7] Letter, Grainger to Herman Sandby, 27 September 1901. Quoted in *The Farthest North of Humanness: Letters of Percy Grainger, 1901–14*, ed. Kay Dreyfus (Macmillan, 1985), p. 4.

[8] Letter, Grainger to Rose Grainger, 14 March 1909. Quoted in ibid., p. 271.

[9] Scott, *The Influence of Music on History and Morals: A Vindication of Plato* (Theosophical Publishing House, 1928), p. 83.

Table 9.1 A comparison of Scott's Sonata in D, Op. 17, with Grainger's arrangement (the *Handelian Rhapsody*)

Sonata in D, Op. 17 (Scott, 1901)					***Handelian Rhapsody* (Grainger, 1909)**		
Form	Key	Bars	Motif		Key	Bars	Motif
A	D	1–32	i	=	D	1–31	i
	C	33–40	ii	=	C	32–9	ii
		[41–73]*					
	F	74–83	iii	≅	F	40–7	iii (altered)
	D	84–105	ii	=	D	48–69	ii
		[106–10]					
B	d	111–19	iv	=	d	70–8	iv
	B♭/D/C	[120–31]					
	B♭	132–6	iv	=	B♭	79–83	iv
	B	137–44	v	=	C#	84–91	v
	E	145–51	vi	=	F#	92–7	v
	E♭	[151–5]					
	D	156–66	iv	≅	D	98–116	iv (altered)
	D	[167–200]	i				
A	D	201–25	i	=	D	117–41	i
	C/D	[226–92]	ii				
	D (fugato)	[293–315]	iv				
	D	316–42	iv/i	≅	D	142–64	iv/i (altered)

* Square brackets indicate the passages excised by Grainger in the *Handelian Rhapsody*.

Ex. 9.6 Scott, Sonata in D, Op. 17, bars 192–200

continuous unfolding through denial of cadence is seen in more than one fanciful excursion in this sonata (bars 169–88, 245–73), and in the unusual juxtapositions of tonality.[10] There is a strong sense – ironically stronger than in Grainger's more cogent arrangement – that an essential 'unity in diversity' informs this work.[11] There is a feeling of simmering sublimity in many passages of this sonata, as it gradually, restlessly and relentlessly builds towards its climactic moments. Even if they fail to reach the heights of a *Liebestod*, the parallels are nonetheless there. Scott tells us that:

> in order to form this great scheme he [Wagner] had to break down many pre-existent musical conventions. In vain did the pedagogues of music look for adherence to their cherished rules of harmony … In place of them they found unresolved discords, false relations, and transitions into keys which had no perceptible connection with the key just abandoned – all was seeming lawlessness, deliberate disregard of rule and precedent – scandalous Freedom! Yet, with this apparent lawlessness, what was Wagner actually accomplishing? In order to attain unity, he was breaking down the barriers to unity, and so setting music free.[12]

Elsewhere, still in reference to Wagner, he says:

> when the ingenuity of a composer is such that he can interblend several beautiful melodies so that they can be played simultaneously to produce one harmonious whole, then the spirituality of his music is assured. But there are yet other ways, one being to clothe his melodic outline in chords, i.e., instead of his melodies being composed of single notes or octaves, like those of Tchaikovsky, they may be composed of chords so that each single note of the chords, when played in succession forms a melody of itself.[13]

This description is an apt summary of what Scott himself strove to do in many of his works, even as early as in this sonata. His notion of *musical flow*, as it pertained to his own works, can be viewed as a product of his admiration for these aspects of Wagner's creative language. Scott's most successful Wagnerian creation is surely the *Andante sostenuto* from the Second Symphony, a work dating from the same year, and known to the world now only as the middle movement of the *Three Symphonic Dances*, Op. 22.

Two large-scale solo piano works in addition to the Op. 17 sonata also date from this time: *An English Waltz*, Op. 15, and the *Scherzo*, Op. 20. They could hardly be

[10] At bar 169, D major slides suddenly into E-flat major, only to return three bars later. At bars 230–1 Scott crossed out two bars in the manuscript, evidently looking for a different approach to the C major at bar 232 from the one employed in the exposition (bars 31–2). The result is jarring, so in my edition and recording of this sonata I supplied a suggested bridge. Both these moments also fell to Grainger's knife.

[11] Scott, *Music: Its Secret Influence Throughout the Ages*, 2nd edn (Rider & Co., 1950), p. 60; 5th edn, titled *Music and Its Secret Influence Throughout the Ages* (Inner Traditions, 2013), p. 93.

[12] Ibid. (1950), pp. 60–1 / (2013), p. 93.

[13] Ibid. (1950), pp. 61–2 / (2013), pp. 94–5.

less alike in style. Both are, like the sonata, technically challenging concert works, the waltz dedicated to Grainger, and the scherzo to Evelyn Suart. Each is absorbed with a different aspect of Scott's creative development as seen in the Op. 17 sonata: *An English Waltz* with its Victorian bravado and its reluctance to veer too far from familiar harmonic and structural paths, while the *Scherzo* is engaged in a level of experimentation that would have bolstered Scott's reputation as an *enfant terrible* of the early twentieth century. It is as if these two conflicting proclivities, inherent in the sonata, divorce themselves to form these two diametrically opposed concert works. That both styles inform the music of Scott's earliest creative life is noteworthy. Caught between *stile antico/stile moderno* worlds, he attempted to enter both with the Op. 17 sonata.

The broad-ranging interests of Iwan Knorr in Frankfurt, and his extensive familiarity with the musical modernisms of his day, no doubt nurtured a curiosity and boldness in his students that few other young musicians studying in Europe in the late nineteenth century would have enjoyed. Algernon Ashton, during the eighteen formative years he spent in Germany, met with nothing comparable in his studies with Raff and Reinecke, and his enormous creative output, though full of integrity, was firmly rooted in a Germanic conservatism that remained with him for life. Indeed, Scott was fortunate in his circles of acquaintance in his youth (Stefan George, Melchior Lechter, Charles Bonnier), which gave him a sense of being a direct, active participant at the cutting edge of modernity, with its concomitant air of superiority.[14] Back in England, Evelyn Suart, herself a fine pianist, also made a deep impression on Scott, introducing him both to the philosophies of Christian Science and to William Elkin, who became his principal publisher throughout his life. The *Scherzo* was the first piano composition of Scott's that Elkin published, and the dedication is a thank you to Suart for having brokered their professional association and friendship. But if Elkin thought he was entering into an agreement with Scott as a purveyor of maudlin miniatures for an undiscerning audience, he was in for a considerable shock! That certainly did not begin with this uncompromising inaugural work, or for that matter the two Op. 24 songs that preceded the *Scherzo* in publication. The group of three pieces of Op. 40, along with several early songs published by Elkin, set that trend in motion late in 1904. Scott always spoke in very grateful tones about William Elkin. Late in life, he reminisced about their working relationship, in a passage informative on many levels:

> Much can be said for the courage of Mr. Elkin senior that he took up a young man who defied the academic traditions and whose adversaries, the teachers and professors, were in far more advantageous positions than were his friends. The whole business meant a long and uphill struggle. Yet my enterprising publisher was to win through in the end; though the policy he adopted to gain that end had certain drawbacks so far as I was concerned. He had stipulated that I should write a certain number of piano-pieces and songs every year, with the result that I composed far too many, and seeing that they deflected attention from my more serious works, I have little doubt that they contributed to my undoing. As to whether I

[14] This was readily acknowledged by Scott himself on many occasions later in life, and is reflected in the very title of his first biography.

> shall live them down when I have ceased to live in my present guilty 'garment of the soul', is a matter about which I would not venture to prophesy.[15]

An English Waltz and the *Scherzo* functioned as vehicles for both himself and his dedicatees. Upon returning to England, Scott strove to carve out a career as a young concert virtuoso while also establishing a reputation as an innovative composer. This was not unusual for the time, and brings to mind other contemporary composer/pianists, such as Busoni, Scriabin, Rachmaninov, Tansman, and Ornstein. Scott arranged to present piano recitals in his home town of Liverpool and in London during the early years of his return to England – a strategy that brought him both piano and composition students, as well as a foot in the door of British society, complete with introductions to influential individuals and invitations to a variety of soirées at which he would invariably be asked to perform. Neither teaching nor socialising was particularly conducive to his temperament, though the latter provided ample fodder for his first autobiography, with its rather self-conscious title, *My Years of Indiscretion*.

The *Scherzo* is a whirlwind of harmonic instability. Its obsessive exploration of repeated figurations up and down the keyboard go further than the similar episodes in the Op. 17 sonata, and at times are so mannered as to seem almost a parody of themselves. The piece is saturated with parallel ninth chords, and unsettling in its ceaseless shifts of tonality. As a student in Germany, Scott had obviously paid close attention to the new tonal experiments in France and Russia, imbibing both their spirit and letter. It is well to keep in mind that this remarkable work pre-dates the early piano works of Ravel (*Jeux d'eau*) and Debussy (*Estampes* and the first book of *Preludes*). What Debussian influence there might have been would have come from the early orchestral works (*Nocturnes, Prélude à l'après-midi d'un faune*), and the opera *Pelléas et Mélisande*.

By contrast, *An English Waltz* is mired in conventionality, effective though it is as a bravura showpiece. But even here there is some tendency to preoccupation with extended transitions (bars 244–68). Grainger, on tour with an aging Adelina Patti:

> played, with success, my showy piece in a large number of towns and thereby brought my name – such as it was – increasingly before the public, and at the same time made people realise that he was a remarkable pianist.[16]

Years later, Scott must have sensed that this piece had worn out its Victorian welcome, as he revised it, shortening it slightly, and added a number of harmonic enrichments and changes in content.[17]

It was at this time that Scott found his mature stride as a composer of piano miniatures in the prevailing drawing-room style of the day. The first of his two *Pierrot Pieces*, Op. 35 – *Pierrot triste* – is today one of his most enduring pieces. Grainger

[15] *Bone of Contention*, p. 94.

[16] *Bone of Contention*, p. 91.

[17] There is reason to believe the revision was done in or around 1920, although the revised publication was released only in 1929.

was in large measure again responsible. The composer credits Grainger for the inspiration:

> The first composition he played to me that afternoon was entitled *A Lot of Rot for Cello and Piano* ... far from being 'rot', it absolutely transported me. There was a painted, powdered pathos about it ... which haunted me with its beauty for weeks afterwards. Grainger had caught something of the sad, sentimental vulgarity of the music-hall. Months later it was still the memory of this music-poem which prompted me to write my *Two Pierrot Pieces*, with their atmosphere of the variety stage, though I doubt whether those who heard them were conscious of my intentions, and the full significance of the 'Pierrot' in this connection.[18]

From a promotional point of view, Grainger always remained an ardent spokesman for Scott's piano music – more so than Scott himself, even. Over forty years later Grainger wrote to Scott, relating an event that sounds as if it came second only to Grainger's own Hollywood Bowl wedding ceremony in ostentation:

> On Sunday I played your slow Pierrot piece to about 7000–8000 people at an outdoor symphony concert (Watergate) in Washington. (I always slightly alter all pieces I play in public.) I was struck by the fact that all my slight changes only worsened the pieces & that your own versions were always better than mine.[19]

Both composers have left recordings of *Pierrot triste* for posterity – Scott's paired with *Pierrot gai* – all dating from 1929.[20] During his one visit to see Gabriel Fauré, Scott chose to play his Pierrot pieces, which were received favourably by the elder composer. Scott returned to the same theme in 1912, with *Pierrette* for piano, the song *Pierrot and the Moon Maiden*, and *Pierrot amoureux* for cello and piano.

Scott's other experimental piano work from this time is an unpublished *Prelude No. 1*, labelled 'Op. 37' on the title page. Two inconsequential miniatures, *At Dawn* and *Shadows*, were published as Op. 37 by Boosey in 1904, a year after the composer's association with Elkin had begun. It seems likely that Elkin balked at his commitment in the wake of the *Scherzo*, at least as far as the piano works, and refused to take a chance on the comparably iconoclastic and ambitious *Prelude*.[21] Who, after all, could and would want to perform these works? Recalling the quote above, regarding a musical public that displayed keen interest in his piano miniatures and

18 *My Years of Indiscretion*, p. 61.

19 Letter, Grainger to Scott, 3 July 1946 (Grainger Museum [02.0069]). The date of the concert was thus 29 June 1946.

20 The enduring popularity of *Pierrot triste* is attested to by strong sales figures, its publication history, and the attention it was given by others. Claude Gonvierre made an early recording of it, and Billy Mayerl featured it in his final BBC recording in 1956. Ian Parrott, however, found it 'sickly': Parrott, *Cyril Scott and his Piano Music* (Thames Publishing, 1991), p. 41.

21 It was certainly intended for publication by Scott, because on page 3 of the manuscript his shorthand marking 'BIS' (= repeat) comes with a marginal note stating 'print in full'.

songs while remaining stoutly indifferent to his more important works, we might well imagine Scott's life-long discouragement as having begun with his experience regarding this *Prelude*. It is indeed unfortunate that it was shunned by publishers, as it is altogether more satisfying a composition than the *Scherzo*. The musical style is as close to Debussy as Scott was to come – with elements of Delius thrown into the harmonic mix as well. From our retrospective critical standpoint, this is an important early piano work, worthy of revival.

Scott's first forays into pianistic exoticism were the *Eastern Dance* from *Three Dances* of 1903, and the Op. 39 pair, *Dagobah* and *Chinese Serenade*, of 1904. Op. 39 was also his last publication with Forsyth. Scott was to explore non-Western themes often, and in the early years especially this does not necessarily reflect his preoccupations with occultism so much as his buying into the public appetite for Eastern and other exotic subject matter – an appetite prevalent in all the arts at the time. *Eastern Dance* distinguishes itself from mainstream European style only by its static, intentionally arbitrary repetition of ideas. There is something of the Tchaikovsky of the *Nutcracker* ballet in it, especially the *Arabian Dance*. A dagobah – for which one of the Op. 39 pieces is named – is a Buddhist shrine that serves as a repository for sacred relics. The luxuriant chromatic harmonies of this work build to an impressive climax (Ex. 9.7). The piece is technically rather demanding, and makes no concession to smaller hands. Ireland and Bax (and later, Warlock) pushed chromatic boundaries in rather different directions from Scott, whose approach seems to have more in common with Delius, at least in *Dagobah*. The tendency to indulge in rapid harmonic rhythm, seen in many of Scott's works, comes from his hallmark harmonisation of every note of a melody. This sophisticated conceit renders the music 'busy' and demanding on the ear in a way that some commentators find tiring and/or cloying.

The serenade in the *Chinese Serenade* can only be the slower middle section, with its picturesque harmonies and lyricism. The busy sixteenth-notes of the outer sections and square-cut repetitive patterns are more reminiscent of a busy city on market day. The unexpected F-sharp major chord on the final chord, after roughly four minutes of D major, is a kind of joke, reminding us perhaps that harmonic structure is not a universal language. Scott will return to eastern themes several times in his later works.

The three pieces that make up Op. 40, also from 1904, are altogether more conventional, and cater to the public demand for ingratiating lyrical miniatures with poignant harmonic touches. The first, *Solitude*, could almost be a song by Quilter. The second, *Vesperale*, with its churchiness and almost maudlin manner, has found some ongoing popularity as service music, and has been transcribed for various combinations, including one for organ. It is an entirely different piece from the song *Vesperal*, Op. 9 No. 3, composed four years earlier. The last piece, *Chimes*, is in Scott's best 'clangy' style (as Grainger would have it), and has the rollicking good humour and musical gestures of the Op. 17 sonata. Later in his piano music Scott would return to the inspiration of bells, with very different results.[22] A passage in

[22] Compare, for instance, *Bells* (from *Poems*), *Angelus* (from *Vieux chine*), *Carillon*, *Twilight Bells* (from *Two Sketches*), and the final pages of the *Theme and Variations* for piano duo.

Ex. 9.7 Scott, *Dagobah*, Op. 39 No. 1, bars 24–9

the middle section of *Chimes*, with its raised fourth degree chord, curiously presages Puccini's *Gianni Schicchi* by some fourteen years.

The last work for piano of 1904, *Impromptu (A Mountain Brook)*, is another concert work – Scott's only one without a dedication to a prominent pianist. Like *An English Waltz*, this piece has two versions, the revised one with significant changes of harmony in keeping with the composer's middle-period style. The pictorial nature of the writing is obvious enough in both, and its rippling figuration provides us with as vivid an insight into Scott's own Chopinesque piano technique as any work he wrote for the medium. Indeed, the composer has left us a Welte-Mignon roll of his interpretation.

With the Op. 47 pair of 1905, we arrive at Scott's signature piece, *Lotus Land*. It was written in the village of Shere, Surrey, where he was staying with the poet Rosamund Marriott Watson and her husband. Scott was to choose her poetry for his songs fifteen times over the next twenty years – more often than any poet apart from Ernest Dowson. This exotic miniature has captured the world's ears in a manner that is, at some level, inexplicable. It is, in its own way, a fine work. But the same, or more, could be said of several other piano miniatures, some of which are hardly known at all. Arguably *Lotus Land* has unfairly eclipsed much of the rest of Scott's piano music, to an extent incommensurate with both its own merit and Scott's estimation of it. He must have been grateful for the recognition *Lotus Land* brought, but he remained remarkably taciturn about his own compositions generally throughout his copious writings. He speaks briefly about it in his 1969 autobiography, only to talk of Kreisler's well-known arrangement for violin and piano, which he preferred to his own original; indeed, he probably would have penned it for that combination himself, had Elkin not discouraged his composing for chamber combinations.[23]

The lotus flower has been loaded with potent symbolism throughout history, in a wide variety of cultures and religions, and it can imply many things. In many eastern cultures the lotus is a symbol of the universe, and of one's awakening to the spiritual reality of all life. It is central to Egyptian, Chinese, Indian, Iranian and Greco-Roman culture, and to Buddhist, Hindu and Taoist teachings. The lotus has been variously the flower of divine birth from which gods sprang forth, the symbol of light and the sun, a lunar emblem, the flower out of which Buddha emerged in flame, the throne of Brahma, and many other things. In Homer's *Odyssey* the soldiers forget everything of the past and present, and live out their lives in languid, idyllic contentment in the 'land of the lotus-eaters', thanks to a single taste of the lotus fruit. The modern composer-critic Ian Parrott was convinced that 'The title, under the influence of Stefan George, must surely refer to the country in Greek mythology where the lotus-eaters lived a life of indolent pleasure.'[24]

By 1905 Scott had become interested in a variety of religions and philosophies, both Western and non-Western, including theosophy, Vedantism and Spirituality. The French periodical devoted to the theosophical movement in France in the days of Blavatsky and Annie Besant was called *Le lotus bleu*. Its German counterpart was a magazine edited by Franz Hartmann, *Lotusblüthen*, and was circulating in Leipzig from 1893 to 1900, Scott's years in Germany. There had been an earlier German magazine on theosophy, *Die Sphinx*, which may have had a part in the naming of Scott's *Sphinx* of 1908.[25]

It is natural enough to wonder about the cross-pollination of ideas between Scott's philosophical beliefs and his composing. He himself wrote extensively about the occult function of music in humanity, in both terrestrial and astral planes of the soul's existence. But ultimately he warns us against delving too deeply into this alleged association. Collins quotes an article from 1950, in which Scott states:

> the assumption that while composing I have, so to say, one ear cocked on the occult, does not and cannot make sense. It is just one of those fables which people (especially journalists) like to create in an attempt to make a composer, artist or whatnot, appear more spectacular or unbalanced than he really is.[26]

By this token, *Lotus Land* may simply imply an unspecified location in 'the East', and announce the exotic harmonic, tonal and figurative gestures in the music itself.

Lotus Land's musical style allows a range of interpretive possibilities, as shown by the many recorded performances that have been released. Scott's own 1928

[23] See *Bone of Contention*, pp. 97–8. Kreisler toured the Orient with *Lotus Land*, where it met with huge success, encored three times on at least one occasion.

[24] Parrott, *Cyril Scott and his Piano Music*, p. 19.

[25] Years later Scott wrote a poem entitled *Lotusland*, which has a Rossettian sublimity.

[26] Sarah Collins, *The Aesthetic Life of Cyril Scott* (Boydell, 2013), p. 172. The article is 'Music and the Occult', *Musical Opinion* 73 (1950), p. 359.

recording on 78 rpm reveals a more pliable pulse than is usually heard in the performances of others. It is also quite fast, probably because of the time limitations of the recording medium. *Lotus Land* is the one composition of Scott's that has made the leap into popular music, having been taken up by a number of popular music groups, especially from 1950 to 1980, and released on LP in a bewildering variety of new clothes.[27]

The other Op. 47 piece, *Columbine*, has no exotic flavour, but is a worthy companion to *Lotus Land*. It is a delightful, if conventional, waltz, not unlike the several *valses* of Cécile Chaminade that were in vogue at the time. The title presumes a return to the *commedia dell'arte* world of the Pierrot pieces, Columbine being a stock servant type – clever and coquettish – the wife of Pierrot, and Harlequin's mistress. If, like *Lotus Land*, the piece was written at Shere, both works may have been in part inspired by an unnamed young lady with whom Scott had a passing romance there.[28]

The piano works of the next two years are all miniatures. *Asphodel*, *Notturno*, and *Two Sketches* are unremarkable productions to fulfil a publisher's contract. The *Sketches* indulge in basic imitative gestures, bird calls and bells – something that Scott returns to on several later occasions in the piano works. Both sketches involve incessant repetitions throughout – cuckoo-calls in the first, and an ostinato left-hand pattern in the second.

Summerland is a set of four miniatures, apparently intended for a younger audience, and indeed dedicated to two children. The titles, and that of the set, may appear to be nothing more than the usual fare for mass-market character pieces. But to an Occultist, Summerland is that place where the soul resides between

[27] Laurie Sampsel, author of *Cyril Scott: A Bio-Bibliography* (Greenwood, 2000), gave an entertaining presentation at the IMS Conference in Melbourne in 2004 on exactly this topic, peppering the talk with a variety of excerpts from these releases. These ranged from ingenious to flabbergasting! The occasion was the 125th anniversary of the composer's birth. It is not known whether Scott in old age received any residuals from such appropriations, or whether he was even aware of them. On the topic of unanticipated and unwanted popularity, Grainger in 1947 had written to Scott the following astounding thought, which reveals more about Grainger's bizarre personal proclivities than anything else: 'One should not be ANNOYED that groups take ones pieces & alter them out of all recognition – one should be grateful and proud; just as a woman should be proud if men want to assault her virtue.' (24 January 1947, Grainger Museum [02.0069]).

The term 'lotusland' has retained its fascination through more than a century now. In 1941 the flambuoyant Polish opera singer and socialite Ganna Walska purchased an estate in California. There she spent the rest of her life engaged in her passion for horticulture, in the garden she named 'Lotusland'. The estate garden has been open to the public since her death in 1984. A now-vintage Japanese video game called *Lotus Land Story* was released in 1998. In contemporary urban jargon, Lotus Land is also the nickname for Vancouver, British Columbia.

[28] *My Years of Indiscretion*, pp. 145–6. Chaminade was also attracted to the *commedia*, and among her piano pieces is a *Pierrette*, an *Arlequine*, and a *Scaramouche*, all predating Scott's contributions by at least fifteen years. Chaminade's lifelong Paris publisher, Enoch, had approached Scott in 1903, asking if they could look at some of his songs. Nothing came of it, but for about a year (1903–4) Boosey had first rights of refusal on the songs and piano pieces (*My Years of Indiscretion*, pp. 71–2).

incarnations, where lessons learned in past lives are understood to be steps on the journey towards unity with the divine. Scott makes the connection clear in two later works. The second piece, *A Song from the East,* was reused, unchanged, as Picture III in his 1924 ballet, *Karma,* in an uncharacteristic instance of musical recycling. And in 1935 he penned a cantata for chorus and orchestra with the same name, and with an explicitly Occult text by the composer himself that equates 'summerland', 'devachan' and 'lotusland'. The didactic *Three Little Waltzes* appeared at this time – a late publication of works written in his earliest years of composing. This may be the case as well with the *Two Alpine Sketches,* as they are dedicated to the son of Scott's piano instructor in Frankfurt, Lazzaro Uzielli, and share the same opus number as the waltzes. There seems to be nothing 'alpine' in the writing in the latter set, so perhaps the title is a topical reference from the time.

Danse nègre can probably be ranked as Scott's second most performed piano piece. It is a high-spirited *moto perpetuo* that is likely to bring to mind Debussy's *Le petit nègre,* though Scott's work is less overtly American in style, and not a cakewalk. Could Scott have known the Debussy piece? It was published a year later than Scott's. Character pieces connecting to black culture, such as black-face minstrelsy, had been in fashion since the mid-nineteenth century, especially in the United States (Gottschalk's concert pieces, Joplin's rags, the negro spirituals of Burleigh and others), and it is possible that Scott knew Samuel Coleridge-Taylor's 1905 *African Suite,* which houses a *Danse nègre.*[29] The composer made a fine two-piano arrangement of the piece in 1935, and his duo partner at the time, Esther Fisher, also published a duet version, derived from the solo original.

With *Sphinx,* Scott returns to the experimental harmonic language of the *Scherzo* and *Dagobah,* and presages things to come in the next few years. The title may remind us of the Sphinxes in Schumann's *Carnaval,* but there the guardian of a secret involves a musical cipher on people's names. Here the sphinx may have a secret, buried in the harmonic parallelisms and unresolved chords, but we are not to divine it. A contrasting section that sounds like a slow, languorous dance enters twice. A copy of the published score with the Scott estate has changes marked in by the composer, presumably for a revised edition. The title and the musical style seem to link the piece with his cycle *Egypt* of 1913, the ideas for which might already have been gestating in his mind.

Scott's piano music is often technically difficult, but it is rarely virtuosic in a 'flashy' surface sense. We might expect to find such writing in his *Two Etudes,* but the target audience there seems to be the intermediate pianist. The tempi are fast, but the texture, harmony and structure are very clear and straightforward, unlike the *études* of Scriabin, Rachmaninov and other contemporaries.

The year 1909 is a landmark in Scott's piano output. Over the next five years he composed his Concerto No. 1, and over fifty works for solo piano, including many of his most important contributions to the medium. The most ambitious of these are his Sonata No. 1, Op. 66, and the *Deuxième suite.*

[29] The *Danse nègre* that ends Scott's *Tallahassee Suite* is a different piece.

10

'Like a Bird Sings': The Piano Works from the Op. 66 Sonata to World War 1

LESLIE DE'ATH

The best traveller has no fixed plans, and is not intent on arriving.

(Lao Tzu)

IT is perhaps fitting that a sentiment expressed by a legendary figure from a distant past, outside the Western tradition, should encapsulate Scott's approach to musical creation, for he was a composer who embraced many different traditions of thought in the formulation of his own aesthetic. If the opening of Beethoven's Fifth Symphony is the iconic example of an entire work emanating inexorably from a pithy nuclear motif, Scott's music often meanders disarmingly, apparently unconcerned with path or quest. This was a defining feature of his writing in connection with works as early as the Sonata in D, Op. 17, and the *Scherzo*, Op. 20. His method was empirical and sensuous rather than orderly and cerebral. Grainger put it most poetically when he remarked that Scott composes 'rather like a bird sings': unpredictable in detail and order, while unified in aesthetic concept.[1] This perhaps also explains why Scott's large quantity of music for piano resists categorisation. Attempts to order his entire piano output into a small number of compositional 'types' invariably founder, faced with some works that seem to straddle two or more categories, and others that fit nowhere.

Stravinsky may have abhorred what he called the 'abyss of freedom', but Scott's music plays itself out and thrives on a loose harmonic, rhythmic and metric framework, in which the listener often has no idea what the next bar will bring. Composing to a rigid framework disenfranchises him. Schönberg, Scriabin and Hindemith may have found composing according to a system the ideal stimulus for the imagination, but Scott's imagination was fired by what he came to call 'musical flow'.[2] This

[1] Percy Grainger, 'The Music of Cyril Scott', *The Music Student* 5, no. 2 (October 1912), p. 31. Grainger's assessment is worth restating here, both for its discernment and as a cautionary note to those inclined to search Scott's scores for occult, representational or philosophical threads:

> Cyril Scott composes rather like a bird sings, with full positive soul behind him, drawing greater inspiration from the physical charm of actual sound than from any impetus from philosophical preoccupations or the dramatic emotions of objective life. Thus, while Strauss is largely concerned with philosophical themes, and Debussy apparently full of pictorial suggestions, and influences, it is mainly the pure delight of the ear in musical sounds (how they sound rather than what they express) that coaxes utterance from Cyril Scott's touching and poetical emotional self.

[2] Cyril Scott, 'Fragments of a Lecture Delivered to the Fabian Society, Summer 1913, IV: Present-Day Changes', *Monthly Musical Record* 44 (1914), pp. 182–3. Quoted in Sarah Collins, *The Aesthetic Life of Cyril Scott* (Boydell, 2013), pp. 186–7.

operates both on the larger and smaller design levels, but does not prevent him from employing standard musical forms such as sonata, ternary form, fugue, and passacaglia, at least nominally. Such flow forms the underlying basis of the two most ambitious and lengthy works for solo piano in his entire output, the first known as Sonata No. 1, Op. 66 (written in the summer of 1908 at Shere), and the second as *Deuxième suite* (published 1910). Although this chapter covers a mere ten years, several of Scott's most significant works for piano were written therein.

Although the Sonata No. 1 breaks new ground in Scott's handling of large pianistic forms, pride of place must rest with the Violin Sonata No. 1, Op. 59, which shares many compositional features with Op. 66, and was written a year earlier. The piano sonata is imposing in its size, musical ideas, and technical demands. Ex. 10.1 illustrates the élan, the lyricism, the whimsy, and the harmonic style.

The work is in four continuous movements, culminating in a fugal Allegro. The writing is harmonically lush in a post-Romantic idiom, often reminiscent of Richard Strauss. The incessant changes of metre are ground-breaking for the time, and serve to accommodate Scott's technique of thematic transformation through a myriad of rhythmic transformations. In this regard, and structurally, the sonata has an affinity with Liszt's sonata. Scott's thought process, however, further blurs the underlying structure, giving the impression more of a symphonic poem than a multi-movement sonata. The fugue of this sonata notwithstanding, Scott's most fundamental compositional trait is his imaginative, complex approach to harmonic colour. It is this aspect of his writing that prompted Grainger to call him a 'perpendicularist'.[3] He is without precedent in this regard, at least among British composers, and even comparisons with Delius are unfitting.

The Op. 66 Sonata presents many problems of chronology and authenticity of text, and underwent several revisions in the decades after its composition. After its first publication in 1909, Elkin issued at least two more musically distinct versions of the work, designated 'revised edition', but all dated 1909.

Critical reception of the published score was mixed. Comments range from 'utter bewilderment', 'the acme of ugliness', 'chaotic stuff' and 'the negative of music', to 'a rich feast' and 'without doubt one of the most significant and important additions to the store of pianoforte music by British composers'.[4] One reviewer, otherwise positive, suggested:

> that the very numerous time figures (they occur almost every bar) be dispensed with altogether, since in advanced works of this sort they are not necessary. These ever changing figures only add to the difficulty of reading; and certainly they would seem, to the eye at any rate, to hinder the natural flow of the music.[5]

[3] Grainger to D. C. Parker, 28 August 1916. In *The All-Round Man: Selected Letters of Percy Grainger, 1914–1961*, ed. Malcolm Gillies and David Pear (Clarendon Press, 2000), pp. 33–5.

[4] George Lowe, writing in *Musical Opinion & Music Trade Review* 33, no. 386 (November 1909), pp. 115–16. Also 'Ampersand' and 'Some New Musical Issues', *Musical Opinion & Music Trade Review* 33, no. 387 (December 1909), p. 181.

[5] 'Ampersand'.

Ex. 10.1 Scott, Piano Sonata No. 1, Op. 66, bars 1–16

By 1909 Elkin had been publishing Scott piano miniatures and songs for five years, and was reluctant to commit to the publishing of such a difficult, modernistic work that was so out of keeping with public expectation. The sonata may never have seen the light, had it not been for the generosity of an anonymous friend with whom

Scott had been rooming at the time, who financed its engraving.[6] The prodigious technical and interpretive challenges of the score did not prevent it from selling well. Thanks in part to the advocacy of Grainger, over 1,200 copies had been sold by 1927, when the first revised edition left the presses.[7] The differences with this version were mainly structural. The Scherzo was changed, and the bridge passage into the third movement was truncated from eighteen bars to four.

The second revision (*c.* 1935) ranks as one of the most singular reworkings of an earlier work by any composer. The revisions are copious and intensely detailed. Many changes are perplexing, and at first glance appear to be an attempt to graft a new level of harmonic complexity onto a lush Romantic score that is arguably better left alone. In short, why did he bother? A comparison of Ex. 10.2 with Ex. 10.1 illustrates this curious metamorphosis. The original score is given cue-sized, and the changes in large notes. Notes omitted from the revised version are in parentheses.

The nature of Scott's revisions are fourfold. First, additional notes are added to chords, to create non-triadic chord structures. These changes often seem harmonically arbitrary, and at times are scarcely noticeable, given the largely chromatic language already present in the original. Second, a greater sense of pulse is created in some passages by the regularising of time signatures, such as 17/16 turned into 4/4. Third, entire passages have been rewritten or drastically altered. Scott provides a new truncated bridge to the third movement, for instance, replacing an eighteen-bar passage with four newly composed bars. The third movement Scherzo contains most of the revisions of this type, although a *tranquillo* passage in the middle of that movement oddly remains completely untouched. The fugal final movement also remains more or less intact, apparently because of the linear writing. Fourth, a sense of tonal centre has often been rendered more abstruse through changes in harmonic progression. This disorientation applies also to melodies, in which individual notes have been chromatically altered. A diatonic melody in which only one note has been chromatically raised or lowered occurs frequently enough in the revision to be considered manneristic. A comparison of bars 6 and 7 of Exx. 10.1 and 10.2 serves to illustrate.

It is tempting to equate constant revision with aesthetic uncertainty. It is more likely that Scott knew exactly what he wanted to do, even if the process was intuitive. In the decades between publications Scott's musical style had changed markedly, and the alterations are in line with his style in other works of the 1920s and 1930s. It has been argued that the attempt to graft a newer language onto an already musically convincing original was ill conceived. Hardy, for instance, finds the interloping chromatic enrichments 'fussy', 'inexplicable', and 'ruining', and one must dance

[6] Scott wrote, 'This was my first (for me) important piano work, and most of it was composed in Shere while I was sharing rooms with an intimate friend, to whom I may only refer as J. B. As Mr. Elkin did not wish to publish such a difficult, "discordant" and unsaleable work without some financial assistance, this generous friend paid for the engraving.' Scott, *Bone of Contention: Life Story and Confessions* (Aquarian Press, 1969), p. 99.

[7] *Monthly Musical Record* 57, no. 678 (1 June 1927), p. 179. Some of this success was due to Grainger, who championed the work both as a performer and teacher throughout his life.

Ex. 10.2 Scott, Piano Sonata No. 1, Op. 66, 2nd revision, bars 1–16

around one's intuitive sense in order to disagree.[8] The most fervent champion of the sonata, Grainger, also had serious reservations about the revisions. He continued to program the work in recitals well past World War 2, but always performed it in its original 1909 version.

Grainger's characteristic inconsistency of opinion is reflected in his commentary on this sonata at different times of his life. In 1947 he wrote to Scott:

> Now, were we (not as individuals, but as race-expressers, period-expressers) not at our prime around 1898–1904? I know, in my own case, that all my best things were penned or sketched by 1904 & after that my compositional life was just a decline. Has that not been equally true of you, Roger, Balfour, etc. How could it be otherwise?[9]

Taken at face value, this would include the Op. 17 sonata in the period of their 'prime', but not the one written in 1908. Yet in 1949 he wrote, 'I never liked the Sonata, Op. 66, personally; but what a Leistung [achievement] it is.'[10] And three years later:

> I was playing in Toronto a week ago. They did my Danish Suite & I played a group of piano solos, and after the solos I played the Scherzo & Finale of your Sonata. <u>It got more applause than anything else I played!</u> And wherever I play it on my recitals it awakens more comments than anything else. So the time is just ripe for this amazing work.[11]

He enthuses over the work in a 1951 letter to Scott: 'I am utterly bowled over by the beauty, the originality & the mental liveliness of the music. I mean the texture of the harmonies, the voice-leadings, the non-architectural flow of the form, the easy but brilliant pianistic style – so typical of your incomparable improvisings.'[12]

A longer letter to Scott, written on 19 June 1956, is most revealing:

> As to the piano sonata, I do not find any great changes from the 2nd to the 3rd version. The great change was from the first to the 2nd edition. I don't suppose you will ever understand my attitude to your sonata or that I will ever understand your attitude. For you it is a work of art, & naturally you are highly justified in making it as good as you can – by revisions or otherwise. For me the sonata gave me the opportunity, as a teacher, to get many copies of a

[8] Lisa Hardy, *The British Piano Sonata, 1870–1945* (Boydell, 2001), pp. 61–5. Hardy itemises all forty-eight minor changes in the first eighteen bars of the first movement, and states that the 'instability of the details confirms weaknesses in Scott's whole approach.'

[9] Grainger to Scott, 19 November 1947. Grainger Museum (02.0069). The references are to two other members of the Frankfurt Group, Roger Quilter and Henry Balfour Gardiner.

[10] Grainger to Scott, 12 August 1949. Grainger Museum (02.0078)

[11] Grainger to Scott, 11 March 1952. Grainger Museum (02.0079)

[12] Grainger to Scott, 1951. Grainger Museum (02.0079)

> major work of yours sold. But that I could only do as long as I could present it as a study in progress – especially progress in free rhythms. But when you regularised the irregular rhythms (notably on page 7) you were repudiating the things I was giving the sonata to pupils for. So much for me as a teacher. Much more serious was my defeat as a composer. I so badly wanted Australia to get the credit for having invented fast-moving irregular rhythms (here again is my evil nature – always wanting one group to triumph over another) & as long as your first edition stood there was I as the originator in 1900, then you, my friend & associate followed in 1908, with Stravinsky coming later. But when you uprooted your irregular rhythms in the 2nd edition there I stood with no bridge between me & Stravinsky – nothing to show that the practice had some connection with me & my fellow-genius-friends. I was so happy, that irregular rhythms had come out of NATURAL PROGR[E]SS (my 1899 study of prose rhythms in speech, the rhythms of that woggley Italian train in Jan 1900) & was not what Balfour called CEREBRAL. We cannot help being what we are. You are a great creative genius, & I am a musical historian. Love to you both
>
> Percy[13]

The first question arising from this letter regards which versions Grainger was referring to. They cannot have been 1909 and the first revision, because page 7 is identical in these two versions. However, page 7 in the second revision is substantially altered, with sections of irregular metres homogenised into 4/8 time. That page in the original had eighteen bars, with seventeen metre changes, but in the final revision there are only twelve metre changes. Thus, the last published version appears to be Grainger's 'second edition', the alterations of the earlier revised publication (assuming he even knew about them) constituting mere tweaking of details. Grainger's reference to a 'third edition' becomes a matter of speculation in consequence, as no further published edition exists. The letter also reveals Grainger's self-absorbed tactlessness (or perhaps tough-love honesty), in implying that his 'defeat' both as a teacher and a composer was a direct result of Scott's misguided revisions. Grainger applauds the unconstrained, irregular flow of the rhythm of Scott's earlier version of the sonata, at the same time taking credit for its invention. Of course neither composer was the first to experiment with changing metres, but the real innovation in this sonata was the pervasiveness of its application. In the 1909 version the continuous four-movement plan unfolds over 582 bars, during which the time signature changes no fewer than 497 times, and twenty-nine different time signatures are represented.[14]

A further unpublished and unknown revised version exists. It is Scott's personal copy of the original 1909 edition, with copious annotations in red ink in the composer's hand, in keeping with his 1930s style of composing. This version involves harmonic enrichments as substantial as those found in the last published revision,

[13] Letter to Scott, 19 June 1956. Grainger Museum (02.0079)

[14] When Grainger complained of Scott's rhythmic regularisation, he exaggerated. The later version still contains 444 changes of metre and twenty-four different time signatures.

Figure 10.1 Changes made by Scott to the published version of Piano Sonata No. 1 (1909)

but differs in many details. It is difficult to know from what year this manuscript revision may stem. A comparison of Fig. 10.1 with Ex. 10.2 reveals that much, but not all of the annotations found their way into the published revision. As one inspects the balance of this annotated copy, many further discrepancies are revealed.[15] The

[15] The composer Ernest Austin, who worked as a copy-editor at Elkin for a number of years, complained generally about Scott's frequent carelessness with his manuscripts, and the difficulty he had in deciphering intended pitches (*Musical Opinion* 62, No. 741 [June 1939], pp. 786–8).

Ex. 10.3 Scott, Piano Sonata No. 1, Op. 66, 4th mvt fugue subject

red-ink copy was undoubtedly a fair copy designed for a revised publication, given its calligraphic tidiness – but not for the final revised version actually published. It is probable that this copy is a first attempt at the last published revision, since some changes are identical to the final published version. Scott's verbal annotations indicate that a proof pull has already been submitted to him. Without further evidence, one can only presume that the published version represents Scott's 'final say' on the matter.[16]

The fugue subject of the fourth movement is unusually chromatic and unlikely (Ex. 10.3), though Scott's *Deuxième suite* of 1910 ends with a much longer, more ostentatious, fugue based on a similarly chromatic subject. In the fugue of this sonata, the unfolding of the counterpoint works remarkably well, and the movement culminates in the reintroduction of themes from the other movements. Scott felt that structural unity in a multi-movement sonata could be achieved if the principal themes of earlier movements were brought back in the Finale as it unfolds.[17] He likens this procedure to that employed in epic forms of literature. (Ex. 10.3 is from the original 1909 Elkin edition; Scott's later versions contain hardly any revisions to this fugue section.)

The Grainger Museum houses Grainger's own working copy of Scott's sonata. This document provides a fascinating performer's insight into the technical aspects of Grainger's pianism. Pedal markings, fingerings, and interpretive annotations abound, and several cuts are indicated which distinguish between 'Scott cuts' and Grainger's own. Fig. 10.2, from the second movement (bars 52–71), is typical, and also illustrates Grainger's fastidious pedalling annotations.

The two spots labelled 'Scott cut' remove seven bars from the second movement. Of the other six Grainger cuts to the first, second and third movements, three are large: 150 bars are removed in total, reducing the playing time according to Grainger

[16] A critical edition of the Op. 66 Sonata, itemising all details of the various versions, would be a welcome addition to Scott scholarship.

[17] *Monthly Musical Record* 47 (1 May 1917), pp. 104–5. See p. 156.

Figure 10.2 Percy Grainger's working copy of Scott's Op. 66 Sonata. 'Scott cut' refers to the published revised edition

Ex. 10.4 Scott, Piano Sonata No. 1, Op. 66, annotated for performance by Grainger, 1st mvt, bars 54–62

from 25½ minutes to 19. Practical considerations were presumably involved, and at one point in the second movement he indicates a 'small cut' and a 'big cut' over the same passage, giving himself flexibility to tailor the performance to suit different concerts. His freedom with the original score in this regard is consistent with his approach in the *Handelian Rhapsody*.

Grainger's imaginative and unusual approach to pedalling, derived from his studies with Busoni and from his own fertile imagination, is distinguished principally by a very liberal use of the middle pedal. The use of all three pedals in this sonata is indicated throughout in great detail. Distinction is consistently made between each of them, and release points are fastidiously notated. In a few places – as in Ex. 10.4, bars 56 and 60 – all three pedals are employed simultaneously. The sound that results from a precise adherence to his markings is lush, orchestral, and entirely convincing.[18] Characteristically, Grainger's approach to pedalling was both iconoclastic and entirely practical – a 'common-sense view of all pedalling', so to speak.[19]

One of Grainger's trademarks – the handkerchief *glissando* – appears in this working copy. At the head of the score Grainger has printed in large letters, 'SILK HANDKERCHIEF – lay silk handkerchief at right end of keyboard for glissando on page 29. Throw handkerchief into lap at end of run.' At what is arguably the climactic moment of the sonata, Grainger indulges in a bit of Horowitz-like showmanship. Since the passage is a black-key glissando, it also has the common-sense advantage of minimising injury. Apparently he had not yet rigged up the elastic device that retracted the handkerchief into the cuff of his sleeve.

Posterity has yet to embrace the revisions of the Op. 66 Sonata, either in performance or on recording. Grainger performed only the original version in his public performing life, and all the four commercial versions available to date are also of that version.

The suite was clearly a structural mould that appealed to Scott. The *Suite (... in the Old Style)*, Op. 71 #1, is the first of seven piano sets with the word 'suite' in the title, though only the earliest two are numbered – this one, and the *Deuxième suite*, Op. 75.[20] Although both were published in 1910, they are diametrically opposed to each other on virtually every level. By that year Scott had come to a cordial understanding with both his regular publishers, Elkin and Schott. The former, being a small firm, could not commit to Scott's more ambitious works, and apart from the subsidised release of the Sonata No. 1, published only his piano miniatures and songs; Schott agreed to issue the more 'serious' works, larger in both design and performing forces.[21] The expectations of the publisher for whom each suite was destined may partly explain the differences between them. The composer may have conceived of them as a study in contrast, and perhaps even gave Elkin first refusal. Had Elkin published it, the title may well have been *Suite (... in the New Style)*.

The first suite is in three movements of modest dimensions, tempi, and technical demands, with dance titles typical for traditional suites. The moniker 'in the Old Style' was common in the day, and implied stylistic homage to the eighteenth century, in neo-Baroque or neoclassical garb. The idea may have come from Fritz

[18] My own recording of this sonata coincidentally follows a pedalling strategy very similar to that in the Grainger copy. This is a serendipitous meeting of minds, as access to Grainger's copy came after the recording sessions.

[19] For more on Grainger's innovative pedalling, see Glen Carruthers, 'The Piano Music of Percy Grainger: A Pianist's Perspective on Pedalling', *Canadian University Music Review* 21, no. 2 (2001), pp. 77–93.

[20] There are also suites for other media, such as the *Tallahassee Suite* for violin and piano, and the *Heroic Suite* and *Lyric Suite* for orchestra.

[21] The Op. 59 violin sonata, although written before the piano sonata, was published a year later by Schott, not Elkin, presumably for want of a financial backer.

Kreisler, famous for his *gemütlich* reworkings of earlier masters, both genuine and sham, for violin and piano, the most famous of which were written between 1900 and 1910.[22] Scott's first suite is characterised by understatement throughout. There are no extremes of tempo, and one soon notices the unusually constrained range of the piano within which almost all the material operates. This feature is so marked that one imagines it having been crafted for young pianists with small hands, or amateurs with limited technical command, or both. Its restraint – unusual for one so preoccupied with harmonic extravagance – may be explained by Scott's dedication of the work to his close friends Hans and Carrie Lüthy, who were avid music lovers. The harmonies are slickly understated as well, achieving a subtle charm within the limits employed, and within a traditional harmonic vocabulary, as Fauré did with such mastery. But the analogy ends there, for the first suite is as un-French as the *Deuxième suite* is immersed in French modernisms.

Seven small piano works were published in between the two suites. Two have remained among Scott's most endearing works: *Water-Wagtail* and *Valse caprice.* In the composer's own recording of *Water-Wagtail* the bird's ubiquitous bobbing is perfectly captured through the subtlety of the rubato, and the understated delicacy of Scott's pianistic sound. The *Soirée japonaise* belongs to the tradition of (often token) emulation of the Far East, a vogue that includes works as disparate as Debussy's *Pagodes* and Puccini's *Turandot.*

The less well-known *Trois danses tristes* are the most interesting piano works from this time. Scott was at the height of his investment in Impressionist musical idioms, and the *Danse orientale* and *Danse langoureuse* are probably the most Debussyan works in his output. By contrast, the opening *Danse élégiaque* continues the indulgent Romanticism of *Pierrot triste* and *Asphodel.*

It is extraordinary that the vast musical canvas of the *Deuxième suite* was almost totally ignored by pianists for the entire twentieth century. Scott himself thought well enough of the suite to record two of its five movements (*Prelude* and *Caprice*), but to date only one commercial recording has been made. Havergal Brian praised it, and Delius called it 'fine, strong stuff'.[23] The French title and the suite's dedication to Debussy reflect its stylistic debts, and probably also at least part of its *raison d'être.* Scott felt strongly enough about the suite to play it for Debussy, and perhaps other French composers, on his visits to France during the pre-war years. 'Of the orchestral compositions he [Debussy] admired most a rhapsody which has since been lost in Petrograd, and of the smaller works the Piano Sonata and the Second Suite. And I think these *were* my best efforts up till the time I last saw him in 1913.'[24] Walter Gieseking performed the *Deuxième suite* in Vienna around 1922, and was surprised when Scott came up to him after the concert, as he did not know the composer was in the city at the time. This ambitious work is at least as technically and interpretively challenging as the Sonata No. 1, and for that reason sales of the printed score were

[22] Scott had known Kreisler as early as 1903, when they joined forces in a performance of Scott's Piano Quartet, Op. 16, at St James Hall in London.

[23] *Bone of Contention*, p. 138.

[24] Scott, *My Years of Indiscretion* (Mills & Boon, 1924), p. 104. The rhapsody referred to is either S 43 or S 44.

likely dismal for both Schott and Scott.[25] Grainger does not seem to have promoted it in his concerts. Indeed, as we have seen, apart from the Sonata No. 1, Grainger was ambivalent about his friend's large-scale and more adventurous works, preferring the miniatures and those that more closely paralleled his own aesthetic.

This suite surprises even today, more by its very oddness than its boldness. Without the title, one would never guess that it is a suite at all. It is certainly not a set of dances, and only the middle movement, *Solemn Dance*, hints nominally in that direction. In its day there was nothing remotely like it in British piano literature, and it must have seemed incomprehensibly modern in the Britain of 1910, not to mention unplayable by all but the most advanced performers. It is interpretively elusive and challenging, and likely to seem rambling and incoherent on first hearing. The writing is as experimentally Impressionistic as the sonata is Straussian. The *Prélude* and *Caprice* that Scott himself recorded are the two shortest, and perhaps least compelling, movements in the suite. He might well have recorded the suite in its entirety, had the technology of the day allowed. The *Air varié*, and the final *Introduction and Fugue* are by far the longest and most ambitious movements.

The opening *Prélude* exploits a single harmonic and rhythmic pattern throughout. The unpublished Prelude, 'Op. 37' (S 171), could well have been an original attempt at beginning this suite, as it exhibits similar compositional traits. The movements of the suite are unified by an arching chromatic motif that is first presented in the fifth bar of the *Prélude* and recurs in all five movements, transformed in detail but always preserving the tritone (Ex. 10.5).

The two lengthy movements also contrast with the other three in terms of their flamboyant writing. The second movement, *Air varié*, subjects the theme to myriad harmonic twists through its four exuberant variations. The final movement, after a sombre introduction, introduces an ambitious fugue with another singular chromatic subject (Ex. 10.6).

Scott had attempted fugal writing for piano twice before – in the final sections of the Op. 17 and Op. 66 sonatas – and was never to return to it. Such contrapuntal processes seem inimical to his musical temperament, and it is not surprising that, after a rigorous exposition of the subject, the writing unfolds in a seemingly endless array of chromatic parallel chord passages, with the subject inserted in long notes reminiscent of *cantus firmus*. This works up to an intense climax, at which point the bustle abruptly ceases, and the main theme of the *Air varié* is brought back to further highlight the interconnectedness of the five movements, a technique already noted in the discussion of the Op. 66 Sonata.[26]

[25] I have never encountered a copy of the 1910 edition outside of library holdings.

[26] Scott spoke in defense of this unifying procedure: 'There is a very simple device which may be employed to establish a unity (leaving aside the most obvious one of joining all the four movements together), for that device is none other than the method which, I dare say, a few composers have already adopted – namely, the introduction of a short recapitulation in the Finale, of all the principal themes exploited in the previous movements. In other words, the free-fantasie section of the Finale should be treated as an arena for all previous themes to re-enter, and so disport themselves once more before their final exit.' Cyril Scott, 'Suggestions for a More Logical Sonata Form', *Monthly Musical Record* 47 (1 May 1917), pp. 104–5.

Ex. 10.5 Scott, *Deuxième suite*, Op. 75, *Prélude*, bars 5–9

Ex. 10.6 Scott, *Deuxième suite*, Op. 75, final mvt chromatic subject

During the years 1912–13 Scott assembled four further piano 'suites' – or at least, multi-movement works with a common theme – all quite different in content and intent: *Impressions from the Jungle Book*, *Poems*, *Egypt*, and *Pastoral Suite*. The first is very much of its time and place, joining in the vogue for Kipling's 1894 set of short anthropomorphic stories; many composers (Bantock, Boughton, Bright, Davies, Delage, Koechlin, Lehmann, Quilter, Shaw *et al.*) exploited the exotic setting for excursions into token musical exoticism. Scott's interest in Kipling may have stemmed from the esteem in which he held Grainger's ability to capture Kipling's world in music. Grainger's own lifelong fascination with Kipling dated from 1897, and resulted in twenty-two settings of stories from the *Jungle Book* composed between 1898 and 1958.[27] Scott said of his friend, 'whenever Grainger elects to produce one of his Kipling settings, be it song or chorus, he *becomes* Kipling in a manner which nobody else in the musical arena can approach.'[28] From our present-day perspective, with its relatively enlightened global awareness, it is hard not to hear Scott's Kipling music as quaint naivety and trite pictorialism, for time has dulled us to the boldness of its harmonic experimentation. This is especially true of the final movement, *Dance of the Elephants*. Its primitive thumpings, it must be remembered, actually pre-date the barbarisms of Stravinsky's and Prokofiev's early works. Other movements are poetic tone pictures, evoking dawn and the jungle. *Rikki-Tiki-Tavi and the Snake* is directly depictive, like a film score to the story.

[27] Edward German had published a cycle of a dozen songs to Kipling's *Just So Stories* in 1903.

[28] Cyril Scott, 'Percy Grainger: The Music and the Man', *Musical Quarterly* 2 (July 1916), p. 93.

Scott's next set, *Poems,* has retained a reputation for being musically perhaps his finest piano set. *Poems* indulges in the penchant of the time, especially in France, for putting poetic captions as a header or footer to each piano 'impression'. Unlike Debussy, who gained inspiration for his instrumental and piano music from famous French poets of the day, Scott was in his youth almost as prolific a poet as he was a composer, having published five books of his own poetry between 1905 and 1915.[29] The five *Poems* are all settings of his own poems (see Catalogue of Cyril Scott's Writings, below, SW 2, 5 and 6), which are printed in the score in their entirety before each piece of music. There is no gainsaying the work's merits, but its popularity is at least partly a by-product of the pairing of poems with music, unique in Scott's output but common in French music of the time. The reality is that many other works from this time are equally worthy yet have been largely forgotten, one example being the *Trois danses tristes* of 1910. The frequent meter changes found throughout *Poems,* and especially in *The Garden of Soul Sympathy* and *Paradise-Birds,* link the compositional process to that of the Op. 66 Sonata. The ecstatic, pulseless, lush harmonies and figuration of *The Garden of Soul Sympathy,* in particular, are also reminiscent of the non-repetitive flow of the *Air varié* of the *Deuxième suite.* Both poetry and music are suffused with the *fin-de-siècle* fragrance of Dowson, Baudelaire, Mallarmé, and Rossetti. There is at least an aesthetic, if not stylistic, rapprochement with the Debussy of *La demoiselle élue* and the Delius of *A Village Romeo and Juliet* to be heard here.

The *Egypt* suite contains arguably the most overt reference in the piano works to Scott's occult beliefs. The dedication reads 'To my Friend Mrs. Marie Russak, that enlightened Seer, who brought back for me the memory of my past Egyptian lives, these impressions are affectionately dedicated.' It is a piano reduction of the orchestral ballet score (S 48). There is no mention of *Egypt* in Scott's chapter entitled 'Experiences with the Theatrical World' in *My Years of Indiscretion,* though he does write of *Electra, Othello* and *The Alchemist.* Evidently never performed, the string parts at least are extant in manuscript.[30] Scott seems to have set out to employ a musical vocabulary altered to suit the exotic subject matter. Figuration involving repeated chromatic, non-functional chord patterns abounds – apparently a kind of slow-moving water imagery, as such patterns are most apparent in the Nile movements. While all the elements of this style can be found scattered throughout earlier works, they come together in a more concentrated, relentless way here, especially in *By the Waters of the Nile.* The grand solemnity of *Funeral March of the Great Ramases* invites comparison with Florent Schmitt's *Cortège des adorateurs de feu* from his *Quatre pièces,* published in 1914.[31]

[29] Scott retained throughout his life a somewhat Wagnerian tendency to set his own prose to music (examples are SS 1, 2a, 11, 21, 22, 24), and more than a dozen songs are settings of his own poetry (see SS 293, 294, 316, 361, 369, 373, 386, 389, 390, 418, 419, 424 and 432). Debussy's fascinating *Proses lyriques* of 1892–3, with poetry by the composer, may have encouraged Scott to try something similar.

[30] The original 1913 edition of the piano score contains a number of questionable note readings, which the performer must come to terms with. The revised Schott edition (1436) presents a slightly different text.

[31] The two composers crossed paths twice, the first time around the outbreak of World War 1, and the second via correspondence thirty-five years later.

With the *Pastoral Suite* of 1913, Scott returns to the idea of a suite as a set of dances, and to his English roots. The rollicking *Rigaudon* and *Rondo* employ piquant harmonies in a fast harmonic rhythm, reminiscent of Warlock. In the *Courante* and *Rigaudon* Scott notes in the score that 'the mood but not the strict form is represented'. The middle section in the *Rigaudon* is less energetic, similar to Ravel's *Rigaudon* from *Le tombeau de Couperin*. Scott may have heard Ravel's suite, though it did not appear in print until a year after his own. The latter half of the *Pastorale* movement is entirely preoccupied with snaky chromatic parallel thirds, which adorn the return of the main theme. This passage is much like the parallelisms found in *Egypt*. The concluding *Passacaglia* repeats an eight-bar modal tune nine times with varied accompaniments, rather in the style of Scott's chromatically exuberant folk-song arrangements.

The other individual slight piano works leading up to World War 1 include the *Mazurka, Serenata, Intermezzo, Chansonette, Berceuse, Pierrette, Autumn Idyll, Barcarolle, Carillon* and *Prelude solennel. Pierrette* looks back to Scott's Liverpool years, providing a supplement to the *Two Pierrot Pieces*. Pierrette rivals Columbine for Pierrot's affections, and we get the sense that, with her skipping rhythms and vivaciousness, courtesy of Scott, they would make a lovely couple.[32] With *Carillon* Scott returns to the fascination with bells that yielded also *Bells* (from *Poems*), *Chimes, Twilight Bells* and *Angelus*. Perhaps the English change-ringing tradition appealed to his artistic instinct. In *Carillon* bells are the gateway to exploration of parallelism and of harmonies based on fourths. There is no clearer example in Scott's music of his theory of harmony deriving from the superimposition of one melody upon itself at various intervals, all in rhythmic unison. Although published as an Elkin miniature, the *Prelude solennel* requires a concert pianist's technique, and at its climax launches into a cascade of sixths rather like the comparable moment in Chopin's famous Etude in E major, Op. 10 No. 3. Its stately chordal unfolding borders on pomposity in the manner of the *Handelian Rhapsody*.

As a pacifist and an artist, Scott's muse was mute, more or less, during times of war, the despair and futility of which he felt profoundly. His reluctance to engage in musical composition is particularly true of the World War 2 years, but even in the first war the composer's pen dried up, apart from texted compositions (both choral and solo song) and a few piano miniatures. The onset of war led to one of Scott's least exemplary works, *Britain's War March*. It exists in both an orchestral and a piano version, and is dedicated to HRH The Prince of Wales. A rather impish medley of popular patriotic tunes (*Rule Britannia, God Save the King, See the Conquering Hero* and *La Marseillaise*), it was written for Henry Wood's 1914 Proms season. Scott's other wartime creations included an *Ode héroïque*, and two musical elegies – *Requiescat* and *Consolation* – for his friend Archibald Rowan-Hamilton, who died in battle in 1915.

[32] Pierrette had already made a flirty appearance in piano music in 1889, with Cécile Chaminade's *Pierrette: air de ballet*. Given Chaminade's fame in Britain, Scott would very likely have been familiar with it. Also perhaps known to him was Joseph Holbrooke's *Pierrot and Pierrette*, Op. 36, an operetta first staged in 1909 at His Majesty's Theatre.

The 1914 *Sea-Marge* has a connection to World War 1 as well. Sea-Marge was the name of a large mock-Tudor home that Scott's friends Sir Edgar and Lady Speyer had built (1908–12) in Overstrand, Norfolk, in the area later known as the Village of Millionaires.[33] Sir Edgar was a music lover, and had, among other things, bailed the Proms out of financial woes leading up to the outbreak of war. In 1914 his wealthy cousin Edward (who figured prominently in Elgar's life) went over the sea to war. Scott responded with a meditation, dedicated to his friends, that evokes 'the falling of a wave on a calm sea' (annotated in the score), and toward the end quotes 'The girl I left behind me', a classic departure song of the British army. Of German heritage, the Speyers were suspected of relaying signals to German submarines from their seaside home, and were obliged to leave Sea-Marge in 1916, never to return.

The rest of the wartime miniatures are a varied mix including the folksong arrangement, *Cherry Ripe*, with its piquant harmonisations; works with national identity (*Russian Dance, Irish Reel, A Little Russian Suite*); light drawing-room miniatures (*Diatonic Study, Danse romantique, Cavatina, Butterfly Waltz, Miniatures*); and an attempt at writing a didactic primer (*Modern Finger Exercises*) with unusual technical exercises (such as whole-tone), focused on the technique required for more contemporary pianistic idioms. One work, however, stands out markedly from the others. *Rainbow-Trout* is as unlikely a composition as is its title. At its most superficial level, one hears the splashing of the fish, perhaps breaching out of the water at times. But this is no trite pictorialisation, nor is it a Schubertian *Forelle.* One senses an arcane dignity – perhaps even wisdom – emanating from this mystical creature. It is perhaps significant in this context that Scott was a believer in the transmigration of souls, and abhorred sport hunting. Exotic harmonies that dwell on ninth chords without resolution throughout make this more a *truite arc-en-ciel,* and it is perhaps odd that Scott did not employ a French title here, as he already had with *Danse nègre, Deuxième suite, Trois danses tristes, Ode héroïque* and other works of the time. The astonishing musical language resonates more with that of Scriabin than with Debussy's. Grainger's own artwork on the front cover of the sheet music does nothing to prepare the unsuspecting public for either the work's iconoclasm or its technical demands. No less surprising is the structure of the music. While there are repetitions of material and contrasting episodes, any attempt to superimpose a form on this piece is rendered null when one listens to Scott's own recording, made thirteen years after its publication. The music is treated like a mosaic of individual phrases that might occur in any order, with passages freely exchanged from their position in the printed score. Comfortable as an improviser, Scott may well have performed this piece differently each time he set out. No other recording of Scott's own playing departs from the published original to the extent this one does. Like Büchner's *Woyzeck,* the tableaux can be freely shuffled without endangering the integrity of the whole – rather akin to how many species of birds sing.

[33] It was at the Speyers' house in London that Scott first met Richard Strauss. He greatly admired Strauss's music, and we can only speculate on how Strauss might have reacted to Scott's most Straussian score, the Op. 66 Sonata.

11

The Later Piano Works

LESLIE DE'ATH

THE Great War fundamentally redefined every aspect of society, seemingly shattering all recollection of what had been important and fashionable in life before. No one was exempt. Those engaged in less utilitarian disciplines, such as the arts, found that the *status quo* had been swept away and many long-established conceits consigned to the past. Conceived in a more innocent era, they were no longer tolerable in a world that had seen such horror, devastation and disillusion. Scott was by no means the only composer to have lost the momentum, in the sense of public awareness and enthusiasm, that he had enjoyed before 1914. The musical bad-boy iconoclast of the Edwardian era was now increasingly perceived as a quaint relic of a former *zeitgeist.*

The Scott piano miniatures and songs continued to appear in about the same quantity, but this production is notable for the absence of any 'signature' works that were to maintain Scott's image during the rest of his life and into posterity. In this regard one is reminded perhaps of other composers who made their fame before 1914 and lived to see the end of World War 2, such composers as Richard Strauss and Florent Schmitt.

The British musical mainstream found Scott's works after 1918 – on the rare occasions when they found them at all – to be mannered, stylistically forced, arbitrary, abstract, gratuitously pseudo-modernistic, or just incomprehensible. Now in his forties and fifties, Scott continued to pen a steady stream of major works, mainly chamber, concertante and orchestral, that remained unpublished and were premiered, if at all, in regional locations on the fringe of general acceptance and publicity. There was an increasing sense in the musical mainstream that he was a composer to avoid, and by the outbreak of the 1939 war, at age sixty, his life was at a critical crossroad, both professionally and personally. He continued to compose prolifically during the interwar years, but then produced virtually nothing from 1937 to 1946.[1]

Scott was attracted to the stage, in its various manifestations, throughout his life. He committed fourteen times to the business of writing music for the stage, from opera and ballet to incidental music and musical plays, and in addition authored a dozen straight plays in the 1940s. But his success in the field was limited. Apart from his opera, *The Alchemist,* few made it past the manuscript page. In his own words, 'It would almost seem that the fates frown disapprovingly at any connection of mine with the stage.'[2]

The earliest stage work of Scott's to reach production was the 1913 ballet score, *Egypt,* discussed in the previous chapter. In 1924, Scott cobbled together new and existing piano works for one of André Charlot's revues at the Prince of Wales Theatre.

[1] Ian Parrott lists a 'Consolation in C' from 1943 in his *Cyril Scott and his Piano Music* (Thames Publishing, 1991), p. 93, which can only refer to the 1918 homage of the same name (S 233).

[2] Scott, *My Years of Indiscretion* (Mills & Boon, 1924), p. 159.

It is likely that the idea for the ballet and its title, *Karma,* came from the composer. The production was lavish and expensive for a revue, and appears to have been well received. It resurfaced four years later in a Dortmund production, and is thus Scott's only stage work to have enjoyed productions in more than one country. Perhaps a tight timeline explains why Scott culled two of the five 'pictures' (*tableaux*) from previously published piano works. The third picture, *A Song from the East,* stems from his 1907 piano set, *Summerland,* with fifty-nine new bars added in the orchestrated version.[3] The final scene recycles his piano miniature *Souvenir de Vienne,* published only a year before the ballet (Fig. 11.1). Whether that waltz was written originally with its future use in *Karma* in mind is unknown. It bears a different dedication from the ballet, and it is quite possible that the ballet's final scene was set in Vienna simply to accommodate the pre-existing popular piano piece. The entire ballet music, reduced for piano, was published by Elkin in 1924 with an exotic cover bordered with ancient Persian script (Fig. 11.2). An incomplete *mis-en-scène* is extant in the piano holograph in Scott's handwriting. It is crossed out, so it is difficult to know whether the version staged conformed to it or not. According to that source the opening scene – strongly reminiscent of Stravinsky's *Rite of Spring* – presents a prehistoric sacrificial site where a maiden is to be sacrificed, to the accompaniment of wild dancing, while her sister weeps over her. Example 11.1 illustrates Scott's take on musical barbarism.

A stranger appears, who calms the dancers with a wave of his wand, then leaves with the lamenting sister accompanying him. The sisters reappear later as rival wives of an Arab sheik, and finally in eighteenth-century Viennese high society. In the penultimate scene, *Before the Church,* one of the reincarnated sisters is determined to become a nun, in spite of a young man's passion for her. A Yogi functioned as narrator for the ballet, tying the tableaux together with text now lost, but presumably demonstrating the effect of karma from one incarnation to the next.

Many of Scott's piano miniatures seem designed to accommodate the technical limits of gifted adult amateur pianists, while other publications are expressly didactic in intent. Several publications attest to his interest in providing pedagogical works for young students. The post-war years include several of the latter: *Young Hearts, Album for Boys, Album for Girls, Zoo, Toy Box,* and the *Nursery Rhymes* for piano duet.[4] To these must be added the *Modern Finger-Exercises* of 1917 and the *Technical Studies* of 1924, which, like his *Pictorial Sketch* of 1913, were designed at least in part to introduce the student to modern compositional styles, as well as to build technique. *Zoo* and *Toy Box* are designed for near-beginners, the former bearing a dedication to Scott's two young children, and the latter 'to Desmond for his seventh birthday'.

The sets of smaller piano pieces published between 1918 and 1926 include *Vistas, Vieux chine, Three Pastorals, A Pageant, Moods, Indian Suite, Three Old Country Dances, Three Dances,* and a set of *Three Dances* for piano duet. The last two sets were both published in 1926, but are distinct pieces in spite of the shared name. While it can be argued that Scott was guided more by contractual responsibility than inspiration in some of these later sets, there are nevertheless some fine moments. The middle *Allegretto molto moderato* of the duet *Three Dances* is as exquisite a miniature

[3] These added bars do not appear in the published piano score of *Karma.*

[4] The ten short pieces of *Young Hearts* (1920) were reissued by Elkin at a later point under the title *For My Young Friends,* with altered ordering of pieces.

Figure 11.1 Cover for the score of *Souvenir de Vienne*, part of Scott's *Karma Suite*

Figure 11.2 Cover for the score of Scott's *Karma Suite*, composed in 1924 for one of André Charlot's revues

Ex. 11.1 Scott, *Karma*, Picture 1, *Prologue and Barbaric Dance*, bars 31–9

as one will find anywhere in his output – one in which his trademark use of piquant chromatic harmonies within a tonal framework is more felicitous and convincing than in many of his more popular miniatures.

The vistas portrayed in *Vistas* are closer to melancholic French impressionist art than to pretty picture postcards. The sylvan landscapes of the first two (*A Lonely Dell* and *In the Forest*) are vivid and imaginative. *In the Forest* opens with a full minute's worth of avian monophony – a bold stroke for 1918, and preceding Respighi's *Gli Uccelli* by a decade. The passage is a remarkable parallel to Vaughan Williams's *The Lark Ascending*, written in 1914. But Scott is unlikely to have known about the Vaughan Williams work, since *The Lark Ascending* had to await a post-war revision before premiering in 1920. A more likely influence is Ravel, whose *Oiseaux tristes* would likely have been familiar to Scott from his pre-war trips to France. Moreover, Scott's style is more French than English in the ensuing music of *In the Forest*, echoing the murmuring ostinati of Debussy's *Poissons d'or*. *Vistas* is dedicated to James Ingall Wedgwood, who was barred from the Anglican church in 1904 for joining the Theosophical Society.[5]

The *Old China* (*Vieux chine*) suite is a diverse set of four miniatures whose title appears to refer only to the final piece, *Willow Pattern* (*Décor de saules*).[6] The first two evoke eighteenth-century European dances – gavotte and minuet – and in the third, *Angelus*, tolling bells proclaim the incarnation prayer, alternating in responsorial fashion with a 'chorale' melody. *Willow Pattern* employs harmonic parallelism, fourths, and repeated rhythmic patterns to provide an eastern tinge. There is likely a narrative pictorialism at play here, too, comparable to that of Scott's *Impressions from the Jungle Book*. The repetitious sequential patterns abruptly cease six bars before the end, and an unaccompanied melody arches twice, bearing no resemblance to anything else in the piece. It is tempting to read into this the flight of the two lovers in the ancient Mandarin tale, Koong-Se and Chang, across the bridge to the safety of the island – a scene often portrayed on willow-pattern chinaware – or perhaps the two doves into which they were transformed by the gods in response to their brutal murder.

The *Three Pastorals* of 1919 would pass without comment, were it not for the extraordinary second piece, *Con delicatezza*, in which a shepherd's pipe improvises over an accompaniment of unobtrusive, sporadic chords. The middle section is more flamboyant, again exploring Scriabinesque harmonies and textures. In a similar improvisatory vein is *Exotic Dance*, the middle movement of Scott's *A Pageant* of 1920. Here the 'exoticism' is geographically undetermined – haunting, pliant and floating – and the overall effect is one of harmonic and melodic experimentation. The concluding *Processional Dance* gives the nod to whatever pageantry there might be in this trio of miniatures. But Scott seems least comfortable stylistically with pomp and solemnity, at least to modern sensibilities, though similar grandiose gestures can be found in his *Prelude solennel* and *Ode héroïque*. Less presumptuous are the wartime laments dedicated to his friends fallen in battle, such as *Requiescat* and *Consolation*. The *Moods* triptych of 1922 carries on in the same experimental vein as the other sets, especially in the first two, *Sadness* and *Lassitude*.

[5] Wedgwood became an Anglican bishop in 1916, and it is possible that *Vistas* was dedicated to him as a congratulatory gesture.

[6] Walter Niemann, who had recorded two of Scott's miniatures on piano rolls, published a set of five miniatures, *Alt-China*, Op. 62 (Peters 3723), in the year following Scott's.

The four pieces comprising the *Indian Suite* reflect the Victorian vogue for *faux* exoticism, still very popular in the light-music commercial orchestral successes of Albert Ketèlbey, written during and after World War 1. The *Indian Suite* possesses a certain ingenuous charm, for those prepared to indulge the period style and listen with the ears of those for whom such exoticism in music was still very new. The idea of 'easternness' was rather vaguely defined in Scott's music, and some passages of the suite (for example, *Dancing Girls* and *Juggernaut*) could well have found a home in his Chinese or Egyptian miniatures.

The *Three Old Country Dances* of 1926, replete with touches of the Lydian mode and musette-like drones, are charmingly unpretentious. The opening of the middle dance, and the coda of the final dance, include some chromatic twists to remind us that these are stylised inventions of Scott's, not straightforward folk dances.

As Scott's harmonic language evolved in the 1920s and 1930s, so did the content of his Elkin miniatures. Elkin's clientele, upon purchasing Scott's 1923 *Arabesque* with perhaps Schumann or Debussy in mind from the title, would have been surprised by the quartal harmonies and the essentially atonal writing, quite unlike anything Scott had produced to date even at his most adventurous. There is a new abstractness here, which reaches forward to the very last works of the 1950s and 1960s. There were perhaps hints of things to come in his 1919 *Caprice chinois*, where the harmonies refuse to settle throughout, and whose middle section sounds like Scriabin. But that difficult work was written for a professional pianist – Mark Hambourg, to be precise – just as the other virtuoso work from the same time, *Rondeau de concert*, was dedicated to Benno Moiseiwitsch. The lure of the orient is still evident in the *Caprice chinois*, but the musical language had changed radically since the *Chinese Serenade*, *Soirée japonaise* and *Lotus Land*.

Scott considered the *Rondeau de concert* one of his most successful and important piano works. He told Grainger enthusiastically that 'I have … bit off rather a brilliant big Rondo de Concert for piano. Harmonically it contains some of the best I have done so far.'[7] It is certainly written on a grander scale than most individual pieces, and presents formidable technical challenges. The right hand engages in chromatic parallel triads almost throughout, even in the more tranquil middle passage. The harmonic language is consistently unsettling, again displaying the influence of Scriabin. This is true also of *Inclination à la danse* of 1922 – a waltz-in-one whose title parodies Weber, and whose middle section is built on a seductive drone akin to the *Arabian Dance* in Tchaikovsky's *The Nutcracker*. The other ambitious concert work from this time is the *Ballad*, 'based on a few bars of an old Troubadour song' (S 240) – the song unidentified, but probably *Ausiment con l'olifant*. Bearing no dedication, this work was likely written to showcase both Scott's pianism and his most recent compositional style on his 1920–1 American tour, where it was received enthusiastically. The work is harmonically adventurous, based largely on the interval of a fourth, and builds through a set of ten variations, juxtaposed so as to maximise the contrast between successive variations, to an impassioned bitonal climax. In structure and style, it foreshadows Scott's next foray into variation form, the *Theme and Variations* for two pianos.

A few of the later one-off miniatures designed for wider public consumption also deserve mention. Some continue in the ingratiating, accessible pre-war style that

[7] Letter to Grainger, 7 December 1916. Grainger Museum 02.0073.

Scott had become known for – specifically, the *First Bagatelle, Spanish Dance, Valse sentimentale* and *Gavotte*. Even in these, however, Scott indulges in a chromatic chordal extravagance that would have taxed both the technical abilities and the stylistic comprehension of even the gifted amateur pianist. Example 11.2, from the *First Bagatelle*, is such a passage, with its rapid rhythm of chord changes and Scott's trademark harmonisation of each melody note, all yet within a tonal context. The title was optimistic: there is no *Second Bagatelle*.

Two worthy pieces from the late 1920s, *Badinage* and *Guttersnipes' Dance*, convince by their rhythmic verve and high spirits, while also being somewhat adventurous harmonically. Both are based largely on chords of fourths, not thirds, in what might be thought of as a neo-classic style, like the *Gavotte*. *Tarantula* (1935) follows in similar vein, and is one of Scott's most fascinating and little-known piano works. He explains that the tarantula is 'a species of spider whose bite was formerly supposed to cause dancing mania, for which the dance "*Tarantella*" was a cure. In this piece both the spider and the cure for its bite are suggested.'[8] The scalar sixteenth-notes are the rapid scurrying of the spider, while the fourths in triplets evoke the tarantella. The piece appears a mere pictorial trifle, but this is misleading: although lasting a mere 90 seconds, it is strangely captivating, and indeed one of Scott's most challenging works to perform.

Miss Remington is unique in its levity and whimsical depiction. The subject is the iconic new young working woman, emancipated from the home in the inter-war years, and rising to the challenges of office labour with enthusiasm, verve, energy and capability – if the Remington typewriter ads were to be believed. The efficient Miss here engages in hectic bursts of typing and carriage returns, interspersed with more wistful, contemplative moments that threaten to compromise her efficiency. Towards the end, her patience seems tested to the limit, though whether this is because of her uncooperative machine or the discomfort of her personal reveries, we do not know.[9] This forgotten comic miniature probably reminds readers of Leroy Anderson's famous orchestral novelty confection on the same subject but, let it be known, Scott's work pre-dates Anderson's by sixteen years.[10]

[8] Note at the beginning of the printed score.

[9] A young Yvonne O'Neill (daughter of Norman O'Neill of the Frankfurt Group) was Scott's model for *Miss Remington*. In correspondence with me (23 January 2017), Yvonne's daughter, Katherine Hudson, states, 'Yes "Miss Remington" was written when my mother taught herself to type in order to type out the letters of the poet Winthrop Mackworth Praed whose biography my father was writing. That would have been in about 1938. However if she ever had a Remington she didn't have it for long as she bought a "Hermes Baby" which she greatly preferred. She was certainly never a professional secretary.'

[10] Given Scott's well-known interest in matters of philosophy, ethics, religion, the occult, medicine and homeopathy in his writings, his lighter side is easily presumed to be insignificant, if not non-existent. His autobiographies, however, are full of breezy anecdotes, often of a humorous nature, and in them he was careful not to take himself too seriously. Humour was to him a 'serious' enough matter to warrant a full monograph on the subject, *Ghost of a Smile* (1939). This singular publication is primarily an analysis of humour, in the tradition of Stephen Leacock's books – *Humour: Its Theory and Technique* (1935) and *Humour and Humanity* (1937) – which Scott cites. Scott's unpublished *The Rhymed Reflections of a Ruthless Rhymer* of 1944,

Ex. 11.2 Scott, , *First Bagatelle,* bars 5–9

A work for two pianos, more popular than any of Scott's original works for that medium, is Grainger's transcription of three movements from Scott's lost Symphony No. 2 of 1901–2. The history of this work is a little convoluted. The original four-movement symphony had premiered successfully at the Proms with Henry Wood in 1903. A few years later Scott reduced it to *Three Symphonic Dances,* eliminating the first movement, and conducted it in Birmingham at the request of Landon Ronald. On the title page of the first movement Scott wrote 'Dance from the ballet *The Short-Sighted Apothecary* (S 6). We shall never know what the opening *Andante* of the original symphony was like, or how heavily (or not) Scott revised the symphony when turning it into *Three Symphonic Dances* in 1907. Grainger's transcription for two pianos was completed in the summer of 1920, and he and Scott recorded the first dance on piano roll in 1922, the same year the score was published. To Grainger's credit, he did not take the knife to these dances as he had done with the Sonata in D, Op. 17 / *Handelian Rhapsody,* and presented them intact in his expertly laid-out transcription. This, after all, was music composed in a style very close to Grainger's own, and one can imagine the combination of enthusiasm and envy he must have had for this music in the course of the labour.

The final product, in both its symphonic and duo-piano forms, ranks as one of the high points of Scott's early style. The spirited first movement unfolds with relentless energy, its modal main theme coming as close to the British folk-song revival tradition as one can find in Scott's music. But it is the poised unfolding of the canvas of the second movement, *Andante sostenuto e sempre molto cantabile,* that is the marvel of this set. Scott had studied Wagner closely, and in no other work does he come

although not a book of humour in itself, adopts the same structure as Leacock's 1936 *Hellements of Hickonomics in Hiccoughs of Verse.* Both are written throughout in rhyming couplets, and it is likely that Scott got that idea too from Leacock. Oddly, those two books were the only works written by each author entirely in verse.

so close to the outpouring of endless melody and denial of cadence that is such a hallmark of Wagner. The music is remarkably diatonic for Scott, but with magical modulations equal to the best moments in Wagner's operas. Perhaps in no other score did Scott succeed in handling large-scale musical architecture so convincingly as here. There are well-placed climactic moments, but the overall impression is one of a remarkable unity of mood. After it, the jig-like final Allegro seems rather forced in its chromatic density.

One of the more rewarding musical experiences of the 1930s for Scott must have been his association with the New Zealand pianist Esther Fisher as a piano duo team. Scott met her at one of her Wigmore Hall recitals in the late 1920s, and they began performing together in London and elsewhere in the early 1930s. The BBC seems to have been more amenable to featuring Scott as a performer than as a composer at this time. Scott had already in 1931 published a solo piano transcription of Bach's *My Heart Ever Faithful*, dedicated to Fisher. He followed this with five published transcriptions for two pianos of other Bach works, and a further transcription remains unpublished. They are light-hearted, and deliciously avoid slavish adherence to the originals. The slow introduction to the *Invention in F*, for instance, employs the theme of the invention, veiled by the tempo and the indulgent harmonies, while the slightly off-tempo middle section introduces chains of very un-Baroque seventh chords.

Although World War 2 brought an end to the duo's concertising, Fisher remained in contact with Scott, paying visits in the 1950s and 1960s to his home in Eastbourne. His last substantial piano works, the *Pastoral Ode* and the Sonata No. 3, were dedicated to and/or premiered by her. For a time in the 1930s, Fisher was also piano tutor to Scott's son, Desmond. Scott also made duo arrangements of his two most successful piano miniatures, *Lotus Land* and *Danse nègre*, probably written as encore pieces for his recitals with Fisher, and also saw fit to transcribe two of the five *Impressions from the Jungle Book*.[11]

One of Scott's most ambitious keyboard works is the *Theme and Variations*, also dedicated to Fisher. This is his only significant duo work in the more modernistic idiom of the 1930s, comparable in style and importance to the Second Sonata. The *Theme and Variations* and *Russian Fair* had to wait until 1947 and 1952 respectively for publication, even though they both appear to have been written much earlier. In 1947, Scott refers to the variations as having been written 'some 18 to 20 years ago'.[12] Scott said of them:

> I cursed myself for having made them unduly difficult, for it meant more practising as far as I was concerned than I altogether relished, the outcome being that Miss Fisher played her part better than I played mine. Indeed, I fear that my conscientious collaborator found me something of a trial at times; composers are apt to be slatternly virtuosi.[13]

[11] Fisher penned an informative (if not always accurate) memoir of her association with Scott in the *Journal of the British Institute for Recorded Sound* 61 (January 1976), pp. 502–10.

[12] Letter, Scott to Percy Grainger, 19 October 1947. Grainger Museum, 02.0069.

[13] Scott, *Bone of Contention: Life Story and Confessions* (Aquarian Press, 1969), p. 202.

The main idea of the 'theme' of the variations is as much a harmonic as a melodic one, given the composer's proclivity for harmonising every note of a melody. A profusion of highly distinct variations ensues, each one adopting a new pattern of figuration and a new mood. The heart of the set is the tenth and last variation, *Andante languoramente*, with its languid melody and murmuring thirty-second-note accompaniment. The writing is particularly imaginative and atmospheric (Ex. 11.3). A grand *Quasi fuga*, followed by an extended working out of ideas complete with a cadenza-like passage for the second piano, ends the variations in a triumphant manner. The writing throughout is expertly disposed for the two pianists, with imaginative contrasts in texture, particularly in Variations five, nine, ten and the extended finale.

Russian Fair is a rollicking duo reworking of Scott's 1915 solo *Russian Dance*. It is based on a popular street song from the Kolomna district, 'Pod yablonyu zelyonoyu', made famous by Tchaikovsky in the finale of his Serenade for Strings. Scott's sometimes astringent harmonic idiom is here put to sustained light-hearted effect, at times bordering on the humorous. After a dreamy, atmospheric slower middle section, there is a delightful extended transition back to the opening material, with the melody gradually resuming its complete statement in an add-on fashion, similar to 'the house that Jack built'.[14]

Two later sonatas, dating from 1933 and 1956, failed to attain the popularity of the Op. 66 Sonata. The obscurity of Scott's second sonata is explained by its having been published by a little-known firm, Universal Music Agencies, which, in spite of its grandiose name, had a small catalogue, was short-lived, and enjoyed but limited success.[15] Scott used them only one other time, for his choral/orchestral *La belle dame sans merci*. It is possible that he also approached them with the score of the *Theme and Variations* duo, and was turned down. That work had to wait until the post-war years, with Elkin's 1947 publication. Two years later Elkin absorbed the UMA catalogue into their own offerings, but they did not reissue the sonata.

The Second Sonata is a long, rhapsodic single movement, fascinating in both its details and its overall effect. There are parallels with Scriabin in the harmonic language, the rhapsodic unfolding of ideas, and more particularly in the '*estatico*' passage near the end – a term employed by Scriabin too on a number of occasions. Scott felt a strong affinity with the artistic principles and aims of his Russian contemporary, and had devoted a chapter to Scriabin's involvement with the occult in his 1928 book, *The Influence of Music on History and Morals*.[16]

As in the Op. 66 Sonata, metres change frequently. To this Scott liberally adds the Scriabinesque feature of polyrhythms, such as 6 against 7 (Ex. 11.4). A loose sonata form structure can be discerned in the work, though the general impression is more

[14] *Russian Fair* makes a fine duo recital encore number.

[15] The owner, Jean Michaud, had provided the poem for Stefan Bergman's song *A Sigh*, published by them in 1935.

[16] Cyril Scott, *The Influence of Music on History and Morals: A Vindication of Plato* (Theosophical Publishing House, 1928), chapter 17, 'Scriabin, the Greatest Deva-Exponent', pp. 132–5. This was later incorporated into his more well-known *Music: Its Secret Influence Throughout the Ages* (chapter 21, 'Scriabin, a Deva-Exponent').

Ex. 11.3 Scott, *Theme and Variations*, Variation 10, bars 306–12

a free stream of ideas with occasional recurrence of material.[17] Harmonies based on the interval of a fourth alternate freely with triad-based harmonies. In Appendix IV of *Bone of Contention*, Scott highlights the 1-4-7 chord (G-C-F) as one which 'I most frequently use, on any degree of the chromatic scale', and follows this with an example from his *Theme and Variations* duo.[18]

A comparison of the printed version with the original manuscript of the Second Sonata reveals some changes in detail, and probably some 'best guesses' on the part of the editor regarding specific pitches. It was Scott's habit in many of his works to make small changes by pasting the new score over the unwanted bars; this occurs

[17] Exposition (bars 1–123), with three principal melodic ideas presented. Development (bars 124–303). Recapitulation (bars 304–410).

[18] Scott, *Bone of Contention*, p. 237. The quote is of the theme as it first appears in piano 1 at the outset, but with some changes. It is closer (although still not exact) to its recurrence at the end (rehearsal 37–8). The 1-4-7 chord is also a prime building block of Scriabin's mystic chord.

Ex. 11.3 continued

Ex. 11.4 Scott, Second Sonata, bars 219–26

with some frequency in this work – a reflection of his characteristic attention to detail when labouring on the major works. The sonata was dedicated to Walter Gieseking, who, according to Scott, sight-read the manuscript 'straight off, making hardly a mistake'.[19] Then the work languished in oblivion until it resurfaced in three early twenty-first-century recordings.

Scott's third and last piano sonata, of 1956, has a multi-movement structure. In fact, it is his only piano sonata so structured, as the Op. 66 Sonata was written in four interconnected movements. The writing is now less flamboyant, and in the harmonically abstract style of his late works for other instrumental combinations. The unifying device of quoting from earlier movements in the final movement is found here, as Scott often did in his larger works throughout his life. Traces of his Romantic roots can still be found in certain passages. The work's detractors find it:

> a lesson in what happens to a composer who overworks a fashionable idiom in his youth. You cannot construct a sonata out of short, very rich harmonic progressions of not more than two or three bars each, with not much logical connection between them, coupled with purely decorative and non-structural passages.[20]

[19] Scott, *Bone of Contention*, p. 138.

[20] Peter Pirie, writing in *Music and Letters* 37 (1956), p. 312.

Ex. 11.5 Scott, *Pastoral Ode*, bars 27–36

Ironically, history has been kinder to this sonata: it was republished in 1981 by the British Music Society, and has been commercially recorded five times – three of them before the year 2000.[21]

The *Pastoral Ode* of 1961 has the distinction of being Scott's last original work for piano. He wrote to Grainger, 'Am getting on with my new piano piece, *Pastoral Ode*, but I find that it takes me so much longer at my age now to get things through. So there is much effort and slow progress.'[22] The musical style of this substantial piece is uncompromisingly meditative and harmonically abstruse, in the style of Sonata No. 3. Example 11.5 illustrates how Scott's writing, while still nominally based on thirds and fourths, has become virtually atonal. It seems appropriate that Scott dedicated the work to his pianistic partner of the last forty years of his life, Esther Fisher. It was written for a chamber concert at Wigmore Hall, organised by William Elkin, to showcase Scott's later style of composition, and was premiered by Fisher on that occasion.

Scott's last piano work to be published, the nostalgic *Victorian Waltz* (1963), is actually a reworking of a vocal duet written thirty years earlier for use in his musical show *Whilom and Whither*.[23] The published copy states that its existence stems 'from a fragment by T. Holland-Smith'. As Holland-Smith was a close friend from Scott's

[21] *British Music Society Journal* 3 (1981), pp. 29–48.

[22] Scott to Grainger, 19 February 1960.

[23] Part I, Scene 5.

youth, one might trace the origins of this waltz back sixty years or more. There is a world-weary, *fin-de-siècle* aura to the piece, not unlike that of *Der Rosenkavalier*. One might even speculate that Scott, after abandoning hope of ever seeing *Whilom and Whither* produced in the 1930s, deliberately withheld publication till late in life, when the aura of the writing might serve as a personal retrospective of his own creative life, a life so centred upon the piano.[24]

Apart from his early Concerto in D, Op. 10 (1900), and the Concerto No. 1 in C major (1914), all Scott's essays in concertante keyboard works fall within the time period of this chapter. There were five. Unfortunately, the two works written for two pianos and orchestra (*Concertino* and *Passacaglia festevole*) in the 1930s appear lost. The 1931 *Concertino* for two pianos and orchestra was premiered by Esther Fisher and Scott with the Bournemouth Municipal Orchestra under Sir Dan Godfrey in December 1931. According to Fisher, Scott also premiered *Early One Morning* with the BMO and Godfrey, and later performed it with Barbirolli.[25] The always enterprising pianist John Ogdon recorded both concerti and *Early One Morning* in the decade following Scott's death, and more recent recordings of the early Concerto in D, Op. 10, and the *Harpsichord Concerto* have rescued these significant scores from oblivion.

Early One Morning, as might be expected, is pastoral throughout, with only one short, unexpected *agitato* outburst in the interior. The mood of the whole is meditative, as befits a song of unrequited love. The folk melody is treated with much harmonic imagination, but is rarely obscured by that. At a surface level, one might be reminded of Delius.[26] There is an extended introductory passage with much improvisatory piano figuration and a solo cadenza. Much writing in parallel fifths and fourths in both piano and orchestra combines with pentatonic melodic figuration. A solo oboe enters, the orchestra hints increasingly at the folk tune, and we finally hear it intact, about 4 or 5 minutes into the piece, in a modest solo piano passage. The diatonic melody is adorned with piquant chromatic harmonies that occasionally threaten to dislocate the tonality – a technique Scott shares with Peter Warlock. One is reminded of Scott's revealing description of his own refractory improvising at a dinner party:

[24] *Danse-Song*, written in 1970, is Scott's last composition, and is sometimes cited as a piano work. It is actually a 'vocalese melodica' [*sic*] for high soprano and piano. The differing calligraphic styles of the manuscript indicate a probable attempt to complete an unfinished song from earlier in life.

[25] Esther Fisher, 'Cyril Scott', *Journal of the British Institute of Recorded Sound* 61 (January 1976), pp. 502–10.

[26] Scott was not an acquaintance of Delius, but he spoke highly of him in *Music: Its Secret Influence* [p. 78 in the 1950 edn]:

'Delius, like all other individualists, developed his style through a selective process – he assimilated certain phases of Grieg, of Debussy and Wagner, and made them his own. He is the poet of *atmosphere*, of the peace-fragranced spirit of the woods, of the freedom of the "cloud-kissing hill", and of the hazy sun-bathed landscape. The folk-song has also played its part in his development.'

(The 'cloud-kissing hill' epithet derives from Wiffen's translation of Tasso's *Jerusalem* [*Jerusalem Delivered* … translated into English Spenserian Verse, 1821].)

> [Mrs. Gardiner, Heddy Gardiner, the wife of Sir Alan Gardiner, Balfour's brother] had invited some friends of a particularly non-Bohemian type to dinner, and had asked me beforehand if I would play. This I promised to do; but when the time came, felt I had dined far too well and was not in the mood, so that a good deal of persuasion was necessary to induce me to keep my promise. Finally, I went with a rather bad grace to the piano and started to play – not Wagner, as I so frequently did, but modernised versions of 'The Honeysuckle and the Bee', and, Hello, my Baby', followed by 'Finiculi, finicula' [Scott spelling], 'After the Ball', 'Lousiana [*sic*] Loo', and many others, ending after about forty minutes with a loud and scandalously harmonised version of 'God Save the King', preceded by an improvised fugue on 'Sailing Away'. But that was not all; when I had played my last chord, I got up from the piano, and without looking at anybody or saying a word, walked straight out of the room.[27]

One can only imagine the impact of the moment, and the exact nature of such an improvisation. But the anecdote reflects well the one feature that seems to permeate all of Scott's piano writing, and his approach to composition generally: the spirit of spontaneity.

[27] Scott, *My Years of Indiscretion*, pp. 123–4. With his examples in this story of a repertoire of the popular stage and music hall numbers of the early twentieth century, Scott was presumably indicating what he thought of his audience. The items he mentions are:
'The Honeysuckle and the Bee', popular song by William H. Penn from the London stage play *Bluebell in Fairyland* (1901) also associated with the Souza Band; 'Hello My Baby' by Joseph E. Howard featured in the show *The Runaway Girl* (1905); 'Funiculì, Funiculà' by Luigi Denza (first published in 1880); and 'After the Ball' by Charles K. Harris (1893). 'Lousiana Loo' probably refers to 'My Lulu Lulu Loo' by Nat D. Mann, published in 1902.

The Twenty-First-Century Orchestral Recordings: The Shock of the Unknown

PETER DICKINSON

CYRIL Scott's centenary in 1979, nine years after his death, was a low moment. Christopher Palmer wrote: 'Few composers of the "lost generation" of English Romantics stand in such urgent need of rehabilitation as Cyril Scott.'[1] The Cyril Scott Society had become defunct even earlier, soon after it was founded in 1964.[2] I was aware of Scott's crippling neglect at a time when I was giving many recitals with my sister, the mezzo Meriel Dickinson, and proposed a modest centenary programme of songs and piano music to BBC Radio 3 – where Scott had been neglected or condescended to for many years. This programme was called Two Post Impressionists and coupled Scott with the American Charles Tomlinson Griffes (1884–1920).[3] They both had anniversaries in the same month; they were pioneers in a modern idiom, especially in harmony; they were involved in oriental thought; and they studied in Germany at a time when their own countries were not regarded as suitable training grounds for composers. They were both professional pianists with important piano works, and Scott's First Sonata (1909) was ground-breaking in both harmony and metre. Thanks to Sarah Collins we now know far more about

[1] Christopher Palmer, 'Cyril Scott: Centenary Reflections', *The Musical Times*, September 1979, pp. 738–41.

[2] A letter to *The Musical Times*, April 1962, p. 250, proposed a Cyril Scott Society. The signatories were a distinguished list including the principals of three London conservatoires and composers Ireland, Goossens, Rubbra and Malcolm Arnold. They lamented that his major works were seldom performed and 'not a single work of his is available in a present-day recording'. W. R. Pasfield, treasurer of the short-lived Society, wrote to me on 12 August 1978: 'In regard to the Cyril Scott Society, its activities reached their zenith in a highly successful performance of his works at the Royal Academy of Music on 1 May 1964, with John Ogdon (Third Piano Sonata), the Alberni Quartet (Third String Quartet) and Pears and Rubbra (Dowson songs). Afterwards the Society unfortunately ceased.' Robert Henderson opened his review: 'Apart from some piano pieces and songs, few of us know anything of the music of Cyril Scott.' He regretted the inclusion of later works which could give 'little indication of what it actually was that attracted musicians to his earlier works'. Henderson ended: 'the feeling persists that there is a good deal still to be discovered in the music of Cyril Scott, when we hear more of it'. *The Musical Times*, June 1964, p. 444. *The Times* ('Music by Scott', 2 May 1964) reported that Cyril Scott, 'a slight but picturesque, bearded, velvet-coated figure, in his eighty-fifth year', acknowledged his own music and Sir Thomas Armstrong, principal of the RAM, spoke of the Society's wish to perform and record Scott's music'. All that had to wait. No wonder that Scott's second autobiography was called *Bone of Contention* (Aquarian Press, 1969). He reports on this concert on p. 231.

[3] Two Post-Impressionists, BBC Radio 3, recorded 23 April 1979, Birmingham, broadcast in September.

Scott's integrated range of activities – literary, philosophical, medical and occult – and his music can be approached from a wider perspective than in the past.[4]

What has transformed the whole climate for Scott's music is the flood of recordings in the twenty-first century. This began after Scott's partner, Marjorie Harston-Scott, died in 1997 and his son, Desmond Scott, came into possession of his father's papers.[5] He found a quantity of unpublished and even unperformed music. Recent recordings allow us to assess much of it for the first time.

The first category contains early works that did achieve performance. The First Symphony in G major was written in 1899 and played the following year by the Darmstadt Opera Orchestra under Willem de Haan.[6] Scott attributed this only known performance to the influence of his friend the poet Stefan George. The score comes from the Grainger Museum and some completion was required. The first two pages of the third movement have been provided from internal evidence by Leslie De'Ath, who has recorded the complete piano works.[7]

After a short introduction, the first movement is in a well-behaved sonata form. The perky first subject is soon upstaged by a lyrical second theme, in the strings, which dominates the development. Echoing Dvořák, the Andante starts with a cor anglais melody; the Allegretto is a nondescript scherzo; and the finale is a theme and ten variations with two solo trombones announcing the melody unaccompanied. It ends with what Scott calls a fugue – not very contrapuntal – and the theme surprisingly becomes a chorale in G minor to finish. Basically this student work is a fluent exercise in orchestration, as was recognised at the time.

The overture *Pelleas and Melisanda*, Op. 5, dedicated to Willem de Haan, was performed at the Palmengarten in Frankfurt in 1900. This was before Debussy's opera or Schönberg's work – Scott knew both Maeterlinck and Debussy, who admired him – but Fauré's incidental music to the play had been used at a production in London in 1898. Scott's overture starts with a modal melody, bassoon against distant tremolando strings, later harmonised, and the scene at first is closer to Sibelius than any of the diverse influences in the early Piano Concerto. It may be possible to identify a programme. The weird unworldly atmosphere persists until some violence – maybe the murder of Pelleas – which stops abruptly. Then the modal material from the beginning recurs – perhaps the death of Melisande.

A second category consists of unperformed works that Scott thought he had destroyed. He said:

> I am one of those people who do not hold with the policy of raking up and performing early and unrepresentative works of composers, works written perhaps long before they had developed their respective styles ... Consequently, unless

[4] Sarah Collins, *The Aesthetic Life of Cyril Scott* (Boydell, 2013).

[5] Desmond Scott, 'Cyril Scott, a Personal Portrait', *Counterpoints, BMIC Friends Newsletter*, July/August 2000. The British Music Information Centre is now located in Huddersfield. See also: Desmond Scott, 'Cyril Scott: A Man whose Time has Come Again?', *British Music Society News* 108 (December 2005), pp. 375–79.

[6] At the Archduke's Court Theatre on 8 January 1900.

[7] See Leslie De'Ath, 'Cyril Scott as Composer-Pianist and Author', *British Music Society News* 106 (June 2005), pp. 304–13.

> they were published and it was already too late, I destroyed practically all my orchestral scores written prior to my *Two Passacaglias* (1912).[8]

Scott showed this early Piano Concerto to Paderewski and said: 'he never played it and I am glad that he did not – for it was a bad work'.[9]

We live in an age when composers who have not finished works are liable to have it done for them. Anthony Payne's edition of Elgar's Third Symphony has been the most successful of all these British completions. Some of Scott's juvenilia have survived. Manuscripts are in the Percy Grainger Museum and Martin Yates has prepared performance materials for the Piano Concerto and Cello Concerto and completed a few passages. There must have been original scores that Scott did destroy, but what survives is extensive and has enabled Yates to put the two concertos into performable shape.[10] Both of them were probably receiving their first performances in these recordings.

The Piano Concerto in D, Op. 10, was begun in 1900. The first movement opens ecstatically with a personality for the soloist derived from Tchaikovsky's First Concerto. Scott's teacher at the Hoch Conservatory in Frankfurt, Iwan Knorr (1853–1916), knew Tchaikovsky and wrote a book about him.[11] Prominent chains of ninth chords may stem from Debussy; Scott's chords drop by semitones, as in Delius; and his chromatic melodies owe much to *Tristan*. The opening movement keeps the soloist constantly engaged where elaborated harmony finally gives way to plain triads of F, G and C major to end. The Intermezzo starts with a modal melody accompanied by the piano. This first section was used again for the song *Evening Hymn*, published in 1904 and dedicated to Scott's parents. Then comes a centrally placed but rather obvious short cadenza before another song-like section to finish, again accompanied by piano flourishes. The melodic efflorescence is comparable to Scott's songs and piano pieces and the movement ends on the major of the initial A minor. The vivace finale has plenty of display. A florid theme comes in the clarinet and is then taken over by the soloist. The continuity is sequential but energetic and the D minor of the opening swells to a triumph on the major. This movement becomes repetitive in a lengthy recapitulation and, presumably after that, Yates had to create an ending. It is hard to see why Scott disowned the Piano Concerto, to which he gave an opus number, so that it waited over a century to be heard. Perhaps he felt that he had suffered from an overdose of Wagner, whom he called 'the Shakespeare of music'[12] and whose technique of continuous flow nevertheless lasted Scott for many years. However, there is here much of what the public expects from a Romantic piano concerto, replete with gestures of the kind that Hollywood would later exploit and media composers still do. Peter Donohoe's performance

[8] Scott, *Bone of Contention*, p. 139.

[9] Scott, *My Years of Indiscretion* (Mills & Boon, 1924), p. 84.

[10] Lewis Foreman. CD booklet, Dutton Epoch CDLX 7302. See also Chapter 8.

[11] Iwan Knorr, *Tchaikovsky* (Berlin, 1900).

[12] A. Eaglefield Hull, *Cyril Scott: The Man and his Work* (Waverley Book Co., 1918), p. 32.

makes a strong case for this to become a repertoire piece if the stranglehold of Grieg, Tchaikovsky and Rachmaninov can ever be broken.[13]

The last of three unknown works on the same CD, the early Cello Concerto, Op. 19 (1902), has also needed some modern surgery, again with materials from the Grainger Museum, completion by Martin Yates and editing by him and Raphael Wallfisch. The official Cello Concerto (1937) also appears never to have been performed.[14] The earlier concerto, in a single movement, opens mysteriously with strings over a low C pedal point plus timpani; the cello rises over characteristic harmonic shifts and, as in the Piano Concerto, there is a cadenza, here exploiting double sixths and thirds. There is an Andante section, attractively scored, and the rest of the concerto is an outpouring of endless melody.

The next category consists of works that were performed in the early decades of the twentieth century, when Scott's reputation was reaching its height. The Second Symphony, Op. 22, originated in 1901–2 and was conducted by Henry Wood at a Promenade Concert on 25 August 1903. The composer's programme-note states significantly that he intended 'to secure a continuous flow, without a cadence from beginning to end of a movement'.[15] Scott then revised and retitled the work *Three Symphonic Dances*; Grainger made an arrangement for two pianos;[16] some movements were performed separately in 1907 and 1912, but in its final incarnation the *Symphonic Dances* is an effective set – the best of Scott's early Romantic style. The syncopated finale is a surprise.

From the same period, the *Festival Overture*, Op. 18, dedicated to Grainger, has had an unstable history. It started out in 1902 as an *Overture to Princess Maleine*, Maeterlinck's first play, published in 1889. Lewis Foreman considers: 'The music is powerfully suggestive of the glorious fifteen-year-old princess over whom men fight, of the sense of foreboding and tragic climax, of the view of land wasted by war and, above all, of the great storm.'[17] The overture was conducted by Henry Wood at a Prom on 22 August 1907 but Scott said it had been performed in the Palmengarten Concerts in Frankfurt earlier.[18] *The Times* reviewer also saw it as programmatic and added: 'The music gives the impression of having been written in the days when admiration for Maeterlinck was still in the unfortunate state of being a cult.'[19] Scott revised the work and added a chorus part for a performance by the Vienna Philharmonic on 22 April 1912 under Franz Schreker. Alban Berg was at the concert and in a letter to Schönberg said it was 'a colossal success' but the overture was

[13] Cyril Scott, Piano Concerto in D, Op. 10. Cello Concerto, Op. 19. Overture to *Pelleas and Melisanda*. Peter Donohoe, Raphael Wallfisch, BBC Concert Orchestra / Martin Yates. Dutton Epoch CDLX 7302.

[14] See Lewis Foreman, CD booklet notes on Dutton Epoch CDLX 7302 (2013).

[15] Quoted in *The Times* review of Symphony No. 2, 26 August 1903.

[16] Recorded by Leslie De'Ath and Anya Alexeyev on Dutton Digital CDLX 7166.

[17] CD booklet to Cyril Scott Volume III. Violin Concerto. Festival Overture. *Aubade*. *Three Symphonic Dances*. BBC Philharmonic / Brabbins, Chandos CHAN 10407.

[18] Scott, *Bone of Contention*, p. 85.

[19] 'Queen's Hall', *The Times*, 23 August 1907.

'never-ending mush, no doubt modern, but it almost made me nauseated'.[20] Then Scott changed the title to *Festival Overture* and submitted it for a *Daily Telegraph* Composition Prize in 1934. There were 223 anonymous entries; the judges were Henry Wood, Hamilton Harty, Frank Bridge and Arthur Bliss. Scott triumphed with first prize (£100); Frank Tapp second (£75); and Arnold Cooke third (£50). This led to a performance of the Scott at Queen's Hall with the BBC Symphony Orchestra under Adrian Boult on 9 May 1934. *The Times* was scathing:

> What we should like to know is whether the judges had the least inkling that they had before them the work of a composer of wide even international reputation: whether any one of them said: 'This must be Cyril Scott.' We should doubt it ... It would be difficult to find any trace of a personal idiom, even with the composer's name to guide to memories of earlier works.[21]

When the overture was given at the Proms on 30 August 1934, along with the other two winners, *The Times* reviewer then said that Scott's work was 'confirmed in first place because it is in no way derivative'.[22] In November 1937 Basil Cameron, director of the Seattle Symphony, performed the overture. Percy Grainger was there and called it 'a work of genius'.[23] Perhaps as a result, in January 1941, Grainger used his influence to obtain a performance with the South Bend Symphony Orchestra in Indiana, USA.[24] The overture was in the Proms again on 20 August 1947 with the BBC Symphony Orchestra under Adrian Boult. *The Times* reviewer described the piece as 'depicting a great gathering of initiates'. That could have been an interpretation of the anonymous text heading the score and obviously printed in the programme. 'And let them be welcomed to the festival with solemn chants and sinuous melodies and a flourish of trumpets, that their hearts may be filled with reverence, sweetness and valour'. However, the review obviously irritated Scott, who wrote to the paper to say that his overture had 'nothing to do with initiates just an overture to a festival'.[25] The piece does raise large issues in a ten minute span; it opens with woodwind choirs alternating with unison low strings; a step-wise rising melody becomes important and recurs; then the organ comes in, soon followed by the brief entry of the voices on a chord of G major alternating with Scott's favourite ninth chords. This is a thrilling moment that is never quite sustained, and the work ends on F major – it was all a long journey from that incidental music in 1902.

The *Aubade* (1905) is another ten-minute piece, premiered in Birmingham in 1906, revised and given in Berlin in 1912, also in Darmstadt and Dresden, and published by Schott in Germany, indicating Scott's standing on the Continent. A performance at the Queen's Hall under Goossens on 23 November 1921 was announced as 'first time'. As with Delius, Scott's music would suffer with the outbreak of World

[20] Berg's letter dated 23 April. Laurie J. Sampsel, *Cyril Scott: A Bio-Bibliography* (Greenwood, 2000), p. 10.

[21] 'A Prize Overture: Mr Cyril Scott's New Work', *The Times*, 10 May 1934.

[22] 'Three Prize-Winning Overtures', *The Times*, 31 August 1934.

[23] John Bird, *Percy Grainger* (Elek, 1976), p. 213.

[24] Ibid., p. 215. In a contemporary music programme that was not well received.

[25] *The Times* review, 22 August 1947; Scott's letter, 30 August 1947.

War 1. In spite of its German connections the *Aubade* is among the most impressionist of Scott's pieces, and one can see why it encouraged his being called 'the English Debussy'.[26] However, Scott thought he had not written 'a (to me) satisfying work' until his *Two Passacaglias on Irish Themes* (1912).[27]

A major landmark towards a new style was the First Piano Sonata, written in 1908 but again revised at various times. Its use of continuously varied metres and its characteristic stream of consciousness continuity relate it to parts of the *Concord Sonata* of Charles Ives, written later. Like Ives, Scott made changes to the work after it was first written. Percy Grainger used to play it into the 1950s and had his own repertoire of cuts, some extensive. Overall the sonata was a remarkable achievement for a British composer at the time, and it presages the improvisatory character of all Scott's larger works to come.[28]

Developing this new style further, the Piano Concerto, officially No. 1, was written in 1913–14 and performed by the London Symphony Orchestra under Beecham at the Queen's Hall with Scott as soloist on 15 May 1915.[29] World War 1 had put an end to a European tour. *The Times* reported favourably:

> In this work Scott seems to have emerged entirely from the experimental stage. The music keeps a straight course; there is not a moment where it drops into commonplace or loses itself in a confusion of ideas. The untiring vitality of his own playing, of course, helped it immensely ... The ordinary listener may have doubts but he could scarcely fail to be carried away by the composer's convictions ... a masterly certainty of handling.[30]

This was an enlightened response to a work which would have seemed avant-garde at the time. Scott himself made some odd remarks, calling the concerto 'not a deep work but an enlivening one'; referring to the first movement 'as if Scarlatti had lived in China'; and mentioning Handel in connection with the continuity of the finale.[31] The

[26] Debussy's testimonial, apparently written for Schott's catalogue, is quoted in Eaglefield Hull, *Cyril Scott*, p. 140.

[27] *Bone of Contention*, p. 92. In spite of his preferring not to conduct his own works, he did conduct the *Two Passacaglias* in America (*Bone of Contention*, p. 163). The first performance was at the Queen's Hall, under Beecham, on 3 November 1914; it was in the Proms on 27 July 1954 with the LSO under Basil Cameron.

[28] Leslie De'Ath has recorded the original version, not the revised edition brought out by Elkin in 1909. Cyril Scott, Complete Piano Music, Volume II, Dutton Digital CDLX 7155.

[29] Scott played the solo part from time to time. His performance with the Philadelphia Orchestra under Stokowski on 5 November 1920 was a highlight of his American tour (see Sampsel, *Cyril Scott: A Bio-Bibliography*, p. 11). *The Times* references include 13 June 1921 at the British Music Society Congress in London; 24 July 1929 at the Festival of British Music in Harrogate; and 15 September 1931 at the Queen's Hall in the Proms. In 1928 the concerto was broadcast by the Polish pianist Stanislas Niedzielski; Scott recalled further broadcasts by Esther Fisher, his piano duo partner, during the 1930s and Kendall Taylor for his seventieth birthday, both with approval (*Bone of Contention*, p. 140).

[30] 'Festival of British Music', *The Times*, 17 May 1915.

[31] *Bone of Contention*, pp. 140–1.

tintinnabulations of piano with celesta and harp created an exotic ambience often based on harmonic chains that prefigure Messiaen. The work's luxuriance recalls what Scott said about Scriabin's *Prometheus*: 'It is an entirely different type of ecstatic element from that produced by Wagner – all sense of the obvious and the diatonic is banished, and with it all sense of the human. It exhales an intense loveliness, but not an earthly loveliness.'[32] This fitted in with Scott's developing occult beliefs.

The first movement starts rhetorically with plentiful decoration from the soloist, who is constantly engaged. The central section is a siciliano, opening on the oboe, in a harmonic idiom close to John Ireland. The finale makes reference to earlier materials, as often with Scott. The overall style is diffuse and discursive – charges also made against Delius, who had a stronger sense of continuity. On 31 October 1969 it was revived at the Queen Elizabeth Hall with the Polyphonia Orchestra under Bryan Fairfax and with Moura Lympany as soloist. It was a tribute to Scott for his ninetieth birthday: he was there, and died just over a year later. In *The Times*, Joan Chissell acknowledged the work's sonorous attractiveness but went on: 'There's a price to pay for self-indulgent beauty. The argument is far too rhapsodic and protracted.'[33]

In the mid-1970s the concerto achieved its first recording and, when it was reissued on CD, I reviewed it in the *Gramophone*:

> This promised to be an exciting reissue thirty years later from the old Lyrita catalogue. It was an example of John Ogdon's generosity when Cyril Scott was forgotten – look at what he did for Sorabji too – and this recording is an important part of the Ogdon discography. You can hear his zealous advocacy with every sumptuous chord. Bernard Herrmann, a genius as a film composer, must have supported the whole idea too in the run-up to Scott's centenary in 1979. Why, then, is it so disappointing? One glance at the playing times tells all. Ogdon is almost nine minutes slower overall than Howard Shelley in the First Concerto and almost five minutes slower in the Second. The entire continuity, under Herrmann, sags and meanders … Shelley and Brabbins get it right and cut nearly five minutes off Ogdon's timing in the first movement alone.[34]

A decade later came the Violin Concerto (*c.* 1925). It inhabits some of the same territory as the Delius Violin Concerto a decade earlier. Delius wrote his concerto for Albert Sammons; Scott sent Sammons an inscribed copy but he did not play it – May Harrison did, with the City of Birmingham Symphony Orchestra under Adrian Boult in 1928.[35] Scott's rhapsodic continuity is based on melodic arabesque coloured by luscious chords: it sprawls languorously in his seductive orchestral

[32] Cyril Scott, *Music: Its Secret Influence through the Ages* (Rider & Co., 1933; 8th impression, 1955), p. 52.

[33] 'Birthday Present', *The Times*, 1 November 1969.

[34] Peter Dickinson, *Gramophone*, May 2007, p. 85. Cyril Scott. Piano Concertos 1 & 2. John Ogdon, London Philharmonic Orchestra / Bernard Herrmann. Lyrita SRCS 251. Cyril Scott, Volume II. Piano Concerto No. 1, Symphony No. 4. Cyril Scott Volume I. Howard Shelley, BBC Philharmonic / Martyn Brabbins. Chandos CHAN 10376.

[35] See Lewis Foreman's notes to this CD and many of the others under discussion.

textures and includes some obvious cadenza material. Not many violin concertos open with a bassoon solo, but this one does. Then the soloist creeps in and there is a lot of slow music. The Largo section opens with the soloist's self-contained melody in C minor characteristically harmonised. It shows the easy melodic flow of Scott, as in his shorter piano pieces and songs. In May 1924 Beatrice Harrison became world famous when she played her cello alongside nightingales in the early days of broadcasting. This was reflected in Scott's *The Melodist and the Nightingales* for cello and orchestra, first performed under Beecham at the Queen's Hall on 14 June 1929.[36] This is a rhapsodic expanse but not as literal in its birdsong as Vaughan Williams's *The Lark Ascending* (1921).

Scott's German connections revived briefly in the later 1920s when his opera, *The Alchemist*, was given three times in Essen in 1925 to a mixed reception, and his ballet *Karma* was hailed at Dortmund in 1930.

Early One Morning (1930–1), a light piece for piano and orchestra, shows Scott improvising on the well-known folk song in his own way, much as he harmonised *Cherry Ripe* for piano. That setting was published in 1915 and dedicated to Granger, who specialised in treating folk songs and making arrangements. Grainger also made several settings of *Early One Morning*, the first in 1899. Scott's *Early One Morning* is a useful case-study in his now mature technique for extended works. It was published by Boosey for two pianos and orchestra in 1931; revised for a single piano in 1962; and at the time of the 1975 recording with Ogdon the version for one soloist had apparently never been performed.[37]

Early One Morning begins casually in the strings over a long low C pedal. Scott said: 'It suggests the quiet mood of sunrise on a peaceful summer morning when there is just a slight haze.'[38] The piano enters with decorative passages not obviously related to the melody. Scott said these figures 'joyously create the impression of songful birds'. Even an oboe solo does not quite get to the melody until the violins enter. Then there are various settings in Scott's characteristic ripe chromatic harmony – he called it 'novel and ingenious' – but still rooted in C major until a sumptuous version in B-flat. Then the soloist raises the temperature with an allegro; the strings have the melody; the brass intervene; and the piano eventually brings the tune back to C major with elaboration like the opening and a protracted ending swathed in added sixth harmony.

Because the melody of *Early One Morning* is so well known, Scott's processes are easily traced. They are comparable to the way Charles Ives quoted or misquoted his hymns and popular songs. Sarah Collins links Scott's practice back to his early years abroad and his friendship with Stefan George:

[36] *The Times* on 15 June 1929 was not impressed. Recorded on Dutton in 2015 with Aleksei Kiseliov and the Royal Scottish National Orchestra / Martin Yates. See *The Cello and the Nightingales: the Autobiography of Beatrice Harrison* (Murray, 1985).

[37] CD booklet notes by Roger Wimbush, Lyrita SRCD 251.

[38] From Scott's own programme note in the Grainger Museum, quoted by Lewis Foreman in the CD booklet to Cyril Scott Volume II: Piano Concerto [No. 1], Early One Morning, and Symphony No. 4. Chandos CHAN 10376.

> The developmental stasis engendered by Scott's 'musical flow' and other techniques designed for undermining any sense of linear progression is entirely consonant with the 'poetic vegetation' of the symbolists. The conversational rupture and emphasis on silence achieved through unfinished sentences and non-sequiturs in Maeterlinck's early dramatic works finds its musical expression in unfinished cadences that segue into new modulations, and surprising juxtapositions of musical ideas and pitch sequences in Scott's music.[39]

Collins perceptively relates these sources as 'a logical prelude to his occult involvement'. Stephen Banfield spotted the influence of these literary sources much earlier: 'Translating Baudelaire must have heightened Scott's awareness of the value accorded by symbolist poetic aesthetics to individual words and phrases prized more for their sensuous properties than their sense.'[40] But Scott can be seen as far ahead of his time if his continuity is compared to the non-sequiturs of Stockhausen's moment form – and they shared occult involvements, too. Scott's output can now be seen in a far broader context than when he was being considered simply as a pioneering modern composer.

Now to another tranche of unperformed works. The fourth volume of the Chandos Scott series opens not only with a first recording, but also a first performance – of the Cello Concerto from 1937.[41] By then Scott had become so unfashionable that, along with at least two unperformed operas, this concerto failed to get performed. It opens with a sixteen-minute movement that is virtually a concerto on its own. Right at the start, the sustained strings, with superimposed celesta, create a magical atmosphere. The cello soloist enters with an arresting melody based on C minor but with chromatic inflections. There are four phrases rising and falling with its reappearances attractively varied as Scott's improvisatory instinct takes over – and the movement ends in D major. The continuity is close to Delius and some of the scoring is as rich as Ravel. The second movement is largely an accompanied cadenza leading directly to the final rondo, where a perky solo bassoon kicks off with a theme that recurs. There is plenty for the soloist to do, and any lapse in continuity is rescued by consistently inventive scoring. Paul Watkins sounds superb and, as before, Martyn Brabbins is an admirable exponent.

The Third Symphony is entitled *The Muses*. There were originally nine muses, ancient Greek goddesses, daughters of Zeus and Mnemosyne, and Scott chose four to portray in music: Melpomene (epic poetry and tragedy); Thalia (comedy and merry verse); Erato (love and poetry); and Terpsichore (dance and song). Written in 1937, the work was dedicated to Beecham, who never performed it: the recording by the BBC Philharmonic under Martyn Brabbins is another first performance.[42] The symphony employs a large orchestra, treats the muses according to their

39 Collins, *The Aesthetic Life of Cyril Scott*, p. 190.

40 Stephen Banfield, *Sensibility and English Song* (Cambridge University Press, 1985), p. 92.

41 Cyril Scott Volume IV. Cello Concerto. Symphony No. 1. Paul Watkins, BBC Philharmonic Orchestra / Brabbins. Chandos CHAN 10452.

42 Cyril Scott Volume I. Symphony No. 3 'The Muses'. Piano Concerto No. 2. Neptune. Chandos CHAN 10211.

specialities, but constantly recalls models – the Debussy of *La mer*; the Ravel of *Daphnis*; the Bax of *Tintagel*; and even triads comparable to Vaughan Williams at climaxes in the first and last movements. The scoring is typically resourceful and even includes a wind-machine. The second movement is a lively scherzo but the improvisatory slow movement lacks focus. The finale uses a mixed chorus and gives it plenty to do, but the use of a chorus cannot have helped to encourage performances.

A work which did get a hearing in this middle period was *Disaster at Sea*, a programmatic work for large orchestra based on the sinking of the *Titanic* in 1912. It was put on at the Queen's Hall – only half full for an unfamiliar programme – by the Royal Philharmonic Society under Albert Coates on 19 October 1933. *The Times* expressed surprise at the idea of an old-fashioned tone-poem with a scenario: 'The whole thing is an extraordinary aggregation of effects which may prevent the realisation of what is undoubtedly the case, that the composer aims at the expression of something deeper.'[43] Scott took this to heart and revised the work two years later, removing some specific effects, minimising the music being played as the ship went down, and retitling it *Neptune*. That version waited for a performance until the first volume of the Chandos series. There are some original atmospheric textures and a pervasive chorale, unusually in parallel triads. There is a waltz – a dance of death. Eugene Goossens remembered Scott working on the score when they were both at Harlech in Wales. He found the subject 'unpleasant but impressive' and added – significantly – that Scott's twenty-minute improvisations were 'as beautiful as any I have ever heard'.[44]

In 1944 Scott said:

> Having reached the age of sixty-five, I had decided that it was best to give up the idea of composing any more … to devote my energies to other possible forms of usefulness. It had become obvious that my more serious compositions were not wanted by the musical powers that be, and it seemed futile to write works unlikely ever to get a hearing, considering the large number I had composed which had not been granted even a single performance.[45]

This attitude changed as a result of Scott's long-established psychic contacts, who urged him to continue to compose. This resulted in the opera *Maureen O'Mara*, to his own libretto. He spent two and a half years on it, without even scoring it. When it was rejected for the Festival of Britain in 1951 Scott referred to his occult sources and was told: 'the first thing is to get the work written; the rest, if needs be, can wait – sometimes even as long as till after the composer's death'.[46] Indeed it did. Scott had been open about his occult interests, first writing about them in 1915;

[43] 'Royal Philharmonic Society', *The Times*, 20 October 1933.

[44] Eugene Goossens, *Overture and Beginners* (Methuen, 1951), pp. 136–7. Grainger also admired Scott's improvisations when they were students together. See Bird, *Percy Grainger*, p. 29.

[45] Scott, *Bone of Contention*, p. 217.

[46] Ibid., p. 222.

in *The Philosophy of Modernism* (1917)[47] he was dogmatic in asserting connections between the occult and music; he published two articles and gave an interview on the subject during his American tour in 1920; and they were the basis of *Music: Its Secret Influence Throughout the Ages*. This was published in 1933 and reached an eighth impression in 1955.[48] In his first autobiography he described the impact of *Rajan Yoga* (1896) by Swami Vivekananda (1863–1902): 'from the day that book came into my hands, the study of all forms of mysticism and transcendental philosophy became a passion; and not only that, but I found in their study a new and great source of musical inspiration.'[49] Eric Blom in *Grove's Dictionary of Music* (5th edn, 1955) realised: 'It is by no means irrelevant to mention the deep interest which the composer began to take in Oriental philosophy and theosophy about this time (1909), for with it his musical style underwent a marked change.' Subsequent editions of *Grove* had far shorter entries on Scott, reflecting his neglect. Scott must be the most versatile composer in the history of music. This of course has been held against him; so have his spiritualist involvements; and both must have been responsible for the decline in his reputation.[50]

These supernatural elements in Scott's work of all kinds since World War 1 can be compared to the visions of Scriabin (1872–1915), who had a far shorter incarnation. But after World War 2, Scott's musical language changed. He regularly used chords based on fourths, when much earlier he employed decorated dominants.[51] Examples are the *Sonata melodica* for violin and piano (1950); the Third Piano Sonata (1956); and the Sonata for flute and piano (1961). The first two have clotted middle-register piano parts, although the Piano Sonata has been recorded five times,[52] but the Flute and Piano Sonata profits from a scintillating variety of textures comparable to Scott's resourceful orchestration.[53]

[47] *The Philosophy of Modernism – Its Connection with Music*, originally Kegan Paul, Trench, Trubner & Co., London, 1917; later published along with A. Eaglefield Hull, *Cyril Scott: The Man and his Works* by The Waverley Book Co., London, n.d.

[48] See the bibliography in Collins, *The Aesthetic Life of Cyril Scott*.

[49] Scott, *My Years of Indiscretion*, pp. 111–12. Vivekananda was responsible for introducing Vedanta and Yogi into the West.

[50] His writings about natural medical remedies came from a genuine concern about mankind and were influential. For example, his booklet on cider vinegar was published in 1948 and had sold over a million copies by 1981.

[51] See Appendix IV in *Bone of Contention*, p. 237.

[52] Raphael Terroni on British Music Society; Evelinde Trenkner on Orion; Eric Parkin on Chandos; Michael Schäfer on Genuin; and Leslie De'Ath on Dutton Epoch.

[53] Peter Dickinson, 'Wind and Piano', *The Musical Times*, March 1962, p. 180. This review shows the situation at that time. 'Cyril Scott's Flute and Piano Sonata is an attractive work with enough trills and melodic embellishments to suggest later Scriabin, a composer equally unfashionable. But the individuality of Scott's music from the early years of the century onwards cannot be denied ... The work plays on the listener's harmonic consciousness in a way familiar through Delius or early Messiaen but referring back to *Tristan* ... As a whole the work is a sensitive and mature example of Scott's under-rated art.' See also my reviews of many of the CDs under discussion in the *Gramophone*.

The Fourth Symphony, completed in 1952, also received its premiere in a recording – over sixty years later.[54] It came from the period after the war when Scott had been writing books rather than music. The first movement of the symphony opens with a rising figure, leading to a major–minor chord, a motif that recurs exactly at the opening of the finale. Lewis Foreman calls the slow movement 'one of Scott's most successful meditations, all colour and atmosphere'.[55] It starts with unison strings in a three-note figure ending with a rising octave. The distinctive chromatic melody that follows contains eleven of the twelve notes. Many composers would have made it a clear basis but, although it does recur, Scott is discursive as usual.

The Second Piano Concerto (1958), like the first, has been recorded twice. Ogdon's recording with the LPO under Bernard Herrmann was the first performance and Howard Shelley and the BBC Philharmonic with Martyn Brabbins followed thirty years later. As with the first concerto, Ogdon and Herrmann are too extended and the best results come from Shelley and Brabbins. But the work is unimpressive. The late style has become a mannerism and it feels as if Scott has lost touch with the live performances that might have kept his imagination alive.

When the First Piano Concerto was revived to mark Scott's ninetieth birthday in 1969, Ronald Crichton criticised it as 'a weird mixture' with 'problems of formal construction too often evaded' but accepted that:

> it is easy to imagine how heady and adventurous this music must have sounded at the time it was written ... compared with the emotional reticence of so much English music of the period ... Though this revival may not start a full-scale revaluation of Scott, it did suggest that his shorter works (the formerly popular piano pieces and songs) may repay examination.[56]

This grudging approach brought up once again the dichotomy between the Scott of the short piano pieces and songs – and some of the chamber works – and the larger works which were mostly unheard until the twenty-first-century recordings. There was little scope for Scott's unworldly improvisation in the easily understood short pieces and songs, but the listener needs to come to the larger works ready to enjoy sensuous textures moving in unpredictable directions. The new recordings, which have garnered some outstanding reviews – the shock of the unknown – have created a new age for the appreciation of a unique figure in twentieth-century British music.

[54] Cyril Scott Volume II. Piano Concerto No. 1. *Early One Morning*. Symphony No. 4. BBC Philharmonic Orchestra / Brabbins, Howard Shelley. Chandos CHAN 10376.

[55] CD booklet notes, Chandos, CHAN 190376.

[56] Ronald Crichton, 'Polyphonia', *The Musical Times*, December 1969, p. 1264.

13

The Chamber Music

KURT LELAND

MOST people familiar with the music of Cyril Scott – from his short piano works to his songs, symphonies and concertos – would agree that he had an extraordinary ear for what musicians call harmonic colour. By half-step alterations of certain notes in a chord, non-diatonic chord progressions, or rapid modulations to distant keys, he could create impressions on the ear that seemed comparatively brighter or darker or that had quasi-kaleidoscopic qualities that cannot be described in words, though they can be easily recognised upon recurrence.

Scott's music was valued in some circles for its harmonic colour. But in others it was denigrated for being nothing more than that. Year after year, critics chided Scott for having no sense of form or logical musical development. Few perceived that he was a revolutionary right to the end of his life, when he was occasionally berated – when noticed at all – for having nothing new to say. The nature of Scott's one-person revolution lies precisely in his lifelong struggle to reconcile expressive colour with logically unfolding form.

Scott's solution bears a resemblance to his Hungarian contemporary Béla Bartók's folk-music-derived method of polymodal chromaticism.[1] Yet Scott arrived at his reconciliation of colour and form by an independent route – thus it merits a distinctive name. I call it *pan-modality*: the juxtaposition or superposition of modes to create functional equivalents for *every* (*pan-*) aspect of traditional tonal music, including melody, harmony, polyphony, tonality and form.

Scott employed modes that included five tones (pentatonic), six (hexatonic, including the whole-tone scale), seven (diatonic, including major and minor scales and the so-called Greek modes encountered in Gregorian chant and folk music), eight (octatonic, including the symmetrical scale of alternating whole- and half-tones), and possibly more, up to twelve (the chromatic scale – but generally not a twelve-tone row as used in the dodecaphonic school of composition). Such modes could be simple (such as those listed above), exotic (as in Indian *rāgas*), or synthetic (self-created by the composer, often through chromatic alteration of a simple mode or by non-tonal doubling of melodic lines in major thirds, perfect fourths, and so on). For Scott, each mode had a colour that the ear could learn to recognise as it was exchanged for other modes to create the illusion of harmonic progression or recurred as a form-generating device, from intervallic cells (modal fragments) to phrases, sections of movements, and unified multi-movement works.

The evolution of Scott's pan-modality may be traced from his first chamber music productions to his last. Let us examine this evolution decade by decade.

[1] See https://en.wikipedia.org/wiki/Polymodal_chromaticism (accessed 9 May 2017) for an introduction to Bartók's method.

BEFORE 1900

Though Scott wished to withdraw the Piano Quartet in E minor, Op. 16 (1899), it had been published in 1903 and therefore was 'safely out of the danger of his fireplace.'[2] Thus it is the earliest of Scott's chamber works to remain accessible and provides the evolutionary beginning point against which his later development may be judged. It is no surprise that the stylistic ambiance of this four-movement work is Brahmsian, given that Scott spent his student years in Germany. However, the brief scherzo is startlingly reminiscent of Fauré. The finale struggles, yet fails, to reconcile pulls toward France and Germany – colour versus form – which is possibly the reason why Scott wished to withdraw the score. A fully integrated mastery of colour and form would not be achieved until a half-century later.

1901–1910

Scott early forged a creative link between harmonic colour and musical mood. For example, *Pierrot amoureux* for violoncello and piano (premiered 1904) is one of several Scott compositions in which the title character appears, others including *Pierrot triste* and *Pierrot gai* for piano, Op. 35 (published 1904).[3] Pierrot's moods – amorous, sad and joyful – could each be called a psychological colour. Scott's task was to evolve in each piece a sound world that reflected its mood. Thus musical colour and psychological colour became analogues of each other. But this was more than mood music.

For Scott the creation of musically projected personae was a lifelong preoccupation. We see it not only in these early works, but also in his many songs, each with a singer cast in the role determined by the speaker of the poem. The value of creating such personae is that they provide a subject experiencing the moods or inner states the composer seeks to project. As we shall see, some of Scott's later works for solo instrument and piano cast the soloist in the role of subjective experiencer, though Scott draws no attention to the fact, perhaps to prevent accusations by critics that he never progressed beyond composing miniatures such as *Pierrot amoureux*.

If the French titles of the Pierrot pieces indicate their reliance on colour, the First Violin Sonata, Op. 59 (premiered 1908; revised 1956) is a quasi-Germanic essay in musical form. Though sometimes said to be in C major because of the lack of a key signature, the sonata is a highly chromatic essay in progressive tonality, winding its way from E-flat major (first movement) to C and D major (slow movement), back to C major (scherzo) and from C to F major (finale). Between each movement's beginning and ending there are rarely moments of arrival in any clearly defined tonality. Yet themes are sometimes restated on the same pitch, providing (for example) the simulacrum of a sonata-form recapitulation.

Commentators have often noted that unity is created across the forty-minute work by persistent sharing of thematic material between movements. What has

[2] A. Eaglefield Hull, *Cyril Scott: The Man and his Music* (Waverly: c. 1917), p. 59.

[3] Except where noted, titles and dates of composition, publication, and first performance are from Laurie J. Sampsel, *Cyril Scott: A Bio-Bibliography* (Greenwood, 2000).

not been sufficiently noticed is that the hexatonic (whole-tone) scale, which Scott used occasionally as a colouristic device in his lesser works, plays a pivotal structural role. The main theme of the slow movement is derived from this mode – a rhythmic augmentation of what seems a merely decorative piece of passage work in the first movement (at letter A).

Regardless of whether we can track the transformed reappearances of other thematic material across the movements, we can recognise this one because of the 'otherwordly' whole-tone colour. Even as Scott was pushing the possibilities of tonal chromaticism to its limits, he discovered what would show the way forward for him in the collapse of tonality that so many Continental composers were struggling with. The arc of his entire composing career can be seen as an exploration of the use of modal colours as a fundamental structural principle.

The three miniatures for violin and piano that comprise Scott's Op. 73 – *Elégie*, *Romance* and *Valse triste* (published 1910) – may serve as points of comparison for the composer's evolution from harmony-based tonal music to colour-based pan-modality. Thus the closing measures of *Elégie* reference the octatonic (symmetrical) scale, but only as a splash of 'local colour' within an otherwise traditionally tonal harmonic texture. Similarly, *Romance* contains hints of the whole-tone scale, primarily ornamental. Once again, the French titles point toward the focus on colour.

Tallahassee Suite for violin and piano, Op. 73 no. 4 (published 1910), is more harmonically and rhythmically adventuresome. The title of the first movement, 'Bygone Memories', indicates that the musical pictures evoked are intended to be nostalgic: presumably, ex-slaves in the American South whistling after work ('After Sundown'), singing spirituals in church, and dancing uninhibitedly ('*Air et danse nègre*').

Scott was never in Tallahassee, Florida. His vision of the South is admittedly racist and wholly mythical. However, the purpose of the work may have been to imagine a place and time where it was possible to shrug off British social conventions, live close to the land, whistle joyfully in public, worship with simple but heartfelt tunes, dance joyfully and unrestrainedly – and above all to counter critics of the Eastern exoticism of his popular piano work *Lotus Land*, Op. 47 no. 1 (premiered 1905), and related works, by evoking a musical landscape located to the west of Great Britain.

Scott's acute criticism of social conventions in his writings, and his attempt to free himself from them in his lifestyle, found musical analogues in his experiments with breaking down the rigidity of regular pulse and metre and the constraints of traditional tonality. In *Tallahassee Suite* these analogues were given an imaginary, peopled locale so they might be more easily grasped by listeners who would otherwise balk at Scott's rhythmic and harmonic freedom. He was not only educating his audience in how to hear his music, but also laying down what became a frequent feature of later compositions, written under the influence of his interest in occultism. The key to the imaginary locale of Tallahassee, like the East evoked in *Lotus Land*, is that Scott evokes it by means of non-British diatonic modes, folk-like instead of exotic.

Later Scott would find similar analogues to portray his spiritual beliefs in musical form. Listeners – and especially critics – might never perceive that his music has symbolic overtones because it functions first and foremost as a perpetual experiment in the juxtaposition and superimposition of modes.

1911–1920

I shall not discuss the handful of chamber compositions that Scott based on British or Irish folk materials. However, *Scotch Pastoral* for flute and piano (published 1914) deserves mention. A set of variations on the tune 'Ye Banks and Braes o' Bonnie Doon', the piece not only offers the flautist an opportunity for brilliant technical display, but also is a veritable catalogue of Scott's rhythmic and harmonic techniques to date. The recognisable tune gives the audience something familiar to cling to while Scott educates them in how to listen to his 'advanced' idiom. He even chaffs his critics by subjecting the tune to what could be called the *Lotus Land* treatment: halving the tempo and shifting the theme's pentatonic mode toward Aeolian or Dorian with occasional 'exotic' inflections.

By contrast, String Quartet No. 1 (premiered 1919) is a suite in five movements: Prelude, Pastorale, Scherzo on an Irish Air, Elegy, and *Rondo retrospettivo*. The retrospectiveness of the final movement consists in the return of themes from the earlier movements. Here the lack of key signature in all but one of the four movements could rightly be interpreted as an indication of a C major tonality for the entire work. The first note we hear is a C in the treble range of the cello, and four of the five movements end on a C major chord (the Pastorale ends on a D-flat major chord). The Scherzo has a key signature of two flats, but the obsessively repeated Irish tune is in the Dorian mode with C as the tonic.

Within the first, second and fourth movements the tonal procedure is nearly identical to that of the brief *Sonnet 1* for violin and piano (1914), which moves from a tonally ambiguous beginning to a fully tonal C major conclusion after many colourful wanderings between apparent atonality and vague tonality. The quartet is also like the sonnet in that, when there is a clearly discernible melody, it is usually diatonic with occasional chromatic inflections, no matter how deeply buried it may be in non-tonal intervallic doublings, non-diatonic chordal slidings, or other tonally disruptive accompaniments.

The Scherzo's modal tune is treated in much the same way as the theme in *Scotch Pastoral*, with constantly varying tonal, modal, chromatic and non-tonal accompaniments – though in the First Quartet, these maniacally inventive colour changes are more of an assault on than an invitation to the ear. At times Scott exploits the tonal ambiguity of the Dorian mode to shift the accompaniment in the direction of F major – without changing a note, the tune is now in the Mixolydian mode. The reinterpretation of notes shared between modes is one of the chief characteristics of Scott's later pan-modality, even when the modes are stranger to our ears than the folk-music modes referenced here.

The final movement attempts to resolve the question of how such contrasting genres, colours, and modal, tonal, or atonal harmonic textures can coexist in the same work. Thus the return of themes from the earlier movements is not merely a mnemonic device exploited to create unity. The juxtaposition of such disparate themes in musical time and space in a way that is satisfying both to mind and ear requires a deft manœuvering of half and whole steps, one becoming the other as we move between fragments of chromatic, modal or tonal scales – another characteristic of Scott's later pan-modality.

Scott does not yet know how to harness these resources to satisfy the developmental demands of the traditional sonata form, hence the First Quartet's being a suite. More than thirty years later he would finally feel adequate to the task of applying these resources to a traditional four-movement string quartet, his second.

The Piano Trio No. 1 (premiered 1920) explores another important technique of Scott's later pan-modality, perhaps the most essential technique: replacing chord-based harmonic rhythm with movement between modes. Whereas in the First Quartet chords often change from beat to beat, in the First Piano Trio they change from bar to bar or phrase to phrase. This more extended harmonic rhythm, which passes fluently from pentatonic to diatonic to hexatonic (whole tone) and octatonic (symmetrical scale) harmonies and lines produces a score practically unequalled in Scott's œuvre for sheer opulence and beauty. Also, there are many adventuresome new sounds resulting from persistent doubling of lines in fourths and the variety of textures and timbres evoked from the strings.

Laid out in the traditional four-movement format, with the scherzo coming second, the work is lyrical and dramatic by turn, but ultimately episodic. It presents listeners with a steady stream of brilliant ideas. Form, however, is merely suggested by their emergence, disappearance, and return. Yet the fluency of the harmonic rhythm creates coherence and results in a unified sound world, startlingly like that of Stravinsky's *Firebird* of ten years before. But the problem of developmental argument remains to be solved.

The Piano Quintet No. 1 (premiered 1920; published 1925) seems to have been conceived originally as a sextet for three violins, viola, violoncello and piano premiered in 1903. It was reworked as a quintet in 1911–12, then further revised for the 1920 premiere, and finally published more than twenty years after conception.[4] I suspect the long gestation period was not merely a result of the stylistic and formal challenges Scott was struggling with. There were other issues he could not easily resolve, such as the musical expression of exalted spiritual states he had personally experienced and the representation of his evolving mystical philosophy in musical form.

The First Piano Quintet may reflect Scott's discovery of Theosophy and Vedanta, an Indian mystical philosophy.[5] In the published version the first movement (of

[4] Reviews indicate that the Sextet was in three movements. A piano quintet, also in three movements, was begun in 1904 and premiered in 1907 alongside the Sextet. It appears that these works were fused to create the four-movement Piano Quintet we know today.

[5] It is not easy to determine the exact date of this discovery from Scott's first autobiography, *My Years of Indiscretion* (Mills & Boon, 1924). Scott wrote of attending a Sunday evening Queens Hall lecture by the theosophist Annie Besant (pp. 95–7), which I believe to have taken place on 29 June 1902. He then states that his discovery of the writings of Swami Vivekananda, first Indian teacher of Vedanta in the West, came soon after the Besant lecture (pp. 97, 111–12). Furthermore, after reading Vivekananda's book *Raja Yoga*, Scott 'began to experience those exalted states of consciousness promised by the author to all faithful practitioners' (p. 112). Vivekananda died in India in July 1902, not long after the Besant lecture. However, evidence points to 1904 as the date of Scott's discovery of Vadanta.

four) is given the unusual tempo marking *Andante con exaltazione*, and the Finale is marked *Allegro con molto spirito*, in which 'much spirit' possibly means not only spirited but also spiritual. Throughout the nearly forty-minute duration of the work the music passes through many psychological states – including spiritually exalted ones – each with its own harmonic colour. The great achievement of the First Piano Quintet is that Scott finds the means to contain so many moods in this vast self-portrait in sound. But it is hardly an essay in logical formal development.

By comparison with the First Quartet and the First Piano Trio, the First Piano Quintet is a stylistically retrospective work. It serves as a fitting close to the first period of Scott's major chamber works – just as the First Piano Trio looks forward and acts as a bridge to the major works of the 1950s. By that time Scott had evolved a repertoire of musical analogues to spiritual states and mystical notions that was sufficiently extensive to allow him at last to solve the problem of how to integrate such autobiographical references into a logically evolving form.

1921–1930

A decade of experiment for Scott, this period is notable for being entirely free of the composer's earlier and later preoccupation with traditional chamber-music genres. Scott was developing the compositional procedures of pan-modality, in which the functions of modulation between keys and movement between chords are taken over by changes of mode coming section-by-section, phrase-by-phrase, or bar-by-bar. This new approach is announced towards the beginning of the decade by *The Extatic* [sic] *Shepherd* (published *c.* 1922). But there are gaps in our understanding of Scott's stylistic evolution because of the number of as-yet unpublished and unrecorded pieces from the 1920s.

The Extatic Shepherd is not as well-known as Debussy's famous 1913 work for solo flute, *Syrinx*. Yet Scott's piece plays a critical role in the development of his later chamber music. It also has the distinction of being one of the few works with overtly theosophical associations. The odd spelling of the title points towards the Greek-derived Latin word *extasis*: displacement from oneself. Though this could be a coy reference to astral projection, there are more important associations.

In the 1920s theosophists were expectantly waiting for the appearance of a World Teacher who would use the young J. Krishnamurti as mouthpiece. The World Teacher was called Lord Maitreya, a figure borrowed from Buddhism. Many theosophists believed that Lord Maitreya was identical with a so-called Christ consciousness that inspired Jesus during the last three years of his life and that he had previously 'manifested as Shri Krishna in India'.[6] Krishna is often depicted as a cowherd playing the flute, causing his listeners to dance in ecstasy; Jesus Christ is often called the Good Shepherd. Thus the 'ecstatic shepherd' is a conflation of these figures. Even the X in the title may be coded reference to Christ (as in the familiar abbreviation for Christmas: Xmas).

Debussy's *Syrinx* is given the key signature of D-flat and eventually ends on that note, by which time all twelve pitches of the chromatic scale have been traversed,

[6] Gregory Tillett, *The Elder Brother: A Life of Charles Webster Leadbeater* (Routledge & Kegan Paul, 1982), p. 105.

some as ornaments and some as indications of movement towards other tonal centres or modes, such as the whole-tone scale at the end. By contrast, Scott's piece has no key signature and few if any tonal references. Yet it constantly departs from and returns to B, where it also finally ends. The ear interprets the notes of any rapid run as a scale with a particular colour. By altering a single pitch in a run, even by just a half step, Scott changes the colour. Some runs sound exotic and vaguely Asian, others bluesy. Obstinate repetition of a series of pitches with longer durations forces us to hear them as a quasi-melody with harmonic implications of a particular colour. Yet they are really nothing more than permutations of either a known and nameable mode or a synthetic one invented by the composer through expanding half steps or contracting whole steps.

From this point forward, Scott's melody and harmony would be determined by his choice of modes, his horizontal and vertical ordering of pitches within them, and his movement between them. With a solo flute line, Scott could only juxtapose modes. But with other instruments, such as the guitar, he could also superimpose them. Thus the pivotal work of this decade for the evolution of Scott's pan-modality is the Guitar Sonatina (1927), written for Andres Segovia. Long thought lost, the work was rediscovered in 2001 and subsequently published.[7]

The sonatina extends the modal processes of *The Extatic Shepherd* into the new sound world opened up by the guitar's ability to move fluently between single lines, lines doubled in various intervals, chordal formations, and melody plus accompaniment. The piece progresses, often disjunctively, between phrases with modal (pentatonic), tonal (functional harmonic), chromatic (nonfunctional harmonic, as in parallel diminished seventh chord references that sound modulatory but never arrive in a key), or atonal construction (as in the opening four-note intervallic cell, which becomes a unifying motive throughout the piece).

The first movement, *Adagio quasi introduzione*, is longer than the second and third movements combined – so Scott's calling it an introduction seems to be an understatement. However, its quasi-improvisatory structure, full of caesuras separating apparently unconnected phrases, functions in much the same way as the opening section of a Bach toccata, as a 'trying out' of the tonality and touch of the key- or fingerboard.

Much has been made of Scott's early use of quartal harmony. The sonatina creates new sounds and colours by focusing on doublings in thirds and sixths. Freshness results from using only major thirds (for example), thus erasing any suggestion of tonality even in quasi-modal or quasi-tonal melodic fragments.

The second movement, *Allegretto pensoso*, is less hesitant, but still 'thoughtful' – as if the possibilities of the instrument were still being tested, yet with greater confidence. We no longer get fragments, but fully formed phrases, increasingly idiomatic for the guitar.

[7] For these factual details and further information, see Allan Jones, 'Cyril Scott, Andres Segovia and the Sonatina for Guitar', in *Symposium of the International Musicological Society* (SIMS 2004), 11–16 July 2004, Melbourne, Australia (http://oro.open.ac.uk/40744/1/Scott%20Segovia%20and%20the%20Sonatina%20for%20guitar.pdf; accessed 15 January 2017).

All hesitancy is gone from the final rushing Allegro, which 'quotes' from traditional guitar textures, *à la espagnol*, though they sound quite different as a result of the intervallic and harmonic procedures to which we have been exposed in the previous movements. Towards the end there is a reminiscence of the opening of the first movement, as if to show how far we have come, before the final impetuous conclusion.

We get a glimpse of Scott's humility and humanity in the progress of the piece, which simultaneously enacts a threefold journey:

> That of a composer diffidently experimenting with the possibilities of writing for a new instrument.
>
> That of a performer learning to apply this unfamiliar new sound world to the instrument while being shown how it could revitalise 'tired and true [*sic*]' guitar gestures and textures.
>
> That of a listener being shown how to 'develop an ear' for new melodic and harmonic processes that operate beyond the range of traditional tonality – and experiencing delight instead of shock when assaulted, as it were, by the rush of notes in the final Allegro.

Thus, the sonatina projects a persona – Pierrot plays the guitar.

1931–1940

Scott published three of his major occult writings during this decade: *Music: Its Secret Influence throughout the Ages* (1933), *An Outline of Modern Occultism* (1935), and *The Greater Awareness* (1936). I discuss these books in a later chapter. Suffice it to say here that Scott implied the existence of a continuum of musical expression comprised of the following levels:

> Human music, dealing with emotions from the lowest passions to the highest forms of romantic love (often chromatically tonal)
>
> Nature music, dealing with human impressions of landscapes, weather, and the elements, as well as the nature spirits (fairies, elves, and the like) said to lie behind natural processes (often diatonically modal or pentatonic)
>
> Lower deva music, dealing with 'desire angels' who express a trans-human love[8] (exotic modes, such as the hexatonic or octatonic scales or Indian *rāgas*)
>
> Higher deva music, dealing with angels of shaping, creation, and the abstract mind (synthetic modes, especially those created by non-tonal intervallic doublings)

[8] 'One of the chief Deva characteristics is Love': Cyril Scott, *Music and its Secret Influence throughout the Ages* [1933], 5th edn (Inner Traditions, 2013), p. 114.

> Buddhic music, which expresses 'that love which *is* God'[9] (possibly pan-modality itself, as an expression of the unifying force of what Scott calls the 'All-Consciousness' or the 'All-Life'[10])

Furthermore, Scott described several states of consciousness in *The Greater Awareness* that could also be linked to music: life consciousness (music of humans and nature spirits), love consciousness (that of humans and lower devas), knowledge consciousness (that of higher devas), and joy or bliss consciousness (buddhic music). It is difficult to imagine that having worked all this out, Scott did not experiment with how it could be applied to his own music. The pan-modal procedures he was developing provided the means.

Thus, of the two miniatures for piano trio published in 1931, *Cornish Boat Song* provides an example of love consciousness. It seems to be a straightforward folksong setting (human realm), but odd non-tonal distortions of the harmony at important cadences suggest a subtle lifting above the ordinary run of human love. *Little Folk-Dance* begins with a banal and childlike tune picked out with one hand in the piano and accompanied by strumming pizzicato in the violin and *col legno* tapping in the cello, but builds ecstatically after the strings take up their bows into what sounds remarkably like a parody of Ravel's *Boléro* (premiered three years earlier), only to end in a whirling dervish dance – all in less than three minutes. That would be joy consciousness. Similarly, the reel of *Pastoral and Reel* for cello and piano (published 1926) exemplifies life consciousness in the human realm; whereas the eerie pizzicato chordal slides in the *Pastoral* suggest the other-than-human inhabitants of the same rural landscape.

The *Ballade* for cello and piano (published 1934) provides a deeper exploration of the continuums described above. The piece is episodic. The episodes are differentiated by modes. Some, like the opening, are solemn and bell-like – a theme that recurs and develops throughout the piece. Others are joyful and pentatonic, perhaps the music of nature or nature spirits. One passage, based on the octatonic scale, expresses terror, as in an encounter with some superhuman figure of darkness. Several sections superimpose modes, one in the cello and another in the piano – with the latter's atonality and mirror-like sequences implying a transhuman being whose nature is peace. In the end, the cello and piano play the bell-like theme in unison, indicating a point of arrival.

Though the title *Ballade* seems not to tell us much, it may perhaps explain the episodic nature of the piece. It is a *story* – at *least* the story of a journey between modes, perhaps also between their associated states of consciousness and the realms and beings encountered in each. The cellist is the subjective experiencer of the journey, the hero of the ballad. The pianist generates the succession of moods/modes through which the cellist journeys. If the bell-like theme is a call from afar, perhaps to a temple and the ordeals of initiation, the cellist passes through these ordeals and

[9] Ibid., p. 94 (original emphasis).

[10] Cyril Scott, *The Greater Awareness* [1936], reprinted edn (Routledge Kegan Paul, 1981), pp. 202, 238. I discuss examples in the chamber music of each level but the last. A possible candidate for Buddhic music occurs in the Second Piano Sonata (published 1935) in the sublime chorale-like Andante beginning at the end of p. 7.

arrives at last at a state of awestruck reverence, at peace (unison) with the summoning call and whatever principle, ideal, or being(s) it represents.

The Serenade for mouth organ and piano (1938) was written for the harmonica virtuoso Larry Adler, who also premiered pieces by Vaughan Williams and Milhaud. Though not commercially recorded, the piece has been recently revived on the internet in a spectacular YouTube performance.[11] It proves to be a single-movement work about four minutes in duration, hauntingly lyrical and technically dazzling by turns. Here the pan-modality operates by phrases rather than by sections or bars, and the continually evolving melody is inflected by the chordal possibilities of the harmonica, including the instrument's characteristic dominant seventh chords, employed for purely ornamental purposes. I place this serenade in the love-consciousness category (the title itself is a clue) – but this is a transhuman love. Theosophists believed that devas (angels) communicated with each other in a language of sound and colour.[12] If Scott ever tried to imagine such a language and portray it in music, it would surely sound like this.

Fantasie orientale for violin and piano (published 1938) is a little gem. Though seeming to hearken back to *Lotus Land*, premiered more than thirty years earlier, it eschews indolent longing in favour of joy consciousness, the spiritual bliss that Scott described in 1936 as the 'one perpetual joy of which all others are but off-shoots and which is not dependent on the world, seeing that it comes from a consciousness within ourselves if we but strive hard enough to attain it.'[13]

Given Scott's 'healthy sense of humour',[14] I suspect the word *orientale* was intended to wave a red flag in front of bullish critics, who were likely to declare the work another example of his wearisome Eastern exoticism – never realising there was a quiet revolution going on in the pan-modal structure of the piece. For listeners wanting to practise how to hear pan-modal music, Scott provides helpful signposts: every change in texture is accompanied by a change in mode, and similar textures – such as the quasi-improvised, incantatory main theme – are usually in the same mode. From time to time there are startlingly percussive chords in the piano part that are vertical versions of the mode generating the melody in the violin. The longer a mode is in force the more its colour takes on the function of a key. Thus modes become the organising principle for sections, and movement between them a replacement for modulation between keys.

Sonata lirica for violin and piano (1937; unpublished)[15] is the one traditionally structured chamber work of the decade (since we know nothing of the as-yet unpublished String Trio No. 1 of 1931). It could be considered an experiment in applying

[11] Visit https://www.youtube.com/watch?v=XXNP4L9ryso (accessed 10 January 2017).

[12] The first appearance of this notion in Scott's books occurs in *The Influence of Music on History and Morals: A Vindication of Plato* (Theosophical Publishing House, 1928), p. 103.

[13] Scott, *Greater Awareness*, p. 225.

[14] Noted by Sampsel in connection with reminiscences of Scott's publisher, Robert Elkin, *Cyril Scott: A Bio-Bibliography*, p. 168.

[15] Not listed in Sampsel. Date of composition from the website of the Cyril Scott estate: http://www.cyrilscott.net/chamber-violin-piano (accessed 15 January 2017).

the still-evolving principles of pan-modality to a multi-movement work. So far these principles had been tried only in short character pieces and the episodic *Ballade*. It may be that Scott was unsure of how successful this experiment would be, hence his not numbering *Sonata lirica* as Violin Sonata No. 2. In fact, the title may have been an attempt to deflect attention away from the form of the piece, often a point of attack for Scott's critics – as well as a coded reference to the love consciousness, whose chief characteristic is soaring lyricism, as in the Harmonica Serenade.

The first of the sonata's three movements frequently employs the octatonic mode, and the third a pentatonic, giving to each a characteristic sound profile, within which phrases and sections proceed with reference to other modes. The tempo marking of the third movement is *Allegro vigoroso*, perhaps a reference to the life consciousness. The haunting middle movement, *Andante tranquillo*, is suffused with transcendental longing. Once again, the solo instrumentalist is made to play a role: the meditating spiritual aspirant.

1941–1950

The paucity of chamber music composed during this decade can be explained by the disruption of the war years, during which Scott was often without a piano, as well as by a decision 'to give up the idea of composing any more'. But he was told by his spiritual Master that '*they* had new work – musical work' for him to do.[16] Apparently this new work involved chamber music, though the two works known to have been completed during the 1940s – String Trio No. 2 (1948) and Violin Sonata No. 2 (1950; unpublished) – have yet to be commercially recorded. Several chamber works published or premiered at the beginning of the following decade probably originated in this one. But, for the moment, there is an unsatisfactory gap in our knowledge of Scott's development in this genre following his compositional hiatus.

1951–1960

This is the decade of Scott's late works. It could also be called the decade of his finally reconciling the German training he received in the 1890s and the formal rigours it demanded with his French-leaning love of colour in sound. For fifty years Scott had been struggling with the problem posed by his Piano Quartet, Op. 16. Now he had collected the tools required for a grand synthesis in which pan-modality took over the functions of generating melody, harmony, harmonic rhythm, modulation and the overall sound world of a section, of a single-movement, or even of a multi-movement work. The problem was to find a pan-modal equivalent to the logical unfolding and development of thematic material within a movement and across the time span of multi-movement works in sonata form. Scott solved this problem in his Viola Sonata, and having mastered the technique produced more than a dozen new works for chamber duos, trios, quartets, and quintets.

The Viola Sonata was apparently premiered in 1939 but did not achieve its present form until 1953. It remained unpublished until recently, and was recorded and

[16] Cyril Scott, *Bone of Contention: Life-Story and Confessions* (Arco, 1969), pp. 210 (no piano), 217, 218 (original emphasis).

released in 2013. It takes the familiar three-movement form that is characteristic of so much of Scott's chamber music: a sonata-like first movement, a scherzo-like second movement – called Humoresque – and a final fast movement that opens with an Adagio introduction fulfilling the function of the traditional slow movement and closes with reminiscences of the themes of the earlier movements. Scott's pan-modality is so seamlessly integrated in this work that it is barely possible to follow changes in mode aurally. Thus the Viola Sonata is perhaps the most demanding of Scott's chamber works to listen to – though it is a compelling, if brooding, production.

I suspect that the work's long gestation was the result of Scott's attempt to tackle the challenge implied in the following statement from *The Greater Awareness*: 'The genuine Occultist ... may be compared to the true artist who aims at creating a perfect work of art; but with the Occultist, that work of art is not an external creation, but is actually his own self.'[17] As the section title that precedes this quotation implies, the procedure, in art as in life, is 'the cultivation of understanding and discrimination [i.e. discernment]', or to 'Know thyself – and – forget thyself'. The result could be called knowledge consciousness: to know something (or oneself) 'in a manner far transcending all theoretical speculation'.[18]

The Viola Sonata culminates Scott's struggle to master the new compositional possibilities opened up by the Guitar Sonatina of 1927. To appreciate this mastery, we must develop new ears and new analytic tools. A thorough analysis of this work would likely provide the key to construction for all that Scott wrote for the remainder of his life. Until such tools have been evolved, performers and listeners are faced with a formidable challenge in the cultivation of understanding and discernment – the development of an ability to track the recurrence of non-tonal melodic and harmonic patterns across the work's nearly twenty-five-minute duration entirely without words. Listening to the piece thus becomes an exercise in self-forgetting. If the tendency I have noted for Scott to project a persona onto the musical protagonists of his works for solo instrument with piano holds true here, the violist is enacting the phrase 'Know thyself – and – forget thyself' in a contemplative process of self-examination, not without drama, that leads from selfish actor/experiencer to selfless knower.[19]

Having completed this process of compositional self-mastery, Scott returned to his First Violin Sonata. His revisions shortened the forty-minute original by ten minutes, not only resulting in a much more structurally integrated work but also opening the way for further numbered violin sonatas.

The Piano Trio No. 2 (published 1951) is one of the most attractive pieces from this decade. A single-movement work of about ten minutes in duration, by turns dramatic, exuberant, mysterious, dance-like and lyrical, the work's pan-modality is strongly influenced by the otherworldly, transhuman sound of the octatonic scale. If the lyrical elements express the love consciousness, the dance elements bring

[17] Scott, *Greater Awareness*, p. 80.

[18] Ibid., pp. 77, 184, 238.

[19] See ibid., pp. 175–84, for the author's thoughts on self-knowledge.

in the life consciousness. Yet both are subsumed into the exuberance of the joy consciousness.

The Quintet for clarinet and strings (premiered 1951) is similarly attractive. Scott dedicated the piece to the British clarinet virtuoso Gervase de Peyer, having been impressed by his playing. I suspect that Scott heard de Peyer play the Brahms Clarinet Quintet in B minor, Op. 115. There is a sly reference towards the end of Scott's quintet to the arpeggiated flourishes of the central section of the slow movement of the Brahms.

Halfway through Scott's quintet there is an eerie passage for high string harmonics. If we think of it as a devic/angelic vision or visitation, we might have a clue to the musical construction of the piece. Sonically, the six or so minutes that precede this visitation would subtly prepare us for the alien sound of the mode that expresses it. Otherwise it would seem like a capricious non-sequitur. The six or so minutes that follow the visitation would then react to and integrate it. Once again, the clarinettist seems to be playing the role of human protagonist receiving this visitation, perhaps by the angel of death. Though Brahms's Clarinet Quintet was one of the composer's final musical testaments, the mood of resignation in its slow movement is turned to triumph in Scott's piece, perhaps reflecting his theosophical beliefs about the afterlife.

Another reflection of these beliefs appears in Scott's String Quartet No. 2 (1951).[20] Scott reported that while working on the piece he received word that a beloved friend, Ena Mathis, had died. So he 'included an *In Memoriam* movement'. Ena had 'a prodigious sense of humour'. She would goad Scott 'to talk about matters occult – in which she did not believe' and then would laugh 'as if the whole thing were a stupendous joke'. Scott claimed that after her death Ena could be seen by a 'clairvoyant acquaintance', who passed on messages from her, including one that his 'occult "revelations"' had 'helped to orientate her in her new though happy surroundings'.[21] These autobiographical details are encoded into the second and third of the quartet's four movements.

The *In memoriam* movement is the quartet's second, marked *Quasi marche funèbre* – but this is no British funeral march. The irregularly repeated open-fifth pizzicati in the cello are like strokes on a temple drum or gong. The mode is Eastern in flavour and seems to rise solemnly and sublimely above mere human grieving. If Scott depicted the afterlife for Ena in speech while she was alive, why should he not attempt to do so in music after her death? One thinks of the famous scene in the Egyptian Book of the Dead where the heart of the deceased is weighed before the gods.

The *col legno* and pizzicato rustlings of the following scherzo sound like the rattling bones of a classic dance of death, swirling beneath and around plaintively bowed solo phrases. Oddly, the tempo marking is *Allegro amabile*. Doubtless, Scott was poking fun at his friend's – and conventional – ideas of death, and the scherzo is an *amiable* jest.

[20] Date of composition from Stephen Lloyd, liner notes for *Cyril Scott: String Quartets* (Dutton CDLX 7138).

[21] Scott, *Bone of Contention*, pp. 207–8.

The outer movements, too, could reflect Scott's beliefs about the afterlife. Thus the theosophical notion of the soul's evolution through lifetime after lifetime finds an analogue in the first movement's opening fanfare, which, like the soul, returns again and again in a variety of forms.[22] The final movement is marked *Allegro con spirito* – and it is after all the *spirit* that is said to reincarnate. Perhaps the hubbub of the finale and the final return of the fanfare from the first movement are yet another amiable message for Ena: Be prepared to come back. Though this interpretation invites the challenge that Scott's typical formal and developmental procedures in his later chamber music always operate in this way, it is possible that he adopted these procedures *because* they provided musical analogues to his beliefs. In any case, the Second Quartet is one of Scott's most lively, colourful, and inventive scores and can be enjoyed purely on the basis of its novel sound world and formal play.

The title of the *Sonata melodica* for violin and piano (premiered 1951) immediately signals a relation between this work and the *Sonata lirica* composed nearly fifteen years earlier. To further underline the relation, both works conclude with a movement marked *Allegro vigoroso*, though a curious element of restraint is added in the *Melodica* with the words *ma non troppo*. Once again, Scott wanted us to know that this work, too, stands outside the series of numbered violin sonatas.

Like its predecessor, the *Sonata melodica* begins with the soaring lyricism of love consciousness. However, this mood is quickly shut down by a noisy peroration in the piano. The dramatic arc of the piece appears to be a struggle to recover and sustain the original mood. Thus what differentiates the *Melodica* from the *Lirica* is this element of contrast and the dramatic arc it makes possible.

The pan-modal language of the *Melodica* is far more integrated than that of the *Lirica*. In fact, a listener coming to Scott's music for the first time with the *Melodica* – and it is an excellent introduction – might assume that it is merely tonal in an unconventional way reminiscent of contemporaneous works by Hindemith, though perhaps more neo-romantic than neo-classical. The title *Melodica* may even be a warning to critics not to be deceived by what appears to be a reversion to tonality. Careful analysis would reveal that the melodies are constructed in the same pan-modal manner as any other chamber work of Scott's from this period. If Scott was bothered by a possible lack of unity in the earlier work, in which the first and third movements differed in modal profile, he has resolved the problem here.

Furthermore, if Scott was interested in creating a non-episodic dramatic narrative, thus resolving issues of continuity raised in the *Ballade*, he was here entirely successful. Indeed, the implied narrative structure of the piece may be the reason why Scott did not number it among his violin sonatas. The lovely and moving central movement seems to portray a person suffering from the loneliness of spiritual isolation, becoming reconciled to it, and finally transcending it. Once again, the violinist is made to play the role of someone experiencing a subjective state.

The single-movement *Aubade* for recorder (or flute or violin) and piano (published 1953) is a good practice piece for training the ear to listen effectively to the colour language of pan-modality. Every phrase is in a different mode, but the

[22] As early as 1917, Hull suggested a correlation between Scott's development of musical themes and the appearance of 'the same soul in successive bodies' (*Cyril Scott*, p. 98).

recorder and piano always share the same mode. Even without being able to name or otherwise identify that mode, the listener can clearly discern the changes in colour from phrase to phrase. An aubade is a love poem associated with the dawn. But the music seems to have the flavour of both the love consciousness and the joy consciousness. The persona established by the unfamiliar sound of the recorder is probably transhuman. Perhaps we have here a desire angel (hence the love) greeting the dawn (hence the joy).

The Violin Sonatas Nos. 3 (1955) and 4 (1956; unpublished) and the Cello Sonata (1958) seem to be more abstract than the works discussed so far. Yet in all three sonatas the interaction between the solo string instrument and the piano sounds almost conversational. Recalling Scott's notion of the colour language of devas, we could perhaps find a way into this elusive music by imagining a conversation between the human emotional warmth of the strings and the nonhuman power and sublime peace and joy that Scott ascribed to devas in the piano.

Such imagery makes it easier to perceive that the two instruments are often in different modes and that the real conversation is between these modes. The solo instrument may express something in one mode and be answered by another mode in the piano, or vice versa. Or both instruments imitate each other with varying degrees of distortion, as if only partially understanding each other. There are cases in which two modes are superimposed, as if these interlocutors were talking at once, and others when both instrumentalists are in the same mode, having fully understood each other.

It is possible that these experiments in musical representation of a transhuman language of colour and sound and of conversation between humans and devas were inspired by the contemporaneous publication of *The Kingdom of the Gods* (1952) by the theosophist Geoffrey Hodson. This described the results of decades of clairvoyant investigation of nature spirits and devas and provided colour illustrations of them. From the middle of the 1950s, Scott seems to be preoccupied with imagining transhuman music and the drama inherent in the possibility of human and transhuman interaction. This was the last stage in the development of Scott's approach to pan-modality: now the modes themselves became personae, not unlike the notion in Indian music that a *rāga* (mode) is the aural embodiment of a god or goddess (deva).

In the slow movement of the Trio for clarinet, violoncello and piano (1955?), Scott may be imagining the possibility of a human being lifted up to experience a transhuman perspective on humanity. It expresses a spiritual sadness beyond self-pity – perhaps a reflection of Scott's concern for suffering humanity. He communicated this concern throughout his literary career in his writings on the occult and his cultural critiques of the selfishness that causes so many personal, national and international problems. *Man, the Unruly Child*, the latest of these critiques, had been published in 1953.

A number of works from the 1950s have yet to be published or recorded commercially, including the Piano Quintet No. 2 (1952; unpublished), Piano Trio No. 3 (1957; unpublished), and String Quartet No. 3 (published 1960).

1961–1970

During the last decade of Scott's long life, his compositional output diminished considerably and consisted primarily of chamber music. Writing in 2018, the following works have yet to be recorded commercially: the Flute Sonata (premiered 1961); the *Trio pastorale* for flute, cello and piano (premiered 1961); and what appears to be Scott's final chamber work, a sonata for two violins and piano (published 1964).

Luckily, we are able to appraise what appears to be Scott's final essay in the genre, his String Quartet No. 4 (published 1968). Here Scott seems to be imagining a transhuman music even more abstract than that in his previous attempts. The human element has been eliminated. The quartet often plays sliding chords in unison rhythm creating chilly yet subtly coloured curtains of sound – the highest angels, perhaps, represented as the shimmering of an aurora borealis.

We do not need to believe in nature spirits, devas, angels or the afterlife to appreciate Scott's music. He was driven by a desire to create a unified language of colour and sound that could replace the melodic, harmonic, tonal and formal procedures of the nineteenth-century musical tradition he inherited – and perhaps to show a way forward for other composers. The great tragedy of Cyril Scott's life was that critics and audiences could not see the musical revolutionary beneath the theosophical trappings.

14

Operas and Music for the Theatre

STEVEN MARTIN

CYRIL Scott was a polymath. Nowhere is this more evident than in his considerable body of works for the theatre, including plays, musical plays, operas, operetta and incidental music. These, more than any single book, poem, painting or piece of music, embody a synthesis of Scott the musician, poet, author, artist, mystic, theosophist, occultist and man. The lure of the theatre or opera house inspired a number of varied and interesting works from Scott's pen; each reflects a different facet of Scott's aesthetic life, beliefs and character, enabling us to paint a fuller picture of this remarkable person.

This chapter is a survey of ten of Scott's musical works for the stage. The process of finding references and scores (or references to scores), and examining these works, has led me to suspect that Scott wrote more incidental music, all traces of which seem to have been irrevocably lost.[1] Of the ten pieces left, only one has been published; only five have been performed; several scores have been lost and one exists only in fragments. Many readers will not have seen or have easy access to the sources (especially the scores), let alone heard or seen performances of these works, so in each case I examine what performance materials exist, and endeavour to give a detailed description of the work in question – both the storyline and music, especially when both were the work of Scott himself. I begin with the operas, moving to the operetta (*Janet and Felix*), then to the musical plays and the incidental music. In dealing with the works in turn, and in this way, I hope that each will reveal another facet of Scott's life and thoughts. Each embodies a different combination, a different synthesis of Scott the composer and occultist, and Scott the artist, or the author, the philosopher, the moralist, or humourist, or all seven.

* * * * *

The first of Scott's major stage works to be performed was his opera *The Alchemist.* In his article 'Some Pitfalls of Operatic Composing', Scott provides an explanation of his approach to opera – a thesis that evolved but never, in essence, changed throughout his life. Written some four months before the premiere of *The Alchemist,* Scott's article claimed that he had created an opera which 'entirely tells its own tale, and which is varied enough in [music and] action to sustain the interest of the beholder'.[2] Although his article is full of advice for would-be opera composers, Scott does not patronise, but rather offers his experience and justifies his method

[1] Considering Scott wrote a number of plays, it is hard to imagine that he did not attempt to add music to them.

[2] Cyril Scott 'Some Pitfalls of Operatic Composing', *The Monthly Musical Record,* 2 February 1925, p. 36.

and approach, in the hope that 'what I can do others can do, and probably do it a good deal better'.[3]

No doubt aware that others may have perceived his musical style as opulent and excessive, Scott believed that a practical and economical approach is essential to writing a successful opera. He stressed the importance of clear word setting but, in addition to this, believed that the music in itself must be sufficient to tell the story on its own. The story must be simple, married to the music with no padding or repeated text, the whole able to maintain the interest of the audience in such a way as to 'make it straight to the human heart and brain'.[4] In order to achieve greater cohesion between drama and music, and to prevent any disagreement about cuts in libretto or music, Scott believed that it was preferable for an opera composer to write his own libretto – a piece of his own advice that he invariably followed.

Achieving the right atmosphere through setting and scenery was also important to Scott, for whom the visual in opera was as significant as the music. Opera, he argued, is an art form capable of revealing great depths of meaning and emotion. He believed that it was preferable for operas to be set in distant (usually past) times, because those set in modern times or presented in modern dress, he observed, were less convincing. The power and meaning of the music and drama is compromised when presented in modern trappings, because operatic conventions, such as the artificiality of sung dialogue (where people express thoughts, feelings and passion in song), seem preposterous when the period and circumstances are immediately familiar to the audience. Scott's operas and other stage works always carried a moral, and it was important that a synthesis, a convincing 'unity of three arts – the musical, the dramatic *and* pictorial' be achieved in order to get that moral across to the audience.[5]

THE ALCHEMIST

Creating an opera to his own exacting specifications was one thing, but securing a performance was another. When Scott finished *The Alchemist* in 1917, the chances of a production of a new opera by a British composer in England were slim. Opera seasons at Covent Garden had been suspended (due to the war) and, although a number of travelling opera companies continued touring, they mainly kept to a repertoire of old favourites or novelties which could be easily staged. According to Scott, Thomas Beecham, at that time running his own touring company, looked at *The Alchemist* and agreed to produce it. Unfortunately, Beecham's company collapsed before the production was planned in detail.[6] Scott's Continental publisher, Schott's Söhne of Mainz, took on the task of securing a premiere, and applied to several German opera houses, eventually coming to an arrangement with Wiesbaden, who agreed to stage it. In the spring of 1923, just before the rehearsals started, the opera house suffered a major fire and the production was abandoned. In October 1923 Scott himself approached Percy Pitt, who was, by this time, chief conductor

[3] Ibid., p. 36.

[4] Ibid., p. 37.

[5] Ibid.

[6] Cyril Scott: *My Years of Indiscretion* (Mills & Boon, 1924), p. 160.

and artistic director of the British National Opera Company, a new touring company formed out of the remnants of Beecham's company in 1921.[7] In his letter Scott suggested a meeting with Pitt, so that he could play through the opera and a ballet, clearly with a view to securing a performance by the British National Opera Company. This meeting may well have taken place, but whatever the outcome, the company never performed *The Alchemist*.[8]

The premiere eventually took place on Tuesday 28 May 1925 at the Essen Stadttheater, conducted by Felix Wolfes (1892–1971), and produced by Dr Alexander Schum. The opera was repeated on Wednesday 3 June. The cast was as follows:

> The Sage: Bruno Bergman (baritone)
> The Young Maid, daughter of the Sage: Sybil Richardson (soprano)
> The Young Man: Walter Favre (tenor)
> The Elemental: Erich Wolfgang Ritz (bass)
> A Jester: Leo de Leeuwe (tenor)
> The Sage's Three Disciples: Eyvind Laholm (tenor), Clemens Pabelick (baritone), Walter Döpp (bass)
> Mixed chorus of flower-gatherers, vassals, gnomes, monks and nuns (Essen Company)[9]

The Alchemist formed the second half of the evening. The first consisted of a performance of three ballets, all performed by the Essen Ballet Company and directed by Hannah Spohr, the resident Mistress of the Ballet.[10] Scott's *Karma* was performed after other ballets by Ernst Toch and Richard Zoellner.[11] Out of the two works by Scott performed that evening, the Essen critics preferred *Karma*, which moved one to write: 'Mr. Scott, seien Sie so lieb, und schreiben Sie recht viel für die Beine. Sie machen das wunderhübsch!' ('Mr. Scott, please be so kind as to write more for the legs. You do it so beautifully!')[12]

7 Their first production was *Aïda* at the Alhambra, Bradford, on 6 February 1922. Herbert Thompson Collection, University of Leeds, MS459/115.

8 Letter from Cyril Scott to Percy Pitt, 1 October 1923. British Library, Egerton MSS, Percy Pitt Papers, vol. 6, fol. 65. In a memo at the BBC dated 28 June 1927 (in Cyril Scott file, BBC WAC), Percy Pitt, discussing a proposed programme of Scott's music, recommended nothing longer than an hour as 'his idiom is a little bit monotonous'.

9 'Tagesprogramm des Stadttheaters', a poster advertising *The Alchemist* in the Franz Feldus Sammuling at the Stadtarchiv, Essen.

10 Spohr also choreographed *The Alchemist*.

11 Cyril Scott implies, in *Bone of Contention* (Aquarian Press, 1969), that *Karma* was not performed during the same evening as the premiere of *The Alchemist*, and that Hannah Spohr did not direct and choreograph *Karma* until 1930, at Dortmund (p. 188). I believe that this is incorrect, as the critic 'W. St.', in his review of *The Alchemist* (*The Monthly Musical Record*, 1 July 1925, pp. 196–7), states that Scott's *Karma* was performed at Essen on 28 May 1925.

12 Marcus Hehemann: 'Cyril Scott: Der Alchimist', *Essener Allgemeine Zeitung*, 29 May 1925. See also: Rolf Cunz, 'Uraufführungsabend der Essener Oper', *Essener Anzeiger*, 30 May 1925.

As with all of Scott's operas, *The Alchemist* is set to a scenario and libretto written by Scott himself. The inspiration for the storyline came, according to some sources, from an Indian folk tale, and to others, from an occult parable.[13] In fact there are probably elements of both, though tending more towards the latter, if we consider Scott's keen interest in the occult and Eastern culture and that the opera was listed as '*Der Alchimist*: Parabel (Oper) in 3 Szenen' in the Essen Stadttheater's *Wochenspielplan*.[14] The label 'parable opera' is appropriate, as it explains both the simplicity of the storyline and why Scott does not give his characters names, but refers to them simply as 'The Young Man' or 'The Sage'. For Scott the moral of the story is paramount; he purposefully negates any pitfalls by ensuring that the storyline and expression are clear and economical, deliberately avoiding any hint of esoteric excess.

The story revolves around the Young Man, who wants everything conducive to a life of materialistic prosperity, ignoring completely his spiritual needs. He approaches the Sage, who offers him the key to spiritual enlightenment, but the Young Man persists in his desire for wealth and possessions and begs the Sage for the magic spell by which the Young Man will be able to conjure a fierce genie (the Elemental), who will grant his every wish. This creature, once he has materialised, must be kept constantly busy with wishes for one hour. If he is not, he will destroy his master.

Needless to say, when the particularly ill-tempered creature appears, the Young Man quickly wishes for all the superficial trappings of happiness and fulfilment he can think of: gold, gems (carried in by gnomes and Orientals), a palace, vassals, dancing fairies, a lavishly decorated oriental robe, etc. The Young Man, running out of ideas, soon asks for a Jester, a fair-weather friend – symbolic of false friendships brought about through the lure of wealth. After suggesting a series of further wishes (prompting the appearance of a troupe of minstrels, a crystal goblet, chanting monks and nuns), the Jester flounders and, sensing impending doom, runs off. The Young Man can think of no more and, fleeing the murderous Elemental, he runs back to the Sage.

As the Sage disposes of the Elemental (by giving him the futile task of straightening a puppy's tail), calm is restored and the Young Man at last understands the folly of his ways and vows to follow the path towards enlightenment. The Sage gathers the Young Man and the disciples, who sit at his feet. He then sings (backed by a luscious orchestral accompaniment that would not be out of place in a Hollywood film score):

SAGE:
Confess to us the truth why thou didst go
in search of all these earthly things!

YOUNG MAN:
'Twas happiness I sought,
And what,
O Master, brings such happiness to birth
save wealth and gold,
aye the choice possessions of the earth?

[13] Jonathan Frank, 'An English Trio', *Musical Opinion*, September 1959, p. 795. This is one of the few sources suggesting *The Alchemist* is based on an Indian story.

[14] *Städtische Bühne Essen*, Spielzeit 1924/25. 8 Heft, p. 9.

SAGE:
'Tis as I thought.
By unreflecting men thou hast been taught
The old, old and barren fallacy
That external things of earth
Bring to birth felicity.
But, O friend! never so;
For know within thyself is ev'ry bliss
And he who chases after joys *without*
Must miss the very thing he seeks
Yea, his own divine and blissful soul,
At one with all humanity.

One of the most striking things about the opera is the simple storyline and tight organisation of the musical material. Each character or idea is given a distinctive theme: The Young Man is given a short four-note (sometimes pentatonic) tune; a regular, bustling ostinato (quavers, leaping in fourths) signifies the magical part and character of the Elemental; the Maid sings a folk-song-like melody, evocative of her calm Pre-Raphaelite coolness.

Throughout the score, Scott has kept to his principle of the audience being able to follow the story through music, independent of the words. To this end he uses his selection of leitmotifs in a clear and flexible way, influenced by an established allegorical musical language. For example, when the Young Man is happy (as he bounds along to the Sage at the beginning of the opera) his motif appears in parallel with itself at consonant intervals (3rds, 4ths). When things go wrong, his simple motif (simple rhythmically and tonally) appears in parallel, jumbled, dissonant intervals (2nds, 7ths). When the Elemental is defeated by the Sage, his bustling ostinato (mostly rising and falling in 4ths), symbolic of the relentlessness of his character and activity, subsides, descending, fragmenting, and gradually disappearing through the orchestration. The music associated with the Young Maid is the most conventionally tuneful, being a gently flowing, measured quasi-folk song (complete with flattened 7th) in triple time. The Sage's music is richer and more expansive, both in rhythm and pitch, incorporating comparatively wider intervals (5ths and 6ths). The Sage's music is the music of wisdom and enlightenment, leading to some very rich orchestrations at the end of the opera, when he promises the Young Man 'higher

Ex. 14.1 Scott, *The Alchemist*, Young Man's theme

Ex. 14.2 Scott, *The Alchemist*, Elemental's theme

Ex. 14.3 Scott, *The Alchemist,* Maid's theme

food, ay gems of wisdom'. All this, plus the fact that there is little musical development, makes for a very direct musical realisation of the story.

* * * * *

In their programme notes, both Felix Wolfes and Alexander Schum wrote enthusiastically about Scott and the opera, and in the reviews Wolfes was praised for his musicianship and Schum for his handling of the wishes sequence. As Scott related (in *Bone of Contention*), they encountered a few difficulties during rehearsals. First, preparations stalled while Scott made amendments to Helmut Andreae's flowery German translation. Scott also hints at another problem:

> At the final rehearsal there was nearly a serious row, though I was not involved in it, and Mrs. Chaplin [a medium and friend of Scott's] had to send a mental S.O.S to Master K[oot].H[oomi]. to come in one of his subtle bodies and diffuse peace.[15]

[15] Scott, *Bone of Contention*, pp. 188–9.

What this 'serious row' concerned is a matter for conjecture. As Scott observed, the Essen critics were still reeling from Debussy's *Pelléas et Mélisande*, which was produced (also by Schum, and conducted by Wolfes) a month before.[16] Out of the two, the critics preferred *The Alchemist*: at least Scott's impressionistic opera was shorter and had more rhythmic vitality! The management was criticised severely for mounting two impressionistic operas in quick succession; Rolf Cunz (a critic writing in the *Essener Anzeiger*) accused them of treating the audience as 'Versuchskaninchen' (guinea pigs) and, in mounting yet another foreign opera, of being unpatriotic.[17] For these reasons, and because the opera was rather unconventional (it did not contain distinctive arias or many chances for the protagonists to shine), the singers may not have been very sympathetic to the work. The demands placed on the two dozen chorus members during the wishes sequence (which must have involved some speedy costume changes, from knights in armour into vassals and monks, from nuns into dancing girls) may also have caused them to grumble.[18]

The performance on 28 May was not sold out, and some people left before the last scene. After the opera the singers refused to appear with Scott on the stage, and although the applause was predominantly enthusiastic, it was mixed with some booing.[19] An English critic, however (perhaps attending the second performance), reported nothing but 'prolonged and exuberant applause'.[20]

Clearly, the reception was mixed. Rolf Cunz begins his article by stating his admiration for Scott and the Essen Stadttheater for having the courage to see through such a ridiculous idea. Yet the simplicity of the story, coupled with the 'jostling numeric' of Scott's ostinatos, proved too much.[21] Both Cunz and another Essen critic, Marcus Hehemann (writing in the *Essener Allgemeine Zeitung*), enjoyed the colour and life of the music, remarking upon the many 'shining' effects in the harmony and orchestration. At times, however, they felt that the speed and intensity of the effects meant that they cancelled each other out, so that 'vor lauter Farben sieht man die einzelne nicht' (in other words, 'one cannot see the wood for the trees').[22]

The score of *The Alchemist* is indeed rich and full of fast-moving bouts of energy and colour; from the buzzing chorus of minstrels strumming on mandolins, to the quasi-*organum* at the entry of the monks, and the unaccompanied, heavenly chorus of nuns. The sequence of seventeen wishes (during which the stage crew must hoist chests full of gems and giant eggs through trap doors, release flower petals and exotic birds from overhead, and let loose casks of vintage wine across the stage, before releasing a large dog), is very chaotic, but there is a clear sense that this mounting disarray is what Scott was after. Following the entertaining climax of the second

[16] Franz Feldens, *75 Jahre Städtische Bühnen Essen* (Essen, 1967), p. 266.

[17] Cunz, 'Essener Kunstanzeiger'.

[18] Franz Feldens in *75 Jahre Städtische Bühnen Essen* (Essen, 1967), pp. 225 & 227, states that during this period there were twenty-two regular chorus members.

[19] See Scott, *Bone of Contention*, p. 189; and Cunz: 'Essener Kunstanzeiger'.

[20] See 'W. St.', '*The Alchemist*', *The Monthly Musical Record*, 1 July 1925, pp. 196–7.

[21] Cunz: 'Essener Kunstanzeige'.

[22] Marcus Hehemann, 'Cyril Scott: Der Alchimist', *Essener Allgemeine Zeitung*, 29 May 1925.

scene, calm is restored and the pace changes. The reappearance of the Maid's folk song reminds us that the Young Man is back to where he started, but this time he is willing to listen to the settling music of the Sage's advice.

Despite the efforts of Wolfes and Schum, there was, as the critics and Scott himself observed, limited enthusiasm among the company. In 1976 Esther Fisher stated that, following the production at Essen, it was 'subsequently to be given three more performances on the continent', but even if these were planned, they do not appear to have taken place.[23] *The Alchemist* has not been staged since, but was heard again in 1995, when the BBC broadcast excerpts on Radio 3.[24]

THE SHRINE

No doubt buoyed up by the prospect of a performance of *The Alchemist*, Scott started work on his second opera in 1924 and completed it in 1926. He chose to write another short opera, *The Shrine*, which is a one-act work divided into four scenes. Scott was no doubt aware of the common practice among travelling opera companies of performing new one-act operas with other, established one-act sureties, thereby enticing the audience to hear a new opera with a guarantee of enjoying at least half of the evening! When touring companies performed new operas by Ethel Smyth, Gustav Holst and Ralph Vaughan Williams, for example, they were often coupled with established box-office favourites, such as Mascagni's *Cavalleria rusticana*, Leoncavallo's *Pagliacci* or Puccini's *Gianni Schicchi*. It is possible that Scott intended for *The Shrine* and *The Alchemist* to follow the same pattern, eventually shedding other stable mates to come together and form an evening's opera.

The Saint of the Mountain and *The Shrine* have often been listed in sources as two separate operas. However, the evidence suggests that the two operas are in fact one and the same work. Scott's own lists of works support this, and the storyline of the one existing libretto renders either title equally appropriate; moreover, there are no definite references to there being two separate works – let alone a second score or separate libretto labelled *The Saint of the Mountain*.[25]

Unfortunately, all that appears to remain of *The Shrine* is the complete libretto and a fragment of music for the first scene. Doubts as to whether or not Scott completed the score are dispelled by examining a variety of sources. In a list of works compiled in 1947 by Robert Elkin for the BBC, *The Shrine* is clearly listed as an

[23] It is possible that Esther Fisher was referring to subsequent performances at Essen in 1925: see Esther Fisher: 'Cyril Scott', *Journal of the British Institute of Recorded Sound* 61 (January 1976), p. 503. Sarah Collins also mentions three more performances: Sarah Collins, *The Aesthetic Life of Cyril Scott* (Boydell, 2013), p. 124. Despite enquiries to several opera houses abroad, I have found no reference to further performances anywhere other than those which took place at Essen in 1925. It should also be noted that Cyril Scott himself was incorrect when he stated that the opera was performed in 1928 (*Bone of Contention*, p. 188).

[24] Part of 'Britannia at the Opera' in the BBC's year-long festival 'Fairest Isle'. Broadcast on 7 August 1995, repeated on 11 November 1995 and now on Oriel OMT 362, see pp. 64 and 587.

[25] See, for example, Laurie J. Sampsel, *Cyril Scott: A Bio-Bibliography* (Greenwood, 2000), pp. 75 & 78; and Michael Hurd, 'Scott, Cyril (Meir)', in *The New Grove Dictionary of Opera*, ed. Stanley Sadie (Macmillan, 1992), vol. 4, p. 273.

unpublished, completed work lasting approximately sixty minutes.[26] The libretto was also translated into German, and Schott's Söhne intended to publish the vocal score.[27] The last of the few surviving pages of the manuscript vocal score breaks off suddenly, in such a way as to suggest that there is (or at least, was) more.

* * * * *

Although cast in a broadly similar stylistic mould to *The Alchemist*, *The Shrine* is a more serious, restrained and deeper piece. The prelude opens very quietly; a sense of unease prevails as slow runs of chromatic parallel chords (typical Scottian chords built on 4ths and 6ths, with added 2nds and 7ths) unfold over a sustained E-flat pedal. The music builds to a brief *forte* before it subsides and thins to a rumbling pedal B-flat, as the curtain rises. The hero (tenor), the Shepherd, aged about nineteen, is seen silhouetted against a dazzling sunset. He is playing on his pipe; rhapsodic and chromatic phrases are answered by similar phrases from a 'distant flute' backstage. After a few exchanges this ceases, leading into a few more bars of descending, rumbling pedal notes, coming to rest on a perturbing dissonance created by a low F-sharp and B chord against an E an octave higher, *tremolando*. Against this, the Shepherd sings a flowing melody in E major (with occasional flattened sevenths), in 6/8 time; the distant pipe plays between phrases. A long cadenza (over a static chord of C in the bass) shared between the two pipes follows, flowing into a faster, fuller section in the accompaniment as the Maid (a soprano, aged about seventeen) enters, and the pair sing of their love for each other, before kissing 'long and ardently' as the scene fades (Ex. 14.4). (The music – in the manuscript vocal score – stops just before the end of the scene, as the Maid rests her head against the Shepherd's shoulder.)

Like *The Alchemist*, the opera is set in the Middle Ages. Again, the characters are not given names, but are referred to as 'The Shepherd', 'The Woodcutter' etc. The plot is similarly straightforward, though the characters are drawn in more detail and are more developed. The story itself is set in an impoverished mountain village, at the centre of which is a shrine to an unidentified male saint, clothed in a jewelled cope. It is the eve of the saint's feast day, and the villagers gather, praying to the saint to help them overcome their latest famine.

As for the Shepherd and the Maid, their relationship appears doomed, as the Maid's father is against the match owing to a long-standing feud with the Shepherd's father, the Woodcutter (according to Scott, a 'genial, devil-may-care type'). The Grandmother – a pivotal character, akin to The Sage in *The Alchemist* – tries to reason with her son on behalf of the young couple, extolling the virtues of mercy, peace, love and forgiveness, but all is in vain as her son, the Maid's father, refuses to listen. The effort proves too much and as she concludes her intercessions at the

[26] The work is also listed as complete in several other lists of Scott's compositions (some of which were compiled by Scott himself).

[27] Although only the last scene of the opera in the German translation is extant, the pagination suggests the scenes on earlier pages have been lost. See also Collins, *The Aesthetic Life of Cyril Scott*, p. 124. Enquires have established that Schott's Söhne did not engrave or publish the opera, and did not keep the manuscript.

Ex. 14.4 Scott, *The Shrine*, duet from opening scene

Ex. 14.4 continued

Ex. 14.4 continued

shrine, she dies. The third scene ends as a celestial chorus of angels surrounds her corpse, laying lilies over it. The light becomes stronger as a miracle occurs: the saint comes to life and hands gems to the angels, who place them on the doorsteps of each cottage.

As dawn breaks, the miracle is revealed and the villagers rejoice. Their joy is short-lived; once the body of the Grandmother is discovered, the chorus intones the Requiem. The father realises the error of his ways and gives his blessing to the Shepherd and Maid. All is forgiven, and all join in a song to the Blessed Virgin Mary, praying for forgiveness. The voice of the Grandmother is then heard again, soaring above the celestial choir (off stage):

> The Name of God is Love, and Love the Fount of Life, There is no death nor strife,
> Below is as above[28]

The opera closes, the Maid, hands clasped, 'looks heavenwards in beatific wonderment' as the Shepherd kneels, head bowed.

* * * * *

Both operas are expressions of Scott's interest in people: their relationships, beliefs and their spiritual journey. Whereas the specific references to a Christian culture are subtle and more superficial in *The Alchemist* – the Maid singing of 'Vesperal airs', the choruses of monks and nuns parading in during the wish sequence, the use of texts from the Ordinary – the Christian elements are more integral to the plot and *mise-en-scène* of *The Shrine.* As Scott later admitted, the Church aesthetic (churches, monks, incense, ceremonial) had a 'poetic appeal', and that up until his twenties he 'imagined that these outward signs of religion had an inspiring effect on my musical activities'.[29] Yet the churchy, distinctly Catholic atmosphere pervading *The Shrine* is a foil for Scott's different ideas: those of the member of the Tantric Order, the author of *The Adept of Galilee* (1920) and *The Vision of the Nazarene* (1933) and the famous *Initiate* series (1920–32).[30]

The idea of using a Christian backdrop for an exposition of his own beliefs about the rights and wrongs of human nature is something that Scott returned to in his last serious opera, *Maureen O'Mara.*

MAUREEN O'MARA

According to Scott (in *Bone of Contention*), in 1935, aged fifty-six, he resolved to give up composing and focus on his other interests.[31] Following his narrative, it was around this time that the Masters encouraged him to write *Maureen O'Mara.* Taking this into account, we can estimate that he completed most of the libretto sometime between 1935 and 1938. In 1945 he related to Percy Grainger that he was writing the opera in conjunction with a fellow-occultist, Mrs Burgess, though her input appears to have been discrete (she may have acted as a medium), and she is not credited as

[28] Cyril Scott, typescript libretto of *The Shrine*, p. 24 (Estate of Cyril Scott).

[29] Scott, *Bone of Contention*, p. 22.

[30] Scott became interested in the Tantric Order during his American tour in 1920. See ibid., pp. 163–8.

[31] Ibid., pp. 217–18.

co-author or composer on the libretto or score.[32] After finishing the libretto, Scott worked on the music and completed it sometime during the second half of 1946.[33]

Maureen O'Mara is set in Ireland during the Napoleonic Wars (*c.* 1803–15). Similar to *The Shrine*, the opera is set in an identifiably Catholic community, one of the main characters being a priest, Father O'Sullivan, and the heroine, Maureen, a devout Catholic. Although written during wartime, Scott did not use the work as a vehicle to explore the rights and wrongs of war to the extent he does in *The Hymn of Unity* (his next large-scale project following the completion of *Maureen*), though there are occasional war-specific references to the need for peace and understanding. Rather, this opera – similar to the others – is primarily about wisdom and goodness: it is a story of jealousy, bitterness and temptation versus the love, winning fidelity and goodness of a soldier's wife.

Conceptually, *Maureen* is the most conventional of Scott's operas. Unlike *The Alchemist* and *The Shrine*, it is of a more standard length (three acts, with an interval suggested after the second). There is less of the 'parable opera' feel of the earlier operas, due in part to the fact that the characters are given names and, although *Maureen* delivers the same broad message as the other operas, the storyline is grittier; there is a greater element of human drama and a more detailed portrayal. There is also a departure from the 'olde-world', Pre-Raphaelite feel of *The Alchemist* and *The Shrine*, as the opera is set during a later, recognisable period and place.

The story centres round Maureen, the wife of Denis, a soldier who goes off to fight with his regiment. The opera opens in the village square, the villagers gathered around singing a mock-Irish song to a pentatonic melody: 'Wind thy river gay / Full of light / Bubbling, bright / joyfully, through the grove / Down to the silver sea'. Among the crowd of villagers, farm-hands and soldiers in this opening scene are: Denis and his wife, Maureen; her brother Shamus; her friend Margaret with her husband, Martin; the priest, Father O'Sullivan; Denis's mother, Mary; and the villain of the opera, Bridget, who is Maureen's widowed sister-in-law.

Maureen is an integral and well-loved part of this close-knit community of family and villagers. In the first act Denis goes off to fight, leaving Maureen distraught. The others rally round her, but the evil Bridget, hell-bent on causing trouble and unrest, plays on Maureen's fear that Denis will be killed in action and further insinuates that Denis has been unfaithful to her. The others see her off and attempt to cheer Maureen. As the day concludes and sunset approaches, Maureen is alone as Bridget reappears to mock her once again. Maureen does not rise to this, but simply ignores Bridget and returns to her house.

The music to Act 2 opens with a low *tremolando* G sharp, then parallel chords in semiquavers climb from it, quickly rising and falling chromatically, as a storm gathers. Safe in her house, Maureen is praying to the Virgin Mary to comfort her in her sorrow, when she hears a knock at her door. It is a wandering piper, Patrick Grady, ill and desperate for shelter. Maureen takes him in and helps him, but is soon discovered by Bridget, who immediately accuses Maureen of infidelity. Maureen

[32] See Collins, *The Aesthetic Life of Cyril Scott*, p. 130.

[33] It is not clear exactly when in that year he finished it, but in March 1946, in a letter to Percy Grainger, Scott remarked that he was still hard at work on the opera. See Collins, *The Aesthetic Life of Cyril Scott*, p. 130.

is distraught, until Shamus (her brother) appears. Although suspicious, he is soon reassured by Maureen and Patrick. Bridget, clearly a lonely, bitter and wretched person, attempts to woo Patrick by offering shelter, but he spurns her and, although still unwell, leaves. Shamus, realising Bridget's malicious intent, sees her off, and Maureen is left alone. She resumes her prayer, praying for an end to war, and asking the Virgin Mary to intercede for Bridget 'who hates me so, that softened be her heart, which God forgive'. A bugle is heard in the distance, but is soon obscured by the sounds of the storm. Patrick returns, staggering in from the storm: he was too ill to carry on. Maureen is distraught: she does not want him back in the house, but feels she must help him, so allows him to stay.

Several weeks pass between Acts 2 and 3. Maureen has nursed Patrick back to health. Inevitably, Patrick has fallen in love with Maureen. He sings of his love for her in a lilting aria in triple time, accompanied by arpeggiated quintuplets. His lyrical outpourings are soon interrupted by Maureen, who is not to be tempted. Patrick persists, trying to steal a kiss from Maureen, but as she resists, Bridget lights upon the scene, delighted at having discovered the pair. After an argument between all three, Patrick begs Maureen's forgiveness and leaves. 'God speed you and forgive you', Maureen sings as he leaves. Bridget sits by the fire as Maureen takes up her usual position, looking out of her window. Suddenly, she sees Denis returning. Bridget wastes no time in telling Denis about Patrick, accusing Maureen of infidelity. Maureen tries to explain, but Denis is furious and vows to go after Patrick and kill him. As he sets off, Maureen attempts to stop him, and a struggle ensues during which Denis throws off Maureen, who hits the ground, unconscious. Denis is utterly distraught. The others fear that Maureen is dead, Patrick is found and exonerates her. To everyone's relief, Maureen gradually comes round and is reconciled to Denis. The crowd now turn their attention to the wicked Bridget, who, sensing their hostility, leaves, crying 'nobody loves or cares for me at all, at all!' as she goes. As the opera ends, Father O'Sullivan prays to God for mercy, and Maureen forgives her.

* * * * *

There are a number of themes and images in *Maureen O'Mara* that are common to all three of Scott's operas. Each carries a moral, and in this way is presented as a parable, warning against the excesses of jealousy, anger and greed. The stories are simply resolved, when goodness and understanding prevail. Each opera has its distribution of attributes: the characters of each could be said to represent souls that are at different stages along the road to enlightenment. Some are almost there. In *The Alchemist,* it is the Sage; in *The Shrine,* it is the Grandmother, and in *Maureen,* it is Maureen herself who sets an example of goodness to the others. Similar to the Sage at the end of *The Alchemist* and the Grandmother in *The Shrine,* Maureen is the protagonist who carries the full, gushing music at the end of the opera: a passage for full chorus and, presumably, orchestra, marked progressively: 'gently flowing', then 'more flowing' then 'very flowing'.[34] Looking more closely at the stories themselves, a number of additional comparisons appear. For example, there is an interesting similarity

[34] In the case of the Grandmother in *The Shrine* there is no score, but the music is described in the libretto.

between the Shepherd, who plays his pipe at sunset at the beginning of *The Shrine*, and Patrick, who plays his pipes as the sun rises at the beginning of Act 3 in *Maureen O'Mara*. Their music is not wholly dissimilar, either. There is also a symbolic connection between Maureen (again, at the beginning of Act 3) and the Maid at the beginning of Scene 3 of *The Alchemist:* both draw water from the well at sunrise.

Compared with the former operas, the musical language Scott uses in *Maureen O'Mara* betrays a more acerbic and uncompromising approach to dissonance, characteristic of his later musical style. Throughout, Scott creates a rich and mysterious unease, often through an uncertain tonality built up of thick parallel chords which oscillate over an underpinning sustained pedal note or *tremolando* chord. An example of this can be found in the prelude to Act 1 of *Maureen O'Mara,* introducing a strong sense of foreboding. This passage reappears in different guises, according to the mood: when the opera ends, the accompanying sequences of parallel chords include dissonances, but these are softened; major become flattened sevenths, etc.

The opening surge of parallel chords at the beginning of *Maureen* (bars 1–3 and 7–13) is similar to those at the opening of *The Alchemist,* but is rendered wilder with added chromaticism and the abandonment of a dominant tonality. In *The Alchemist* Scott portrays the Young Man's confusion and unease by adding dissonances (chromatically altered 2nds, 7ths etc.) to his theme; a similar technique is found in *Maureen,* as can be seen in the prelude (e.g. bars 16–33). This theme recurs when Maureen's honour is doubted, or if she has a difficult decision to make. The contrasting, brightly decorated motif of bars 33–7 often appears at moments in the story where love is portrayed. This rhapsodic, flexible theme sometimes suggests Patrick's piping, but the way in which the motif progresses (to a light or melancholic melody), and the nature of the accompaniment (consisting of loyal, parallel chromatic chords for Denis, forbidding *tremolando* pedal notes for Patrick), signal how this expression of love should be read. Another recognisable motif is the pentatonic 'Irish tune' sung by the chorus at the beginning of the opera. The tune (in its complete eight-bar form, or snatches of it), reappears occasionally, often when an 'Irish' touch is warranted.

The musical characterisation in *Maureen* is as direct and logical as in the other operas, but more subtle – not least because there is a greater measure of tonal ambiguity throughout the score. The canvas is larger, too, owing to the more complex storyline – which, as Scott intended, dictates the musical characterisation. Similar to *The Alchemist, Maureen O'Mara* is a very focused piece of work; Scott never wastes time, and is always intent on what is happening on stage and on ensuring that the music conveys the story. Given the scale of *Maureen,* such economy of means is no bad thing, yet it is a shame that, as in *The Alchemist,* the accompaniment often contains the majority of the interest. Similarly, *Maureen O'Mara* lacks variety in the vocal writing, and contains few moments for the singers to shine: there are too few true duets, and no small ensemble numbers. Such inclusions would ease the intensity of the piece.

That said, there are several moments when the music relents and the writing becomes more lyrical. Such is the case in Act 2, when Maureen despairs at the nature of war and man's inhumanity to man (Ex. 14.6). How this aria, or any part of the opera, would sound with full orchestra is a matter for the imagination, for Scott never orchestrated it. He did, however, finish the vocal score, and waited for an opportunity to secure a production. Such an opportunity arose when, in February 1949, the Arts Council announced an opera-commissioning scheme whereby composers first

Ex. 14.5 Scott, *Maureen O'Mara*, prelude

Ex. 14.5 continued

Ex. 14.5 continued

submitted the outline of an opera. Scott later recalled: 'I am reminded of the implication that I was a better librettist than a composer. For when the 1951 Festival of Britain was pending, I sent the piano score to the Arts Council *after*, in accordance with the ruling, first having submitted the libretto.'[35]

The judges of the competition were Steuart Wilson (chairman), Edward Dent, Lawrance Collingwood, Constant Lambert and Frederic Austin. John Dennison (Head of Music at the Arts Council) and Eric Walter White (Secretary) whittled down the initial 117 applications to 61, of which Scott's was one.[36] Although the librettos and operas were submitted anonymously, each author adopting a *nom de plume* (Scott's was 'Charles Lundy'), it is clear that the true identities of the entrants were known.[37]

Despite this, no documentation exists to tell us which judges looked at *Maureen O'Mara*, or what they thought of it. We do know that the man behind the opera competition, Eric Walter White, was aware of *The Alchemist*, and that Edward Dent was too, and a few years earlier had considered it as a possible work for revival at Covent Garden.[38] In contrast, it is likely that other committee members were not sympathetic towards Scott. Steuart Wilson (also Director of Music at the BBC) did not reveal himself to be a particular admirer of Scott's music when he delivered the BBC's seventieth-birthday tribute to the composer in 1949.[39] But whether the panel judges expressed themselves keen on *Maureen O'Mara* or not, the work was not taken up by the Arts Council, but was rejected at the judges' meeting in September 1949.

35 Scott, *Bone of Contention*, p. 220.

36 For a detailed history and analysis of the Arts Council Opera Competition, see Nathaniel Lew, 'A New and Glorious Age: Constructions of National Opera in Britain, 1945–1951' (PhD thesis, University of California at Berkeley, 2001).

37 Although some sources have it as 'Grundy', Scott's writing on the vocal score (submitted to the Arts Council) looks more like an 'L' than a 'G'. Arts Council records have it as 'Lundy'. Scott wrote plays under the name 'M. Arkwright Lundy' to avoid confusion with another playwright, Noel Scott (1888–1956).

38 *The Alchemist* is mentioned in both Dent's and Walter White's respective opera books (*Opera* and *The Rise of English Opera*), and is listed in a two-page typescript dated 1944 (perhaps compiled by Dent) and titled 'Operas Suitable for Covent Garden', found among Dent's papers concerning his membership of the Royal Opera House Control Committee. King's College, Cambridge, EJD/2/7/4.

39 Scott, *Bone of Contention*, p. 223.

Ex. 14.6 Scott, *Maureen O'Mara*, Act 2 (vocal score), Maureen's aria, p. 156

As it turned out, this was not a great calamity. If *Maureen O'Mara* had been chosen as a winning opera, Scott may well have been the richer by £300, but, ironically, the chances of a staged performance would have been slim, considering the fate of the operas that were chosen. There were four winning operas: Arthur Benjamin's *A Tale of Two Cities*, Alan Bush's *Wat Tyler*, Berthold Goldschmidt's *Beatrice Cenci*, and Karl Rankl's *Deirdre of the Sorrows*. Though the British Council had intended

Ex. 14.6 continued

the winning compositions to be performed, a lack of funding and political upheaval within the institution prevented this from happening. As it was, Scott was saved the uncertainty and frustration suffered by the winners, and was able to look forward to a performance of his own Festival of Britain commission: the *Irish Serenade* premiered by the Riddick String Orchestra in June 1951. *Maureen O'Mara* was set aside, unorchestrated and unperformed.

JANET AND FELIX

In 1954, while compiling a list of his works, Scott wrote to the BBC enquiring about a work he had written for them twenty years before, but had since forgotten all about.[40] The work in question was his radio operetta, *Janet and Felix*, which the BBC commissioned from him in 1931.[41] *Janet and Felix, or Singing Sickness*, was broadcast on Thursday 26 November 1931 on London Regional, and again the day after on National. The operetta was one of a series of short operas adapted and produced by Gordon McConnel during a period when the BBC were looking to develop its own studio-opera organisation, alongside its commitment to broadcasting outside relays from opera houses.

The story of *Janet and Felix* is a farcical tale involving a mischievous Sprite (played by soprano Wynne Ajello) who, in the first scene, puts a spell on Felix Fairchild (John Armstrong), which affects his voice. After consulting a nose and throat specialist, Dr Kurtz (played by J. Hubert Leslie), Felix is enrolled, by his mother (played by Ann Stephenson), at Signor Pindello's Operatic Academy. After an adventure involving a Wishing Seat in a cave 'somewhere on the Yorkshire Moors', the story is resolved, and the operetta ends back in Signor Pindello's rehearsal room.

In the absence of a score, libretto, full synopsis or recording (all of which, despite an extensive search, appear to be lost), information regarding the character of the music and storyline must be gleaned from various other sources.[42] From these, we learn that the operetta consisted of a short overture followed by six scenes. The piece contained spoken dialogue, especially in the second scene (the consultation with Dr Kurtz). As with all his stage works, Scott was his own librettist.

The *Radio Times* described the music of the overture to *Janet and Felix* as 'whimsical', and noted that in Scene 3 the students of Pindello's Operatic Academy have fun while trying to rehearse a section of Scott's *The Rat-Catcher*, a piece for male chorus and flute obbligato (Fig. 14.1). In a similar vein, Scott parodies a duet from an 'operetta by Sauerbier', rehearsed by the heroine, Janet Suckling (Tessa Dean), and Signor Pindello (played by Bertram Binyon).[43] The atmosphere of the piece appears to have been comic and otherworldly, with the ghostly singing of the Sprite running as a thread throughout the piece. The impression one gets from various BBC internal memos and correspondence is that both the work and the performance were successful, and that those involved enjoyed working on it: Scott related that his good friend Bertram Binyon's performance as Signor Pindello 'so amused

[40] Cyril Scott, Letter to Richard Howgill, 11 November 1954. Cyril Scott Composer File 2, BBC WAC.

[41] For *Janet and Felix* see also Chapter 3, above.

[42] The performance materials for *Janet and Felix* were in the BBC's possession in November 1954, when, prompted by enquiries about the work from both Scott and Robert Elkin (who suggested it for television broadcast), the score was examined by Kenneth Wright (then Head of Music Programming for BBC TV). In an internal memo Wright seems to have responded favourably to the suggestion, but there the trail goes cold, and whatever his assessment, no further broadcast resulted.

[43] *Radio Times*, 20 November 1931, p. 633.

THURSDAY

LONDON REGIONAL (356.3 m.)

SEXTET
Waltz Song, Musetto .... *Leo Peter*
Aubade .... *D'Ambrosio*
Serenade .... *Schubert*
Canzonetta .... *Mendelssohn*

IDA GEDDES
Sleep .... *Parry*
Quick! we have but a Second .... *Stanford*
There are seven that pull the Thread .... *Elgar*

SEXTET
Fantasy, The Mastersingers *Wagner, arr. Weninger*

ORCHESTRA
Bacchanale (Samson and Delilah)

9.15 'Janet and Felix' or 'Singing Sickness'

An Operetta by CYRIL SCOTT

Characters in the order of their appearance:—
Janet Suckling
Felix Fairchild
Mrs. Fairchild (his mother)
Dr. Kurtz (the nose and throat specialist)
Students at Signor Pindello's Academy
Signor Pindello (the maestro)
John McKay (coach and accompanist)
Kiddle (a student)
The Sprite (cause of all the trouble)

Scene 1. The Drawing-room of Janet Suckling's Flat
Scene 2. Dr. Kurtz' Consulting Room
Scene 3. Signor Pindello's Operatic Academy — the Practise Room
Scene 4. Pindello's Academy —The Garden
Scene 5. The Wishing Seat in a Cave on the Yorkshire Moors
Scene 6. Pindello's Academy —the Practise Room

Adapted and produced by GORDON McCONNEL
THE WIRLESS CHORUS and THE B.B.C. THEATRE ORCHESTRA
Conducted by LESLIE WOODGATE
(*For cast see page* 638.)

'JANET' 'FELIX'
CYRIL SCOTT
Tessa Dean and John Armstrong who play lead in Cyril Scott's operetta 'Janet and Felix,' which is being broadcast tonight at 9.15

IDA GEDDES
Silver .... *Hely-Hutchinson*
A Christmas Carol .... *Bax*
The Windmill (Words from an old Sussex Mill Post) .... *Colin Taylor*

SEXTET
A Song of Farewell .... *Vidal*
Serenade .... *Rachmaninov*
Bourrée and Gigue .... *Edward German*

8.0 Saint-Saëns Programme

ASTRA DESMOND (*Contralto*)
THE B.B.C. STUDIO SYMPHONY ORCHESTRA
Conducted by PERCY PITT

ORCHESTRA
Overture to an unfinished Comic Opera
Prelude, Le Deluge

ASTRA DESMOND and Orchestra
Aria, O Love, from thy Power (Samson and Delilah)

ORCHESTRA
Symphony No. 2, in A Minor
Allegro marcato; Adagio; Scherzo; Presto; Prestissimo

ASTRA DESMOND and Orchestra
Ballade, La Fiancée du Timbalier

THE overture of this whimsical operetta, whose text and music are both Cyril Scott's, with its distant fairy voices, and its hints of the uncanny, prepares us at once for the mood in which to listen, and then, in the first scene, we are introduced to the heroine practising her singing. The unlucky hero appears later. In the second scene his mother is consulting a Harley Street specialist about her son's sad case; this is dialogue until near the end, when music leads into the third scene—a school of singing. There, everything, even conversation, must be sung, and the music is typical of Cyril Scott's whimsical fun, including a rehearsal by male voice chorus with flute accompaniment—in which he makes merry over his own 'Rat-catcher'—and a brilliantly comic burlesque of an operatic duet by Sauerbier, sung by the heroine and the maestro of the school. Scene IV is the garden of the school, where no better fortune attends a second proposal by the hero, and the fifth is the cave of the sprite, who was the innocent cause of all the trouble. What befell there and afterwards must be left to unfold itself, as it does unmistakably. And all through the piece, the laughter of the unfeeling sprite can be heard breaking in and fading away again.

10.15 'The Second News'
WEATHER FORECAST, SECOND GENERAL NEWS BULLETIN

10.30 Regional News

10.35-12.0 DANCE MUSIC
JACK PAYNE and his B.B.C. DANCE ORCHESTRA

Figure 14.1 Billing for *Janet and Felix* in the *Radio Times*, November 1931

the orchestra that they could hardly rehearse'.[44] The orchestra in question was the BBC Theatre Orchestra, which was augmented for the broadcast by the addition of a harp, flute and piano.[45]

The operetta ran for approximately thirty-five to forty minutes, and was followed by a selection of songs and other works by Scott: *Blackbird's Song* performed by

44 Cyril Scott, Letter to Richard Howgill, 15 November 1954. Cyril Scott Composer File 2, BBC WAC. See also Scott, *Bone of Contention*, pp. 206–7.

45 Scott was commissioned and wrote the opera just before the formation of the BBC Theatre Orchestra, which is why extra players were required. See also p. 59.

Wynne Ajello, *Souvenir de Vienne* (No. 5 from the *Karma* suite) by the BBC Theatre Orchestra, and a full performance of *The Rat-Catcher* and *Huntsman's Dirge* performed by members of the BBC Wireless Chorus, who also provided the chorus in *Janet and Felix*. Leslie Woodgate conducted.

During February 1932 the score was returned to Scott for a short period, perhaps in order for him to interest another group in performing it, but no further performances resulted, so the score was returned to the BBC Music Library. Twenty-two years later, correspondence resulting from an enquiry about the first performance of *Janet and Felix* sparked interest in the work within the BBC, and the scores were retrieved with a view to performing it on BBC Television, but no further broadcast took place.[46]

BACKWARDS AND FORWARDS

Another work of this period that shows Scott in a somewhat lighter vein is his music for a show co-written with his wife, Rose, and two other friends around the same time, or slightly before, Scott set to work on *Janet and Felix*.[47] There was some (apparently unresolved) indecision over what the title of the work should be: *Backwards and Forwards, Forwards and Backwards,* or *Whilom and Whither*; I shall use the former title.[48] Scott later explained how *Backwards and Forwards* came to be written:

> One capricious summer, while passing a holiday with my wife and two friends, we decided to pass the time in an amusing manner by concocting a Musical Show, which was to be distinguished from the customary Revue … by a plot … Having between us devised … a suitable humorous and dramatic theme, I then set about writing a certain proportion of the dialogue, the lyrics, and finally the music, which was of by no means high-brow quality.[49]

The 'two friends' were Brian Ross (otherwise known as 'David Anrias') and Melanie Mills (known by her pen name, H. K. Challoner). Although described as a 'Musical Show', it is more correctly a musical revue, consisting of eighteen sketches with music. Scott wrote the words and music for twelve musical numbers (including an overture and finale), and the script for eleven scenes. Rose and Brian Ross wrote three scenes each, and Mills a further scene, together with one co-written by Scott and Mills. *Backwards and Forwards* appears to have been the only occasion when these four friends collaborated and produced a joint work.

46 Memo from Kenneth Wright to R. J. F. Howgill, 7 December 1954. Cyril Scott artists file, BBC WAC.

47 The typed script dates from 1932, leading to the conclusion that the piece was complete and being sent to potential producers/interested parties.

48 Chosen because *Backwards and Forwards* is the title Scott handwrote on the cover of one of the songs, and it makes more sense when one considers the chronology of the story (the characters first go back before going forward in time).

49 From Cyril Scott's unpublished memoir, *Near the End of Life*.

Although all four believed in, and wrote serious books about, reincarnation, *Backwards and Forwards* is a series of comic skits based on the theme of previous lives. The main characters – the elderly Lord Sepsis Pancreas and his younger wife, Lady Pancreas – visit Dr Impasse, a quack who specialises in enabling people to dream (and relive) previous incarnations. The following scenes take the couple back in history to the nineteenth, sixteenth, fourteenth and eleventh centuries, and into prehistoric times. Amid much farce the folly of human nature is explored, as Lady Pancreas falls in love with her husband's secretary, and Lord Pancreas is frustrated through jealousy and amorous misadventures of various kinds.

In the second act the scenes move progressively forward in time (including, interestingly, a scene based in London in 1940 during 'a war'), until the serious message behind the satire starts to emerge in the penultimate scene, set in a beautiful garden in the year 2350. One of the characters reads from an 'ancient book' (written in the 1930s) and discusses the way people behaved then:

> Yes, they were so busy rushing after happiness in every conceivable and inconceivable place, that they quite forgot to look for it inside themselves. And in the process, what with their rush and their noise and their machinery and their smoke, they turned this beautiful earth into a perfect hell.[50]

Scott then introduces one of his favourite themes – the concept of perfect freedom in marriage – as Lady Pancreas tells her husband she has fallen in love with his secretary. Lord Pancreas has no doubt read Scott's *The Art of Making a Perfect Husband* (1928), because when asked if he minds, he replies: 'Not if it makes you happy, my dear. After all, just because I'm your husband, I'm not so conceited to think I'm the only man worth falling in love with – or that no other man would ever fall in love with you!'

The music for *Backwards and Forwards* survives in vocal score. It is doubtful, considering that the work has never been staged, that Scott ever orchestrated it, though he sometimes indicates instrumentation here and there. The songs themselves are straightforward strophic settings, mainly in unison, with simple accompaniments (Ex. 14.7). Most of the songs are solos and duets; those for more singers divide into simple two-part writing. The general musical style reflects the Cyril Scott of the simpler early piano works, with occasional moments of greater complexity. Apart from the short overture (124 bars of music), there are also a few instrumental sections incorporated into the songs and during the finale. (One of these, a 'Victorian parlour song', was later published separately as *Victorian Waltz* by Elkin in 1963.)

Scott's friend and fellow composer Pedro Morales (1897–1938) endeavoured to help Scott secure a production of *Backwards and Forwards* by arranging an interview with the impresario Charles B. Cochran. His musical director thought well of it, but Cochran himself was not convinced. Sir Oswald Stoll (1866–1942) was also approached but turned it down, as he considered it contained an element of impropriety.

[50] Typescript of *Backwards and Forwards*.

Ex. 14.7 Scott, 'Auntie be a sport', from *Backwards and Forwards* (vocal score)

NEPHEW INTO AUNT

Nephew into Aunt: A Boccaccio Touch! is a comic play with music, 'adapted from the Italian of Leonardo Sighieri' by Scott himself. Who Sighieri was is a matter for speculation. The reference to Giovanni Boccaccio's *Decameron* in the title leads us to the fictional character called Leonardo Sighieri, mentioned in one of the episodes (Day 4, Story 8), but not to an Italian author of the name. Nor do the characters in *Nephew into Aunt* appear in the *Decameron*. It is possible that, in adding a reference to Sighieri, Scott wanted to add a layer of mystique, deflecting authorship to Sighieri

Ex. 14.7 continued

15
S.
cresc.
when all is said, you're a hun - dred and fif - ty and so, al -
Pno.
cresc.
20
S.
tho' we don't want to loose you
Pno.
23
S.
p
poco rit.
a tempo
we think you ought to go.
Pno.
etc.

as a conceit to cover his own, sole authorship; or perhaps he believed that the work was dictated to him. The 'Boccaccio touch' reflects the character of the storyline and the setting of the piece (Italy, 'any attractive period between 1350 and 1750'), rather than any connection to a particular story from Boccaccio's work. The story of *Nephew into Aunt* can therefore be regarded as original.

The play is a farce in three acts. The plot revolves around the amorous adventures of the nephew, Enrico di Parma, and a number of others, whose efforts are confounded when Enrico uses a love potion in order to secure the affections of his intended, Cecilia di Vinciolo. Other interested parties (brother and sister Fedora and Guido, who are in love with Enrico and Cecilia respectively) enlist the help of a magician, who takes Enrico out of the equation by rendering him unconscious and transports his spirit into the body of his aunt, Angelina del Tesco (who is at that moment also conveniently unconscious, in the midst of a swoon). After various complications and antics, all is resolved when the love potion is used again, and each character is matched to a suitable paramour.

The precise date of composition is uncertain, but, judging by the look of the score and comparing it with the more assured style of *Backwards and Forwards*, it is possible that *Nephew into Aunt* pre-dates *Janet and Felix* and *Backwards and Forwards* by at least a few years. Both the music and story are similar to *Backwards and Forwards* in approach, though there are fewer musical numbers in *Nephew into Aunt*: ten songs for solo and vocal ensemble (there is no overture or finale). *Nephew into Aunt* only exists in piano/vocal score; some further songs are indicated in the script, but are missing or were never written. The work has not yet been performed.

SCOTT'S INCIDENTAL MUSIC

One of Scott's earliest incidental scores was written for Matheson Lang's production of *Othello* at the New Theatre, London, which ran from 11 February to 19 May 1920. Nothing survives of the music; all that remains are a few references to it in reviews. The production itself was successful, and the critics generally praised Lang's interpretation, judging Scott's music as a 'fitting part of the noble scheme'.[51] Shortly after, in March 1920, Scott provided the music for a production of Kenneth Hare's *Return to Nature*, performed by the Curtain Group at the Lyric Theatre, Hammersmith on 14 March 1920. Again, the score has not survived, and few reviews mention the music in any detail. Those that do are complimentary: *The Stage* critic praised the music, commenting that it worked well with the Futurist conception of the decor. This production included 'delicious singing of old French and English Songs by Mlle. Raymonde Collignon',[52] but considering her rendition of similar songs on recordings from the same period, it is doubtful that these were settings arranged by Scott.

In late September 1937 Scott stepped in at short notice to compose the incidental music for a production of James Bridie's *Susanna and the Elders*, produced at the Duke of York's Theatre, London, which ran from 31 October to 14 November 1937.[53] Yet again, the score is lost, and our only clue to the music is found among press snippets; from these we learn that the music was well regarded, and that Olive Dyer sang 'one or two Psalms, to which suitable music has been compiled by Cyril Scott'.[54]

[51] 'Flaneur', *The Globe*, 12 February 1920. New Theatre, St Martin's Lane, *Othello* production file, V&A Theatre Archive.

[52] *The Times*, 15 March 1920, p. 14.

[53] Letter from Cyril Scott to Herbert Murrill, Monday 4 October 1937. Cyril Scott file, BBC WAC.

[54] *The Stage*, 4 November 1937, p. 10.

SMETSE SMEE

Although he made some attempt to get *Backwards and Forwards* and *Nephew into Aunt* staged, playwriting was more of a pastime for Scott, providing relaxation between demanding compositions. He wrote around fifteen plays during his lifetime, almost all during the early 1940s, after which he returned to writing music and books. Having seen shows where the musical songs were thrown into the script arbitrarily, Scott set himself the challenge of creating a play with a score that flowed logically from the script.

The most significant incidental music Scott composed was for his own adaptation of Charles de Coster's *Smetse Smee*.[55] Compared with *Backwards and Forwards* and *Nephew into Aunt*, *Smetse Smee* benefits from being less consciously comical or earnest in either plot or language. As a result there is the sense that, relieved of the responsibility of writing a story which must be funny or aid moral enlightenment, Scott can relax, and focus on creating a piece of interesting and colourful theatre. It is possible that Scott realised this too, as he worked hard to complete and secure a performance of *Smetse Smee*. Given the quality of Scott's script and music, it is a shame that its performance history consists of a series of unfortunate near-misses.

Scott worked on the script and music during the mid-to-late 1920s. In 1929 *The Times* announced that Maurice Browne had acquired the play for a production in London, and that he intended to produce it in 1931. Unfortunately, Browne ran into financial difficulties and the production never went ahead. The script was translated into German for another production, planned for 1939, but this also failed to materialise, as a result of World War 2.

Plans to produce *Smetse Smee* at a West End theatre in July 1945 also stalled, as did an idea to turn it into a film.[56] At the end of September 1945, Scott's friend Walter Rilla, then working as a producer at the BBC, was asked by them to adapt Scott's script for radio broadcasting. In February 1946 the BBC examined the music, which they had located at Schott's German office the previous December (presumably it was stored there in readiness for the German production that never took place).[57] Scott made a list of cuts suitable for the broadcast version, but it was around this time that Rilla gave up much of his work to look after his wife, who had developed cancer.[58] *Smetse Smee* remains, as yet, unperformed. Thankfully, all of the performance materials have survived, including the original full script, Rilla's adaptation script for broadcast, and the full score and orchestral parts.

The Faustian storyline of *Smetse Smee* clearly appealed to Scott, with its clear moral message of good over evil. The goodly philanthropic blacksmith Smetse Smee has happened upon hard times and is on the brink of suicide. An Envoy from the infernal regions appears at the last moment and persuades Smetse Smee to enter a pact, thereby securing him more time and money to sort out his problems. This

[55] Charles de Coster, *Flemish Legends* (Chatto & Windus, 1920), pp. 103–71.

[56] Letter to Percy Grainger, 19 July 1945, cited in Collins *The Aesthetic Life of Cyril Scott*, p. 130.

[57] Memo from Miss L. A. Duncan to Miss Reeves, 4 December 1945. Cyril Scott file, BBC WAC.

[58] Letter to Val Gielgud, 14 April 1948. Walter Rilla file, BBC WAC.

Smee agrees to, and he continues in his charitable works. He outwits the Devil on numerous occasions before the final reckoning, where his good deeds and defiance are recognised, and he is welcomed into heaven.

As it stands, *Smetse Smee* is undoubtedly Scott's most convincing script. It stands above his other plays in terms of quality, balance, and the general appeal of the storyline. Scott's adaptation of the story is balanced and well judged: he has selected just the right number, and sort, of episodes from de Coster's story, the result being a coherent, clear and colourful piece of theatre. The characterisation is consistent and, to provide more contrast and depth, Scott has accentuated the personality of Susannah Smee, to make her a feistier, slightly darker figure. Comparing the book with the play, it is clear that Scott felt this greater definition necessary in order for the story to work effectively on stage.

The score is substantial, but, for a three-act play, not overbearing. The balance between unaccompanied spoken dialogue and musical background has been carefully thought out; the two elements are dependent on each other, forming a homogeneous piece of theatre. Scott's score is all one would imagine of his orchestral style of this period (1920s/1930s). His use of colour, both in the orchestration and the music itself – especially his characteristically deft handling of mood and contrast through chromatic and non-functional harmonies – means that his score is ideally suited to the episodic storyline. The musical portrayal of the action in the play (the bustles and fights during which Smee and his smiths outwit the Devil) is carefully restrained: characteristically Scottian ostinato passages build to occasional, tight bursts of full orchestra. Simple phrases are repeated and developed (reharmonised, or flowed into imitative passages) as the story demands, as with a phrase Scott uses to open both Act 2 and Act 3, but takes in different directions in each act (Exx. 14.8a/b). The whimsical, quixotic, slightly picaresque nature of the story is an excellent match to Scott's music.

Similar to his other pieces of musical theatre, *Smetse Smee* no doubt appealed to Scott because it is a story of a man who resolves to lead an improved, enlightened way of life. It is interesting to consider why Scott did not use *Smetse Smee* as the basis of an opera, as his acquaintance Franz Schreker did in 1929.[59] It is possible that Scott never even considered it, or that the two men had discussed the matter (Schreker appears to have started work on his adaptation slightly after Scott), and Scott decided not to make an opera out of it for that reason. Given Scott's account of his inspiration for *Maureen O'Mara*, however, and considering his deep spirituality, it is likely he felt that the sole purpose of his operatic work was to reveal occult wisdom, and therefore must be based on original stories inspired by, or even given to him, by his spiritual Masters.

* * * * *

Apart from *The Alchemist*, *Smetse Smee* is the only piece of Scott's music for the theatre to have survived complete, with all of the materials necessary for the complete

[59] Schreker worked on his opera from 1929 to 1932. *Der Schmied von Gent* was first performed in Berlin on 29 October 1932. See Christopher Hailey, *Franz Schreker (1878–1934): A Cultural Biography* (Cambridge University Press, 1993), p. 256.

Ex. 14.8a Scott, *Smetse Smee*, opening of Act 2

Ex. 14.8b Scott, *Smetse Smee*, opening of Act 3

Ex. 14.8b continued

performance that Scott himself would no doubt have envisaged. There is a strong case for revisiting these two important works with a view to performances or at least full recordings; *The Alchemist* is an entertaining and colourful work, full of life (as the excerpts recorded by the BBC in 1995 show), and *Smetse Smee* is unique in his œuvre as the only complete example of Scott as a writer of incidental music.

It is difficult to see how some of the other works discussed here could be brought to life. Leaving aside the music that is lost, such pieces as *Backwards and Forwards* and *Nephew into Aunt* would not be commercially viable on stage – if indeed they ever were. That said, they are important documents and worthy of closer attention. Musically, they are not complex and do not stand out as innovative, but they do show Scott in a distinctly different, perhaps rather surprising light. The storylines and themes both reflect Scott's serious, deeply held beliefs concerning moral and spiritual truths, which are married to scores that display his ability to write amusing lyrics set to simple, catchy 'light' music. They also enable us to consider what the lost score of *Janet and Felix* – clearly a similar piece, roughly of the same period – may have sounded like. The existence of *Backwards* and *Nephew* demonstrates Scott's practical application of his belief in the spiritual benefit of laughter; these works are testament to the theory and philosophy he explored in his book on the subject, *The Ghost of a Smile* (1939). Furthermore, it is interesting to note that, apart from *The Shrine* and *Maureen O'Mara,* all of Scott's works for the stage (meaning those for which he wrote the libretto/script and music: *Janet and Felix, The Alchemist, Smetse Smee, Nephew into Aunt*) contain an element of humour or farce.

Along with the *Hymn of Unity* (1946), *Maureen O'Mara* is one of Scott's last major works and one of his few extended, large-scale vocal pieces. Musically it reflects his later compositional style, embodying a Romantic austerity in its uncompromising acerbic yet rich harmonic palette. Similar to *The Shrine,* it also reflects the interests of Scott the author of *The Initiate, The Vision of the Nazarene* and *The Adept of Galilee,* in its juxtaposition of Christian and occult influences and aesthetics. A performance of *Maureen O'Mara* would be achievable on a small scale. The case for orchestrating and fully staging the opera is weak; it would not be practical, unless the work found a suitable stage, or was arranged for small forces (e.g. chamber orchestra). If a performance opportunity arose, a semi-staged production, using Scott's piano accompaniment (perhaps adapted for two pianos to add depth and more textural variety) would seem the most pragmatic approach. It is, after all, only in performance that the full impact of Scott's creative diversity can be fully appreciated.

15

The Choral Works

LESLIE DE'ATH

ALTHOUGH Scott is not known for his choral works, twenty of them survive, half for chorus with orchestra, and half unaccompanied or with keyboard. His interest in the medium spanned most of his creative life, from the very early setting of the *Magnificat* to the post-war *Hymn of Unity*, his ultimate musical mission statement for mankind.

MAGNIFICAT

Scott came to consider his early 1899 *Magnificat* 'pretentious', and duly consigned it and other works 'to the crematorium, which is the best and safest place for them.'[1] Evidently he had yet to appreciate fully the curatorial instincts of Grainger, who arranged a piano reduction of the work and kept it safe in the museum for posterity, where it remains today. Scott's aim in his early large-scale works was 'to invent a species of Pre-Raphaelite music, to consist mostly of common chords placed in such a way as to savour of very primitive church music, thereby, as I thought, reminding its listeners of old pictures'.[2]

LA BELLE DAME SANS MERCI

Like the members of the Pre-Raphaelite Brotherhood, Scott found inspiration in medieval legend, especially in his early years. His own home in London, with its Burne-Jones stained-glass window, its custom furniture and austere interior appointments, was tailored to that aesthetic. Several of his vocal and choral works are settings of medieval literature, or of more modern authors with similar artistic orientation. Among the choral works, there are his *La belle dame sans merci*, *Mirabelle*, *The Emir's Serenade*, *The Huntsman's Dirge* and *The Rat-Catcher*. His unpublished stage adaptation of Charles de Coster's *Smetse Smee* similarly belongs loosely in this group, though it is a comedy in the tradition of the Belgian author's most well-known work, *Till Eulenspiegel*.

Keats's succinct poem of tragic love, *La belle dame sans merci*, elicited from Scott one of his most sensual scores. Written during World War 1, it was not published until 1935. It was first conceived (*c.* 1913) as a dialogue between the hapless knight and the beautiful fairy maiden, and revisited two years later with a chorus providing commentary, as the poem invites. Scott's adventurous, Frenchified harmonic language of this period is deftly employed to suggest the nuances of the poem, which

[1] Cyril Scott, *My Years of Indiscretion* (Mills & Boon, 1924), pp. 25–6. He includes the Symphony No. 1 along with the *Magnificat* in this assessment – a work which likewise owes its continued existence to Grainger. It was performed once, in Darmstadt in 1900, and recorded in 2008.

[2] Ibid. p. 25.

alternates between amorous sensuousness and the despair of love deceived. Much use is made of chordal parallelism, first encountered in the orchestral prelude (Ex. 15.1), and then recurring in the chorus to suggest the seductiveness of the maiden upon encountering the knight (Ex. 15.2).

Ex. 15.1 Scott, *La belle dame sans merci*, bars 18–25

18
Tranquillo (quasi tempo I.)
p espr.
22
pp

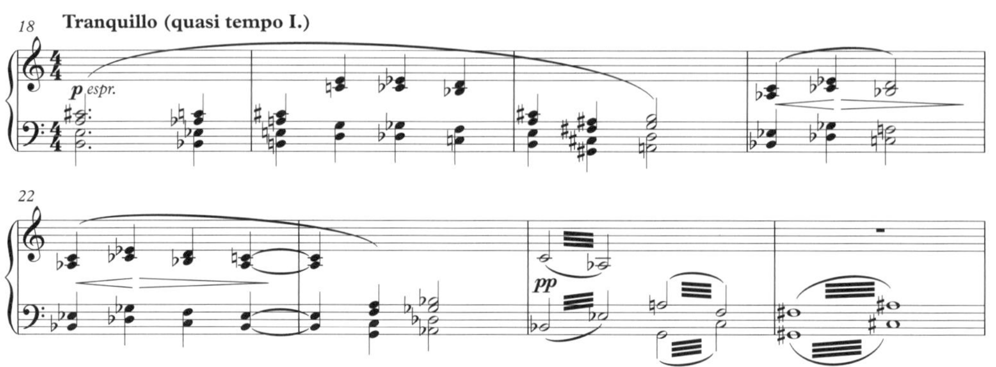

Ex. 15.2 Scott, *La belle dame sans merci*, bars 208–25

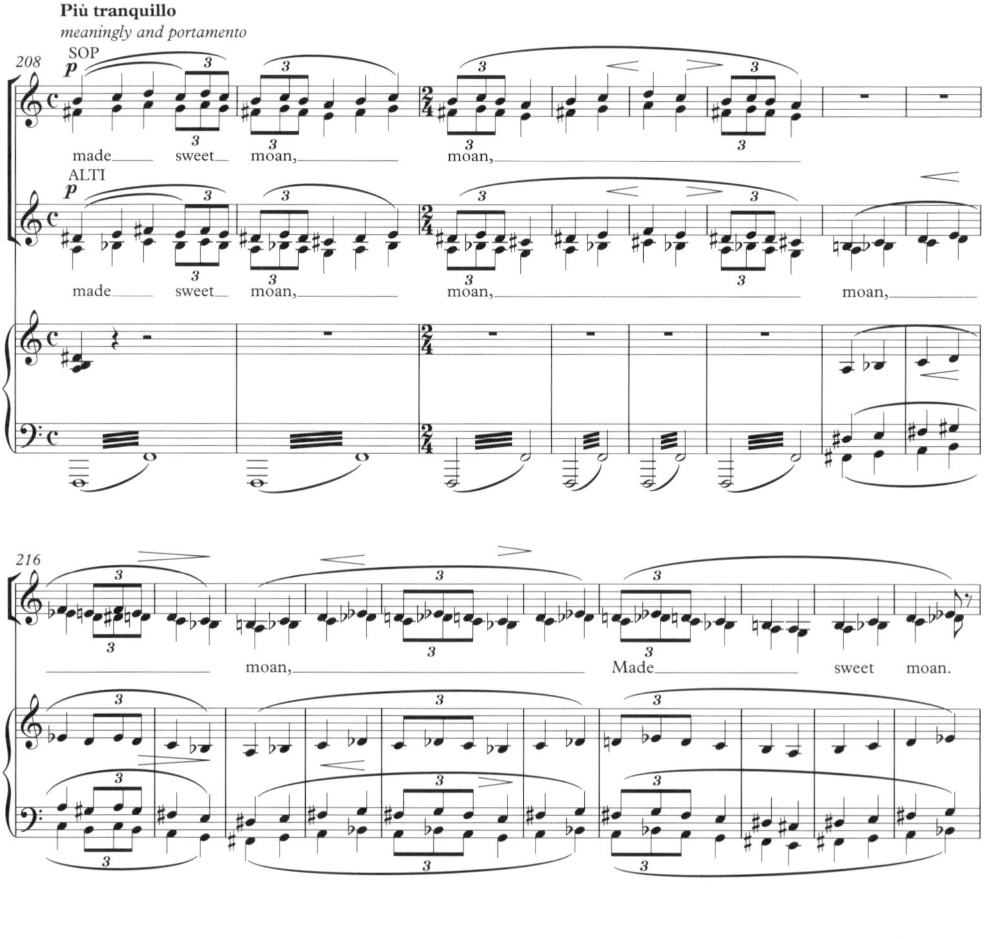

Più tranquillo
meaningly and portamento
208
SOP
p
made sweet moan, moan,
ALTI
p
made sweet moan, moan, moan,
216
moan, Made sweet moan.

The ecstasy of the knight as he kisses the maiden to sleep, and their intimacy, is echoed by a wordless chorus of split altos and tenors, in close chromatic seventh chords (Ex. 15.3, bars 260–5). The challenging choral writing here is essentially *a cappella*, accompanied only by a pedal in the low strings. The slithering chromatic major triads in the orchestra (bars 250–3) that accompany the words 'She took me to her elfin grot and there she gazed and sighed deep' are strongly reminiscent of the figuration that pervades Scott's concert piano work of 1916, *Rondeau de concert*.

The writing throughout demands a highly adept chorus, and the chromatic harmonies demand precise intonation, as further seen in Example 15.4. Scott's choral writing is often adventurous and unconventional: here the writing is eight-part, and at one point both tenor lines lie above the altos, by as much as an octave, while a range of 2½ octaves separates the first tenors from the second basses. As the chorus laments

Ex. 15.3 Scott, *La belle dame sans merci*, bars 249–65

249 Baritone Solo *mp* *poco animato*
She took me to her
p

251
elf - in grot And there she gazed and sigh - ed deep And
8va

15 *linger* *sosten.*
254 *tranquillo* *p*
there I shut her wild sad eyes so kissed to

Ex. 15.3 continued

the knight's unhappy fate, the choral writing becomes contrapuntal and disjunct, in addition to the involved vertical and horizontal chromatic movement (Ex. 15.5).

Measures 100–3 and 109–12 exhibit other unusual features of Scott's choral writing – specifically, the simultaneous declamation of separate texts, the chorally precarious group *portamento*, and the crescendo to sudden silence.

Ex. 15.4 Scott, *La belle dame sans merci,* bars 44–57

Ex. 15.4 continued

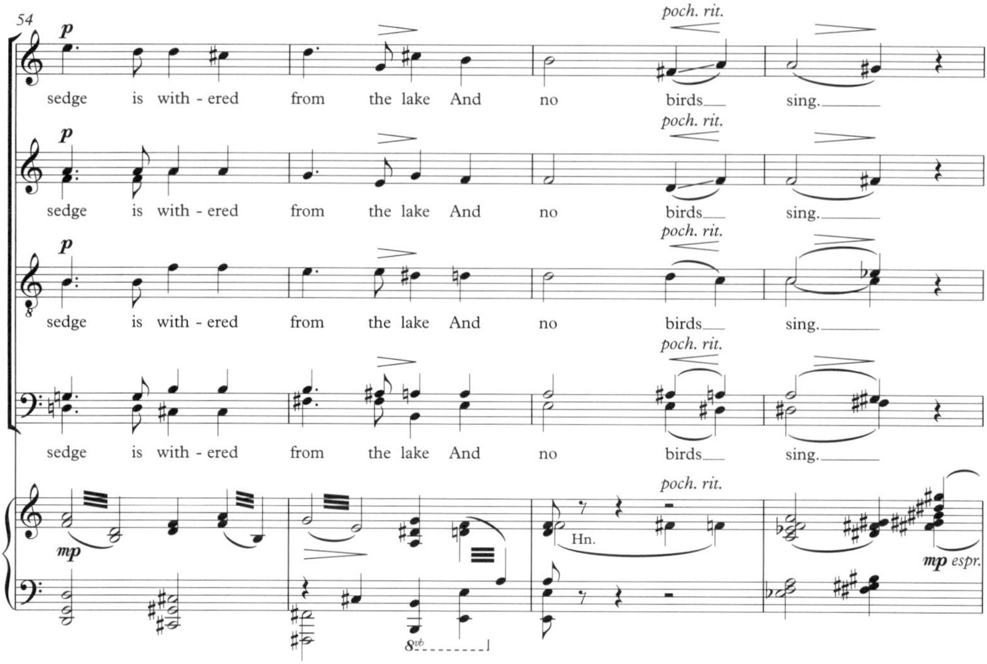

54 *p* sedge is with - ered from the lake And no *poch. rit.* birds sing.

p sedge is with - ered from the lake And no *poch. rit.* birds sing.

p sedge is with - ered from the lake And no *poch. rit.* birds sing.

sedge is with - ered from the lake And no *poch. rit.* birds sing.

mp Hn. *poch. rit.* *mp espr.* 8vb

Ex. 15.5 Scott, *La belle dame sans merci*, bars 95–112

Ex. 15.5 continued

100 *f poco ten.*

squir-rel's gran - ar - y is full and the har - vest's done, Ah, wretch - ed wight Ah,

f poco ten.

pale - ly loi-ter-ing, loi - ter-ing,

f poco ten.

lone and loi - ter-ing,

poco ten. *mf* Ah

sedge has with - er'd from the lake

7

f poco ten.

Ped. *

105

wretch - ed wight So hag - gard and so woe be - gone

A - lone A -

A - lone A -

wretch - ed wight wretch-ed wight So hag-gard, so

Ah, wretch - ed wight

5 5 *f* 5

Ex. 15.5 continued

PRINCESS MALEINE / FESTIVAL OVERTURE

Collins discusses this work at some length, in the context of Scott's emerging early musical style.[3] The original form of this work, now lost, was an orchestral overture from 1902 entitled *Princess Maleine*. It was revised ten years later with an expanded orchestra and the addition of a mixed chorus and organ *ad lib*, and was performed in Vienna in 1912. Scott returned to the work in 1929, renaming it *Festival Overture* and dedicating it to Grainger. Scott's eager absorption of Grainger's criticisms of the orchestration, and his revisions for a further version in 1933, say much about the esteem in which Scott held his friend's opinions, their often disarming candidness notwithstanding.[4]

[3] Sarah Collins, *The Aesthetic Life of Cyril Scott* (Boydell, 2013), pp. 182–4. Collins states that it is 'difficult to ascertain how much of the *Festival Overture* was written in the earliest years of the century', since the 1902 *Princess Maleine* overture upon which it is based was destroyed by the composer. Her ensuing discussion emphasises how different in style this work is from the conventional musical language of the Symphony No. 1 of 1900, quoting the extravagant choral interjections of the *Festival Overture*. The chorus was not added to the work, however, until *c.* 1912. Scott's harmonic and metric experimentation certainly dates from the turn of the century, but is more definitely traceable in other early works still extant, such as the *Scherzo*, Op. 25.

[4] When Scott was living at Pevensey Bay, Grainger posted the following suggestions to him:

2 bars before 4 – I don't like the flute with horn. All too loud & thick between 4 & 5. Between 6 & 7 all too thick & heavily scored (more like Strauss than CS). 7, melodic outline lost again, breaking the continuity. Feel that the strings ? (check this!) [*sic.*] / 8 should start p – and go to mf. 9 is too loud & should not work up to ff. 8 bars after 9 (Piu tranq) is also too loud. The 2 flute passages are disturbing & seem superfluous. / 8 bars after 10 (? check) [*sic.*] melodic outline lost in mere chords brass reeds all 1st violins. Contra fag. better out. Too thick. / 6 bars after 11 would prefer triangle not

Table 15.1 The various versions of *Princess Maleine / Festival Overture* and *Nativity Hymn / Noël: Christmas-Overture*

Princess Maleine / Festival Overture			
Version	original	revised	final
Title	*Princess Maleine*, Op. 18 (S 40)	*Princess Maleine* (S 16)	*Festival Overture* (S 19)
Date of composition	1899–1902	1912	May 1929–1933
Scoring	orchestra	chorus, organ, orchestra	orchestra
First performance	22 Aug. 1907, cond. Henry Wood, Queen's Hall	22 Apr. 1912, cond. Franz Schreker, Vienna Phil. Orch.	9 May 1934, cond. Adrian Boult, Queen's Hall
Notes	withdrawn	withdrawn	–
Nativity Hymn / Noël: Christmas-Overture			
Version	original	revised	final
Title	*Christmas Overture*, Op. 10 (S 47)	*Nativity Hymn* (S 18)	*Noël: Christmas-Overture* (S 55)
Date of composition	*c.* 1900	1913	1930
Scoring	orchestra	soli, mixed chorus, orchestra	orchestra, organ, chorus *ad lib*
First performance	13 Nov. 1906, cond. Landon Ronald, London SO	April 1914 (cancelled because of WW1)	20 Sept. 1932, cond. Sir Henry Wood, Queen's Hall
Notes	–	PV score 1923, Stainer & Bell, continuation of *Christmas Overture*	optional ending, *Nativity Hymn*, adds soli/chorus

NATIVITY HYMN / NOËL: CHRISTMAS-OVERTURE

The *Nativity Hymn* is Scott's second-longest choral work, only exceeded by the *Hymn of Unity*. Chronologically its history roughly parallels that of the *Festival Overture*. Table 15.1 serves to clarify the confusing history of these two works. Both date from the turn of the century in their original orchestra-only form, then were revised and expanded roughly a decade later. When the war intervened, both works were shelved, to be revisited only in the late 1920s.

The orchestra-only original *Christmas Overture*, Op. 10, laced *Good King Wenceslas* and *See the Conquering Hero Comes* into the score, dressed up with characteristic flamboyant harmonies. When Scott returned to a Christmas theme in 1913, he decided to pen a cantata that would be a continuation of the overture. The seventeenth-century metaphysical poet Richard Crashaw provided Scott with an appealing text for musical

trilling. Am doubtful about celesta with all those chords & continuing so long. Think it best for it to come in 4 bars before 13 as in my score. Passage starting 2 bars after 13 too heavy. Does not sound joyous & dance-like & should not work to ff at Allegro con spirito. And the latter should start mp & work up. The whole section is too much on the [same?] level of loudness. 5 bars after 19 surely you mean [minim] = 80 not [crotchet] = 80. 8 bars after 21 ff for flute seems too loud. (Letter with estate.)

Such frank criticism is in keeping with Grainger's reworking of the Op. 17 piano sonata into the *Handelian Rhapsody*, and reflects the strength of their friendship. Perhaps such critical intimacy can be achieved only between those who have been friends from school days.

setting. The two pastoral characters of the poem, Tityrus and Thyrsis, are given to baritone and tenor soli respectively, while the chorus both outlines the narrative and functions responsorially. Tityrus chastises the World for choosing so lowly a place as the manger for Christ's birth, and contrasts the darkness of the night with the bright dawn of redemption. Scott's setting responds accordingly, making good use of celesta, piano, harp and organ to suggest celestial joy. Thyrsis likens the story-to-be of the newborn Christ to the fable of the phoenix, and wonders whether the warm down of the Seraphim will 'pass for pure'. Scott employs large orchestral forces, but the scoring is delicate and restrained – perhaps he took his cue from Berlioz's *L'enfance du Christ*.

It is difficult to know how much of the early *Christmas Overture* informs the writing of his 1928 *Noël*. *Noël* was designed as the new overture to the *Nativity Hymn*. It is a substantial overture in which four seasonal carols and songs are laced into the fabric towards the end: *The Twelve Days of Christmas, In dulci jubilo* (fourteenth-century melody), *Ehre sei Gott in der Höhe* (1668), and *Die heilige Nacht* (Gruber, 1818). These short interjections are given to the organ alone, or can be sung by the optional mixed chorus.

MYSTIC ODE

The *Mystic Ode* of 1932 is a short paean of praise to the ultimate deity, for male chorus and orchestra, with a text by the composer beginning 'Hail to Thee, the ONE, the Changeless, in Whom are all things, Who art in all things, yet beyond all things.' Such phrases as 'The spirit of Fraternity', 'Because man, in his pride and nescience, hath turned his face away from Thine effulgence', and 'Because the nations have walked in the valleys of separateness' portend the textual style and message of the post-war *Hymn of Unity*. The dense writing for six-part male chorus is deftly handled, and modal parallel major triads in second inversion prevail, particularly in the laudatory climactic moments. The orchestra, rather than attempting to compensate for the absence of female voices, is pared down to join in the texture of the male voices. The string section consists only of celli and double basses, and bassoons are the only woodwind instruments. There is, however, a full complement of brass, which predominate in the instrumental interludes and dramatic moments.

MIRABELLE

The cantata *Mirabelle*, for soli, mixed chorus and strings (or *a cappella*), was published in the same year as *Mystic Ode* but belongs to an entirely different tradition – that of Tennyson's *Enoch Arden*, which may have served as a model for the subject matter and narrative style. Its counterparts in Scott's output are his incidental music to *Smetse Smee*, and the trilogy of narrative choral works from 1924 for male chorus (*The Emir's Serenade, The Huntsman's Dirge*, and *The Rat-Catcher*). The text is poetic throughout, and likely to be by Scott himself. The story unfolds in ten short vignettes covering the eighteen years of Mirabelle's life. The first two celebrate her birth, and the fuss the entire town makes over what to name her. By the time she is six years old Mirabelle is seen by the townsfolk as a 'scurvy maid' who plays mean tricks on her playmates. Soon enough, the parents lament the passing of the years, their three children having grown up. Mirabelle, now seventeen, is the youngest, and within a year the women of the town gossip over Mirabelle, who has pledged her troth to a sailor who was passing through. It is not long before she is lamenting the absence of her sailor, and has developed a reputation in town of being 'a baggage'. The other lads in town ('Seven Swains') all vie vainly for her attention. No sooner has one, Pat, seemingly won her heart than her sailor returns to marry her. In a fit of jealousy, Pat stabs her while on her way to the wedding.

Scott makes effective use of split chorus for the dialogues between the townsfolk, and between Mirabelle and her suitors. One of the most effective vignettes is the fifth, 'Told While Spinning'. Here Chorus 1 divulges the gossip while the women of Chorus 2 spin.[5] Unlike in Wagner's and Gounod's spinning scenes, Scott has the singers themselves imitating the sound of the spinning wheel, on gentle 'rr' melismas. As the vignette unfolds, both choruses involve themselves in spinning and gossiping, in a variety of imaginative combinations. The ensuing 'Mirabelle's Love Plaint' is Mirabelle's *Gretchen am Spinnrade* moment. But here the lament is stylised, with the entire chorus singing on her behalf (Ex. 15.6). In 'Seven Swains' Mirabelle thwarts the ardour of her suitors by revealing to them all that she loves none of them, but rather a sailor who is now returning to marry her (Ex. 15.7).

The musical language of *Mirabelle* displays little of the modernity of Scott's other works from the 1930s. He has tempered his language as he endeavours to paint a stock legendary narrative in quaint hues. The harmonies are almost uniformly diatonic, even in the quarrels and the final stabbing scene, and hover between tonality and modality. Perhaps he was also catering to a wider choral tradition here than in many of his other choral works. *Mirabelle* is a dated work belonging to the genre of narrative cantata so popular in Victorian and early twentieth-century England, but it has some beguiling moments and can still be effective for an audience prepared to indulge its period conceits.

SUMMERLAND AND ANTHEMS

The 1935 choral *Summerland* has no musical connection to the eponymous set of piano miniatures written almost twenty-five years earlier. Indeed, the two works provide a good example of the transformation in Scott's harmonic language from 1907 to 1935. The choral work depicts a Utopian astral realm where all is bliss, love and harmony. With much repetition, the text is non-narrative, and functions as a scaffold for purely musical depiction and elaboration. The tripartite mantra, 'Summerland, Devachan, Lotusland', confirms the identity of these concepts in Scott's mind, and suggests what he probably had in mind in 1905 when composing his signature piano work, *Lotus Land*. Devachan derives from theosophical precepts and is roughly analogous to the Christian idea of purgatory, referring to a dwelling place after death and before reincarnation into the physical world. The music unfolds in a mosaic of tonal sections, effective in its unexpected juxtaposition of disparate tonal centres. The musical flow is akin to *The Garden of Soul Sympathy* (S 210), but with a later harmonic language involving free interplay of chords based on thirds and fourths. There is no development of material, as befits the timeless nature of the poetry. Like other later choral works of Scott's, the eight-part writing for the choir is challenging and demands fine musicianship in all parts.

It is odd to find Scott in the mid-1930s penning four short works for the Anglican liturgy, for chorus and organ. They were all published in 1935 in Stainer & Bell's

[5] Such scenes are conventional in stage works and opera; this one is reminiscent here of the Spinning Chorus in Wagner's *Der fliegender Holländer*, or the chorus of seamstresses in Charpentier's *Louise*.

Ex. 15.6 Scott, *Mirabelle*, bars 13–40

Ex. 15.6 continued

Ex. 15.7 Scott, *Mirabelle*, bars 58–74

Ex. 15.7 continued

'Modern Church Services' – a series featuring *Te Deums*, 'Mags & Nuncs', masses and services by a host of minor composers, but also Stanford and Dyson. This was the only association Stainer & Bell had with Scott, apart from the *Nativity Hymn*. These anthems perhaps originated from a commission, and stand in marked contrast with his *Summerland* for chorus and orchestra, published in the same year. The four Scott anthems are *Benedicite omnia opera Domine*, *Benedictus es Domine*, an Evening Service, and *Jubilate Deo*. The Evening Service was not the first Scott setting of the *Magnificat* and *Nunc dimittis*, as West had published an earlier setting twenty years before.[6]

To think of these liturgical works as hackwork for Scott is as misleading as it is for the piano miniatures and songs. *A propos* of this, a most interesting orchestral version of the *Benedicite* in Scott's hand is extant, implying that the work may have been intended originally for the concert hall, that the published organ version is a reduction for liturgical use, and that the other three anthems may also have had a parallel existence, with their orchestral versions now lost. The only reason we still have the *Benedicite* in its orchestral version is that Novello returned it via registered mail to Marjorie Hartston

[6] The only other work of Scott's published by West is the odd *Dorothy Waltz* for piano of 1916, which (if by Scott at all) may well have been penned out of financial need, and presumably stemmed from their recent association regarding the present choral work. See Catalogue of Scott's Music, below, at S 449.

in Eastbourne in July 1985. Unfortunately there is no date on the manuscript, so it is possible that it was expanded from an original organ version sometime after 1935.[7]

Scott eschews the more adventurous compositional features of his other works from the 1930s in these settings, presumably in consideration of their expected use by parish choirs, organists and music directors. All are conveniently in C, and unfold in straightforward diatonic fashion, after the manner of so many other anthems of this kind. The occasional foray into chromatic parallelisms reveals a more authentic Scott voice, albeit found primarily in the organ interludes rather than in the choral writing.

ODE TO GREAT MEN

The libretto of this 1936 ode was assembled by Scott from three sources – Ecclesiasticus 44, J. R. Lowell's *Ode recited at the Harvard Commemoration, 1865*, and Shelley's *Prometheus Unbound* – linked by their common adulation of all those who have passed on, famous and otherwise. The text is entrusted entirely to the tenor soloist, with the women's chorus entering wordlessly only at the end of the ode. The score in fact calls for nine altos only, who enter on the words of Prometheus, 'The wand'ring voices and the shadows there of all that man becomes'.

Their low register harkens back to the first of Shelley's lines, 'The echoes of the human world which tell of the low voice of love, almost unheard.' This commemoration of lost lives from a pacifist is echoed, after World War 2, in the *Visitation* and *Miserere* from the *Hymn of Unity*.

HYMN OF UNITY

The World War 2 years were difficult ones for Scott. The family unit split apart in 1939, and Scott spent the war lodging in several places, as he could afford them, in southwest England, without access to a piano much of the time. As a pacifist, he was profoundly disillusioned by events in Europe. As an itinerant misfit, he must have felt a strong sense of alienation on many levels – personal, social, political and artistic. He felt that he would not live much longer, as is reflected in the title of his unpublished memoir, *Near the End of Life: Candid Confessions and Reflections*. He stopped composing, and turned to other pursuits, including alternative medicine and the writing of plays and poetry. The catalogue of musical works is vacant from 1940 to 1946, and publication ceased entirely from 1939 to 1953. It was presumably during these years that he also wrote *Health, Diet and Commonsense*, *The Christian Paradox* and *Medicine, Rational and Irrational* – all of which were published – and *The Poems of a Musician* and *The Rhymed Reflections of a Ruthless Rhymer*, which were not. A dozen straight plays, all written under the pseudonym M. Arkwright Lundy, were written during these years, though none has ever reached the stage.

For these reasons, two substantial works of the immediate post-war period are of considerable interest: the opera *Maureen O'Mara*, and the oratorio *Hymn of Unity*. Scott tells us that it was through Master Koot Hoomi that he came to understand that he had more to contribute musically to the world in this lifetime. These works,

[7] It is also possible that the works were written much earlier, perhaps contemporaneous with the 1900 *Magnificat* (S 15) or the *Magnificat and Nunc Dimittis* of 1915 (S. 448).

and presumably those that followed, all owe their existence to this conviction.[8] In 1944, Mahatma Koomi had reactivated his occult communication with Scott, through Scott's partner Marjorie Hartston, who received visits from him. It was then that the Master advised the composition of a new opera, which occupied Scott for much of 1946. The *Hymn of Unity* was the product of the latter portion of his productive stay at Ella Grainger's Sussex cottage the following year.

There is good reason to believe that Scott considered the *Hymn of Unity* to be his *magnum opus* as a composer. The only other work in his œuvre of comparable dimension is the opera *The Alchemist*, which similarly deals with lofty philosophical, spiritual and ethical matters. The text of the *Hymn* bears the message of universal brotherhood and peace more insistently and ardently than any of Scott's other texted works. Its inherent preachiness is perhaps less to modern taste than it might have been in 1947, and it remains unperformed. This was predicted by Scott:

> While living in Pevensey Bay, it happened that after completing some shorter works, I suddenly had the urge to write a non-sectarian Oratorio, otherwise a universalist choral work, which I thought to call *Hymn of Unity*. But being uncertain whether my urge could be 'trusted', I did not actually engage on it till I had received the assurance that the undertaking was approved of; whereafter I wrote the libretto in about three weeks and finished the whole work in around six months. Not that I hoped for a performance of it in the near future, since I fully realised that until the Aquarian Age – the Age of unification we have just entered – had got more under way, it might be asking too much of any British choral society to produce an English Oratorio which embraced other religions besides the Christian. Thus I do not expect my *Hymn of Unity* will be either performed or published during my life-time ...
>
> Why, I questioned, should The Masters, who know all about the influence of the stars, bother to use me, or any other receptive composer, for the creation of some lengthy musical work at a time when the prospects for its performance were not at all favourable, or were even definitely bad? And the reasonable answer I received was; that although the astrological aspects at a given time might be excellent for the inspiring and composing of a particular kind of music, it by no means follows that they must also be good for its getting a hearing. From The Masters' point of view the first thing is to get the work written; the rest if needs be can wait – sometimes even as long as till after the composer's death.[9]

The prose of the *Hymn* indulges in an archaic King James religiosity that may strike a modern ear as being affected, misplaced, or even comical or blasphemous. Whatever Scott's reasoning, he felt compelled to lift the text out of colloquial commonplace, and this was to his mind the most convincing, if not the only available manner of doing so.[10] It is entirely possible that he reasoned that the familiar Biblical English would engage the traditional Christian fold, and that the depiction of an alterna-

[8] Scott, *Bone of Contention* (Aquarian Press, 1969), pp. 215–16.

[9] Ibid., pp. 220–2. Scott lived at Pevensey Bay from 1945 to 1947.

[10] The unpublished performing edition of the score that exists includes an altered rendering of some parts of the text, created by Desmond Scott and myself, and designed to render the text more natural to modern audiences. It is available through the Fleisher Collection at Philadelphia Public Library.

tive interpretation of morality and ultimate truths lying in the *Hymn*, employing the same sanctified archaic literary style, would not be lost on the attentive.[11] He had already indulged this literary predilection in *The Alchemist* and other vocal works. The musical structure also borrows from liturgical ritual, as in the two *Chorales*, the *Litany*, and *Invocation*. The text – Scott's own – concerns the universal brotherhood of mankind, as espoused in several of his published books, and must have seemed particularly urgent in 1947, as the full horrors of World War 2 continued to emerge. The message is universally timely, and has become, if anything, even more compelling today.

The work lasts over an hour and unfolds in fifteen parts, with chorus present in twelve of them. Mezzo-soprano and baritone soli function as Dame Nature and as the Sage respectively. In the first *Prelude*, the chorus identifies the essential message: 'Alone through Unity can come our salvation … Truly is separateness the deadliest of all sins … But through the joyous bond of Brotherhood all may be achieved.' The opening, 'Unity! Unity! Unity!', immediately evokes the *Sanctus* from the Mass, and perhaps also the tripartite repetitions of Masonic symbolism. Harmonies become more austere and dissonant as the text warns of the dangers of separateness (Ex. 15.8). A jubilant C major, peppered with 7th and 9th chords, underscores the concluding text, 'Unity, Brotherhood, Fraternity! The names are three, but the truth is one. Let there be Unity among all the peoples of the world so that the Kingdom of Heaven may be established on earth!'

The ensuing *Confession* is a choral lament, with tenor and soprano soli, for the errors of mankind. 'Civilisation! – a long and lofty-sounding word it is; but how can there be civilisation when there lacketh the essential thing … civility?' The harmonic austerity of Example 15.9, with its tritones and augmented chords, typifies Scott's handling of texts concerned with human transgression.

The *Visitation* comes next. It is sung by a Sage 'from another planet', who is visiting earth to dispense ultimate wisdom, and is delivered in part by unaccompanied recitative: 'I am aeons older than ye, and have outgrown your follies and your limitations … Strangely childish are ye who deem yourselves enlightened' (Ex. 15.10).

The postlude leads *attacca* into a *Chorale* in the Protestant service tradition, 'May the High Powers enlighten mankind!' (Ex. 15.11).

The allusions to war in the *Visitation* become more prominent in the following *Miserere*, a lament that puts a twist on received dogma: 'Ah, we who wrangled and fought as to the manner God should be worshipped, Were we so sure that He yearned to be worshipped at all? Because we created our God in our own image, Therefore did we endow him with our own vanity.' The movement concludes with a lament for all those who have perished in war, and for those whose lives have been forever altered because of it, though it ends on a more uplifting tone (Ex. 15.12).

Part 6, *Exhortation*, is Dame Nature's warning to humankind that free will without wisdom will be its undoing. This text reflects Scott's view – remarkably prescient,

[11] Scott's own book *The Adept of Galilee* lends additional force to this interpretation. The majority of the book is a complete rewriting of the Gospel narrative according to Occult precepts. Christ, for instance, does not die on the Cross, but enters a state of Samadhi. Cyril Scott, *The Adept of Galilee: A Story and an Argument, by the Author of 'The Initiate'* (George Routledge & Sons, 1920), p. 390.

Ex. 15.8 Scott, *Hymn of Unity*, 'Prelude', bars 118–29

Ex. 15.8 continued

Ex. 15.9 Scott, *Hymn of Unity*, 'Confession', bars 74–89

Ex. 15.9 continued

Ex. 15.10 Scott, *Hymn of Unity*, 'Visitation', bars 94–134

Ex. 15.10 continued

Ex. 15.10 continued

Ex. 15.11 Scott, *Hymn of Unity*, 'Chorale I', bars 175–84

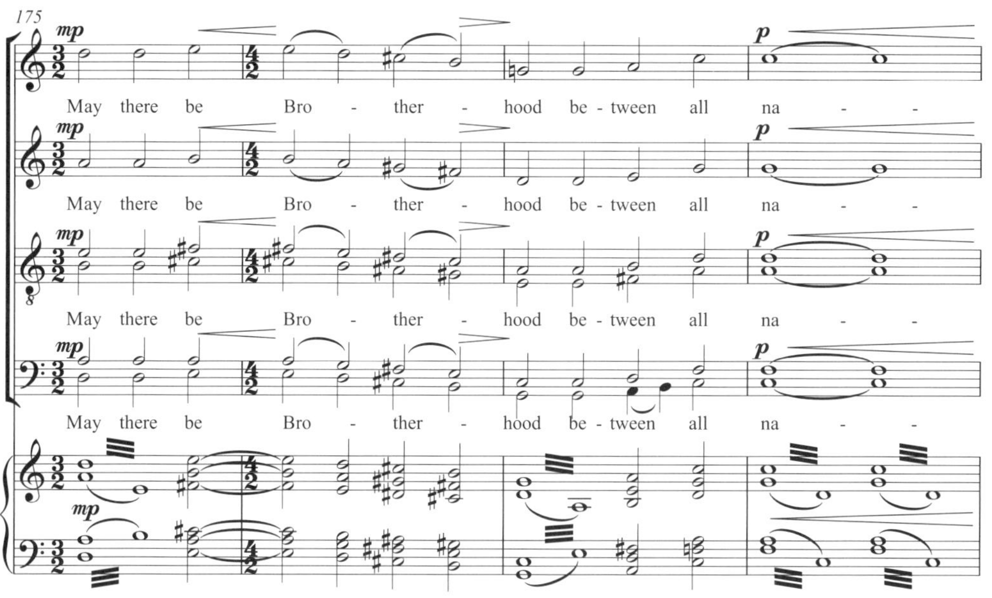

Ex. 15.12 Scott, *Hymn of Unity*, 'Miserere', bars 101–15

106

ff

pp sub. *mp*

12

Life more a - bun-dant in the Realm of spir-its____

Life more a - bun-dant in the Realm of spir-its____

Life more a - bun-dant in the Realm of spir-its____

Life more a - bun-dant in the Realm of spir-its____

12

5

pp sub.

ff

Ex. 15.12 continued

given the challenges of our own century – that ignoring the imperative of Unity does not merely put humanity in jeopardy, but is also a cosmological concern. The prose unfolds in dramatic, scolding, dissonant recitative virtually throughout (Ex. 15.13). Nature then implores humanity to return to her axioms in a brief, more conciliatory passage, but returns at the end to fire and brimstone: 'Oh arrogant, presumptuous children … Try me not too far, lest it be needful that I should destroy you, as aeons ago I did destroy Atlantis!' Humanity is cowed into humiliated self-reproach in the ensuing choral lament, *De profundis* (Ex. 15.14).

The larger cosmological view of Unity made explicit in *Exhortation* continues in *De profundis*: 'The saying runs that man hath conquered Time and Space. Ah, would that first he had achieved the conquest of himself! A fatal victory, this: for lo! A neighbour now is every nation, and therefore a potential foe.' This lengthy collective sigh of despair begins and ends with the sense that we are 'beyond all hope', setting up the response of the believers in the ensuing *Jubilate I* – a sudden transformation of mood reminiscent of the *Crucifixus / Et resurrexit* of Bach's Mass in B minor.

The chorus in the ensuing *Jubilate I* provides the rejoinder: 'Away with your despondency! – those mighty Souls who have <u>attained</u> do work for your redemption. Unto the fold of Unity They lead the way.' It is a message of hope and joy, if only mankind will be receptive. 'They work for your emancipation. Repent, rejoice! Unto the fold of Unity they lead the way.' Although they are not named, the allusion is to the Great White Brotherhood of ascended masters, a cornerstone of Theosophical thought, to whom there is a reference in Revelation, Chapter 7.

Ex. 15.13 Scott, *Hymn of Unity*, 'Exhortation', bars 160–86

What think ye would come to pass if the migh-ty for-ces I do
wield should choose to pull their dif-fer-ent ways, and so de-
fy the Law of U-ni-ty? Ah, ver-i-ly, then the cos-mos would be
shat-tered! and ev-'ry liv-ing thing would per-ish!
ten.
marcato e rubato
agitato

Ex. 15.13 continued

Ex. 15.14 Scott, *Hymn of Unity*, 'De profundis', bars 19–33

Ex. 15.14 continued

Part 9, *Colloquy*, is the heart of the oratorio. The choral dialogue in the previous two movements is now identified as having been between the Sceptics (*De profundis*) and the Disciples (*Jubilate I*). A Sage (baritone), or enlightened seer, explodes the specious logic of the chorus of Sceptics, who declaim in short outbursts ('Impossible, we say!') and snaky, derisive polyphonic lines ('Fantastic dreams of idle dreamers'). The calm response of the Seer is summed up by the Disciples' chorus at the end, in flowing, harmonious phrases. 'He speaketh wisdom doth our Master: Well-being-for-all, and brotherhood. No idle sentimental dream of morbid souls is brotherhood, no sickly pious concept – it is the very flower of good sense.'

A further *Chorale* ensues, and the rest of the *Hymn of Unity* is a paean of joy, hope and reverence, increasingly adopting liturgical conventions familiar to Anglican congregations. The text and music of the *Litany* is responsorial, between the two soloists and the chorus functioning now as disciples. The alto soloist declaims the first five lines, with the choral response 'O pow'r of love in our hearts henceforth deliver us.' She is joined by the baritone soloist for the final four lines, with the choral response 'O spirit of brotherhood henceforth deliver us.' The *Jubilate II* is a chorus of those who have passed on and now inhabit an astral realm of peace and unity. In perhaps the most joyous moment in the score, they deliver a message to humanity: 'Although ye know it not, we strive for you, we joyful ones; we seek to whisper wisdom in your ears and guide you unto Unity.' The movement ends triumphantly (Ex. 15.15).

Before the final two choruses of joy and praise, the mezzo-soprano solo returns, as the Angel of Mercy, and exhorts humanity to embrace compassion as the ultimate virtue, and the path towards a perfect culture. The preachy scolding of Dame Nature earlier on finds only a distant echo in *The Angel of Mercy*, where the message is about clemency and kindness (Ex. 15.16).

Ex. 15.15 Scott, *Hymn of Unity*, 'Jubilate II', bars 114–26

Ex. 15.15 continued

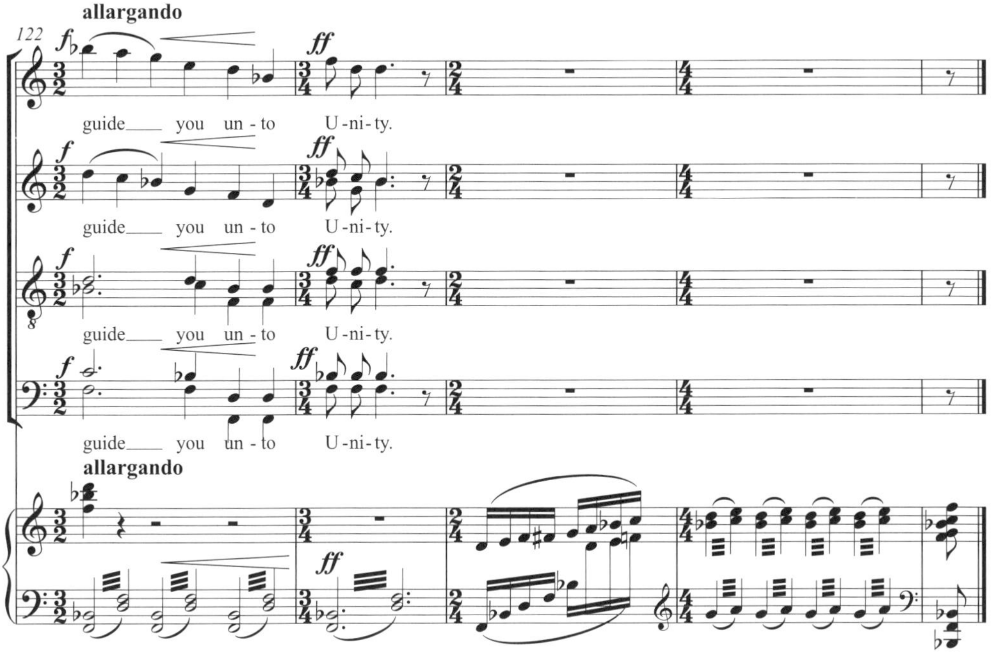

allargando
122
f
ff
guide you un - to U - ni - ty.
guide you un - to U - ni - ty.
guide you un - to U - ni - ty.
guide you un - to U - ni - ty.
allargando
ff

Ex. 15.16 Scott, *Hymn of Unity*, 'The Angel of Mercy', bars 115–32

12
115
(warmly)
C.
Com - pas - sion com -
mp
118
C.
pas - sion O ye im - mor - tals,

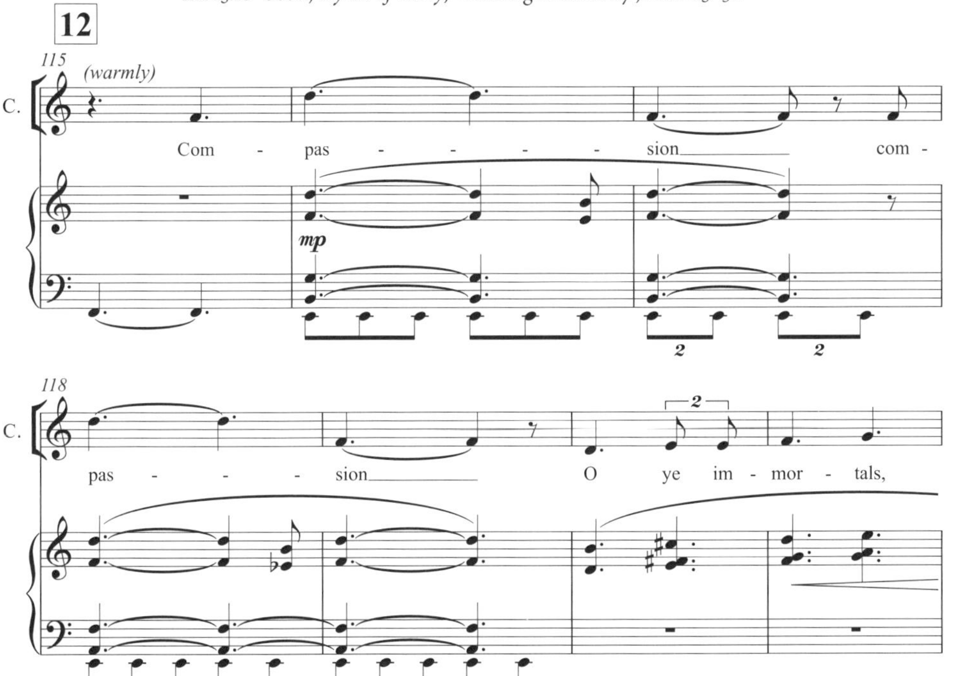

Ex. 15.16 continued

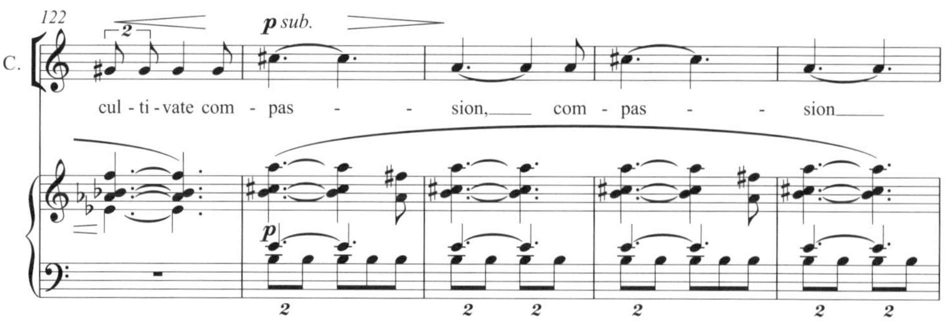

The penultimate chorus, *Invocation,* is a series of eight supplications unto the Great White Spirit to provide the world with the building blocks of brotherhood. The various sections of the chorus take turns pronouncing the first five invocations, and the baritone solo invokes the final three, concluding with, 'May our hearts be suffused by the golden light of Brotherhood, so that we may regard all the nations of this earth as one family and as one kin.' Each of the supplications has an 'Amen' response from the chorus, each one musically unique, increasing in musical elaboration and ecstasy, and abounding in florid triadic triplet melismas. The fourth 'Amen' (Ex. 15.17) features the sopranos and tenors, the latter singing almost two octaves higher than the altos. Chorus 'Amens' then meld with the final baritone supplication to end the movement (Ex. 15.18).

The *Final Chorus* is a formal choral anthem, a pantheistic summation of all that has gone before, and with the chorus declaiming throughout in exact rhythmic unison. The oratorio ends with 'may the spirit of Unity irradiate our hearts, so that the dark and deadly sin of separateness may vanish like the night when morning wakes, and that the Age of Brotherhood may dawn and may endure for Man.' Indeed.

Ex. 15.17 Scott, *Hymn of Unity*, 'Invocation', bars 45–8

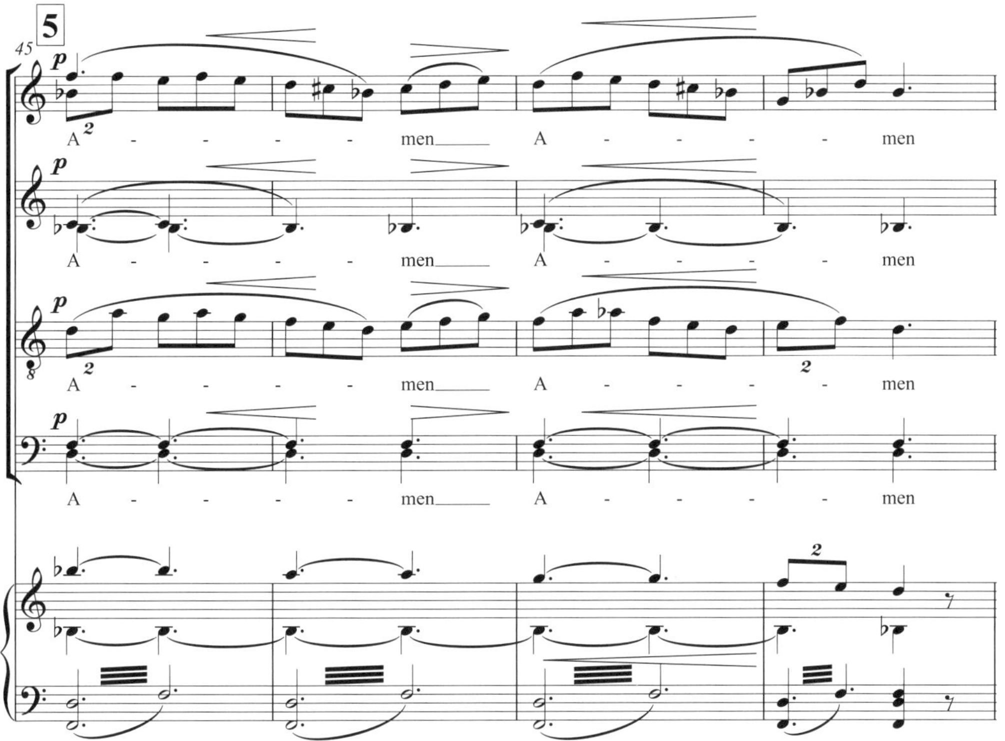

Ex. 15.18 Scott, *Hymn of Unity*, 'Invocation', bars 90–113

Ex. 15.18 continued

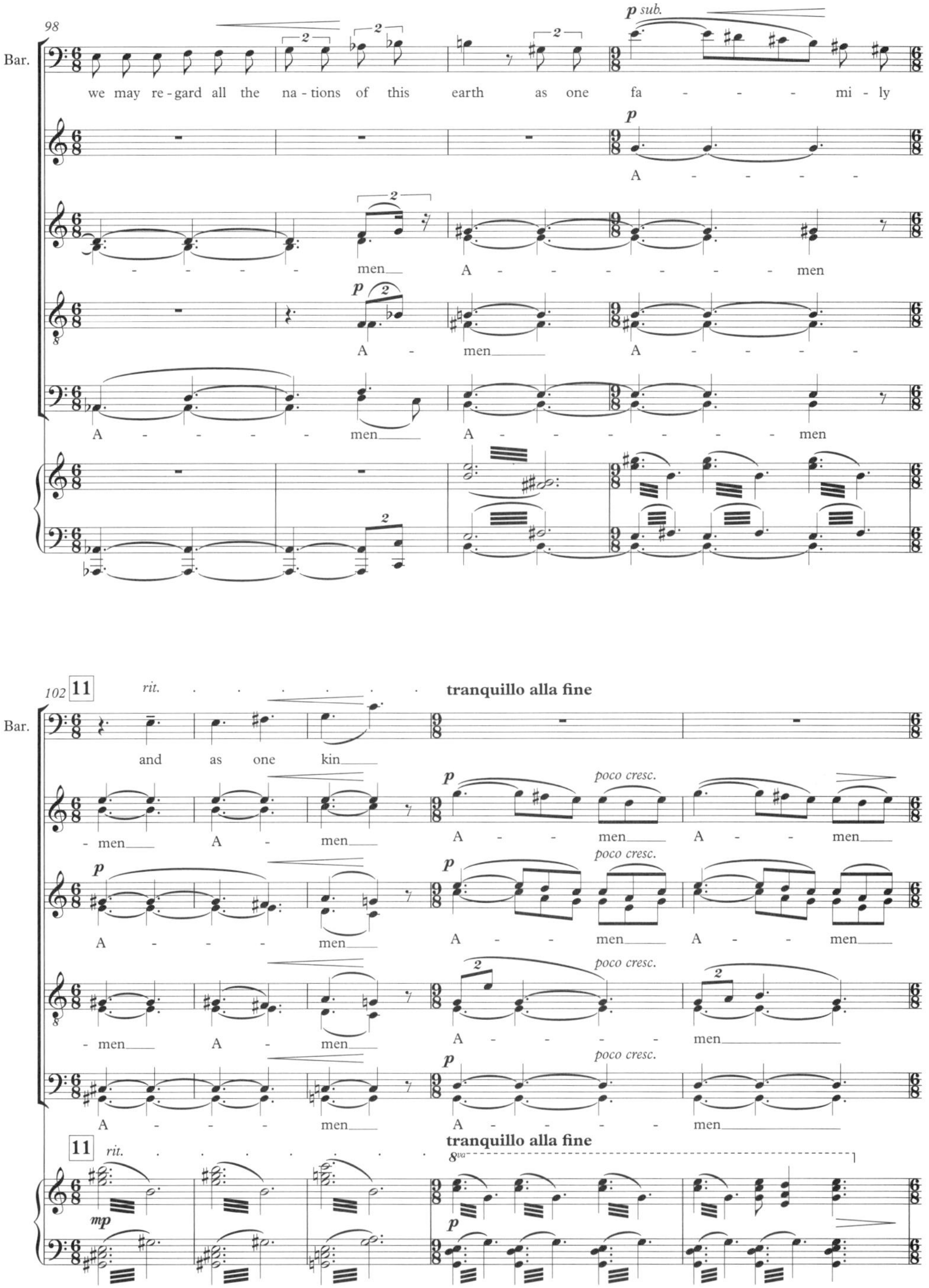

102 **11** *rit.* . . . . **tranquillo alla fine**
Bar.
and as one kin
p *poco cresc.*
- men A - men A - - men A - - men
p *poco cresc.*
A - - - men A - - men A - - men
p *poco cresc.*
- men A - men A - - - - men
p *poco cresc.*
A - - - men A - - - - men
11 *rit.* . . . . **tranquillo alla fine**
8va
mp
p

Ex. 15.18 continued

16

The Songs

VALERIE LANGFIELD

THESE are not parlour songs, easy on the ear, easy to absorb, passing through voice or fingers and making little impression *en route*. The best create an individual sound-world, but some singers will find them hard to grasp; their angularity and chromaticism mean that they are demanding to sing, and they require singers willing to put their technique and artistry fully at Scott's disposal, to enable the musical painting to come alive. The songs do not set the precise meaning of the words: they are not settings of the poems as such, but rather, settings of the sense behind the poems, of the images that these evoke. This is why Scott's settings of Dowson and Watson, especially, are so effective: the words are in themselves almost irrelevant, but Dowson's and Watson's gift of evoking emotions and memories provided the means within which Scott could create a private world.[1]

It is of course not possible in a chapter of this scale to examine all Scott's songs, so I have limited myself to most of the settings of Ernest Dowson, Rosamund Marriott Watson, and Scott himself; the folk-song settings; and those that I consider of particular interest. It is therefore a personal choice. Appendix 1, at the end of this volume, gives details of where I have found occasional misprints (through examination of high- and low-voice versions of the same song); this is a brief and by no means complete list. In giving an overview, I have also endeavoured to give enough information to enable performers to decide which songs to seek out and explore further. A few songs are available only in manuscript; I have only mentioned these where they shed light on Scott's development.

Scott was commissioned to write songs and piano pieces on a regular basis; this provided an income, but their brevity and need for accessibility coloured their composition and their reception. An undated press notice from the *Daily Telegraph* is illuminating: 'Mr. Cyril Scott's music is fresh and pleasing, and the writing shows no sign of effort.' Some of Scott's 150 or so songs are distinctly unremarkable, but the majority are very fine and many are exceptional; that these remain unknown is not

[1] I am delighted to acknowledge the enthusiastic assistance of Louis Hurst (bass-baritone) and Timothy Langston (tenor), at the time both post-graduate students at the Royal Northern College of Music, Manchester, England, for singing the majority of the songs through with me over a sustained period, and for making pertinent comments from the singer's viewpoint. Leslie De'Ath generously made available to me his copies of many of the songs. Tessa Sutcliffe helped me to find a way in to writing about them, when I was becoming somewhat swamped. Stephen Shutt read through early drafts in detail; I am deeply grateful for his invaluable comments and thoughtful insights. Above all, my greatest thanks are due to Desmond Scott: he made his copies of songs available to me, throughout has encouraged me and answered with enduring patience my constant questions, and, by his initial request, has made it possible for me to discover many wonderful songs.

justifiable. It does not help that so few are still in print; the rest are to be found in various libraries, in secondhand shops, on internet sites, and through inter-library loan. About fifty songs have been recorded or broadcast, some many times, but very few recordings are readily available now.

Although it is the poem that engenders the song, thereafter the words are the least important aspect, and in Scott's finest songs it is the image conjured by the words, rather than the words themselves, to which he reacts. This was recognised in 1909, when George Lowe wrote 'After hearing some of Cyril Scott's best settings of the various lyrics that he has chosen, one feels that he has caught the true inner and pictorial meaning of the poem set.'[2] Even if the text itself is maudlin or trivial, or simply indifferent, it can inspire an effective song. This text (by Irene McLeod, a contemporary of Siegfried Sassoon) is not a promising one, but Scott responds to the mood, and the repetition of 'O', often placing it on the first beat of the bar to emphasise it:

O deep mysterious face
Of vast slow-breathing night!
O dim clouds drifting far!
O passionate still space,
O rising deathless star,
O purple infinite.

The song, dating from 1926, relatively late in Scott's song-writing oeuvre, opens with slow chords, marked *adagio*, pivoting about E and alternating C-sharp minor and C major; it is bold to continue such a relentless, hypnotic march, but it results in a serene, spacious song, supported by the use of the piano's wide compass (Ex. 16.1). The middle section changes speed and texture, illustrating the fire in the words, and the parallel chords maintain and make no attempt to settle the indeterminate key. Not until the end, following a return to the opening chord pattern, does Scott finally resolve onto C major. This is a large-scale song, needing courage on the part of the singer to hold the measured tempo. On the page, it looks awkward and contrived, and the vocal line crosses registers and is typically angular, but its elegiac quality is Schubertian in scale.

Many songs have descriptive accompaniments: in 'Rain' (published in 1916; Ex. 16.2), we hear plenty of musical precipitation; in 'Dairy Song' and 'Song of Arcady' (alternative settings of the same text), we hear the butter being churned; we hear the waves in 'Sea-Song of Gafran', and the moan of the wind in 'Night-Wind'.

These soloistic accompaniments – works of art in themselves, often difficult, always pianistic – enable the voice to be projected over the top with a degree of independence, while being well supported. Other songs have a more obvious interdependence between voice and piano: 'My Captain' (text by Whitman, published in 1914) and 'Trafalgar' (text by Thomas Hardy, published in 1904) are in this vein, though they are not otherwise typical of Scott; generally the voice is treated as a

[2] George Lowe, 'The Songs of Cyril Scott', *The Musical Standard* (13 March 1909), pp. 165–6.

Ex. 16.1 Scott, 'Aspiration', bars 3–6

Ex. 16.2 Scott, 'Rain', bars 7–12

means to an end, as another strand in the construction of the work. Scott drives his songs forward with the musical ideas, not by virtue of a particular vocal line. 'Lullaby' (Christina Rossetti) and 'Blackbird's Song' (Rosamund Marriott Watson), published in 1908 and 1906 respectively, were very well-known and are readily found secondhand; my first encounter with Scott's music was with his 1905 song 'Don't Come in Sir, Please!', also very popular, and given to me by my then singing teacher. As a niece of Alec Rowley, she was of a generation that had grown up with Scott's reputation as a composer of such items, and of little else. The words for 'Lullaby' (Christina Rossetti) are almost doggerel, those for 'Don't Come in' (text from the Chinese, by H. A. Giles) twee, but those for 'Blackbird's song' (Watson again) are of much better quality; all three are transformed by their accompaniments, 'Lullaby' hypnotically soothing (Edmund Rubbra described 'the perfectly matched vocal line and piano' as '[hiding] a good deal of artifice'),[3] 'Don't Come in' simple and appealing – despite its arch coyness, the song remains surprisingly fresh – and 'Blackbird's Song' with a decorative right-hand part, imitating birdsong, and full of Scott's typical arabesques. Scott came to bear a grudge against the song, written out of guilt at not having 'fulfilled [his] duty to the good Mr Elkin, having long kept him waiting for an item to publish.'

Exact composition dates are generally not known but are likely to be close to the date of publication; except where otherwise stated, all dates given here are dates of publication. Scott assigned opus numbers to the earlier songs, until confusion arose when different publishers became involved and began assigning duplicate numbers. Consequently, from around 1911, his songs were un-numbered.

Beyond a growing confidence, Scott's song-writing style developed little over the years; it is fundamentally diatonic, despite a rich chromaticism. Throughout the entire output run several common threads: a lesser use of irregular time-signatures than in other works; the use of music to portray the mood of the poem; a sense of detachment, as if he is exploring the harmonies as a technical exercise, to see what he can do with them, rather than involving them with the poetry; and an angularity of vocal line. The angularity is largely explained in a document that Scott wrote in 1942, entitled *Near the End of Life, Candid Confessions and Recollections*:

> To me, the words have been of such equal importance as the music, that I have usually endeavoured to imitate in the melodic curve the inflections of the voice as they would naturally occur if the verses were recited.

The consequence of this, however, is that the vocal lines can be hard to place in the voice: not impossible, but they need an accomplished singer to manage them. The hymn-like 'Invocation' (Margaret Maitland Radford, 1916) has difficult downward leaps, though its breadth of sound has an Elgarian touch. Songs such as 'Lullaby' and 'Arietta' (Duffield Bendall, 1910) need less technical ability, a significant factor in their popularity, and one that overrides the quality of the song, particularly in the case of the latter.

[3] 'Composer Portrait of Cyril Scott', BBC Network Three, 26 April 1967, introduction by Edmund Rubbra. See p. 403.

'Meditation' (1915) has an even more angular line than 'Invocation', with falls of 6ths, 7ths, octaves and 9ths, usually in accordance with the falling cadence of the word – for example, 'after', 'roses', 'closes'. It is a setting of Dowson's poem 'Vitae Summa Brevis Spem Nos Vetat Incohare Longam' (a quotation from Horace, 'The brief sum of life forbids us the hope of enduring long'). The full text is:

> They are not long, the weeping and the laughter,
> Love and desire and hate:
> I think they have no portion in us after
> We pass the gate.
>
> They are not long, the days of wine and roses:
> Out of a misty dream
> Our path emerges for a while, then closes
> Within a dream.

Scott opens the song with a tonic pedal under oscillating dominant chords with added 7ths, 9ths and 13ths, a hazy sound, which he uses at the points in the poem that are impersonal (Ex. 16.3). The third line has simple chords, before a return to the oscillating chords on 'after'. A break in the vocal line here could seem odd, but instead produces a sense of suspension, and the chromatic introduction to the second verse contributes to the tonal instability. The song is marked 'Andante semplice'; it is not a simple song, but its trance-like colours need a simple touch. Quilter, Scott's compatriot at Frankfurt Conservatory, set the poem too, calling it 'Passing Dreams', the second of the *Four Songs of Sorrow*, Op. 10, dating from 1904 but revised in 1907. His through-composed setting is marked 'Andante serioso'; his text setting is similar rhythmically to Scott's, but rather than create a sound world in the way that Scott does, he develops a three-note motif, E-flat–D-flat–B-flat, which appears in both accompaniment and vocal line, and with the same intervallic relationships, but at a different pitch, elsewhere. Quilter uses the harmony to indicate the movement within the poem: the end of the first verse ends on the dominant chord and we are left waiting for the resolution on to the tonic at the beginning of the second.

Scott repeats the first verse, as an echo. The extension allows the atmosphere to develop a little more, even though the echo is exact until the final phrase, and he uses

Ex. 16.3 Scott, 'Meditation', bars 1–3

texture to indicate which part of the poem we are in. His setting is strophic, but the second verse has adjustments to accompaniment and vocal line – 'roses' is a semitone higher than 'laughter'. Both Quilter's and Scott's settings are thoughtful and expansive, with wide tessituras in both voice and piano.

The air is dark and sweet
  This wet Spring night –
Spring, of the wand'ring feet,
  The secret flight,
Call'd through the slow, soft rain –
  O voice of gold!
Calls to me once again,
  As oft of old.

These words – by Rosamund Marriott Watson, whose work was published in the *Yellow Book* – were set as 'Nocturne' (1913; the original poem lacks the final 'e'). It was a popular song, its flowing accompaniment of three-part chords in quavers accessible and familiar in texture, and it is a substantial and effective song with which to end a group (Ex. 16.4). Its frequent changes between 2/4 and 3/4 allow an ebb and flow that mirrors the imagery in the text – not of the sea, but of the night. Watson had a felicitous ability to hint at long-lost memories; Scott's accompaniment of continuous quavers, punctuated by occasional low 5ths or octaves, matches her mood perfectly. The texture changes at the third verse (only the first is shown above) to a more declamatory sound, with a tonic and dominant pedal under the words 'Deep under graveyard grass it could not be / The Spring could never pass and I not see'; the piano takes over when the voice rests, and pauses when the voice becomes almost *recitativo*. The accompaniment uses the full range of the piano, so much so that in the lower-voice version, the left-hand octaves have had to be transposed up an octave. The vocal line is angular even by Scott's standards, but is expansive and makes musical sense.

Scott set Ernest Dowson twenty-two times, more than any other poet, and he set poems by Rosamund Marriott Watson fifteen times, all thirty-seven songs dating from around 1899 to 1927. Scott wrote of Stefan George that he:

> awakened in me a taste for poetry, and introduced me to the poems of Ernest Dowson, which he had lately discovered and greatly admired. He quite rightly maintained that the musician who only cared for music and neglected other branches of art and learning would only end in being a very poor composer; and although I was reading a good deal of science and philosophy at the time, this was not enough, and I must study poets and painters as well.
>
> The effect of my introduction to Ernest Dowson's poems was remarkable. Previous to that, poetry had not interested me in the least, but henceforward it became almost a passion.[4]

[4] Cyril Scott, *My Years of Indiscretion* (Mills & Boon, 1924), p. 32.

Ex. 16.4 Scott, 'Nocturne', bars 14–20

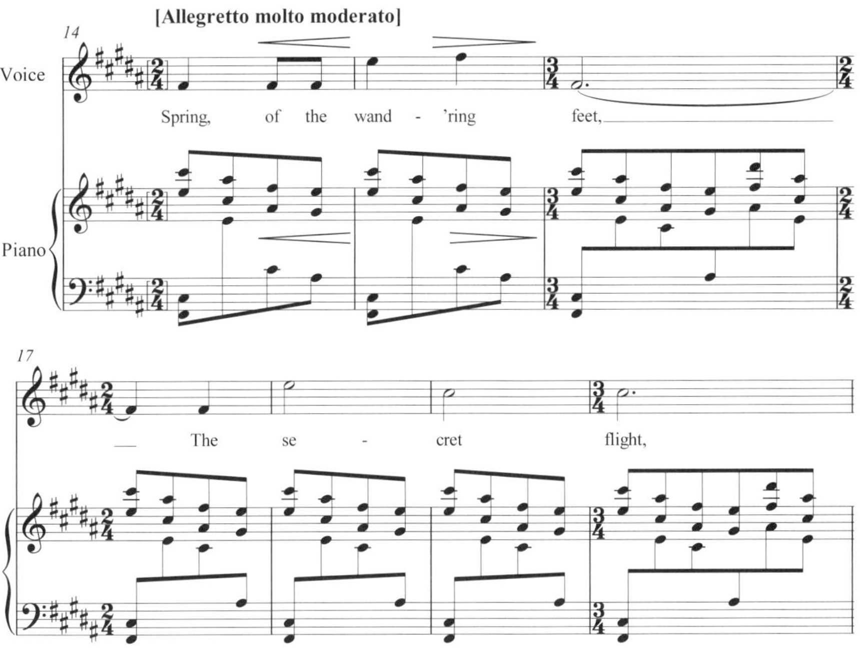

Dowson, one of the *fin-de-siècle* decadents, generally wrote in melancholy vein, but his 'Soli Cantare Periti Arcades' is much lighter and Scott set it twice but with different titles. In both settings the vocal line sits squarely, and independently, above the accompaniment. In the first, 'Dairy Song' (1903; Ex. 16.5a), dedicated to Roger Quilter, the sustained dominant pedal under a constant semiquaver movement imitates the milk-churning in the outer verses; when the environment moves to the town, the churning ceases; the second setting, 'A Song of Arcady' (1914; Ex. 16.5b), maintains the churning motif throughout (marked *quasi concertina* in the piano part). Both songs are light and attractive; both omit a verse from the original text. The later setting also alters the text at the end from 'I will live in a dairy' to 'I would live in a dairy'.

An undated manuscript, probably dating from around 1899, contains one song, though four are listed on the cover as a group of Dowson settings: 'April Love', 'Ad Domnulam [*sic*] suam', 'Sole Cantare Periti Arcades' and 'Yvonne of Brittany'. 'April Love' and 'Ad Domnulam (Little Lady of My Heart)' were published by Metzler, without a date, and are identified as Op. 3 Nos. 1 and 2 respectively. 'Sole Cantare' is the first setting of 'Dairy Song'; it and 'Yvonne of Brittany' were published by Boosey in 1903, as Op. 5 Nos. 1 and 2 respectively. The manuscript that survives is of 'April Love'; there are some small differences between it and the published version, chiefly to do with layout and with fullness of chord (Ex. 15.6a and b). It is a simple song, very direct, but is clearly a work in which Scott is finding his compositional feet.

Ex. 16.5a Scott, 'Dairy Song', bars 49–51

Ex. 16.5b Scott, 'A Song of Arcady', bars 61–3

'Ad Domnulam' is undistinguished, but 'Yvonne of Brittany' is the surprise. For such an early song – even if we may assume that Scott revised it in some measure between manuscript and publication, as he did with 'April Love' – it shows a real understanding of the text, a confident handling of the vocal line and a bold harmony. For the verse set in the past, Scott moves to the flattened submediant, E flat major in high voice version against the tonic G major (and omits the fourth of the original five verses), treating it as an extended German 6th, and for the last two lines of the verse, moving briefly to its own flattened submediant, B major, before finally returning to the tonic G major and the present; it ends with a chord distinctly reminiscent of Wagner's *Tristan* (Ex. 16.7a and b).

The sentiment of Dowson's voice clearly appealed to Scott, but not all the settings are successful: 'There Comes an End to Summer' (1903) is somewhat mechanical, following the word rhythm rigidly, and 'A Last Word', subtitled 'Ma Mie' (1903), after starting with some promising harmonies resorts to self-indulgent, and unsuccessful, repetition. Curiously, Scott himself felt that this was one of the best examples of his style, from among his early songs.

Scott all too often falls into the trap of writing steady crotchets, where simplicity becomes only dullness. In these Dowson settings, 'Asleep' (1903) is not exempt; it is slow, and enjoys its harmonies more than it should, though this is another song

Ex. 16.6a Scott, 'April Love' MS, bars 1–9

Ex. 16.6b Scott, 'April Love' published version, bars 1–9

Ex. 16.7a Scott, 'Yvonne of Brittany', bars 49–56

Ex. 16.7b Scott, 'Yvonne of Brittany', last 4 bars

that Scott liked. 'Autumnal' (1904) is disappointing for the same reason. 'Sorrow' (1904) misses the point too; though thoughtful and reflective, it is also conventional. 'Pierrot and the Moon Maiden' (1912), however, is pleasingly unpretentious, the conversation between the eponymous characters treated very lightly. Although the vocal line is angular and set very high in the voice, it is manageable, and the opening quintuplets make the song flow simply (Ex. 16.8).

'The Valley of Silence' (1911) is also treated lightly; it has similarities with Quilter's setting, arising largely from the three-syllable anacrusis; Quilter's, of 1908, is the more direct setting (Ex. 16.9a and b).

Ex. 16.8 Scott, 'Pierrot and the Moon Maiden', bars 1–8

In the atmospheric and simple 'And so I made a Villanelle' (1908; Ex. 16.10), Scott builds layers of independent but co-existing textures over an ostinato piano accompaniment, a device he employed frequently. It is a very attractive song and Scott to an extent reflects the two-rhyme requirement of a villanelle in musical terms by using just two chords in each section, though this largely disintegrates for the last seven lines.

Scott wrote four songs with 'Villanelle' in the title, three of them to words by Dowson. The fourth song, 'Villanelle of Firelight', to words by Naomi Carvalho, is undistinguished. 'Villanelle' (1904), which only has four tercets, not the normal five, is another song with an ostinato-like, rocking accompaniment, set almost entirely over a dominant pedal, even ending on it, the dominant seventh leaving the song suspended in mid-air – and since it is marked 'Slowly as if a lullaby', we may assume the child has gone to sleep.

The final Dowson villanelle, 'Villanelle of the Poet's Road' (1911; Ex. 16.11) is mesmerising; in 12/8 with long, lilting lines, diminished chords predominate in the right hand and their inherent instability over an almost continuous tonic and dominant pedal in the left hand produces a haunting effect.

'A Valediction' (1904) reveals its delights slowly – at first hearing it seems somewhat saccharine, but when performed simply it becomes a fine song. In the low transposition, the final piano note, the G 3½ octaves below middle C, is beyond the range of most pianos.

Ex. 16.9a Scott, 'The Valley of Silence', bars 1–11

Ex. 16.9b Quilter, 'A Land of Silence', bars 1–3

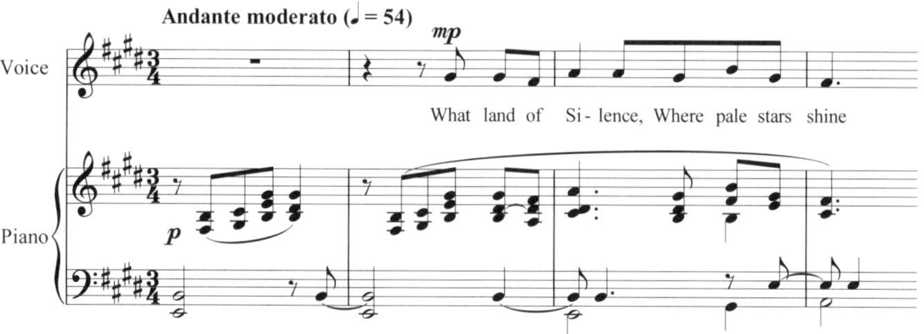

What are in some songs faults become in others virtues. A third of Scott's songs are in 2/4 and many suffer from it; the consequent short rhythms and frequent quavers restrict ingenuity. However, in 'A Gift of Silence' (1905), also in 2/4 time, Scott has a variety of rhythms in the piano and uses much of its keyboard, and the chromatic chords fit comfortably under the hand. The vocal line follows, more or less, the natural voice inflection, and avoids a regular phrase length. The high-voice version has a slightly altered ending (Ex. 16.12a and b).

'Vesperal' (Dowson's title) exists in manuscript and was dedicated 'For Percy Grainger. My dear friend – in all affection and friendly love. April 1900' (Ex. 16.13a). It was revised as 'Evening' (Ex. 16.13b), now dedicated to Walter and Ella Pearce,

Ex. 16.10 Scott, 'And so I made a Villanelle', bars 1–6

Andante
Voice
p
I took her dain ty eyes as well As silk-en ten drils of her hair,
Piano
p semplice

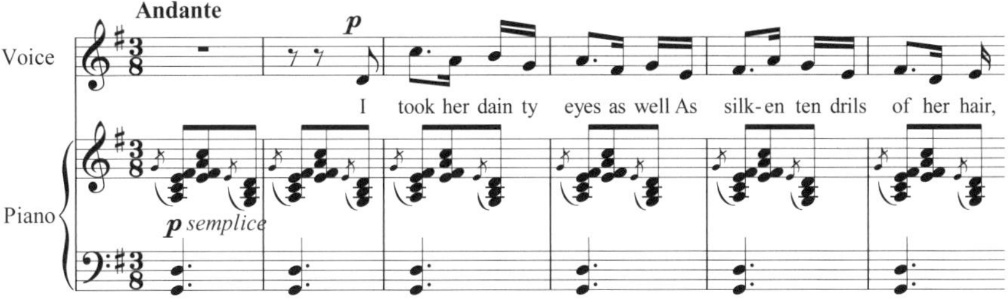

Ex. 16.11 Scott, 'Villanelle of the Poet's Road', bars 1–5

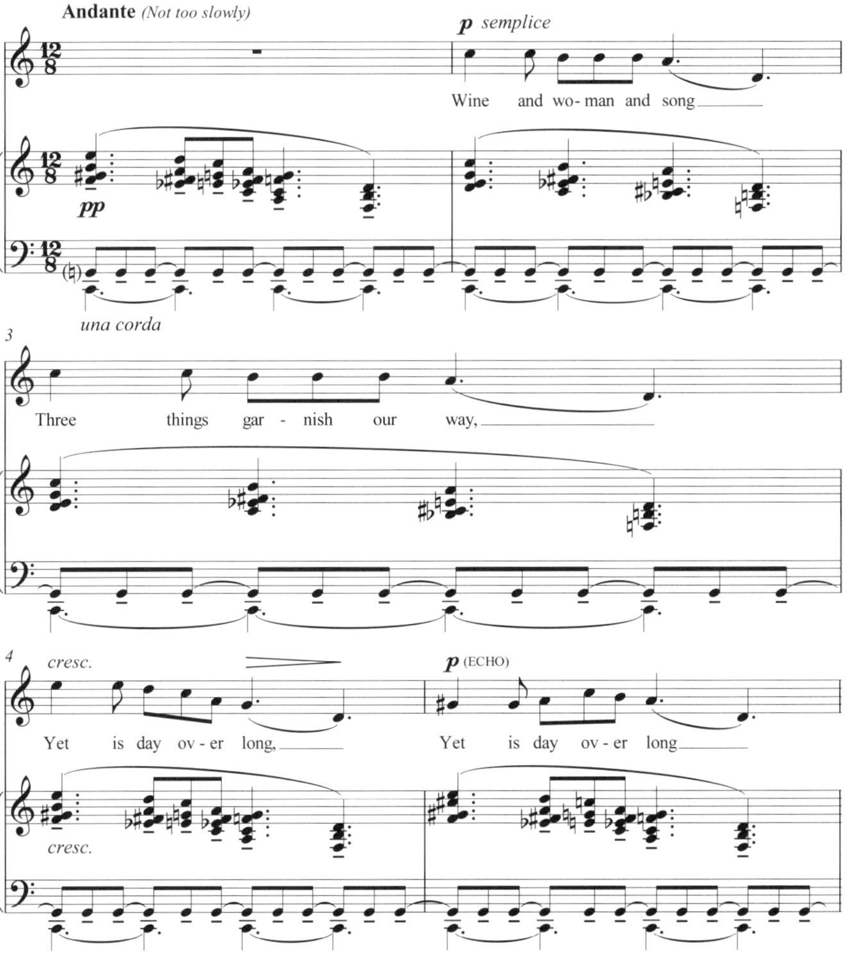

Andante (Not too slowly)
p semplice
Wine and wo-man and song
pp
una corda
3
Three things gar - nish our way,
4
cresc.
Yet is day ov - er long,
p (ECHO)
Yet is day ov - er long
cresc.

Ex. 16.12a Scott, 'A Gift of Silence', low voice, last 6 bars

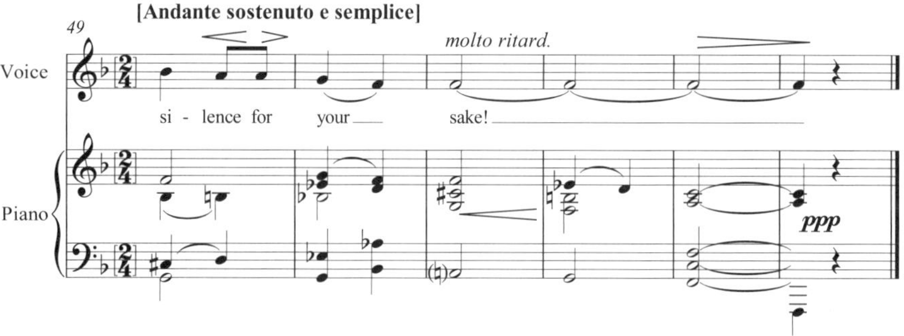

Ex. 16.12b Scott, 'A Gift of Silence', high voice, last 4 bars

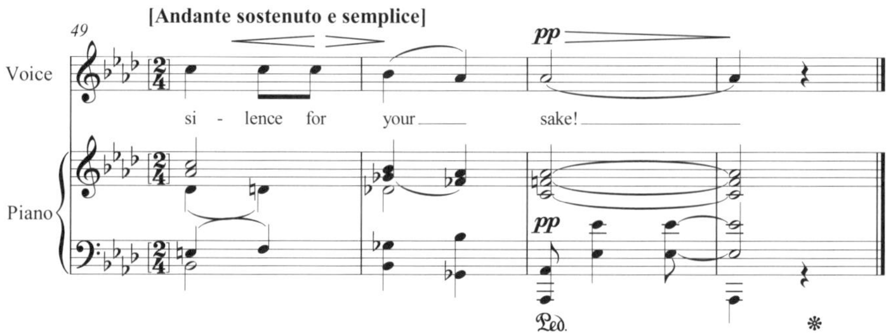

and published in 1910. By that time Scott had written fifty further songs (about a third of his total song output; he wrote about fifty more songs in the second decade of the century) and honed his skills considerably. The revisions are more than cosmetic: there is now a short introduction, a break between verses 2 and 3, syllable-setting is improved, and the vocal lines are smoothed, particularly under the text 'are the day's evil things'. As with many of Scott's songs, it looks simple on the page, but it is very moving and beautiful; in performance it should not be overdone, but be allowed to speak for itself.

'Retrospect' (1913; Ex. 16.14) follows voice inflection, in shape rather than rhythm; its coloured harmonies twist and turn the tonality, matching the sorrow in the poem and its ultimate resignation.

'Love's Aftermath' (1911; Ex. 16.15) is arguably one of Scott's finest songs, its free, almost conversational, phrasing engendering frequent but uncontrived changes of time signature: 2/4, 3/8, 5/8, 1/4 and so on. The warmth of the added 6th chords at the beginning gives way to an oscillation between black- and white-note keys (whether in low or high voice); the slipping from one key to that of the adjacent semitone is at one level Scott exploring harmonies, but at another rocks with an anguish that matches the poem, and produces a distinctly impressionistic sound.

Ex. 16.13a Scott, 'Vesperal', ms bars 9–17

Ex. 16.13b Scott, 'Evening', bars 13–22

Ex. 16.14 Scott, 'Retrospect', bars 16–24

Dowson's delicate poetry can easily be swamped with mawkish settings, Scott's and others. At their best, however, Scott's Dowson settings are superb, displaying the sentiment without sliding into sentimentality.

Scott's earliest songs date from 1893, when he was just fourteen; 'The Time I've Lost in Wooing' (Thomas Moore) was probably revised before its publication in 1904, but is unremarkable; 'Damon' (Goethe), unpublished and the manuscript dated 17 August 1895, is Schubertian in texture; the *Six Songs* of 1895–6, again unpublished, are variable but attractive, without the technical vocal difficulties presented in later songs. Once Scott had met Stefan George, however, his approach began to change; George's works affected him very deeply and in due course he translated some of them. The *Sänge eines fahrenden Spielmanns* (Songs of a Travelling

Ex. 16.15 Scott, 'Love's Aftermath', bars 19–24

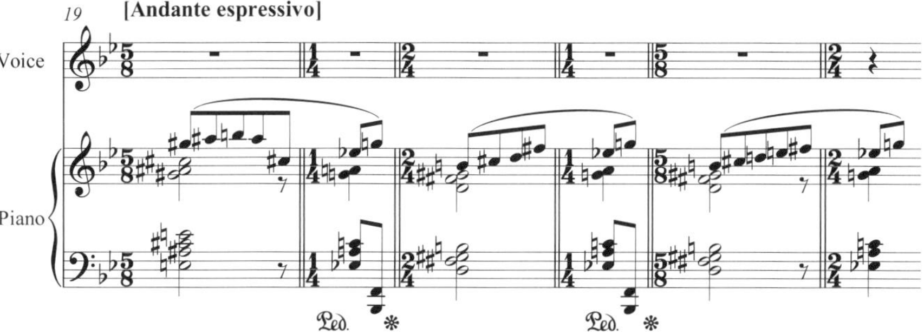

Minstrel), dated April 1898, an unpublished set of six songs with the first described as a Prelude, frequently show a new approach to the accompaniments, though in many other respects they are very static. The set as a whole has a full sound, and the piano gives a good deal of help to the voice, something Scott did much less in later work. 'Heißt es viel dich' has an ostinato piano part characteristic of many later accompaniments, providing a background cushion over which the voice lifts (Ex. 16.16).

In *Candid Confessions*, Scott wrote:

> Harmony is the great medium for emotional expression, a medium so elastic and unlimited that it serves to express almost every conceivable shade of feeling; and that four verses all depicting varying emotions should be sung to precisely the same harmonies … is altogether wrong from the dramatic outlook. How is it possible for a singer to give expression to those harsh emotions demanded by the words, when in the accompaniment is some inappropriately sweet or trivial chord which at once detracts from the effect the singer is at pains to produce?

In the George songs, Scott was beginning to put this into practice, though he did not always do so: in the strophic 'The White Knight' (1905), the first of his settings of Rosamund Marriott Watson, he placed the significance of the piano part, evocative of galloping horses, over the meaning of the poetry. 'A Song of London' (1906) is

Ex. 16.16 Scott, 'Heißt es viel dich bitten', ms bars 1–4

quite another matter. The vocal lines vary slightly from verse to verse and the piano texture varies depending upon whether the words speak of London or the country; when in London, the flowing quavers (with bars that would otherwise repeat, shifting by a semitone) indicate that a big city is never still. The almost monotone vocal line makes its own contribution to the continuity of the song, voice and piano independent but the whole greater than the sum of the parts.

The next group of songs are to texts by Rosamund Marriott Watson. 'Mirage' (1910; Ex. 16.17) is a more nuanced song. The voice largely follows the natural speech inflection, with a consequent sense of intimacy; the bass line underpins the song, oscillating at the beginning between the dominant E-flat and E-natural before resolving on to a long tonic pedal that itself oscillates between A-flat and its enharmonic G-sharp. With its alternately rich and predictable harmonies, this is a strange but curiously effective song.

'In the Valley' (1912) again has unprepossessing words, and Scott again goes beyond the obvious images of birds and the seasons to conjure something rich and strange. The high-voice version is given three flats, but whether the key is E-flat major or C minor is indeterminate. The opening motif may imitate birdcall but has more than a hint of a shepherd's pipe about it, and the sense of stillness, created within the singer's first nine bars by a combination of a pedal B-flat and a largely whole-tone line, is highly potent. The song ends in a clear F major, with added 7ths; but there are so many accidentals, one wonders why Scott bothered with the three-flat key signature in the first place. No matter; this is a very fine song.

'Autumn's Lute' (1914; Ex. 16.18) has words that at first sight seem trivial and contrived; but Scott achieves a Blake-like spareness and lightness. Phrases of irregular length fall entirely naturally, and the 'Follow now' lines are set in compound rhythms, evoking barely glimpsed and not entirely benevolent sprites. Parallel chords, moving chromatically, add to the unsettled mood; for the final line, 'Follow through the sunset gold', the voice is in simple time, while the piano escapes into compound time for the ending.

By now Scott was very confident in his handling of text and voice – he was always confident in his handling of piano textures – and unafraid of silence and stillness. His next Watson setting, 'Night-Song' (1915), is bold, the tonic pedal chiming throughout almost the whole song, moving away only for the brief final verse. The song is largely diatonic, though with plenty of added 6ths and 7ths, and the fluid quaver rhythm creates a haunting sound. For the occasional 6/8 bars (a gentle sighing of the wind?), Scott does not specify whether it is the quaver that is constant, or the pulse; the latter flows better. Its matter-of-fact lack of sentimentality is highly effective.

Scott's final Watson song was published nine years after 'Night-Song'; perhaps he had had enough of Watson's archetypal memory images and nostalgia. However, 'The Garden of Memory' (1924; Ex. 16.19) inspired a heavily speech-inflected and very free melodic line, and Scott gives the listener many pianistic clues to the 'hidden lute' before its mention in the last line.

Watson appears to have been set by only one other composer, Arthur Foote. In 1896 his setting of her poem 'In Picardie' was published, with Watson writing under

Ex. 16.17 Scott, 'Mirage', bars 1–9

Ex. 16.18 Scott, 'Autumn's Lute', bars 1–11

Ex. 16.19 Scott, 'The Garden of Memory', bars 9–12

her pseudonym Graham R. Tomson.[5] Scott set the same text, calling it 'A Little Song of Picardie' (1912), but neither song is notable.

Scott was attracted to folk song. Quilter and their fellow student at Frankfurt, Percy Grainger, both arranged folk songs, and treated them carefully and respectfully. Scott, by contrast, often leapt in where others feared to tread, with varying results: in 1925 Joseph Holbrooke, in *Contemporary British Composers*, wrote acerbically 'Of … his harmony to our old songs I do not wish to speak.'[6] The set of three *Old Songs in New Guise* (1913) – 'Where be going?', 'Drink to me Only' (Ben Jonson) and 'Summer is acumen in' – need to be treated lightly, but it is a good group, the middle song making an excellent if somewhat purple-harmonied alternative to Quilter's arrangement. In 'All Through the Night' (1921), one in Scott's series of eight *British Songs*, his harmonies are too self-indulgent for the simplicity of the words, smothering the melody with overladen chords. This was the first of the collection, however, and the later arrangements are far more telling. 'The Minstrel Boy' (Thomas Moore, 1922) is very simple, with an improvisatory feel, and 'Blythe and Merry was She' (Burns), 'By Yon Bonny Banks' and 'Comin' Through the Rye', all published in 1922, are covered with just a thin blanket of Scott's sound, but retain the simplicity of the originals. 'Cherry Ripe' (Herrick, 1922) goes off at a harmonic tangent, relying for its considerable effect on the audience knowing the tune extremely well. 'I'll bid my Heart be Still' (Thomas Pringle, 1922) goes to the other extreme – for Scott, very simple and direct, scarcely any chromaticism, and exquisitely poignant.

By the time of 'Lord Randal' (1926), Scott had learned that he had no need to hammer home his point. Much is accompanied by straightforward chords, revealing the story without let or hindrance; but even though we know there is bound to be a surprise at the words 'A rope from hell to hang her!' (this is Scott after all),

[5] Tomson was her second husband's name, and she left him for Henry Brereton Marriott Watson, the Australian novelist, whom she never married. Scott met the couple in around 1900 and wrote about them in *My Years of Indiscretion* (pp. 74–5).

[6] Joseph Holbrooke, *Contemporary British Composers* (Cecil Palmer, 1925), p. 90.

Ex. 16.20 Scott, 'Lord Randal', bars 120–34

the impact is immense (Ex. 16.20).[7] Ethel Smyth used the melody very effectively in her delicious one-act comic opera *The Boatswain's Mate* of 1915, an opera noted for its use of familiar tunes (including 'Three Blind Mice' and her own *March of the Women*, as well as a brief quote from Beethoven's Fifth Symphony). The leading character Mrs Waters takes the melody of 'Lord Randal' for her Part One aria 'What if I were young again'.

A group of any of these folksong settings would be welcome in a concert programme, particularly 'Lord Randal'.

[7] John Charles Thomas recorded a memorable and intensely dramatic performance in 1938: it can be heard at http://www.youtube.com/watch?v=HbxDOIXSoKo. The recording by Gerald Finley and Julius Drake is also finely characterised (*The Ballad Singer*, Hyperion CDA67830, track 11).

Scott set his own words on occasion, and in two songs dispensed with words entirely. Setting his own texts allowed him free rein, and since he played with the words as he played with chords and harmonies, the results are sometimes wayward and uncontrolled. Although some are unstylistic and can be dismissed, some are extremely effective. 'Voices of Vision' (1903), the first of the *Two Poems*, is a remarkable song, a well-judged match between mood of text and colour of music, and stretches tonality with chains of chromatic chords. The arpeggio figurations emerge entirely naturally. However, the second song, 'Willows', also published by Elkin in 1903 (and published in German translation by Schott in 1911 as 'Trauerweiden'), meanders harmonically and lacks the imagination of 'Voices of Vision'. 'Afterday' (1906), setting Scott's text in homage to Dowson, is too similar to 'Lullaby', but might have worked better had he orchestrated it. 'Spring Song' (1913) is disappointingly predictable, but the richness of 'Evening Melody' (1914) is such that it can easily overpower everything within reach. 'In the Silver Moonbeams' (1923) is an unbridled harmonisation of the melody 'Au Clair de la Lune', set to new words. 'Little Foreigner' (1932), subtitled 'A Character Song', is an uncharacteristically obvious but delicious arrangement of the Neapolitan song 'Santa Lucia', intended for a soubrette soprano.

The 'Idyllic Fantasy' (1921) and 'Idyll' (1923) both set Scott's own words and both have instrumental accompaniments to the soprano line, the former with oboe and cello, the latter with flute. They are extremely free rhythmically, the bar lines present merely for convenience. The oboe and cello are marked 'to be played behind a screen at the side of the stage or in the ante-room with door ajar', an instruction that suits the geography of the ante-rooms at the Wigmore Hall, London, where it was first performed on 12 May 1919 (by its dedicatee, Astra Desmond), the instruction presumably arising from the circumstances of the performance. Both oboe and cello have lines with a mournful and highly chromatic fall, partly reminiscent of Wagner's use of the oboe and cor anglais, but in their sometimes sparse sound also looking ahead to Vaughan Williams's use of the oboe in his *Ten Blake Songs* for voice and oboe, of 1958. In the 'Idyll', Scott builds the flute's melodic lines by expansion or contraction of intervals – F–D followed by G-flat–D-flat, for example – with generally simpler semitonal movement for the voice: the melody, constantly returning into itself, is unable to escape, despite the flute's florid cadenzas, and the sinuous chromaticism is claustrophobic, sinister and utterly mesmerising.[8] Both works are well worth seeking out.

The two *Songs without Words* (both 1919) are variable; the first, 'Tranquility' [*sic*], a woman's song, makes a useful addition to the wordless song repertory, but the second, 'Pastorale', seems to be a sketch for 'Have Ye Seen Him Pass By?' and is disappointingly repetitious.

Scott's description of 'Rima's Call to the Birds' as a scena indicates its scale. It was written originally for soprano and string quartet, and performed on 4 May 1927; Scott orchestrated it and Basil Cameron conducted it at the Harrogate Festival

[8] A review in *The Times*, 18 February 1924, p. 17, refers to the 'Idyllic Fantasy', though since it describes a flute and voice work, it evidently means the 'Idyll'. Percy Scholes reviewed the 'Fantasy' for *The Observer* on 15 January 1922, p. 8, and was somewhat scathing about everyone and everything.

of British Music in July 1929, both times with the Australian coloratura soprano Gertrude Johnson, to whom it was dedicated, as soloist. The vocal score was published in 1933. Rima is a character in W. H. Hudson's *Green Mansions: A Romance of the Tropical Forest*, published in 1904; she is alleged to have the ability to communicate with the creatures of the forest. The words in the song are Scott's (and there is a German translation), but it is generally wordless (and, indeed, the text is largely irrelevant), free melodically and rhythmically, with lush musical colours. There are some reminders of Vaughan Williams's *The Lark Ascending*, but these soon dissipate as pentatonic vocal lines blend with an improvisatory piano part, and the trills and chirruping motifs expand and thicken the texture, as a dawn chorus of birds gathers. It is a splendid showpiece for the singer.

A number of the remaining songs stand out or are at least worth investigation, and are discussed here in chronological order. Scott set an eclectic range of poets, from early settings of Shakespeare, Longfellow and Goethe, to Duffield Bendall, George Darley, Dorothy Grenside, Thomas Hardy, Teresa Hooley, Charles Kingsley, Thomas Moore, William B. Rands, Charles Sayle, Walter Scott, Arthur Symons, and many others, mostly from the late nineteenth century.

'The Ballad of Fair Helen' (Ex. 16.21), a man's song, was published as a song for voice and piano in 1925, but the original version – for baritone and orchestra – was written in 1900 and performed at the Bechstein Hall (later the Wigmore Hall) in 1905 by its dedicatee, Frederic Austin, conducted by Thomas Beecham. It relies on a dominant pedal and fluid changes of time-signature for its indefinite and scene-setting effect, over a D minor then D major tonality. It moves to augmented chords over an ostinato bass line, and almost a monotone for the voice, as the point of murder, the climax, is reached. The final, declamatory ending has a remarkably wide-ranging vocal line, marking the singer's deep anguish. Grainger wrote of this very memorable song 'This I consider one of the greatest ballads ever written.'[9]

The five *Songs of Old Cathay* date from 1906–19; all five are to texts translated by Herbert Allen Giles. The two designated Nos. 4 and 5 are the earliest and were published in 1906 as Op. 46 Nos. 1 and 2; they were dedicated to R. R. Vamam Shankar Rav Pandit. In these early songs, Scott's style is clearly apparent: chromatic, a hazy

Ex. 16.21 Scott, 'The Ballad Of Fair Helen', bars 1–4

[9] 18 October 1958, in *The All-Round Man: Selected Letters of Percy Grainger, 1914–1961*, ed. Malcolm Gillies and David Pear (Clarendon, 1994).

Ex. 16.22a Scott, 'A Picnic', bars 1–2

Ex. 16.22b Scott, Piano Concerto in C, 1st mvt, Fig. 45

sound, pianistic. 'Waiting' is brief and luscious (with brief word-painting on 'lute'), and 'A Picnic' shows off Scott's colours with pentatonic patterns for piano (and a black-note glissando at the end) and whole-tone scales for voice; it must have been a luxurious picnic. Scott clearly thought well of it, since he used it substantially, and memorably, in the first movement of his Piano Concerto No. 1 in C, of 1913–14.

'A Song of Wine', Op. 46 No. 3, was dedicated to Frederic Austin; again a mixture of pentatonic and whole-tone scales, with augmented chords and amusing word-painting on 'tipsy', and more black-note glissandi, this is a strong song, great fun and most effective. Of it, Scott wrote in *Candid Confessions*:

> The accompaniment is far from straightforward, and at one point involves a glissando up and down the black keys extremely painful to persons with a delicate skin!

The remaining two songs, written twelve years after 'A Song of Wine', continue the opulent sound of the first three, tempered with a maturity of style, perhaps less fresh and youthful, but assured. 'Alone' (1919; Ex. 16.23) has a French liquidity and freedom of sound, perfumed, often whole-tone, while 'In Absence' is almost oppressive in its richness. The group deserves to be heard in its entirety.

'Daffodils' (Ella Erskine, 1909; Ex. 16.24) is too light to work with a baritone voice; it is one of a few that succeed with one type of voice but not another, and is best sung by a soprano. It suffers much from its text, but is retrieved by a very attractive setting and a piano texture of dancing chords, and it favours Scott's common device of chromatic lines. It was published in three keys: the higher two are substantially the same but the low-voice version has differences that go beyond textural differences relating to tessitura, and rather as if the transposer was in a hurry. These differences are detailed in Appendix 1, below.

Ex. 16.23 Scott, 'Alone', bars 1–8

'My Lady Sleeps' (Duffield Bendall, 1910) is of its time but shows Scott in fluid style, the 7/8 (notated as 2/4 and 3/8) breathing easily. It is unpretentious, needs to be sung with an awareness of the text – it is unusual for Scott to need quite so much flexibility – and is altogether an attractive and useful song.

'A Birthday' (1913) is a setting of words by Christina Rossetti that were made famous in a setting by Parry; Scott's version provides a more than satisfactory alternative, rather more muted and less overtly a woman's song than the Parry. It is harmonically less extreme, too, than some of Scott's other songs, and the voice is more closely connected to the accompaniment than is usual.

'Lilac-Time' (1914; Ex. 16.25), on the other hand, is unequivocally a woman's song, a vehicle for a singer with a brilliant, agile tone and an exuberant style. Set to Walt Whitman's words and dedicated to Maggie Teyte, it is fast-moving, highly chromatic with a very angular line, and set high in the voice; a very useful song with which to end a group. Scott was pleased with it.

Ex. 16.24 Scott, 'Daffodils', bars 1–4

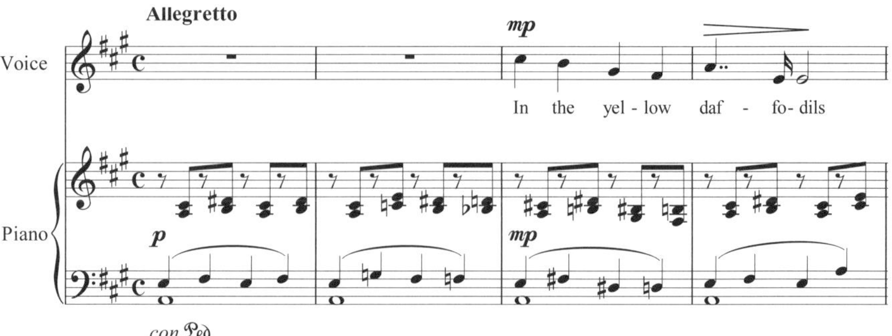

Ex. 16.25 Scott, 'Lilac-Time', bars 6–9

'A Prayer' (1914), best sung by a woman, was very popular, and rightly so. It is a setting of Kingsley's 'The Summer Sea', from *The Water Babies*, and was set by Holst too, as 'Slumber Song'. Based for once around 6ths rather than 4ths, the piano sound is open despite the low tessitura (even in high voice); the 6/8 rocking metre is calm. Note that the low-voice version goes out of range of the piano: the low A-flat in the seventh bar from the end can be put up the octave. A smooth, lyrical line makes this a very attractive song.

The hearty 'Tyrolese Evensong' (Felicia Hemans, 1916; Ex. 16.26) is, in its jolliness, somewhat untypical of Scott; but it is too attractive to omit. Much of the piano part (marked 'Tempo di Mazurka') is set over a tonic and dominant drone, with the right hand mostly in 6ths, acting as a countermelody to the sustained vocal line.

Ex. 16.26 Scott, 'Tyrolese Evensong', bars 9–16

'The Pilgrim Cranes' (Lord de Tabley, 1917; Ex. 16.27a) is another fine example of the whole being greater than the sum of the parts. Neither piano nor voice dominates; the words are a vehicle for the overall colour, and the combination is simple and soothing, almost Brittenesque in its oscillation of sound; one wonders whether John Ireland knew the song when he wrote 'The Trellis' in 1920 (Ex. 16.27b).

'The Sands of Dee' (Kingsley, 1917; Ex. 16.28) has a similar simplicity, despite the chromaticism. A distinct melody, in folk-song vein, with a piano part that accompanies rather than paints a picture in Scott's usual manner, enables a highly emotive setting of Kingsley's words. It is strophic, the middle verse harmonised rather differently from the outer verses (bass lines falling chromatically, reflecting Mary's hair floating in the water), with piquant adjustments between the harmonies in the first and last verses; the variety is telling. The song needs to be sung very simply, with no adornment, and would fit very well with a group of folk songs. Scott himself felt that this was the best of his folk-song, or folk-song-like settings.

Many of Scott's songs have pictorial elements: 'Sea-Fret' (Teresa Hooley, 1919, dedicated to Granville Bantock) is one such. The accompaniment is specifically marked 'Quickly, like falling waves in the distance', a marking which would verge on the pretentious, save for the lightness and effectiveness of the colouration. The demanding vocal line is more than usually difficult to place in the voice, with wide leaps and long phrases, but the result is a finely judged miniature. In the low-voice version the piano part juxtaposes clusters of black and white notes, and the song is consequently best performed in this key.

Ex. 16.27a Scott, 'The Pilgrim Cranes', bars 1–4

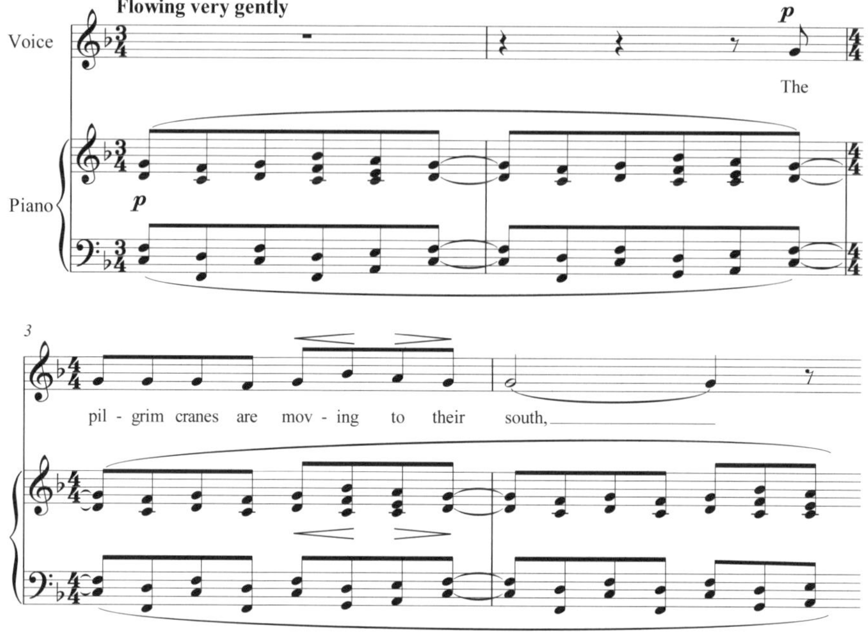

Ex. 16.27b Ireland, 'The Trellis', bars 1–3

'Sundown' (Dorothy Grenside, 1919), perhaps best suited to a woman's voice, ought to be trite and superficial, but the delicacy of the piano figuration overrides any such considerations. The two tempi, almost conversational, with two textures – murmuring piano quavers plus mordents, and sustained chords – and an often monotonal vocal line make this a gentle song, fully in keeping with the mood one might expect from the title.

'The Watchman' (Jean Hyacinth Hildyard, 1920) is Scott in milder harmonic mood. The two-chord ostinato in the piano builds, through fuller chords, until the dawn arrives against a vibrant sunburst of (in the middle-voice version) chords of F major, A-flat major and second-inversion F-sharp major with added 7th and 9ths, finally resolving on to C major (Ex. 16.29).

Ex. 16.28 Scott, 'The Sands of Dee', bars 31–6

Ex. 16.29 Scott, 'The Watchman', last 9 bars

Ex. 16.30 Scott, 'The Huckster', bars 13–15

'The Huckster' (Edward Thomas, 1921; Ex. 16.30) is unpretentious, unsubtle, busy, and a good ending song for a group. The words clearly caught Scott's fancy; it is brief, and unusually jolly, and he surely dashed it off very quickly. The piano texture makes it easy to play, as required, 'in a rather bumpy manner', and the vocal lines are suitably inebriated.

The sighing, chromatic motif of the highly dramatic 'Have Ye Seen Him Pass by?' (1921; Ex. 16.31) pervades the entire song; there is a memorable recording by Peter Pears. The words come from the story of Tyl Ulenspiegel (as translated by Geoffrey Whitworth), where they are spoken by Nele to a stranger as she seeks her love, Tyl. She does not know that she is in fact speaking to Tyl himself, and he plays a trick on her by calling out in a drunken tone, 'In a shaky old cart, with age all green, Your feckless lover I have seen.' In Scott's setting the last verse is treated cynically and bitterly, somewhat differently from the tone of the story (though marked 'with a change of voice'), but in the context, highly emotive. Although nominally set in A minor, there is considerable play between chords of A/E, A/E-flat and A-flat/E-flat, and, as with many of Scott's songs, the tonality is ambivalent and shifting. The result is a melancholy and haunting song. Scott thought it the finest of his later songs and wrote of it that 'the opening and frequently recurring phrase with its harmonic turn ... is both my saddest and happiest effort.'

In 'Mist' (Marguerite E. Barnsdale, 1925; Ex. 16.32), dedicated to Astra Desmond, Scott gives free rein to his fondness for parallel chord clusters, though he varies the textures throughout. The voice is often monotonal and treated as recitative, over an evocative accompaniment; in the hazy sound of this song one can hear a distinctly French tone. This is a delicate poem about mists on the moors, and it is treated in a delicate manner.

Ex. 16.31 Scott, 'Have Ye Seen Him Pass by?', bars 9–12

Spare chords, often matching guitar tuning (inexplicable but resonant), and an open texture anticipating Britten, mark 'A March Requiem' (Norah Richardson, 1928) out from many other songs. The chords rely on stacked 4ths for creating their effect of a tolling bell; the atmosphere is one of calm resignation.

The text for 'Lady June' (Elizabeth Haddon, 1935) begins unpromisingly:

> Lady June she is fair,
> And the gold from her hair
> Shines over the land, while the joy of her smile
> Is re-born in a bud, and will early beguile
> The shy birds to our isle.

But the later mention of the thrush trilling brings clever and unconventional word-painting from the piano part, which is highly pianistic and lies easily under the hand. It is a gentle song that repays time spent on rehearsal. 'Arise, my Love, my Fair one' (Song of Solomon, 1939), full of variety of texture and vibrant musical colours, suits a female voice. Scott has finally learned to be kinder to the singer: the vocal lines are shaped to a singer's way, with room to breathe, and contain melismas that lie well in the voice, suiting the ecstatic mood of the text.

There is no doubt that Scott is often self-indulgent: the piano figurations can be repetitious and clichéd, the dreamy harmonic colours of some songs please for a while, but can soon pall, and his judgement over which songs are his best is sometimes questionable, though he was right in his opinion of 'Love's Aftermath' and 'The Pilgrim Cranes'. Percy Grainger described the Frankfurt Group (he

Ex. 16.32 Scott, 'Mist', bars 9–16

excluded Norman O'Neill, leaving Scott, Quilter, Balfour Gardiner and himself) as 'Prerafaelite', though in Scott's case attempting a 'CONSCIOUS charm from what is archaic'[10] sometimes produced distinctly uninspiring results. The variability in quality also arises in part from his treating piano and voice as vehicles for his exploration of mood and harmonic colour (leaving it to the performers to manage the consequent technical demands): the experiments may work, but can be overladen rather than nuanced, and sometimes the poetry is simply irredeemable – but on the other hand, bills need to be paid. Against this, his frequent use of an ambivalent tonality is often highly concentrated and engaging, his sound often exotic and sometimes ravishing, and his interpretations can be boldly handled, purposeful and individual. Others might set words as one hangs clothes on a washing line; Scott interpreted the texts via the music. It takes time to work one's way into Scott's approach to songwriting, and to work the lines into the voice, but the harvest is a very rich one indeed.

[10] 18 October 1958, ibid.

III

THE WRITINGS

17

The Poetry

DESMOND SCOTT

At first glance, the poetry of Cyril Scott would seem to be the antithesis of his music, which was considered advanced in his day. In music he was thought of as an iconoclast, breaking all the rules and flouting convention. His poetry, by contrast, harks back to the Victorian era in which he grew up, abides by all the rules, and would not be out of place beside the poems of Swinburne, the Rossettis (Dante Gabriel and Christina), or his favourite, Ernest Dowson, twenty-two of whose verses he set to music.[1]

Even so, Scott stated that 'were he not a musician he could not be a poet, and were he not a poet he would compose a very different sort of music.'[2] It was the German poet Stefan George, whom Scott had met while a music student in Frankfurt, who introduced him to the poetry of Dowson, and, but for that, Scott wrote, he might never have become a poet. Until that time poetry had not interested him in the least, but thereafter it became almost a passion.

For ten years, between 1905 and 1915, he was a prolific poet. He published *The Shadows of Silence and the Songs of Yesterday* (*c.* 1905),[3] *The Grave of Eros and the Book of Mournful Melodies, with Dreams from the East* (1907),[4] *The Voice of the Ancient* (1910),[5] *The Vales of Unity* (1912),[6] and *The Celestial Aftermath* (1915).[7] In addition, he translated Charles Baudelaire's *Les fleurs du mal* in 1909,[8] and in 1910 a selection of poems by his friend Stefan George, 'The Awakener within me of all Poetry', as Scott's dedication to him in *The Grave of Eros* reads.

In 1915 he ceased writing poetry altogether for almost thirty years, but in 1943 he selected what he felt were his best poems, taken mainly from *The Shadows of Silence* and *The Grave of Eros*, added sixteen new ones and completed a final collection, *The Poems of a Musician* (unpublished). A short note at the beginning reads:

> This volume contains, apart from my latest poems, a selection of those experiments in rhythm that I made in my early years. But as even those I consider worth retaining were marred by many imperfections, they are here given out in an amended form. Sept. 1943.

[1] Algernon Charles Swinburne (1837–1909), Dante Gabriel Rossetti (1828–1882), Christina Rossetti (1830–1894), Ernest Dowson (1867–1900).

[2] A. Eaglefield Hull, *Cyril Scott: Composer, Poet, and Philosopher* (Kegan Paul, Trench, Trubner, 1918) p. 147.

[3] Published by George Fraser, n.d.

[4] Published by The Lyceum Press, n.d.

[5] Published by J. M. Watkins.

[6] Published by David Nutt.

[7] Published by Chatto & Windus.

[8] Cyril Scott, *The Flowers of Evil* (Elkin Mathews, 1909).

His views on what constitutes poetry and its relation to music were very definite. First, it must rhyme. Blank verse was merely where:

> indolent minded persons could express themselves without putting their brains to the trouble of mastering the technique of versification or of displaying sufficient inventiveness to write in rhymed verse in an un-trivial manner.[9]

Language had to be elevated in order to become poetic. Scott never used colloquialisms because they lowered the tone and debased his Romantic ideal of poetry as simply another form of music. The nearer it came to being music, he felt, the more it could stir the soul. Indeed, one might argue that his insistence that poetry be as melodious and as musical as possible meant his verse had no place in the discordant, jangling twentieth century. He said as much in his disparaging of modern verse: 'As in the ultra and consistently discordant phase, melody had been banished from the art of music, so rhyme and metre – the melodies of poetry – were banished from the poetic art.'[10]

As for his own verse, following the advice of his friend Charles Bonnier,[11] Scott said he strove to find new rhythms and unusual rhymes, and to invent new 'poetic melodies', but experimenting with language was not for him. Compared with some of his contemporaries – Gerard Manley Hopkins or Ezra Pound, for instance – he never advanced beyond the late nineteenth century. That said, he should not be criticised for not doing something he had no wish to do.

The first section of *Poems of a Musician*, entitled 'Nature Lyrics and Songs of the Heart', adheres strictly to the rules Scott set himself. Reading a number of these poems in quick succession is like inhaling deeply some exotic perfume, like the incense that Scott was so fond of burning. The language creates a very distinctive and evocative atmosphere: the prevailing mood is contemplative, occasionally joyful or ecstatic but more often poetically melancholy. The tempo throughout is consistently *legato*, never *staccato*. The setting is rural, mostly with murmuring streams and waving trees as a backdrop, with autumn and dawn being the favoured subjects. Here Scott is entirely successful. By contrast, when he moves from the rural to the urban, and finds beauty in a heavily polluted industrial town, the measured rhyming stanzas and use of unfamiliar words, such as 'dern', lessen the impact.

There is no denying his versifying skills. For example, the villanelle is a poetic form that demands much ingenuity. It requires a series of five three-line verses ending with a quatrain. The first line is repeated at the sixth, twelfth and eighteenth lines, and the third line is repeated at the ninth, fifteenth and nineteenth lines. Scott used the form at least three times, in the 'Villanelle of Spring', the 'Villanelle of Dead Love', and the 'Villanelle of Autumn'.

This is 'Villanelle of Spring':

[9] Cyril Scott, *Near the End of Life, Candid Confessions and Reflections*, 1942–4 manuscript in the possession of the Estate of Cyril Scott.

[10] Ibid.

[11] Quoted by Hull in *Cyril Scott*, p. 148.

The first vernal kiss hath blest the hopeful heather,
And Winter's tears and woes across the plains dissolve;
Forgiven and forgotten is the wintry weather.

In mellow moods our hearts are closer twined together,
Whilst long embittered chords in sweeter strains resolve:
The first vernal kiss hath blest the hopeful heather.

Some early violets 'midst the celandines we gather,
And from their tender perfumes gentle dreams evolve:
Forgiven and forgotten is the wintry weather.

Have done with gloom! Have done with all that's dark and nether!
Away with empty grievings and with lost resolve!
The first vernal kiss hath blest the hopeful heather.

Again bedeck thy frozen heart with flower and feather,
And in the magic rays of sun thy soul absolve;
Forgiven and forgotten is the wintry weather

No longer now thy soaring spirit earthwards tether,
But with the Shining Ones in joyous dance revolve:
The first vernal kiss hath blest the hopeful heather,
Forgiven and forgotten is the wintry weather.

'Have done with all that's dark and nether' is awkward, but apart from that the poem is a beautiful and successful example of a most difficult art form. It was revised from the original in *The Grave of Eros.*

Another, much simpler, example showing what a change in rhythm can do is this final stanza of 'Song of Dawn', revised from *The Shadows of Silence*:

Morning's light grows,
  warblers trill now anew,
Silver-gold gems
  Prink the stream's babbling mirth.
Rich with magic perfumes thrills the morn-glad earth,
As the Sun-God's face appears
  in the myriad gems of dew;
For the Lords of Earth and Sky, in mystic union blent,
Again a new morning bless
  for their children's ravishment.

Scott could have written the poem with six lines of equal length. The rhyme scheme is not unusual: abbacc, but simply by breaking up the stanzas and indicating where the pauses come, he creates an entirely different effect.

It is amusing to look back and note what a critic of the day had to say about Scott's second volume, *The Grave of Eros.* In Scott's press-cutting book there is a review headed 'Notes on New Books'. The date, the paper in which it appeared, and the author all remain unidentified, but it has to have been written in 1907 or 1908. It begins:

> The book before us contains some five hundred lines of poetry varying in beauty, rhythm and value ... most of the lines are original, rich in imagination and spiritual fragrance and if the faults of construction were removed might easily be transformed into poems of the highest order of merit.
>
> ... Where he fails is ... in the violation of accepted canons of poetical composition. Not only is there a lack of rhythm and cadence in the author's lines but the meaning is sometimes obscure.

Being criticised for lack of rhythm and cadence would not have pleased Scott, for whom, as we know, they were the essentials of verse. He delighted in violating accepted canons in music but not in poetry. He enjoyed challenges. In his little book on humour[12] he illustrated a parlour game where contestants had to write a story using only words of one syllable, then of two syllables, then three. He soon discovered that constructing sentences of four-, five- and six-syllable words taxed his ingenuity to the utmost.

As well as setting many of Dowson's verses to music, Scott also wrote a poem 'To the Memory of Ernest Dowson'; when he set it to music, he called it 'Afterday'.[13] His Victorian poetic sensibilities accorded well with Dowson's, and in that vein he loved to indulge in pleasurable feelings of sadness, though he was, in reality, the least melancholy of men. He echoed the older man's most famous verse in a poem he called 'Meditation'.[14]

Dowson wrote:

> They are not long, the days of wine and roses:
> Out of a misty dream
> Our path emerges for a while, then closes
> Within a dream.

Scott's version reads:

> They are but brief, these languid laughing hours,
> Dying before the daily course is run;
> Few dreamy forms, few dimly fading flowers,
> Then set of sun.
>
> They are so short, those darksome days of anguish,
> Looming across the pathway of the soul;
> Few fleeting years our weary shadows languish,
> Before the Goal.

[12] *The Ghost of a Smile* (Andrew Dakers Ltd, 1939).

[13] Scored for voice and piano (Elkin, 1906).

[14] For the Dowson see No. 914, in *The Oxford Book of English Verse* (Oxford University Press, 1948), p. 1087.

Awake, arise! And through this realm of sorrow
Let us then turn at last our lives away,
And from the glories of the Goal just borrow
  One sacred Ray!

Dowson's verse is melancholy, without hope, but Scott's is exultant, focusing on whatever may lie beyond.

William Wordsworth, in his Preface to *Lyrical Ballads* (1798), stated that poetry should be as close to everyday language as possible. Scott, as we have noted, thought otherwise. He delighted in obscure and beautiful-sounding words, such as 'complores', 'lassitude' and 'morient'. Later, in his unpublished memoir, *Near the End of Life*,[15] he recanted, saying: 'Being mostly intent on creating new rhythms and new "verbal music", I became too preoccupied with sound and insufficiently with sense, and employed words in a grandiloquent manner without appreciating their precise meaning and manner of use.'

Scott was very severe about his early work, rejecting all but one of his first forty-six poems. 'Willows', the one he kept, considering it his best, he set to music shortly after writing it. In a revised form he both typed it out in the *Near The End of Life*, and added it to *Poems of a Musician*. Here is the first verse:

These mournful trees, caressed in the ancient poets' dreams,
That weep their trembling leafy tears along the silver streams;
Christened by the clear waters, swaying in the breeze:
Willows weeping, wailing – Nature's sorrow-stricken trees.

In my opinion a much better example, both in mood and atmosphere, is 'Valediction'. This was a new poem in *Poems of a Musician*, and echoes Thomas Gray's 'Elegy in a Country Churchyard'. Every detail – the distant church-bell, the solitary figure, the setting sun and the cry of the curlews – contributes perfectly to the feeling of melancholy at the thought of parting. Even the unusual word 'morient' (dying) seems fitting in this context:

From over the snow-capped darkening rugged peaks now
The song of twilight softly floats to us,
The roseate hue of the morient sunlight streaks now
The delicate despised convolvulus.

Afar in the valley a churchbell gently chimes still
Amidst the gem-like twinkling village lights,
One shadowy figure we faintly see who climbs still
The path towards his home among the heights.

The hour has struck when we must say goodbye here;
Ah, if it could only be unsaid! But no;

[15] Scott, *Near the End of Life.*

For I am left to hear the curlews cry here
Whilst you into the dark Unknown must go.

At his best Scott was a fine lyric poet. Here is the first verse of 'Invocation', revised from *The Voice of the Ancient*:

Autumn love, re-live again in me
I who turned my heart away erstwhile from thee;
These echoes whisper words that bring thee back with a broken song:
My mood is sadness – and the days are long.

Now the summer suns have set for thee,
Faded visions softly rise to sink in me;
Oh let thy radiance bathe me ere the plains be oversnowed,
And Summer's leaves lie dead upon the road.

Those last two lines are surely among Scott's most evocative. The poem ends:

Autumn love, turn not thy face from me,
Let thy gentle spirit sing again through me!
Thy scentless asters shall replace the rose and fragrant nard
And robin's chirp the throstle's rich aubade.

Let us return to Scott's fondness for unusual words. We have mentioned 'lassitude' before; on at least one occasion it caused him problems. 'Bells', one of the five poems accompanying the musical items in the piano suite *Poems* (Schott, 1912), includes the line 'Bells across the lone lassitude'. But lassitude is a state of mind – it means weariness, or torpor. Purists would argue it makes little sense in this context, though others would retort that poetry should transcend the literal. Scott later changed the line, perhaps because of adverse comments, but the revisions were not universally considered an improvement. In *The Grave of Eros* the first stanza read:

Through the limitless years of sad silent loneliness tolling,
With infinite sorrow, surging sounds of changeless might;
Bells across the lone lassitude, rising, swelling, endlessly rolling
Over the wasteland-solitude lost into the cold chaotic night.

The 1943 revision in *Poems of a Musician* has:

Through the unremembered years of long desolate loneliness, tolling
With poignant sorrow, surging sounds of changeless might;
Bells across the vast solitudes, rising, falling, endlessly rolling
Over the peaks and plainlands lost within the cold chaotic night.

Percy Grainger expressed best the objection to the change, complaining:

> Cyril has allowed himself to be drawn out of a vague, eerie EMOTIONAL landscape into a reasoning, concrete GEOGRAPHICAL landscape. 'lone lassitude' is a condition of the soul, from which all we over-fed middle-class continually suffer, as Tolstoy pointed out.[16]

Scott could be very severe on himself, and rejected most of his early poetry as immature. The title of his first volume, *The Shadows of Silence,* he later said was meaningless; he thought it would have been marginally better reversed, to *The Silence Of Shadows,* but would then have been self-evident. And anyway, as he saw it, almost nothing in the volume was worth keeping, for the whole was:

> Merely indicative of a young romantic intent on expressing himself in metre without the essential literary equipment for that desideratum and who, as Bernard Shaw later on pointed out, was 'too fond of beauty', or at any rate of the type of beauty which appealed to certain poets and painters (Burne-Jones for instance) towards the end of the last century.[17]

Two of the new poems in the *Poems of a Musician* sound a note of genuine melancholy, as opposed to the 'poetic melancholy' of earlier verses. From the first section, this is the second and final stanza of 'Morning Melancholy':

> Soon, the moon, resembling but a small white cloud,
> Will behind the snowy mountain peaks have slunk away.
> Whence comes this wealth of memories that unrequested crowd
> Round me now that I am old and soon must say
> Farewell to all the fields of life that I have ploughed
> Through sun and shadow in my dappled day?
> Who knows – when summer comes again, 'tis I who may
> Have sunk away.

In the second and final verse of 'Song of Twilight', he writes,

> My life has passed its Spring now,
> Not long, and Autumn will be near,
> The over-laden songs I used to sing, now
> Already foolish seem and somewhat sear,
> For many dreams that brought me joy or pain, now
> Have lost their old delight or shed their sting;
> And though each year its blossomtide will bring, now
> *My* Spring can never bloom again.

With these two poems we are reminded that the older, revised ones were originally written when Scott's career was in the ascendant. He was a young man in his twen-

[16] Round letter to composer-friends, 15 August 1947.

[17] *Near the End of Life.*

ties and the world was before him. Now, in the middle of World War 2, he is at the nadir, over sixty, unwell, and ignored as a serious composer.

Scott was fortunate in that he never saw active service. For World War 2 he was too old, and for World War 1 he was considered unfit for duty and made himself useful, as he remarks in the autobiography *Bone of Contention*, by giving concerts for wartime charities.[18] He considered war a colossal waste, an appalling stupidity that made nothing better and everything worse. He even chastised those poets who coated its ugliness with a semblance of beauty, thinking obviously of Rupert Brooke, the epitome of Romantic youth dying for his country. One wonders if he ever read Wilfred Owen!

The Poems of a Musician has five sections, but the fifth one, Scott's 'Translations from the German' of poems by Goethe, Heine, Hebbel, Eichendorff and others, will not be discussed here. We are concerned only with his original poems.

All the poems we have been looking at are in the first section, 'Nature-Lyrics and Songs of the Heart'. The second section, 'Through Other Eyes', has only three poems, all called 'Lamentation.' They are powerful and moving verses, but what is most striking, given that they were written when the war was occupying everyone's thoughts and the outcome was still in doubt, is that Scott takes the German point of view, defending in all three the innocence of the German people. In 'Lamentation I', the parents of a dead soldier mourn the loss of their only son and place the blame squarely on Adolf Hitler.

> They called him Leader, but he led us only to our doom,
> For what? Alone to glorify his now accursèd name.

In 'Lamentation II' a woman forlornly watches the ship carrying her lover away to war, and cries:

> What care they for the simple husbandman,
> Save this – to use him for their evil ends?
> And we who lead our unoffending lives from day to day.
> With blood or tears must pay.

In 'Lamentation III' a soldier returns only to find his home destroyed, his parents and his sweetheart all dead. He confesses that at first he was happy and proud to serve the Fatherland because:

> He played upon our patriotism and our pride,
> He told us that we were the highest-raced
> Of all the peoples, and alone were qualified
> This world to lead and rule:
> And I – oh fool –
> Because he asked from us the best,
> Worshipped him as hero and as saint,
> Only in the end to learn – how bitterly –

[18] Cyril Scott, *Bone of Contention* (Aquarian Press, 1969), p. 142.

That everything was but a feint
To bring us into thrall.

The speaker is left disillusioned, a bitter orphan without hope.

In the fourth section, 'Miscellaneous Poems', there are several where it is hard not to see at least some reference to Scott's own situation at the time. We have to sympathise with 'Le Vieillard', an old man who looks back over his life and complains that everything has changed – he is living in a world he can no longer understand:

I have lived to see
All loveliness despised in noble Art.
And what erewhile caressed the heart,
Debased to mockery.

And music pure
That once the soul to lofty ethers could entice,
Today, what is it but a vice
That everywhere I must endure?

He cries bitterly that no one pays any attention to him, or wants to meet him any more, and feels that secretly they wish he were dead.

In 'Envoy', the final poem of this section, the speaker admits he has had some success in earlier days, but not with his more serious works, the ones he laboured over longest:

They took my trifles
And they spurned the rest;
Those deeper things the soul creates
They wanted not to hear.
They only asked for honeyed song
Which gently titillates
A hardly heeding ear.

Hitherto Scott's poems had mainly been lyrical and sensual expressions of mood and atmosphere, but now he turns to more mundane issues. 'The Misogynist' believes he is free of all emotion concerning his lover who has left him, but in reality has become a hate-filled refugee from life, who only loved himself through her. 'The Laggards' are hidebound slaves to tradition who refuse to see that change is inevitable.

Another poem voices one of Scott's most cherished ideas, that of complete freedom in marriage. 'A Husband To His Wife', is a revision of a poem that first appeared in *The Voice of the Ancient* in 1910. It would have been shocking then, and even today its idealism, or some might say its naivety, could still raise an eyebrow. The verses speak of jealousy as childishness, and maintain it is a compliment to the woman when a man loves her so much that he always puts her happiness before his own. The husband whose wife has taken a lover insists her passion for the new man cannot destroy the love they share together.

What do they understand, the cynic and the sneerer,
Who falsely cry that love in wedlock never can be free?
Nay, just this love for him has brought you still a little nearer
By weaving one more bond for us of joy and sympathy.

The ideas expressed did not originate with Scott, as he explains in his autobiography *My Years of Indiscretion.*[19] He was introduced to them around 1903 by Mrs Robert Stevenson, a relative of novelist Robert Louis Stevenson. What is interesting is that he adopted them so completely that they became part of his core beliefs, and we find them again in many of his books: *The Real Tolerance* (1913),[20] *The Initiate* (1920),[21] *My Years of Indiscretion* (1924)[22] and *The Art of Making a Perfect Husband* (1928),[23] and also in a satirical revue (never produced) called *Backwards and Forwards.*

We now turn to the third section of *Poems of a Musician*, 'Rhetorical and Mystical Poems'. Because of its significance these poems have been left to the last. They deal with ideas and beliefs that engaged Scott for most of his life, and that he expressed throughout his prose writings as well as in his verse. Several, including the one called 'Karma', deal specifically with reincarnation, but the fullest exposition of his whole philosophy comes in the longest poem of the entire book, written while the war was raging, and titled 'If He Should Speak Today'.

This is a rhetorical work in which Scott asks: if Christ were to return today, what would he have to say? Perhaps:

Death and destruction sweep through every land,
At last man reaps the baneful harvest he hath sown
These thousand years.

Christ continues, after regretting that his precepts have never been followed except by a few:

'Tis ye who, having broken every Law of Unity,
This desolation on yourselves have brought.
Blame not God or me
Because ye listened not to what I taught.
For in that God gave man a measure of free-will,
So gave He for all time to men the choice
'Twixt good and evil, and their cups to fill
With drops that are as poison or with precious wine.
And ye have chosen ill:
Fraternity was God's Design,
But ye have gone the way of separateness.

19 Cyril Scott, *My Years of Indiscretion* (Mills & Boon, 1924), pp. 77–9.

20 Anon. [Cyril Scott], *The Real Tolerance* (A. C. Fifield, n.d. [1913]).

21 Anon. [Cyril Scott], *The Initiate, by his Pupil* (Routledge & Kegan Paul, 1920).

22 Scott, *My Years of Indiscretion*, pp. 62–5.

23 Cyril Scott, *The Art of Making a Perfect Husband* (Harper & Brothers, 1929).

The Unity and Separateness referred to in the poem are the positive and negative of Scott's entire philosophy, or, to put it another way, the whole and the part. His motto was Unity in Diversity, of which he himself was a prime example, his manifold interests finding expression in a variety of different ways, but all being part of the one man.

The poem continues with a passage on reincarnation:

> Be comforted!
> The evil that besets you all around
> Is fraught with hidden good,
> ... no soul can suffer what it hath not earned,
> Born many times before, it will be born again
> To reap what it has sown of joy or sown in pain;
> For on the doer every action must rebound.
> No debts man pays save those he hath incurred
> In this or in a former span of life upon this globe.
>
> Such is the perfect if mysterious Law
> Of action and re-action
> All things are destined to obey,
> And which no soul can circumvent upon the pilgrim-way
> That ye must tread, and I myself have trod,
> From imperfection unto perfect everlasting Bliss.

Christ then declares that it was wrong to call him the *Only* Son of God, for all are sons of God and are all divine potentially, differing not in kind but only in degree. From the earliest times, he says, Jesus has been misinterpreted, his teachings disregarded, and Christianity, instead of being a guidance and a blessing, has been, for the most part:

> but as a blot
> Upon the scroll of history,
> So little have ye let the loving spirit of the Christ
> Amongst yourselves prevail.

To those who long for the second coming, the speaker asks what would be the point of returning to give a new lesson, when the lessons he gave over 2,000 years ago have still to be learned. Despite that, the poem ends on a most positive and joyous note and expresses perfectly the essence of Scott's philosophy:

> Yet be not comfortless,
> Through all uplifting things my Spirit breathes,
> Through every rite that nobly stirs the heart,
> Through wisdom-pregnant word of scribe and orator,
> Through soul-exalting music, through the highest Art
> And garlands rich in rhythmic beauty that the poet wreathes.

So am I always nigh to those who seek for me
Upon the plains or scan the mountain's peak for me,
It matters nothing what their creed or caste may be,
All noble strivings lead at last to me.
Some selfless souls I guide have hardly heard my name,
No man, however often he has erred, I blame;
For Love Divine all things forgives because it comprehends
Those sins that fret the pilgrim ere his arduous journey ends.
And if I do not stand before your errors dumb,
'Tis this and only this –
That through self-knowing all the swifter ye may come,
Responsive to my call,
To share that never-to-be-quenchèd Bliss
Which is the heritage of all.

This is followed by an ecstatic mystical poem called 'The Voice'. It speaks of love, life and bliss. All these words are in upper case, in order to emphasise the degree of the rapture. Each of the three verses ends 'For I am LIFE, the ONE; For I am LOVE, the ONE; for I am BLISS, the ONE.' This is the complete last verse.

The One, the only Self in man am I,
From birth to birth he goes yet cannot die;
Denying Me, he cannot flee from Me,
Divided never can he *be* from me.
In his beloved's eyes he looks for Me,
He scans the mountains, dales and brooks for Me,
In wisdom or in foolishness he craves for Me,
He fights through passions' dark and turgid waves for Me,
Yea, urge to every action is the search for Me,
Even his crystal soul he would besmirch for Me,
For I am BLISS
The ONE.

Scott has much in common with the seventeenth-century mystics Thomas Traherne and Henry Vaughan, who saw beyond any creed or religion to the unity of all things and were inspired by a spiritual concept of the world that informed every line they wrote.

The Poems of a Musician contains some fine poems, and a few would grace any anthology of English poetry. If Scott had continued writing in a similar vein to those in the 'Nature Lyrics' section, the book would stand simply as the record of a poet-musician over a forty-year span; the war poems and the more personal pieces give us a glimpse into his views on war and provide some insight as to his state of mind at the time; but it is the philosophical and mystical verses that give the book its importance, raising it to a new level and contributing significantly to a fuller understanding of the man himself.

I Scott's mother, Mary, as a young woman

II Scott's father, Henry, aged forty-seven

III 'The Laurels', Oxton, Cheshire, where Scott spent his infancy and childhood

IV Scott aged five

V Scott aged fifteen

VI Scott aged eighteen

VII Scott aged twenty-eight; compare with frontispiece drawing by Jane Emmet de Glehn

VIII The poet Stefan George; Scott always kept a framed photograph of George in his study

IX The composer Percy Grainger; Scott always kept a framed photograph of Grainger in his study

X Lazzaro Uzielli, Scott's piano teacher at the Hochs'che Conservatorium in Frankfurt, who became a friend; the greeting reads 'To my dear friend Cyril Scott with warm regards, Feb. 1951'

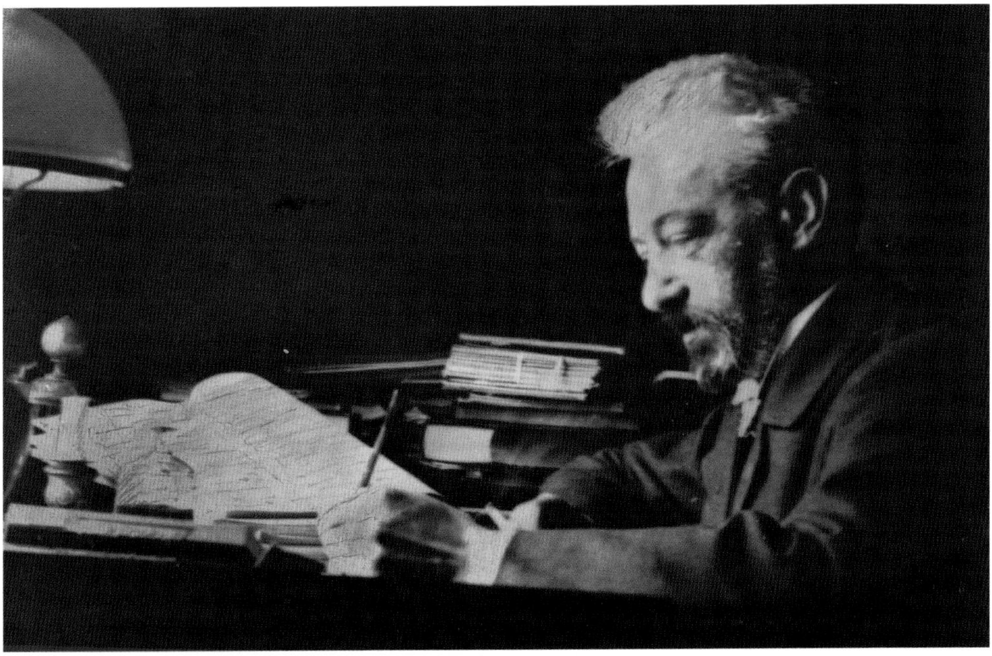

XI Iwan Knorr, Scott's composition teacher at the Conservatorium in Frankfurt

XII Four members of The Frankfurt Group at the Harrogate Festival in 1929 (*left to right*)
Cyril Scott, Roger Quilter, Percy Grainger, Norman O'Neill; the fifth member, Balfour Gardiner, is missing

XIII Swami Vivekananda, whose book Raja Yoga caused Scott to abandon his agnosticism

XIV Robert Elkin, Scott's long-term publisher and friend

XV Scott at the piano; postcard used by the music publisher Augener as a promotional tool (*c.* 1913)

XVI Scott in Toronto in 1921, during a tour of the USA and Canada, a few months before he returned home to marry Rose Allatini

SECOND NEW YORK RECITAL

Aeolian Hall, Friday Afternoon

FEBRUARY 4th

The program will include songs interpreted By Mme. EVA GAUTHIER

CYRIL SCOTT

IN

New York Boston Philadelphia

Philadelphia Record:

Scott is a man of great versatility, a musician, pianist, poet and philosopher, a sort of modern Leonardo da Vinci. His piano concerto in C major presented him as the interpreter of the most advanced work done by the orchestra in some time. Unlike much of modern composition, however, it is a work abounding in beauty—beauty of effects rather than of melodic design. Dissonances, consecutive fifths, in fact all the combinations regarded as dangerous and undesirable by the conservative element, are used with a facility of workmanship that makes them beautiful as they are refreshing to hear.

Boston Transcript (H. T. Parker):

Mr. Scott has ability to write largely, variously, freely within a wide-stretched frame. He compasses no small sweep and power and large imagination sustains his music. In all his shorter pieces he makes his imagination a poetry in tones.

New York Post (H. T. Finck):

Mr. Scott has been characterized as Debussy's English double, but this generalization is neither fair nor completely true. He has something original to say in music and he says it in a distinctly individualistic way, with the stamp of his own personality. These short piano pieces and songs show a command of diversity and variety in delicate and fastidious workmanship, glints of rare tonal beauty, novel harmonic effects, and considerable skill in evoking the mood. As compared with some of the ultra modern music, Cyril Scott's pieces are lucidity itself.

Boston Herald (Philip Hale):

There was much to enjoy in his recital. It is the easiest thing in the world to say that he has been somewhat influenced by Debussy; but to be influenced and to imitate are not the same thing. He has his own idiom, an idiom not borrowed, not affected. His technical proficiency is suited to his music. He showed himself a colorist, rhythmically sure, and with range of dynamic gradations from poetic delicacy and refinement to force. The Passacaglia was brilliantly conceived.

Boston Post (Olin Downes):

Mr. Scott is a personality on the stage—an admirable pianist. He has been accused of imitating Debussy, but it must be recalled that Ravel also owed much to Debussy, that few moderns have failed to respond to his influence. Scott has a poetic talent, an exotic imagination. He writes music which recoils from the beaten path. He also has genuine force. As a whole, he is Byronic in his music as in his personality, which is the quality which quite convincingly affects his hearers.

Philadelphia Evening Ledger:

The workmanship of the concerto is of a high order. The orchestration is original. As a pianist, Mr. Scott showed talents of a high order especially in the softer passages, although he has ample power when required. His touch is firm but gentle, and he frequently brought a delicious quality of tone from the instrument. His technic is ample, but he has apparently not made a fetish of this too often abused facility.

Management: LOUDON CHARLTON, Carnegie Hall, New York

XVII Publisher's press release, with notices of Scott in Boston, Philadelphia and New York

18

The Occult Writings

KURT LELAND

IN 1950, Cyril Scott wrote a cranky letter to *Musical Opinion* in which he defended himself against a critic who (in Scott's words) 'put forward my interest in the occult as a reason for my shortcomings as a composer'. Scott complained that:

> The assumption that while composing I have, so to say, one ear cocked on the occult, does not and cannot make sense. It is just one of those fables which people (especially journalists) like to create in an attempt to make a composer, artist or whatnot, appear more spectacular or unbalanced than he really is. To be quite candid, I have always and merely written the sort of music *I like* to write and which seems for me natural to write.[1]

He further indicated not only that 'I have never attempted to be a practising mystic' but also that 'my musical characteristics' had developed '*before* my interest in such matters was aroused'.[2] Such an avowal implied that his music should be judged without regard for his immensely popular occult writings, some of which are still with us today, having been continuously in print for nearly a century.

Yet, as I pointed out in my chapter on Scott's chamber music, there is indeed a connection between Scott's musical practice and his occult beliefs. They evolved in parallel and interacted with each other. But the music was also the result of an evolution that had begun, as Scott stated, before his interest in the occult developed. Thus Scott's answer to his critic should be understood to imply that there is no easy, simple, or superficial relationship between the two. The evolution of his chamber music over half a century indicates how sophisticated was Scott's development of musical analogues for mystical experiences and notions. Here we shall examine in greater detail just what those notions were.

In *An Outline of Modern Occultism*, Scott defined occultism as 'the synthesis of Science, Mysticism, Philosophy, Psychology and Religion, in their purest forms'.[3] He elaborated on this definition as follows:

> It is to those who find orthodox religious creeds too illogical or sentimental, and materialism too unsatisfactory and negative, that occult philosophy should prove acceptable, for it renders life vastly more interesting, more intriguing and more romantic. It shows cosmic life to be other than that mechanical 'order of things' which the materialist postulates, and shows personal life as the 'adventure magnificent' which does not merely begin with the cradle and end with the grave.

[1] 'Letters to the Editor: Music and the Occult', *Musical Opinion* 73 no. 870 (March 1950), p. 359 (original emphasis).

[2] Ibid.

[3] Cyril Scott, *An Outline of Modern Occultism* (George Routledge & Sons, 1935), p. 17.

> Furthermore, it shows the *raison d'être* for all religions worthy of the name, for cults, movements, philosophies, arts and sciences, their evolution and various phases. It explains the apparently unexplainable without making impossible demands upon faith, advocating *reason* as the most reliable stepping stone to knowledge.[4]

It is possible to tease out from this statement a diagnosis of the intellectual plight of Western civilisation in the late nineteenth and early twentieth centuries, and a prescription that could just as well be labelled modernism as occultism:

- rejection of orthodox religion as illogical and sentimental
- anxiety over the implication of scientific materialism that human existence is the result of chance and ultimately without purpose or meaning
- need for some form of belief, not necessarily religious, to restore a sense of meaning to life (hence the notions of 'romance' and the 'adventure magnificent' in Scott's phrasing)
- resolution of this need by discovering, revealing, or creating a comprehensive (if syncretic) explanation of world conditions and cultural projects that might include the possibility of faith, but must be answerable to reason and explain even the 'apparently unexplainable' (running the gamut, for example, from creative genius to the behaviour of ghosts)

Current scholarship has begun to reveal just how indebted modernism was to a wave of interest in esotericism by intellectuals and artists at the turn of the twentieth century – a wave in which the Theosophical Society (TS), founded in 1875 in New York but headquartered in India since 1879, played a critical role.[5] Historians have long been aware of the impact of a book entitled *Thought-Forms,* published in 1905 by the theosophical clairvoyants Annie Besant and Charles Webster Leadbeater, on the development of modernism in the arts.[6] Its ideas about the clairvoyant perception of thoughts and emotions in terms of shape and colour were taken up by the Russian painter Wassily Kandinsky in *Über das Geistige in der Kunst* (On the Spiritual in Art; 1912) and in the evolution of his approach to painting, in particular on the development of abstraction and non-objective art.[7]

By dint of Scott's many theosophical writings – he joined the TS in 1914[8] – he is perhaps the most visible example of the influence of the TS on a musical modernist. He himself linked theosophical ideas to the development of modernism in a book of essays published in 1917, *The Philosophy of Modernism – Its Connection with Music,* which included a chapter entitled 'The Hidden Side of Music' (referencing

[4] Ibid., 4–5.

[5] See Alex Owen, *The Place of Enchantment: British Occultism and the Culture of the Modern* (University of Chicago Press, 2004), pp. 11–50, for an excellent introduction to the subject.

[6] A misprint in later editions of *Thought-Forms* has led to a persistent scholarly misdating of the first edition to 1901.

[7] Owen, *Place of Enchantment*, pp. 229–30.

[8] Jean Overton Fuller, *Cyril Scott and a Hidden School: Towards the Peeling of an Onion,* Theosophical History Occasional Papers 7 (Theosophical History, 1998), p. 8.

illustrations of clairvoyantly perceived thought-forms produced by music in *Thought-Forms*) and an appendix called 'The Occult Relationship between Sound and Colour'.[9]

Scott listed the fundamental tenets of occultism as follows (I have added notes in brackets to clarify connections to the issues discussed above and to provide amplifications based on Scott's theosophically informed worldview):[10]

1. Humanity 'is in a process of evolving from comparative imperfection to much higher states of physical and spiritual existence'. [Thus Darwin's originally materialistic theory of evolution has been applied to social and religious progressivism along the lines of human perfectibility, not as a metaphor, but as a truth that operates identically in both the physical and the spiritual universe.]
2. 'The evolutionary process in all its phases is directed by a Great Hierarchy of Intelligences who have themselves reached those higher states.' [Among these intelligences are Masters, devas (Sanskrit for 'shining ones' or gods – something like Jewish, Christian, and Muslim angels), and the 'founders' of world religions, such as Buddha, Christ, Krishna, Muhammad, Zoroaster. These higher beings provide models and standards of moral and ethical perfection that would otherwise be absent from a purely mechanistic universe, as well as inspiration and instruction in individual and collective betterment along physical, emotional, intellectual, and spiritual lines.]
3. 'The world that is perceptible to normal sight is only a small portion of a much greater world which is perceptible to the trained occultist, and comprises the inner and higher planes of consciousness.' [Thus the scientifically measurable outer/material world perceived with the physical senses is linked with a number of intuitively perceived subtle/inner worlds in a continuum ranging from lowest matter to highest spirit. This continuum is said to pass through seven stages or planes – physical, astral/emotional, mental, buddhic/intuitional, nirvanic/spiritual, monadic, and divine – thus erasing the troubling boundaries between inner and outer experience, objective and subjective realities, and physical and (assumed) nonphysical universes while unifying science, religion, and psychology under the aegis of consciousness.][11]
4. 'The physical body is not the *generator* of consciousness, as many biologists assert, but only the densest vehicle of consciousness or a "garment" of the immortal soul.' [Thus all is consciousness, which creates one or more bodies as focal points for experience (i.e. vehicles) on each plane. These vehicles of consciousness include, on the physical plane, the dense physical body and the subtler etheric body (the energetic model upon which the development of the physical body is based); on the astral plane, the astral or emotional body (the self we usually experience when dreaming); on

[9] Cyril Scott, *The Philosophy of Modernism – Its Connection with Music* (Waverly, *c.* 1917), pp. 97–109; pp. 111–18.

[10] Scott, *Modern Occultism*, pp. 11–12.

[11] For an explanation of these planes and their associated subtle bodies and types of clairvoyant vision by Annie Besant, see Kurt Leland, *Invisible Worlds: Annie Besant on Psychic and Spiritual Development* (Quest, 2013), pp. 229–45.

the mental plane, the mental body (what we call the mind) and the causal body (what we call the soul, which is said to hold the *causes* of our frequent reincarnations); and so on. By positing bodies on nonphysical planes that are experienced from what scientific materialists would call a subjective state in the physical body, occultists reify the contents of these planes.]

5. 'Interpenetrating and surrounding the physical body are subtler bodies composed of rarefied matter, which are also garments of the soul. These likewise are perceptible to the trained occultist.' [The manner of perception is called clairvoyance and the aggregate of these subtle bodies is called the aura. Each body has its own form of clairvoyant vision, which allows it to observe the contents of its respective plane. Thus etheric vision allows us to perceive beings who operate at that level, including fairies and nature spirits; astral vision allows us to perceive the denizens of the astral plane, which include dreamers, the so-called dead, and angels or devas who operate at that level; and so on.]
6. 'The whole universe is an expression of energy ... not only the elements, but all beings both embodied and disembodied are storehouses and transformers of energy.' [The word *energy* may be defined as follows: 'the capacity for work or vigorous activity'; 'exertion of vigor or power'; 'vitality and intensity of expression.'[12] These definitions could be equally applied to inorganic elements or organic beings. Thus the notion of physical laws guiding the work or expressions of purely physical elements is linked with the psychological or spiritual laws of how beings work or express themselves. If all is consciousness, including so-called inorganic elements, then physical laws and psychological laws must be identical, thereby suggesting another means of unifying objective and subjective realities.]
7. 'A Law of immutable justice and fundamental beneficence, i.e., the law of cause and effect, governs the entire Cosmos, both visible and invisible.' [Thus the ancient Hindu notion of karma is equated with Newton's third law of motion. If every action has an equal but opposite reaction on the physical plane (the firing of thrusters in a rocket propels the rocket in the opposite direction), then something similar must occur in the moral universe (e.g. a selfish action on my part intended to create personal happiness at the expense of another's suffering draws to me suffering of the same type and degree in the present or a subsequent lifetime; or if I perform an action of selfless service for others' benefit in a previous lifetime, something similar may be done for me in the present lifetime). This equation of karma with Newton's law is not intended as a metaphor, but is believed to demonstrate that a single law operates equally in the physical universe and the moral/spiritual universe, thereby revealing their fundamental unity.]

With these views in mind, we are ready to consider Scott's occult writings, five published anonymously (either by 'the author of the Initiate' or by 'his [the Initiate's] pupil) and three under his own name.

[12] *The American Heritage College Dictionary*, 4th edn (Houghton Mifflin, 2007), s.v. 'energy'.

THE INITIATE: SOME IMPRESSIONS OF A GREAT SOUL (1920)

Scott's most successful literary endeavour was a series of three semi-autobiographical occult novels published anonymously and referred to collectively as the Initiate series: *The Initiate: Some Impressions of a Great Soul* (1920); *The Initiate in the New World* (1927); and *The Initiate in the Dark Cycle* (1932). He revealed his authorship of these popular books (which are still in print) in *An Outline of Modern Occultism.*[13] The premise of the series is that enlightened beings in human form, whether Masters or Initiates who are passing through a graded series of tests of their spiritual evolution in service of humanity on their way to becoming Masters, are present among us.[14] The author, identified as the poet Charles Broadbent – a stand-in for Scott's literary side (Scott had published several volumes of poetry before 1920), knows such an Initiate and is recording this Initiate's doings and teachings. Indeed, the book is dedicated to 'That Great Soul whose identity is concealed under the name of Justin Moreward Haig'.

Readers and scholars alike have speculated on the identity of the Initiate for decades without coming to a conclusion. Indeed, he may be a composite of all of the spiritual teachers who impressed Scott as 'great souls'. He is called Moreward in *The Initiate,* MH in *The Initiate in the New World,* and JMH in *The Initiate in the Dark Cycle;* for simplicity's sake, I refer to him as JMH throughout.

Many of Scott's writings indicate that his *bête noire,* both personally and professionally (as a composer) was the individually and collectively repressive social and spiritual climate of Victorian and post-Victorian England, which he called Phariseeism: 'that mental indolence which prompts people to conform to ready-made customs and ready-made opinions' resulting in 'the conventional, the orthodox, the sticklers who refuse to move with the times' and who 'do everything because it is the supposedly right thing to do'.[15] In *The Initiate,* Scott poses the question: what would happen if a spiritually advanced soul were to enter the staid drawing rooms of England in the early years of the twentieth century and gently, lovingly, persuasively pick apart the cherished conventions by which the occupants regulated their physical, emotional and moral lives?

Regardless of what we might think about the existence of theosophical Masters, Scott answers this question with a brilliant and hilarious comedy of manners. Thus the first half of *The Initiate* collects a number of vignettes in which we witness JMH's handling of people in various social stations and personal difficulties. The individual chapters are more like a series of linked short stories than the cohesive plot of a novel. JMH's character and the consistency of his principles in attacking the conventions from which people were suffering provide a thematic link, and the gradual expansion of Broadbent's awareness of JMH's spiritual superiority provides a sense of progression in time.

[13] Scott, *Modern Occultism,* pp. 231–4.

[14] I retain Scott's use of upper case to distinguish the words *Master* and *Initiate.*

[15] Cyril Scott, *The Greater Awareness* [1936], reprinted edn (Routledge & Kegan Paul, 1981), pp. 14–15.

Neither purely fictional nor purely autobiographical, this category-defying piece of writing could perhaps be called a memoir of spiritual unfolding. Furthermore, the portions focused on JMH relate the process of spiritual unfolding to events in the outer world that have some (not clearly defined) basis in fact; the portion entitled 'The Circuitous Journey', by contrast, relates this process to events in the inner world of archetypes and allegory that may have some basis in (presumably) past-life events, whether real (if we are believers in reincarnation) or imaginary.[16] Thus, in a memoir of spiritual unfolding, the facts are the *stages* in which that unfolding takes place. In *The Initiate*, Scott demonstrates that outer-world narrative and inner-world allegory are equally viable means of portraying such stages.

THE ADEPT OF GALILEE: A STORY AND AN ARGUMENT (1920)

Touted as 'by the author of the Initiate', Scott's next book, published in the same year, seems like an aberration. Gone are the sparkling wit of JMH's comedy of manners and the atmospheric, though sometimes plodding, allegory of 'The Circuitous Journey'. Instead, we have a wholesale remake of the gospels whose intention seems to be the creation (Scott would say restoration) of Jesus's life story and character along the lines of a vegetarian Eastern adept. This adept is not the son of God, but a highly evolved human whose practice of yoga results in quasi-miraculous feats that obey lesser known laws of nature instead of upending those laws, as in traditional Christian teachings. Furthermore, this adept's teaching reveals depths of common sense and illuminative wisdom not immediately apparent in biblical accounts and exegesis. Finally, the lost years of Jesus's life, from age twelve to age thirty, have been filled in with extravagant detail.

We know that Scott was brought up in the Anglican faith and that he lost his religion as a young man. We also know that his spiritual quest began in the first years of the twentieth century in conjunction with reading Christian Science literature at the behest of a friend, attending a lecture by Annie Besant that first exposed him to theosophy, and encountering Swami Vivekananda's 1896 book *Raja Yoga*, which became a lifelong influence.[17] Around 1907, Scott came under the influence of Swami Abhedananda, an associate of Vivekananda who had studied under the same guru, Sri Ramakrishna. In 1902, Abhedananda published a book, *How to Be a Yogi*, which included a chapter entitled 'Was Christ a Yogi?'[18] A ten-page excerpt appears in the introduction to *The Adept of Galilee*.[19] Perhaps Abhedananda's book

[16] Cyril Scott, *The Initiate: Some Impressions of a Great Soul* [1920], reprinted edn (Weiser, 1995), pp. 213–381.

[17] Cyril Scott, *Bone of Contention: Life Story and Confessions* (Arco, 1969): Anglican upbringing, pp. 20–2; development of agnosticism, pp. 60–3; further developments, pp. 114–16. Swami Vivekananda's *Raja Yoga* (as it is presently known) was first published under the title *Yoga Philosophy: Lectures Delivered in New York, Winter of 1895–6, by the Swâmi Vivekânanda on Râja Yoga, or Conquering the Internal Nature* (Longman, Greens, 1896).

[18] Swami Abhedananda, *Vedânta Philosophy: How to Be a Yogi* (Vedânta Society, 1902), pp. 163–80.

[19] Cyril Scott, *The Adept of Galilee: A Story and an Argument* (Routledge, 1920), pp. 6–15.

prompted Scott to reassess his relationship to the Christian faith of his youth along theosophical and occultist lines.

Adept draws upon a number of peculiar beliefs about 'the Master Jesus' that were held by some members of the TS in the early years of the twentieth century, such as that he was born a hundred years before the officially given date and that he was presently incarnate in a Syrian body and living near Mt Lebanon.[20] Scott folded these beliefs into the traditional gospel stories along with details from several non-traditional, 'rediscovered' (i.e. channelled) tracts from the early 1900s to create a unified narrative of the spiritual development of Jesus.[21]

The publication of *Adept* had little impact inside or outside the TS. As Scott noted in his second autobiography, *Bone of Contention,* a bombing shortly after the book's publication destroyed most of the stock.[22]

THE INITIATE IN THE NEW WORLD (1927)

Whereas *The Initiate* focused on JMH's teachings as applied to individuals in one-on-one encounters, its sequel, which I will call *New World* for short, focused on these teachings in the social context of a closed group of personal students. Scott calls this group an ashram, using the Sanskrit term for the often live-in community of devotees that develops around a guru in India. Though the book is set in Boston, the likely model for this community was the ashram of Pierre Bernard in Nyack, New York, which Scott visited on his five-month American concert and lecture tour of 1920–1.[23] Bernard was a teacher of Tantra, an ancient Indian form of spiritual practice intended to harness the polarity of male and female sexuality through meditation, breath control, and various physical means (not necessarily sexual) to achieve physical well-being and spiritual ecstasy and enlightenment.[24]

The book reads more like a novel than its predecessor in the series, its plot developing from a choice Broadbent must make between two young women, one attractive physically and emotionally (Clare Delafield), the other intellectually and spiritually (Viola Brind). JMH is strongly in favour of marriage to Viola, whereas Broadbent prefers Clare. The romantic triangle affects each member inwardly (spiritually) and outwardly (socially) and causes various strains between them, as well as with their teacher.

The chapters alternate in function between those that further the plot or delineate JMH's character in personal encounters with his students, and JMH's lectures on various topics, such as morality, love, egotism, marriage, sex, the causes of war, and 'the

[20] Josephine Ransom, *A Short History of the Theosophical Society, 1875–1938* [1938], reprinted edn (Theosophical Publishing House, 1989), pp. 52–3.

[21] Among others, Scott cites Levi H. Dowling, *The Aquarian Gospel of Jesus the Christ* (1908) and Gideon Jasper John Ouseley, *The Gospel of the Holy Twelve* (1901).

[22] Scott, *Bone of Contention*, 146.

[23] See Scott's autobiographical version of this visit ibid., pp. 165–8.

[24] For further information, see Robert Love's biography of Pierre Bernard, *The Great Oom: The Improbable Birth of Yoga in America* (Viking, 2010), especially p. 141, which provides a general idea of the teachings Scott would have encountered during his visit to Bernard's ashram.

permanent love consciousness', which returns as a major theme of a later book published under Scott's own name, *The Greater Awareness*.[25] A lecture by JMH on the philosophy of humour also anticipates further explorations of the subject in *The Greater Awareness* (in a spiritual context) and *The Ghost of a Smile* (in a social context).[26]

Though the book could be read as a demonstration of JMH's teachings on unconventional relationships (Clare and Viola transcend the socially conventional roles of jealous romantic rivals to become friends and confidantes), Viola has been identified as Rose Laure Allatini (1890–1980), a novelist who wrote prolifically under various pseudonyms and who married Scott in 1921, after he returned from his American tour. According to Scott, this was an 'occult marriage', one in which 'two pupils engage to marry at the suggestion of the Master, that in conjunction they may the better carry out his work and also provide the finer type of bodies for certain souls who, under his guidance, may wish to reincarnate'.[27] Clare has not been identified.

New World ends with a New Year's talent show in which JMH demonstrates several apparently miraculous occult phenomena, such as reduplicating himself and levitating a music box. Bernard was known to hold such festivities for the students at his ashram – though contemporary reports mention nothing so extraordinary.[28] Scott may have attended such a programme during his American tour. In the book a pianist named Hausmann, possibly a stand-in for Scott, plays Debussy, Ravel and Scriabin before and after JMH's performance.[29]

THE INITIATE IN THE DARK CYCLE (1932)

The final instalment of the Initiate series is less successful than the other two as a stand-alone work of literature. It is directed to fans of the previous books as a means of answering the many letters Scott had received from them asking for marital or other advice, interviews, opportunities to meet JMH, or demanding that he reveal JMH's identity and miraculous methods for the personal good of the correspondent or that of humanity.[30] It is also directed to members of the TS who were undergoing a crisis of belief: J. Krishnamurti, who had been trained and touted by TS leaders to become the spokesperson of a new world religion as if he were Christ come again, had repudiated the notion of Masters, occultism, and the TS itself.[31] Thus Scott packed JMH off to an unknown destination where he would meditate

[25] Scott, 'The Cultivation of Love-Consciousness', *Greater Awareness*, pp. 3–76.

[26] 'The Philosophy of Humour', in Cyril Scott, *The Initiate in the New World* [1927], reprinted edn (Weiser, 1991), pp. 72–81; 'The Value of Humour', in Scott, *Greater Awareness*, pp. 162–74; and Cyril Scott, *The Ghost of a Smile* (Andrew Dakers, 1939).

[27] Scott, *Bone of Contention*, p. 177; Scott, *Modern Occultism*, p. 232.

[28] In *The Great Oom*, pp. 142, 158, Love indicates that many of the residents and guests at Bernard's ashram were talented performers. In *Bone of Contention*, pp. 166–7, Scott briefly describes a few 'miracles' for which Bernard was known – though nothing as spectacular as those recounted in *New World*.

[29] Scott, *New World*, pp. 282, 288.

[30] Cyril Scott, *The Initiate in the Dark Cycle* [1932], reprinted edn (Weiser, 1992), pp. ix–xi.

[31] Ibid., pp. 65–77, 133–43.

for an unspecified length of time for his own personal development and the better to help the larger world. In the meantime, Scott included many conversations and teachings designed to reassure TS members of the existence and ongoing support of the Masters in the lives of their personal students, the TS and the world.

The autobiographical elements of *Dark Cycle* include a moving tribute to Nelsa Chaplin (here called Christabel Portman), the medium Scott worked with from about 1919 until her death in 1927. She was a source of many of the Master-derived teachings used by Scott in *Music: Its Secret Influence throughout the Ages* (1933). Scott hints that a book on music has been commissioned by the Masters, thereby partially giving away his identity as the author of the Initiate series.[32] Scott conveys something of the atmosphere in which these teachings were received at the Firs (here called the Pines), a healing retreat centre in Crowhurst, Sussex, England, run by Nelsa and her husband.[33]

We also meet a new real-life character, an eccentric and amusing astrologer-cum-artist named Brian Anrias Ross, who wrote under the name David Anrias.[34] As 'the author of *The Initiate*', Scott had written a long introduction about the Masters for Ross's book of channelled messages from them, *Through the Eyes of the Masters* (1932), which included portraits of them drawn by Ross. The notion of a dark evolutionary cycle lasting from 1909 to 1944 may have originated with Ross in his capacity as an astrologer.[35]

The ontological status of another new character, Sir Thomas, is less easy to determine. He is said to be JMH's teacher – a Master rather than an Initiate, as was JMH. Theosophical lore posited the existence of two English Masters, identified as Sir Thomas More (1478–1535; executed for defying Henry VIII on the immorality of divorce and remarriage) and Thomas Vaughan (1621–1666; an alchemist writing under the name Eugenius Philalethes, and the twin brother of the poet Henry Vaughan).[36] It may be that the old-fashioned skullcap worn by Sir Thomas in *Dark Cycle* is intended to suggest that More was still embodied centuries after his alleged physical demise.[37] In this instalment the character of JMH himself seems to be determined more by the exigencies of Scott's plot and message than by the words and deeds of a real-life model.

The composer Lyall Herbert represents Scott *in propria persona*[38] – though one hopes that the praise and glorious predictions of his future lavished on him by JMH and Sir Thomas were offered tongue in cheek, or at least were reports of channelled

[32] Ibid., pp. 3–19 (portrait of Nelsa Chaplin), 205, 213 (book on music).

[33] See Scott, *Bone of Contention*, p. 158, for confirmation of these details; see also Fuller, *Cyril Scott*, pp. 13–14, for further corroborative details. Scott wrote that Chaplin died around 1930 (*Bone of Contention*, p. 198), but 1927 was the date of her death record at Ancestry.com.

[34] Brian Anrias Ross's name appears in this form in the TS General Membership Register at http://tsmembers.org/. See book 4, entry 49417, file 4C/33 (accessed 22 September 2016).

[35] Scott, *Dark Cycle*, pp. 13n and 118–20.

[36] Ransom, *Short History of the Theosophical Society*, p. 54.

[37] Scott hints at the longevity of the Masters in *The Initiate*, pp. xiii–xiv.

[38] See Scott, *Modern Occultism*, p. 231, for a hint to this effect.

messages from Masters rather than self-advertisement.[39] In any case, Scott makes his alter ego say: 'Occultism's so marvellously full of surprises and romance ... how dull ordinary life must seem without it', and 'Composing without any ideal behind it – what is it? ... Art for Art's sake is all very well as a high-sounding catchphrase, but Art for the Masters' and Humanity's sake is much more romantic.'[40]

THE VISION OF THE NAZARENE (1933)

Scott seems to have felt some urgency about getting humanity to cease behaving in childish ways, hence his several critiques of Western civilisation, such as *Childishness: A Study of Adult Conduct* (1930). By the early 1930s, well into the Great Depression, it was clear that no one was listening and nothing had changed. What was left but for Scott to appeal to a higher authority, such as the Master Jesus?

I cannot vouch for Scott's having arrived at such a conclusion in connection with *The Vision of the Nazarene*, but I can at least suggest that what might seem to be Scott's most embarrassing book developed from self-consistent thought processes and beliefs. What, after all, are we to make of these 'utterances', said to be impressions received during deep meditation during which the Master Jesus (supposedly alive and well in Syria) took the author on an out-of-body tour of the world and commented on its ills and wrongs in quasi-biblical language?[41] We might note politely that the book is not unlike Kahlil Gibran's *The Prophet* (1923), which similarly treats a variety of subjects pertaining to outer and inner life in poetic prose as teachings of a spiritual (though non-theosophical) Master – and pass on without further comment.

Yet it is possible to see *Vision* as Scott's most extreme experiment with the guiding statement behind so much of his literary work in prose, first articulated in *The Real Tolerance*: 'A point of view is a prophylactic against all evil: hence the science of happiness consists in one's ability to construct the most peace-inspiring point of view.'[42] Indeed, the first words JMH speaks in *The Initiate* are: 'A certain point of view ... is a prophylactic against all sorrow.'[43] The theme appears again in *New World* in a chapter entitled 'The Tyranny of View-Points', which opens with JMH quoting from *The Real Tolerance*.[44] Finally, more than thirty years after the publica-

[39] However, these predictions may also have provided advance notice of a 1932 composition Scott was working on at the time – *Mystic Ode*, for men's or mixed chorus and small orchestra –listed in Laurie J. Sampsel, *Cyril Scott: A Bio-Bibliography* (Greenwood, 2000), p. 59.

[40] Scott, *Dark Cycle*, p. 166.

[41] Cyril Scott, *The Vision of the Nazarene* [1935; rev. edn 1955], reprinted edn (Weiser, 2000), pp. xiii–xv, 3. This revised edition expands the introductory material, drops four sections, and adds two new ones.

[42] Cyril Scott, *The Real Tolerance* (A. C. Fifield, 1913), unpaginated. The book was published anonymously (though it is attributed to Scott on the 'Also by Cyril Scott' page in *Music and Its Secret Influence*, probably on the authority of Desmond Scott, who wrote the introduction). The sentence cited appears on the first page.

[43] Scott, *Initiate*, p. 11.

[44] Scott, *New World*, pp. 260–77.

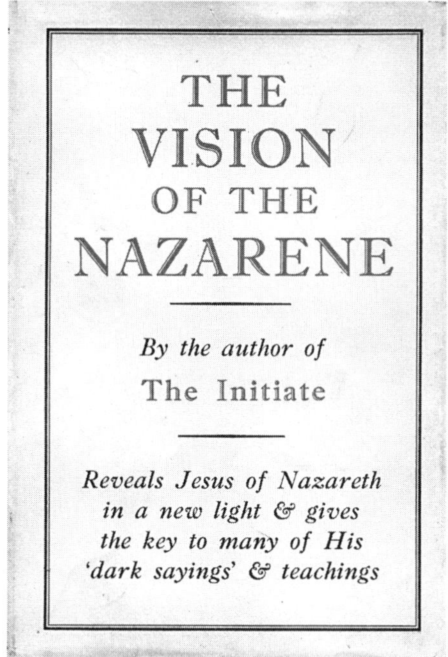

Figure 18.1 Dust jacket of *The Vision of the Nazarene*

tion of *The Real Tolerance*, Scott suggests that a method of breaking down hatred and developing tolerance 'consists in altering the point of view; seeing that a certain point of view is a prophylactic against almost anything.'[45]

We could think of the contents of *Vision* as spiritual teachings, but then we must wrestle with questions such as, did they come from a higher plane, Scott's higher self or soul, his creative subconscious, or any combination of these? Or we could think of them as topical commentary cast in literary form by a writer's conscious mind as an exercise in writing from an altered point of view. But perhaps the best way to think of this book is as yet another instalment in a vast memoir of spiritual unfolding that began with *The Initiate* and includes each of the books discussed so far.

The experiments in points of view in these books split Scott into a poet (Broadbent), a composer (Herbert), a more advanced version of himself (JMH), a childhood version of the JMH self (*The Boy Who Saw True*, a semi-autobiographical diary of a clairvoyant child)[46], the most advanced version of himself he could conceive (the Jesus of *Vision of the Nazarene*), and an archetypal soul on the journey

[45] Scott, *Greater Awareness*, p. 24.

[46] *The Boy Who Saw True* (1953) was published anonymously, with an introduction by Cyril Scott. Jean Overton Fuller demonstrated that the book draws heavily on an earlier, anonymously published book, subsequently banned as obscene, entitled *The Autobiography of a Child, Written from the Psycho-Sexual-Analytical Standpoint for Doctors, Parents, Teachers and Psychologists* (1921) and that Scott was the author of the latter – and therefore of both. See Fuller, *Cyril Scott*, pp. 17–24, 47–51.

from man of the world to initiate ('The Circuitous Journey' in *The Initiate*). Thus this great narrative of spiritual unfolding covers every stage of human growth and evolution from child to wise elder and from unconscious sensualist to all-seeing, all-helpful Master.

MUSIC: ITS SECRET INFLUENCE THROUGHOUT THE AGES (1933)

Perhaps the best way to introduce *Music: Its Secret Influence*, published under Scott's own name, is to provide his own summary from *An Outline of Modern Occultism*:

- 'Music affects the minds and emotions of mankind.'
- 'It affects them through the medium of suggestion and reiteration [as of feelings, moods, or states of consciousness].'
- 'It affects them either directly, indirectly, or both.' [Direct effects occur during a performance one is attending; indirect effects radiate outward from that performance as thought-forms that influence people within a radius of several miles, as illustrated in Besant and Leadbeater's *Thought-Forms*.][47]
- 'Hence, as in music, so in life.'[48]

Scott asserts that: 'Of all the arts, music is, from the occult standpoint, by far the most potent; so potent indeed that it has been instrumental in moulding thought and morals, influencing its sister arts and even to some extent history itself.' Furthermore, 'The prevalent idea is that certain types of music have been the outcome of the characteristics of the age in which they appeared, but, astonishing though the statement may seem, the reverse is the truth.'[49] In support of this statement, Scott makes reference to Plato's remarks on music in *Republic* and *Timaeus*.[50]

Thus, 'practically each great composer has been definitely used to bring about certain effects in the domain of thought and morals, and consequently as a factor in the furthering of the evolutionary Plan.' The means whereby this 'use' occurred involved the gradual impression of a style upon the great composers 'by the Master, or the *devas* working under that Master, who used him as a medium.'[51] Conductors and performers, too, can be 'used and inspired' by Masters and devas; as well as performers, who may 'derive their inspiration from their Higher Self, sometimes

[47] See Annie Besant and C. W. Leadbeater, *Thought-Forms*, 2nd edn, abridged (Quest Books, 1999), plates M [Mendelssohn], G [Gounod], and W [Wagner], and explanations on pp. 66–76.

[48] Scott, *Modern Occultism*, pp. 159–60. See also Cyril Scott, *Music and Its Secret Influence throughout the Ages*, 5th edn (Inner Traditions, 2013), p. 41. Note the slight change in title for this edition.

[49] Scott, *Modern Occultism*, p. 157.

[50] See *Republic* 398c–404e (on music and morals) and 424b–425b (on the emotional effects of modes and rhythm; and *Timaeus* 47c–e (on music creating harmony on the soul).

[51] Cyril Scott, *An Outline of Modern Occultism*, rev. edn (Routledge & Kegan Paul, 1950), p. 144 (original emphasis).

from the *devas* or even from the "spirits" (to use the language of Spiritualism) of celebrated executants who have "passed over" yet wish to help their *confrères* still on the earth'. Sometimes it even 'happens that a Master wishes to use an executant as his medium'.[52]

Thus *Music: Its Secret Influence* demonstrates what Scott's alter ego, Lyall Herbert, meant when he said, 'Art for the Masters' and Humanity's sake is much more romantic' – because service to the Masters and humanity provided what Scott believed to be a genuine 'ideal' to which he could aspire, while inspiring other musicians to do the same. What made the great music of the past so great? – composers using their art to change the morals and spiritual ideals of humanity, whether consciously or unconsciously, as mediums for higher powers. Yet, given Scott's frequent diatribes against Phariseeism, his notion that jazz and rock music are vehicles for the 'Dark Forces' to encourage the erosion of sexual morality seems inconsistent and overstated.[53] His screed against such music could perhaps be attributed, along with the mildly misogynist remarks and ambivalent attempts to be tolerant of homosexuality scattered throughout his literary œuvre, to a not entirely successful attempt to rise above the classist, racist, sexist, and homophobic biases of his time.

Of the many new ways of experiencing and thinking about music to be encountered in Scott's book, perhaps the most intriguing is his notion of inspiration by devas. According to Scott, the word *deva* refers to a nonhuman and largely nonphysical evolutionary hierarchy that ranges from simple 'smallest nature spirit' (elves, fairies, brownies, and the like) to 'loftiest cosmic archangel'.[54] Devas have no human 'passions or sorrows' and no moral sense, but express *joie de vivre*.[55] Furthermore, 'One of the chief Deva characteristics is Love'.[56] The lower rungs of the deva evolution, represented by nature spirits, delight in song and dance, reveries in nature, the play of sunlight and moonbeams, playing pranks, idly shaping clouds, and playfully transforming themselves into various shapes.[57] They have a childlike naiveté. Music expressing these characteristics is deva music – more specifically, nature-spirit music. In such music, as in the sounds of nature, everything is 'enchantingly indefinite, between the notes, varied, yet in a sense charmingly monotonous', as well as 'subdued, delicate, nebulous'.[58] It often sounds as if improvised.[59]

In ballet and opera, nature-spirit music may accompany storylines based on fairy tales and mythological subjects.[60] There are also higher levels of inspiration by devas.

52 Scott, *Modern Occultism* (1935), pp. 160–1.

53 Scott, *Music and Its Secret Influence*, pp. 136–9. It is worth noting that Scott was one of the few serious composers of his generation who seems not to have experimented with the incorporation of jazz elements into his music – and in this he was indeed consistent.

54 Scott, *Music and Its Secret Influence*, p. 104.

55 Ibid., p. 124.

56 Ibid., p. 114.

57 Ibid., p. 124.

58 Ibid., p. 123.

59 Ibid., pp. 114–15.

60 Ibid., p. 124.

Table 18.1 Deva music according to Cyril Scott

Plane	*Deva type*	*Composer*
physical/ etheric	nature spirits	Tchaikovsky (no examples)[a] Grieg, 'In the Hall of the Mountain King' (*Peer Gynt Suite* No. 1) Delius (no examples)[b] Debussy, *Jardins sous la pluie* (*Estampes*); *La Mer*; *Nuages* (*Nocturnes*); *Pelléas et Mélisande*; *Prélude à l'après-midi d'un faune*'; *Reflets dans l'eau* (*Images*) Ravel, *Ondine* (*Gaspard de la nuit*); *Histoires naturelles*
astral	lesser emotional devas	Ravel, *Le Gibet* (*Gaspard de la nuit*); *L'heure espagnole*
lower mental	national (lesser mental) devas	Wagner (no examples)[c]
upper mental	higher mental devas	Franck, Piano Quintet Scriabin, *Prometheus*
buddhic	buddhic devas	Wagner, *Tristan und Isolde* ('Liebestod');[d] *Die Meistersinger* ('Preislied');[e] *Parsifal* ('Karfreitag-zauber')[f] Franck, *Les béatitudes*

[a] Tchaikovsky's *The Nutcracker*, Op. 71, as a ballet with fairy elements, would certainly fit in here.

[b] Perhaps following Scott's lead, the British theosophist/composer John Foulds listed a number of works by Delius as examples of deva music. See John Foulds, *Music To-day, Op. 92* [1934], reprinted edn (Noverre Press, 2010), pp. 311–13. Foulds cites *Music: Its Secret Influence* in a footnote on pp. 281–2.

[c] Possibly Wagner's *Ring* cycle would fit in here, since it deals extensively with German folklore.

[d] 'Love-Death', *Tristan*, Act 3, finale; also performed as a stand-alone concert piece (often combined with the Prelude to Act 1), with or without the vocal part.

[e] 'Prize Song', *Die Meistersinger*, Act 3, scene 2.

[f] 'Good Friday Spell', *Parsifal*, Act 3; often performed as a stand-alone concert piece without the vocal part.

The highest is called seraphic or buddhic music. *Buddhi* is a Sanskrit word meaning 'illuminated' or 'enlightened' and refers, in Scott's words, to a 'state of Unity, of selfless, unconditional Love',[61] as well as to the fourth of the seven planes described in theosophical literature. Buddhic music reflects the influence of angels rather than nature spirits. It expresses 'not love *for* God' but 'that Love, which *is* God, the Divine Love'.[62] Scott provides a number of musical examples of nature-spirit and buddhic music. Table 18.1 demonstrates how these examples relate to the theosophical planes listed earlier.

We have seen how the notion of nature spirits and devas inspired some of Scott's chamber music. If I had to nominate one of Scott's orchestral works as an example of deva music, it would be *Early One Morning* for piano and orchestra, composed in 1930–1. Whatever its relation to the eponymous folk song, this heavily pentatonic score is a perfect embodiment of Scott's description of deva music as enchantingly indefinite, charmingly monotonous, and sounding as if improvised.

[61] Ibid., p. 94.

[62] Ibid. (original emphasis).

AN OUTLINE OF MODERN OCCULTISM (1935)

I turn now to two of Scott's books published under his own name, but related by many themes to the Initiate series: *An Outline of Modern Occultism* and *The Greater Awareness*. These books could perhaps be described as nonfictional reflections of the fictionally portrayed teachings in the Initiate series. The first is a serviceable introduction to the theosophical worldview. It is clear, concise, not overly technical, and focuses on the practical application of theosophical teachings in daily life. Subjects covered include:

- Masters
- reincarnation, spiritual evolution, and karma
- subtle bodies
- Christianity, spiritualism, Christian Science, and theosophy
- The arts (poetry, fiction, drama, painting, composing and performing music)
- science and healing
- clairvoyance
- the occultist's path of spiritual attainment

Here Scott was vocal about his intention to do away with what he must have considered a theosophical form of adult childishness: 'In this book the author endeavours to present an outline of Occult Science divorced from all sectarianism and the differing opinions of the various schools', decrying the 'policy of rejecting all statements, books, doctrines, teachings, etc., unless they have emanated or been sanctioned by one particular leader or teacher'.[63]

Thus the expanded 1950 edition of the book discusses the work of two theosophists who had left the TS and become important spiritual teachers in their own right: Rudolf Steiner and Alice Bailey.[64] The earlier edition includes an afterword, absent from that of 1950, in which Scott admitted to being the author of the Initiate series, claiming that already in 1935 this authorship was 'now an open secret'.[65]

THE GREATER AWARENESS (1936)

Relatively unknown and difficult to find, this sequel to *Modern Occultism* was intended 'to offer some suggestions which may prove useful to the aspirant [spiritual seeker]', which is to say, advice on how to apply occult ideals to daily life. It was also intended to update various theosophical terms and views since 'much of the Occult literature published during the last fifty years bears certain Victorian characteristics

[63] Scott, *Modern Occultism* (1935), pp. 3, 7.

[64] The 1935 edition discusses Bailey only. As explained in a footnote in the 1950 edition, the chapter on Steiner was intended for, but not included in, the earlier edition (Scott, *Modern Occultism* (1950), p. 128n). The 1950 edition also adds two new chapters on Bailey's teachings.

[65] Scott, *Modern Occultism* (1935), p. 231.

which either do not appeal to or tend to antagonise the present generation.'[66] Scott mentions in particular the notion of purity, by which was meant sexual celibacy – then proceeds to drag the TS into the Freudian age, frankly discussing homosexuality, lesbianism, masturbation, female orgasm and their karmic implications.

But the book does more than deliver on these intentions. Its notion of the greater awareness could perhaps be seen as the key to Scott's lifework. In the concluding chapter Scott breaks down this greater awareness into the following components, which reveal not only the structure of the book but also the categories into which Scott's literary works may be sorted:[67]

- Love: covered in part 1, 'The Cultivation of Love-Consciousness'. Here Scott refers to love as 'the fundamental law', indicating that intolerance, hatred, selfishness, and vanity are transgressions against it. Thus *The Real Tolerance* and the series of books on adult childishness, such as *Man is my Theme* (1939) and *Man, the Unruly Child* (1953), come under this heading, as well as *The Initiate* and *The Initiate in the New World*, the latter containing a chapter entitled 'The Permanent Love-Consciousness',[68] with its railing against the conventionality of musical audiences and its suggestion of musical inspiration by devas who are beings of love and of a higher music that expresses 'that Love, which *is* God', *Music: Its Secret Influence* also belongs here.
- Knowledge: covered in part 2, 'The Cultivation of Understanding and Discrimination [i.e. discernment]'. This section discusses such topics as self-knowledge, matrimony (understanding between the sexes, especially in connection with sexuality), humour, spiritual organisations (including the TS), Krishnamurti and misunderstood or misapplied teachings of occultism (such as those on virtue and renunciation), indicating that books such as *The Art of Making a Perfect Husband* (1928),[69] *The Ghost of a Smile*, *The Initiate in the Dark Cycle*, and *An Outline of Modern Occultism* come under this heading.
- Life: covered in part 3, 'The Cultivation of the Life-Consciousness'. From his remarks under the subsection entitled 'Karma and Ill Health', including advice on diet, exercise and the use of mental suggestion to effect cures, it becomes clear that Scott's early interest in Christian Science and his later writings on diet and health, such as *Victory over Cancer* (1939) and *Health, Diet, and Commonsense* (1940), come under this heading.
- Joy: covered in part 4, 'The Cultivation of the Joy-Consciousness'. From remarks in this section (such as, 'unless religion made people joyous, there was either something wrong with it or something wrong with their interpretation of it') and the interpretation of Jesus's teaching that 'The kingdom

[66] Scott, *Greater Awareness*, pp. vii–viii.

[67] Ibid., pp. 238–9.

[68] Scott, *New World*, pp. 175–81.

[69] Scott confessed to having written this anonymously published book in *Greater Awareness*, p. 84n.

of heaven is around you and within you' (Luke 17:21) as 'another expression of the Absolute-Existence-Knowledge and Bliss of the Vedantist', it becomes clear that *The Adept of Galilee* (to which a footnote directs the reader)[70] and *The Vision of the Nazarene* come under this heading.

- Freedom: the result of achieving the consciousness of love, knowledge, life and joy is the spiritual liberation of the Vedantist, which Scott defines as 'an expansion of consciousness freed from the limited consciousness of the lower self' and 'the plenitude of awareness which has been termed Cosmic Consciousness, and which, since words are inadequate, cannot be described but only experienced'. *The Greater Awareness* itself comes under this heading.

I have used the terms *love, knowledge, life,* and *joy consciousness* as a means of categorising Scott's musical and literary work to suggest the consistency of aims in each – aims that could be said to transcend those of modernism, as outlined at the beginning of this essay, in the same way that the 'greater awareness' of Vedanta could be said to transcend occultism's preoccupation with clairvoyant perception of auras, thought-forms, higher beings and planes. However, for Scott, joy was 'the unification of Life, Love and Knowledge' and therefore the most important.[71] 'Let us have no illusions about joy', he wrote, 'for it is the one thing before all others worth possessing.'[72]

Perhaps here we have the key to Scott's irritation at the suggestion that his alleged shortcomings as a composer resulted from his interest in occultism. Starting with his first exposure to the teachings of yoga and Vedanta in Vivekananda's *Raja Yoga*, Scott was following a path of liberation from social convention and 'the limited consciousness of the lower self'. For millennia, Eastern yogis have taught that such a path exists and that its goal is a joyful freedom that can not only 'transform the world into a garden of endless delights' but also make 'those who possess it quite independent of external circumstances'.[73] For Cyril Scott, composing music and writing about occultism were ways of exploring this joy consciousness without regard for critical aspersions and public neglect.

[70] Scott, *Greater Awareness*, p. 229n.

[71] Ibid., pp. 238–9.

[72] Ibid., p. 225 (original emphasis).

[73] Ibid.

19

The Purpose of *The Boy Who Saw True*

Desmond Scott

CYRIL Scott wrote a number of books on the occult, beginning in 1920,[1] and by 1950 had become fairly well known as a writer on the subject. He was therefore not surprised one day to receive an unusual document on an occult topic that aroused his curiosity and interest.

Unlike other unsolicited manuscripts, this one was not asking him to suggest a publisher, nor was the author in any way seeking publicity, wishing instead to remain anonymous. The manuscript had been sent to him, he maintained, by the author's widow, with a note explaining that the author asked only that it be given to someone with a known interest in the occult. Scott decided it should be published, wrote an Introduction, Notes and Afterword, and sent it to Neville Spearman, who produced the first edition in 1953. What intrigued him, he explained, was that the manuscript was in the form of a diary – a diary written by a boy who, judging from the vocabulary, was about eleven or twelve years old and who initially had no idea his ability to hear and see spirits was anything out of the ordinary.

The date of the diary is 1885, making Scott and the Boy very close in age. Scott was born in 1879, and even the most cursory examination reveals many other parallels. Both came from conventional, middle-class, church-going families from the north of England; both were extremely sensitive to music and prone to weeping at sad hymns in church. Both had sisters three or four years older (Mildred in the Boy's case, Mabel in Scott's), who liked to tease and torment them. More significantly, there is a spirit that frequently visits the Boy, whom he originally thinks is Jesus. This highly evolved individual later suggests the Boy call him E. B. or Elder Brother – the same name Scott used for such souls in his *An Outline of Modern Occultism*.[2] Obviously, the author of *The Boy Who Saw True* is Cyril Scott himself.

Scott's *An Outline of Modern Occultism* was published in 1935. Since then, World War 2 had intervened and attitudes had radically changed. Maybe Scott felt that it was time for another book on the subject, and, instead of revising the old one, decided he would try an entirely new approach.

The Boy Who Saw True can be read simply as chronicling the normal, everyday existence of a young lad growing up in a conventional church-going Victorian family. It can also be taken as yet another of Scott's occult books, but one presented from a different angle. The idea of using a boy as the hero, a boy ordinary in every way except for having been born with clairvoyance or second sight, is nothing less than brilliant. Setting the story in the late Victorian era also has certain advantages.

[1] See Chapter 18 (above).

[2] *An Outline of Modern Occultism* (George Routledge, 1935).

The distance lends it charm and the feeling of a period piece, while Scott's intimate knowledge of the time provides authenticity, and he could flesh out the story when needed with details from his own childhood. He cleverly introduces the occult and esoteric content only gradually, and increases its complexity as the book proceeds.

Scott was fascinated by clairvoyance, which he considered a talent like any other. Some people are born with it, as others are born with an aptitude for maths or football, and, like all talents, clairvoyance had to be nurtured and exercised or else it would wither and die. Lacking that ability himself, he needed a medium to enable him to receive the teachings of his guru, Master K. H. He often worked with the very talented psychic and healer Nelsa Chaplin for that purpose.

Scott held a number of occult beliefs, many of which are discussed in *The Boy Who Saw True*. He was in complete agreement with evolution, not only in the Darwinian sense but also in the spiritual one. Reincarnation, the means by which the soul attains greater and greater states of physical and spiritual perfection, is part of evolution. The process, he believed, is governed by a hierarchy of Initiates, souls who, after countless incarnations, have reached a point where they no longer need to reincarnate, but who choose of their own volition to return and assist others along the path they themselves have walked. The elder brother, E. B., in the book is one such, as is Scott's own guru, Master K. H., and also Moreward Haigh (JMH) in his Initiate trilogy.

Another of Scott's occult tenets is that the physical body is merely the densest of several bodies – emotional, mental and spiritual – each composed of finer and finer material, all of which surround and interpenetrate the physical.

Parallel with the human is the Deva evolution. Each element – Air, Earth, Fire, Water – is governed by a hierarchy of devas ranging from little elves and fairies to entities of enormous power and beauty. Christians know them as angels and archangels, but they are recognised under different names by many other faiths as well. This is a subject explored in detail and beautifully illustrated by H. K Challoner in *Watchers of the Seven Spheres*. Published *c.* 1936, it had an introduction by Scott. In 1966 a revised edition appeared with a new title, *Regents of the Seven Spheres*.[3]

But to return to *The Boy Who Saw True*. The Boy's diary, written between 1885 and 1887, is divided roughly into three sections, the first concerned solely with the Boy's ordinary life, plus the problems his clairvoyance causes him. There are also occasional remarks by the diarist as an adult, commenting on things his younger self had written.

The Boy can see the aura, the gold halo around saints' heads found in most religious paintings, which the Boy initially refers to as 'lights': 'Pa got up on the wrong side of the bed this morning and complained of his liver … I always know when Pa has liver because his lights are all dirty.' He discovers it also changes colour according to the health and character of the individual. While on holiday he takes an instant dislike to a very pretty little girl because of her aura, which he describes as being 'like dirty blood'. All the grown-ups, including his mother, speak of her as a little angel. She is his own age and is introduced to him as a playmate, but when she takes him behind the sand dunes where no one can see them, she exposes herself and tries to

[3] *Regents of the Seven Spheres* (Theosophical Publishing House, 1966).

persuade him to do the same, deeply offending his delicate Victorian sensibilities. By contrast the aura of 'Jesus' (later to be revealed as E. B.) is bright gold with all the colours of the rainbow.

In 1911, Dr Walter Kilner, a respected English physician, published a book in which he claimed the chemically treated glass screens he had invented allowed anyone to see the human aura. It is not known whether Scott used them himself, but he did believe they worked and described them once to me.

The Boy's mother is implacably hostile to anything psychic, and his distress at never being believed no matter what he tells her, whether it is of fairies playing by the sea shore, an old gnome in a tree, or his Uncle Willie sitting in the chair where his father is about to sit, is a theme that runs through the entire book. One occasion concerns a letter. The Boy can, like many psychics, sense things from letters. His cousin Agnes sends him a note enclosed in a letter to his mother from which he intuits she is soon to marry. When he tells his mother this she demands to see the note, and finding nothing in it about a new romance, accuses him angrily of disgraceful mischief-making. Later he overhears her telling his father that Agnes will indeed soon marry, but for now they must tell no one, leaving the Boy feeling understandably aggrieved.

There are many touches of humour in the book. The Boy wonders how much dead people can see: 'I wonder if they see us when we are having our bath or in the closet? I am sure mamma would be very put out if grandpa or Uncle Willie was to turn up when she was in one or tother place. But I suppose neither of them would do that, because it would be rude.' One morning the Boy becomes alarmed on finding his stool to be filled with what looks like blood. His mother calls the doctor. Some foul-tasting medicine is prescribed, with another dose to be taken the following day. Later the spirit of his grandfather, who often comes to visit and comfort him after especially distressing days, appears and asks if he has been eating beetroot. When the Boy answers yes, Grandfather laughs, calls the doctors nincompoops, always looking for trouble where there is none, and advises the Boy to throw the medicine down the sink and pretend he has taken it.

A proper diet, as we know from Scott's many books on the subject, was very important to him.[4] He suffered from the deficiencies of the Victorian diet himself. The adult diarist comments:

> All the inmates of our house were constipated with the exception of the cat and the parrot; the consequences being that my mother and myself suffered from horrible fits of depression, my father was always complaining of liver and indigestion, the cook was afflicted with pronounced dyspepsia … whilst the parlour maid suffered from the most embarrassing form of flatulence.

The second year of the diary introduces Mr Patmore, who is to tutor the Boy at home. A conscientious but open-minded teacher, he is sceptical at first but in due course accepts and is fascinated by the psychic talents of his pupil. Since he can neither see nor hear what the Boy reports, Scott provides him with a knowledge of

[4] See Chapter 21 (below).

shorthand. He becomes the amanuensis, taking down everything the Boy reports, then gives it back to him as dictation which the youth subsequently writes in his diary.

His grandfather is by now a frequent visitor. He has become the Boy's friend, and together they discuss matters that puzzle the lad, such as what life is like in the afterlife and on the 'astral plane.' This introduces one of Scott's most deeply felt occult beliefs, namely that death, far from being the final cessation of being, is no more than the transition from one state of existence to another, equivalent to little more than the exchange of one garment for another. Earth is the only place providing the opportunity for working through karma, both good and bad, and for making the spiritual progress that must be made if the soul is to evolve.

The spirits who visit the Boy are all on the astral plane, a resting place or interim between incarnations, a 'celestial holiday' where souls go as a relief from the stress and turmoil of life on earth, to reflect on that past life and, when ready, to prepare for a return to earth in a further incarnation. Grandfather tells the Boy that on the astral plane there are so few changes that many people do not realise they are no longer on earth, and so they need a lengthy period of adjustment. He cites a clergyman who loved to preach. On the astral plane he continues to do so to anyone who will listen to his long-winded and platitudinous sermons. Change, it seems, happens only when the individual is ready to change. Grandfather gives his wife as an example. On earth she believed she was one of the elect and that only she, and a few who thought exactly like her, would be saved. He tells the Boy that she lives now in a world of false thoughts she has created for herself; being a very stubborn woman, in death as in life, she is destined to remain there until she grows tired of it and begins, of her own volition, searching for something better.

Toward the end of this section 'Jesus' appears and suggests the Boy think of him simply as an elder brother, or E. B. He discusses reincarnation and states that the three of them – he, the Boy and Patmore – have been together in many previous lives. He refers to passages in the Bible that seem to agree with the theory, so that the Boy can begin to reconcile reincarnation with the orthodox religious teaching he has so far received. The Boy is intrigued. When next his grandfather appears, he and Patmore decide to ask Grandfather his views on reincarnation. To their surprise, he retorts that he does not believe in it and most certainly does not want to return to earth again. This is probably the most frequently expressed rationale for those who are averse to the idea. One life with all its sorrows and hardships is more than enough for most people.

Later, the E. B. sends them one of his pupils, who explains about the additional and interpenetrating bodies that everyone has. He tells them that only someone with second sight can see these bodies, because they vibrate at a higher rate than can be perceived by the ordinary eye.

The third section brings us to the main purpose of the book, namely to introduce more people, young and old, to the beliefs of occultism. Two lectures are delivered by a character who was a scientist on earth. He begins by echoing what E. B.'s pupil said earlier, that every single thing in the universe vibrates, and vibrates on a multitude of different frequencies, very few of which can be seen by those not gifted, like the Boy, with 'second sight'. Scott cleverly gets around the problem of having someone discussing quantum physics in 1887 by having the man remark that the concept will not be fully understood for another hundred years. The scientist goes on to talk about space and matter, insisting that there is no such thing as empty space and that it appears to be empty simply because of the distance between the molecules and the rapidity of their vibration. Even in the densest material there is always space between the molecules and that is how, according to the scientist, he can occupy the same space as, for instance, a chair – its molecules are far enough apart to permit his doing so.

All religions, all systems of belief, demand a leap of faith. Occultism, on the other hand, seeks to prove that its beliefs are based on established scientific fact rather than on faith.

The second lecture moves onto more debatable ground. The scientist begins with a *mea culpa*, confessing that much of what he learned on earth was false. Darwinian evolution, he now believes, ends up drawing the wrong conclusions. He agrees that the more evolved the form, the higher the degree of consciousness or life, and from that, therefore, one can posit that the form is the *creator* of life. The form is the cause, and the consciousness, or life, is the effect. That omits the fact, claims the scientist, that Life exists entirely *independent* of form. He illustrates his point by explaining that the sun's light is different according to the colour of the glass through which it shines, but the glass does not create the light, for the sun exists entirely apart from it. Though it manifests itself in untold millions of forms, Life itself remains unchanging and eternal. The scientist argues that there is no life without a degree, however small, of consciousness, a concept that many people are now beginning to find entirely possible.

The scientist again mentions the function of the Devas, both the little nature sprites and those that govern the Seven Spheres, and concludes by giving a talk on the history of civilisation and the beginning of the machine age, hinting at new inventions inconceivable to their forefathers. Not surprisingly, the Boy finds some of this tedious, and Scott has him complain to his diary about it.

On Grandfather's last appearance, he stresses to the Boy the importance of love, the essence of Scott's entire credo, expressed in the following three lines near the end of the diary:

> There is but one LIFE manifesting through all forms.
> There is but one SELF manifesting through all selves.
> There is but one LOVE manifesting through all loves.

In the same way that Life is evident in numberless different forms, yet Life itself is unchanging and eternal, so the SELF is present in every living creature, but the SELF too is unchanging. Love your neighbour as yourself, says the Bible. Scott goes further: Love your neighbour as yourself because he *is* yourself.

The diary ends abruptly before the end of the year. One assumes Scott decided he had by then said all that he wanted to say. It is followed, however, by an Afterword containing details supposedly supplied by the Boy's widow, in which we learn what happened to him after he became an adult. Perhaps Scott wanted to make a point concerning karma, and so needed the epilogue. The Boy makes a disastrous first marriage and berates E. B., who has remained his guru, for not warning him about it. E. B. replies that there was karma to be worked out between the Boy and his wife and that no one, no matter how evolved he might be, is permitted to subvert the working of it.

With '*The Boy Who Saw True*', Scott created an entertaining and entirely believable character whose problems caused by clairvoyance in his everyday life rouse sympathy in the reader. Children readily identify with the goblins and fairies he reports seeing, while adults can focus on the more difficult concepts in the book. It is both a serious guide to occultism and a beguiling fictional account of an unusual Victorian childhood. It succeeds on both counts.

20

Near The End of Life: Candid Confessions and Reflections: A Discussion of the Memoir

Desmond Scott

CYRIL Scott wrote this memoir between 1942 and 1944. It exists, like *The Poems of a Musician*, only in typescript. That he was unable to find a publisher for it is not entirely surprising, for while the material itself is of great interest, it is also excessively long-winded and self-conscious. Though some of the content was used in the later 1969 autobiography, *Bone of Contention*, much of it is new and does not feature in any of his other writings, making it, despite the style, an essential document for any serious student of Scott's work.[1]

The war years, 1939–1945, were a very bleak period for Scott. He was almost sixty-five, depressed and unwell, firmly convinced he would not live to see seventy. He had been largely passed over as a serious composer, remembered for short piano pieces but not for any of his major compositions.

When the war began he and his wife, Rose, separated, leaving their London home to avoid the bombing. He went for a short time to his sister Mabel's in Somerset, while Rose went to stay with Melanie Mills in Sussex. After leaving his sister's home Scott spent the rest of the war in a series of guest houses, rootless and restless. He had little money, no piano on which to compose, and lacked the guidance and support of his spiritual master, which had always been so important for him. Nevertheless, he managed to continue working as hard as ever. He completed not only the volume of poetry referred to above, but also a sixty-three page document, *The Rhymed Reflections of a Ruthless Rhymer*, written entirely in rhyme on one of his favourite topics: adult childishness. He also wrote four full-length plays and two adaptations of well-known novels.

Near The End of Life is not, as he said in his Introduction, an autobiography in the sense of being a history of life events; it is concerned more with his mental and creative attitude during a difficult period. It is not a diary hastily scribbled in moments of anger or depression, but a carefully composed document intended for publication. He wished, he said, to 'express myself relative to matters concerning my creative efforts and my many transgressions, before I arrive at that state of disembodiedness which will render such an undertaking no longer possible.'

A measure of fame followed by almost total neglect cannot be an easy experience with which to reconcile oneself. Scott in that situation is greatly to be admired, for though there is regret in these writings, there is rarely any bitterness.

[1] *Bone of Contention* (Aquarian Press, 1969).

One incident, though, did rankle – so much so that he recounted it over twenty-five years later in *Bone of Contention*.[2] There it was reduced to one short paragraph, but here he devotes several pages to it, heading the discussion 'Reflections of a Musician in an Unmusical Milieu', and following it with a section titled 'An Art which has Become a Bad Habit.'

On New Year's Eve 1941, Scott was in Minehead, Somerset, hoping to listen to the first BBC broadcast of his *Ode to Great Men*. This was a major event for him, particularly since such occasions had grown so rare. There was but one single radio, and that was in the bar. To his chagrin, the manageress made no attempt to tell the patrons about the broadcast. No one paid the slightest attention, and they carried on laughing and dart-playing entirely oblivious to the music.

Either to conceal the depth of his feelings or simply because it amused him to do so, he sometimes adopted the style of his favourite author, Charles Dickens. Here, referring to his reception in the bar, he is in full Dickensian mode:

> although a certain Biblical saying of an uncomplimentary nature relative to pearls and pigs did not noticeably intrude on my, I hope, charitable mind, the circumstance tended to strengthen my conviction … that what was anciently regarded as an art has now assumed the proportions of, or degenerated into, a vice.[3]

He went on to explain why he felt the ubiquity of music had become detrimental to it. Though it was not nearly as pervasive then as it is now, the idea of music simply as background noise appalled him.

In no particular chronological order, Scott wrote on subjects that mattered to him. Music, naturally, predominates, and occupies more than two thirds of the typescript. On being largely ignored as a serious composer, he comforted himself by remarking that few composers are appreciated in their lifetime, and blamed himself for composing too many small pieces and not concentrating on larger and more ambitious ones. He described the problem of getting new works accepted by an audience that would rather hear a Beethoven Symphony for the hundredth time than listen to a piece that was unfamiliar to them. How is it, he asked plaintively, that people rush to read the latest novels and book tickets to the latest plays, but fail to embrace anything new musically?

It would be nice to think that audiences are more receptive now, but one suspects most composers today would agree that little has changed. Another plaint, still sadly familiar to all composers and musicians, was the lack of rehearsal time. Referring to England, he wrote:

> Seeing that for the majority of concerts in this country there are merely two rehearsals and very often only one, nearly all first performances of new works are so inadequately rehearsed that a composer has almost to consider himself fortunate if the orchestra contrives to get through his composition without a noticeable breakdown … it can not be expected that new works should obtain perfect per-

[2] Ibid., pp. 213–14.

[3] Also echoed in his poem 'Le Vieillard' in *The Poems of a Musician*.

> formances, unless repeated at close intervals, so that the players, having become adequately familiar with the notes, can then be directed towards a consideration of the *nuances*, in which, of course, dynamics play so important a part.

He gave a personal example. The sole performance of his 1933 tone poem on the sinking of the *Titanic*, *Disaster at Sea*, was a disaster in more ways than one. The climax was intended to feature a choir singing a version of the hymn 'Nearer my God to Thee'. There had not been a full rehearsal with orchestra, and the choir was distantly placed in the organ loft in London's Queen's Hall. At the crucial and dramatic moment when their voices should have greatly moved the audience, they were almost inaudible. The work, intended by Scott to be partly impressionistic and partly a realistic portrait of the sinking, was savaged by the critics. On the one hand they condemned it as 'film music', and on the other they complained about the unusual harmonies he had used in the hymn. Scott later rewrote the piece, removing all overt reference to the *Titanic* and renaming the work *Neptune, Poem of the Sea*. As such it was accorded excellent notices when it was recorded in 2004. Regrettably he destroyed the original. Now that the climate of opinion on Scott has changed so radically, and as the sole example of his writing 'programme music', it would be fascinating to know how it would be received today had it survived.

Scott discussed technical problems, too, such as whether the score of a particular instrument or group of instruments should be marked *forte*, *mezzo forte*, *piano* or *pianissimo*, and how crucial that could be. Orchestras differ in size. One might have six first and five second violins; another might have sixteen first and sixteen second violins. That, obviously, makes a huge difference to the sound. He gave as an example his Christmas overture, *Noël*, written for a medium orchestra. In this piece:

> there is, at the beginning, a little figure for solo viola, which in a medium-sized orchestra would be heard as I intended it *should* be heard; but when it had to penetrate through an accompaniment of thirty-two violins together with a formidable number of cellos and bases, it became well-nigh inaudible and hence ineffective.

Another example was his *Festival Overture* (1934) and a normally very minor instrument, the triangle. Scott reported that, either foolishly or carelessly, he had marked the score *mf* instead of *p*, and so the triangle became quite offensively obtrusive. Had he been able to be present at the rehearsal, Scott said, he would have realised a few alterations were needed. As it was, an easily adjusted matter became a major menace to his already insecure reputation. One also wonders why the conductor had not dealt with it when he heard it, ignoring the score's *mf* instruction to the player. Scott forestalled similar problems by advising future conductors to disregard the expression marks and make their own judgement. Perhaps that was the case when Martyn Brabbins and the BBC Philharmonic Orchestra recorded the *Festival Overture* in 2006. In the excellent reviews it received, there is no mention of the triangle!

Around the turn of the century Scott was much attracted to the Victorian Pre-Raphaelite painters Millais, Holman Hunt, Rossetti and Burne-Jones, and under their influence he wrote a *Magnificat* (1899), composing what he thought of as 'Pre-Raphaelite' music. Yet he soon discovered it was a mannerism he had adopted, not a genuine expression of his musical creativity, and he abandoned both the idea and the piece.

The years between 1899 and 1905 were a very creative time for Scott: he completed two symphonies, three overtures for plays by the Belgian playwright Maurice Maeterlinck, two orchestral rhapsodies, a cello concerto, a piano concerto, his *Idyllic Suite*, a string quartet, the *Heroic Suite* and the *Magnificat*. But had it not been for Percy Grainger's demanding the scores for his Melbourne Museum, every one of these pieces would have been lost. With the exceptions of the Second Symphony, which was heavily abridged and reworked as *Three Symphonic Dances*, and the overture that later became the *Festival Overture*, Scott rejected them all. Why? The answers he gives in the memoir are revealing. It was not that he considered them worthless, but, with the arrogance of the young artist, he had been confident he would go on to produce works of greater maturity and depth, and wanted to be judged not on ones he considered immature but on those major works he would undoubtedly compose in the future. Seventy-five years after the writing of *Near the End of Life*, most of the juvenilia are available on CD. The recordings have left people shaking their heads, wondering why Scott chose to withdraw such gorgeous pieces.

Scott mentions Debussy in both the memoir and the 1969 *Bone of Contention*, and how kind the composer was to him as a young man, inviting him to dinner whenever he was in Paris. On these occasions Scott always played or showed him the recent scores of his more serious compositions, such as the Piano Sonata No. 1, the First Violin Sonata and the Second Suite for piano, which is dedicated to him. The last time he visited Debussy, in 1913, Scott found that his English publisher had just sent the Frenchman a collection of the smaller works. After leafing through a few of them, he told Scott that he found most of them very trite, and asked why he occupied himself with such trifles when he could write works of the distinction he had earlier played him. For some reason this incident is omitted in the later autobiography, which is curious because Scott was delighted to have Debussy's praise of his larger works at a time when he was already starting to worry that he was considered as a composer solely of songs and piano miniatures. His inability to get a hearing for his major works is a constant theme running through the entire typescript. It occurs yet again in *Bone of Contention*, where there is a chapter headed 'How I Gained my Undesired Reputation'.[4]

Both in this memoir and in the later book Scott mentions Debussy's surprising views on other composers, particularly Beethoven:

> revealing him to be unusually deficient in that veneration for the classics which the looked-up-to representatives of music and musical culture in England displayed and regarded as musical blasphemy not to display. Whilst the English bigwigs almost bowed their august heads at the sacred name of Beethoven, Debussy uncharitably and irreverently referred to him as '*le vieux sourd*'.

[4] *Bone of Contention*, pp. 89–94.

Another composer Scott felt was in the same predicament as himself, known for small piano pieces such as *Molly on the Shore* or *Handel in the Strand*, but not for his larger works, was his fellow-student and lifelong friend, Percy Grainger. They first met in Frankfurt and their friendship and mutual admiration lasted for over sixty years. Scott was not exaggerating when he wrote: 'It would be difficult to find in the whole course of musical history a man so generous and so uneconomical with his praise and admiration of such composer friends he genuinely admires and likes.' In the memoir he devoted ten times the space to his friend as he had in his autobiographies, which makes this an important document for understanding both men. Scott noted Grainger's idiosyncrasies, his 'blue-eyed English', his generosity and his boundless energy, but also insisted he could be a stern taskmaster, who often censured him for not working harder to get his larger works performed. In his eagerness to get a piece 'right', as he saw it, Grainger could apparently be downright tyrannical!

Grainger's selfless desire to make a score the best it could be extended as far as spending hours, or even days, altering it himself. Scott points out that for an orchestral work this meant not merely altering the score, but laboriously correcting all the orchestral parts as well. Today, even with computers and music apps, it remains, as every musician knows, tedious and painstaking work, but Grainger was doing it by hand, and not even for himself but for his friend!

During his time in Frankfurt, Scott met another man who was to have a great influence on him: the poet Stefan George. He was the complete opposite of Grainger, maintaining that one should never allow oneself to be influenced by the public, or pay any heed to adverse criticism. He was, said Scott, 'an intellectual aristocrat' who divided mankind into two categories: on one hand the few cultured and discerning persons; and on the other the innumerable bourgeois, who were undeserving of any consideration on the part of the artist, and should simply be left to wallow 'in the refuse of their own mediocrity'. Scott insists that this was not an uncommon attitude among artists at the time. He confesses it had even affected his own outlook to some extent, as Grainger often pointedly told him. For if George was the aristocrat, Grainger was the complete democrat, even going so far as to insist, as Scott noted in *Bone of Contention*, that a concerto was undemocratic because the soloist got more attention than the other players.

Scott and Grainger were youths when they first met, Scott sixteen, Grainger thirteen. The latter's much-discussed peculiarities were pronounced even then. He was always testing his powers of endurance, Scott reported, for instance by opening his window in winter, taking all his clothes off, and lying nude on the rented grand piano for hours until he was chilled to the bone.[5]

Scott and Grainger played their compositions to each other in Frankfurt, and to anyone else they could persuade to listen. They were always told they were going through their *Sturm und Drang* period and that, as they matured, they would surely tone down. Scott comments that this never happened, and that the things Bernhardt Scholz (the ultra-conservative head of the Frankfurt Conservatory) objected to only grew more pronounced over the years. Before he was twenty, wrote Scott, Grainger

[5] John Bird recounts that anecdote, which Scott had told him, in his book on Grainger: *Percy Grainger* (Elek, 1976).

was abolishing bar lines and thinking about writing in irregular rhythms. Scott initially felt this was nonsense, but some ten years later, in his Piano Sonata No. 1, he began writing that way himself. He explained that the old manner of writing in uniform bar-measures restricted creativity. He felt he was trapped by regular rhythms, and that the only way out of the impasse was to adopt Grainger's method. Grainger had hoped to be the first to startle the musical world with his innovation, and was distressed to find not only Scriabin and Stravinsky using versions of it, but also his closest friend. Despite his chagrin at not being acknowledged, Grainger played that sonata constantly for the next forty years. Though he was genuinely concerned he had upset Grainger, Scott wrote: 'Verily the way of composers is hard: for I think it often happens that we imagine we have invented a thing when either we have merely foreseen a short distance into the future or else absorbed an idea already floating about on the mental plane.'

He spends several pages discussing Grainger's museum in Melbourne, which he viewed with amused tolerance, unaware of how vitally important it would become for his own legacy by safeguarding his manuscripts, letters and other memorabilia. He also discussed Grainger's horoscope, astrology being a subject he took seriously, and noted that Grainger was a Cancerian. This meant, he said, having an eye towards the future but a soul focused on the past. According to Scott, the museum was a perfect example of that. He went on to discuss Grainger's 'blue-eyed English' and his desire to return to an Anglo-Saxon English free of Latin or French words – using, for example, 'toothsmith' for dentist, 'louden lots' for fortissimo, and 'hoardhouse' for museum that, Scott insisted, was not only an example of his love of the past, but also showed Grainger the democrat, not wanting to appear superior to his fellows by using long words of foreign derivation. He went on to talk about Grainger's intense love of detail, and his complaint that no one wanted to hear any of his major works (sounds familiar?), before ending with a most generous and sincere tribute to his friend.

> Future generations will do him a gross injustice if, apart from his eccentricities and his valuable bequests in the realm of music, they fail to appreciate that he was also one of the most humanity-loving souls who graced this globe at a time when mortals were contriving their mutual destruction, and that he was one of the most generous friends who trod the rich pastures of ever blessed friendship.

Perhaps reacting against the many unfavourable reviews he received, Scott discussed success – success as distinct from popularity. Popularity he thought was not altogether desirable, for if you were in favour with the people, you tended to be dismissed by the discerning. No composer, he insisted, was ever 'classical' in his own day – he was a law-breaker, a revolutionary who defied the conventions and only came to be accepted after repeated hearings of his work. At the first performances of his Piano Sonata No. 1 the discords were considered almost unbearable, but twenty-five years later, he said, audiences did not even notice there were any!

To make his point, Scott remarked that even Mozart was guilty of writing discords and that the publishers returned the proofs of his scores, asking if they could possibly be correct. He continued:

> The composer who first discovered the sugary dominant seventh chord, was censured for having invented an ear-splitting discord. Newness in music is often merely a novel way of using the old in a different manner.
>
> Consecutive 5ths were used frequently in ancient music, as were bare 4ths. They subsequently fell out of favour for many years but now 5ths and 4ths used in a fresh way have become a musical commonplace and form part of our harmonic vocabulary.

Another example Scott gave was *false relations*. For those unfamiliar with the term, a *false relation* is when, for instance, a C-sharp in one part of the score is followed closely by a C-natural in another part. For many years, that was considered ignorant or amateurish, but Scott discovered a new way to use it, and produced what he considered some of his happiest effects with it. The first time was in a short violin piece, *Sonnet 1* (1914); he also thought of this work as a study for the piano concerto, composed around the same time.

From discords in his own work, Scott turned to ultra-discordant composers, such as Boulez, Honegger and Webern, who were just then coming into favour and whom he regarded as all head and no heart. About them, he wrote:

> The protagonists of that exclusively cacophonous phase had decided that anything remotely resembling a melody or even the most unconventional conceptions of beauty must be avoided as something disastrously disfiguring or indicative of the worst forms of musical senility. The problem with unrelieved discordancy was that it inevitably led to monotony. The true keynote in art is variety. Unless discord be varied by concord, ugliness relieved by periods of beauty, tempestuousness by peacefulness, the final outcome is nothing but tedium.

Writing in the 1940s, Scott maintained that he and a number of his contemporaries (whom he does not name, but it can be assumed he meant composers such as Granville Bantock, Joseph Holbrooke, Gustav Holst, or John Ireland) were in an unenviable position. They were considered too discordant for the traditionalists yet not discordant enough for the modernists, who regarded them as laggards who had not kept up with the times. At the performance of *Disaster at Sea* a critic was overheard to say that 'Scott was the *enfant terrible* of the Edwardian age, and he has not come up to our expectations.' To which Scott, with some justification, demanded how an accurate assessment of any composer could be made when so few of his major works had been heard.

He also insisted that for a new work to be fully appreciated it must be given more than one hearing – a point with which every composer past and present would surely agree. That led him to discuss the predicament of the critics, who have to pronounce judgement after only one performance, and for whom he seems to have had a grudging sympathy. For their part, Ernest Newman, the foremost music critic of the day and a great Wagner scholar, showed great understanding of the composers' situation when he wrote to Scott (who had appealed to him after receiving some particularly adverse criticism, perhaps for *Disaster at Sea*):

> Dear Scott,
> Don't take that appalling drivel too seriously. What is one to say about a new work that comes and goes in a moment, and of which one doesn't know a note in advance and in connection with which one cannot even be sure that it is sounding as the composer meant it to sound?
>
> In general God help the poor composer! … I ask myself what right we have to assume that any <u>first</u> performance is technically and mentally adequate.
>
> The upshot of it all is that the musical world is quite mad, always has been and always will be!

First impressions can prove misleading, not only for the critics. Scott, citing *Carmen* as a personal example, confessed that when he first heard the opera he thought the melodies too obvious, and only after repeated hearings began to appreciate the skill of the orchestration and the exquisite refinement of the melodies and how perfectly they fitted the drama.

It is always interesting to discover what an artist selects as his best work. Of his major compositions Scott picked out the Piano Concerto (1913), the Cello Concerto (1937), the Violin Concerto (1926), and the Concerto for two violins (1931). In these he felt were his happiest moments of melodic or thematic creativity. Of the shorter piano pieces, *Lotus Land* (still the piece for which he is best known) is not at the top of Scott's list. It comes third, after *Sphinx* (1908) and *Pierrot triste* (1904). *Sphinx*, he said, appealed to Ravel when they were a 'Mutual Encouragement Society'. In *Pierrot triste* he was striving for the pathos that underlies the clown, and it was the first time he felt he had enlarged his harmonic vocabulary. His list also includes *The Twilight of the Year*, *Poppies* and *Bells*, all from the suite called *Poems* (1912), and finally *Rainbow-Trout*, which he considered the most colourful and opalescent of his short-form piano works.

Scott does not list his favourite songs, but he wrote over 150, so his opinions are worth considering, particularly since they are as applicable today as when he first set them down seventy-five years ago. He felt song-writing was both the easiest and the hardest thing for a composer:

> The easiness lies in the fact that it requires no outstanding musical ability to superimpose a melody on top of an accompaniment of the simplest variety, whilst the difficulty lies in the fact that it requires much ingenuity and an original turn of mind to invent a melody containing an element of newness, and an accompaniment rich in harmonic device yet not so elaborate as to place the vocal part in the shade …
>
> Harmony is the great medium for emotional expression, a medium so elastic and unlimited that it serves to express or emphasise almost every conceivable shade of feeling.
>
> The entire character of a melody may be changed by altering the harmonization … I regard harmonic change (not to be confounded with *enharmonic* change) as the surest means of assisting the singer to express at a given moment the emotional content of the words. That four verses, all depicting various emotions, should be sung to precisely the same harmonies is both unsuitable and altogether wrong from the dramatic outlook.

Valerie Langfield discusses the points he raises here in her detailed discussion of the songs in Chapter 16 (above).

Towards the end of the memoir Scott describes the technical innovations he felt he had made throughout his musical career:

> I have in my major compositions made a novel use of *False Relations*.
>
> I have evolved new scales.
>
> I have employed descant in a novel manner.
>
> I have enriched the harmonic 'vocabulary' without uninterruptedly having to resort to ear-drum shattering discords.
>
> Partly by irregular rhythms and partly by unusual scales I have created new turns of melody.
>
> I have discovered that a certain chord (D.G.C. on any degree of the scale) when employed as a base allows for almost endless possibilities and is productive of new effects even when applied in the ordinary diatonic mode.
>
> This chord I have also used in the treble as a descant i.e. moving parts in similar motion as opposed to contrary motion.
>
> I have used sixths in an unusual manner.
>
> I have occasionally written melodies in bare 11ths ('Trio No 1 for violin, cello and piano' 1922) and used 9ths as part of my musical language.

In the latter part of his life, and for several decades after, there were those who felt Scott's music to be too 'occult', and that that prevented it from being more widely accepted. He took issue with that idea in the memoir, insisting there was no didactic intention behind a single bar of his music, though, as with any composer, he said, listeners were free to attribute any meaning they wished to it. He objected to Scriabin, whose music he loved, attaching a kind of theosophical programme to some of his best works instead of letting them be enjoyed simply as 'pure music'.

The memoir also contains a somewhat discursive chapter giving an account of Scott's spiritual journey from the low-church religion of his parents to becoming an occultist. This differs from what he wrote in *My Years of Indiscretion*[6] and *Bone of Contention.*[7] There is no mention here, for instance, of Evelyn Suart or Christian Science, and Annie Besant only appears at the end. Scott writes that he first took aversion to his parents' conventional Christianity because whenever he questioned anything they intimated that 'the greater the demand made upon one's credulity, the greater the merit in believing the unbelievable!'

In his seventeenth year, in Liverpool, after deciding not to become a professional pianist but before returning to Frankfurt to study composition, Scott met Hans Lüthy, a married man who was a great lover of music, as was his wife. Lüthy took a great interest in him and invited him to their *soirées.* Scott speaks warmly of him in

[6] *My Years of Indiscretion* (Mills & Boon, 1924), pp. 94–8.

[7] *Bone of Contention*, pp. 114–16.

both his autobiographies, but only here admits that Lüthy had sublimated homosexual feelings for him. Lüthy also decided to complete Scott's education, and when Scott was in Frankfurt sent him, unknown to his parents (who would have strongly disapproved), many books on Victorian rationalist thinking and current scientific thought. The result was that Scott soon became a committed agnostic. A great reader, he read all the books Lüthy sent him and would have remained an agnostic had he not also read books on the science of the mind and on spiritualism, which was a vogue in the early 1900s. He clung to his agnosticism, though with increasing doubt the more he read; then, when he encountered the work of Swami Vivekaneda on Raja Yoga he abandoned agnosticism, becoming first a Vedantist and then an occultist. Those interested in reading further are directed to Sarah Collins's very scholarly and absorbing book, *The Aesthetic Life of Cyril Scott*.[8]

He seemed reconciled, at least on paper, to being disregarded as a serious composer, and wondered if he would have devoted as much time to his other writings if more of his larger works had been accepted. As it was, in the 1940s he felt he would likely spend what he thought would be the short remainder of his life on literary matters, leaving the composing of music to his 'more competent and fortunate confrères'. This is curious, because, apart from a passing remark that *Doctors, Disease and Health* was the best book he ever wrote, there is scarcely a mention of his writings in the memoir, though he derived the major part of his income from them, not from his music.[9]

Composer, pianist, author, playwright, librettist, philosopher, therapeutist, mystic, occultist, yogi and poet. That was how Scott described himself, noting that painting, in particular, was a relaxation and that he delighted, like a small child, in creating landscapes out of his own imagination. In *Bone of Contention*, many years later, he wrote:

> Holding the belief that the more subjects one can, within limits, become interested in, the less time and inclination one has to be unhappy, I will make no excuses for what the friends of my music call my versatility and its detractors the dissipation of my energies, for … in a sad plight is the composer who has no side line or pastime to turn to during those desolate periods when musical ideation gives out, leaving but that painful sense of emptiness and frustration so familiar to all creative artists.[10]

After his music, next in importance for Scott was his poetry. For a decade between 1905 and 1915 he was equally poet and musician. During that period he published a total of five volumes of his own verse, and two books of translations. He then turned to prose, and began writing his occult and therapeutic books. Not until nearly thirty years later did he return to poetry, with *The Poems of a Musician*. As a dramatist he wrote a total of sixteen straight plays, six of them, as previously noted, during this 'dry' period. He also wrote several with music. None was ever produced, though

[8] Sarah Collins, *The Aesthetic Life of Cyril Scott*. Woodbridge, The Boydell Press, 2013.

[9] Cyril Scott, *Doctors, Disease and Health* (Methuen and Co., 1938).

[10] *Bone of Contention*, p. 11.

several came close to it. For a full description of his theatrical excursions and misadventures, see Chapter 14 (above).

For most people, astrology is a subject that rouses scepticism. Scott, who had two respected professional astrologers as friends, thought the 'recondite science' (as he termed it) deserved not to be dismissed out of hand. Towards the end of the memoir he talked of his horoscope. By that he did not mean the forecasts found in the gossip columns of the daily papers, which deal only in vague generalisations. He knew that a serious astrologer needed not only the date of birth, but the hour and minute, plus the longitude and latitude, from which he would calculate with the aid of an astronomical almanac the exact position of every planet in the zodiac at the precise moment of the individual's birth. Only then would he be able to predict the character and possible future of his subject.

Despite the bleakness of his situation at the time, there is a sense of optimism in the writing of this memoir, as if Scott somehow knew that his music would eventually be heard. It was his optimism, surely, that caused him to discuss his horoscope and leave it for future readers to discover. He had Virgo rising, he reported, and that indicated much labour with little reward during lifetime, but a belated recognition thereafter. Whatever one's personal thoughts on astrology, considering the unprecedented revival that has taken place in the present century, that prophecy has turned out to be remarkably accurate.

21

The Therapeutic Books

DESMOND SCOTT

The cause of disease is a simple one, so is the method for its prevention and cure.

Unless things of the spirit are taken into consideration as well, medical science can never be complete and the doctor will search in vain for truth.

THOSE two quotes from *Doctors, Disease and Health* sum up almost everything Cyril Scott had to say in all the books he wrote on the subject.[1] He not only provided advice on medical matters, but also offered a spiritual answer to the troubling question of why one person could be healed and another not. One may think it unusual to find philosophy and therapeutics together in the same volume, but Scott was a most unusual man, whose philosophy embraced both the physical and the spiritual and whose motto was Unity in Diversity.

Over a period of thirty years, beginning in 1939 and ending in 1968, he published a total of ten books and pamphlets: four books on doctors and medicine, a book and a pamphlet on cancer, and four pamphlets on a variety of other health topics. The first book, *Doctors, Disease and Health*, was by far the most comprehensive, and Scott thought it the best book he wrote. The other volumes are mainly shorter and revised versions of this first publication or, in the case of the booklets on black molasses, cider vinegar and constipation, variations of passages within it.

The book includes chapters on the cause of disease, on diet and nutrition, on vaccination and inoculation, on constipation, on commercialism and on alternative systems of medicine, and also has one chapter on astrology and another on reincarnation, because the human body, in Scott's view, was an instrument of the soul, 'to be made as efficient as possible for preliminary steps towards mental and spiritual evolution'.[2]

What caused him to turn to writing therapeutic books Scott explained in his *Simpler and Safer Remedies for Grievous Ills*:

> As a child, despite the fact that I was blest with the most considerate and understanding parents, my health was very poor indeed. Although my mother had no faith in ordinary doctors, she nonetheless waived her prejudices, and physician after physician was called in to prescribe for me, but without any noticeable results. Only when I grew older did my condition somewhat improve. Even so I was never really well, my chief misery being 'nerves', exhaustion, horrible fits of depression, recurring attacks of agonising neuralgia, and sundry other afflictions

[1] *Doctors, Disease and Health: A Critical Survey of Therapeutics Modern and Ancient* (Methuen, 1938; rev. edn True Health Publishing, 1946). All quotes are taken from the 1946 edition.

[2] Ibid., pp. 5–6.

> that need not be mentioned … And then in my twenty-fourth year came my salvation. I heard of Naturopathy (not that this is a treatise on that cult) and even after adopting its dietetic principles to only a limited extent I felt a transformed being within a few days. The explanation is quite simple; hitherto I had been living on the usual English type of food [that is] so deficient in vitamins and mineral salts. My self-cure created the beginning of my interest in unorthodox methods of healing. Thereafter I read scores of books on Therapeutics; English, German, French, American; books on Yoga, on Osteopathy, Homeopathy, the Biochemic System of Medicine, on Herbalism and even on Mental Therapeutics. Whenever I heard of a new method of healing the sick, I set to work to study its claims, so as to sift 'the tares from the wheat'.[3]

When Scott said scores of books he was not exaggerating. He had seventy entirely on medical subjects in his library, ranging from Robert Burton's famous *The Anatomy of Melancholy*, first published in 1621, to *Pears Medical Encyclopaedia, Blacks Medical Dictionary* and three volumes of the homeopathic *Materia Medica*. There are four books on cancer, eight on biochemics, eleven on homeopathy, thirty on such miscellaneous subjects as arthritis and rheumatic diseases, and two on healing and prayer.

Before discussing Scott's own books it is important to note that he wanted it clearly understood that he was not himself a medical practitioner. His suggestions come from his wide reading, his own experience, and from discussions with a great number of professionals, not only highly qualified MDs with strings of letters to their names, but also the more unorthodox, including naturopaths, homeopaths and osteopaths.

It is not surprising, given that he began writing these books some seventy-five years ago, that he was not always right in his assertions. He was mistaken about the cause of cancer, for instance, and his dislike of vaccination and inoculation was unfounded, but those who think of Scott as someone with his head in the clouds, preoccupied with music or other-worldly matters, will be surprised to discover not only how pertinent much of what he wrote still is, but also how eminently practical and reasonable he could be. There are passages in the books that deserve to be quoted simply for their common sense: 'The only rational way to cure and prevent disease is consistently to live in a manner that does not cause disease.'[4] 'The prime cause of disease is the absence of substances that should be in the body and the presence of substances which should not be in the body.'[5] 'The golden rule regarding the law of nutrition is that our diet must contain a sufficiency of vitamins, roughage and mineral salts, but apart from that the golden rule is that there is no golden rule.'[6]

Two main themes run throughout, the first being the need for the right diet, and the second the absolute necessity that the physician treats the whole patient. The caring physician – concerned with the entire well-being, both mental and physical, of his patient – provides a perfect example of Scott's mantra 'Unity in Diversity', in contrast to the specialist, obsessed with only one particular part, who represents the

[3] *Simpler and Safer Remedies for Grievous Ills* (Athene Publishing Co., 1953).

[4] *Health, Diet and Commonsense* (Andrew Dakers, 1940).

[5] *Doctors Disease and Health*, epigraph.

[6] *Health, Diet and Commonsense*, p. 41.

reverse – separateness. Scott believed the body, under right conditions, was well able to heal itself, and that the main requirement was proper nutrition, with the nutrients and vitamins coming from natural fruits and vegetables, not from synthetic or chemical supplements. He insisted over and over again that 'right food is the basis of all good health and wrong food the basis of all ill health; for given this everything else will look after itself'.[7]

If medicine had been his profession instead of his hobby, he would most likely have been a homeopath. He considered surgery should be used only as a last resort when all else had failed; it must be remembered that when he was writing *Doctors, Disease and Health* in 1937 the surgical removal of tonsils, adenoids or the appendix was a routine and everyday occurrence.

Nowadays, when all food is labelled with every ingredient listed, and newspapers print daily articles on nutrition, we can clearly see that Scott was far ahead of his time. The average diet consisted largely of white bread, meat, potatoes and the few greens, the latter cooked until all goodness had been boiled out of them. Fresh fruit was seldom eaten and, of course, was available only in season. Scott felt eating too much red meat was unhealthy, but he was not in favour of total vegetarianism.

What one notices above all is the reasonableness of his approach:

> A man may eat a few useless if pleasant things without appreciable harm, provided the remainder of his diet be intrinsically conducive to health.
>
> In other words, the human body is so constructed that it will tolerate a few unsalubrious articles of food as long as it is supplied with the essential amount of salubrious ones ...
>
> A wise doctor instead of forbidding certain cherished foods would say, 'You may occasionally have your special fancies, and your little glass of wine and your little smoke.[8]

He was not, of course, including chain smokers in that remark, nor in all probability was he aware in 1938 of the carcinogenic and addictive properties of tobacco. He was a moderate pipe-smoker himself well into his seventies, and smoked both a herbal mixture and a brand of tobacco called Three Nuns, but nevertheless lived to be over ninety.

In his book Scott listed a few of the requirements for a healthy diet. He did not advocate that a heavy meat eater give up meat altogether, but he did insist the diet had to include wholemeal cereals, bran, plenty of raw fruit (especially apples), honey rather than refined white sugar, green salads and vegetables. It was not the eating of one particular unwholesome food that caused the trouble, he said, but 'the not eating as a daily habit' the foods he had listed. He remarked that the cure was 'Nature in combination with your own efforts' rather than a prescription from a doctor.

Many pages were devoted to constipation. In 1956 he published an entire pamphlet on the subject, *Constipation and Commonsense*.[9] In it he argued against the

[7] *Doctors, Disease and Health*, p. 27.

[8] Ibid., pp. 121–2.

[9] *Constipation and Commonsense* (Athene Publishing Co., 1956).

use of violent purgatives that produced a movement of the bowels but were no help in identifying the cause. Moderation in all things was his creed. Too much of a good thing was detrimental, however beneficial the substance might normally be. A healthy bowel, he maintained, was the basis for good health, and a faulty one the prime cause of innumerable ailments, and he lamented the fact that that most people had not the slightest idea of what went on in their own insides:

> If man were a wise and inquiring mortal he would know that the rightness of what he puts into himself may be judged from what proceeds from himself.
>
> Yet so ignorant are most people of the most elementary laws of colonic hygiene that they think their nutritional habits are perfectly right and wholesome when they are very much the reverse.[10]

As always, the proper diet, with a sufficient amount of roughage and the right balance of mineral salts, was the answer.

Two systems of alternative medicine, biochemics and homeopathy particularly appealed to Scott because both are concerned with treating the whole patient. Biochemics is based on the tissue salts (such as calcium, potassium, sodium) found naturally in the blood and in the food we eat. They are considered essential to good health by homeopaths and biochemists because a deficiency or excess of one or more of them causes an imbalance in the body that could lead to disease. One example is sodium chloride, common salt, which in excess is thought to cause high blood pressure. The biochemical remedy would be to moderate the excess and supply the lack, thus restoring the balance. Given the right diagnosis by the biochemist, the cure would then be largely in the hands of the patient, a method that Scott, who was strongly in favour of patients being their own physicians, firmly endorsed.

'Homeopathy', wrote Scott tartly, 'is in many quarters still regarded as a species of faith-cure by a public which knows nothing about it, and by orthodox doctors who condemn it prior to investigation.'[11] The British Homeopathic Association describes it on its website as 'a form of holistic medicine used to treat both acute and chronic conditions. It is based on a system of "like cures like" – in other words, a substance given in very small doses will cure those same symptoms that it causes if taken in large amounts.' Homeopathy is much more widely recognised now than it was in Scott's day, but the reasons he gave for it not being universally adopted are probably still applicable now. He said that it took a homeopathic doctor far more time and skill to find the exact 'like' for a number of 'perhaps complicated and sometimes apparently irrelevant symptoms ... than just to prescribe a text-book remedy for some tabulated disease'.[12] Homeopathy uses medicines largely made from natural sources, not synthetic ones, giving yet another reason for Scott as naturopath to advocate it so strongly.

The second theme that occurred again and again was Scott's unfavourable opinion of the average medical professional of his day. A fair man, though, he was eager in his introductory remarks to single out and praise those 'wise and enlightened physicians ... who command our greatest respect and admiration both as men and

[10] *Doctors, Disease and Health*, p. 29.

[11] Ibid., p. 194.

[12] Ibid., p. 195.

savants'. He added 'Indeed it is with the discoveries and contentions of these wise physicians of whatever school that we are largely concerned in this book.'[13] His quarrel, as we have noted, was that doctors for the most part were too concerned with effects, and not enough with causes. His aversion to specialists who tended to know everything there was to know about a disease except how to cure it is a recurring theme. Here he cites Hippocrates to bolster his argument:

> From the time of Hippocrates, wise physicians have maintained that there is only one scientific way of treating a disease and that is by treating the whole body; but the specialist thinks he knows better and so he ignores the wisdom of the wise and his patients are the sufferers.
>
> Indeed, specialism is a medical fashion based on a contradiction of ordinary scientific logic; it presupposes that one organ of the body works independently from the other organs or ... that it leads a life of its own.[14]

He believed that fashionable specialists, instead of searching for the cause, simply cut out the offending organ and charged a huge fee for doing so. The knife, Scott felt, was only to be used in the most extreme cases, as all an operation could do was to remove the tumour or ulcer. It failed, in his opinion, to rid the body of its poisons, or to correct its nutritional deficiencies:

> All Nature's processes are gentle and gradual ... surgical methods in relation to disease are violent and mutilative ... destructive of tissue and hence opposed to Nature's beneficent designs.[15]

Scott investigated both the new and the old. Part II is headed 'Medical Knowledge of the Ancients'. His research was wide. In order to write the chapter, which he began by remarking that many discoveries were merely rediscoveries, he consulted a number of texts including *Outlines of Greek and Roman Medicine* by Sir James Elliott,[16] *Greek Medicine in Rome* by Sir T. Clifford Allbutt,[17] *Notes on the History of Military Medicine* by F. H. Garrison[18] and the *Journal of Tropical Medicine*, edited by Dr F. W. Sambon.[19] From them Scott noted a number of surprising things that were known long before our time. In to the pre-Christian era, for instance, Indian doctors knew the effects of opium and cannabis. They knew mosquitoes caused malaria and that rats were carriers of bubonic plague. They knew about diabetes. The Egyptians knew about cancer. The Greeks used anaesthetics and operated on cataracts, and Scott quotes from Hippocrates's *Ancient Medicine*: 'All organs cooperate in their

[13] Ibid., p. x.

[14] Ibid., pp. 40–1.

[15] Ibid., p. 65

[16] Published by The Medical Heritage Library.

[17] Published by Macmillan & Co. (1921).

[18] Published by National Capital Press Inc. (1922), reprinted from the journal *The Military Surgeon* (1921–2).

[19] Published by Blackwell Scientific Publications (1910).

functions, being united to form an harmonious whole.' He had great respect for the Greek physician and referred to him several times, but unfortunately he did not tell us which translation he was using or the name of the publisher.

Throughout his book Scott insisted there was only one disease and that it was caused either by dietary deficiency or, as he called it, by self-poisoning. That being so, he asked, why does disease manifest itself in so many different ways, as diabetes in one, angina in another, arthritis in a third? His answers to that question bring us to Chapter XXI, 'Astrology in Relation to Disease'.

Well aware that most people consider astrology superstitious nonsense, he nevertheless maintained that the body-type of an individual was governed by the planets at the moment of birth, as were the types of diseases from which he or she would likely suffer. As there are twelve signs of the Zodiac, so there are twelve body-types, each with its own strengths and weaknesses. Moreover, each sign governs one or more parts of the body, so that someone born under Taurus, which governs the throat, might suffer from laryngitis or diphtheria, while someone born under Sagittarius, which governs hips and thighs, might suffer from sciatica. Scott concluded this chapter with a passage that deserves to be quoted in full:

> There is no doubt as to the interconnexion between the stellar influences and the treatment of disease. This fact will of course be challenged by those upon whose credulity it makes too great a demand. For although they are doubtless ready to admit the influence of the moon upon the tides, they will argue that to ascribe influences from stellar bodies billions of miles away, and influences, moreover, that diversely affect individuals, is surely to stretch imagination to breaking-point. Let them, however, realize that the Cosmos is a unity and that space and time, as we know them, are illusory ... Are we not apt to forget that some of the most commonplace facts are still mysteries; that although we may place a seed in the ground, we only know that it becomes a plant but cannot say why?[20]

Scott considered there was a spiritual component to health and disease, and he elaborated on that in the chapter 'What Reincarnation Explains'. There he discussed the spiritual cause of disease and stated that astrology could say why one person was prone to a certain complaint, and another not; it could also, to a certain extent, predict the possible path an individual might take. What it could *not* do, however, was explain why the individual was born at that particular moment to be subject to that particular destiny. Reincarnation, however, does provide the answer. It could explain whether that particular life was likely to confront the obstacles it had to face or would be defeated by them, always taking into account the exercise of free will.

This is explored fully in Scott's occult books, namely the *Initiate* trilogy,[21] *An Outline of Modern Occultism*[22] and *The Greater Awareness*.[23] He believed firmly in an immortal

[20] *Doctors, Disease and Health*, pp. 224–5

[21] *The Initiate, by His Pupil* (1920); *The Initiate in the New World, by his Pupil* (1927); *The Initiate in the Dark Cycle, by his Pupil* (1932). All published by Routledge & Kegan Paul; all reissued and published by Red Wheel / Weiser, *The Initiate* in 1979, and the other two volumes in 1991.

[22] *An Outline of Modern Occultism* (Routledge & Kegan Paul, 1935).

[23] *The Greater Awareness* (George Routledge & Sons, 1936).

soul, and that when it was on what he called its 'celestial holiday', it reviewed its previous existence with other souls more advanced along the path and chose where it would reincarnate next, selecting not necessarily the most easy life, but one that would afford it the best opportunity to make progress spiritually. It was part of his 'Unified Theory of Everything', as Einstein put it, or 'Unity in Diversity', as Scott has it.

Two years later, in 1940, came another book, *Health, Diet and Commonsense*. Many of the same subjects are covered as in *Doctors, Disease and Health*, and in the Introduction Scott wrote that he had been asked to write it. Though he had insisted he was not a doctor, he had received countless letters from people asking him to recommend treatment for their particular ailment – advice, he remarked with an understandable touch of irritation, he had already given, had they troubled to read the book more carefully. The first chapter reiterated his two main contentions: that the primary cause of disease was faulty nutrition, and that most doctors were concerned only with effects for, as he put it:

> Until the public realise once and for all that doctors are more interested in studying disease than health there will be little hope of a state of collective well-being, for the assumption will persist that to cure a given disease is necessarily to cure a given patient ...
>
> Drugs prescribed by the orthodox may suppress or divert a particular ailment, but that is not the same thing as a permanent cure.[24]

The title *Health, Diet and Commonsense* was descriptive, as the book is largely a commonsense manual on diet. There is sensible advice on not drinking scalding hot liquids, on chewing more thoroughly, and on the lack of vitamins in the average diet – a lack to be supplied, of course, by natural foods. He listed foods under various categories, dividing them into calcium foods, iron foods, potassium foods, and gave the benefits they conferred. Nuts, oats, lettuce, rich in potassium, helped stimulate brain and cell activity and heal injuries; mushrooms, artichokes, green beans and garlic were rich in iodine. Garlic helped prevent hardening of the arteries and was good for lungs and chest.

There was advice on diet for fat people and thin. For obese people who might be quite small eaters, he suggested the problem could be caused by some of the glands being undernourished and therefore not functioning properly. The solution was to feed the glands but not fatten the patient, and he prescribed plenty of steamed (not boiled) vegetables, salads and low-acid fruits, and no white bread, only wholemeal. Meat should be limited to one serving a day. Potatoes, jams, sweet cakes and sugar were to be avoided. In a later pamphlet he insisted cider vinegar was the best and safest cure for obesity.[25] For thin people he suggested dairy produce, wholemeal bread, vegetables (particularly carrots, celery, onions and peas), lentils and potatoes baked in their jackets and buttered. None of this would alarm a nutritionist today, and the only noteworthy point is that in 1940 dietary habits were such as to need Scott to comment on them.

[24] *Health, Diet and Commonsense*, p. 15.

[25] *Cider Vinegar: Nature's Great Health-Promoter and Safest Cure of Obesity* (True Health Publishing, 1948).

The chapter on constipation lists the causes of the complaint, along with the biochemic salts needed to remedy it. The salts, Scott remarked, would supply the deficiency and alleviate the problem, but he warned that the cure would be permanent only if there were no return to the old wrong feeding habits. Scott was a great believer in roughage, particularly bran, to scour the bowel and get rid of faecal matter that might otherwise be absorbed into the system and cause toxaemia. He gave several recipes for bran – bran biscuits, bran cookies, and a bran and ginger cake – crediting for them Mr J. Ellis Barker, a homeopath for whom he had great respect and whom he quoted several times in his books.

Health, Diet and Commonsense also brings in astrology, in relation to biochemic salts. Each salt corresponds to a particular sign of the Zodiac. Scott considered knowing the sign a person was born under could be of help to doctors in the diagnosis and treatment of disease, because it indicated to a certain extent not only the foods most suited to that person, but also the biochemic salt needed to maintain the necessary balance. All the salts are needed for good health, but a person born under Aries, for instance, needs more of a particular salt than one born under Libra or Gemini. Scott then gave a table listing the dates of the astrological signs, the parts of the body they governed and the salts, the 'birth salts' as they are called, that corresponded to them. He was not alone in making an astrological connection, for the American Biochemical Association on its current website states the same thing, linking each salt to a particular sign in the Zodiac.

In 1946 Scott published his third book on the subject *Medicine Rational and Irrational*.[26] Its thesis can be summed up in a single sentence: 'In its highest aspect Medicine is an art, in its lowest aspect it is merely a means of making money.' His aversion to specialists and the fees they charged remains, his contention being that the more the specialist concentrated on a part, the less he knew about the patient as a whole. He felt medicine had been corrupted by pharmaceutical companies, whose chief concern was to make huge profits from their products. He complained that most doctors ignored the simpler, far less expensive and safer remedies both homeopathy and biochemistry could provide. He did not suggest they should replace allopathic medicine entirely, but pleaded for a wider outlook where orthodox doctors accepted and acknowledged that homeopathy and biochemistry were powerful and effective weapons in the communal fight against disease and ill-health, not spurious methods only used by quacks and charlatans.

The fourth book on the subject, published in 1953, was *Simpler and Safer Remedies for Grievous Ills*, which is largely a summing-up of the previous three. Scott suggested alternative remedies for a number of ailments including arthritis, thrombosis, duodenal ulcers and cancer. He concluded by insisting 'that until the universal principle of unity in diversity is accepted there can be no victory over disease'. No system of medicine was applicable to all, 'because of the differing kinds and nature of human afflictions'.

We have not mentioned Scott's second book, *Victory Over Cancer* (Fig. 21.2)– a title that was to have a sad irony.[27] He had based the book on the theories of several

[26] *Medicine, Rational and Irrational* (True Health Publishing, 1946).

[27] *Victory Over Cancer* (True Health Publishing, 1939).

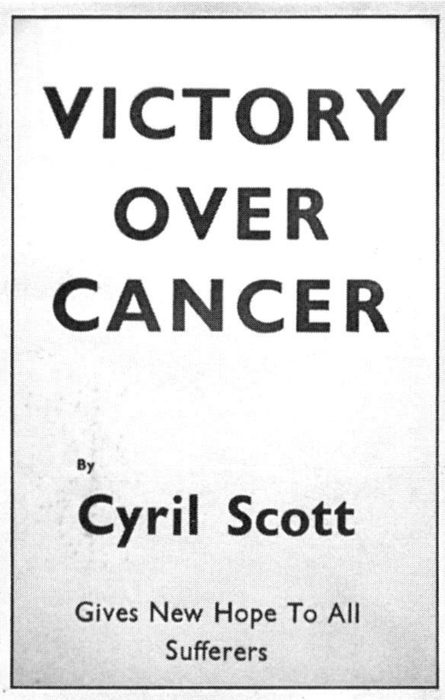

Figure 21.1 Dust jacket of *Victory Over Cancer*

distinguished doctors, chief among them Dr William Forbes Ross,[28] but also Dr Robert Bell,[29] Sir William Arbuthnot Lane[30] and Mr J. Ellis Barker.[31] If I may simplify, their basic contention was that in many cases cancer is due to a dietary deficiency and a lack of potassium. It is now accepted that it is caused by cells growing out of control, that it can happen in any part of the body, and that there are at least a hundred different types of the disease. Nearly thirty years later Scott published his final booklet, called *Cancer Prevention: Fallacies and some Reassuring Facts*.[32] By 1968 it was known that cancer was caused by the proliferation of cells, which Scott acknowledged, but he stuck to his main point:

> surgery has made spectacular strides during the last few decades. And yet it is unreasonable to suppose that a disease can be permanently cured merely by cutting away its *effect* instead of removing its cause. Granted that a cancerous growth

[28] Dr William Forbes Ross, Scottish physician and surgeon, wrote *Cancer: The Cause of its Genesis and Treatment* (Methuen, 1912).

[29] Dr Robert Bell, Scottish physician and surgeon, wrote *Cancer: Its Cause and Treatment without Operation* (1913). Publisher not known.

[30] Sir William Arbuthnot Lane (1856–1943), physician and surgeon, initiated programmes of health education that are still in use today. He founded the New Health Society (1925) to publicise his views on healthy diet and life.

[31] J. Ellis Barker (1870–1948), a German-born homeopath, emigrated to Engand and wrote several books on homeopathy. The most famous is *My Testament of Healing* (John Murray, 1936).

[32] *Cancer Prevention: Fallacies and some Reassuring Facts* (Athene Publishing Co., 1968).

> occurs when a number of cells in the body run riot and proliferate, yet that does not explain *why* they should proliferate, and so we are still left in ignorance of the prime cause of the disease.[33]

Proper nutrition – a natural and varied diet providing the right combination of mineral salts (especially potassium) and feeding all the various parts and functions of the body – was, he continued to insist, essential for perfect health.

It is amusing to note, in hindsight, how reluctant Scott was to allow that heavy smoking was a major cause of lung cancer, though he did admit it was not harmless. He certainly noted the difference between 'the smoke taken into the lungs and that same smoke breathed out again; a difference that can only mean that some of its denser particles have remained in the lungs.'

The booklet ended with his reasons for writing it:

> [Nowhere] in this digest of the various and varied theories, pronouncements and opinions regarding cancer, have I myself presumed to be able to explain that mystery. But if I have succeeded in adding any useful information to this bone-harassing subject, I shall consider my effort well rewarded.[34]

Apart from the matter of the pipe-smoking, Scott followed his own dietary advice to the end. As an adult his health was in general very good. He ate plenty of fresh fruit, vegetables and fish, and as he grew older he consumed very little red meat. He seldom had colds, exercised regularly and the only time he was ill was during the very low period of his life during World War 2, when he was in hospital for a short time with severe influenza; one suspects the strain that brought this on was as much mental as it was physical.

In 1949 and 1948 Scott published two booklets. One was *Crude Black Molasses*,[35] the other *Cider Vinegar*. In *Cider Vinegar* he credited Dr D. C. Jarvis for much of the material he used. In 1958 Dr Jarvis had produced a book titled *Folk Medicine* that became a best seller. Scott's booklets also became hugely popular, went into multiple editions, were translated into German, Spanish, French, Italian and Hebrew and sold in their hundreds of thousands all over the world. Reiterating his thesis that most diseases were caused by years of wrong feeding and a deficiency of mineral salts and vitamins, he claimed that black molasses and cider vinegar used either separately or together supplied those missing salts and vitamins, thereby promoting general health and relieving many ailments, including arthritis (which he considered was largely due to a lack of potassium in the body).

The final pamphlet we will look at is *Sleeplessness: Its Prevention and Cure by Harmless Methods*.[36] Scott began by giving commonsense advice on relaxing techniques for the mind, and decried the use of sleeping pills because they only treated

[33] Ibid., pp. 14–15.

[34] Ibid., p. 46.

[35] *Crude Black Molasses, a Natural 'Wonder-food'* (Athene Publications, 1949).

[36] *Sleeplessness: Its Prevention and Cure by Harmless Methods* (Athene Publishing Co., 1955).

the symptoms and not the cause. The physical cause, he insisted again, was improper nutrition, and here too he extolled the virtues of black molasses and cider vinegar to remedy dietary deficiencies. He ended by listing a number of homeopathic and biochemic remedies including arnica, coffee and aconite, each one for a specific problem. Arnica was for fearful people, particularly the aged, afraid of death; coffee (the homeopathic version, naturally) was for when the brain becomes intensely active upon getting into bed.

Scott was no TV evangelist making millions peddling the latest 'Wonder Cure'. His sole aim was to make known to those who might be unaware of them the many alternative methods of treatment available. He believed if he learned something that could be of value it was incumbent on him to share that knowledge; for knowledge in itself was worthless unless the experience could be used to benefit others. If a few people found his recommendations valid he was happy he had been of use. One may not agree with everything he wrote, particularly in regard to astrology and reincarnation, but there is no disputing his sincerity and genuine desire to be of help.

22

Childishness or The Moron Mind

DESMOND SCOTT

CYRIL Scott produced five volumes all on the same subject. They are *The Way of the Childish* (1916); *Childishness: A Study in Adult Conduct* (1930), *Man is my Theme* (1939), *The Rhymed Reflections of a Ruthless Rhymer* (unpublished but completed *c.* 1943–4) and finally *Man the Unruly Child* (1953). In addition to these five books, there is another one to be considered: *The Real Tolerance*. The question arises as to what induced him to repeat the same basic premise for almost forty years? The answer could be he was so aware that the problems he pointed out in the first book had been totally ignored, as had his suggestions for resolving them; perhaps he saw himself as a present-day prophet crying in the wilderness, compelled to proclaim his warnings even though his audience was heedless to them.

Despite the devastation and horrors of World War 1, adults, Scott insisted, continued to behave like children. Could a post-war generation do better? The basic argument never alters. It can be summed up in a passage from *The Way of the Childish*:

> Mankind has never grown up. With few exceptions, lost like needles in haystacks, the world is peopled by millions of souls who, despite their age and stature, behave like children in the nursery. The only difference is that, whereas the nursery behaviour of children may be on a small and comparatively harmless scale, the nursery behaviour of mankind is on an extensive and devastating one.

Scott published a number of books anonymously and sometimes a little detective work is needed to ascertain if he is the author. For instance, *The Way of the Childish* appears to have been written by Shri Âdvaitâchârya, but on the flyleaf below the title in smaller letters we find: 'Written down by the author of *The Real Tolerance*'. Five years later, in 1921, it ran to a second edition, but this time the flyleaf read 'Written down by the author of *The Initiate*'. Clearly both books were written by Cyril Scott.

The Way of the Childish is significant because it is the first notice we have of Scott's interest in theosophy. He explains that the book had been dictated to him and states: 'The great Initiates, known as "Masters" in the Theosophical literature, instruct their pupils mostly from another plane but there are lesser Initiates who instruct them by word of mouth.' This is the first reference we have to his being a pupil of an Initiate; published in 1916, it pre-dates the first *Initiate* book by four years.

The importance of *The Real Tolerance*, published anonymously in 1913, is that not only is it the first book Scott wrote but also that his entire philosophy is laid out within it. In all his subsequent writings that philosophy is simply expanded and developed. In the Foreword to *The Real Tolerance*, Scott wrote his aim was to:

> attempt to show how the true Charity, set forth in all Divine Philosophies may be adjusted to the spirit of the age and brought to bear on the manifold circumstances of Life ... much which the world calls sin when looked at with the further-seeing eyes of wisdom can be called sin no longer – for there is no such thing

as virtue in itself … the great proclamation 'Forgive unto seventy times seven' is not an upholdment of sin, but unlimited forgiveness; and above all, were there nothing to be tolerant about, there could be no tolerance.

That shows a considerable shift in Scott's thinking, both from the orthodox Christianity of his parents, which he had abandoned long ago, and from the agnosticism he later adopted.

The book is divided into short chapters and aphorisms titled 'Friendship', 'Parenthood', 'Love' and 'Conjugality'. Each chapter consists of short paragraphs, two or three to a page. From the chapter on friendship, for instance: 'Happy is the man who makes many friends, for each new being whom one learns to love is one step nearer to Universal Love, which is the goal of all Humanity.' From that on love: 'Happy is the man who realises that it is more blessed to love than to be loved.' And: 'Deluded is the man who professing great depth of love, puts not the Beloved before his own happiness: for that man does not love his Beloved but merely himself through her.' From 'Conjugality':

If you possess a wife whom you do not truly cherish, and she falls in love with another man, do not upbraid her, or stand in the way of her love; for your pain arises alone from vanity, which is ignoble, while her pain arises from love which is the highest thing on earth.

Covering much of the same ground, also made up of aphorisms, and published anonymously fifteen years after *The Real Tolerance* is another book, a genuine curiosity, that deserves a mention. *The Art of Making a Perfect Husband* (Fig. 22.1) deals with love and marriage, and what it has to say is both provocative and controversial.[1] It is an illusion that two people in love know each other, Scott insists. They only know what they think of each other, and if they marry, they often find they have married strangers. He reiterates the concept of complete freedom in marriage, and goes so far as to suggest that if a wife desperately yearns to have a child and her husband is sterile, he should allow her to be impregnated by another man. To many this would seem unconventional even today. Scott remarks truthfully that marriage is not a rose-garden but a school with hard and difficult lessons, and that mutually enjoyable love-making is a skill that has to be learned like any other. His attitude to women is ambivalent, forward-looking in the above examples but patronising when he claims women think with their emotions rather than their intellect, revealing that he is still basically a Victorian.

In 1930, fourteen years after *The Way of the Childish*, Scott published *Childishness: A Study in Adult Conduct*.[2] Like the other books we have been discussing, it is divided into short chapters no longer than two or three pages, with titles such as 'Love of Power', 'Money and Greed' and 'Democracy'. On democracy he is surprising, saying it is beautiful in theory, but that government by the populace is like

[1] Scott acknowledges it as his in *The Greater Awareness* (George Routledge & Sons, 1936).

[2] Cyril Scott, *Childishness: A Study In Adult Conduct* (John Bale, Sons & Danielsson, 1930).

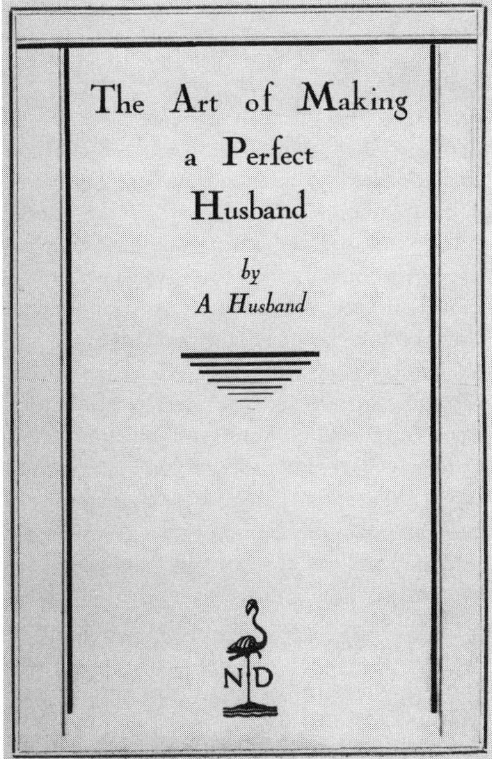

Figure 22.1 Dust jacket of *The Art of Making a Perfect Husband*

hoping that one can somehow multiply ignorance into knowledge. Towards the end of this book comes, so far as I am aware, the very first mention of the phrase that was to become Scott's guiding principle and motto, and which was eventually engraved on his tombstone. He was speaking about religion and insisting that not until we discard the naïve belief that there is but one true religion (that being the one we ourselves happen to believe in) will we 'attain the realisation of unity in diversity'. At that point the phrase was not capitalised. Eight years later *Man is my Theme* was published, and it is here (apart from a reference in the first edition of *An Outline of Modern Occultism*)[3] that we find Unity in Diversity defined as a complete philosophy.

Put briefly, Unity in Diversity means acknowledging and respecting differences, be they racial, religious, political or familial, endeavouring to understand rather than hastily to condemn. It demands great tolerance and respect for other religions, viewpoints and attitudes:

> People who can only see one point of view, their own, be it religious or political, are usually those who think with their emotions instead of their reason. There can

[3] *An Outline of Modern Occultism* (George Routledge & Sons, 1935), p. 8.

> be no such thing as a point of view common to all, for temperaments differ and circumstances differ. Therefore the wisest way to solve all problems is to recognise the principle of Unity in Diversity.

In *Childishness: A Study in Adult Conduct* Scott declares that 'we are apt to think that childishness is incompatible with so-called civilisation', but insists that 'Civilisation has made us more sanitary and more ingenious ... but not less childish.' The so-called 'War to end all Wars' had ended a decade earlier, and though Scott chose not to spend time discussing it specifically, it provided a perfect example of his entire thesis. Most of the world's problems, he believed, are due to childish behaviour. He then proceeds to enumerate those behaviours and points out the havoc they cause in the adult world when not recognised as such. Wars begin in the nursery. Children are selfish, but so are adults. Children 'quarrel crudely and noisily about toys, about cakes, about everything and nothing'. Adults quarrel about money, they cheat, lie, brag, steal and jostle for power. Many of those adult characteristics are hangovers from the nursery. When children display such behaviour, their concerned parents chide and punish them; yet that same behaviour when carried out on a global scale by organisations and nations is not condemned, but rather is widely encouraged and applauded, recognised as childish only by very few.

Man is my Theme (Fig. 22.2) is dedicated to Scott's friend the novelist Doris Langley Moore, who, having admired *Childishness: A Study in Adult Conduct*, urged him to write a more comprehensive book on the same subject. Scott said he originally wanted to call it *The Moron Mind*, using the word exactly as the dictionary defines it – 'a person with the mental age of eight to twelve' – but he doubted if the average reader would know the meaning of the word. The book was written in 1938, when it looked for a short time as though World War 2 had been averted, but it was not published until September 1939, by which time war had been declared. Having lived through the 1914–1918 war, the conflict just beginning was, naturally, very much on Scott's mind. He begins by repeating what he said in the earlier book, namely that we delude ourselves by thinking that childishness augmented to great proportions ceases to be childish. He goes on to say:

> This delusion is so prevalent that when the bulk of Mankind exhibits nursery behaviour on a gigantic scale, only the few are clear-sighted enough to realise it is nursery behaviour at all. Squabbles and altercations of great magnitude which when sanely examined prove to be the result of greed, wounded vanity, lust for power ... seem to be invested with a pseudo dignity which obscures their true nature.

Love of power, he insists, shows itself very early in the kindergarten, and is closely linked to boasting and bullying. A child will not allow others to play in the sandbox where he is building his castle. As an adult he glories in being in command and refuses to accept advice; as an aging CEO, he clings obstinately to power long after he should have stepped down.

Conventionality, according to Scott's somewhat harsh assessment, is a combination of mimicry, cowardice and mental inertia. Mimicry, he points out, is an essential learning tool for the child but in the adult it consists in copying the ideas and

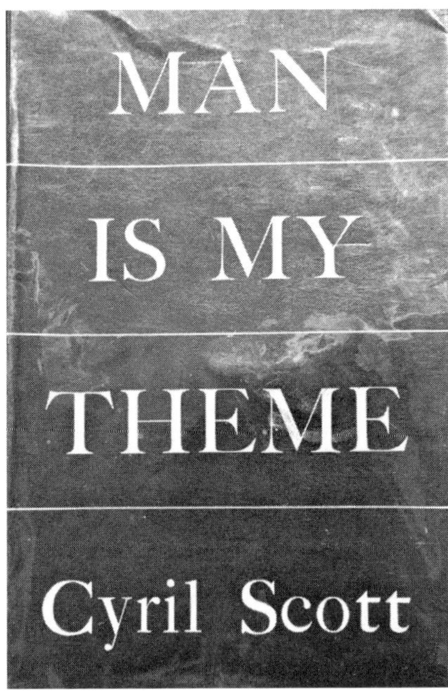

Figure 22.2 Dust jacket of *Man is My Theme*

opinions of others. As children grow older it becomes essential for them to be part of a group. With adults it becomes a need to conform and a fear of doing anything out of line, and the mental inertia comes from always accepting and never challenging existing norms.

Scott is more concerned with the institution of war in general than with the specific conflict of 1939–1945, but World War 2 does provides yet another illustration of that thesis he never tired of reiterating: '*we are in general far more childish than children*' (his italics). He continues:

> Instead of cultivating those more beautiful elements in the child nature, one of the most graceful being affection (the augmentation of which would be universal brotherhood and neighbourly love), Mankind, to the contrary, has developed insidious forms of greed, lust for power, vanity (personal, national or both) and contentiousness. What, in fact, does a study of past history and contemporary international politics reveal? It reveals Mankind in such an unfavourable light that the most charitable explanation is the simple fact that it has never grown up.
> (pp. 15–16)

The first twelve chapters of *Man is my Theme* are devoted to politics and government. One of the first subjects discussed is lying. We teach our children the importance of telling the truth, yet governments tell diplomatic lies to gain an advantage, and political parties tell political lies, making promises they know they cannot keep. Scott gives examples from his own times, but incidents just as egregious are, sadly, not lacking today, over seventy-five years later. Spying he considered even worse than lying, and illustrative of a perfect double standard: children caught spying or eavesdropping are punished by their peers or their parents; but an adult who spies for 'our' side is brave, fearless and a patriot; and someone caught spying for the 'other' side deserves to be shot.

The book is full of topical references that are no longer relevant, but it is interesting to note that Scott admired Neville Chamberlain, the British Prime Minister at the time, who was, he believed, truly a man of peace. Briefly lauded when it was thought he had averted the war, he was then reviled for having made a treaty with Hitler that proved worthless. Shortly after war was declared he resigned, disgraced, but later historians have given him credit, pointing out that Britain was totally unprepared for war in 1938, and that Chamberlain's actions allowed Britain a year in which to mobilise.

The League of Nations was created after World War 1 in 1920, with the laudable intention of creating world peace. Unfortunately it provided a perfect example of the childishness Scott so deplored. When a nation found itself at odds with the League, instead of trying to find a solution to the problem it simply walked away, like a pouting child throwing down his toys and refusing to play anymore. Indeed, in the section 'Nationalism versus Unity' Scott insisted that nationalism also begins in the nursery. It starts with *my* toys, *my* school, *my* team, *my* family, *my* political power and *my* country. Hitler, with his *Deutschland über alles,* was the prime example of extreme nationalism, and Scott writes: 'Great and wise statesmen think internationally, but demagogues think nationally, and this, as we have all had to realise only too forcibly is one of the causes of the present state of affairs' (p. 52). Notice that he says 'one of the causes'. This is no accident, for he felt the Treaty of Versailles, in putting the entire blame for the conflict on Germany, was far too punitive (as do a number of historians now). He was greatly in favour of US President Wilson's 'Fourteen Points', which Britain and France rejected as being too idealistic. Scott then continued:

> As long as a continent is divided up into separate monarchies … there is … nothing but strife, but as soon as it has become united into an Empire or a United States, such inordinations automatically cease. When Mankind has grown up and shed most of its moronistic traits, when the nations have ceased to keep apart, hugging their sovereignty, only then will they appreciate the principle of Unity in Diversity.
>
> (p. 52)

With World War 2 starting and World War 1 ending only twenty years earlier that must have seemed to many an idealistic hope, if not a totally naive one. The world Scott was advocating did not exist then, does not exist now, but he was prepared to take the long view. He was an idealist and an optimist and believed that his dream of unity would eventually prevail, while accepting that the growing up and maturing of humankind is a painfully slow process, and has still a long way to go.

Part II of *Man is my Theme* is headed 'Pertaining to Religion', and chapter XIII is titled 'Religion neither Understood nor Followed'. Scott begins by pointing out that although religion is a household word, very few people can explain exactly what they mean by it. The dictionary defines it as 'conduct indicating a belief in, reverence for, and desire to please a divine ruling power'. For Scott, the best definition was a Buddhist one: 'a knowledge of the laws of life that lead to happiness'. He frequently takes issue with the Christian religion. 'Christian nations', he says provocatively:

> do not believe in their religion, they merely imagine they do. For except in the imagination there is no such thing as believing in Christ and not believing in His teachings; the more so if the Christians really believe he was the Son of God. Christ unequivocally laid down the principles of human conduct by which man would attain harmony and peace and happiness in this world and felicity in the next. But instead of applying those principles, man for the most part disregards them.
>
> (p. 160)

He cites the biblical injunction to love your enemies and then says (referring to wars past and present) that each side instead tries as hard as possible to demonise the other. The combatants all pray for victory; none of them prays for peace. What is God to do with all these demands for victory, he asks? Even He cannot give it to both, and if He gives it to one, that is showing favouritism, surely unthinkable for the Supreme Deity!

Scott argues that the Old and New Testaments should never have been combined, because Jehovah was basically a tribal god whose warlike and vengeful characteristics are utterly at variance with those of the Heavenly Father of the Christians. Christ came to repudiate Jehovah and denounce war, holding out the idea of Heaven and the Peace of God. The two opposing concepts were thrown together, Scott maintains, because 'Man created God in his own image', not the other way around. In this way Westerners have been able to behave more or less as they wished and still call themselves Christians:

> Should he [Western man] want to go to war, there was the Old Testament to justify him, should he want to be vengeful and have an eye for an eye could he not point to a vengeful Jehovah who set him an example? And, of course, if he sinned he knew there was the God of the New Testament always ready to forgive him.
>
> (p. 163)

Scott was, however, opposed to the doctrine of forgiveness of sins, by which anyone, whatever their crimes and misdeeds, has only to accept Jesus as Christ the Saviour in order to be saved. That is too easy, says Scott, who now introduces the concept of karma. This is simply the law of cause and effect, or, as the New Testament clearly states (Galatians 6:7), 'Be not deceived; God is not mocked for whatsoever a man soweth, that shall he also reap.'

Scott believed in reincarnation and also that there are many souls who, through countless incarnations, have progressed to a point where they choose of their own free will to return to earth to help the rest of us make spiritual progress. Among those initiates he counts Buddha, Mohammad and Jesus.

No single religion, Scott felt, could have a monopoly on truth. Pure white light refracted in a prism splits into all the colours of the rainbow. So too with religion; each contains some of the truth, but none can possess all of it because each one is filtered not only through its founder (whether it be Buddhism, Judaism, Christianity, Islam, and so on), but also by the characteristics of each country and the historical period in which it takes hold. In addition, and adulterating truth even further, there are differences within the same religion – Catholics and Protestants, Sunni and Shia, to cite two obvious examples – each one claiming that it and it alone it is the one true faith. The further it is removed from the source, Scott felt, the more contaminated a religion becomes.

He believed wholeheartedly in the teachings of Jesus, but felt the Church, or 'Churchianity', had misinterpreted and perverted them, and that the idea of an all-merciful God demanding the sacrifice of his only Son was a complete misconception. Christ did not die to save sinners; he *lived* to show sinners how to save themselves from the results of wrong thought and wrong action. Jesus, like Buddha, showed them the way, and it was 'not the way of Judaism but the way from Judaism to a much higher conception of God'. Indeed, Scott had much to say about the Church. The book includes sections called 'Churchianity versus Christ', 'Belief versus Proof', 'Yoga versus Childishness' and, finally, 'Moron Attitude Towards God' (pp. 171–83). They contain many provocative remarks that, if nothing else, provide material for great disagreement and discussion. His final paragraphs in particular are worth noting, where he writes:

> The cultivation of certain virtues and the eradication of certain vices, chief among which is hypocrisy are indispensible to success, hence did Jesus speak so strongly against hypocrites. He said, in effect, 'You cannot expect to attain the goal if you worship God on Sundays and worship Mammon all the week. You cannot expect to contact the Unconditional Happiness if your minds are filled with gloom and doom … And you cannot expect to contact the Universal Love-Consciousness if your minds are poisoned with rancour towards your neighbour or towards your national neighbour. In fine, if you want to be like children and expect to eat your cake and still have it, you will never succeed.' And so it is the old story of lip-service; men treat their Heavenly Parent as children treat their earthly parents; they think that all they have to do is to beg fervently and long enough and their parents will eventually yield to their importunities … even if they have not been 'good children' and have little intention of being good children. Christians pray 'Thy Kingdom come on earth', yet make little attempt to hasten its advent; they merely demand that God should do everything whilst they do nothing.

Readers interested in learning more about Scott's views on Christianity are directed to a separate book, *The Christian Paradox: What is, against what should have been*, which he published in 1942.[4]

The next book in the series, *The Rhymed Reflections of a Ruthless Rhymer*, was completed in late 1944, when the war in Europe was still raging.[5] It is a sixty-three page document written entirely in doggerel. He hoped to print it and even had someone draw cartoons to accompany the text, but it was never published. He claimed to

[4] Published by Rider & Co. Ltd.

[5] *The Rhymed Reflections of a Ruthless Rhymer*, unpublished manuscript in possession of the Cyril Scott Estate.

be writing it solely for his own amusement, but clearly there was a serious purpose behind it, the same one as in the previous books but with a new approach:

> In short, that every reader at the start should know it,
> I only claim herein to be a rhymer, not a poet.
> In hopes that what I have to say through rhyme may be accentuated
> And hence more pleasantly and quickly be assimilated.

One can admire his skill in rhyming 'heartsease' with 'Nazis' ('those miscreants the Nazis / Who over years deprived us of our heartsease'), or 'Mussolini' with 'evil genie'. When speaking of the dangers of extreme nationalism, he gives us:

> 'Tis strange no single noun is yet included in our nomenclature
> For men whose cleverness exceeds by far their moral stature.
> Like – well – the Fuehrer, yes, and why exclude Napoleon?
> Who bent their strong but ill-directed powers wholly on
> Exalting self and nation high above the others.

The message remains unchanged:

> What use are laws and schemes and conferential
> Assemblies if we still ignore this one essential
> Prerequisite to peacefulness? What use the loud petitioning
> For this and that until we turn our hands to re-conditioning
> Our inner selves, and rid us of that infantile myopia
> Through which we make of earth a hell instead of a Utopia?

The doggerel, though amusing to begin with, soon becomes tiresome, and the demands of rhyme lessen the impact of the message. Composing a serious sixty-three page treatise entirely in doggerel is a considerable achievement, and credit must given him for attempting it, but it is, in my own opinion, the least successful of the five books.

Nine years later, in the aftermath of the war and after the shock of the atomic bomb, the final book, *Man the Unruly Child*, was published.[6] Like the other books, with the exception of *Man is my Theme*, *Man the Unruly Child* is short. It reads like a summing up, a restatement of what has come before. The message is unchanged, though less topical, and the writing is simpler, but Scott felt the subject was so important that it needed to be repeated again and again, particularly because, as he remarks in the Aphorisms that end the book:

> Political Man is more childish than children. Unless complete nitwits, children learn from bitter experience, political Man does not.
>
> After one war, disastrous both to vanquished and victors, he immediately starts preparing for the next!

[6] *Man the Unruly Child* (Aquarian Press, 1953).

And:

> It has become a commonplace to say that another war would mean the end of civilisation; but how can there be an end to something that doesn't as yet exist – except in name?

Scott speaks of the devastation caused by love of power, whether in individuals or in nations playing power politics and trying to maintain a balance of power. He insists that the human race has to mature and come to realise that the world 'can never be saved through the love of power but only through the power of love' (p. 16).

There is a chapter in *Man the Unruly Child* where he insists that 'Unselfish children are very rare, unselfish adults are comparatively rare, unselfish politicians are extremely rare and unselfish nations are practically non-existent.' He contends that nations, when they make pacts and form blocs, do so not to work for the common good but selfishly, simply to protect themselves from an opposing bloc of other nations. This may be because of fear, nations being obsessed by the fear of aggression, and then he asks what aggression is, if not an aspect of selfishness, since 'no nation aggresses another nation just for fun; it does so because it wants something for itself'. The fear, he concedes, may be delusional, but he insists that the astronomical sums being spent on defence would be much better used to foster amity and trust among the nations, resulting in the making of the only worthwhile pact, a Pact of Universal Fraternity (his capitals).

Scott felt the times he was living through also provided an unprecedented opportunity for a change of attitude. Unfortunately the attainment of his ideal appears even further away now than it was when he published *Man the Unruly Child* in 1953. He would have been saddened but not overwhelmed by the world today, and would remain essentially optimistic, reminding himself, as he wrote in his first book, *The Way of the Childish*: 'A true philosopher is one who advises but seldom commands and if his advice is not followed he is not resentful, but proceeds calmly along his way.'

23

A Note on the Plays*

DESMOND SCOTT

ADAPTATIONS excepted, Cyril Scott wrote plays with one thought uppermost: how to expand his audience by presenting his ideas in a different format, a format that gave him scope to write prefaces and programme notes to amplify his message. He wrote thirteen plays and three adaptations. His first original play *Prigs in Clover*, written 1926–7, was set to be produced in the West End the following year with one of the leading actors of the day, Dennis Eadie, but circumstances prevented that from happening, and Eadie unexpectedly died before it could be rescheduled.

A Victorian comedy set in the 1880s, the play's major theme is 'What will people *think*?' It deals with a stereotypical Victorian couple who demonstrate many of the qualities the Victorians were thought to have, among them conventionality, sanctimoniousness and hypocrisy. Scott's 'ideal' man, a character who also features in some of the later plays, makes his first appearance. Tolerant, easy-going, totally unprejudiced, eminently reasonable and unconventional, he is always in contrast to the rest of the cast. Here called John, he discovers that his wife, Evelyn, has fallen in love with another man. He is unperturbed:

> Evelyn: Aren't you the least bit angry or jealous? I thought all men were jealous?
>
> John: My dear, jealousy is all very well for primitive people who haven't the brains to know better – and it may be excusable to some extent in persons who've only been married a week; but under all other circumstances it is childish and after some years, that wild romantic passion that so often seems to inspire jealousy, simmers down into a calm affectionate friendship or love like ours, now doesn't it?

He then gives Evelyn a speech that has real feeling and is the most genuine in the whole play:

> Evelyn: Ah, but it's just that simmering down which is so hard for a woman … Do you know what it's like to sit in front of a low fire late at night, and gradually watch it die – feel all its lovely glow fading and leaving you chilled and sad? That's what a woman feels like when she realises that the glow has gone out of her husband's love, and that never again will she hear him say 'I love you' as he used to when he was first in love with her.

* A complete list of the plays can be found in the catalogues at the end of this volume (Cyril Scott's Writings). His views on alternative medicine can be found above, in Chapter 21; his views on childishness in Chapter 22. For a discussion of Scott's ideas on occultism, see Chapter 18

All Scott's plays were written between *c.* 1936 and *c.* 1946, with the exception of *Prigs in Clover* and *Smetse Smee*. Two of them are set in 1937, perhaps because in retrospect 1937 seemed a halcyon year when hope still remained that World War 2 could be averted.

The war years, 1939–1945, were a difficult time for Scott.[1] Nevertheless, during this period he wrote four plays and two adaptations. His first one, written in the late 1920s and the only one to be published, was *Smetse Smee*, a play with music from a story by Charles de Coster. It is discussed fully by Steven Martin in an excellent contribution to this volume (Chapter 14, above).

A second adaptation was of *The Moonstone* by Wilkie Collins, a Victorian novelist contemporary with Charles Dickens and, in his day, almost as popular. Scott's third adaptation was of *Barchester Towers* by Anthony Trollope, another highly respected late-Victorian novelist who wrote a series of novels about the fictional county of Barset, *Barchester Towers* being the second. Scott had recognised its dramatic and comedic potential many years before the BBC produced its very successful series on TV.

Drama tends to be very much a product of its time. The interest for us today is not so much in Scott's plays themselves, but in noting the ways he used drama to spread his ideas. In 1940, when *Bad Samaritans* was written, cancer was such a dreaded disease it could not even be named. Scott had to refer to it as 'krebus', and to radium, the only known orthodox treatment at the time, as 'xadium'. He advocated in the play, as he did in *Victory over Cancer* and other books, a healthy diet and homeopathic or herbal medicines rather than surgery.[2] One of the characters even quotes directly from *Victory over Cancer*: 'What's the cause of most diseases? Faulty nutrition. We eat too many of the wrong things and starve ourselves of the right ones.' In the programme note Scott complained:

> In 1919 a London doctor, since deceased, published a book on the cause and cure of a dreaded disease. But although he substantiated his claims by numerous cures, he was disregarded and neither the hospitals nor any of his colleagues could be induced to take up his simple treatment, based on an observable law of Nature. In more recent times, physicians of various schools have discovered many effective cures for the same dreaded disease. Yet far from receiving any support for their valuable discoveries, they have either been ignored, scoffed at, or even persecuted.

The weakness of *Bad Samaritans* is that neither the argument for, nor that against Scott's view is presented strongly enough; both lack conviction. The physician-hero is far too easily turned from orthodoxy towards embracing more natural remedies for it to be a real contest. Scott, unlike Bernard Shaw, lacked the ability to take two opposed positions and make both equally persuasive.

[1] See Chapters 7 and 20, above.

[2] Books including *Victory over Cancer* (Methuen & Co., 1939); *Childishness* (John Bale, Sons & Danielsson, 1930); *Man is my Theme* (Andrew Dakers Ltd, 1939); *Man the Unruly Child* (Aquarian Press, 1953).

In 1943 Scott wrote *Mrs Maplewood, M.P.* Despite the title this is not primarily about politics, but is a play on two of his recurring themes: childishness[3] and perfect freedom in marriage.[4] In the Preface he reiterated his contention that 'until we begin to realise that our international conduct is nothing short of nursery-behaviour on a gigantic scale – only worse – we cannot hope to have peace and security on the war-ridden globe'.[5] He continued:

> In the world of international politics, for years we have often been faced with the curious fact that a statesman may be 'the most perfect gentleman' in his private life, and yet the most unscrupulous shuffler in his capacity of diplomat. The result of this absurd convention has been inevitable; we have landed ourselves in the abyss. As we cannot hope to govern our individual affairs on a system of lying and cheating, still less can we hope to govern the world.

The play takes place in 1937, when the only professions commonly open to women were teaching or nursing. Having the heroine, Nora, not only an M.P. but an Independent to boot, owing allegiance to no political party, singled her out as a comparative rarity – a career woman with a mind of her own. Sadly, Scott misses the opportunity to explore that aspect. Though there is a short discussion on the childishness of nations and the threat of war, the play hinges not on politics but on personal freedom, and a woman not practising what she preaches. Nora takes a lover, her adoring husband allows it (though it drives him to drink), yet when he, in turn, falls in love and wants a divorce it is another matter. Nora has written books decrying conjugal jealousy and her constituents, she says, would be appalled at a divorce. Her friend, a wise old doctor sums up the situation. 'You have chosen', he says:

> to be one of those many women of the present day who is suspended between the horns of a dilemma; the choice between her married life and her career. But can the two be efficiently combined? Alas, I think not; either the one will have to suffer, or else the other. As women come more and more to be independent ... this is the problem which will increasingly have to be faced in the future.

Whether that problem has been faced is a matter of opinion, but thousands of women today have learned brilliantly how to juggle both marriage and a career.

Throughout the 1940s and for two decades more, the Censor was an important and literally forbidding figure. D. H. Lawrence's *Lady Chatterley's Lover*, for instance, was not allowed unexpurgated in the bookshops until 1960. Every script had first to be submitted to the Censor for approval before it could be performed in public, and it was not uncommon for a play to be banned entirely.

[3] Cyril Scott, *My Years of Indiscretion* (Mills & Boon, 1924), chapter 7. Cyril Scott, *Bone of Contention* (Aquarian Press, 1969), chapter XVIII. See also above, Chapters 17 and 22.

[4] Cyril Scott, *The Art of Making a Perfect Husband* (Harper Brothers, 1929).

[5] See above, Chapter 20.

Not All Men Know also takes place in 1937. Scott is to be commended for daring to tackle the subject with delicacy and understanding. He felt it important enough to warrant two Prefaces. The first begins:

> Psycho-analysis and the modification of prudery relative to matters of sex have brought many startling things to light. One of them is that hundreds of women – strange though it may be – can pass their entire married lives without that satisfaction to their sex nature which, when two people are harmoniously united, is a concomitant of conjugal life. Why this should be so is due to the simple but curious fact that 'not all men know' that lovemaking is more than an instinct, it is also an art; and one, moreover, that requires a due understanding of the opposite sex, particularly on the part of men … countless men are lacking in any real comprehension of women, not only in regard to sex relations but also as regards those psychological differences pertaining to their more delicate organisms. This is one of the reasons which go to create so many unhappy alliances.

Or, as one of the women in the play remarks: 'Just because thousands of men think only of themselves while making love thousands of women go through their married lives thinking men are coarse brutes and wondering what it's all about.' Preface Two repeats much of the above and then refers to censorship, complaining that almost anything was permitted on stage so long as it was not to be taken seriously. In other words, one could write a farce to make people laugh, but not a drama to make them think.

The subject is yet another variation on freedom in marriage, and that in itself would have made the Censor uneasy; the Prefaces most certainly would have given him cause to ban the work, and he promptly did so.

In the play Sybil and James run a guest house and are happily married. When one of their guests, Maisie, confides in Sybil about her unsatisfactory sex life, Sybil suggests her husband make love to Maisie to show her what good sex could be. He obliges and Maisie tells Sybil how much better she feels from the experience. Another guest, Jeanne, also encouraged by Sybil, coaxes her reluctant partner, Maurice, into making love to her. Today the sex would be graphic and would possibly take place in full view, but here all the love-making happens offstage. Nothing in the dialogue is remotely titillating or provocative. There are comedic complications, but finally everything is resolved to the satisfaction of all concerned.

The next play, *Though This Be Madness*, concerns clairvoyance, a subject dear to Scott's heart. Not clairvoyant himself, he depended on those who possessed this ability to keep him in touch with his spiritual master. In the play's Preface he wrote:

> a large section of the public still believes that all psychics are either frauds or charlatans or poseurs, or that clairvoyance and the capacity to see the disembodied are nothing but figments of the imagination. Clairvoyance in its many and varied aspects is a *talent*, like a talent for music, painting and poetry; and a talent, moreover, with which one may be born and which either may be developed or suppressed according to volition or circumstances.

The few clairvoyants seen on stage, he complained, were there either to be exposed or ridiculed, probably having in mind Noel Coward's Madame Arcati in *Blithe Spirit*, which premiered in 1941. But whereas Coward's intent was solely to amuse, Scott's comedies were also designed to encourage his audiences to think, so there are references to reincarnation, another of his core beliefs.[6]

The hero of the play is George Winslow, a psychic who can see the spirits of the dead and correctly predict the future. He is another version of Scott's idealised man, to be set in opposition to the rest of his family. As the play opens the old butler is taken ill and needs an operation, whereupon George declares that: 'Surgery is a monument to medical incompetence. When doctors can't cure an organ they frighten us into having it out and say God didn't know his business when he put it there in the first place.'[7] The butler subsequently dies. In the last act George tells his mother and sister, Gladys, that he sees the dead butler frequently and that he often comes to visit them, whereupon Gladys says: 'Often comes to see us? Good Lord, that means he might see us in our bath or God knows where!' The idea of disembodied spirits seeing us in inconvenient places was one that clearly amused Scott, for he used the same joke years later in *The Boy Who Saw True*.[8]

The final play to be considered, and probably the last one Scott wrote, is *Malice in Blunderland*. Undated, the action takes place in 1945. It is a sprawling, loosely structured play with too many characters and lacking a firm dramatic arc. Indeed, it is more of an illustrated lecture on Scott's core philosophy than it is a regular play. He called it a Diversion, perhaps signalling that it was not to be taken too seriously, but from our point of view it is an important work because the form allows him to give free rein to all his deeply felt occult and spiritual beliefs. Reincarnation, karma and the evolution of the soul, love, religion, childishness and politics are all thrown into the mix. One might think of it as a present-day version of Dante's *Inferno*.

A major part of the action takes place on the Astral Plane, as Scott referred to it, which is where everyone goes when asleep and dreaming, though most people cannot remember their experiences when they wake. It is a spirit world similar to the Catholic Purgatory. As in Dante, there are various levels in this realm, but we are concerned with just two. The first seems to be where the average person with a normal mixture of virtues and vices goes. The other is a lower region, closer to what we might think of as hell. Our guides on this Astral Plane are Bill and his girlfriend, Julia, who are among the few who can recall their dreams when awake. After a series of emotional, spiritual and medical problems they have achieved a degree of enlightenment.

There is a sub-plot concerning Bill and the dysfunctional marriage to Susan, his unloving wife, and the play jumps back and forth between their problems on earth and the surreal activities on the Astral Plane, where we find broad caricatures of Hitler, Mussolini and Goebbels, who all blame each other for their defeats and refuse to accept culpability for the atrocities they have committed. They are suffering the effects of their actions on earth and the bad karma these have generated for them.

[6] Cyril Scott, *An Outline of Modern Occultism* (Routledge & Sons, 1935).

[7] Cyril Scott, *Doctors, Disease and Health*, 2nd edn (True Health Publishing, 1946).

[8] Cyril Scott, *The Boy Who Saw True* (Neville Spearman, 1953).

We meet a variety of characters; some do not realise they are dead, others are bewildered, looking for friends to help reorient them in their unfamiliar surroundings.

Among these characters is Queen Victoria, who insists that nations must stop thinking only of themselves and learn to act for the good of all nations, or else civilisation will perish. She is joined by Bismarck and Napoleon, who are there to demonstrate Scott's belief in reincarnation and the evolution of the soul. We see how their attitudes have changed. Bismarck still holds that his unification of Germany was a good thing but concedes that the extreme nationalism of Hitler was disastrous. Napoleon hopes that in his next incarnation he may return not as a conqueror, but as a warrior of peace.

A Sage appears, says his sole aim and those of his brother Initiates is to help their fellow creatures, and voices Scott's views that: 'Had Man shed his childishness and grown to years of wisdom he would long since have known that only through brotherhood and good-will among the nations could peace and security be attained. It was not wisdom to desire peace, yet *do* all the things that create wars.'

Looking over at Hitler and Mussolini, who appear to be in agony, the Sage says there is no evading the law, and that those who caused suffering to others must suffer themselves. Though he feels compassion for them, he is powerless to help. He tells Bill and Julia, who have witnessed it all, that nothing is due to chance in the cosmos, and reminds them that the purpose of reincarnation is to acquire through countless lives the lessons and experiences necessary for the evolution of the soul. He ends his homily by explaining that:

> as Man evolves from the material to the more spiritual, the great gulf between the embodied and the disembodied will become increasingly narrowed … death will lose its sting and its terrors and Man will come to *know*, and not merely to hope or believe, that he is truly immortal.

He encourages them by pointing out that having acquired a measure of knowledge and some memory of the afterlife they can be of great help to their less enlightened fellow pilgrims.

Cyril Scott in his many and varied writings was also trying to help his fellow pilgrims, and his plays were yet another way of doing that. As he wrote in one of his notebooks: 'Everything has been said before many times, so all an author can hope for is to make people heed it by saying it differently.'

XVIII Rose Scott, *née* Allatini, a.k.a. novelist Eunice Buckley, A. T. Fitzroy etc.

XIX Rose and Cyril on holiday in the Harz mountains

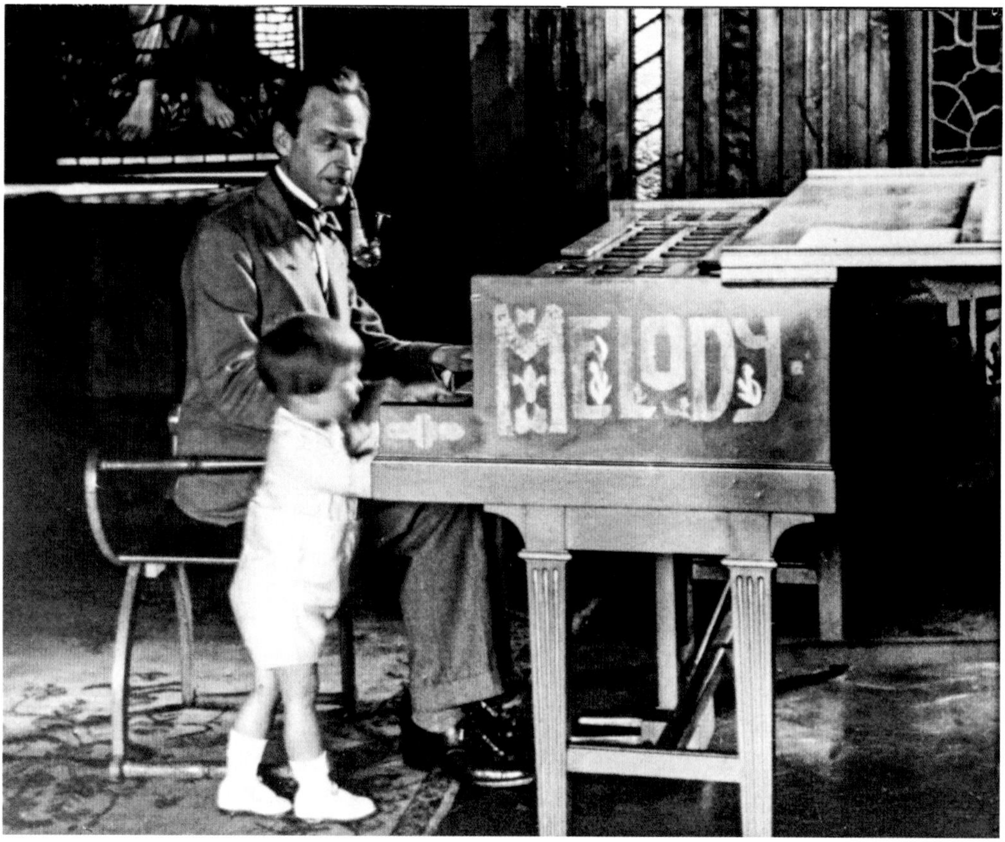

XX Scott at the piano with his son, Desmond; the lettering on the piano, designed by Melchior Lechter, reads 'Melody is the cry of Man to God'; round the other side is written 'Harmony is God's answer to Man'

XXI The Scott family with Taurus the cat

BEATRICE HARRISON

WILL GIVE

A

'Cello Recital

AT THE

WIGMORE HALL

ON

WED., MARCH 15, at 7 p.m.

The programme will include

First performance of

Sonata for 'Cello and Piano — *Cyril Scott*

ASSISTED AT THE PIANO BY

MARGARET HARRISON

AND

CHARLES LYNCH

Management: HAROLD FIELDING AGENCY DIVISION

TICKETS: 9/-, 6/- and 3/-

May be obtained from Wigmore Hall (Wel. 2141); Chappell's Box Office (May. 7600), and all Ticket Agents

PORTRAIT BY FRANK O. SALISBURY, G.V.O., LL.D., R.P.

XXII Programme of Beatrice Harrison playing Scott's Cello Sonata

XXIII The house in Eastbourne, 53 Pashley Road, where Scott moved with Marjorie in 1955

XXIV Marjorie and Scott with Scott's grand-daughter Amanta, aged five

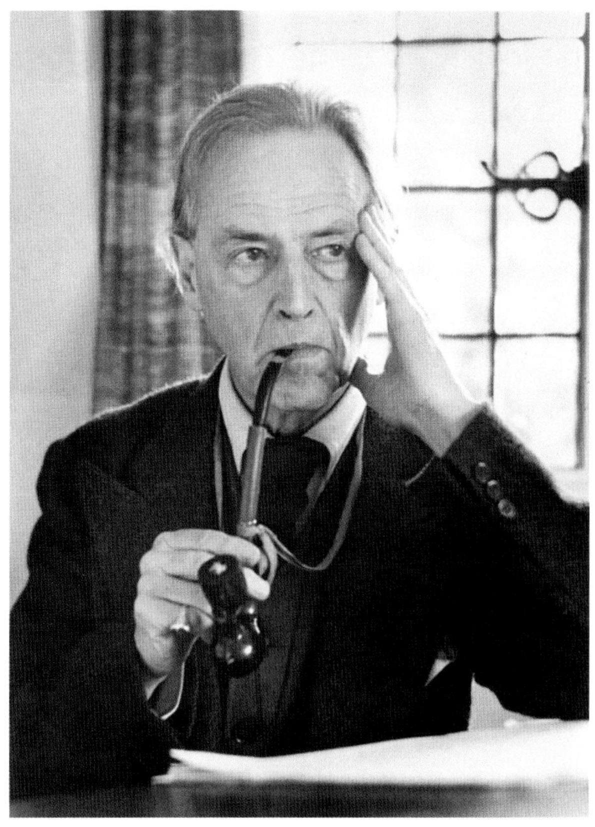

XXV Scott smoking the special pipe with the water-filled glass bowl he designed and had made

XXVI Scott in his eighties, still composing

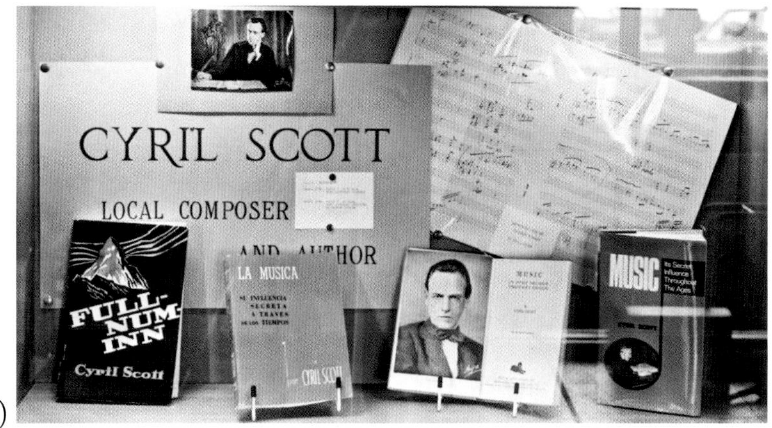

(i)

(ii)

XXVII (i and ii) Display in Eastbourne celebrating Scott's ninetieth birthday

Plate XXVIII (i) Desmond Scott with conductor Martin Yates and pianist Peter Donohoe at Watford after completing their recording of the Piano Concerto in D (1900) in November 2012

Plate XXVIII (ii) Martin Yates with pianist Peter Donohoe during their recording session for the Piano Concerto in D (1900) discuss a point of interpretation

CYRIL SCOTT SOCIETY

President : SIR THOMAS ARMSTRONG

A Concert of Music

BY

Cyril Scott

in

The Duke's Hall, Royal Academy of Music

on Friday, May 1st, 1964 at 8 p.m.

Artists will include

JOHN OGDON, PETER PEARS, EDMUND RUBBRA AND THE ALBERNI QUARTET

Admission by programme - price 7/6

(Full-time music students 3/9)

Obtainable at the door, or from the Secretary of the Cyril Scott Society, c/o London College of Music, Great Marlborough Street, London, W1.

(After April 23rd)

XXIX Programme for 'A Concert of Music by Cyril Scott', 1 May 1964, at the Royal Academy of Music

XXX Montage of covers for Cyril Scott recordings, specially created for this book by Amanta Scott

(i)

XXXI (i–iii)
Three of Scott's landscape paintings featuring rocks, trees and water – some of his favourite subjects

(ii)

(iii)

IV

PERSONAL REMINISCENCES

24

Cyril Scott: A Personal Memory

KATHERINE HUDSON

CYRIL Scott (1879–1970) had already been a friend of my mother, Yvonne O'Neill's, family for sixty-five years when I was sent to stay with him and his partner, Marjorie Hartston-Scott, at their home in Sussex in the spring of 1961. I was seventeen and it was the first time we had met. Cyril was of course part of the mythology of my childhood: his genius, his music, his unorthodox beliefs, his cloaks and wide-brimmed hats – all this I knew. So it was with some curiosity that I packed my bag and took the train to Eastbourne during the spring holiday from the London Academy of Music and Dramatic Art, where I was training to become an actress.

My grandfather, the composer Norman O'Neill, had first met Cyril in Frankfurt, where both were pupils of the composer Iwan Knorr at the Frankfurt Conservatory of Music. My grandmother, Adine Rückert, who had been a pupil of the pianist Clara Schumann, had met and become engaged to my grandfather while both were still students there. Clara Schumann's death in 1896 required that Adine returned home to Paris – but her absence prompted a long correspondence between the engaged couple, exchanging news of the musical world in Frankfurt, Paris and London (now in the British Library).

Norman's first meeting with Cyril, in 1896, was actually recorded in one such letter to Adine:

> I had the little English boy to tea on Monday – I told you about him I think. He has a very great talent for composition – and such good fingers! It was rather nice to see a regular English schoolboy again and to hear all those old school expressions again![1]

That was probably the last time Cyril was so described. The regular English schoolboy was soon to be introducing my grandfather to the poet Stefan George (an hilarious encounter for Norman), writing poetry himself, and adopting the flamboyant costume that became his hallmark.

In 1897 my grandfather left Frankfurt and returned to London; but in the following year Adine visited her friends still studying at the Conservatory – sending a lively report back to Norman on the progress of Cyril and of his new friend, Percy Grainger. Her command of English was not yet perfected at this time:

[1] BL 71456–71472, O'Neill Papers. These two letters are from the correspondence of Norman and Adine O'Neill contained in the collection presented to the British Library in 1994. They were transcribed for this article from a recorded talk I gave to the Delius Society in 1991, and the punctuation may not therefore be identical to the original. Other letters presented by Mrs K. Jessel (Katherine Hudson) have been kindly made available by the British Library.

> Today the little Scott came. He played me an amount of work. Not *all* Knorr says that the quantity of things he has done since the summer is quite wonderful. A Trio, a String Quartet, a Sonata piano and violin, a Sonata piano etc. He played me Preludes for the piano – some of them are nice but others I did not care. The Trio is awfully nice – but the String Quartet is really the best – and so clever too – I know you would like it. He gets so excited at the performance of his works! After we went together to the Graingers and we made Percy play some of his compositions. It's awful! And sounds so queer! The Themes are nice but spoiled by awful discordings, harmonies – the little chap – he enjoys that! We had tea – and Scott went to the piano and for an whole hour played Tristan and Isolde – but perfectly wonderful the way he did it and he got more and more excited – got quite mad, and we really were obliged to stop him otherwise we should still be there![2]

Norman and Adine were married in 1899 and settled down in London, where eventually O'Neill was made Musical Director of the Theatre Royal, Haymarket – creating incidental music to such plays as J. M. Barrie's *Mary Rose* and Maeterlinck's *The Blue Bird*, which was to make his name. Adine founded the music department at St Paul's Girls' School in 1903, and was responsible for the appointment of Gustav Holst as Music Director, a post he held until his death in 1934. Adine herself became a well-known pianist and teacher, famous for her pioneering piano recitals on the BBC from the 1920s onwards. It was on these programmes that she played much of Cyril's piano music, including, famously, *An English Waltz*. These pieces gave Cyril an early reputation as a miniaturist and led to his becoming well known as 'the English Debussy'.

Indeed, at the turn of the twentieth century Cyril was in fact the most successful member of the 'Frankfurt Gang' – as the Frankfurt friends became known. By 1903 his *Heroic Suite* had been conducted by Richter in Liverpool and Manchester, and his two symphonies had already been performed in Darmstadt and London. Scott and Grainger, together with Balfour Gardiner and Roger Quilter (also members of the Frankfurt Gang), were remarkable in remaining lifelong friends, as a group photograph taken at the 1929 Harrogate Festival confirms (Plate XII). However, while Cyril saw more of Norman once they had all settled in London, it is certain that my grandfather did not have as much in common with him as he did, say, with Balfour Gardiner (who lived opposite to the O'Neills in Pembroke Villas, Kensington) or Roger Quilter. Cyril's eventual embracing of occultism, to which Adine, who had been brought up in Burma, was probably more sympathetic, simply reduced Norman to gales of laughter.

'Although serious *au fond*', Cyril recalled, he appeared to take nearly everything in life as a joke, including myself. My philosophical outlook, my interest in Occultism, almost everything I said or did, he treated as subjects of intense amusement.' With Adine, however, he felt he could 'discuss serious matters seriously, whereas with her husband never'.[3] Yet Adine had her own wry detachment. A letter dated

[2] As above.

[3] From Cyril Scott, *Bone of Contention* (Aquarian Press 1969).

2 November (in the year 1922, since it mentions Norman's visit to America) had been carefully preserved to demonstrate Cyril's curious attitude of mind: 'Rose [his wife] is expecting a baby in January. It is a premeditated event. Master requested us to have it to provide a vehicle for a particular ego that wanted to come to us.' My grandmother placed an asterisk above the word 'have' and wrote in the margin: 'to *have it* is glorious!! Adine.'[4]

That 'ego' was Cyril's daughter, Vivien, born in 1923: her brother, Desmond, was to venture a similar incarnation three years later.

Norman actually took Cyril a good deal more seriously than perhaps he realised. 'Scott seems to be getting on awfully well & getting his things played', Norman wrote to his friend Carlo Fischer in 1900: 'I tell everybody (not HIM) that he is the most talented person in England! And I really begin to think he is! Tho' you will say perhaps that that is not saying much!!'[5] Nevertheless, Cyril's many other interests were to mean a neglect of his music. Norman doubtless felt he was wasting his talents through his involvement with occultism, diet and so forth – what we would now call his 'lifestyle' – and hence my grandfather's stubborn refusal to concern himself with it.

Over the years Cyril came to have a special relationship with my mother, Yvonne – whom he called 'Greta' after the celebrated film star. (Unfortunately, since Garbo famously 'never smiled', very few photographs survive of my mother looking even reasonably cheerful.) When Yvonne fell ill in 1932 with rheumatic fever, which necessitated her being confined to bed for a long period, Cyril walked over to Kensington from his home in Ladbroke Grove every week to see her, bearing a large bunch of Lily of the Valley. These she was instructed to sniff deeply as they were *Convallaria* and good for the heart.

Cyril accepted death in accordance with his philosophy – and so he comforted my mother on the demise of both her parents with the certainty of the life – indeed lives – to come. Norman had been the first to go, very suddenly, as the result of a road accident on 3 March 1934. 'Darling Greta', wrote Cyril to my mother:

> All my sympathy dear. I wish you could have been spared such a loss at your age, but there it is, & perhaps you will get a little comfort if you try and realise that your father will be happier in a world that is so much more joyful than this one. When you feel you want to see me I will come. Meanwhile many many loving thoughts my dear.
> Always your friend.
> Cyril[6]

The death of Adine, however, in 1947 clearly came as a more personal shock:

[4] Letter from Cyril Scott to Adine O'Neill. BL Ms Mus 932, fols 84–5.

[5] From copies of letters from Norman O'Neill to Carlo Fischer, 'statements about Cyril Scott's music'. Unknown source. Typescript in my possession.

[6] Letter from Cyril Scott to Yvonne O'Neill, n.d. [March 1934], in my possession.

> My dear, it is a hard thing to lose one's mother, as there is such a strong link between parent & offspring & one feels the separation very acutely. As for myself, I have lost a very old friend and a strong link with the past. Your mother was a great personality & I knew no one at all like her. She has gone to a more joyous plane & I am sure with her views & tastes she will enjoy a richer life. But we shall miss her very much & the world of music has lost a fine artist.[7]

I knew no detail of this rich hinterland as the taxi propelled me from Eastbourne station to 53 Pashley Road. Indeed, it had been very courageous of Cyril and Marjorie to have me to stay with them at all: a week would have been a long time to suffer an uncongenial guest in their very exceptional household – but I was Adine and Norman's grand-daughter, and that I suppose was enough.

The house – *Santosa* – was a reassuringly ordinary detached home looking out across the Downs to the sea. Inside some attempt had been made to recreate the neo-Gothic style of Cyril's youth. Wall cupboards and other green-painted furnishings turned out on closer inspection to be little more than theatrical scenery – but the refectory table in the dining room was solid enough. It was here that I was startled one lunchtime to find Cyril in a yoga headstand beside his chair as I brought in the tray for our vegetarian meal.

The sitting room was cosy with pictures and books and contained Cyril's piano – painted green with trails of flowers around the case. At a desk by the window he worked on his compositions every morning before marching me briskly out across the Downs, swinging his stick. Cyril whistled as he strode along – he was an excellent *siffleur* – and this was a pleasant and soothing accompaniment to our walk.

My own simple room was at the back of the house, looking onto the garden which sloped up the Down. A portrait of a spirit guide hung over the mantelpiece.

I had not been long in the house when a rather unfortunate incident took place. Cyril was exceedingly fond of Siamese cats and at that time owned three. I loved animals, and to my delight they settled on my lap and on my shoulders. But not for long. Soon my face was swelling uncontrollably; my eyes watered and my nose ran. The cats were banished to a room of their own for the duration of my stay, homoeopathic remedies were sought, and I was taken by Marjorie into the garden to be hoovered thoroughly on the end of a long flex. The pair of us laughed uncontrollably over this unexpected activity – but tears welled up in Cyril's eyes at the sight of my distressed condition and it looked for a moment as if my stay was over before it had begun.

In fact we were to spend many happy hours walking, reading and taking trips out to the local countryside in a taxi. In the evenings Cyril played the piano to Marjorie and me, and we explored his library. I had brought with me my recorder, which I was learning for a Shakespeare performance at LAMDA, and a fellow student, John Toye (the son of my grandfather's assistant at the Haymarket, the composer Geoffrey Toye), had obligingly written a descant part for the Bach two-part Invention in C major as an exercise. This we tried out together, and rather to Cyril's surprise it was quite successful. 'Yes! It works!'

[7] Letter from Cyril Scott to Yvonne Hudson. BL Ms Mus 933, fol. 91.

He also read from *The Ghost of a Smile* (1939) – a book that he wrote because 'Life is too serious to be taken seriously' (thus perhaps endorsing my grandfather's own outlook). It is dedicated to his Frankfurt friends – Grainger, Quilter and Gardiner. The reading took place at the kitchen table – Cyril on one side and me on the other, as Marjorie prepared the dinner. Under the heading 'Unintentional Humour in Poetical Utterance', Cyril started to read:

> What I would emphasise is, that a cake of butter (though it may be curiously reminiscent of 'the moon and green cheese') appears to be so common a simile in India that even I have had it applied to my unillustrious self. Indeed the passage from the article in which it occurs is typical enough to be quoted; the writer of the said article, after having described at some length how he called at my house, goes on to say:
>
> 'Meanwhile in the cool shade of this closet, a treasure-house so to term it, of the devices of the Goddess of artistic inspiration, drinking in the nectar of its peacefulness and tabulating in my memory its multitudinous objects of beauty – I awaited the arrival of the proprietor' [Cyril looked up – we were coming to the denouement]. 'Then unostentatiously, *like a cake of butter,* Musician Scott entered the closet [really these archaisms!] and graciously saluted me.'

It was hilarious – and highly appropriate to our culinary setting. It was some time before I could look at butter in the same way again.

My stay was gentle, funny and fun. 'I enjoyed every minute of my visit', I wrote to them both afterwards, 'and loved your home, and the countryside – and even your cats!!!'[8]

We were not to meet again for another four years, though Cyril kept in touch with lively responses to our postcards. 'How nice of you to remember us on your holiday', he wrote in 1962, 'You may be amused to hear that there is an agitation afoot to form a "Cyril Scott Society". None of my doing. I feel honoured, but I also feel rather embarrassed at being the subject of a Society, at any rate while still alive to some extent!'[9] The Cyril Scott Society in fact did come into being, championed by Sir Thomas Armstrong, with a concert in the Duke's Hall at the Royal Academy of Music – but it did not flourish. Nevertheless, during these years Cyril, with the wonderful support of Marjorie, continued to compose – and his compositions of that time are finding favour now.

Despite my happy association with Cyril, it amazes me that, with the audacity of youth, I invited myself to stay again. I was by now working professionally in the theatre, and finding that a touring production I was appearing in was to include a week at the Congress Theatre, Eastbourne, I wrote to Cyril and Marjorie suggesting myself as a theatrical lodger. I dare not think of the consternation this must have created in their quiet, well-ordered home: I was not a young student any more but a noisy theatrical, banging home late at night, lounging around during the day – the cats!

[8] Letter from me to Cyril Scott and Marjorie Hartston-Scott, n.d., thanking them for my stay in April 1961; in my possession (given by Desmond Scott).

[9] Letter from Cyril Scott to D. and Y. Hudson. BL Ms Mus 936, fol. 7.

13.9.64

My dear Dilly.
I am writing for Marjorie whose life is even more hectic than my own!

Although we both love you dearly, and are happy to hear we will have the chance of seeing you here – and in your professional capacity at that – I'm afraid your proposal is not quite as simple as it sounds. We live a long way from the Congress theatre, and it is a good distance walk even to reach the nearest bus, which only runs infrequently to that theatre. This would mean that you would have to take taxis every night to and from the theatre.

Also, of prime importance, is that you are allergic to cats, of which we have now 4, and they are in full Autumn molt [*sic*]. You may have forgotten the dire effect that had on your charming face (wealds [*sic*] swelling etc) the last time you stayed with us. This would be a major disaster for you in the present circumstances and one for which we would feel terribly responsible (or terribly anxious all the time lest it <u>should</u> happen again.)

So all in all we reluctantly feel it would be distinctly unwise for you to put up here – though needless to say there is no question of us not wanting you. I'm sure you'll agree it is better not.

Glad the show is a success, and we look forward to seeing you in it.[10]

'My dear Cyril', I hastily replied from Cardiff:

> 'Many thanks for your sweet letter. <u>Of course</u> I quite understand: you are right – it would be much easier to stay in 'digs'.
>
> Actually, I had forgotten how far you were from the theatre – and had temporarily forgotten the cats: although the memory will never entirely be eradicated![11]

True to their word, Cyril and Marjorie duly turned up at the Congress Theatre for an evening performance of *No! No! Nanette!* I do not recall that they let me know which night they were coming – and it was something of a shock when, after the show, an excited colleague popped her head round the dressing-room door: 'Kate! There's an *incredibly* old man wandering about the corridors – and he says he is looking for *you*!' Cyril!

Somehow farce was never far away when Cyril, Marjorie and I were together. Having escorted them down to the stage door, where a taxi was waiting, I was relieved to see them safely installed and to be waving them away without apparent mishap. I turned to find a puzzled Larry Drew – our leading man – standing on the pavement. He too was waiting for his taxi, which had not yet turned up. My heart sank. Yes – moments later Cyril's own taxi arrived, by which time he and Marjorie had vanished into the night towards Mr Drew's theatrical lodgings on the opposite side of town. Larry was annoyed, the taxi driver was annoyed, and we all hung around the stage door waiting for Cyril's return. After an agitated ten minutes or so

[10] Letter from Cyril Scott to Katherine Jessel. BL Ms Mus 936, fol. 16.

[11] Letter from me to Cyril Scott, 16 September 1964; in my possession (given by Desmond Scott).

they came into view – Marjorie roaring with laughter and Cyril (who did not find *this* so amusing) extricated himself from Larry's taxi and clambered into his own. After fresh 'goodbyes' they set off again, this time in the right direction. Two things puzzled me about this incident. Had anyone paid for the unscheduled 'Eastbourne-by-night' excursion? (I didn't like to ask.) And how could even a taxi driver have imagined that such a very elderly gentleman as Cyril Scott be starring in a touring production of *No! No! Nanette!*

Since my relations with Cyril were almost familial – I still have a nursery song book signed 'from "Uncle Cyril"', and he had clearly become a father-figure to my mother – I was never consciously storing up memories for the future (like the journalist for whom Cyril was *a cake of butter*). I can say, however, that I was aware of his being a unique human being – an almost Sarastro-like figure at this stage – and if his beliefs were unusual, then they certainly had a calming and broadening influence on his spirit. Cyril enjoyed the company of young people, and was generous and uncritical towards their gaiety and aspirations. I do regret that at the time of life that I knew Cyril I was inclined, like my grandfather before me, to take life as a joke – but perhaps by then even this characteristic had come to have something to be said for it.

Cyril and I last met on 31 October 1969, shortly after his ninetieth birthday, at a concert at the Queen Elizabeth Hall, London. I was by then twenty-six years old and my touring days were behind me. Cyril, alas, was very frail, and his sight was beginning to fade. He had been accompanied to London by Marjorie and his godson, Rohinten Mazda.

Bryan Fairfax conducted the Polyphonia Orchestra in a mixed programme of Milhaud, Debussy, Prokofiev and Britten. Cyril's first piano concerto was the penultimate item, with Moura Lympany as soloist. It was thrilling to hear this seldom-performed work (which Cyril himself had dismissed as 'lengthy and pretentious'.) I hope he had more cheerful feelings towards it on that occasion, close as he seemed to a renewed success, with his many friends about him. Yet as he appeared on stage in a velvet smoking jacket – joined by his old associate Lionel Tertis – a curtain seemed to be coming down.

After the concert I made my way through the throng of people gathering round him: 'Cyril – it's me!' He looked up into my face and lifted a hand – his eyes filling with tears. And I had the strange feeling that it was not myself who was standing there at all, but my own grandfather – and this was not 1969, but a long, long time ago in a misty past, when all was young and ready for discovery, poised to create a brand new world.

25

Reminiscences

ROHINTEN DADDY MAZDA

I was about eight years old when the name Cyril Scott registered with me. My maternal grandfather had been a theosophist and was acquainted with some of C.S.'s works, and so from an early age my mother had been familiar with these teachings.[1] Moreover, Mr Mehta, an old family friend and theosophist, had acted as an elder brother or mentor to my mother from early womanhood. From all accounts he was a fine and noble soul who had introduced my mother to a wider range of C.S.'s writings and other occult and esoteric works. From childhood my sister and I had been introduced by our mother to cider vinegar, crude black molasses, other health foods and alternative medicines, as advocated by C.S. in his publications.

Theosophy literally means 'Divine Wisdom', from the Greek *theosophia*: *theos*, divine; and *sophia*, wisdom. It may be described as the science of invisible forces. It is the synthesis of philosophy, science and religion – a seeking of knowledge of the Divine Principle, of man's relations to it and nature's manifestations of it. Reincarnation, karma and spiritual evolution are central to theosophy. Theosophy teaches universal brotherhood and the divinity of man. It is a knowledge of 'being' at all levels, which governs the evolution of the physical, astral, psychical and intellectual constituents of nature and of man. This ageless wisdom is synonymous with everlasting truth.

Mr Mehta was a great admirer of C.S. and had been in correspondence with him for many years. So when it was decided that I should be sent to boarding school in England, Mr Mehta wrote to C.S. asking if he could help a dear friend find a suitable preparatory school for her only son. He must have agreed.

By way of brief family background, my paternal grandfather left his home in Yazd in the 1890s, at the age of sixteen, to make a new life and seek his fortune in India. Yazd, an ancient city in the centre of Persia, was always a stronghold of the ancient Zoroastrian religion. On both sides of the family we had always been Zoroastrians – the only religion in the world that does not take converts. My grandfather had come from a poor rural background and died in Calcutta in 1969, having accumulated a self-made fortune through various business enterprises, beginning with a chain of provisions stores. He had taught himself English and some Indian languages. Both my parents and my sister and I usually spoke English at home. Through my grandfather's business contacts, both in Britain and India, and because he held in high esteem the 'sterling qualities of the British', he decided to send my father to boarding school in England in 1927. In 1937, at the age of eighteen, my father returned to Calcutta and joined his father in business.

[1] I have referred to Cyril Scott as C.S. (at Marjorie's suggestion), as this is what I called him in his lifetime. 'Cyril' would have been disrespectful owing to my age, and 'Mr Scott' too formal. Even after C.S.'s passing, both with Marjorie and other friends who knew Cyril Scott, it was always C.S. in conversation and in writing.

Having been so impressed by his years in England, and thinking the British boarding-school education the best in the world, my father decided to send me to school in England too. I never returned to settle in India, but made England my home. My mother and I landed in London on 9 June 1956. We flew from Calcutta in an Air India four-propellered Constellation. I was then aged ten, and this was my first international flight and, indeed, my first trip abroad. I recall we had several stops to refuel and take on new passengers, and it felt exciting to be in transit at all the stopovers. The entire journey took approximately thirty-six hours.

Soon after landing we travelled to Eastbourne by train, and then took a taxi to meet Cyril Scott at his home: 53 Pashley Road (the house was called Santosa). I was destined to make this journey on several occasions until 1967; thereafter, I drove down in my first car – a Vauxhall Viva, which was a twenty-first-birthday present from my parents.

Before I met Cyril Scott I had the strong impression that he was a famous and accomplished man, and it was clear to me that my mother held him in high regard. Under my mother's protective wing, I was not at all daunted by the occasion. My first meeting with him was in June, and I was oblivious of all the adult conversation that must have ensued regarding my boarding school to be. I recall being most warmly greeted by C.S. and Marjorie Hartston-Scott. I felt totally at ease in their company.

Marjorie always exuded great affection and had a lovely smile. She had met Cyril in 1943 through occult and karmic links, and lived with him and cared for him most lovingly as a companion; she helped in every way the furtherance of his life's work. Whenever I met C.S., Marjorie was always there.

On this visit I was thrilled to play with Bobo, the Siamese cat at Santosa. At home in Calcutta we also had a Siamese cat. Through a surfeit of affection and stroking, I must have irritated Bobo, who promptly scratched my hand, drawing blood, much to the consternation of C.S. and Marjorie! During the afternoon Marjorie served us a wonderful selection of sandwiches and cakes, which was the case on all my subsequent visits. We returned to London that day, and I was not to see C.S. and Marjorie again till my mid teens, by which time I was at Milton Abbey public school in Dorset. Through C.S.'s efforts and contacts I was to begin at Little Abbey preparatory school near Newbury, Berkshire, in September 1956. I seem to recall that my mother told me that the second headmaster, a Mr Lock, knew Cyril Scott through his writings and had corresponded with him. So that was the link to my joining Little Abbey, where I was very happy until I left in 1959. Furthermore, Dr Mary Austin, a medical practitioner in alternative medicines who knew Cyril Scott, had agreed to act as my guardian in England, in spite of leading a busy professional career in London. She looked after my needs, *in loco parentis,* along with her partner, Brigadier R. C. Firebrace, CBE who, unusual among military men, was an expert astrologer.

When I was sixteen, in Calcutta during my long summer holidays, my mother gave me the *Initiate* trilogy, which she said had had a profound impact upon her life, and so it proved to be with me too. I well remember my father repeatedly calling for me to join him and my mother at the dining table, and my being quite unable to put down the first volume, so absorbed was I. I devoured these books, my first introduction both to C.S.'s writing and to the world of the Masters. This awakening was like sudden light, reminding me of a line from a Dante Gabriel Rossetti poem, 'some veil did fall, – I knew it all of yore'. I felt a new dimension had been added to my life.

At the age of eighteen, in 1964, I had published in our school magazine an article entitled 'Theosophy: An Introduction to "The Great Ones"', much to the amusement of some, who probably thought that either I was very impressionable or I had lost my marbles! I sent a copy to C.S. and Marjorie. Marjorie wrote me a wonderfully warm and encouraging letter on behalf of C.S. and herself, which sadly I cannot now find.

I visited C.S. and Marjorie on several occasions at their home in Eastbourne after having left school at the end of 1964, and was always treated with great love and affection. I would visit for the day, either for tea with the usual wonderful array of sandwiches and cakes that Marjorie would prepare, or on occasion to lunch in the dining room midst C.S.'s Pre-Raphaelite oak furniture, some of which was designed by him. Our conversations circled around the occult and music and poetry to some extent, but C.S. and Marjorie were always interested to hear how my life and studies were progressing. I was studying for the Bar exams as a member of the Inner Temple.

It was the world of the occult and that Hierarchy of Initiates known as the Mahatmas, Masters of Wisdom or The Great White Brotherhood that occupied my thoughts. One of the highest Initiates among them, known as Master Koot Hoomi (K. H. for short), had been C.S.'s main guide. C.S. had first made conscious contact with him in the flesh in 1920. I had always understood that this link through several previous lives had been a cornerstone of inspiration and deep belief for both himself and Marjorie. K. H. was also Marjorie's Master. Marjorie told me that she had acquired the ability to hear Master K. H.'s voice 'as clear as a bell' whenever he wished to communicate regarding C.S.'s work, or for whatever reason, without his actually materialising. Marjorie was to be C.S.'s final link with Master K. H. He and Marjorie had also told me that since 1944 Master K. H. had appeared often to give guidance or suggestions relevant to C.S.'s work or other mundane matters connected with it. One day in the late 1960s, when Marjorie had left the room to make tea, C.S. told me 'I can't see, but she can.' Much has been written in occult literature as to the reason for these things, which C.S. too has fully covered in his works.

After April 1967, when I acquired my first car, I would meet C.S. and Marjorie at Victoria Station on their various visits to London and drive them to their destination. On one occasion I well remember C.S. was in the front passenger seat with Marjorie seated behind him. I had recently re-read the *Initiate* trilogy and was persistently probing as to his true identity in that narrative. This was the only time I ever saw C.S. lose his equilibrium – he got quite irritated with me. Marjorie soon diffused the situation and all was calm once again.

Incidentally, long before *Bone of Contention*, C.S.'s last autobiography, was published, he had told me that Master K. H. had informed him that he had been a musician in his past two lives. As to the detail, this could not be divulged, though he had been out of incarnation for thirty years after his previous life. According to C.S., he derived some pleasure from hearing the works he wrote in his more recent existence, and with a few exceptions was bored by those of his earlier one.

A few other specific memories stand out for me. On one occasion when I had driven down in the late 1960s, having been invited for tea, C.S. was at his Broadwood baby grand piano in the bay window, working on a composition. Old and frail as he was, the sheer speed and agility of his Chopinesque hands in their movement across the entire keyboard amazed me. This facility and fluidity belied his age, and this image remains in my mind's eye.

My mother had always kept in contact with C.S. and Marjorie. She had also been back to Eastbourne with me on her visits to England in the late 1960s, and had met C.S. and Marjorie on more than one occasion. On one of these visits to Santosa, on 30 July 1969, C.S. had warmly inscribed my copies of the *Initiate* trilogy. I still have the photographs of all of us together in the front garden of the house, which I treasure. On another occasion, shortly before C.S. died, we had met him and Marjorie for tea at the Grosvenor Hotel in Victoria. That was the first time I met Lady Baron, the wonderful New Zealand-born concert pianist Esther Fisher, who had been a lifelong friend of C.S.'s from the time they met in the late 1920s. C.S., I well recall, was silent most of the time, and being very frail was leaning with his head on his folded hands upon his walking stick. Esther asked Marjorie if he was well, and Marjorie assured her that he was fine, could perfectly well hear and follow our conversation too.

Another time, in the autumn of 1970, I met C.S. and Marjorie at Victoria and drove them to their hotel. My mother was in London then, and together we drove to the Festival Hall to attend a performance of *Swan Lake* with the great Russian ballerina Natalia Makarova from the Leningrad Kirov Ballet in the role of Odette. (She was soon to defect from her native Russia as Rudolf Nureyev had done in 1961, and Mikhail Baryshnikov was later to do in 1974.) For some reason we were slightly late and arrived after the performance had begun. We entered the Festival Hall and seated ourselves at the first vacant seats, which happened to be near the entrance in the gangway, so as not to disturb anyone. I could observe C.S. a few seats away, with his chin resting on the back of his hands, which were folded on his walking stick. I had to admire his sheer concentration and the way in which he was unperturbed by our late arrival and our having to sit apart until the interval. When we then went into the foyer we encountered a distinguished looking John Denison CBE, who was general manager of the Royal Festival Hall. He politely but pointedly told Marjorie that there was 'a lift for the use of invalids'. Marjorie at once retorted, 'He is not an invalid; this is Cyril Scott you know.' I have rarely seen anybody so contrite and apologetic, and clearly Mr Denison was honoured to have met C.S.. I believe they kept in touch thereafter.

Another vivid memory belongs to 18 October 1969. I had, as usual, met C.S. and Marjorie at Victoria, and driven them to the old Howard Hotel on the Embankment. That evening the celebrated English pianist Moura Lympany was to play C.S.'s Piano Concerto No. 1, with Bryan Fairfax conducting the Polyphonia Orchestra at the Queen Elizabeth Hall. This was on the occasion of C.S.'s ninetieth birthday celebration. I was at the hotel before the start of the evening and Marjorie had asked me to assist in dressing C.S. for the occasion. I will always remember his gentle smile of gratitude for the assistance.

From my school days onwards I had a passion for poetry. I had in the past shown C.S. some of my amateurish attempts at writing poetry, and he had been most encouraging. On this evening he suddenly mentioned the *fin-de-siècle* poet Ernest Dowson (1867–1900) and told me that he was 'the last of the great lyric poets'. He then recited flawlessly from memory Dowson's 'The Villanelle of the Poet's Road'. I was utterly moved. I had never heard of Dowson before. As long as I live, I will always remember C.S.'s beautiful recitation. The music, the rhythm, the pathos and sheer poetical feeling he brought to that poem can never again be equalled for me. It was the love and distillation of a life's experience that resounded in his voice. Dowson at once struck a chord in me, just as he did for C.S., who set twenty-five of his poems to music.

For the concert itself, there I was, aged twenty-three and placed in a position of honour. We were somewhere in the middle of the auditorium. Marjorie was seated to the left of C.S., and I was seated to his right. Immediately to my right was the famous English viola player Lionel Tertis, who was an old friend and musical collaborator, and his wife. Tertis was ninety-two years old. There they were, two old friends greeting one another and chatting excitedly with me in the middle. Their boyish exuberance and joy in this meeting was truly something to behold. The performance went beautifully, and Marjorie had asked me to accompany C.S. to the stage so that he could receive his well-deserved accolade from a jubilant audience. He was visibly moved by the appreciative applause. I recall how nervous and self-conscious I was, realising the importance of the occasion. The walk to the stage and back to our seats seemed to last forever!

Although I had read several books on occult and esoteric subjects by the end of 1969, and knew something of C.S.'s prodigious output and achievements in various fields, it was not until the publication in September 1969 of his second autobiography, *Bone of Contention*, that I realised so many other facets of his remarkable life. Many years later I chanced upon his first autobiography, *My Years of Indiscretion*, published in 1924, and finally realised the full stature of the man, who along with Marjorie had made such an indelible mark on my life, never to be forgotten.

I would like to recall an event that took place in 1975. A Greek lady anonymously and generously funded a recording of C.S.'s Piano Concerto No. 1. Marjorie had entrusted the original score to me, which I personally delivered to the home of the pianist John Ogdon, joint winner of the International Tchaikovsky Piano Competition at Moscow in 1962. Marjorie later invited me to accompany her to the live recording in London, where Ogdon recorded the concerto with Bernard Herrmann conducting the London Philharmonic Orchestra. This was perhaps the first commercial recording of a major orchestral work by Cyril Scott.

After C.S. died on the last day of 1970, I went down to see Marjorie at Eastbourne. She confided to me two things that stand out in my memory. First, that all one's knowledge and philosophy diminished little the pain and poignancy of a physical separation. Also, that at the end Master K. H. had himself come in one of his subtler bodies to take C.S. across the veil. He told her that in this incarnation C.S. had truly achieved everything that could be expected of him, and had really won his laurels.

Marjorie also presented me with a copy of C.S.'s book of poems entitled *The Vales of Unity*, with an enclosed note which perhaps explains many things. She wrote:

For Rohinten –
Known to us in other
lives than this –
With the affection
of
C.S. & Marjorie

26

BBC Ninetieth-Birthday Tribute[1]

EDMUND RUBBRA

THIS ninetieth-birthday tribute to Cyril Scott isn't for me just the usual laudatory anniversary talk, for it's based on a friendship which beginning as a master and pupil relationship has lasted for over fifty years. It was in 1918, when I was 17, that my enthusiasm for Scott's work led to my giving a public concert of his music in my home-town of Northampton. Unknown to me, the programme of this concert was sent to Cyril Scott by one who was interested in my welfare, the Reverend S. J. Hooper, and although Scott's activities didn't include teaching, he responded to my enthusiasm by agreeing to give me some composition lessons. So began my long association with him.

I shall never forget that first meeting in London. Imagine a boy brought up in an ugly working-class area of an industrial Midlands town being ushered into a house where every object was strange, the heavy gothic furniture, the stained glass, the faint smell of incense, the writing pad containing an austere quotation from the Indian Song Celestial 'To work thou has the right, but not to the fruits thereof', and the piano with another quotation in large lettering painted in gold, a quotation that I couldn't complete because the end of it was lost in the curve of the instrument. At this first meeting, and after he had looked at my work, Scott played some of his music to me. Not the popular pieces such as *Lotus Land* or *Water-Wagtail*, but such pieces as *Bells* from the set of *Poems*, and the then recent *Rainbow-Trout*.[2]

Cyril Scott first became known here in his own country at the beginning of the century when British music was still largely in the academic rut it had been in for a number of years, the influence of which he had escaped because he had studied in Frankfurt under a most excellent and broadminded teacher, Iwan Knorr.

Knorr used to tell those of his pupils who showed real talent and originality 'you must learn the rules, not slavishly stick to them, but be able to break them with good taste if inspiration demands it'. And Cyril Scott did break the rules, as they then were.

In any case the professors highly disapproved of him, said he was a bad influence and refused to teach any of his songs and piano pieces. It even happened that after the noted singer Frederic Austin had sung a group of those songs, Sir Charles Villiers Stanford went up to him and indignantly exclaimed 'Those songs are simply blasphemous!' It is difficult for us today to believe how such an adjective could ever have been hurled at Scott's music, considering that he had never been an exponent of unrelieved dissonance. As an American writer worded it, 'Scott has never been one of the boys of the sour chords.'

Cyril Scott is one of those rare composer-pianists who, like Scriabin, is able by a highly personal touch and tone quality to reveal unsuspected qualities in his music.

[1] Broadcast talk on 'Music Magazine', BBC Radio 3, 28 September 1969. Reprinted by kind permission of Adrian Yardley and the Edmund Rubbra Estate.

[2] Paragraphs 3 to 5 are from Rubbra's introduction to 'Composer's Portrait: Cyril Scott' broadcast on BBC Network Three on 26 April 1967.

Its idiom isn't revealed by an external examination of the notes on paper, but by a hyper-sensitive regard for the colour of his thought, and it's not sufficiently realised how much this thought is rooted in things other than music. For instance, the piece *Bells,* which Scott played to me on my first visit, is part of a set of five pieces, each of which is prefaced by a poem written by the composer. Scott has published many volumes of poetry and his fine translations from the German of the poems of Stefan George have won high praise from such an authority as Sir Maurice Bowra. Again, his immersion in the occult, and his unorthodox but sanely argued booklets on the healing of disease point to an unique personality whose creativeness hasn't been channelled in only one direction. This breadth of outlook makes him entirely free from the bitterness that might so easily have resulted from the neglect of his biggest and best work, and it gives him a detachment that frees him from the egotism so common in one-pointed creative artists.

The strong bias toward literature in Scott's creative output makes his contribution to song-writing of unique importance.

In his best songs, and his output in that field is very large, one sees how his sensitiveness to words results in a naturalness of vocal line that at the same time is completely in tune with both the rhythm and the mood of the words.

These virtues shine through the utterly simple texture of such an early song as *Invocation.* In a second and much later example of his song writing, *Have Ye Seen Him Pass By?,* the harmonic language has become fully personal, yet nothing of the early naturalness has been lost. The result is a song of haunting poignancy.

Scott at ninety is still creative, and if opportunities could be given for the late works to be heard he would again be viewed, as he once was in the early years of this century both here and on the Continent, as a composer unique in English music.

APPENDIX 1

The Songs: Misprints and High/Low Voice Variants

VALERIE LANGFIELD

There are some misprints in the songs as published, generally established by comparison between high and low voice versions. This is not an exhaustive list.

'Autumn's Lute' high voice

Bar 20: the 3/4 time signature is missing; on the second beat in the piano right hand, insert a natural in front of the F
Bar 21: the 2/4 time signature is missing
Bar 28: the piano right hand E should be E-flat
Bar 30: as for bar 28

'A Birthday' high voice

From the first quaver in the piano in the 3rd bar from the end, up to and including the 2nd crotchet in the 2nd bar from the end: add a slur

'Daffodils'

The plate numbers for the low and high voices (A and C, 515 and 516) indicate that these were published first, with the middle-voice (B-flat, 515a) version published later. Small differences are tabulated below; where the differences in the low-voice version are too significant to be reliably described, new versions are given. These are transposed from the high voice version; it is up to performers to decide whether they wish to use these.

Table A.1 Misprints and voice variants in 'Daffodils'

Bar	*Low (A major)*	*Medium (B♭ major)*	*High (C major)*
1 piano	***p***	***pp***	***pp***
10 piano, last beat	missing crescendo hairpin under the crotchet D	hairpin present	hairpin present
15 voice	decrescendo hairpin over whole bar	decrescendo hairpin over whole bar	crescendo hairpin over whole bar
20–1; see Ex. A.1	different from medium and high	matches high voice	matches medium voice
26–8; see Ex. A.2	different from medium and high	matches high voice	matches medium voice
32 piano right hand, last beat	C♯/G♯	E♭/A; E♭ should be D	E/B
34–6; see Ex. A.3	different from medium and high	matches high voice	matches medium voice

Ex. A.1 Scott, 'Daffodils', low voice, bars 20–1, transposed from high voice

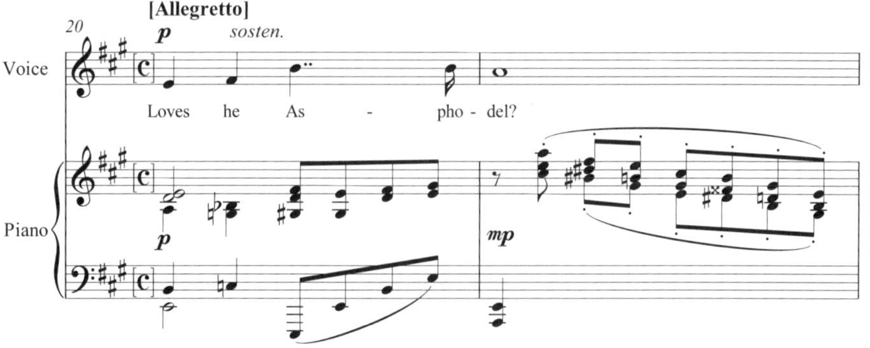

Ex. A.2 Scott, 'Daffodils', low voice, bars 26–8, transposed from high voice

Ex. A.3 Scott, 'Daffodils', low voice, bars 34–6, transposed from high voice

'Evening' high voice

Bar 63: piano left hand, the F should be an E-flat, so: E/A-flat/B-flat, not F/A-flat/B-flat

'A Gift of Silence' high voice

Bar 29: the last chord in the piano right hand needs a natural in front of the lower B-flat (but not the upper)

'In a Fairy Boat' low voice

Bar 33: piano, add slur from 2nd to 3rd crotchet in both hands
Bar 38: piano right hand, add slur over last 2 quavers
Bars 47–50: add slurs over piano both hands, to match those in bar 4

'Love's Aftermath' high voice

Bar 10: piano right hand, add slur over the 2 quavers
Bar 35: piano right hand, add slur over the 2 crotchets
Bar 38: piano right hand, add slur over the 2 crotchets

'Love's Quarrel'

The plate numbers for the low and medium voices (G and B-flat, 403 and 404) indicate that these were published first, with the high-voice (C, 404a) version published later.

Table A.2 Misprints and voice variants in 'Love's Quarrel'

Bar	*Low (G major)*	*Medium (B♭ major)*	*High (C major)*
16 piano right hand	no tenuto lines	has tenuto lines	has tenuto lines
18 piano right hand	no hairpin	decrescendo hairpin over middle two quavers (starting on the 1st of these and ending on the 2nd)	as medium voice
21–2 piano left hand	2nd crotchet of bar 21, 1st crotchet of bar 22, no tenuto lines	2nd crotchet of bar 21, 1st crotchet of bar 22, no tenuto lines	2nd crotchet of bar 21, 1st crotchet of bar 22, have tenuto lines
22–3 piano left hand	slur starts on 2nd crotchet and continues to end of bar 23	slur starts on 2nd crotchet but does not continue	slur starts on 2nd crotchet and continues to end of bar 23
26–7 piano left hand	no slur	no slur	slur starts on 2nd crotchet and continues to end of bar 27
35 piano left hand	last quaver has tenuto line	last quaver has tenuto line	last quaver does not have tenuto line
Bar 37 piano; see Ex. A.4	different from medium and high	matches high voice	matches medium voice

Ex. A.4 Scott, 'Love's Quarrel', low, medium, high voice, bar 37 (piano only) matching medium voice

'Lullaby' medium voice

Bars 21–2: the decrescendo hairpin below the piano left hand should be placed between the piano staves
Bar 26: piano right hand, add slur over first 3 quavers, as in previous bar
Bar 33: piano right hand has a tenuto line not present in high voice version

'Lullaby' high voice

Bar 21: piano right hand, add slur over first 3 quavers
Bar 22: as bar 21

'Mirage'

Bar 36: the 7th semiquaver in the left hand should read G-flat, not G-natural

'My Captain'

6th page of music: 4th system, 2nd and 3rd bars, under the words 'Exult O shores!' The high voice has accents in the piano left hand on the first quaver of each of these two bars; the accents are absent in the low-voice version

'Nocturne' low voice

Bar 77: the last page of music, 1st system, 2nd bar (under the word 'hear'), 2nd crotchet, piano both hands should have a flat before the E
Bar 87: 2nd crotchet, piano left hand possibly should have a C-sharp below the chord, to make it a 1st inversion, not a 2nd inversion chord. Scott may have intentionally omitted it, in the interests of texture

'Osme's Song' low voice

Bars 32–3: piano left hand, add tenuto lines over the minims

'A Prayer' high voice

Bar 6: the first right-hand crotchet should read a 3rd lower, high C/A, not E/C

'Serenade'

The early edition of this song spells the librettist's name 'Ruffield Bendall'; 'Duffield Bendall' is correct. The later edition is dedicated to Theodore Byard, and has the following variants:

Bar 4: vocal line has decrescendo hairpin over first minim
Bar 20: vocal line is marked 'pochiss. animato'
Bar 34: vocal lines is marked 'poco stringendo'
Bar 39: over the hairpin in the vocal line, marked 'string'
Bar 41: before the hairpin in the vocal line, marked 'ritard'
Bar 43: marked 'tranquillo' over the vocal line

'A Song of Arcady'

Bar 18: vocal line, high voice shows 'mp'; low voice shows 'p'

'The Unforeseen'

The plate numbers for the low and high voices (B-flat and D, 611 and 612) indicate that these were published first, with the medium-voice (C, 611a) version published later.

Bars 1–4: medium and high, voice has tenuto lines over piano right hand (8 notes in all), not present in low version
Bars 8, 12, 26, 30: low voice has arpeggiato sign on crotchets on 1st beat piano left hand, not present in medium and high voice versions.

There are variations between high and low voice versions in the following songs: these are to do with texture, arising from the piano tessitura and details are therefore not given.

'Arietta',
'Cherry Ripe',
'From Afar' ('D'Outremer')

APPENDIX 2

Chronology of Works Published during Scott's Lifetime

LESLIE DE'ATH

This is a chronology of publication, not of composition, and thus includes only works that found their way into print during Scott's lifetime. A brief glance reflects the years in which Scott had an association with his various publishers, and in which years he was most active and successful in getting works published. Anomalies occur, with presumed numbering errors on the part of publishers. This list cannot be construed as a chronology of composition, because unpublished works are not included, and some works waited years before they found their way into print.

Elkin forged associations with both Galaxy in North America and Ricordi in Europe, for the broader dissemination of Scott's works. Galaxy and Ricordi are names often found together with Elkin on Scott's music. The Elkin plate numbers are always used. Some plate numbers have proven elusive, in which cases only the publisher's name appears. 'Schott' indicates both Schott of London and B. Schott's Söhne of Mainz. The chronology is arranged by publishers' numbers.

1903							
Title	**S**	**Opus**	**Date**	**Elkin**	**Schott**	**Boosey**	**Other**
Three Frivolous Pieces	164	2	1903				267 (Forsyth)
Six Pieces	166	4	1903				(Forsyth)
April Love	282a	3/1	1903				M.8162 (Metzler)
Little Lady of My Heart	283a		1903				M.8163 (Metzler)
An English Waltz	163	15	1903				11663 (Jaeger)
Yvonne of Brittany	285a	5/2	1903			H.3966	
Piano Quartet	86	16	1903			H.3969	
Dairy Song	284a	5/1	1903			H.4031	
Three Dances	168	20	1903			H. 4074	
There Comes an End to Summer – C	297	30/2	1903			H.4124	
A Last Word – C	296	30/1	1903			H.4125	
Asleep	298	31/1	1903			H.4228	
A Last Word – B-flat	296	30/1	1903			H.4297	
Voices of Vision	293	24/1	1903	181			
Willows	294	24/2	1903	181			

1904							
Title	**S**	**Opus**	**Date**	**Elkin**	**Schott**	**Boosey**	**Other**
Scherzo	169	25	1904	222			
A Valediction – G	302	36/1	1904	256			
A Valediction – B-flat	302	36/1	1904	257			
My Captain – F	304	38/1	1904	258			
My Captain – G	304	38/1	1904	259			
Sorrow – E-flat	303	36/2	1904	262			
Sorrow – F	303	36/2	1904	263			
Two Pierrot Pieces	170	35	1904			H.2498 /99	
Daphnis and Chloe	286	9/1	1904			H.4304	
The Time I've Lost in Wooing	273		1904			H.4307	
There Comes an End to Summer – A-flat	297	30/2	1903			H.4310	
Autumnal	299	32/1	1904			H.4336	
Villanelle	300	33/3	1904			H.4423	
Two Piano Pieces	172	37	1904			H.4453	
Trafalgar	305	38/2	1904			H.4462	
The Ballad Singer	307	42/2	1904			H.4497	
Eileen	306	42/1	1904			H.4498	
Mary	308	42/3	1904			H.4499	
Evening Hymn	301	34	1904			H.4532	
Dagobah	173	39/1	1904				Forsyth
Chinese Serenade	174	39/2	1904				Forsyth
Solitude	175	40/1	1904	264			
Vesperale	176	40/2	1904	265			
Chimes	177	40/3	1904	266			
Impromptu: A Mountain Brook	178	41	1904	269			

1905							
Title	**S**	**Opus**	**Date**	**Elkin**	**Schott**	**Boosey**	**Other**
Don't Come in Sir, Please! – D	310	43/2	1905	296			
Don't Come in Sir, Please! – E	310	43/2	1905	297			
A Gift of Silence – F	309	43/1	1905	304			
A Gift of Silence – A-flat	309	43/1	1905	305			
The White Knight – D	311	43/3	1905	310			
The White Knight – E	311	43/3	1905	311			
A Reflection – D	312	43/4	1905	312			
A Reflection – F	312	43/4	1905	313			
Columbine	180	47/2	1905	321			
Lotus Land	179	47/1	1905	322			

1906

Title	S	Opus	Date	Elkin	Schott	Boosey	Other
Afterday – G	316	50/1	1906	338			
Afterday – C	316	50/1	1906	339			
Asphodel	181	50/2	1906	340			
Waiting	313	46/1	1906	344			
A Picnic	314	46/2	1906	344			
A Song of London – e	317	52/1	1906	355			
A Song of London – g	317	52/1	1906	356			
A Blackbird's Song – D	319	52/3	1906	357			
A Blackbird's Song – E-flat	319	52/3	1906	357a			
A Blackbird's Song – F	319	52/3	1906	358			
A Roundel of Rest – C	318	52/2	1906	359			
A Roundel of Rest – E-flat	318	52/2	1906	360			

1907

Title	S	Opus	Date	Elkin	Schott	Boosey	Other
Lovely Kind and Kindly Loving – G	321	55/1	1907	389			
Lovely Kind and Kindly Loving – B-flat	321	55/1	1907	390			
Why So Pale and Wan? – F	322	55/2	1907	391			
Summerland	182	54	1907	393			
Love's Quarrel – G	323	55/3	1907	403			
Love's Quarrel – B-flat	323	55/3	1907	404			
Love's Quarrel – C	323	55/3	1907	404a			
A Song of Wine	315	46/3	1907	406			
Two Sketches	183	57/4-5	1907	411			
Atwain – low/med	324	56/1	1907	416			
Insouciance – F	325	56/2	1907	416			

1908

Title	S	Opus	Date	Elkin	Schott	Boosey	Other
Lullaby – D-flat	327	57/2	1908	431			
Lullaby – E-flat	327	57/2	1908	431a			
Lullaby – F	327	57/2	1908	432			
Prelude – B-flat	326	57/1	1908	433			
Prelude – C	326	57/4	1908	433a			
Prelude – D	326	57/4	1908	434			
Two Alpine Sketches	184	58/4	1908	443			

1908 (continued)							
Title	**S**	**Opus**	**Date**	**Elkin**	**Schott**	**Boosey**	**Other**
Danse nègre	185	58/5	1908	446			
Notturno	186	54/5	1908	471			
In a Fairy Boat – C	330	61/2	1908	472			
In a Fairy Boat – E-flat	330	61/2	1908	473			
A Serenade – D	329	61/1	1908	474			
A Serenade – F	329	61/1	1908	475			
Sphinx	187	63	1908	479			
A Lost Love – E-flat	331	62/1	1908	481			
A Lost Love – F	331	62/1	1908	481a			
A Lost Love – A-flat	331	62/1	1908	482			
A Vision	332	62/2	1908	483			
Etude No. 1	188	64/1	1908	485			
Etude No. 2	189	64/2	1908	486			
An Eastern Lament – c	333	62/3	1908	487			
An Eastern Lament – e	333	62/3	1908	488			
And So I Made a Villanelle – G	335	65	1908	489			
And So I Made a Villanelle – B-flat	335	65	1908	490			

1909							
Title	**S**	**Opus**	**Date**	**Elkin**	**Schott**	**Boosey**	**Other**
Sonata for piano No. 1, Op. 66	190	66	1909	511			
Daffodils – A	336	68/1	1909	515			
Daffodils – B-flat	336	68/1	1909	515a			
Daffodils – C	336	68/1	1909	516			
Serenata	192	67/2	1909	517			
Mazurka	191	67/1	1909	518			
Osme's Song – D	337	68/2	1909	519			
Osme's Song – F	337	68/2	1909	520			
Handelian Rhapsody (Grainger)	T58	[17]	1909	537			

1910							
Title	**S**	**Opus**	**Date**	**Elkin**	**Schott**	**Boosey**	**Other**
Intermezzo	193	67/3	1910	540			
Mirage	339	70/2	1910	543			
Suite … in the Olden Style	195	71/1	1910	544			
Evening	340	71/2	1910	545			
Evening	340	71/2	1910	546			
My Lady Sleeps – D	338	70/1	1910	549			
My Lady Sleeps – F	338	70/1	1910	550			
Water-Wagtail	196	71/3	1910	570			
A Spring Ditty – D	341	72/1	1910	571			
A Spring Ditty – F	341	72/1	1910	572			
Scotch Lullabye – D	328	57/3	1910	575			
Scotch Lullabye – F	328	57/3	1910	576			
Soirée japonaise	194	67/4	1910	577			
Arietta – C	342	72/2	1910	584			
Arietta – E-flat	342	72/2	1910	585			
Violin Sonata No. 1	119	59	1910		28818		
Elegie	120	73/1	1910		28928-1		
Romance	121	73/2	1910		28928-2		
Valse triste	122	73/3	1910		28928-3		
Tallahassee Suite III – Air et Danse nègre	123	73/4	1910		28928-4		
Trois danses tristes	197	74	1910		28989-91		
Blackbird's Song (Amsel-Lied)	319	52/3	1910		28996		
Deuxième suite	200	75	1910		29050		

1911							
Title	**S**	**Opus**	**Date**	**Elkin**	**Schott**	**Boosey**	**Other**
Aubade	45	77	1911		29143		
Tallahassee Suite I – Bygone Memories	123	73/4	1911		29290		
Tallahassee Suite II – After Sundown	123	73/4	1911		29291		
Blackbird's Song (Chanson du merle)	319	52/3	1911		29299		
And So I Made a Villanelle (Und so macht ich ein Villanelle)	335	65	1911		29301		
Sorrow (Chagrin)	303	36/2	1911		29302		
Willows (Trauerweiden)	294	24/2	1911		29364		

1911 (continued)

Title	S	Opus	Date	Elkin	Schott	Boosey	Other
And So I Made a Villanelle (Ainsi fis-je une villanelle)	335	65	1911		29365		
Sorrow (Kummer)	303	36/2	1911		29366		
Cherry Ripe, vln/pf	124		1911		29441		
Mirage (Traumbild)	339		1911		29637		
The Valley of Silence – C	344	72/4	1911	589			
The Valley of Silence – E-flat	344	72/4	1911	590			
The Trysting Tree – C	343	72/3	1911	591			
The Trysting Tree – D	343	72/3	1910	592			
Chansonette	199	74/8	1911	601			
Valse caprice	198	74/7	1911	602			
Villanelle of the Poet's Road – C	346	74/5	1911	609			
Villanelle of the Poet's Road – E-flat	346	74/5	1911	610			
The Unforeseen – B-flat	345	74/4	1911	611			
The Unforeseen – C	345	74/4	1911	611a			
The Unforeseen – D	345	74/4	1911	612			
The New Moon – E	347	74/6	1911	613			
The New Moon – G	347	74/6	1911	614			
Berceuse	201		1911	617			
Love's Aftermath – B-flat	348		1911	618			
Love's Aftermath – D-flat	348		1911	619			
Over the Prairie	202		1911	631			
An Old Song Ended – E-flat	349		1911	633			
An Old Song Ended – F	349		1911	634			

1912

Title	S	Opus	Date	Elkin	Schott	Boosey	Other
Pierrette	203		1912	643			
For a Dream's Sake – A-flat	350		1912	644			
For a Dream's Sake – B-flat	350		1912	644a			
For a Dream's Sake – C	350		1912	645			
A Little Song of Picardie – D	351		1912	646			
A Little Song of Picardie – E	351		1912	647			
Autumn Idyll	204		1912	653			
Barcarolle	205		1912	681			
Pierrot and the Moon Maiden – D-flat	352		1912	682			

1912 (continued)							
Title	**S**	**Opus**	**Date**	**Elkin**	**Schott**	**Boosey**	**Other**
Pierrot and the Moon Maiden – E	352		1912	683			
In the Valley – med	353		1912	684			
In the Valley – high	353		1912	685			
Sleep Song – d	354		1912	686			
Sleep Song – f	354		1912	687			
British Melodies 1 & 2	206–7		1912	692			
Summer is Acumen In							
(British Melodies 3) – C	208		1912	693			
Pierrot amoureux	138		1912		29537		
Impressions from the Jungle Book	209		1912		29538-42		
Deux préludes	125		1912		29644 / 29645		
The Gentle Maiden	126		1912		29646		
A Little Song of Picardie							
(Ein kleines Lied von der Picardie)	351		1912		29669		
For a Dream's Sake							
(Durch ein Traumbild)	350		1912		29670		
Poems	210		1912		29695-99		

1913							
Title	**S**	**Opus**	**Date**	**Elkin**	**Schott**	**Boosey**	**Other**
Drink to Me Only With Thine Eyes – A-flat /							
Where Be Going? – G	356–8		1913	699			
Autumn Song – B-flat	359		1913	709			
Autumn Song – D	359		1913	710			
[6 organ arrangements]							
[arr. Arthur Pollitt]	T70–5		1913	711			
A Birthday – C	360		1913	717			
A Birthday – D	360		1913	718			
Prelude solennel	213		1913	719			
Spring Song – low/med	361		1913	740			
Spring Song – high	361		1913	741			
Nocturne – A-flat	362		1913	745			
Nocturne – B	362		1913	746			
[Scott soprano album]			1913	749			
[Scott contralto album]			1913	750			

1913 (continued)							
Title	**S**	**Opus**	**Date**	**Elkin**	**Schott**	**Boosey**	**Other**
[Scott tenor album]			1913	751			
[Scott baritone album]			1913	752			
Retrospect – C	363		1913	756			
Retrospect – D	363		1913	757			
Pastoral Suite – Courante	214		1913	758			
Pastoral Suite – Pastorale	214		1913	759			
Pastoral Suite – Rigaudon	214		1913	760			
Pastoral Suite – Rondo	214		1913	761			
Pastoral Suite – Passacaglia	214		1913	762			
Carillon	211		1913		29837		
Egypt	212		1913		29889		
Pictorial Sketch	215		1913				APS 504

1914							
Title	**S**	**Opus**	**Date**	**Elkin**	**Schott**	**Boosey**	**Other**
A Song of Arcady – D	366		1914	770			
A Song of Arcady – F	366		1914	771			
Autumn's Lute – low/med	367		1914	787			
Autumn's Lute – high	367		1914	788			
Cavatina	217		1914	789			
A Prayer	368		1914	806			
Evening Melody – low/med	369		1914	809			
Evening Melody – high	369		1914	810			
Sea-Marge	218		1914	814			
Lilac-Time – med	370		1914	816			
Lilac-Time – high	370		1914	817			
Alpine Sketches [arr. Lange]	T65		1914	822			
Mazurka [arr. Lange]	T67		1914	823			
Intermezzo [arr. Lange]	T31		1914	826			
Diatonic Study	219		1914	828			
Britain's War March, pf	216		1914		3269		
Sonnets I & II	127–8		1914		29982		
Scotch Pastoral	139		1914				1613 / 15674 (W. Hansen)

1915							
Title	**S**	**Opus**	**Date**	**Elkin**	**Schott**	**Boosey**	**Other**
Ode héroïque	223		1915	835			
Danse romantique	224		1915	838			
Meditation – B-flat	375		1915	839			
Meditation – C	375		1915	840			
Russian Dance	225		1915	849			
Night-Song – D-flat	376		1915	859			
Night-Song – E-flat	376		1915	860			
The Alchemist	1		1924		30891		
Rainbow-Trout	228		1916		31026		
Butterfly Waltz	221		1915		31027		
Miniatures	220		1915		31028		
Cherry Ripe, pf	222		1915		3290		

1916							
Title	**S**	**Opus**	**Date**	**Elkin**	**Schott**	**Boosey**	**Other**
Irish Reel	226		1916	865			
Rain – low/med	377		1916	870			
Rain – high	377		1916	871			
Invocation – D	378		1916	873			
Invocation – F	378		1916	874			
Tyrolese Evensong	379		1916	895			
Tyrolese Evensong	379		1916	896			

1917							
Title	**S**	**Opus**	**Date**	**Elkin**	**Schott**	**Boosey**	**Other**
Looking Back – D-flat	381		1917	908			
Looking Back – E-flat	381		1917	908a			
Looking Back – F	381		1917	909			
The Sands of Dee – C	382		1917	910			
The Sands of Dee – E-flat	382		1917	911			
The Little Bells of Sevilla – med	383		1917	913			
The Little Bells of Sevilla – high	383		1917	914			
Modern Finger Exercises	229		1917	916			
[6 organ arrangements]							
[arr. Arthur Pollitt]	T76–81		1917	918			
Requiescat	230		1917	919			
Rondeau de concert	231		1918	933			

1917 (continued)

Title	S	Opus	Date	Elkin	Schott	Boosey	Other
The Pilgrim Cranes – F	384		1917	934			
The Pilgrim Cranes – G	384		1917	935			
Requiem – C	385		1917	936			
Requiem – E-flat	385		1917	937			
Irish Suite, vln/pf	129		1917				27046-4 (Schirmer)

1918

Title	S	Opus	Date	Elkin	Schott	Boosey	Other
Sunshine and Dusk – low	388		1918	947			
Sunshine and Dusk – med	388		1918	948			
Lullaby, arr. Evans	T39		1918	952			
Lullaby, arr. Barns	T34		1918	952a			
Twilight-Tide	232		1918	953			
Oracle – E-flat	389		1918	958			
Oracle – F	389		1918	959			
Consolation	233		1918	975			
Vistas – A Lonely Dell	235/1		1918	979			
Vistas – In the Forest	235/2		1918	981			
Vistas – The Jocund Dance	235/3		1918	982			
Old Loves – G	390		1918	988			
Old Loves – A	390		1918	989			
Old China, suite	234		1918		3655-58		

1919

Title	S	Opus	Date	Elkin	Schott	Boosey	Other
First Bagatelle	236		1919	990			
Time o' Day – C	391		1919	992			
Time o' Day – D	391		1919	993			
Caprice chinois	237		1919	996			
Sea-Fret – C	392		1919	1003			
Sea-Fret – E-flat	392		1919	1004			
A Little Russian Suite	227		1919	1010			
Three Pastorals – Allegretto	238/1		1919	1012			
Three Pastorals – Con delicatezza	238/2		1919	1013			

1919 (continued)							
Title	**S**	**Opus**	**Date**	**Elkin**	**Schott**	**Boosey**	**Other**
Three Pastorals – Pensoso	238/3		1920	1014			
Alone	393		1919	1015			
In Absence	394		1919	1016			
She's But a Lassie Yet – E-flat	395		1919	1016			
She's But a Lassie Yet – F	395		1919	1017			
Tranquility	396		1919	1034			
Pastorale	397		1919	1035			
Sundown – D	398		1919	1046			
Sundown – D	398		1919	1047			

1920							
Title	**S**	**Opus**	**Date**	**Elkin**	**Schott**	**Boosey**	**Other**
Water-Lilies – C	400		1920	1066			
Water-Lilies – D-flat	400		1920	1066a			
Water-Lilies – E-flat	400		1920	1067			
An English Waltz, rev.	163		1919	1071			
Immortality – E-flat	401		1920	1073			
Immortality – F	401		1920	1073a			
Immortality – G	401		1920	1074			
Intermezzo [arr. F. Howard, pf/ str.qtt.]	T49		1920	1075			
Pastoral Suite – Passacaglia [arr. Howard]	T50		1920	1077			
Three Little Waltzes No. 1 [arr. F. Howard, pf/str.qtt.]	T51		1920	1078			
Pastoral Suite No. 5, organ [arr. P. J. Mansfield]	T85		1920	1079			
Young Hearts I	239		1920	1088			
Young Hearts II	239		1920	1089			
The Watchman – B-flat	402		1920	1100			
The Watchman – C	402		1920	1101			
The Watchman – D	402		1920	1101a			
Night Wind	403		1920	1141			
Our Lady of Violets – C	404		1920	1157			
Our Lady of Violets – D	404		1920	1158			
Pastoral Suite	214		1920	1161			
String Quartet No. 1 (parts)	104		1920	1164			

1920 (continued)							
Title	**S**	**Opus**	**Date**	**Elkin**	**Schott**	**Boosey**	**Other**
Ballad on a Troubadour Air	240		1920	1165			
Three Little Waltzes No. 3							
[arr. F. Howard, pf/str.qtt.]	T52		1921	1176			
Three Little Waltzes	165		1906	1178			
A Pageant	241		1920		3765-67		

1921							
Title	**S**	**Opus**	**Date**	**Elkin**	**Schott**	**Boosey**	**Other**
All Through the Night – G	405		1921	1202			
All Through the Night– B-flat	405		1921	1203			
The Huckster – B-flat	406		1921	1204			
The Huckster – C	406		1921	1205			
Have Ye Seen Him Pass By?	407		1921	1206			
Vesperale [arr. B. Hambourg, vc/pf]	T40		1921	1238			
String Quartet No. 1 (score)	104		1921	1239			
Idyllic Fantasy	112		1921	1240			

1922							
Title	**S**	**Opus**	**Date**	**Elkin**	**Schott**	**Boosey**	**Other**
Inclination à la danse	242		1922	1241			
Moods	244		1922	1244			
Villanelle of Firelight – B-flat	408		1922	1257			
Villanelle of Firelight – C	408		1922	1258			
Cherry Ripe – C	409		1922	1262			
Cherry Ripe – E-flat	409		1922	1263			
The Minstrel Boy – E-flat	410		1922	1264			
The Minstrel Boy – F	410		1922	1265			
By Yon Bonnie Banks	411		1922	1266			
I'll Bid my Heart be Still	412		1922	1267			
Blythe and Merry was She	413		1922	1268			
Coming thro' the Rye – G	414		1922	1269			
Coming thro' the Rye – A	414		1922	1270			
Lotus Land [arr. Kreisler, vln/pf]	T35		1922	1303			
Piano Trio in C	92		1922		30740		
Piano Concerto No. 1	70		1922		30764 (2-pf) 30765 (parts)		
The Extatic Shepherd	153		1922		30766		

1922 (continued)							
Title	**S**	**Opus**	**Date**	**Elkin**	**Schott**	**Boosey**	**Other**
Two Passacaglias	52		1922		30769		
Indian Suite	243		1922		30802		
Three Symphonic Dances [arr. Grainger, 2 pfs]	T62		1922		30826		

1923							
Title	**S**	**Opus**	**Date**	**Elkin**	**Schott**	**Boosey**	**Other**
Reconciliation – G	415		1923	1327			
Reconciliation – B-flat	415		1923	1328			
From Afar – C	416		1923	1343			
From Afar – E	416		1923	1344			
In the Silver Moonbeams – G	417		1923	1347			
In the Silver Moonbeams – A	417		1923	1347a			
Souvenir de Vienne	246		1923	1358			
Vistas	235		1923	1360			
Idyll, voice & flute	418		1923	1378			
Arabesque	245		1923		31066		
Lotus Land (arr. Kreisler)	T35		*c.* 1923		31143		
Nativity Hymn	18		1923				2405 (S&Bell)

1924							
Title	**S**	**Opus**	**Date**	**Elkin**	**Schott**	**Boosey**	**Other**
Technical Studies	247		1924	1379			
The Garden of Memory	420		1924	1401			
Karma, pf	248		1924	1441			
The Emir's Serenade	27		1924			H.11121	
The Rat-Catcher	28		1924			H.11122	
The Huntsman's Dirge	29		1924			H.11313	

1925							
Title	**S**	**Opus**	**Date**	**Elkin**	**Schott**	**Boosey**	**Other**
The Ballad of Fair Helen	422		1925	1448			
Mist	423		1925	1449			
Spanish Dance	249		1925	1465			
Lullaby (SSA, arr. Kramer)	T19		1920	1476			
Angelus – A	424		1925	1494			
Angelus – C	424		1925	1495			

1925 (continued)							
Title	**S**	**Opus**	**Date**	**Elkin**	**Schott**	**Boosey**	**Other**
Three Old Country Dances	250		1925		31354		
Piano Quintet in C	93		1925				3048 (S&Bell)

1926							
Title	**S**	**Opus**	**Date**	**Elkin**	**Schott**	**Boosey**	**Other**
Album for Boys	251		1926	1532			
Album for Girls	252		1926	1533			
Aspiration	425		1926	1565			
Lord Randal	426		1926	1572			
Three Dances, pf duet	265						TD-18 (Presser)

1927							
Title	**S**	**Opus**	**Date**	**Elkin**	**Schott**	**Boosey**	**Other**
Lullaby [arr. R. Elkin, pf]	57/2		1927	1582			
To-Morrow	427		1927	1619			
Sea-Song of Gafran	428		1927	1645			
Suite fantastique	53		1927				Universal/ B&H

1928							
Title	**S**	**Opus**	**Date**	**Elkin**	**Schott**	**Boosey**	**Other**
Badinage	253		1928	1667			
A March Requiem	429		1928	1674			
Bumble-Bees	157		1928		32023		
Idyll, vln	158		1928		32178		

1929							
Title	**S**	**Opus**	**Date**	**Elkin**	**Schott**	**Boosey**	**Other**
Vesperale [arr. F. Howard]	T55		1929	1701			
Valse sentimentale	255		1929	1732			
Guttersnipes' Dance	254		1929		32272		

1930							
Title	**S**	**Opus**	**Date**	**Elkin**	**Schott**	**Boosey**	**Other**
Mermaid's Song	431		1930	1757			
Zoo: Animals	256		1930		32619		
The Melodist and the Nightingales	142		1930		BSS 32697		
Noël	55		1931		32461/32462		

1931							
Title	**S**	**Opus**	**Date**	**Elkin**	**Schott**	**Boosey**	**Other**
My Heart Ever Faithful [Bach, arr.]	442		1931	1795			
Vesperale / Danse nègre							
[arr. orch, Newman]	T8–9		1931	1808			
First Suite for strings	54		1931				H.7031 (Hawkes)
Cornish Boat Song	94		1931		BSS 32946		
Little Folk Dance	95		1931		BSS 32947		
Early One Morning	75		1931				7020 (WR / B&H)

1932							
Title	**S**	**Opus**	**Date**	**Elkin**	**Schott**	**Boosey**	**Other**
A Song from the East / Water-Wagtail							
[arr. orch, Newman]	T10–11		1932	1816			
Gavotte	257		1932	1820			
The Little Foreigner	432		1932	1831			
Mirabelle	20		1932				H.13694 (B&H)
J. S. Bach – Three Pieces [arr. Scott, 2 pfs]	444		1932				4707 (WR)

1933							
Title	**S**	**Opus**	**Date**	**Elkin**	**Schott**	**Boosey**	**Other**
Mystic Ode	21		1933	1842			
Rima's Call to the Birds	85		1933	1852			
Toy Box	258		1933		33849		
Neptune	57		1933		hire		

1934							
Title	**S**	**Opus**	**Date**	**Elkin**	**Schott**	**Boosey**	**Other**
Blackbird's Song [arr. P. J. Mansfield]	T20		1934	1885			
Miss Remington	259		1934		33960		
La belle dame sans merci	17		1934				UMA 3
Ballade, vc & pf	143		1934				10.584 (Universal)
Nursery Rhymes	266		1935	1892			

1935							
Title	**S**	**Opus**	**Date**	**Elkin**	**Schott**	**Boosey**	**Other**
Lady June	433		1935	1905			
Danse nègre [arr. A. W. Kramer, vln/pf]	T37		1935	1908			
Danse nègre [arr. E. Fisher]	T68		1935	1909			
Danse nègre [arr. 2 pfs]	268		1935	1910			
Tarantula	261		1935	1917			
Piano Sonata No. 2	260		1935				UMA 13
Summer Gardens	58		1935		DSO 390		
Summerland (choral)	22		1935				10233 (Universal)
Benedicite, omnia opera Domine	30		1935				4569 (S&Bell)
Benedictus es Domine	31		1935				4570 (S&Bell)
Jubilate Deo	32		1935				4571 (S&Bell)
Evening Service	33		1935				4572 (S&Bell)

POST-1935							
Title	**S**	**Opus**	**Date**	**Elkin**	**Schott**	**Boosey**	**Other**
Andante in F [Bach, arr. Scott]	445		1936	1928			
Jig Fugue [Bach, arr. Scott]	443		1936	1929			
Pierrot triste	T63		1936			H.12543 (B&H)	
Impressions from the Jungle Book, Nos 1 & 5 – 2 pfs	269		1938		35367		
Arise, my Love, my Fair One	434		1939	2026			
String Trio No. 1	105		1940		35962		
Theme and Variations, 2 pfs	267		1947	2093			
Lotus Land, arr. 2 pfs	270		1948	2128			
Concerto, oboe & strs	81		1949	2169			
Piano Trio No. 2	96		1951		S&C 5591		
Russian Fair, 2 pfs	272		1952	2253			
Sonata melodica	132		1953	2289			
Aubade, rec & pf	148		1953		S&C 5669		

POST-1935 (continued)							
Title	**S**	**Opus**	**Date**	**Elkin**	**Schott**	**Boosey**	**Other**
For My Young Friends	239		1953	2291			
Invention in F [Bach, arr. Scott]	441		1955	2404			
Sonata No. 3, piano	262		1956	2406			
String Quartet No. 2 (score)	108		1958	2530			
String Quartet No. 2 (parts)	108		1958	2531			
Neapolitan Rhapsody	66		1959			B&H 18521	
String Quartet No. 3	109		1960	2577			
Pastoral Ode	263		1961	2589			
Sonata, flute & pf	150		1961	2617			
Early One Morning, rev.	75		1962			B&H 18602	
Victorian Waltz	264		1963	2656			
Sonata, 2 violins & pf (scribal score)	151		1964	2696			
Rural Intermezzo	152		1965				DOR 340
String Quartet No. 4	110		1968	2718			

Scott's autobiographies are full of lively anecdotes and character portraits about the people he was acquainted with, both famous and otherwise. He seems to have deliberately avoided using the medium to showcase his own creativity, both as a composer and as a writer. References to music or to his compositions are notable by their relative absence. This diffidence is striking, for one who took the trouble to pen three autobiographies over his long lifetime (if one includes the unpublished *Near the End of Life*). It is sometimes presumed that Scott had neither the knack nor the predisposition to self-promote aggressively. A communication to the editor from Peter Marchbank provides a lively, somewhat different, take:

> Giles Easterbrook worked for Novello's while CS was still alive. He told me that CS would hawk his scores around the London publishing houses, leave them like confetti and then forget where they were. He also told me that CS would harangue the staff of the Novello showroom in Wardour Street if his music was not prominently displayed and then demand the MSS back.
>
> (communication to the editor, 23 April 2017, with permission)

CATALOGUES, DISCOGRAPHY & BIBLIOGRAPHY

i

Catalogue of Cyril Scott's Music

COMPILED BY LESLIE DE'ATH, WITH THE ASSISTANCE OF DESMOND SCOTT

A new classified index of Scott's works is provided here, with compositions identified as S 1, S 2, etc. Works are listed by genre in the first instance, and then chronologically according to composition (when known) or publication date, within each genre. Timings are taken from existing recordings of the work. The exact timing is given when only one recording exists. When two or more exist, an average is chosen, or the extremes given in the event of a significant variation among two or more. For the piano works, Scott's own recorded timings are given in {curly brackets}. He provided his own estimated timings for a number of works – often well wide of the mark – which are indicated as [00' CS]. Number of pages and measures are also indicated after works and movements. Repeats, which are not common in Scott, are indicated in the totals by (parentheses). First performances are only provided in isolated instances. For more complete data, see Laurie J. Sampsel, *Cyril Scott: A Bio-bibliography*.

Titles have been provided with the spellings and diacritical marks of the original editions, whether linguistically defensible or not (i.e. *patético, mysterioso, giacoso, gracioso, extatic,* etc. are reproduced as published, without an identifying [*sic*]).

Scott's earliest works were published by Forsyth, Boosey & Co., Jaeger and Metzler. In 1903, Elkin became Scott's principal publisher, a close relationship that endured throughout his life. Initially Ricordi was Elkin's distributor in North America, a function that Galaxy Music assumed in the mid-1930s. Thus, editions of Scott's piano music and songs can be found with any of those publishers' names on the front cover (also Elkin/Ricordi, or Elkin/Galaxy). Elkin were interested primarily in the smaller genres – piano miniatures and songs. From 1910, Schott (i.e. both Schotts Söhne, Mainz, and Schott of London) became Scott's publisher of the larger works, while also obtaining rights to some of the Elkin miniatures, and issuing some songs with German and French texts.

Scott provided a date at the end of the manuscript for most of his scores. Sometimes just a year, and sometimes an exact day. Such dates indicate the completion date, without further specification.

Information is provided as available.

ABBREVIATIONS

b	bars
BC	*Bone of Contention*, 1969 autobiography
Comp	date of composition
Ded	dedication
Dur	duration
FP	first performance
FS	full score
LE	later editions
LS	literary source (poet)
m	measure(s)
MS	holograph or other manuscript source
MYI	*My Years of Indiscretion*, 1924 autobiography
Orch	orchestration [fl(utes) . ob(oes) . cl(arinets) . bsn (bassoons) / hn (French horns) . tpt (trumpets) . trom(bones) . tuba / timp(ani) . perc(ussion) . hp (harps) . pf (piano) . org(an) / strs (strings)]
Publ	publication data
PV	piano/vocal score
Ref	references
S	Scott (new numbering system)
T	Transcriptions
W	Works numbers from Laurie Sampsel, *Cyril Scott: A Bio-bibliography*

INDEX OF CONTENTS
(references are to S numbers)

A STAGE

i – opera, musical theatre

S 1 W 6 **The Alchemist** [*Der Alchimist*], opera in three scenes [PV, 150p]

Prelude: Allegro con molto spirito – Più mosso [4p / 74m]

Scene I – *A cottage in a wood* – Allegretto [maid / young man / Sage / flower-gatherers] [38p / 691m]

Scene II – *A moonlit glade* – Con moto [young man / Elemental / vassals / jester / Nuns] [63p / 1066m]

Scene III – *A cottage in a wood* – Moderato [maid / young man / Sage / Disciples / flower-gatherers] [44p / 560m]

Cast: A maid, daughter of the Sage (mezzo) / The young man (tenor) / The Sage (baritone) / The Elemental (bass-bar) / A jester (tenor) / Three Disciples of the Sage (TBB soli) / Flower-gatherers (SSA chorus) / Vassals (SSATB chorus) / Nuns (SSSAA chorus)

Time: The Middle Ages

LS: Cyril Scott; German translation Helmut Andreae.

Comp: 1917–18

Publ: 1924 Schott [30891]

Dur: [*c.* 90']

Orch: [4(2/3/4pic).3(3ca).3(3E♭cl).bcl.3.cbsn / 6.4.3.1 / timp / 5perc / 4gtr / 3mand / 2hp / cel / pno /strs] stage music (minstrels): 3mand / 2gtr / org / str(3vn.va.vc)

FP: 28 May 1925, Essen (cond. Felix Wolfes)

MS: full score with Schott, London. FS/parts on hire, Schott.

Ref: *MYI*, 160, 202, 235, 281

BC, 67, 146, 154, 157, 181, 188

Note: The Schott plate number [30891], assuming sequential numbering, puts the date at 1915/16 (prior to composition), and is likely an error.

S 2 W 304 **The Saint of the Mountain**, opera in one act

Comp: 1924–25

Publ: unpublished

FP: unperformed.

Note: No score or libretto has survived.

S 3 W 319 **The Shrine**, opera in one act, four scenes

Scene I – *On the heights at sunset*

Scene II – *Cottage interior*

Scene III – *The village street*

Scene IV – *The same*

LS: Cyril Scott (Scene 4 in German).

Comp: *c.* 1925

Publ: unpublished

FP: unperformed

MS: Piano score of a Prelude, and PV score to Scene I exists.

Ref: *MYI*, 235 – a likely reference to the libretto of this opera

Note: Likely the same work as S 2, either revised or simply retitled.

S 4 – **Whilom and Whither** *[Backwards and Forwards / Forward and Backward]: A Musical Show*

Overture – Moderato

Part I – Scene 1 – A street in London

1, song, *Worry, Rush, Excitement, Noise* – Allegro con spirito

Scene 2 – Hernia's house

Scene 3 – Dr. Impasse's waiting room

2, song (Pamela) with chorus, *You Can't Tell I'm a Girl by my Hair* – Moderato

Scene 4 – Dr. Impasse's office

3, song (women's voices), *Sleep and Remember* – Allegretto molto moderato e legato – Andantino [attacca into No 5]

4, song (3 yogis), *Salaam, sahibs, salaam!*

Scene 5 – Victorian era, 1850

5, song, *But Say the Word, Beloved* – Appassionata

6, instrumental, then duet, *Victorian waltz song and polka* – Slowish valse time (original version of S 264)

Scene 6 – An Italian bedroom, 1500

Scene 7 – Spain, 1300 – play within a play (cf. *Hamlet*)

Scene 8 – A Norman castle, 1070

Scene 9 – A prehistoric cave, characters now Neanderthals

Scene 10 – Dr. Impasse's office, present day

Scene 11 – A street outside Dr. Impasse's office

7, duet (Lady Pancreas, Arthur), *I Have Transferred Every One of my Affections*, then chorus, *Dreams, Dreams, Soft and Revealing* – Moderato

8, song (Pamela) with chorus of constables, *Here is a Fine Opportunity* – Alla marcia: Con spirito

Part II –Scene 12 – A nursing home

9, solo with chorus, *This is the Perfect Nursing-home* – Allegretto

Scene 13 – Same. Reprise of No. 4, *Salaam, sahibs, salaam!*

Scene 14 – A street, 1940 crowd scene

10, chorus, *War is a Great and Glorious Thing!* – Quick march

Scene 15 – A scene of horror as war comes

Scene 16 – A room, 2200

11, song (Bright young things), *Auntie be a Sport* – Moderato con moto

Scene 17 – A beautiful garden, 2350

Scene 18 – Farther in the future; wordless, music plays throughout

12, instrumental, *Scene and Finale* (chorus not extant)

LS: Cyril Scott – Scenes 1, 4–7, 10, 11, 13, 17 / Rose Allatini – Scenes 3, 12, 14 / Brian Ross [= David Anrias] – Scenes 2, 8, 16 / J. M[elanie] A. Mills [= H. K. Challoner] – Scenes 9, 15

Comp: *c.* 1933?

Publ: unpublished

FP: unperformed

Note: Ross and Mills were neighbours and friends of the Scotts for several years in the 1930s, and Scott penned introductions to three of Ross's and Mills's occult books. CS states, 'One capricious summer, while passing a holiday with my wife and two friends, we decided to pass the time in an amusing manner by concocting a Musical Show, which was to be distinguished from the customary Revue … by a plot. Having between us devised … a suitable humorous and dramatic theme, I then set about writing a certain proportion of the dialogue, the lyrics, and finally the music, which was of by no means high-brow quality.' CS's self-conscious foray into a lighter musical style in this work lends some weight to the authenticity of the earlier *Dorothy Waltz*, S 449, written in similar vein. Music No. 6 is the source, previously unrecognised, of his last published piano composition, S 264.

S 5 W 196 **Maureen O'Mara**, opera in three acts

Act I – Con spirito

Act II – Quickly & stormily

Act III – Andante sostenuto

Scene: A farmyard in Ireland; the Napoleonic wars

Comp: 1946

Publ: unpublished

FP: unperformed

LS: Charles Lundy [= Cyril Scott]

MS: PV score [282p] and typescript libretto with estate.

Ref: *BC*, 218

Note: Unsuccessful in the Festival of Britain opera competition.

ii – ballet

S 6 W 158 **The Incompetent Apothecary: A Brueghel Comedy** (elsewhere known as **The Short-Sighted Apothecary**)

Comp: 1923

Publ: unpublished

Dur: [40' CS]

FP: one movement only, *Dance of the Citizens*, in Harrogate, Royal Hall, 26 July 1929, cond. Scott

Note: The first movement of Three Symphonic Dances, S 46 (qv), appears to have been employed for this ballet.

Ref: *MYI*, 279 / *BC*, 157

MS: Autograph MS to have been sold in the Novello auction sale (15 May 1996), but withdrawn.

S 7 W 167 **Karma: A Fantasy in Mime & Music in Five Pictures** – *Suite*

Prologue

Andante sostenuto [7p / 29m]

Picture I. *Barbaric Dance*

Allegro – Adagio maestoso e sostenuto – Allegro – A little broader [29p / 116m]

Picture II. *A Piper in the Desert*

Lento (– Much quicker – Lento) [18p / 68m (50m without middle section)]

Picture III. *Song from the East*

Allegro non troppo / Lebhaft! – Molto maestoso – A tempo – Con molto spirito [21p / 90m]

Picture IV. *Before the Church*

Adagio [95p / 18m (incomplete)]

Picture V. *Souvenir de Vienne*

Andante sostenuto

Ded: André Charlot

Comp: *c.* 1924, St Leonards on Sea

Publ: unpublished (see S 248)

LE: Novello (hire, facsimile of holograph of FS)

FP: 23 September 1924, London, Prince of Wales Theatre

Orch: [1.1.1.1 / 2.2.1.0 / perc / cel / pf / harmonium / strs] The score calls for 'Mustel & celeste'. Evidently Charlot had at his disposal both a Mustel harmonium and a celesta – probably also a Mustel. Written on the same staff, the harmonium is indicated 'organ'. A Mustel harmonium is implied by the registration in the score. For instance, the score begins with a Mustel solo, marked 'con metaph' (= metaphone), 'harpe eol' (= eolienne), and 'cor Ang.' (= cor anglais), all stops on the Mustel harmonium. The score seems to call for a separate celesta, rather than the 'celeste' stop on the harmonium.

Ref: *BC*, 189

Note: Holograph of FS (82p) with estate. For holograph of piano draft, see S 248. The following notes relate to the FS:

An 18-bar return of Picture I material in the middle of Picture II may have been cut in performance.

A 6-bar transition from Picture II to III is excised in the holograph.

Picture IV (IV Bild) is incomplete. The manuscript has the first 18 bars only, corresponding to S 248, bars 1–16.

Picture V is missing, except for a 20-bar piano sketch, the music of which is not found in the piano version (S 246 / 248). It served as an introduction to the scene, and is labeled '*Souvenir de Vienne – Prelude.* Andante sostenuto (very tranquilly).'

Review commentary, from *The Stage*, 25 September 1924: 'The ballet depicts "the working, in five stages, of the Buddhist doctrine of reincarnation."' Pictures I & II: 'the attempted sacrifice of one Prehistoric sister by another, their rivalry, later on, as wives of an Arab Sheik'.

S 8 W 195 **The Masque of the Red Death**

LS: Edgar Allan Poe

Comp: *c.* 1930

FP: 4 September – 15 November 1930, London, Cambridge Theatre, in André Charlot's *Masquerade*

Ref: *BC*, 189

Note: score lost

iii – incidental music

– – **Electra**

Comp: *c.* 1905

Publ: unpublished

MS: lost

Note: Reference is made in *MYI* to a projected overture and incidental music to Arthur Symons's adaptation of *Elektra*.

It seems as if composition was aborted in consequence of a vitriolic correspondence, but Scott quotes one of his own letters: 'As I cannot accept your terms, and as I *am* glad to have the opportunity to write this overture, I shall be delighted if you will accept it from me for nothing.' This leaves open the possibility that he had finished at least an overture, now lost.

S 9 W 231 **Othello**

LS: Shakespeare

Publ: unpublished

FP: 11 February 1920, London, New Theatre

MS: lost

Ref: *MYI*, 159

S 10 W 290 **The Return to Nature**

Publ: unpublished

FP: 14 March 1920, Hammersmith, Lyric Theatre

MS: lost

S 11 W 324 **Smetse Smee: A Bizarre Comedy in Three Acts**

Act I – [57p / 490b]

Moderato – Tempo poco scherzando – Molto cantabile e dolce – Tempo I [18p / 124b]

Lento e triste [10p / 108b]

Allegro moderato – Poco meno mosso – Andante espressivo – Energico – Meno mosso [8p / 71b]

Lento e misterioso – Tranquillo – Allegro ma non troppo – Poco meno mosso – Energico [19p / 187b]

Act II – [61p / 618b]

Andante religioso – Più mosso – Moderato – Vivace [13p / 120b]

Moderato – Lento [7p / 64b]

Andantino – Allegro non troppo – Allegro con spirito – Poco meno mosso [13p / 179b]

Allegro – Con anima – Andante sostenuto – Energico [28p / 255b]

Act III – [35p / 359b]

Adagio religioso – L'istesso tempo [6p / 68b]

Andantino – Adagio – Tristamente – Allegro moderato – Poco meno mosso – Andante [29p / 291b]

LS: Cyril Scott, theatrical adaptation after Charles de Coster's short story

Comp: *c.* 1925–6

Publ: n.d. Schott (scribal orchestral score on hire. No. 414)

Orch: 1.0.2(=bcl).1 / 0.2.1.0 / perc / hpd / pf / strs (4.4.2.2.2)

FP: unperformed

MS: An orchestral autograph score, titled 'Prelude to Act I', and residing with the estate, is almost certainly meant for *Smetse Smee*. It is perhaps an unfinished draft, as the scoring is very light.

Note: Scott's script is a self-standing literary work, the typescript (29+31+33 = 93p) duplicated in facsimile by Ethel Christian (London, n.d.).

S 12 W 364 **Susannah and the Elders**

Publ: unpublished

FP: 31 October – 14 November 1937, London, Duke of York's Theatre

MS: unknown

S 13 – **Nephew into Aunt: A Boccaccio Touch!** – *A Light Comedy. In Three Acts, with Incidental Music. Adapted from the Italian of Leonardo Sighieri by Cyril Scott*

Cast: Fedora, 37, a well-to-do widow / Guido, 45, her brother / Cecilia di Vinciolo, 21, an orphan, and Guido's ward / Enrico di Parma, 26, a young man / Rinaldo del Tesco, uncle to Enrico / Angelina del Tesco, aunt to Enrico / A magician / Pizzetti, his apprentice / Maria, a sort of baby farmer / Alberta, a maid / Giorgio, a man-servant / Karlukarlu, an invisible voice.

Era: Any attractive period between 1350 and 1750. Italy.

Act I

1, 'While 'neath my parents' roof I dwelt, I fared on good macaroni', Gently flowing [Cecilia, with minstrels] [5p / 63b]

2, 'O lusty lavish lady mine, so hale and full of ardour' Allegro [Enrico] [4p / 90b]

3, 'O juice of jovial Bacchus' [music not extant][servants]

4, Love potion chant, 'O precious, most expensive love-potion. Infallible in cases of unrequited devotion', Recitative / Slow [Enrico] [4p / 30b]

5, 'How shall I bid my heart to cease from flutt'ring in my breast', Andante / Allegro moderato [Enrico] [5p / 102b]

6, 'I've dreamed of princely enchanters', Languorous (andante) [Cecilia] [5p / 77b]

7, reprise, 'O lusty lavish lady mine' [Enrico]

Act II – Scene 1

8, Maria's song, 'Everyone loves Maria', Andante sostenuto [Maria] [4p / 71b]

Scene II

9, 'When a wizard of some reputation goes forth to pursue his vocation', Allegretto [Apprentice and maidens] [4p / 89b]

10, reprise, 'I've dreamed of princely enchanters' [Cecilia]

Scene III

11, Lullaby [music not extant] [Cecilia]

12, 'Who would be a maid? Always circumspect and staid', Time of slow waltz [Maid's song] [5p / 83b]

13, 'Oh, were my soul a butterfly I'd wing the wide world over', Allegretto [Cecilia] [3p / 46b]

Act III – Scene 1 (The Priest of Napoli)

14, 'Now 'tis only in dream, beloved' (reprise of end of 'I've dreamed of princely enchanters') [Cecilia]

15, 'To shrive myself one morning I hasten'd to a priest of Napoli', Moderato [Guido with minstrels] [10p / 91b]

Comp: early 1940s

Publ: unpublished

FP: unperformed

MS: Full script and ten musical numbers extant (PV), with estate.

Note: On the title page to Act I, 'Into' is crossed out, and the title changed to *Nephew cum Aunt*.

S 14 – **Janet and Felix, or 'Singing Sickness': A Musical Satire for the Radio**

Scene I – the drawing-room of Janet Suckling's flat

Scene II – Dr Kurtz's consulting room

Scene III – Signor Pindello's Operatic Academy – the practice room

Scene IV – Pindello's Academy – the garden

Scene V – The wishing seat in a cave on the Yorkshire moors

Scene VI – Pindello's Academy – the practice room

Comp: 1931

Publ: unpublished

MS: lost

Note: First broadcast on 27 November 1931. Adapted and produced by Gordon McConnel. Alan Paul at the piano. The Wireless Chorus and the B.B.C. Theatre Orchestra (cond. Leslie Woodgate).

Cast included Tessa Dean (Janet Suckling), John Armstrong (Felix Fairchild), Ann Stephenson (Mrs. Fairchild, his mother), J. Hubert Leslie (Dr Kurtz and John McKay), and Bertram Binyon (Signor Pindello). Billing in the *Radio Times* calls it an operetta.

B CHORAL

i – with orchestra

S 15 W 192 **Magnificat** for soli, chorus, organ and orchestra

Comp: November 1899

Ded: Percy [Grainger], Roger [Quilter], Eric [Harben], Agnes [Harben], Hans [Lüthy], Carry [Carrie Lüthy]

MS: Grainger Museum [MG C2/SCO-113], PV score by Grainger

Ref: *MYI*, 25–6, 39, 68–71

Note: withdrawn by Scott; preserved by Grainger

S 16 W 264 **Princess Maleine** [Op. 18], overture for chorus, organ and orchestra

LS: anon. (Scott?), based on play by Maurice Maeterlinck

Comp: 1912

Publ: unpublished

Ref: *MYI*, 200–1

Note: Revision of S 40, and performed in Vienna, 1912. Further revision, 1929, as *Festival Overture*, S 19.

S 17 W 44 **La belle dame sans merci** for chorus (SSAATTBB), baritone solo and orchestra [36p / 425m]

Andante sostenuto – Moderato – Tranquillo – Allegretto – Moderato – Più tranquillo – Tempo più animato – Tranquillo – Allegro con passione – Moderato – Quietly flowing – Tempo quasi andante – Molto sostenuto e tranquillo

LS: John Keats

Ded: Roy Henderson

Comp: *c.* 1913 / 1915–17

Publ: 1934 Universal Music Agencies (U.M.A. 3)

Dur: [25' CS]

Ref: *MYI*, 202, 235 / *BC*, 146

Note: orig. *c.* 1913 version was for soprano and baritone soli, without chorus.

S 18 W 213 **Nativity Hymn**, cantata for soli, chorus [SSAATTBB] and orchestra [67p / 976m]

Andante sostenuto – Andante – Sostenuto e tempo animato – A tempo agitato – Con moto – Sostenuto e religioso – Con moto – A tempo energico – Tranquillo – Poco più mosso – Molto maestoso e meno mosso

LS: Richard Crashaw, 'In the Holy Nativity of Our Lord'

Comp: March 1913, London

Publ: 1923, Stainer and Bell [S. & B. 2405] (PV only; Carnegie collection of British music)

Published under the scheme of the Carnegie United Kingdom Trust, 2017, printed FS available through estate

Dur: [60' CS]

Orch: [2.picc.2.ca.2.bcl. / 4.3.3.1 / timp / perc / hp / pf (upright will suffice) / cel / org / strs

MS: with estate [141p / 975m]; score was lost for 4 years, & discovered after the war 'in a cellar in Great Marlborough Street'.

Ref: *MYI*, 201

Notes: *Christmas Overture*, S 47, intended as beginning of this work.

Optional ending for *Noël*, S 55.

Some instrumental and expression markings in score are in German.

WW1 precluded a Vienna premier performance.

S 19 W 121 **Festival Overture** for full orchestra and chorus and organ ad lib

Tempo tranquillo – Con moto tranquillo – Con moto – Allegro poco moderato – Più tranquillo – Allegro con spirito – Meno mosso – Maestoso – Molto tranquillo – Molto moderato – Con moto – Allegro agitato

LS: anon. (Scott?)

Ded: Percy Grainger

Comp: May 1929 / December 1933

Publ: 2005 Novello (special order edition)

Dur: [10' 34"] [*c.* 10' CS] [*c.* 12' CS] [16' CS]

Orch: [2(=picc).2(=ca).1.bcl.3(=cbsn) / 4.2.3.1 / timp / perc / hp / pf(cel) / strs] [optional: fl3. ca(extra player). clar2 / tpt3 / extra perc / org]

MSS: Grainger Museum [MG C2/SCO-70], FS, parts & chorus parts

May 1929 holograph with estate [54p]. Front cover states 'for control only', and 'N.B. This score is incorrect in some details and should not be used except for balance and control.' Underneath, in Grainger's writing, '& it's no use for that'.

December 1933 holograph with estate [33p]. This MS has much taping-over of sections and individual parts, perhaps indicative of Grainger's suggested revisions.

Undated letter to Scott from Percy Grainger with estate, containing 5 loose sheets with suggested revisions to scoring of 1929 version.

Ref: *BC*, 69, 138, 165

Note: Revision of *Princess Maleine*, S 16.

Grainger further revised the work in the early 1930s, to make it 'fool-proof' (i.e. scored so that it will sound well even with insufficient rehearsal).

Won the £100 *Daily Telegraph* prize for orchestral works, and premiered in 1934 (Queen's Hall, Sir Adrian Boult).

S 20 204 **Mirabelle: A Quaint Cantata** for soli, mixed chorus and strings (or a cappella) [102p / 858m]

I – *Lullabye* Moderato [7p / 64m]

II – *The Colloquy* Allegretto con moto [16p / 97m]

III – *Six Years Old, Come Friday* Quietly flowing [12p / 107m]

IV – *Parents Lament* Andante sospirando [9p / 63m]

V – *Told While Spinning* Allegro vigoroso [17p / 90m]

VI – *Mirabelle's Love-plaint* Poco tranquillo, e semplice [4p / 51m]

VII – *Mirabelle is a Baggage, We Know* Larghetto [4p / 86m]

VIII – *Seven Swains* Poco allegretto – Con moto [8p / 74m]

IX – *To the Wedding* Allegretto con moto [12p / 114m]

X – *Tragedy* Con spirito [13p / 112m]

LS: anon. (probably Cyril Scott)

Publ: 1932 Boosey & Hawkes [H. 13694] (score/parts on hire)

Dur: [30' CS]

Orch: strs / soli / mixed chorus

FP: radio broadcast, 13 or 14 April 1933, The Wireless Chorus

Notes: The 1929 score identifies text as 'anon.'

Julius Harrison refers to this cantata as containing 'some very nice moments' (letter to Leslie Boosey, 29 October 1931).

S 21 W 212 **Mystic Ode** for male chorus (or mixed chorus ad lib) and chamber orchestra [19p / 146m]

Slowly & gravely – Più animato – Con moto / Andante tranquillo

LS: Arkwright Lundy (= Cyril Scott)

Comp: November 1932

Publ: 1933 Elkin [1842]

Dur: [7' CS]

Orch: [0.0.0.2 / 4.2.3.1 / timp / perc / hp / org / vc / db (no vln or vla) / male chorus (SA ad lib)]

MS: holograph of PV score [17p] with estate.

Notes: The original title, *Ode to Unity*, was crossed out on the title page of the manuscript, and replaced with *Mystic Ode*. The title on p. 1 of the score is *Mystical Ode to Unity*, with the <-*al*> and <*to Unity*> excised. Cf. S 24

'It is recommended that the parts for soprano and contralto be used when such voices are available; the work is, however, complete without them.' The optional SA parts enter appear intermittently, and simply double the TB lines up an octave.

Autograph MS to have been sold in the Novello auction sale (15 May 1996), but withdrawn.

S 22 W 360 **Summerland (Devachan)** [*Sommerland (Devachan)*] for chorus (SSAATTBB) and orchestra [27p / 264m]

'Summerland, Devachan, Lotusland. O blessed land!'

['Sommerland, Devaland, Lotusland. O sel'ges Land.' – transl. R. S. Hoffmann]

Andante sostenuto (Lontano, misterioso) – Poco più animato – Tempo tranquillo – Gently flowing – Con moto

LS: Cyril Scott

Publ: 1935 Universal [10233] (PV score)

Dur: [16' CS]

S 23 W 225 **Ode to Great Men** for tenor solo or orator, orchestra and women's voices

Maestoso: Andante – Poco più tranquillo: Misterioso – Tempo poco più animato – More tranquil – Twice as quickly – Gently flowing

LS: Ecclesiasticus, Chapter 44 / James Russell Lowell, *Ode recited at the Harvard Commemoration, 1865* / Percy B. Shelley, *Prometheus Unbound*, III, iii

Comp: February 1936 and premiered at the Norwich Festival, 24 September 1936

Publ: Elkin/Novello (score/parts)

Dur: [15' CS]

Orch: [3.2.ca.2.bcl.3 / 4.3.3.1 / timp / perc / hp / pf / cel / org / strs + speaker (tenor solo) / AAA chorus]

MS: Grainger Museum [MG C3/SCO-98A], photoprint of FS [34p / 207b]
Ref: *BC*, 213 (referred to as *Ode to Famous Men*)

S 24 W 142 **Hymn of Unity** for chorus [SSAATTBB], contralto, baritone and orchestra [FS / PV]

I – *Prelude* [Chorus – 'Unity, Unity! Of that do we sing'] [I / I]

Adagio – Maestoso – Poco più mosso – Moderato – Maestoso [183m] [37p / 17p]

II – *Confession* [Chorus, – 'Not only to God, but to each other let us confess our sins'] [II / II]

Andante – Tempo poco rubato – Tempo I [121m] [30p / 18p]

III – *Visitation* [Baritone – 'Ask me not who I am – for ye would not understand.']

Con spirito – Moderato – Poco più mosso – Più tranquillo (Andante) [III / III] [162m] [34p / 13p]

IV – *Chorale I* [Chorus – 'Oh may the High Powers enlighten mankind'] [IV / IV]

Adagio maestoso [22m] [4p / 3p]

V – *Miserere* [Chorus – 'Have mercy upon me, O God!'] [V / V]

Andante – Tempo poco più mosso [115m] [32p / 18p]

VI – *Exhortation* [Contralto – 'Erewhile ye chose to christen me Dame Nature'] [V / VI]

Moderato – Allegretto / Molto moderato (quasi recit.) – Aria [141m] [37p / 14p]

VII – *De profundis* [Chorus – 'Woe is man! For he doth seem to be, alas, beyond all hope'] [VI / VII]

Adagio lamentoso – Pochissimo più mosso [174m] [35p / 20p]

VIII – *Jubilate I* [Chorus – 'O ye despondent ones – ye err!] [VII / IX]

Allegro [83m] [19p / 13p]

IX – *Colloquy* [The Sage (Baritone) – 'Reason and logic! / the Skeptics (chorus) – 'Impossible! Do we retort! / and the Chorus of Disciples – 'He speaketh Wisdom doth our Master'] [VIII / X]

Fluente tranquillo – Vigoroso – Meno mosso (quasi tempo I) – A tempo, vigoroso – Più tranquillo, quasi tempo I – A tempo molto moderato [214m] [45p / 22p]

X – *Chorale II* [Chorus – 'Oh may we more and more respond unto the pow'r'] [IX / XI]

Maestoso – Adagio, quasi chorale [22m] [4p / 2p]

XI – *Litany* [Contralto/baritone soli and chorus – 'From our great and long-harboured illusions'] [X / X]

Allegretto – A tempo, ma poco meno mosso – Poco meno mosso; somewhat lingeringly [110m] [22p / 12p]

XII – *Jubilate II* [Chorus – 'We are the joyous ones, the free and joyous ones'] [XI / XIII]

Allegro - Somewhat lingeringly – Grazioso – Con moto; quasi tempo primo – Allegro [126m] [29p / 15p]

XIII – *The Angel of Mercy* [Contralto – 'Culture – ye pride yourselves upon its attainment'] [XII / XIV]

Lento – Poco più mosso – Poco tranquillo [132m] [23p / 10p]

XIV – *Invocation* [Chorus – 'Unto the Great White Spirit, unto the Forces of Light'] [XIII / XV]

Allegro moderato [113m] [24p / 15p]

XV – *Finale* [Chorus – 'O life – The one that doth inform the heavens and the earth'] [XIV / XVI]

Con moto – Poco meno mosso, molto maestoso – Con riverenza – Più allargando [115m] [26p / 14p]

LS: Cyril Scott

Comp: PV – March 1947

FS: July 1947

Publ: unpublished; see Note *infra*

Orch: [3.2.eh.2.3 / 4.3.3.1 / timp / perc / hp / pf / org / strs]

Dur: *c.* 75 minutes

MS: Holograph of FS [401p] and PV [211p] with estate. A separate 19-page typescript by Scott of the libretto also exists.

Notes: Scott's most ambitious choral/orchestral work, written in response to Mahatma Koot Hoomi's plea to Scott to return to composition, after the long break from composition during the war years. Scott began with the libretto, then wrote out a piano-vocal score, and orchestrated lastly. The FS/parts and the PV score, in computer-generated form (Trevor Wagler/Graham De'Ath, ed. Leslie De'Ath) are available through the Fleisher Collection in Philadelphia [U-6106].

After the first five movements, confusion prevails in the numbering of movements in the FS and PV. The FS inadvertently has two movements numbered 'V', while the PV score omits 'VIII' and numbers the *Litany* 'X'. The result is that neither manuscript labels the movements correctly from *Jubilate I* to the end, nor are they in agreement with one another except on 'X' – which actually should be 'XI'. Fortunately both manuscripts agree on the ordering of movements, implying that the problems are confined to numerical labels and do not implicate the actual order.

ii – unaccompanied, or with keyboard

S 25 W 188 **Lucy I Love You**, for voice, chorus and piano

Comp: 16 February 1899

LS: Sydney Jones

Ded: Percy Grainger

MS: Grainger Museum [MG C2/SCO-49]

S 26 W 97 **Dixit Dominus** [*Psalmus David CIX*], Op. 27, for male chorus a cappella

LS: Bible (Psalm 109)

Comp: 29 April 1903

MS: Grainger Museum [MG C2/SCO-57]

S 27 W 108 **The Emir's Serenade**, for TTBB soli (or chorus), a cappella [11p]

LS: Ferdinand Irby

Ded: De Reszke Singers

Publ: 1924 Boosey [H. 11121] (Modern Festival Series 314)

LE: Boosey & Hawkes [BH 83480]

Note: All vocal lines have tonic sol-fa notation as well as standard pitch notation.

S 28 W284 **The Rat-Catcher**, for TTBB soli (or male chorus) and flute [12p / 59m]

LS: unknown (prob. Cyril Scott)

Publ: 1924 Boosey [H. 11122] (Modern Festival Series 315)

Ded: De Reszke Singers

Note: Flute part may be played on piano, or flute stop of organ. Wordless humming predominates throughout.

All vocal lines have tonic sol-fa notation as well as standard pitch notation.

S 29 W 141 **The Huntsman's Dirge**, for male chorus (TTBB) a cappella

LS: Sir Walter Scott

Publ: 1924 Boosey [H. 11313] (Modern Festival Series 321)

LE: Boosey & Hawkes [BH 83479]

MS: with estate [3p / 41b]

Note: All vocal lines have tonic sol-fa notation as well as standard pitch notation.

S 30 W 45 **Benedicite, omnia opera Domine**, for chorus (SAATTBB) and organ [11p / 186m]

Con spirito

Publ: 1935 Stainer & Bell [S. & B. 4569] [Modern Church Services No. 286]

Dur: [6' CS]

Note: unpublished version for chorus and orchestra exists (MS with estate) [25p / 186m] [3.2.2.bcl.3 / 4.3.3.1 / timp, perc, hp, pf ('upright will suffice'), celesta / strs]

S 31 W 46 **Benedictus es Domine**, for chorus (SSAATTBB) and organ [7p / 74m]

Maestoso ma con moto

Publ: 1935 Stainer & Bell [S. & B. 4570] [Modern Church Services No. 287]

S 32 W 166 **Jubilate Deo**, for chorus (SAATB) and organ [7p / 71m]

Moderato con moto

Publ: 1935 Stainer & Bell [S. & B. 4571] [Modern Church Services No. 288]

S 33 W 115 **Evening Service**, for chorus (SSAATTBB) and organ [12p / 262m]

1 – *Magnificat* Moderato ma con spirito [7p / 180m]

2 – *Nunc dimittis* Andante sostenuto [4p / 82m]

Publ: 1935 Stainer & Bell [S. & B. 4572] [Modern Church Services No. 289]

C ORCHESTRAL

S 34 W 366 **Symphony No. 1 in G major**

I – Allegro frivolo – Andante – Allegro assai [6' 36"]

II – Andante con moto – Grazioso – A tempo I [6' 18"]

III – Allegretto [Trio I, Poco meno mosso / Trio II, Moderato] [4' 57"]

IV – Finale: Tema con variazioni – Molto moderato – Fuga: Pochissimo più mosso – andante [12' 37"]

Comp: April 1899

Publ: unpublished. Score available through the Fleisher Collection in Philadelphia [U-6481].

Ded: 'In the truest friendship and admiration to the poet Stefan George to whose art I am indebted for many of my best and most religious ideas.'

Dur: [30' 44"]

Ref: *MYI*, 25–6, 31, 36–9, 115 / *BC*, 76

Notes: According to Scott, the symphony was rewarded 'by exciting the admiration of both Quilter and Grainger.' (*MYI*, 25). 'I have since consigned them [S 34 and 15] to the crematorium, which is the best and safest place for them.' (*MYI*, 26)

Third movement completed and edited for performance by Leslie De'Ath.

S 35 W 234/244 **Pelleas and Melisanda** – overture, Op. 5 / Op. 20 [315m]
Andantino – Andante con moto – Più allegretto – Andante doloroso
Comp: 1 February 1900 (rev. *c.* 1902 as Op. 20)
Ref: *MYI*, 39–41, 59, 68
Dur: [17' 21"]

Note: score edited by Martin Yates, 2012

S 36 W 190 **Lyric Suite**, Op. 6
Comp: 1900
Ref: *MYI*, 68 (referred to as 'Idyllic')

Note: unpublished; MS lost'

S 37 W 138 **Heroic Suite**, Op. 7
1 – *Solemn Prelude*
2 – *Legend*
3 – *Capriccio and Andante*
4 – *Theme with Variations*
Comp: 1900
Ref: *MYI*, 68, 80–83, 92 / *BC*, 85–6

Note: unpublished; MS lost

S 38 W 118 **Symphonic Fantasia**, Op. 12
Comp: *c.* 1900

S 39 W 367 **Symphony No. 2 in A minor**, Op. 22
1 – Andante
2 – Allegro con brio
3 – Andante
4 – Finale: Allegro
Comp: 1901–02
Publ: unpublished
Ref: *MYI*, 68, 115 / *BC*, 91

Note: Revised as *Three Symphonic Dances*, S 46. See also T.62.

S 40 W 263 **Princess Maleine** – overture, Op. 18
Comp: 1899–1902
Ded: Clemens von Franckenstein
Ref: *BC*, 138 (referred to as *An Overture to Princess Maleine*)

Note: Not premiered until 22 August 1907 (Queen's Hall, Henry Wood). Destroyed by Scott. Reworked in 1912 as S 16.

S 41 W 3 **Aglavaine et Sélysette** – overture, Op. 21

Comp: *c.* 1901

Note: Overture to the Maurice Maeterlinck play. Scott refers to it as the Prelude.

S 42 W 14 **Arabesque**

FP: Birmingham, *c.* 1910 (conducted by Scott)

S 43 W 292 **Rhapsody No. 1**, Op. 32

FP: London, Queen's Hall Promenade Concert, 10 September 1904 Queen's Hall Orch. (cond. Sir Henry Wood)

Ref. *MYI*, 104.

Note: Scott states that Debussy admired this work, and that it later was lost in Petrograd.

S 44 W 293 **Rhapsody No. 2**

Comp: *c.* 1904

Ref: *MYI*, 81–2

Note: Never performed. Score destroyed by Scott.

S 45 W 22/23 **Aubade**, Op. 77, for large orchestra [35p / 226m]

Andante sostenuto – Poco più mosso – Allegro – Tempo de l'Andante

Ded: 'To my friend Landon Ronald'

Comp: 1905 / rev. *c.* 1911

Publ: 1911 Schott [29143] Score available through the Fleisher Collection in Philadelphia [4550].

LE: n.d. Schott [ED 3372, FS & parts on hire]

Dur: [10' 50"] [10' CS]

Orch: [3(=picc).2.ca.2.bcl.2 / 4.2.3.1 / timp / perc (1) / 2 hp / vla solo / strs]

MS: Schott, London

Ref: *BC*, 124

S 46 W 365 **Three Symphonic Dances**, Op. 22

1 – Allegro con brio – Vivace [4' 45"]

2 – Andante sostenuto e sempre molto cantabile [8' 47" – 9' 11"]

3 – Allegro energico – Grazioso – Sostenuto [4' 25"]

Comp: *c.* 1907, from S 39

Dur: [17' 59" – 18' 29"] [25' CS]

Ref: *BC*, 91 (referred to as *Three Orchestral Dances*)

Orch: [3.3.2.2 / 4.3.3.1 / timp / perc / 2 hp / strs]

Note: Revision of Symphony No. 2, S 39, omitting the first movement. On the title page of 1 – Allegro con brio, Scott has written 'Dance from the Ballet the "Short-Sighted Apothecary"' (S 6, qv). See also T.62.

S 47 W 65/66 **Christmas Overture**, Op. 10

Comp: *c.* 1900; rev. *c.* 1910

Note: withdrawn

Cf. S 18 & 55

S 48 W 104 **Egypt**

1 – *In the Temple of Memphis*

2 – *By the Waters of the Nile*

3 – *Egyptian Boat Song*

4 – *Funeral March of the Great Raamses*

5 – *Song of the Spirits of the Nile*

Comp: 1913

Publ: (Schott)

MS: string parts (1926) extant, with Schott Music, Mainz. Score and other parts missing.

Note: See also S 212.

S 49 W 256 **Poems – No. 4 – Twilight of the Year**

Comp: arr. *c.* 1913 from S 210

Publ: Schott

MS: Schott (parts only)

S 50 W 257 **Poems – No. 5 – Paradise-Birds**

Comp: arr. *c.* 1913 from S 210

Publ: Schott

Dur: [3' Sch]

Orch: [2.picc.2.ca.2.bcl.2.cbsn / 4.3.3.1 / timp / perc / 2 hp / strs]

MS: Schott London (FS/parts)

S 51 W 51 **Britain's War March**

Comp: 1914

Ded: HRH The Prince of Wales

Dur: [*c.* 3' 30"]

FP: 23 October 1914, Promenade Concert, Queen's Hall Orchestra (cond. Sir Henry Wood)

Note: cf. S 216

S 52 W 236 **Two Passacaglias on Irish Themes** [36p / 305m]

I – Allegretto alla breve [23p / 20m] [6' 33"]

II – Andante sostenuto [13p / 99m] [4' 44"]

Comp: 1914 / rev. 1916

Publ: 1922 Schott [30769]

Dur: [11' 17"] [7' CS]

Orch: [4(=picc).3.ca.4.bcl.4.cbsn / 6.4.3.1 / timp / perc (3) / cel / org / pf / 2 hp / strs]

Ref: *MYI*, 164 / *BC*, 85, 92, 139, 163

S 53 W 353 **Suite fantastique** for chamber orchestra

I – *Fata morgana* Tranquillo e poco rubato [7' 22"]

II – *Fire Dance* Allegro [1' 25"]

III – *Dance of Spectres* Allegretto poco moderato [5' 03"]

IV – *Goblins and Elves* Con moto [3' 33"]

Publ: 1927 Universal (B&H)

Dur: [17' 23"] [16' CS]

Orch: [1.1.1.1 / 1.0.0.0 / timp / perc / hp / strs]

S 54 W 356 **First Suite** [*Suite No. 1*] for string orchestra

I – *Silver Threads Among the Gold* [3' 47"]

II – *Long, Long Ago* [2' 42"]

III – *Oh, Dear, What Can the Matter Be?* [2' 27"]

Publ: 1931 Hawkes & Son [H. 7031]

Dur: [8' 51"] [8' CS]

Orch: strs

S 55 W 221 **Noël: Christmas-Overture** for large orchestra with mixed choir ad lib [64p / 397m]

Misterioso: Lento – Più mosso – Andante amabile – Allegro – Poco meno mosso – Tranquillo – Allegro – Tempo di chorale – Molto cantabile – Molto tranquillo

Comp: 1930 (November 1928 on holograph)

Publ: 1931 Schott (hire) [32461, score / 32462, parts]

LS: Richard Crashaw

Ded: Sir Thomas Beecham

MS: with estate

Dur: [10' CS] [7' Schott]

Orch: [3(=picc).2(=ca).2.bcl.3.cbsn / 4.3.3.1 / timp / perc (5) / 2 hp (2nd ad lib) / cel / pf (upright) / org / strs]

LE: Schott [3329]

Notes: Title page of holograph has title 'Nowell', crossed out and replaced with 'Noel'. See also S 18 and S 47.

S 56 W 95 **Disaster at Sea**

Comp: begun 1918

FP: London, Queen's Hall, 19 October 1933, London Philharmonic Orch. (cond. Albert Coates)

Ref: *BC*, 204

Note: music reworked into S 57

S 57 W 215 **Neptune: Poem of the Sea**, for large orchestra

I – Andante – Molto maestoso [5' 34"]

II – Con moto – Largo [1' 40"]

III – *Tempo di valse.* Molto cantabile – Wistfully [3' 39"]

IV – Allegro agitato [9' 28"]

V – Adagio molto – Tristamente [4' 00"]

Comp: 1933 (rev.1935)

Publ: Schott (hire)

Orch: [4(=picc).2.ca.3.bcl.3.cbsn / 6.4.3.1 / timp / perc / 2 hp / cel / pf / org / strs]

Dur: [24' 21"] [16' CS]

Note: revision of S 56

S 58 W 359 **Summer Gardens** [*Sommer-Gärten*]

1 – *Reverie in the Rose-Garden*

2 – *Where the Bee Sucks*

3 – *Raindrops*

Publ: 1935 Schott [Domesticum-Salon-Orchester 390]

Dur: [8' Schott]

Orch: [1.1.1.1 / 1.0.0.0 / perc / hp / strs]

S 59 W 368 **Symphony No. 3, *The Muses***, for orchestra, SATB chorus and organ

1 – *Melpomene: Muse of Epic Poetry and Tragedy*, Andante sostenuto [346m] [14' 33"]

2 – *Thalia: Muse of Comedy and Merry Verse*, Allegro con spirito [192m] [5' 40"]

3 – *Erato: Muse of Love and Poetry*, Molto tranquillo [90m] [6' 43"]

4 – *Terpsichore: Muse of Dance and Song*, Molto moderato e ritmico [231m] [7' 55"]

Comp: 1937

Publ: 2000 Computer score by Colin Rae. Schott (hire)

Ded: Sir Thomas Beecham

Dur: [34' 45"] [35' – CS]

Orch: 4(4.pic).2.ca.2.bcl.3.cbsn / 4.3.3.1 / timp / perc / 2hp / pno / cel / org / strs

MS: with estate

S 60 W 223 **Ode descantique**, for string orchestra

I – Maestoso poco rubato

II – Tranquillo

III – In the folk dance manner

Comp: *c.* 1940

Publ: Schott (hire)

Dur: [15' Schott]

MS: with estate (*Serenade*), & Schott (*Ode*)

Ref: *BC*, 205

Orch: strs

Note: alternative title is *Serenade for strings*

S 61 – **Five Preludes for orchestra** [92p / 435m]

1 – *Reverie* Quietly flowing [18p / 86m]

2 – *Invigoration* Vigoroso (alla Marcia) [21p / 83m]

3 – *Romance* Andante tranquillo – Con moto ma tranquillo (Tempo 2) [15p / 64m]

4 – *Jocundity* Allegro non troppo [22p / 116m]

5 – *Lamentation* Grave / Maestoso [16p / 86m]

Comp: May 1949

Publ: unpublished

Printed score available through estate.

Orch: 2.1(ca).2.2 / 2.2.3.1 / perc / hp / strs

Note: Discovered 1 June 2017 among MSS belonging to the estate.

S 62 W 139 **The Hourglass**, suite for small orchestra

I – Night [5' 00"]

II – Dawn [5' 30"]

III – And then the day [4' 00"]

IV – Evening [4' 00"]

Comp: *c.* 1949

Publ: unpublished

Orch: [1.1(=ca).2.1 / 2.1.0.0 / timp / perc / pf / strs]

Dur: [18' 30"]

Ref: *BC*, 224

Note: The suite was premiered posthumously at the Queen Elizabeth Hall (Polyphonia Orchestra, Bryan Fairfax cond.) on 21 May 1971.

All attempts to locate a score have been unsuccessful.

Data is from an old Keith Prowse catalogue.

Frank Bridge's 3-movement piano suite *The Hour Glass* (1920; H.418), with its

Debussyan sonorities, may have served as a model for this suite, unless the title is mere coincidence. The Bridge titles – *Dusk / The Dew Fairy / The Midnight Tide* – follow a similar diurnal pattern.

S 63 W 164 **Irish Serenade,** for string orchestra

Comp: *c.* 1951

Publ: n.d. Novello (FS & parts)

Dur: [16' CS]

Orch: strs

S 64 W 369 **Symphony No. 4** [133p / 579m]

1 – Adagio – Vigoroso – Grazioso – Andante poco rubato – Grazioso [47p / 204m] [9' 31"]

2 – Molto tranquillo [17p / 104m] [7' 03"]

3 – *Scherzo*: Allegro – Allegro non troppo – Cantabile con amore [29p / 108m] [3' 53"]

4 – *Rondo retrospettivo*: Adagio – Energico – Estatico, con amore [40p / 163m] [7' 53"]

Comp: *c.* 1951–52

Publ: 2000 Computer score by Colin Rae

Dur: [28' 21"]

Orch: 2.1.ca.2.3 / 4.3.3.1 / timp / perc / hp / pno(cel) / str

MS: with estate

Note: labeled 'Symphony No. II' in the autograph MS, which was to have been sold in the Novello auction sale (15 May 1996), but withdrawn.

S 65 W 302 **Russian Fair**

Comp: *c.* 1952

Publ: Novello (FS & parts)

Orch: [3.2.2.2 / 4.2.3.1 / timp / perc / 2 xyl / glock / cel / hp / strs]

Dur: [20' CS]

Note: See also S 227 and S 272.

S 66 W 214 **Neapolitan Rhapsody** [66p / 292m]

Tranquillo – Energico – Tempo poco sostenuto – Allegro moderato – Vigoroso – Tranquillo – Andante tranquillo – Tempo meno tranquillo ma rubato – Allegro – Cantab. amabile – Giocoso – Maestoso

Publ: 1959 Boosey & Hawkes [B. & H. 18521]

Dur: [13' 15"] [12'–12' 30", B&H]

Orch: [3.2 + ca.2.3 / 4.3.3.1 / timp / perc / hp / strs]

S 67 W 320 / 321 **Sinfonietta** for string orchestra, organ and harp

I – Misterioso. Molto tranquillo – Poco meno tranquillo – Più tranquillo – Gently flowing but rubato and a shade lingeringly at times – More flowing – A tempo – Poco meno mosso – Tempo II –Ben fluidamente – Maestoso [47p / 174m]

II – *Scherzo*: Energico – Allegro moderato – Pochissimo meno mosso – A tempo, grazioso – Flowing [26p / 68m]

III – *Fine retrospettivo*: Adagio – Allegretto – Pochissimo meno mosso. Grazioso – Con moto – Tempo di Mve.1 – Tempo di Scherzo – More flowing [47p / 151m]

Comp: September 1964

Publ: unpublished

Score available through the Fleisher Collection in Philadelphia [U-6433].

MS: with estate [121p]

Orch: [org / hp / strs]

Note: Scott's last work for a large ensemble, written at age 84. The manuscript now reveals a certain tremulousness in the handwriting, while still being quite legible. The *Sinfonietta* for string orchestra (W321 in Sampsel) appears to be non-existent.

D CONCERTANTE WORKS

i – instrumental

S 68 W 73 **Concerto in D**, for piano and orchestra, Op. 10

I – Adagio maestoso [10.53]

II – *Intermezzo*: Andante espressivo – Cadenza – Andantino [10.02]

III – *Finale*: Vivace [9.40]

Comp: 1900

Dur: [30.35]

MS: Grainger Museum [MG C2/SCO-46]

Ref: *MYI*, 68

Notes: CS showed it to Paderewski *c.* 1901, but he never played it.

'Destroyed', according to Scott (*MYI*, 83–4). One melody from it was incorporated into S 301.

Performing edition realised and completed by Martin Yates from surviving sketches in the Grainger Museum, 2012.

S 69 W 79 **Concerto for violoncello and orchestra**, Op. 19

Largo misterioso – Quasi cadenza – Andante cantabile – Allegro con brio

Comp: 1902

Dur: [20' 52"]

MS: Grainger Museum

Note: Completed and revised by Martin Yates, 2012.

Cello part edited by Raphael Wallfisch, 2012.

S 70 W 74 **Concerto No. 1 in C major for piano and orchestra** [59p]

I – Allegro maestoso – Allegro – Molto tranquillo – Andante quasi allegretto – Allegro [29p / 670b] [12' 46"]

II – Adagio [7p / 137b] [7' 55"]

III – Allegro poco moderato – Estatico – Andante e improvizatore – A tempo [23p / 586m] [10' 00"]

Comp: 1913–14

Publ: 1922 Schott [30764], 2-pf reduction. Schott [30765], parts. Score also available through the Fleisher Collection in Philadelphia [86p].

Orch: [2.1.2.2 / 0.0.0.0 / timp / perc (2) / hp / cel / harmonica? / strs + piano solo]

Dur: [30' 42" – 39' 24"] [25' CS]

Ref: *MYI*, 83–4, 164, 201 / *BC*, 79, 138–41, 163

S 71 W 76 **Concerto for violin and orchestra** [68p]

I – Larghetto [4' 12"]

II – Adagio – Allegro con spirito [7' 12"]

III – Largo [4' 44"]

IV – Allegro [5' 46"]

Comp: 1927

Publ: Schott [ED 12828], pf reduction
Schott, FS (hire)

Dur: [21' 55"] [25' CS]

Orch: [2(=picc).2.2.2 / 4.2.3.1 / timp / perc / hp / strs + vln solo]

Ref: *BC*, 206

S 72 W 245 **Philomel,** for violoncello and orchestra

Comp: *c.* 1925

Score lost

Note: Early version of S73?

S 73 W 77 Concerto for violin, violoncello and orchestra

Comp: 1926

MS: full score lost; 2 solo parts at Royal Academy of Music

Note: written for May and Beatrice Harrison

S 74 W 199 **The Melodist and the Nightingales** [*Der Musikant und die Nachtigallen*], for violoncello and orchestra

Comp: *c.* 1929

Publ: Schott (hire)

Dur: [19' 28"] [16' CS]

Orch: [2.1.2.3 / 4.(3).0.0 / timp / perc / hp / pf / strs + vc solo]

Note: see S 142.

S 75 W 101 **Early One Morning: Poem,** for piano and orchestra

Andantino – Senza misura – Allegretto – Tempo moderato – Tempo poco più mosso – Tempo agitato – Idealmente e poco meno mosso – Tempo più tranquillo al fine [35p / 280m]

Comp: June 1930, rev. September 1958

Publ: 1931 Winthrop Rogers / Boosey & Hawkes [7020], 2-pf reduction 1962 Boosey & Hawkes [18602], 2-pf reduction

Dur: [13' 54" – 14' 48"] [16' CS]

Orch: (1962) [2.2.2.3 / 4.0.3.0 / timp / perc / hp / strs + piano solo]

S 76 W 78 **Concerto for two violins and orchestra**

Comp: 1931

Publ: Novello

Dur: [25' CS]

Orch: [2.2.2.2 / 4.2.3.0 / timp / perc / hp / strs + 2 violins soli]

Note: Autograph MS to have been sold in the Novello auction sale (15 May 1996), but withdrawn; score subsequently lost.

S 77 W 70 **Concertino for two pianos and orchestra**

Comp: *c.* 1931

Publ: unpublished

Dur: [16' CS]

Orch: [1.0.0.0 / 2.2.3.0 / timp / perc / strs + 2 pfs soli]

Note: score appears to be lost.

S 78 W 235 **Passacaglia festevole** for two pianos and orchestra

Comp: *c.* 1935

Dur: [20' CS]

MS: unknown

S 79 – **Concerto for violoncello and orchestra**

I – Molto tranquillo – Allegro [16' 41"]

II – *Intermezzo pastorale.* Andante molto sostenuto [3' 59"]

III – *Rondo giocoso.* Maestoso [6' 22"]

Comp: 11 May 1937

Publ: unpublished

Dur: [27' 08"] [25' CS]

Orch: [2.2.2.2 / 4.2.3.0 / timp / perc / hp / cel(pf) / strs + vc solo]

S 80 W 71 **Concerto for harpsichord and orchestra** [117p / 462m]

I – Allegro vigoroso – A tempo ma poch. meno mosso – Sostenuto tranquillo – Molto moderato – Quicker, con moto – Vigoroso [62p/251m] [8' 11"]

II – *Pastorale orientale*. Andante [20p/72m] [4' 44"]

III – *Finale*. Allegro con spirito – Cantabile con grazia – Nearly twice as quick [35p/139m] [3' 57"]

Publ: 2008 (rev. 2009) Novello [NOV 958100] (FS). Modern print of the full score by Jory Vinikour.

Dur: [16' 52"] [25' CS] [*c*. 18', Novello FS]

Orch: [1.0.1.1 / 0.0.0.0 / hp / pf / str / + harpsichord solo]

FP: London, Wigmore Hall, 8 April 1938 (Lucille Wallace, harpsichord, Grande Chamber Orchestra conducted by Angel Grande; modern revival: 2008, London, St. John's Smith Square (Jory Vinikour, harpsichord / Orion Orchestra / Toby Purser, cond)

Ref: *BC*, 204

Note: Autograph MS to have been sold in the Novello auction sale (15 May 1996), but withdrawn.

S 81 W 72 **Concerto for oboe and strings**

I – Molto vigoroso – Andante [7' 24"]

II – *Pastorale*. Tranquillo [5' 20"]

III – *Rondo giocoso*. Allegro non troppo [6' 43"]

Comp: 1946

Publ: 1949 Elkin [2169]

Dur: [19' 27"] [17' Elkin]

Orch: [strs + oboe solo]

Note: Autograph MS to have been sold in the Novello auction sale (15 May 1996), but withdrawn at the sale. With estate.

S 82 W 69 **Concertino for flute, bassoon and string orchestra** (in one movement) [MS: 32p/253m]

Con moto tranquillo – Tranquillo e poco rubato – With more movement – Poco maestoso e sostenuto – Broader in tempo e sostenuto – Andante (but don't drag) – Vigoroso – Quasi tempo primo – Pochissimo meno mosso – Maestoso e poco rubato – Quasi cadenza: Tranquillo – Double as quick – Maestoso e rubato – Con moto

Comp: 4 March 1951

Publ: unpublished

Printed score/parts by Graham De'Ath, available through estate [29p]

MS: holograph in the University of Michigan library system

Orch: strs + flute & bassoon soli

Note: Facsimile score available through the Fleisher Collection, Philadelphia[U-6435].

S 83 W 75 **Concerto No. 2 for piano and orchestra**

I – Con moto e poco rubato – Meno mosso – Vigoroso [9' 46"]

II – Molto tranquillo – Adagio – Tempo I [4' 49"]

III – Energico – Grazioso – Moderato – Tempo I [5' 43"]

Comp: 1958

Publ: Schott (hire)

Dur: [20' 14" – 25' 00"]

Orch: [3.2.ca.2.3 / 4.3.3.0 / timp / perc (2) / hp / strs + pf solo]

ii – vocal

S 84 W34 **The Ballad of Fair Helen of Kirkconnel**, Op. 8, for baritone and orchestra

Ded: Frederic Austin

Comp: 1900

Note: Balfour Gardiner rescored it in 1911

See also S 422

S 85 W296 **Rima's Call to the Birds**, scena for soprano and orchestra [16p / 233 (252)m]

Moderato – Allegro con spirito – Allegro moderato ed improvisatore – Allegro con spirito – Broadly

'Oolah, oolah / Oh, ye lovely ones' ['Ulah, ulah … / Kommt, Ihr Lieblichen']

LS: Cyril Scott? (from W. H. Hudson, *Green Mansions*)

Ded: Gertrude Johnson

Comp: *c.* 1929

Publ: 1933 Elkin [1852 – pf reduction]

Dur: [15' CS]

MS: holograph of PV score with estate

Ref: *BC*, 203

Note: The PV holograph contains the text in English and German. Although no German title is found, many musical markings also appear in German, as well as Italian. Scott may have hoped that Schott would pick up the score, too, but no score is known to have been published by them. The original title in holograph is *Rima*, which is crossed out and replaced with the full title.

E CHAMBER

i – piano and strings

S 86 W 265 **Quartet in E minor**, Op. 16, for piano and strings [36+8+8+8p]
I – Allegro maestoso con spirito [15p / 280m] [6' 45"]
II – Andante molto espressivo [7p / 77m] [4' 33"]
III – Allegretto amabile e sempre con sordini [5p / 52m] [3' 07"]
IV – Allegro non troppo [9p / 287m] [5' 05"]
Ded: 'To William Henry Leslie in friendship and gratitude'
Comp: 1899–1901
Publ: 1903 Boosey [H. 3969]
Dur: [19' 30" – 21' 50"]
Ref: *MYI*, 68–72
BC, 84, 87–8

S 87 W 383 **Trio in E minor**, Op. 3, for violin, cello and piano
Ded: Iwan Knorr
Comp: *c.* 1899
Ref: *MYI*, 13
BC, 64

S 88 W 275 **Quintet in E minor for piano and strings**
Comp: *c.* 1900
Note: withdrawn
MS: National Library of Scotland

S 89 W 317 **Sextet for piano and strings**, Op. 26 (3 vlns, vla, vc, pf)
Comp: *c.* 1903
Ref: *MYI*, 92, 148. 156
Note: withdrawn

S 90 W 276 **Quintet for piano and strings**
Comp: *c.* 1907
Note: withdrawn; perhaps a revision of S 89, further revised as S 91.

S 91 W 277 **Quintet for piano and strings**

Comp: 1911–12

Publ: unpublished

Dur: [*c.* 40.00]

Note: revision of Sextet, S 89.

Ref: *MYI*, 71

Note: 'Op. 57', according to Fuller-Maitland (Grove, 1914 – an unusual claim, given that Op. 57/1–5 had all been published between 1907 and 1910. Opp. 53 or 60 seem far more likely, neither number having been claimed.

S 92 W 384 **Trio in C major** [No. 1] for violin, cello and piano [56p / 914m]

I – Allegretto moderato – Allegro con spirito [23p / 372m] [13' 22"]

II – Sostenuto misterioso – Allegro con molto spirito [10p / 198m] [5' 56"]

III – Andante sostenuto [10p / 150m] [8' 54"]

IV – *Rondo giocoso*. Allegro ma non troppo [13p / 194m] [5' 27"]

Comp: *c.* 1920

Publ: 1922 Schott [30740]

LE: Schott [ED 3110]

Dur: [33' 48"] [25' CS]

Ref: *BC*, 212, 224

S 93 W 278 **Quintet in C major** [No. 1] for piano and strings [85+19/19/19/19p / 883(+7)m]

I – Andante con esaltazione [28p / 254m] [13.11]

II – Allegro grazioso ma non troppo [13p / 133m] [4.19]

III – Adagio con gran espressione [15p / 193(+7)m] [9.25]

IV – *Finale:* Allegro con molto spirito [27p / 303m] [10.51]

Ded: Evyln Howard-Jones

Comp: 1920

Publ: 1925 Stainer & Bell [S. & B. 3048]

LE: 2003 Maecenas Music [MM 0522], 2011 Peters [EP 71595]

Dur: [37' 46" – 39' 20"] [25' CS]

Ref: *BC*, 92–3, 229

Note: won the Carnegie Trust Award in 1924.

S 94 W 81 **Cornish Boat Song** [*Schifferlied aus Cornwall / Chant du marin de Cornwall*], for violin, cello and piano [3+1+1p / 37(46)m]

Languido, poco lento

Ded: Cecil Holmes Waghorn

Publ: 1931 Schott [B.S.S. 32946]

LE: Schott [ED 2181]

Dur: [3' 00"]

S 95 W 174 **Little Folk-Dance** [*Englischer Volkstanz / Danse paysanne anglaise*] for violin, cello and piano

Moderato

Ded: Grace Thynne

Publ: 1931 Schott [B.S.S. 32947]

LE: Schott [ED 2182]

S 96 W 385 **Trio** [No. 2] in one movement, for violin, cello and piano [26p / 250m]

Grave – Molto moderato – Fließend – Amabile – Con moto – Molto maestoso e sostenuto

Publ: 1951 Schott [S & C. 5591]

LE: n.d. Schott [ED 10416]

Dur: [10' 08"]

S 97 W 279 **Quintet** [**No. 2**] **for piano and strings** [91p]

I – Grave, maestoso – Andante fluidamente – Allegretto amabile – Tranquillo – Tempo primo [41p / 219m]

II – *Humoresque* – Allegro moderato – Maestoso e poco rubato – Tranquillo – Tempo primo [20p / 125m]

III – Adagio – Poco più mosso – Maestoso (attacca IV) [11p / 83m]

IV – *Finale* – Energico – Allegretto – Maestoso e poco rubato – Tempo primo – Molto maestoso [21p / 136m]

Comp: 23 November 1952

Publ: unpublished

MS: holograph with estate

Note: In the holograph, black ink changes to blue ink toward the end of the third movement.

S 98 W 386 **Trio** [No. 3] for violin, cello and piano

Comp: 1957

Publ: unpublished

ii – strings

S 99 W 266 **String quartet**, Op. 12

Comp: November 1901

Publ: unpublished

Ref: *MYI*, 43, 68

Notes: 'I sent it to a certain violinist in Manchester, and either he lost it or it got lost in the post. In either case I bear him no ill-will – he saved me the trouble of burning the work, which was an immature one.' The manuscript nevertheless is extant in the Liverpool Central Library,

Repository 74-D4. A note with the manuscript indicates it was written for 'Mr F. J. Hall of Liverpool and performed once in his home'.

S 100 W 267 **String quartet**, Op. 28

Comp: *c.* 1903

S 101 W 268 **String quartet in F major**, Op. 31

Comp: *c.* 1904

S 102 W 280 **Quintet for two violins, viola, and two celli**

Comp: 1919

Publ: unpublished

Ref: *MYI*, 235

S 103 W 96 **Divertimento for string quartet**

Comp: *c.* 1920

Publ: unpublished

Dur: [16' CS]

S 104 W 269 **Quartet for strings** [No. 1] [76p]

I – *Prelude*. Molto moderato – Molto tranquillo [18p / 176m] [10' 31"]

II – *Pastorale*. Allegro moderato – Tempo tranquillo – Tempo I [12p / 100m] [5' 40"]

III – *Scherzo. On an Irish Air*. Vivace – Più mosso – Presto [10p / 82(114)m] [3' 05"]

IV – *Elegy*. Andante sostenuto con molto espressione – Poco animato – A tempo primo [6p / 68m] [4' 33"]

IV – *Rondo retrospettivo*. Allegro con spirito – Animato [29p / 230m] [7' 40"]

Comp: 1918–19

Publ: 1921 Elkin [1239]

Dur: [31' 49"] [25' CS]

Ref: *MYI*, 235

S 105 W 387 **String trio No. 1** [12/12/12p]

I – Allegretto cantabile, ma poco rubato – Quasi Tempo II – Tempo I – Maestoso [177m]

II – Allegro con spirito – Tranquillo – Tempo I [150m]

III – Andante ma con moto (quietly flowing) – Poco più animato, ma con rubato – Tranquillo [124m]

IV – Allegro vigoroso – Tranquillo – Tempo I – Quasi tempo of Move[ment] 1 [141m]

Comp: 1931

Publ: n.d. [1940] Schott [B.S.S. 35962a-c], set of parts

Dur: [25' CS]

S 106 W 388 **String trio No. 2** [37p]

I – Molto moderato e poco rubato [13p / 179m]

II – Larghetto [7p / 111m]

III – Con spirito [6p / 77m]

IV – Moderato, maestoso e poco rubato – Energico – Poco meno mosso – A tempo. Energico [11p / 191m]

Ded: 'In memory of Iwan Knorr'

Comp: January 1948

Publ: unpublished

S 107 W 281 **Quintet for two violins, 2 violas and cello** [66p / 399m]

I – Tranquillo – Andante – Moderato – Poch. più mosso – A tempo – Quasi Tempo I – Amabile, flowing – Con moto [28p / 165m]

II – Adagio – Poco più mosso [9p / 59m]

II – Energico – Poco meno mosso – Poco maestoso – Meno mosso – Poco più animato – Poco maestoso – Più mosso – Amabile – Quasi Tempo I – Grazioso – Maestoso [19p / 175m]

Comp: 3 July 1953

Publ: n.d. Novello (facsimile of MS)

MS: with estate

S 108 W 270 **String quartet No. 2** [47p]

I – Allegro moderato e maestoso – Slightly quieter – Quasi andante – Tempo primo [20p / 238m] [9' 08"]

II – *In memoriam E.M.*: Quasi marche funèbre – A shade quicker – Tempo I [3p / 51m] [3' 11"]

III – Allegro amabile – Andante con moto – Tempo I [6p / 116m] [4' 11"]

IV – Allegro con spirito [16p / 155m] [6' 16"]

Ded: Percy and Ella Grainger

Publ: 1958 Elkin [2530]

Dur: [22' 46"] [25' CS]

Ref: *BC*, 207, 231

S 109 W 271 **String quartet No. 3** [36p]

I – Con moto poco tranquillo – Con amore [17p / 157m]

II – Adagio ma non troppo – Cantabile – Più sonoro [8p / 105m]

III – Energico – Gracefully flowing – Con moto [11p / 102m]

Publ: 1960 Elkin [2577]

S 110 W 272 **String quartet No. 4** [16p]

I – Allegretto amabile [8p / 112m] [6' 00"]

II – Adagio non troppo – Pochissimo più mosso – Tempo 10 [3p / 58m] [3' 48"]

III – Allegro assai – Allegretto amabile – A tempo primo [5p / 93m] [3' 42"]

Comp: June 1965

Publ: 1968 Elkin [2718]

Dur: [13' 30"]

iii – mixed chamber

S 111 W 407 **Two Villanelles,** for vocal quartet, viola and pianoforte [32p / 182m]

1 – *Villanelle of Autumn*

'Our dreams are dead for summer suns are spent'. Andante [17p / 111m]

2 – *Villanelle of Spring*

'The first vernal sighs caress the hopeful heather', Allegretto molto moderato [15p / 71m]

Comp: 1911

Publ: unpublished

Note: MS (copyist's hand) with estate

S 112 W 145 **Idyllic Fantasy,** for voice, oboe and cello [11+7+7p / 149m]

[no marking] – Animato – A tempo

'What plaintive melodies are these / Sighing 'mid the shadowy trees?'

LS: Cyril Scott

Ded: Astra Desmond

Publ: 1921 Elkin [1240]

LE: Masters Music Publications (= Elkin [1240])

Performance note: 'The oboe and 'cello to be played behind a screen at the side of the stage or in the ante-room with door ajar.'

S 113 W 294 **Rhapsody arabesque,** for flute, harp and string trio

Comp: *c.* 1925

Publ: unpublished

Dur: [12' CS]

Note: René Le Roy, flautist, founded the *Quintette instrumental de Paris* (fl / hp / string trio) in 1922. The group also received works by d'Indy, Jongen and Roussel. S 113 & 114 were both composed for this group. No extant copy of the score is known.

S 114 W 274 **Quintet for flute, harp and string trio**

Ded: René Le Roy

Comp: 1926

Publ: unpublished

Note: See note under S 113.

S 115 W 295 **Rima's Call to the Birds**, for soprano and string quartet

Comp: *c.* 1927

Publ: unpublished

S 116 W 273 **Quintet in one movement**, for clarinet and string quartet

Molto moderato e maestoso e poco rubato – Grazioso (con moto) – Maestoso – Andante, but don't drag – Con moto – Poco largamente (1951)

Grave, maestoso e poco rubato – Tranquillo, flebile – Moderato, amabile – Cantabile – Con moto – Molto tranquillo – Cantabile grazioso – Quasi Tempo II – Giubilante (1953)

Comp: 15 April 1951

Revised version, 24 December 1953

Publ: 2008 Peters [EP 71594] (facsimile of 1953 holograph, with copyist's printed parts [8+7+8+7+7p])

Dur: [13' 13"]

MS: with estate (1951) [27p / 283m] / with estate (1953) [24p / 269m]

The 1953 holograph score comes with a clarinet part (only). Elkin is written on the title page, indicating the intended publisher, but the score was not published in any form in Scott's lifetime.

S 117 W 382 **Trio in B-flat**, for clarinet, cello and piano [37p / 353m]

I – Moderato [22p / 196m] [9' 54"]

II – *Intermezzo*. Adagio espressivo [5p / 55m] [4' 37"]

III – *Rondo capriccioso*. Allegro amabile [10p / 102m] [3' 29"]

Ded: Gervase [de Peyer] and Sylvia [Southcombe]

Comp: 1955

Publ: 2003 Maecenas Music [MM 0523]. 2008 Peters [EP 71596]

Dur: [18' 04"]

MS: Royal Academy of Music Library

S 118 W 381 **Trio pastorale,** for flute, cello and piano [48p]

I – Allegro – Andante – Poch. più mosso – Allegretto amabile e poch. rub. – Maestoso – Andante – A tempo [26p / 278m]

II – Tranquillo poco rubato – Poco più mosso – Quasi Tempo I [8p / 100m]

III – Energico – Poco meno mosso – Più tosto lente – Quasi tempo I [13p / 124m]

Comp: I – 19 April 1959. II/III – 12 July 1960

Publ: unpublished

iv – chamber duo, violin and piano

S 119 W 334 **Sonata No. 1,** Op. 59, for violin and piano [64+19p]

I – Allegro moderato [20p / 224m] [9' 48" – 11' 52"]

II – Andante [12p / 203m] [7' 44" – 10' 56"]

III – Allegro molto scherzando [10p / 108m] [2' 46" – 4' 15"]

IV – Allegro maestoso [21p / 288m] [8' 30" – 12' 47"]

Ded: Miss Ethel Barns

Comp: 1908

Publ: 1910 Schott [28818]

LE: Schott [ED 1449]

Dur: [28' 48" – 39' 50"] [25' CS]

Ref: *MYI,* 104, 197–99 / *BC,* 121, 136–7

S 120 W 107 **Elégie,** Op. 73 No. 1 [7+3p / 111m]

Andante

Ded: 'To my Friend Paul Stoeving'

Publ: 1910 Schott [28928–1]

LE: Schott [VLB 163], in *Trois pièces lyriques*

Dur: [4' 16" – 5' 02"]

S 121 W 297 **Romance,** Op. 73 No. 2 [6+3p / 92m]

Lento

Ded: 'To my Friend Paul Stoeving'

Publ: 1910 Schott [28928–2]

LE: Schott [VLB 163], in *Trois pièces lyriques*

Dur: [3' 38" – 4' 11"]

S 122 W 398 **Valse triste,** Op. 73 No. 3 [7p / 156m]

Allegretto moderato

Ded: 'To my friend Paul Stoeving'

Publ: 1910 Schott [28928–3]

LE: Schott [VLB 163], in *Trois pièces lyriques*

Dur: [3' 19"]

S 123 W 370 **Tallahassee: Suite**, Op. 73 No. 4 [21+7p]

I – *Bygone Memories*

Andante molto sostenuto – Poco più mosso [5p/70m] [2' 54"]

Publ: 1911 Schott [29290]

II – *After Sundown*

Allegretto – Andante [5p/68m] [2' 33" – 3' 24"]

Publ: 1911 Schott [29291]

III – *Air et danse nègre*

Allegro – Andante – Allegro con spirito [11p/ 243m] [4' 02" – 4' 22"]

Ded: Efrem Zimbalist

Publ: I – 1911 [29290] [29290.1] / II – 1911 [29291] [29290.2] / III – 1910 [28928.4] [29290.3]

LE: Schott [1450]
Masters Music Publications [M 3544] (= Schott [1450])

Dur: [9' 30" – 11' 38"]

Ref: *MYI*, 199

BC, 137

Note: The *Air et danse nègre* was issued first, at the same time as S 120–S 122. The other movements followed in 1911. A later reissue renumbered the plates [29290.1–3].

S 124 W 61 **Cherry Ripe: Morceau**

Molto sostenuto – Allegretto molto moderato [4+1p / 88m]

Ded: Fritz Kreisler

Publ: 1911 Schott [29441]

Dur: [4' 00"]

LE: Schott [ED 1948]

Note: Cf. also S 222 and 409.

S 125 W 262 **Deux préludes** [13p]

Prelude No. 1 – *Poème érotique*

Andante – Poco più mosso – Tempo I [7p / 108m] [5' 10"]

Ded: 'An Herrn Adolf Rebner'

Prelude No. 2 – *Danse*

Allegro [6p / 88m] [2' 24"]

Ded: 'For Miss Daisy Kennedy'

Publ: 1912 Schott [29644 / 29645]

LE: 1991, Masters Music Publications

Dur: [7' 34"]

S 126 W 129 **The Gentle Maiden (Irish Air)** [3+1p / 46m]

Andante

Ded: Max Mossel

Publ: 1912 Schott [29646]

Dur: [2' 10"]

S 127 W 344 **Sonnet 1**

Allegretto molto moderato – Poco meno mosso [5+1p / 56m]

Ded: Daisy Kennedy

Publ: 1914 Schott [29982–1], rev. edn 1956

Dur: [3' 45"]

Note: Jean Paul quote precedes the score: 'And from the whole of nature around me flowed peaceful strains, as if from distant evening bells.'

S 128 W 345 **Sonnet 2** [4+1p]

Ded: Fritz Rothschild

Publ: 1914 Schott [29982–2]

Dur: [4' 49"]

S 129 W 165 **Irish Suite**

I – *Irish Lament* Moderato – Andante – Tempo Io [5+1p / 56m]

II – *Irish Dance* Allegretto [7+3p / 125m]

Ded: Francis Macmillan

Publ: 1917 G. Schirmer [27046–27047]

S 130 – **Sonata lirica** [48p]

I – Allegro moderato [23p / 179m] [9' 44"]

II – *Pastorale*: Andante tranquillo [6p / 100m] [4' 17"]

III – Allegro vigoroso [19p / 158m] [6' 25"]

Comp: 3 December 1937

Publ: unpublished

Dur: [20' 26"] [20' CS]

FP: May Harrison & Scott, 7 February 1938

MS: holograph with estate

S 131 W 120 **Fantasie orientale**

Ded: Jascha Heifetz

Comp: 1938 Elkin

Dur: [8' 07"]

S 132 W 327 **Sonata melodica** [28p]

I – Moderato – Più mosso – Energico – Andante sostenuto / Poco più mosso – Tranquillo semplice – Andante senza trascinare – Con moto – Tempo primo – Con moto [14p / 213b] [10' 32"]

II – Adagio ma non troppo – Poco più mosso – Andante sostenuto [4p / 55b] [5' 19"]

III – Allegro vigoroso, ma non troppo – Poco meno vigoroso – Allegretto – A tempo ma poco rubato (quasi allegretto) – Con moto – Tranquillo (lingeringly) – Quasi tempo I [9p / 122b] [6' 26"]

Ded: François d'Albert

Comp: 1950

Publ: 1953 Elkin [2289]

Dur: [22' 17"]

Ref: *BC*, 225

S 133 W 335 **Violin sonata No. 2**

Comp: 1950

Note: Unknown. Probably the same work as S 132.

S 134 W 336 **Violin sonata No. 3** [33p]

I – Tranquillo [15p / 190m] [11' 03"]

II – *Pastorale*. Andante amabile [8p / 152m] [6' 13"]

III – *Rondo capriccioso*. Energico e poco rubato [10p / 137m] [6' 07"]

Comp: 22 February 1955

Publ: unpublished by Elkin (but title page of holograph has Elkin stamp) 2008 Novello (special order edition) [29+15p]

Dur: [23' 23"]

MS: with estate [33p]

S 135 W 337 **Violin sonata No. 4** [35p]

I – Andante tranquillo [15p / 165m] [7' 46"]

II – Allegretto moderato e amabile [7p / 89m] [2' 42"]

III – Energico [13p / 125m] [5' 47"]

Comp: 2 July 1956

Publ: unpublished by Elkin (but title page of holograph has Elkin stamp)

Dur: [16' 15"]

MS: with estate

Note: Metronome marking at top of score indicates 'pocket tape metronome' (see Note, S 262)

v – chamber duo, other

W 136 – **Sonata for cello and piano**

Comp: *c.* 1899

Publ: unpublished, withdrawn

Ref: *MYI*, 28

S 137 W 119 **Fantasia for viola and piano**

Comp: *c.* 1911

MS: Incomplete [11p] holograph in the Curtis Institute of Music Library. Photocopy [10p / 173m], signed 'gift / Cyril Scott / Jan. 24, 1930' appears to have been donated to a different library (copies with estate and at Curtis).

Note: 'N.B. Some of this work has been embodied in my Concerto for violin & orchestra' (S 71)

S 138 W 251 **Pierrot amoureux**, for cello and piano [7+3p]

Andante

Comp: 1912 Schott [29537]

S 139 W 310 **Scotch Pastoral**, for flute and piano [11+4p / 173b]

Andante – Allegro scherzando ma non troppo – Halbes Zeitmass – Tempo I

Ded: 'À Monsieur Louis Fleury'

Publ: 1914 Wilhelm Hansen [1613 / 15674]
Masters Music Publications [M 1692]

S 140 W 130 **The Gentle Maiden (Irish Air)**, for cello and piano

Comp: *c.* 1925

Publ: unpublished

MS: Royal Academy of Music [MSS 2A]

Note: arrangement of S 126

S 141 W 237 **Pastoral and Reel**, for cello and piano [6+4p]

Comp: 1926

Publ: 1926 Schott [31834]

LE: Schott [1992]

Dur: [3' 32" – 5' 01"]

S 142 W 200 **Poem: The Melodist and the Nightingales** [*Der Musikant und die Nachtigallen*], for cello and piano [15+8p]

Ded: Baba [Beatrice] Harrison

Publ: 1930 Schott [B.S.S. 32697]

LE: Schott [2130]

Note: arrangement of S 74

S 143 W 39 **Ballade for cello and piano** [16+3p / 260m]

Adagio – Etwas bewegter – Tempo agitato – Allegro non troppo – Tempo primo

Ded: 'to Madeleine'

Publ: 1934 Universal [10.584]

Dur: [15' 17"] [16' CS] [11' Universal]

FP: Tony Close and Scott, Wigmore Hall, 14 October 1930

S 144 W 40 **Ballade for viola and piano**

Ded: Lionel Tertis

Comp: *c.* 1934

Publ: unpublished

MS: Royal College of Music Library

Note: arrangement of S 143

S 145 W 315 **Serenade for harmonica and piano**

Andante – Poco più animato – Quasi tempo I

Ded: Larry Adler

Comp: 1938

Publ: unpublished

MS: with estate [8p / 95m]

S 146 W 333 **Sonata for viola and piano** [50p / 465m]

I – Allegretto – Grave e molto espressivo – Con moto – Tempo I [22p / 217m]

II – *Humoresque*: Allegro – Poco sostenuto e poco maestoso – Tempo primo [12p / 96m]

III – Adagio – Energico – Poco meno mosso – Maestoso / Molto maestoso [16p / 152m]

Comp: 1 November 1953

Publ: 2015 EM Publishing [EMP SP006] (ed. Rupert Marshall-Luck)

Dur: [23' 57"] [20' CS]

MS: with estate [53p]

Note: The recent first publication of this sonata is the first Scott score to be critically annotated in print (cf. S 156).

S 147 W 339 **Sonata for cello and piano** [33+14p]

I – Andante, rubato [10' 43"]

II – Allegretto scherzando [3' 01"]

III – Grave [3' 54"]

IV – Rondo gioviale animato [5' 13"]

Comp: 1948–50

Publ: 2003 Schott [ED 13081 / 7754]

Dur: [22' 51"]

S 148 W 24 **Aubade,** for recorder (or flute or violin) and harpsichord (or piano) [14+3p]

Molto moderato

Ded: Carl Dolmetsch

Publ: 1953 Schott [S&C 5669]

LE: Schott [ED 10330]

Dur: [8' 29" – 8' 56"]

Note: Requested by Dolmetsch for a 1952 Wigmore Hall recital.

S 149 W 299 **Rondo serioso,** for viola d'amore and piano [15p / 157m]

Tranquillo – Meno mosso – Maestoso, quasi Tempo I – Poco più mosso

Ded: S. Montagu Cleeve

Comp: 1957

Publ: 2007 Bardic Edition [BD0936]

S 150 W 328 **Sonata for flute and piano** [30+11p / 304m]

I – Tempo molto moderato e sempre poco rubato – Poco meno mosso. Cantabile – Quasi Tempo Io ma non allentato – Quasi doppio tempo [134m]

II – Andante tranquillo – Grave – Tempo Io [77m]

III – *Rondo frivolo*: Animato, giocoso – Quasi a tempo, elegante, cantabile – Tempo Io [93m]

Publ: 1961 Elkin [2617 – scribal score]

S 151 W 338 **Sonata for two violins and piano** [41+9+9p / 352m]

I – Poco tranquillo – Tempo moderato poco rubato e grazioso – Meno mosso – Tempo I – Molto tranquillo, and lingeringly [13p / 107m]

II – *Elegy*: Andante sostenuto [10p / 106m]

III – *Finale frivolo*: Energico [18p / 139m]

Publ: 1964 Elkin [2696 – scribal score]

MS: with estate

S 152 – **Rural Intermezzo,** for flute and piano [3+1p]

Publ: 1965 Doric Music [340]

vi – instrumental solo

S 153 W 117 **The Extatic Shepherd** [*Der extatische Schäfer / Le berger extatique*], for solo flute [2p]

Comp: 1921

Publ: 1922 Schott [30766]

Schott [FTR 142]

Dur: [3' 20" – 6' 22"]

S 154 W 179 **Londonderry Air**, for harp

Comp: *c.* 1922

Publ: unpublished

S 155 – **Celtic Fantasy**, for harp [20p]

Ded: Sidonie Goossens

Comp: 1926

Publ: 2016 Schott [ED 13301]

Dur: [10' 01"]

Note: premiered on 20 October 1999, Wigmore Hall, London (Hugh Webb).

S 156 [W 291] **Sonatina for guitar** [15p / 233b]

I – Adagio quasi introduzione – Molto moderato [7p / 104b] [6' 10" – 8' 09"]

II – Allegretto pensoso [2p / 61b] [2' 04" – 1' 51"]

III – *Finale*: Allegro – Tempo di movimento I – Tempo I (Allegro) [6p / 68b] [2' 36" – 2' 52"]

Ded: Andrés Segovia

Comp: June 1927

Publ: 2002 Bèrben [E. 4760 B.]

Dur: [10' 50" – 13' 25"]

Note: Segovia named the first movement *Reverie*. The score was presumed lost until 2001, when Angelo Gilardino found the holograph among Segovia estate papers in Linares. Segovia said he was 'not too keen about it', and appears only to have performed it once. The Bèrben edition (ed. Angelo Gilardino and Luigi Biscaldi) includes a facsimile of the entire holograph. Scott's manuscript calls the work 'Sonatina' on the title page, and 'Sonatine' at the head of the score. Oddly, one text directive in the score is in German '(ein wenig zögern)'; elsewehere in Italian.

The recent first edition of this sonatina is the first Scott score to be printed in conjunction with a facsimile of the complete autograph manuscript.

S 157 W 53 **Bumble-bees** [*Die Hummeln*], for solo violin [3p / 50m]

Quickly – Poch. meno mosso

Ded: May Harrison

Publ: 1928 Schott

Dur: [1' 22"]

LE: Schott [ED 1949]

MS: with estate

S 158 W 143 **Idyll,** for solo violin [5p]

Ded: Isolde Menges

Publ: 1928 Schott

LE: Schott [ED 1950]

F PIANO

i – solo

S 159 W 399 **Variations on an Original Theme**

Comp: *c.* 1898 (Frankfurt-am-Main)

Pub: unpublished

FP: 1898, at an examination concert in Frankfurt-am-Main, by Scott

HM: no longer extant

S 160 W 38 **Klavierstucke: 1ste Ballade in D moll** [4p / 97b]

Allegro energico

Ded: 'This to my fellow student Percy Grainger in remembrance of the 'Pfeifender Reiter. Frankfurt-Main 1898.'

Comp: May 1898 (Frankfurt-am-Main)

Publ: unpublished

Dur: [3' 30"]

HM: Grainger Museum, Melbourne [MG C2/SCO-49]

Note: Together with the *Ballade* in the holograph is a one-page, 8-bar fragment of a vocal solo with chorus, labeled 'Sydney Jones & Meir Scott. To Percy Grainger', and dated 16 February 1899. The text is 'Lucy, I love you. Don't cry, I'll meet you in the morning.' See S 25.

Two Studies for a Slow Movement

S 161 W 352 No. 1 – *Andante* Andante espressivo (B-flat major) [4p / 57m]

S 162 W 352 No. 2 – *Largo* Maestoso (B-flat major) [3p / 66m]

Comp: *c.* 1900

Publ: unpublished

Dur: No. 1 – 4' 34" / No. 2 – 4' 18"

MS: No. 1 – Grainger Museum, Melbourne [MG C2/SCO-219–1] / No. 2 – Grainger Museum, Melbourne [MG C2/SCO-219–2]

S 163 W 109 **An English Waltz,** Op. 15 [Orig. 11p / 328m] [Rev. 11p / 294m]

Con spirito

Ded: 'To Percy Grainger in friendship and admiration'

Comp: Original version – Dec. 1901 / Revised version – 1919

Publ: Original version – 1903 A.J. Jaeger [11663] / Revised version – (1920) / 1929 Elkin [1071]

Dur: Original – [6' 44"] / Revised – [6' 06"]

MS: Grainger Museum, Melbourne

Ref: *MYI*, 73 / *BC*, 90

Notes: Elkin [1071] is dated MCMXXIX, but the catalogue number places the revision at 1919. The score should undoubtedly have read MCMXIX. This bravura piece contains many repeat marks. If all are observed, the 1903 edition contains 418 bars, and the 1929 edition 366 bars. Timings are given with all repeats observed.

S 164 W 124 **Three Frivolous Pieces**, Op. 2 [11p / 457m]

1 – *Allegretto grazioso* [4p / 194m] [3' 06"]

2 – *Andante pastorale* [3p / 95m (105m with repeats)] [2' 54"]

3 – *Valse scherzando* [4p / 158m] [2' 17"] {1' 59"}

Ded: Herbert Golden

Comp: 1898–99

Publ: 1903 Forsyth [267]

Dur: [8' 17"]

Ref: *MYI*, 73

Note: Scott's own piano roll of *Valse scherzando* adds an unpublished 20-bar postlude,for a total of 178 bars.

S 165 W 178 **Three Little Waltzes**, Op. 58 [14p / 274m]

1 – *Allegretto poco scherzando* [4p / 84m] [1' 22"]

2 – *Andante languido* [4p / 102m] [2' 21"]

3 – *Allegretto gracioso* [4p / 88m] [1' 40"]

Ded: 'For my little cousins, Dudley, Laurence and Barbara.'

Comp: 1898–99

Publ: 1906 Elkin [1178]

LE: n.d., Elkin [26 1178 03]

Dur: [5' 23"]

Note: Also published separately by Elkin, as [1178]. The plate number would indicate a 1920 publication date, and is presumably an error.

S 166 W 248 **Six Pieces,** Op. 4 [11p / 354(414)m]

1 – *Valse* Allegretto grazioso [2p / 61(69)m] [1' 22"]

2 – *Adagio serioso* Adagio [1p / 32(40)m] [2' 40"]

3 – *Étude* Allegro molto grazioso [3p / 166(194)m] [2' 30"]

4 – *Folk-song* Andante con moto [1p / 39(55)m] [1' 40"]

5 – *Scherzino* Allegretto [2p / 34m] [0' 56" – 1' 10"]

6 – *Andante maestoso* Con espressione [1p / 22m] [1' 37" – 1' 52"]

Ded: 'To Professors Iwan Knorr and Lazzaro Uzielli in grateful remembrance of my student days.'

Comp: 1898–99

Publ: 1903 Forsyth [none]

Dur: [10' 44" – 11' 14"]

Ref: *MYI*, 73

S 167 W 329 **Sonata for pianoforte in D,** Op. 17 [14p / 341b]

Allegro molto moderato e maestoso – Andante doloroso – A tempo primo – Fugato

Ded: 'To Percy Grainger as a token of intense admiration and love and in remembrance of the days of youthful inspiration. November 1901'

Comp: 1900 – 11 September 1901, Vevey, Switzerland

Publ: unpublished

Dur: [12' 59"]

MS: Grainger Museum [MG C2/SCO-195]

Notes: cf. T.58.

S 168 W 87 **Three Dances,** Op. 20 [9p / 203m]

Gavotte Allegro moderato [2p / 30m] [1' 44"]

Eastern Dance Andante con moto [4p / 112m] [2' 23"]

English Dance Vivace [3p / 61m] [1.17']

Ded: 'To my little friends Tertie, Louisi and Oscar'

Comp: 1902?

Publ: 1903 Boosey [H. 4074]

LE: Well-Tempered Press, *c.* 1969 [WTP W1001]

Dur: [5' 24"]

S 169 W 308 **Scherzo,** Op. 25 [11p / 260m]

Vivace

Ded: Evelyn Suart

Comp: 1902?

Publ: 1904 Elkin [222]

Dur: [3' 42"]

S 170 W 253 **Two 'Pierrot' Pieces,** Op. 35 [14p / 342m]

No. 1 – Lento *(Pierrot triste)* [5p / 49m] [2' 42" – 3' 31"]

No. 2 – Allegro *(Pierrot gai)* [9p / 293m] [3' 25" – 3' 50"]

Ded: No. 1 – Ernest Thesiger / No. 2 – T. Holland-Smith

Comp: 1901?, Liverpool

Publ: 1904 Boosey – No. 1 [H.4298] / No. 2 [H.4299]

1929 (No. 2, revised edition) Boosey [H.4299])

LE: No. 1 – Boosey & Hawkes [1457–4] / Boston Music [13743] / Boosey & Hawkes [M051280087] / Schott [BH 83477 / BH 83478]
No. 2 – Boosey & Hawkes [M051280070]

Dur: [6' 29" – 6' 56"]

Ref: *MYI*, 61, 94, 99, 125

BC, 91, 93

Note: Revisions to No. 2 in 1929 are limited to occasional harmonic enrichments of the original.

S 171 W 261 **Prelude No. 1** ['Op. 37'] [11p / 234(249)m]

Comp: 1904

Publ: unpublished

Dur: [6' 49"]

MS: British Library [Add. MS 69447]

Notes: This substantial unpublished work bears Scott's designation 'Op. 37' on the title page. S 172 however was published in 1904 with the same number,which may indicate either that Scott withdrew S 171 from possible publication or that it was rejected by Elkin, in the wake of the recently published Scherzo [S 169]. Boosey's interests lay in dissemination of drawing-room miniatures and 'ballads', and would have been unlikely to have promoted a work such as S 171.

There appear to be two versions. The BL manuscript comprises 11 pages of music, but the last page of music is numbered '9'. The original page numbering did not include b.76–130 of the revision. The additional pages (between numbered pages 3 and 4) provide a contrasting middle section to the prelude.

S 172 W 249 **Two Piano Pieces,** Op. 37 [6p / 90b]

No. 1 – *At Dawn* Andante semplice [2p / 47m] [2' 16"]

No. 2 – *Shadows* Allegro molto moderato [3p /41m] [2' 10"]

Publ: 1904 Boosey [H.4453]

Dur: [4' 26"]

S 173 W 83 **Dagobah**, Op. 39 No. 1 [4p / 47m]
Andante
Ded: Jacques Blanche
Publ: 1904 Forsyth [none]
Dur: [4' 01"]
Ref: *MYI*, 118, 144

S 174 W 64 **Chinese Serenade**, Op. 39 No. 2 [8p / 177m]
Allegretto
Ded: Jacques Blanche
Publ: 1904 Forsyth [none]
Dur: [4' 34"]

S 175 W 326 **Solitude**, Op. 40 No. 1
Andante sostenuto [5p / 38m]
Ded: Henry Balfour Gardiner
Publ: 1904 Elkin [264]
LE: 1913 Elkin [753], *First Album of Pianoforte Pieces*
Dur: [2' 18"]

S 176 W 401 **Vesperale**, Op. 40 No. 2 [5p / 58m]
Andante
Comp: ?, prob. Shere
Publ: 1904 Elkin [265]
Dur: [2' 14"]
Ref: *MYI*, 241
BC, 97

S 177 W 63 **Chimes**, Op. 40 No. 3 [7p / 146m]
Allegro moderato
Publ: 1904 Elkin [266]
Dur: [3' 58"]
LE: n.d. Kalmus (CPP/Belwin) [K 09966] / 1994 Masters Music Publications [W7120]

S 178 W 152 **Impromptu (A Mountain Brook)**, Op. 41
Prestissimo Original [11p / 399m] Revised [11p / 398m]
Publ: Original edition – 1904 Elkin [269]
Revised edition – [1904] Elkin [269]
LE: n.d. Kalmus (CPP/Belwin) [K 09966] – original version / 1994 Masters Music Publications [W7120] – original version
Dur: Original – [4' 08" – 4' 46"]

Revised – [3' 52"]

Note: The difference in length of one bar between the two versions occurs at b.159 – a figure repeated for 3 bars in the original edition, and for 4 bars in the revision. In that the rest of the piece is organised in 4-bar units practically throughout, the original edition may be in error, with the intention being a 4-bar repeated figure.

S 179 W 183 **Lotus Land**, Op. 47 No. 1 [7p / 67m]

Andante languido

Ded: Henry Hadley

Comp: 1905, Shere

Publ: 1905 Elkin [322]

LE: 1962, Galaxy [GMC 2262] / 1962, Fischer [P.3059] [S 8010] / 1989, Alfred [AP455], in *Masters of Impressionism* / 1997, MMP

Schott [ED 1804]

Dur: [2' 58" – 5' 45"] {2' 57"}

Ref: *BC*, 88, 97

S 180 **W 67** **Columbine**, Op. 47 No. 2 [7p / 263m]

Allegretto

Publ: 1905 Elkin [321]

Dur: [4'09 – 4' 40"]

S 181 W 19 **Asphodel**, Op. 50 No. 2 [6p / 53m]

Andante semplice

Ded: Robert King

Publ: 1906 Elkin [340]

LE: 1919 Elkin [1011], *Second Album of Pianoforte Pieces*

1992 Masters Music Publications [MMP 1915]

Dur: [3' 06"]

S 182 W 361 **Summerland: Four Little Pieces**, Op. 54 [14p / 170m]

1 – *Playtime* Allegretto scherzando [3p / 35m] [1' 20"]

2 – *A Song from the East* Allegro non troppo [3p / 45m] [1' 41"]

3 – *Evening Idyll* Allegretto non troppo [3p / 39m] [2' 08"]

4 – *Fairy Folk* Allegretto grazioso [3p / 51m] [1' 29"]

Ded: 'To my young friends Honey & Peter Harris'

Publ: 1907 Elkin [393]. *A Song from the East* also published separately (1907 Elkin)

LE: n.d. Kalmus (CPP/Belwin) [K 09966] / No. 3 – 1968 Larrabee Publications

Dur: [6' 38"]

Note: *A Song from the East* was later used as Picture III in *Karma*, S 248.

S 183 W 322 **Two Sketches**, Op. 57 Nos 4 & 5 [7p / 99(117)m]
Cuckoo-call Andante languido [3p / 67m] [1' 59" – 2' 54"]
Twilight Bells Allegro moderato [2p / 32(50)m] [1' 50"]
Ded: Landon Ronald
Publ: 1907 Elkin [411]
Dur: [3' 49"]

S 184 W 10 **Two Alpine Sketches**, Op. 58 No. 4 [7p / 76m]
No. 1 – Rather slowly [3p / 45m] [1' 39"]
No. 2 – Allegretto non troppo [2p / 31m] [1' 04"]
Ded: 'For my young friend Alberto Uzielli'
Publ: 1908 Elkin [443]
Dur: [2' 43"]

S 185 W 89 **Danse nègre**, Op. 58 No. 5 [7p / 68m]
Molto vivace
Ded: Adine & Norman O'Neill
Publ: 1908 Elkin [446]
LE: 1962 Galaxy [GMC 2262] / 1992 Masters Music Publications [MMP 1915]
Dur: [1' 28" – 2' 02"] {1' 39" / 1' 55"}
Ref: *BC*, 91

Note: See also S 123, III.

S 186 W 220 **Notturno**, Op. 54 No. 5 [6p / 70m]
Andante con espressione
Publ: 1908 Elkin [471]
Dur: [3' 10"]

S 187 W 348 **Sphinx**, Op. 63 [6p / 71b]
Andante
Ded: John Sargent Esq.
Publ: 1908 Elkin [479]
Dur: [4' 11" – 4' 27"]

Note: A copy of Elkin [479] with the estate has a few bars added and tempo markings changed, in the composer's hand. Rewrites in b.11–13, 15–17, 43, 46–9.

S 188 W 110 **Etude I**, Op. 64 No. 1 [7p / 118b]
Allegro
Ded: Jack Bradshaw Isherwood
Publ: 1908 Elkin [485]
LE: 1962, Galaxy [GMC 2262]
Dur: [2' 40"]

S 189 W 111 **Etude II**, Op. 64 No. 2 [7p / 127b]

Allegro con brio

Ded: Jack Bradshaw Isherwood

Publ: 1908 Elkin [486]

LE: 1962, Galaxy [GMC 2262]

Dur: [2' 20"]

S 190 W 330 **Sonata No. 1**, Op. 66 [38p]

1st movement - Allegro con spirito – Double as quickly [14.5p / 238b] [8' 15" – 10' 57"]

2nd movement - Adagio [revised: Adagio ma non troppo] –

Tempo of 1st movement [5.5p / 106b] [5' 19" – 6' 52"]

3rd movement - [no marking] – Tranquillo [8p / 132b] [4' 58" – 6' 50"]

4th movement - *Fugue*: Allegro / Molto maestoso e sostenuto [8p / 106b] [3' 51" – 4' 34"]

Ded: Alfred Hoehn

Comp: summer 1908, Shere

Publ: 1909 Elkin [511] 5/- net, Beak St.

LE: n.d. Elkin [511], 5/6 net, Beak St.

n.d. Elkin [511] 5/6 net, Kingly St.

n.d. Elkin [511] 5/6 net, Kingly St., 'revised edition'

n.d. [*c.* 1935?] Elkin [511] 10/- net, Kingly St., 'revised edition'

Kalmus (CPP/Belwin) [K 09966] = 1909 version, with a few corrections

Masters Music Publications (W7121, = 1909 version)

Dur: [22' 14" – 28' 27"] [20' CS]

Ref: *MYI*, 104, 205, 209

BC, 70, 83, 99, 121, 138

Note: A troublesome work in establishing an 'authentic' version, or versions. Elkin [511] released at least three distinct versions, all dated 1909, and with plate number [511], but with differing prices and addresses. Two are labeled '(Revised Edition)', but are different from each other as well as from the original 1909 text. The first revised edition involves changes to the 1st movement (mm.89–106), a truncated bridge to the third movement (18 bars reduced to 4), and substantial changes to the 3rd movement, particularly in meter. A second revised version (price 10/-), probably from the 1930s, retains the revised bridge to the third movement, and makes drastic revisions in detail to the 1st and 3rd movements in particular.

A copy of the original 1909 issue resides with the estate, in which Scott has added many red-ink revisions, designed for an Elkin reprinting. Its interest lies in the fact that it corresponds to neither published 'revised edition', but represents yet another revision, not necessarily last in chronology.

Percy Grainger's personal copy of the original 1909 edition exists in the Grainger Museum [MG C3/SCO-196], with copious annotations to the score, including elaborate markings for all three pedals, and cuts that reduce his performance time, as he states, from 25½ minutes to 19 (cf. S 167 and T.58).

The later revised editions refer the tempo markings to the 'pocket tape metronome' (see Note, S 262).

S 191 W 197 **Mazurka**, Op. 67 No. 1 [7p / 114m]

Allegretto

Publ: 1909 Elkin [518]

LE: 1913, Elkin [753], *First Album of Pianoforte Pieces*

Dur: [2' 53"]

S 192 W 316 **Serenata**, Op. 67 No. 2 [7p / 150m]

Allegretto

Publ: 1909 Elkin [517]

LE: 1913, Elkin [753], First Album of Pianoforte Pieces

Dur: [3'04]

S 193 W 161 **Intermezzo**, Op. 67 No. 3 [6p / 51m]

Gently flowing

Ded: Adine O'Neill

Publ. 1910 Elkin [540]

LE: 1919 Elkin [1011], *Second Album of Pianoforte Pieces*

1992 Masters Music Publications [MMP 1915]

Dur: [2' 21"]

S 194 W 325 **Soirée japonaise**, Op. 67 No. 4 [7p / 109b]

Allegretto

Publ: 1910 Elkin [577]

Dur: [2' 43" – 3' 09"]

Note: Scott's opus number assignment implies that this was composed contemporaneously with S 191–193. But its publication was delayed until after S 195 and 196, to judge by the Elkin catalogue numbers.

S 195 W 354 **Suite … (in the Old Style)**, Op. 71 No. 1 [15p / 382m] [= Suite No. 1]

I – *Prelude* Allegretto [5p / 120m] [3' 05" – 3' 55"]

II – *Sarabande* Adagio [4p / 86m] [3' 46" – 4' 21"]

III – *Minuet* Allegretto [5p / 176m] [3' 31" – 3' 59"]

Ded: 'for Hans & Carrie Lüthy, in long and deep Friendship.'

Publ: 1910 Elkin [544]

Dur: [10' 25" – 12' 15"]

Note: The editor owns 3 copies of Elkin [544], each different in details but with identical music. One has a plain brown cover, while the other two have a cut-out through which a photograph of Scott on the title page shows.

S 196 W 414 **Water-Wagtail** [*Bachstelze / Bergeronnette*], Op. 71 No. 3

Allegretto [7p / 118m]

Ded: ' For S'

Comp: *c.* 1910

revised 1915

Publ: 1910 Elkin [570] / *c.* 1915 Elkin

LE: 1992, 94? Masters Music Publications [MMP 1915]

Dur: [2' 13" – 3' 17"] {2' 09"}

Ref: *BC*, 91, 138

S 197 W 92 **Trois danses tristes**, Op. 74 [17p / 327m]

I – *Danse élégiaque* Molto tranquillo [4p / 83m] [4' 21" – 4' 42"]

II – *Danse orientale* Allegretto moderato [8p / 154m] [3' 56" – 4' 25"]

III – *Danse langoureuse* Andante / Rather slowly [5p / 90m] [3' 30"]

Ded: 1 – Herbert Fryer / 2 – Maude Roosevelt / 3 – unspecified

Publ: 1910 Schott [28989 / 28990 / 28991]

LE: Augener [14067] (No. 3 is pp 32–5) / Schott [ED 1801 / 1802 / 1803]

Dur: [12' 10"]

S 198 W 396 **Valse caprice**, Op. 74 No. 7 [7p / 195m]

Allegro moderato

Publ: 1911 Elkin [602]

Dur: [3' 32"]

S 199 W 59 **Chansonette**, Op. 74 No. 8 [6p / 113m]

Poco allegretto

Publ: 1911 Elkin [601]

Dur: [2' 26"]

S 200 W 355 **Deuxième suite**, Op. 75 [43p / 635m]

1 – *Prélude*

Allegretto moderato [5p / 75m] [3' 01"]

2 – *Air varié*

Andante sostenuto – Poco più mosso – Allegro con brio – Andante – Molto scherzando – Tempo I [15p / 222m] [8' 48"]

3 – *Solemn Dance*

Andante semplice [5p / 86m] [3' 51"]

4 – *Caprice*

Tranquillo – Allegretto scherzando [5p / 68m] [1' 57"]

5 – *Introduction & Fugue*

Adagio – Fugue – Adagio [13p / 184m] [10' 36"]

Ded: 'À Monsieur Claude Debussy'

Publ: 1910 Schott [29050]

LE: Schott [1443]

Dur: [28' 13"]

Ref: *MYI*, 104

BC, 138

Note: The *Air varié* can benefit from a piano with a bass extension (to A-flat) in b.218.

One of the most overlooked landmarks of early twentieth-century British piano music.

S 201 W 47 **Berceuse** [7p / 95m]

Andante sostenuto

Publ: 1911 Elkin [617]

LE: 1913, Elkin [753], *First Album of Pianoforte Pieces*

Dur: [3' 18"]

S 202 W 233 **Over the Prairie: Two Impressions** [7p / 102m]

1 – Andante [3p / 50m] [2' 38" – 2' 56"]

2 – Allegretto [3p / 52m] [1' 47" – 1' 56"]

Publ: 1911 Elkin [631]

LE: No. 2 – 1913, Elkin [753], *First Album of Pianoforte Pieces*

Dur: [4' 34" – 4' 43"]

S 203 W 250 **Pierrette** [6p / 89m]

Allegretto

Ded: William Lamont Shand

Publ: 1912 Elkin [643]

LE: 1913, Elkin [753], *First Album of Pianoforte Pieces*

Dur: [1' 56" – 2' 34"]

S 204 W 25 **Autumn Idyll** [6p / 56m]

Andante

Publ: 1912 Elkin [653]

Dur: [2' 45"]

S 205 W 41 **Barcarolle** [7p / 109b]

Allegretto moderato

Ded: Miss Soutter

Publ: 1912 Elkin [681]

Dur: [4' 04"]

British Melodies

S 206 W 71 1 – *All Through the Night*

Andante sostenuto [4p 41m] [2' 09"]. Publ: 1912 Elkin [692]

S 207 W 419 2 – *The Wild Hills of Clare*

Lento [3p 45m] [2' 01"]. Publ: 1912 Elkin [692]

S 208 W 357 3 – *Summer is acumen in (Old English air)*

Allegro [7p 120m] [2' 21"]. Publ: 1912 Elkin [693]

Ded: 'To my friend Edward Goll'

Dur: [6' 31"]

Note: No. 3 published separately from the first two. See also S 358 & 405.

S 209 W 149 **Impressions from the Jungle Book** [19p / 401(408)m]

1 – *The Jungle*

Adagio [4p / 92m] [3' 17" – 3' 31"]

2 – *Dawn*

Andante semplice [2p / 48m] [2' 20"]

3 – *Rikki-Tikki-Tavi and the Snake*

Poco allegretto [6p / 107m] [4' 00"]

4 – *Morning Song in the Jungle*

Andante sosten. [2p / 47m] [2' 17" – 2' 37"]

5 – *Dance of the Elephants*

Allegro [5p / 107(114)m] [2' 30"]

Publ: 1912 Schott [29538 / 29539 / 29540 / 29541 / 29542]

LE: Schott [1437] / Masters Music Publications [M 2963]

Dur: [14' 20" – 14' 59"]

Ref: *MYI*, 199

S 210 W 255 **Poems** [27p / 328m]

1 – *Poppies*

Lento: Very languidly but with expression [3p / 50m] [2' 36" – 3' 22"]

2 – *The Garden of Soul-sympathy*

Andante amabile [5p / 63m] [2' 55" – 3' 22"]

3 – *Bells*

Moderato [4p / 93m] [3' 00"]

4 – *The Twilight of the Year*

Andante sostenuto [3p / 46m] [2' 55" – 3' 53"]

5 – *Paradise-Birds*

Andante [6p / 76m] [3' 21" – 4' 08"]

Publ: 1912 Schott [29695 / 29696 / 29697 / 29698 / 29699]

LE: Schott [1440]

Dur: [14' 55" – 17' 33"]

Notes: A unique example in Scott's piano music of poems (his own) published preceding each of the pieces. Performances of the cycle, with poetic readings prior to each movement, have been given. Whether this was the composer's intention or not remains an open question.

Poetic sources: Nos 1, 3 & 4 – *The Grave of Eros and the Book of Mournful Melodies with Dreams of the East* (Liverpool: Lyceum Press, 1907) / No. 2 – *The Vales of Unity* (London: David Nutt, 1912) / No. 5 – *The Voice of the Ancient* (London: J.M. Watkins, 1910)

Schott [ED 1440] has German renditions of the poetry as well, translated by Alfred Kayser.

S 211 W 57 **Carillon** [3p / 65m]

Allegro moderato

Ded: Herr und Frau Robert Kaufmann

Publ: 1913 Schott [29837]

LE: Schott [ED 1797]

Dur: [2' 00"]

S 212 W 105 **Egypt: An Album of 5 Impressions** [21p / 308m]

1 – *In the Temple of Memphis*

Adagio mysterioso [3p / 45m] [2' 52"]

2 – *By the Waters of the Nile*

Tempo tranquillo (Allegretto) [6p / 96m] [3' 09"]

3 – *Egyptian Boat Song*

Lento e molto languido [4p / 45m] [3' 35"]

4 – *Funeral March of the Great Raamses*

Adagio [3p / 54m] [4' 38"]

5 – *Song of the Spirits of the Nile*
Allegretto amabile [5p / 68m] [3' 26"]

Ded: 'To my Friend Mrs. Marie Russak, That enlightened Seer, who brought back for me the memory of my past Egyptian lives, these impressions are affectionately dedicated.'

Comp: 1913

Publ: 1913 Schott [29889]

LE: [n.d.] Schott [ED 1436]

Dur: [17' 40"]

Note: The earliest edition has the title of No. 4 as *Raamses*, while [1436] has *Ramses*, along with a number of corrections in notation. See also S 5, S 48.

S 213 W 260 **Prélude solennel**

Andante maestoso [7p / 75m]

Ded: Paul Otto Möckel

Publ: 1913 Elkin [719]

Dur: [4' 28"]

S 214 W 239 **Pastoral Suite** [27p / 372m]

1 – *Courante* Allegretto amabile [4p / 76m] [2' 10"]

2 – *Pastorale* Andante pastorale [5p / 76m] [2' 58"]

3 – *Rigaudon* Allegro non troppo [6p / 85m] [2' 27"]

4 – *Rondo* Allegro con energico [5p / 56m] [1' 47"]

5 – *Passacaglia* Allegro con spirito [5p / 79m] [2' 39"]

Publ: 1913 Elkin [758 / 759 / 760 / 761 / 762]

LE: 1920 Elkin [1161]

Dur: [11' 56"]

Note: Originally published separately. A performance of a two-piano arrangement of the *Passacaglia* took place on 31 July 1950, as part of a festival devoted to Scott's music at the University of Canterbury, Christchurch, NZ, with pianists Dale Mancer and Vernon Griffiths. The arranger is unknown, and the music of that arrangement appears to be lost.

S 215 W 247 **Pictorial Sketch** [4p / 78m]

Andante non troppo

Publ: 1913 Art Publication Society [504] (Modern Composers' Series)

LE: [1913] Art Publication Society [714] [908]

Dur: [3' 36"]

Note: Didactic annotations by Scott on the style and form of the work. One of only two compositions published exclusively in the United States (cf. S 265). Scott was probably commissioned by the publisher to contribute to their series of pedagogical piano works. The score appears to have been given three different catalogue numbers over its publication life.

S 216 W 52 **Britain's War March** [4p / 94m]

Moderate marching time

Ded: HRH The Prince of Wales

Publ: 1914 Schott [3269]

LE: Schott [ED 12795]

Dur: [3' 20"]

S 217 W 58 **Cavatina** [5p / 98m]

Andante sostenuto

Ded: Herr und Frau Heinrich von Kuh

Publ: 1914 Elkin [789]

LE: 1919, Elkin [1011], *Second Album of Pianoforte Pieces*

Dur: [4' 13"]

S 218 W 312 **Sea-Marge: Meditation** [6p / 73m]

Rather quickly (Like the falling of a wave on a calm sea.)

Ded: Sir Edgar and Lady Speyer

Publ: 1914 Elkin [814]

Dur: [2' 30" – 3' 20"]

Note: Cf. S 392.

S 219 W 94 **Diatonic Study** [6p / 61m]

Tranquillo – Allegro poco moderato

Publ: 1914 Elkin [828]

Dur: [2' 10"]

S 220 W 202 **Miniatures** [9p / 142m]

To an Old Miniature [*A une miniature ancienne / An ein altes Miniaturbild*] Allegretto [3p / 54m] [1' 45"]

A Ballad Told at Candle-light [*Une ballade contie à la chandelle / Eine Ballade, beim Licht der Kerze erzählt*] Tempo di Marcia [2p / 37m] [1' 18" – 1' 30"]

A Little Dancer from Spain [*Un petit danseur d'espagne / Ein kleiner Tänzer aus Spanien*] Andante – Allegretto [4p / 51m] [1' 31"]

Ded: 'To the winsome Bobberty (Robin David Tate) for when he will be old enough'

Publ: 1915 Schott [31028]

LE: Schott [ED 1439]

Dur: [4' 34"]

S 221 W 54 **Butterfly Waltz** [*Valse des papillons / Schmetterlings Walzer*] [7p / 147m]

Allegretto

Publ: 1915 Schott [31027]

LE: Schott [1800, Eng] [3289]

Dur: [2' 55"]

S 222 W 60 **Cherry Ripe** [4p / 72m]

Andante

Ded: Percy Grainger

Publ: 1915 Schott [3290]

LE: Schott [ED 11977]

Dur: [1' 33" – 3' 19"]

Notes: Cf. also S 124 and 409. The arrangement for violin and piano came first. The piano solo omits the first repeat of the tune (b.21–40), during which the violin supplies a counter-melody. The solo version also enlarges upon the link passage back to the final statement of the tune (cf. S 222, b.40–44 with S 124, b.60).

Scott wrote, 'Re. Cherry Ripe. About crotchet = 80 when it gets going – say between 80 & 88 rubato in parts' (letter to Grainger, 11/4/26, Grainger Museum (02.0076).)

S 223 W 224 **Ode héroïque** [6p / 57m]

Andante sost. e maestoso

Ded: George Davidson

Publ: 1915 Elkin [835]

LE: 1919, Elkin [1011], *Second Album of Pianoforte Pieces*

Dur: [3' 01"]

Ref. See *BC*, 155–56

Note: The French diacritics do not appear on the published edition.

S 224 W 91 **Danse romantique** [7p / 157m]

Allegretto poco languido

Ded: Ernesto Consolo

Publ: 1915 Elkin [838]

Dur: [2' 42"]

S 225 W 301 **Russian Dance** [7p / 144m]

Allegro con spirito

Ded: Benno Moiseiwitsch

Publ: 1915 Elkin [849]

LE: 1919 Elkin [1011], *Second Album of Pianoforte Pieces*

Dur: [2' 05"]

S 226 W 163 **Irish Reel** [7p / 95m]

Allegro non troppo

Ded: Mrs. [Charlotte] Milligan-Fox

Publ: 1916 Elkin [865]

Dur: [2' 08"]

S 227 W 176 **A Little Russian Suite** [12m]

1 – *Russian Air* Andante e poco semplice [4p / 42m] [2' 20"]

2 – *Siberian Waltz* Allegretto [4p / 106m] [2' 00"]

3 – *Dance* Allegro con brio [4p / 71m] [1' 25"]

Publ: 1916 Elkin [1010]

Dur: [5' 45"]

Note: The main theme of No. 3 also used in *Russian Fair*, S 272.

The Elkin plate number would indicate a publication date of 1919. The 1916 date on the sheet music may be an error.

S 228 W 283 **Rainbow-Trout** [*Truites / Forellen*] [10p / 89m]

Andante languido e poco rubato

Ded: Percy Grainger

Publ: 1916 Schott [31026]

LE: Schott [ED 1799]

1994 Masters Music Publications [??]

Dur: [3' 53" – 5' 16"] {3' 04"}

Ref: *MYI*, 182

Note: Footnote to the first page of music states 'This piece requires very careful pedalling.'

S 229 W 208 **Modern Finger-Exercises** [12m]

1–5 *Right hand exercises*

6–9 *Left hand exercises*

10–14 *Exercises for two hands*

15–30 *Exercises for both hands – in double notes*

Publ: 1917 Elkin [916]

S 230 W 288 **Requiescat** [7p / 59m]

Largo

Publ: 1917 Elkin [919]

Ded: 'In memory of Archibald Rowan Hamilton (Died of wounds, October, 1915)' (cf. S 233)

Dur: [3' 12"]

S 231 W 298 **Rondeau de concert** [17p / 272m]

Vivace

Ded: Benno Moiseiwitsch

Comp: 1916

Publ: 1918 Elkin [933]

Dur: [5' 25"]

MS: fragment with estate (see note with W 386)

S 232 W 390 **Twilight-Tide** [6p / 65m]

Andante (not too slowly)

Publ: 1918 Elkin [953]

Dur: [2' 37"]

S 233 W 80 **Consolation** [7p / 76m]

Slowly and wistfully

Ded: 'For Lena Rowan Hamilton in memory of Archie James Rowan Hamilton' (cf. S 230)

Publ: 1918 Elkin [975]

Dur: [3' 47"]

S 234 W 403 **Old China: Suite** [*Vieux Chine: Suite / Altes China*] [15p / 169m]

1 – *Old World Gavotte* [*Gavotte du bon vieux temps / Gavotte aus alter Zeit*]

Moderato [3p / 29m] [1.13']

2 – *Old World Minuet* [*Menuet du bon vieux temps / Menuett aus alter Zeit*]

Rather slowly and stately [3p / 48m] [1' 37"]

3 – *Angelus*

Andante [3p / 51m] [2' 00"]

4 – *Willow Pattern* (*A Little Study in Fourths*) [*Decor de saules* (*Petite étude en quartes*) / *Weiden-Muster* (*Kleine Etüde in Quarten*)]

Allegro poco moderato [4p / 41m] [1' 23"]

Publ: 1918 Schott [3655 / 3656 / 3658 / 3657]

LE: Schott [1435]

Dur: [6' 13"]

Note: The Schott catalogue numbers may reflect a change in ordering of the movements. Perhaps *Willow Pattern* was originally conceived to be third, and *Angelus* last.

S 235 W 409 **Vistas: Three Pieces** [17p / 189m]

1 – *A Lonely Dell*

Andante (Not too slowly) [5p / 61m] [2' 57"]

2 – *In the Forest*

Light and capricious, like birds – Con moto. Murmuringly like the leaves of beeches [6p / 40m] [2' 47" – 3' 28"]

3 – *The Jocund Dance*

Allegro giacoso [5p / 88m] [1' 36"]

Ded: J[ames] I[ngall] Wedgwood

Publ: 1– 1918 Elkin [979] / 2 – 1918 Elkin [981] / 3 – 1918 Elkin [982]

LE: [1923] Elkin [1360], published together / 1991, Masters Music Publications

Dur: [8' 01"]

S 236 W 31 **First Bagatelle** [5p / 60m]

Allegretto

Ded: Mary Hunter

Publ: 1919 Elkin [990]

Dur: [1' 50" – 2' 14"]

Note: No further bagatelles exist, published or otherwise.

S 237 W 56 **Caprice chinois** [7p / 92m]

Allegro leggiero

Ded: Mark Hambourg

Publ: 1919 Elkin [996]

Dur: [3' 15"] {2' 49"}

S 238 W 242 **Three Pastorals**

1 – *Allegretto*

Allegretto [4p / 71m] [1' 59"]

Publ: 1919 Elkin [1012]

2 – *Con delicatezza*

Quickly [5p / 73m] [1' 57"]

Ded: No. 2 – Adine O'Neill

Publ: 1919 Elkin [1013]

3 – *Pensoso*

Allegretto moderato [4p / 58m] [2' 26"] {2' 19"}

Publ: 1920 Elkin [1014]

Dur: [6' 22"]

Note: Published separately. No. 2 titled *Con delicatessa* in the American Ricordi edition of Elkin [1013].

S 239 W 421 **Young Hearts** [10p + 7p]

Series I

1 (2) – *See-saw* Allegretto [1p / 31m]

2 (9) – *Lament for a Broken Doll* Adagio [2p / 38m]

3 (6) – *Musical Box* Allegro poco moderato [2p / 24m]

4 (3) – *Evening Prayer* Quasi chorale (not too slowly) [1p / 18m]

5 (10) – *Quick March* Con brio [2p / 24m]

Series II

1 (1) – *March of a Tin Soldier* Alla Marcia [2p / 57m]

2 (7) – *Sunday Morn* Allegretto [1p / 37m]

3 (4) – *Concertina* Allegretto [1p / 15m]

4 (5) – *Loneliness* Andante sostenuto [1p / 24m]

5 (8) – *The Boy with the Pipes* Allegro [1p / 16m]

Publ: 1920 Elkin [1088 / 1089]

Ded: 'To Mrs. Kendal, my first Teacher'

LE: 1953, Elkin [2291], under the title *For My Young Friends: Ten Pianoforte Pieces* (bracketed numbers above indicate revised order) [15p]

Dur: [9' 30"]

Note: Holograph of *Evening Prayer* with estate. [1p / 18m]

S 240 W 32 **Ballad** [11p / 252m]

Andante

Publ: 1920 Elkin [1165]

Dur: [6' 52" – 7' 36"]

Note: 'Based on a few bars of an old Troubadour song.'

S 241 W 234 **A Pageant: Three Dances** [*Pompe*] [15p]

1 – *Sentimental Waltz*

Rather slowly and sentimentally / Sostenuto e con sentimento [4p / 54m] [1' 49"]

2 – *Exotic Dance*

Not quickly / Non vivo [5p / 64m] [2' 18"]

3 – *Processional Dance*

Slowly and solemnly / Lento e solenne [4p / 41m] [2' 22"]

Ded: No. 1, 'For my friend Herbert Fryer' / No. 2, 'For my friend Pedro Morales' / No. 3, 'For my friend Renton Sprange'

Publ: 1920 Schott [3765 / 3766 / 3767]

LE: Schott [ED 1442]

Dur: [6' 29"]

S 242 W 157 **Inclination à la danse** [7p / 207m]

Allegro scherzando

Ded: Mme. H[ermann] de Pourtalès

Publ: 1922 Elkin [1241]

Dur: [3' 35"]

Note: The title is a word play on Weber's *Invitation to the Dance.*

S 243 W 159 **Indian Suite** [14p]

1 – *The Snake Charmer*

Andante [3p / 44m] [2' 14"]

2 – *Juggernaut*

Andante religioso [3p / 60m] [2' 15"]

3 – *Indian Serenade*

Andante sostenuto [3p / 28m] [1' 56"]

4 – *Dancing Girls*

Allegro [4p / 52m] [1' 48"]

Ded: Marjorie Forsyth Barlow

Publ: 1922 Schott [30802]

LE: n.d., Schott [ED 1438]

Dur: [8' 13"]

S 244 W 209 **Moods (Three Pieces for the Pianoforte)** [11p]

1 – *Sadness*

Slowly and plaintively [3p / 47m] [2' 54" – 3' 26"]

2 – *Lassitude*

Allegro poco moderato [4p / 81m] [2' 23" – 2' 41"]

3 – *Energy*

Allegro, poco moderato [2p / 47m] [1' 29" – 1' 37"]

Publ: 1922 Elkin [1244]

Dur: [7' 04" – 7' 26"]

S 245 W 15 **Arabesque** [7p / 87m]

Vivace

Publ: 1923 Schott [31066]

Dur: [3' 00"]

S 246 W (168) **Souvenir de Vienne** [7p / 113m]

Poco allegretto, con grazia – Allegro con moto

Ded: 'à Madame la Comtesse Hermann de Pourtalès

Publ: 1923 Elkin [1358] 2' 37" {2' 25"} / Schott

MS: holograph with estate [4p / 113b].

Note: Employed unchanged the following year as the finale to *Karma*, S 248.

A version for orchestra exists (T2), and is available through the Fleisher Collection in Philadelphia [2962].

S 247 W 372 **Technical Studies** [22p]

Allegro [3p / 34m]

Allegro [4p / 44m]

Allegro scherzando. not staccato [3.5p / 58m]

Andante (Study in finger shifting – speed may be increased, if desired) [1.5p / 22m]

Scherzando (Exercise in hand shifting) [2p / 38(54)m]

Allegretto grazioso [2p / 35(47)m]

Allegro [1p / 23(39)m]

Allegro [3p / 45m]

Ded: 'To my friend Edward Goll'

Publ: 1924 Elkin [1379]

Ref: *MYI*, 274

S 248 W 168 **Karma: A Ballet in Five Pictures** (from 'Charlot's revue') [24p / 402m]

Picture I: *Prologue and Barbaric Dance*

Andante sostenuto – Allegro – Adagio maestoso e sostenuto – Allegro – A little broader [8p / 141m] [4' 44"]

Picture II: *The Piper in the Desert*

Larghetto – Poco più animato – Tempo I [4p / 52m] [2' 24" – 2' 50"]

Picture III: *A Song from the East*

Allegro non troppo [3p / 45m] [1' 42"]

Picture IV: *Before the Church*

Adagio – Poco più animato – Maestoso – Semplice – Tempo adagio [3p / 51m] [3' 33"]

Picture V: *Souvenir de Vienne*

Poco Allegretto, con grazia [5p / 113m] [2' 37"] {2' 25"}

Ded: André Charlot

Publ: 1924 Elkin [1441]

LE: *A Song from the East* – 1962, Galaxy [GMC 2262] / *Souvenir de Vienne* – 1962, Galaxy [GMC 2262]

Dur: [15' 00"]

MS: holograph of piano draft with estate

Notes: Pictures III and V previously published as S 182 No. 2 and S 246 respectively.

Picture III was also published separately (see S 182).

Elkin published the piano suite in the same year as the Charlot ballet was produced. Perhaps it served rehearsal purposes.

Comparison of holograph of S 7 (Charlot ballet) with published piano score, S 248, Elkin [1441]:

Prologue [21m] is a truncated version on that in S 7.

Barbaric Dance ends slightly differently in S 248, adding 3 measures (m.56 is also an added bar).

The Piper in the Desert, marked 'Lento' in S 7, has been reworked considerably in S 248, omitting an 18-bar return of the *Barbaric Dance* in the middle section of S 7. This passage was scored, but may also have been cut from the original revue. The opening of S 248 is marked 'languidly and flute-like', but is scored for clarinet in S 7.

A Song from the East – The first 31 bars of both S 7 and S 248 correspond. The balance of S 7 repeats previous material, while the ballet score continues with 59 bars of material not found in the piano score.

Before the Church – The holograph of S 7 is incomplete, and m.17–51 of S 248 provide the only clue as to how the ballet music might have continued.

Description of holograph of piano version:

This manuscript consists only of Pictures I, III and IV. The published score follows this manuscript precisely. Picture II is lost. For the holograph of Picture V, see S 246.

A *mise-en-scène* has been provided in Scott's handwriting for the three new numbers, as below. It has been crossed out, but presumably represents Scott's initial conception of what the music depicts, whether the realised ballet conformed to it or not.

Prologue [2p / 21m] *and Barbaric Dance* [7p / mm.22–121] – After m.121, a 16-measure sketch is crossed out, with the indication 'to page 10' (missing from holograph).

m.22 – 'Picture I. Prehistoric scene. A sacrificial site in wild craggy place. A girl is lying on a stone slab. Another girl, her sister is weeping over her. A wild dance is in progress.'

m.87 – 'A mysterious stranger appears. He commands a halt.'

m.95 – 'The dancers talk angrily among themselves. They disagree and a struggle ensues – some would attack the stranger – others seek to defend him. The struggle waxes very hot & the stranger is in danger. '

m.116 – 'Suddenly he lifts up a magic wand. They are rendered powerless & he proceeds to lead the girl away. Her sister begs him to allow her to follow – he acquiesces – awe-struck the crowd watch them go.'

The Piper in the Desert [3p / 52m]

Before the Church [5p / 51m] – The beginning of the *mise-en-scène* is missing.

m.17 – '… now appears & C. passionately entreats her. She is torn between love & religion, but bids him a last farewell, for she is not to be turned from her purpose.'

m.26 – 'She enters the church, kneels before the Madonna, then is lost to view. C. shows the grief of a strong man.'

S 249 W 347 **Spanish Dance** [10p / 122b]

Allegro con spirito

Publ: 1925 Elkin [1465]

Dur: [3' 44"]

S 250 W 226 **Three Old Country Dances** [*3 Vieilles danses Anglaises / 3 altenglische Tänze*] [7p / 140(198)m]

1 – Allegretto [2p / 60(76)m] [1' 07"]

2 – Andante cantabile [2p / 31(49)m] [2' 47"]

3 – Allegro [2p / 49(73)m] [1' 02"]

Publ: 1925 Schott [31354]

LE: Schott [1441]

Dur: [4' 56"]

Note: In No. 2, m.17(30) repeats to m.13(26) – the repeat sign is missing.

S 251 W 4 **Album for Boys** [10p]

I – *The Cossack* Like a horse's trot [32b] [0' 30"]

II – *By the Fishing Stream* Fairly fast, murmuringly [17b] [0' 30"]

III – *Christmas Morning* Rather quickly [58b] [1' 00"]

IV – *Lazing* Slowly and dreamily [26b] [1' 15"]

V – *The Hunt* Gaily [43b] [0' 45"]

Publ: 1926 Elkin [1532]

Dur: [4' 21"]

S 252 W 5 **Album for Girls** [12p]

I – *Walking from School* Rather briskly [69b] [1' 00"]

II – *Dreaming* Slowly and delicately [38p] [1' 25"]

III – *On the Swing* Fairly fast [27b] [0' 50"]

IV – *Harebells* At moderate speed [36b] [1' 10"]

V – *The Poor Organ-grinder* Waltz-time [37b] [0' 35"]

VI – *Once Upon a Time* (Wistfully) [17b] [0' 50"]

Publ: 1926 Elkin [1533]

Dur: [6' 25"]

S 253 W 30 **Badinage** [7p / 130m]

Allegro scherzando

Publ: 1928 Elkin [1667]

Dur: [3' 39"]

S 254 W 133 **Guttersnipes' Dance** [3p / 82m]

Vivace

Publ: 1929 Schott [32272]

LE: Schott [32272]

Dur: [1' 41"]

S 255 W 397 **Valse sentimentale** [7p / 116(133)m]

Slowly

Publ: 1929 Elkin [1732]

Dur: [4' 08" – 5' 08"]

S 256 W 423 **Zoo: Animals** [19p]

The Elephant [*Der Elefant*] Allegretto [1p / 21m] [0' 50"]

The Squirrel [*Das Eichhörnchen*] Moderato [1p / 23m] [0' 46"]

The Bear [*Der Bär*] Allegretto [1p / 25m] [0' 52"]

The Monkey [*Der Affe*] Moderato [1p / 24m] [0' 37"]

The Snake [*Die Schlange*] Andante [1p / 15m] [1' 10"]

The Giraffe [*Die Giraffe*] Allegro non troppo [1p / 16m] [0' 37"]

The Tortoise [*Die Schildkröte*] Adagio [1p / 16m] [1' 20"]

The Rhinoceros [*Das Nashorn*] Allegretto [1p / 25m] [0' 36"]

Ded: 'To my children Vivien Mary, and Desmond Cyril Scott'

Publ: 1930 Schott [32619]

LE: Schott [ED 2115]

Dur: [6' 48"]

Note: Illustrations by Willy Harania

S 257 W 128 **Gavotte** [6p / 67m]

Allegretto con grazia

Publ: 1932 Elkin [1820]

Dur: [2' 28"]

S 258 W 378 **Toy Box: Ten Easy Pieces** [*Spielkiste: 10 leichte Stücke für Klavier*] [11p]

The Boot-black [*Der Stiefelputzer*] Allegro [1p / 12m]

Teddy-bear's Headache [*Teddy-Bär hat Kopfweh*] Andante [1p / 15m]

The Little Round-about [*Das kleine Karussel*] Allegretto non troppo [1p / 22m]

Jumbo [*Jumbo*] Moderato [1p / 24m]

The Little Highland Piper [*Der kleine Schotte*] Allegretto [1p / 17m]

The Strutting Sergeant [*Der tapfere Sergeant*] Alla Marcia [1p / 25m]

Grandma [*Großmama*] Andante [1p / 10m]

The Clockwork Mouse [*Die Spielmaus*] Allegro moderato [1p / 15m]

The Prancing Horse [*Ein stolzes Pferd*] Allegro moderato [1p / 33m]

The Russian Dancer [*Der russische Tänzer*] Allegro non troppo [1p / 19m]

Ded: 'to Desmond [Scott] for his seventh birthday'

Comp: 1932

Publ: 1933 Schott [33849]

LE: 2004, Schott [ED 2334], ed. Rainer Mohrs, as *The Toy Box*

Dur: [5' 11"]

S 259 W 206 **Miss Remington: Scherzo** [7p / 120m]

Vivace (like a typewriter)

Ded: Yvonne O'Neill

Publ: 1934 Schott [B.S.S. 33960]

LE: n.d. Schott [2344]

Dur: [3' 24"]

S 260 W 331 **Second Sonata** [33p / 410m]

Maestoso – Moderato e con poesia – Andante – Tempo tranquillo e poco rubato – Con moto – Tempo vivace – Linger somewhat – Andante ma non senza moto – Con spirito – Estatico – Più sostenuto

Ded: Walter Gieseking

Comp: 1933, Rye

Publ: 1935 Universal Music Agencies [U.M.A. 13] (The Plain Cover Edition)

LE: 2007 Novello (Special order edition)

Dur: [14' 33" – 18' 27"] [16' CS]

MS: with estate

Ref: *BC*, 138

Notes: In one movement. There are many notational discrepancies between the holograph and the UMA edition.

S 261 W 371 **Tarantula** [5p / 59m]

Molto vivace

Publ: 1935 Elkin [1917]

Dur: [1' 35"]

S 262 W 332 **Piano Sonata No. 3** [20p / 410m]

I – Molto tranquillo – Poco più mosso – Adagio ma non troppo

[10p / 201m] [9' 12" – 10' 15"]

II – *Scherzo patético*: Allegretto [4p / 88m] [3' 30" – 4' 00"]

III – *Finale*: Grave – Con moto [5p / 121m] [4' 17" – 4' 55"]

Publ: 1956 Elkin [2406]

LE: *Journal of the British Music Society*, Volume 3 (1981), pp. 29–48, as *Piano Sonata III*, with an introduction by W. R. Pasfield, and employing the same engraving plates as Elkin [2406].

Dur: [17' 15" – 20' 10"]

Ref: *BC*, 229

Note: The metronome mark given for the first movement is measured by a 'pocket tape- metronome', a device that had been in existence since the mid-nineteenth century. It was advertised in *The Musical Times* 4 (1 November 1850), p. 92, as follows: 'The Patent Portable Metronome, is a very complete and perfect instrument for measuring time in music. It is the size and form of a small watch, and may be carried in the waistcoat pocket, being similar to a spring measuring tape, on one side of which are marked the vibrations in one minute (as in Maelzel's Metronome), and on the other the Italian musical terms in general use.'

S 263 W 238 **Pastoral Ode** [12p / 188m]

Ded: 'To Esther' [Fisher]

Comp: 1960 (finished by 4 April)

Publ: 1961 Elkin [2589]

Dur: [9' 09"]

Note: Scott's last composition for piano.

S 264 W 402 **Victorian Waltz** [5p / 113m]

In slow waltz time – Poco più mosso (Tempo II)

Comp: *c.* 1933?

Publ: 1963 Elkin [2656]

Dur: [3' 05" – 3' 34"]

Notes: 'from a fragment by T. Holland-Smith'

Although this was Scott's last piano work to be published, its provenance is from the 1930s, having been written originally as a vocal duet in Scene 5 of *Whilom and Whither*, S 3.

ii – piano, 4-hands

S 265 W 88 **Three Dances** [19p / 261m]

I – Slow waltz time [4p / 78m] [2' 35"]

II – Allegretto molto moderato [10p / 124m] [3' 37"]

III – Allegro scherzando [4p / 59m] [0' 47"]

Ded: Mr. James Francis Cooke

Publ: 1926 Presser [T.D.–18]

Dur: [6’ 59”]

Note: One of just three Scott works published only in the United States. See also S 130 & 215.

S 266 W 222 **Nursery Rhymes** [13p]

1 – *My Daddy and Mammy are Irish* Allegretto [2p / 21m] [0’ 35”]

2 – *Polly Put the Kettle On* Moderato [2p / 26m] [0’ 41”]

3 – *Sing a Song of Sixpence* Moderato [2p / 22m] [0’ 28”] (alla marcia)

4 – *Little Bo-Peep* Andante con moto [2p / 24m] [0’ 43”]

5 – *I Saw Three Ships* Con spirito [2p / 24m] [0’ 32”]

6 – *Yankee Doodle* Allegro non troppo [2p / 15m] [0’ 34”]

Publ: 1935 Elkin [1892]

LE: Augener

Dur: [3’ 33”]

Note: Designed for teacher (secondo) and student (primo).

iii – two pianos

S 267 W 373 **Theme and Variations** [52p / 465m]

Tema Adagio ma non troppo [13m] [0’ 44”]

Variation I Poco allegretto [17m] [0’ 34”]

Variation II Allegro moderato. Con spirito [18m] [0’ 37”]

Variation III Adagio [26m] [1’ 29”]

Variation IV Con vigore [29m] [0’ 47”]

Variation V Allegretto [68m] [3’ 01”]

Variation VI Allegro scherzando [45m] [0’ 51”]

Variation VII Tempestosamente [36m] [1’ 13”]

Variation VIII Andante espressivo [20m] [1’ 04”]

Variation IX Vivace [33m] [1’ 06”]

Variation X Andante languoramente [49m] [3’ 00”]

Quasi fuga Nearly twice as quickly [111m] [3’ 55”]

Ded: Esther Fisher

Comp: *c.* 1933

Publ: 1947 Elkin [2093]

Dur: [18’ 28”] [25’ CS]

Ref: *BC*, 202

Note: Letter to Grainger, 19 October 1947, referring to the variations as having been written ‘some 18 or 20 years ago’. [Grainger Museum, 02.0069]

S 268 W 90 **Danse nègre,** Op. 58 No. 5 [13p / 69m]
Publ: 1935 Elkin [1910]
Dur: [2' 08"]

Note: This version repeats b.57 of the solo version (S 185). Cf. T.66.

S 269 – **Impressions from the Jungle Book** [16p / 202(206)m]
W 150 1 – *The Jungle* Adagio [6p / 96m] [3' 34"]
W 151 5 – *Dance of the Elephants* Allegro [8p / 106(110)m] [2' 20"]
Publ: 1938 Schott [B.S.S. 35367]
LE: Schott [2647]
Dur: [5' 54"]

S 270 W 184 **Lotus Land,** Op. 47 No. 1 [8p / 67m]
Andante languido
Publ: 1948 Elkin [2128]
Dur: [4' 20"]

S 271 – **Pastoral Suite**
W 240 5 – *Passacaglia*
Publ: unpublished
Dur: [2' 40"]

S 272 W 303 **Russian Fair (A Dance-Fantasy on Two Russian Folk-Tunes)**
Con moto – Allegro [24p / 310m]
Publ: 1952 Elkin [2253]
Dur: [6' 34"]

Note: Arranged for 2 pianos from the orchestral work, S 64.
See also S 227.

G SONGS

S 273 W 375 **The Time I've Lost in Wooing**
Allegretto [B-flat / C] [5p / 60m]
'The time I've lost in wooing'
LS: Thomas Moore
Ded: Hans and Carrie Lüthy
Comp: July 1893
Publ: 1904 Boosey [H. 4307 (C)]
MS: holograph with Leslie East

S 274 W 85 **Damon**
Largo [d] [2p / 32m]
'Bei dem Glanz der Abendröthe'

LS: J. W. von Goethe
Ded: Hans Lüthy, Esq.
Comp: 17 August 1895; Disley (Cheshire)
Publ: unpublished
MS: holograph with Leslie East

S 275 W 343 **Sigh No More**
Moderato [e] [4p / 69m]
'Sigh no more ladies, sigh no more'
LS: William Shakespeare
Ded: Miss Edith Rutherford
Comp: 8 November 1895
Publ. unpublished
MS: holograph with Leslie East

S 276 W 343 **What Win I if I Gain**
Andante [C] [4p / 45m]
'What win I if I gain'
LS: William Shakespeare
Ded: Mrs. G. Hall-Neale
Comp: 1 December 1895
Publ: unpublished
MS: holograph with Leslie East

S 277 W 343 **Under the Greenwood Tree**
Moderato [F] [3p / 76m]
'Under the greenwood tree / Who loves to lie with me'
Ded: Mlle. A.M. Sylvestre
Comp: 7 December 1895
Publ: unpublished
LS: William Shakespeare (*As You Like It*)
MS: holograph with Leslie East

S 278 W 343 **Beware**
Allegro [a] [5p / 91(133)m]
'I know a maiden fair to see'
LS: Henry W. Longfellow
Ded: G. Hall-Neale Esq.
Comp: 1895–96
Publ: unpublished
MS: holograph with Leslie East

S 279 W 343 **Hark! Hark! The Lark!**

Allegretto [d] [2p / 23m] 'Hark! Hark the lark at heaven's gate sings'

LS: William Shakespeare (Cloten's song)

Ded: 'Dedicated to Herr L. Uzielli', crossed out in holograph

Comp: 1895–96

Publ: unpublished

MS: holograph with Leslie East

S 280 W 343 **Sleep Little Baby Sleep**

(none) [C] [2p / 48mm]

'Sleep! Sleep little baby sleep'

LS: Caroline Southey

Comp: 1895–96

Publ: unpublished

MS: holograph with Leslie East

S 281 W 307 **Lieder aus 'Sänge eines fahrenden Spielmanns' von Stefan George**, Op. 1 (*componiert für mittelstimme und Clavier*)

Prelude: Worte trügen Worte fliehen Sehr langsam [e to G] [1p / 25m]

No. I – *Heisst es viel dich bitten* Sehr langsam [C] [2p / 30m]

No. II – *So ich traurig bin* Sehr langsam [F] [1p / 20m]

No. III – *Dieses ist ein rechter Morgen* Langsam [G] [1p / 24m]

No. IV – *Aus den Knospenquellen* Allegretto molto moderato [C] [2p / 26m] No.V – *Sieh mein Kind ich gehe* Langsam und einfach [C] [2p / 24m]

LS: Stefan George

Ded: Hans Lüthy, Clemens Franckenstein, Balfour Gardiner, T. Holland-Smith, & Roger Quilter

Comp: April 1898

Publ: unpublished

MS: holograph in Grainger Museum

Note: *Prelude* moves *attacca* into No. I. No. III is set strophically.

S 282 W 13 **April Love**, Op. 1 No. 1

Andante [C] [3p / 34m] 'We have walkd in love's land a little way'

LS: Ernest Dowson

Ded: Stefan George

Comp: 1900, with S 283, 284 & 285, Oxton

Publ: 1903, as S 282a

MS: holograph (1900) with Leslie East

Ref: *MYI*, 39

Note: Scott collected four Dowson poems ('April love', 'Ad Domnulam suam', 'Soli cantare periti arcades' and 'Yvonne of Brittany') into a set of songs, Op. 1 (S 282–285), and dedicated them 'to those who are the cause of these songs as I hope they may be the cause of many others.' All were later published by Metzler and Boosey as Opp. 3 and 5, the Latin-titled ones renamed (S 282a, S 283a, S 284a, and S 285a). 'Those' are presumably the four dedicatees of the published 1903 versions.

S 282a W 13 **April Love**, Op. 3 No. 1

Andante e molto semplice [C] [3p / 34m]

'We have walk'd in Love's land a little way'

Comp: 1900

Publ: 1903 Metzler [M. 8162]

LS: Ernest Dowson

Ded: Frederic Austin

Ref: *MYI*, 149

Note: published version of S 282. The dedicatee had changed between the manuscript and the published version.

S 283 W 1 **Ad Domnulam suam**, Op. 1 No. 2 [A]

'Little Lady of my heart!'

LS: Ernest Dowson

Comp: 1900, with S 282, 284 & 285, Oxton

Publ: 1903, as S 283a

MS: holograph with Leslie East

Note: see Note, S 282

S 283a W 1 **Little Lady of My Heart** (*Ad Domnulam suam*), Op. 3 No. 2

Andante e molto semplice [A] [4p / 59m]

'Little Lady of my heart!' LS: Ernest Dowson

Ded: Stefan George

Comp: 1900

Publ: 1903 Metzler [M. 8163] (Metzler's Royal Edition No. 8)

Note: published version of S 283.

S 284 W 84 **Soli cantare periti arcades**, Op. 1 No. 3

'Oh, I would live in a dairy'

LS: Ernest Dowson

Comp: 1900, with S 282, 283 & 285, Oxton

Publ: unpublished

Note: see Note, S 282

S 284a W 84 **Dairy Song**, Op. 5 No. 1
Allegro con grazia [F / G] [5p / 60m]
'Oh, I would live in a dairy'
LS: Ernest Dowson
Ded: Roger Cuthbert Quilter
Comp: 1900
Publ: 1903 Boosey [H. 4031 – F]
Note: Published version of S 284.

S 285 – **Yvonne of Brittany**, Op. 1 No. 4
'In your mother's apple orchard'
LS: Ernest Dowson
Comp: 1900, with S 282, 283 & 284, Oxton
Note: see Note, S 282

S 285a W 422 **Yvonne of Brittany**, Op. 5 No. 2
Andante [F / G] [7p / 76m]
'In your mother's apple orchard'
LS: Ernest Dowson
Ded: Walter Crook
Comp: 1900
Publ: 1903 Boosey [H. 3966 – G]
Note: The fourth verse of the original setting is omitted in the published version.

S 286 W 93 **Daphnis and Chloe**, Op. 9 No. 1
Andante [G] [5p / 74m] 'White Chloe lay sleeping / Under a beechen shade'
LS: Selwyn Image
Ded: Francis Korbay
Comp: *c.* 1900
Publ: 1904 Boosey [H. 4304]

S 287 W 116 **Exile**, Op. 9 No. 2
Comp: *c.* 1900
Publ: unpublished

S 288 W 400 **Vesperal**, Op. 9 No. 3
Andante con moto ma molto semplice [E-flat] [5p / 73m]
'Strange grows the river on the sunless evenings'
LS: Ernest Dowson
Comp: 23 April 1900, Walton on Thames

Publ: unpublished

Ded: 'For Percy Grainger, my dear friend – in all affection and friendly love. April 1900'

MS: holograph with Leslie East

Note: Not to be confused with *Vesperale*, S 176

S 289 W 29 **Autumnal**, Op. 11 No. 1

'Pale amber sunlight falls across the reddening October trees'

LS: Ernest Dowson

Comp: *c.* 1900

Publ: unpublished

Note: 1st version of S 299.

S 290 W 305 **The Sands of Dee**, Op. 11 No. 2

'O Mary, go and call the cattle home'

LS: Charles Kingsley

Comp: *c.* 1900

Publ: unpublished

Note: See S 382.

S 291 W 33 **Ballad of Dark Rosaleen**, Op. 13

'O my dark Rosaleen'

LS: James Clarence Mangan

Comp: *c.* 1900

Publ: unpublished

S 292 – **Let Be at Last**

Andante sostenuto [D]

LS: Ernest Dowson (*Venite descendamus*)

Comp: 11 December 1907?

Publ: unpublished

MS: with estate [4p / 64b]

Note: Holograph is in two parts. A single-folio, 2-page fragment of the first 34 bars of the song, including roughly half the Dowson poem, is written in the calligraphic style consistent with that of his earliest works. A second folio, containing the last 30 bars of the song, is written in the more cursive scrawl typical of his drafts.

Two Poems, Op. 24 [11p]

S 293 W 410 No. 1 – *Voices of Vision*

Slowly and intensely [range: C–F] [8p / 84b]

'These are the voices from the vale of twilight hours.'

LS: Cyril Scott

Comp: 11 March 1903

Publ: 1903 Elkin [181]

Ded: Aimée & Robin Legge

MS: holograph (6p) with estate

Ref: *MYI*, 92

Note: Scott's personal copy has additional French text penned in ('Ce sont les voix du val de l'heure du crépuscule'). Unlike S 294, Schott did not issue this song in German or French.

S 294 W 420 No. 2 – *Willows* [*Trauerweiden*]

Moderately [range: C–F] [3p / 48m] Moderato [range: C–F] [3p / 48m]

'These mournful trees caressed in the ancient poets dreams' ['Ihr Trauerweiden weint schon in alter Dichter Traum']

LS: Cyril Scott

Ded: Aimée & Robin Legge

Comp: 11 March 1903

Publ: 1903 Elkin [181]

1911 Schott [29364] – transl. A. M. von Blomberg

MS: holograph (3p) with estate

Ref: *MYI*, 92

Note: Scott's personal copy has additional French text penned in ('Arbres mornes frôlés de poétiques rêves'). No French edition was published.

Holograph has 'mourneful' and 'carressed'.

S 295 W 132 **Greek Song**, Op. 29

Comp: *c.* 1903

Publ: unpublished

Note: No trace of this song has been forthcoming.

S 296 W 171 **A Last Word** [*Ma mie*], Op. 30 No. 1

Andante [B-flat / C] [5p / 46m]

'All that a man may pray'

LS: Ernest Dowson

Ded: David Bispham

Publ: 1903 Boosey [H. 4297 (B-flat) / 4125 (C)] Ref: *MYI*, 94

Note: Scott's own personal copy of H.4297 has French text penned in ('Ne t'ai-je pas prié autant qu'homme supplie'), not found in Boosey.

S 297 W 374 **There Comes an End to Summer**, Op. 30 No. 2

Allegretto [A-flat / C] [5p / 55m]

'There comes an end to summer'

LS: Ernest Dowson

Ded: Charles Bonnier

Publ: 1903 Boosey [H. 4310 (A-flat) / H.4124 (C)]

MS: with estate

Note: Title page of holograph labels H.4124 'For tenor'.

S 298 W 18 **Asleep**, Op. 31 No. 1

(none) [C] [5p / 60m]

'Sleep on, dear, now'

Ded: Agnes and Eric Harben

LS: Ernest Dowson

Publ: 1903 Boosey [H. 4228]

Ref: *MYI*, 94

S 299 W 28 **Autumnal**, Op. 32 No. 1

Andante semplice [B-flat] [5p / 54m]

'Pale amber sunlight falls across the reddening October trees'

LS: Ernest Dowson

Ded: Rosamund Marriott Watson

Comp: *c.* 1900

Publ: 1904 Boosey [H. 4336]

Note: Revision of S 289. The dedication to 'Rosamund and Marriot Watson' in Boosey is an error.

S 300 W 404 **Villanelle**, Op. 33 No. 3

Slowly as if a lullaby [G] [5p / 39m]

'Come hither, child, and rest,'

LS: Ernest Dowson

Ded: Mabel and Edwin Lee

Publ: 1904 Boosey [H. 4423]

Ref: *MYI*, 94

S 301 W 113 **Evening Hymn**, Op. 34, for voice and pianoforte with violin *ad lib*
Adagio [D] [7p / 107m] 'The sun is sinking fast, / The daylight dies'
LS: Edward Caswall (translated from the Latin)
Ded: 'To my Father and Mother' (Henry & Mary Scott)
Publ: 1904 Boosey [H. 4532]
Ref: *MYI*, 84
Note: Material derived from *Piano Concerto* in D, Op. 10, S 68. The violin *ad lib* plays only in the final verse, bars 74 – end.

S 302 W 394 **A Valediction**, Op. 36 No. 1
Andante [G / B-flat] [6p / 49m]
'If we must part, Then let it be like this'
LS: Ernest Dowson
Ded: Gervase Elwes
Publ: 1904 Elkin [256 / 257]
Ref: *MYI*, 98 (probable reference)

S 303 W 346 **Sorrow**, Op. 36 No. 2
Very slowly with simple pathos [E-flat/F] [3p / 43m] / [*Kummer*] [3p] / [*Chagrin*] [4p]
'Exceeding sorrow / Consumeth my sad heart!'
Ger. transl. A.M. von Blomberg
LS: Ernest Dowson
Ded: Melchior Lechter
Publ: 1904 Elkin [262 / 263] / 1911 Schott [29366] (*Kummer*) / 1911 Schott [29302] (*Chagrin*)
Ref: *MYI*, 99
LE: 1913, Elkin, contralto album [750, in E-flat]

S 304 W 210 **My Captain**, Op. 38 No. 1
Allegro con brio [F / G] [9p / 114m]
'Oh Captain! my Captain! our fearful trip is done'
LS: Walt Whitman
Publ: 1904 Elkin [258 / 259]

S 305 W 379 **Trafalgar**, Op. 38 No. 2
Con spirito [C] [5p / 80m]
'In the wild October night-time, when the wind raved round the land'
LS: Thomas Hardy (*The Dynasts*)
Publ: 1904 Boosey [H. 4462]

S 306 W 106 **Eileen**, Op. 42 No. 1
LS: Ellen Mary Rowning
Publ: 1904 Boosey [H. 4498]

S 307 W 37 **The Ballad Singer**, Op. 42 No. 2
Andante sostenuto [D-flat] [5p / 80m]
'Down where the lotus perfume sighs'
LS: Eric Harben
Ded: 'To Eric and Agnes [Harben], as an attempt at the true English pathos'
Publ: 1904 Boosey [H. 4497]

S 308 W 194 **Mary**, Op. 42 No. 3
Moderato [G] [5p / 51m]
'I'm sitting on the stile, Mary'
LS: Helen Selina, Lady Dufferin
Publ: 1904 Boosey [H. 4499]

S 309 W 131 **A Gift of Silence**, Op. 43 No. 1
Andante sostenuto e semplice [F / A-flat] [4p / 52m]
'A Gift of Silence sweet!'
LS: Ernest Dowson
Ded: Heddie & Alan Gardiner
Publ: 1905 Elkin [304 / 305]
LE: 1913 Elkin, contralto and baritone albums [750 & 752]

S 310 W 98 **Don't Come in Sir, Please!**, Op. 43 No. 2
Allegretto grazioso [D / E] [7p / 36m]
'Don't come in, sir, please!'
LS: Herbert A. Giles (from the Chinese)
Ded: Walter Crook
Publ: 1905 Elkin [296 / 297]
LE: 1913 Elkin, soprano album [749]
Note: Text change penned into CS's personal copy of [296], 'What would the world say!', (instead of 'What the world would say!'), bar 30. Elkin [297] and [749] were published correctly.

S 311 W 417 **The White Knight**, Op. 43 No. 3
Allegro [D / E] [7p / 55m]
'Gallants, riding to the war, / Riding o'er the lea'
LS: Rosamund Marriott Watson (Old French, 1600)
Ded: Rosamund Marriott Watson
Publ: 1905 Elkin [310 / 311]
MS: with estate [in D]

S 312 W 286 **A Reflection**, Op. 43 No. 4

Andante [D / F] [6p / 30m]

'Let us bathe; on our brows let us twine'

LS: William Roger Paton (from the Greek)

Ded: Henry Hadley

Publ: 1905 Elkin [312 / 313]

LE: 1913 Elkin tenor album [751]

Two Chinese Songs, Op. 46 [7p]

S 313 W 411 1 – *Waiting*

Adagio [C# to E] [3p / 45m]

'The sun has sunk behind the western hill'

LS: Herbert A. Giles (from the Chinese)

Ded: 'To my friend R.R. Vamam Shankar Rav Pandit'

Publ: 1906 Elkin [344]

LE: 1919, Elkin, 'Songs of Old Cathay' (No. 4)

Ref: *MYI*, 72, 179

S 314 W 246 2 – *A Picnic* (from the Chinese)

Allegro [C to G-flat] [4p / 70mm]

'The sun is setting as we loose the boat'

LS: Herbert A. Giles (from the Chinese)

Ded: 'To my friend R.R. Vamam Shankar Rav Pandit'

Publ: 1906 Elkin [344]

LE: 1919, Elkin, 'Songs of Old Cathay' (No. 5)

Dur: [2' 22"]

Ref: *MYI*, 72, 179

S 315 W 342 **A Song of Wine**, Op. 46 No. 3

Allegro [C to F#] [7p / 83m]

'What is life after all but a dream'

LS: Herbert A. Giles (from the Chinese)

Ded: Frederic Austin

Publ: 1907 Elkin [406]

LE: 1919, Elkin, 'Songs of Old Cathay' (No. 3)

Dur: [2' 34"]

Ref: *MYI*, 179

S 316 W 2 **Afterday**, Op. 50 No. 1
Andante [G / C] [6p / 32m]
'They are but brief those languid laughing hours'
LS: Cyril Scott
Publ: 1906 Elkin [338 / 339]
LE: 1913, Elkin baritone album [752]

S 317 W 341 **A Song of London**, Op. 52 No. 1
Allegro con spirito [e / g] [7p / 67m]
'The sun's on the pavement, The current comes and goes.'
LS: Rosamund Marriott Watson
Ded: H.G. Wells
Publ: 1906 Elkin [355 / 356]
LE: 1913 Elkin contralto and baritone albums [750 & 752]
Dur: [1' 42"]

S 318 W 300 **A Roundel of Rest**, Op. 52 No. 2
Andante sostenuto [C / E-flat] [6p / 58m]
'If rest is sweet at close of day'
LS: Arthur Symons
Ded: Arthur Symons
Publ: 1906 Elkin [359 / 360]

S 319 W 49 **Blackbird's Song** [*Amsel-Lied / Chanson du merle*], Op. 52 No. 3
Allegretto [D / E-flat / F] [7p / 42m]
'Sweetheart, I ne'er may know
['Chère, je ne sais ni ne le verrai' – transl. unnamed]
LS: Rosamund Marriott Watson
Publ: 1906 Elkin [357 / 357a / 358]
1910 Schott [28996, in D, Ger/Eng]
1911 Schott [29299, in D, Fr/Eng]
Dur: [2' 57"]
Ref: *MYI*, 276
BC, 91, 98

S 320 W 42 **La belle dame sans merci**, duet
'Oh what can ail thee, knight-at-arms'
LS: Keats
Comp: *c.* 1907
Publ: unpublished

Two Old English Lyrics

S 321 W 187 No. 1 – *Lovely Kind and Kindly Loving*, Op. 55 No. 1
Andante [G / B-flat] [7p / 44m]
'Lovely kind and kindly loving'
LS: Nicholas Breton
Publ: 1907 Elkin [389 / 390]
LE: 1913 Elkin, tenor album [751, B-flat]

S 322 W 418 No. 2 – *Why so Pale and Wan?*, Op. 55 No. 2
Allegro con spirito [F] [7p / 11m]
'Why so wan and pale fond lover'
LS: Sir John Suckling
Publ: 1907 Elkin [391]

S 323 W 186 **Love's Quarrel**, Op. 55 No. 3
Andante [G / B-flat / C] [7p / 46m]
'Standing by the river, gazing on the river'
LS: Lord Lytton
Ded: Cara and Austin Harris
Publ: 1907 Elkin [403 / 404 / 404a]
LE: 1913, Elkin, tenor album [751, in C]

Two Songs, Op. 56 [7p]

S 324 W 21 1 – *Atwain*, Op. 56 No. 1
Moderately [low-med, C] [4p / 32m]
'Shades of eve assemble / Softly o'er the plain'
LS: F. Leslie
Publ: 1907 Elkin [416]

S 325 W 160 2 – *Insouciance*, Op. 56 No. 2
Allegretto amabile [high, F] [3p / 35m]
'I wander north, I wander south'
LS: Herbert A. Giles (from the Chinese)
Publ: 1907 Elkin [416]

S 326 W 259 **Prelude**, Op. 57 No. 1
Andante semplice [B-flat/C/D] [6p / 42m]
'The blossom-snow begins to blow'
LS: Rosamund Marriott Watson
Ded: A.J. Rowan Hamilton (cf. S 230 & 233)
Publ: 1908 Elkin [433/433a/434]
Dur: [1' 43"]

S 327 W 189 **Lullaby** [*Berceuse*], Op. 57 No. 2
Allegretto grazioso [D-flat / E-flat / F] [6p / 45m]
'Lullaby, oh lullaby!'
LS: Christina Rossetti
Ded: Guy and Marie Harben
Publ: 1908 Elkin [431 / 431a / 432] / 1911 Schott (Ger,Fr,Eng)
Dur: [2' 25"]
Ref: *BC*, 91, 98, 157
Note: The earliest printings state 'Not too slowly' instead of 'Allegretto grazioso'.

S 328 W 309 **Scotch Lullabye**, Op. 57 No. 3
Allegro non troppo [D / F] [7p / 104m]
LS: Walter Scott
Comp: *c.* 1908?
Publ: 1910 Elkin [575 / 576]

S 329 W 314 **A Serenade**, Op. 61 No. 1
Allegretto amabile [D / F] [6p / 48m]
'Will thou not wake? Alone between The dawn and darkness'
LS: Duffield Bendall
Ded: Theodore Byard
Publ: 1908 Elkin [474 / 475]
LE: 1913 Elkin tenor and baritone albums [751 & 752]

S 330 W 153 **In a Fairy Boat**, Op. 61 No. 2
Gracefully [C / E-flat] [7p / 52m]
'In a fairy boat on a fairy sea'
LS: Bernard Weller
Publ: 1908 Elkin [472 / 473]

S 331 W 182 **A Lost Love**, Op. 62 No. 1
Andante sostenuto [E-flat / F / A-flat] [6p / 39m]
'Too late, alas! I came to find'
LS: Herbert A. Giles (from the Chinese)
Publ: 1908 Elkin [481 / 481a / 482]
LE: 1913 Elkin soprano and contralto albums [749 & 750]

S 332 W 408 **A Vision**, Op. 62 No. 2

Allegretto [A] [7p / 118m]

'The dust of the morn had been laid by a shower'

LS: Herbert A. Giles (from the Chinese)

Ded: Mrs. Rowan Hamilton

Publ: 1908 Elkin [483]

S 333 W 103 **An Eastern Lament**, Op. 62 No. 3

Slowly [*c* / e] [6p / 73m]

'Alone I mount to the Kiosque which stands'

LS: Herbert A. Giles (from the Chinese)

Ded: Swami Abhedananda

Publ: 1909 Elkin [487 / 488]

Dur: [2' 08"]

S 334 – **Lone Summer**

Moderato [F] [4p / 39m]

'You are far from me Dearest, my lover

LS: Ella Erskine

Comp: 16 March 1909

Publ: unpublished

MS: with estate

S 335 W 11 **And So I Made a Villanelle** [*Und so macht' ich ein Villanelle / Ainsi fis-je une villanelle*], Op. 65

Andante [G / B-flat] [7p / 65m]

'I took her dainty eyes as well' ['Ich dacht' an ihre Augen hell' – transl. A.M. von Blomberg] ['Je pris ses chers yeux B ma belle' – transl. unidentified]

LS: Ernest Dowson

Ded: Mr. & Mrs. H. W. Darvell (Darwell in Schott [29301])

Publ: 1908 Elkin [489 / 490] / 1911 Schott [29301, Fr/Eng] [G] [6p] / 1911 Schott [29365, Ger/Eng] [B-flat] [5p]

S 336 W 82 **Daffodils**, Op. 68 No. 1

Allegretto [A / B-flat / C] [7p / 39m]

'In the yellow daffodils Sunshine seems to dwell'

LS: Ella Erskine

Publ: 1909 Elkin [515 / 515a / 516]

LE: 1913, Elkin, soprano album [749]

S 337 W 230 **Osme's Song**, Op. 68 No. 2

Fast [D / F] [7p / 97m]

'Hither! Hither! / O come hither!'

LS: George Darley (from *Sylvia, or The May Queen*, 1827)

Ded: Astra Desmond

Publ: 1909 Elkin [519 / 520]

MS: with estate

Note: original title in holograph [in F] is '*O Come Hither*'.

S 338 W 211 **My Lady Sleeps**, Op. 70 No. 1

(none) [D / F] [6p / 65m]

'My lady sleeps: no murmurs rise'

LS: Duffield Bendall (from *The Idler* magazine)

Ded: Landon Ronald

Publ: 1910 Elkin [549 / 550]

LE: 1913 Elkin, tenor album [751, in F]

S 339 W 205 **Mirage** [*Traumbild / Mirage*], Op. 70 No. 2

Andante [A-flat] [7p / 46m]

'I dreamed the peach trees blossomed once again' (Ger. transl. A.M. von Blomberg)

LS: Rosamund Marriott Watson

Ded: 'For M.' [London]

Publ: 1910 Elkin [543] [7p / 46m] / 1911 Schott [29367 – Ger/Eng] [5p] / Schott

LE: 1913 Elkin, soprano album [749]

MS: with estate

S 340 W 112 **Evening**, Op. 71 No. 2

Andante sostenuto [C / E-flat] [7p / 81m]

'Strange grows the river on the sunless evenings'

LS: Ernest Dowson

Ded: Walter & Ella Pearce

Publ: 1910 Elkin [545 / 546]

LE: 1913 Elkin, contralto album [750, in C]

S 341 W 349 **A Spring Ditty**, Op. 72 No. 1

Allegretto [D / F] [7p / 96m]

'In the Spring, ah happy day!'

LS: John Addington Symonds (from the Latin)

Publ: 1910 Elkin [571 / 572]

Ref: *MYI*, 187

S 342 W 16 **Arietta**, Op. 72 No. 2

Andante [C/E-flat] [5p]

'I made a song of tears and fire'

LS: Duffield Bendall

Publ: 1910 Elkin [584 / 585]

LE: 1913, Elkin, tenor album [751]

S 343 W 389 **The Trysting Tree**, Op. 72 No. 3

Quickly [C / D] [7p / 71m]

'Meet me, love, where the woodbines grow'

LS: Charles Sayle

Publ: 1910 Elkin [591 / 592]

MS: with estate

Notes: Elkin [591] is dated 1911.

Holograph (in D) states Op. 72 No. 2. [3p]

S 344 W 395 **The Valley of Silence**, Op. 72 No. 4

Rather slowly [C / E-flat] [7p / 82m]

'What land of Silence, / Where pale stars shine'

LS: Ernest Dowson

Publ: 1911 Elkin [589 / 590]

MS: with estate [5p]

S 345 W 393 **The Unforeseen**, Op. 74 No. 4

Andante sostenuto [B-flat / C / D] [6p / 61m]

'How could I dream a day would ever dawn'

LS: Rosamund Marriott Watson

Ded: Miss Grainger Kerr

Publ: 1911 Elkin [611 / 611a / 612]

Ref: *BC*, 98

Note: Elkin indicates this song as Op. 74 No. 3, a number also used by Schott a year earlier for *Danse langoureuse* from *Trois danses tristes*, S 197. This appears to be an Elkin error, and the correct number should have been Op. 74 No. 4, as this is otherwise unknown, and Op. 74/5–6 are both songs.

S 346 W 406 **Villanelle of the Poet's Road**, Op. 74 No. 5

Andante (Not too slowly) [C / E-flat] [6p / 29m]

'Wine and woman and song'

LS: Ernest Dowson

Ded: Charles Dyer

Comp: 5 July 1910?

Publ: 1911 Elkin [609 / 610]

MS: with estate – holograph [4p] has *Wine & Woman & Song* as original title, crossed out. Tempo marking is simply 'Andante'

S 347 W 216 **The New Moon**, Op. 74 No. 6

Allegretto moderato [E / G] [7p / 59m]

'Beyond the crooked apple-bough'

LS: Rosamund Marriott Watson

Ded: Miss Jean Waterston

Publ: 1911 Elkin [613 / 614]

LE: 1913 Elkin, soprano album [749, in G]

S 348 W 185 **Love's Aftermath**

Andante espressivo [B-flat / D-flat] [7p / 58m]

'Love's aftermath! I think the time is now'

LS: Ernest Dowson

Publ: 1911 Elkin [618 / 619]

LE: 1913, Elkin, contralto album [750]

S 349 W 228 **An Old Song Ended** [*Ein altes Lied beendigt*]

Slowly and simply [E-flat / F] [6p / 47m]

'How should I your true love know from another one?' (Ger. transl. A.M. von Blomberg)

LS: Dante Gabriel Rossetti

Ded: Miss Maggie Teyte

Publ: 1911 Elkin [633 / 634] / 1912 Schott [6p]

MS: with estate [3p]

S 350 W 122 **For a Dream's Sake** [*Durch ein Traumbild*]

Andante [A-flat / B-flat / C] [7p / 32m]

'The hope I dreamed of was a dream' (Ger. transl. A.M. von Blomberg)

LS: Christina Rossetti

Ded: Beryl Freeman

Publ: 1912 Elkin [644 / 644a / 645] / 1912 Schott [29670, Ger/Eng] [6p]

S 351 W 177 **A Little Song of Picardie** [*Ein kleines Lied von der Picardie*]

Allegretto grazioso [D / E] [7p / 80m]

'Pale leaves waver and whisper low' ['Silberpappeln am Ufer stehn']

LS: Rosamund Marriott Watson

Publ: 1912 Elkin [646 / 647] / 1912 Schott [29669 (Ger/Eng), transl. A.M. von Blomberg] [D]

LE: 1913 Elkin soprano album (749)

S 352 W 252 **Pierrot and the Moon Maiden**

Allegretto moderato [D-flat / E] [7p / 52m]
'What is love? / Is it a folly'
LS: Ernest Dowson
Ded: 'For Wiesi & Klemens'
Publ: 1912 Elkin [682 / 683]
MS: with estate [4p]

Note: See *In the Silver Moonbeams*, S 417, for another poem related to Pierrot.

S 353 W 156 **In the Valley**

Allegretto [med / high] [6p / 72m]
'Myriad birds in the thicket sing'
LS: Rosamund Marriott Watson
Ded: Hubert & Kitty Eisdell
Comp: 1 April 1912 (?)
Publ: 1912 Elkin [684 / 685]
MS: with estate [4p; medium key]

S 354 W 323 **Sleep Song**

Andante semplice [d / f] [7p / 56m]
'The wind whistled loud at the window pane'
LS: William B. Rands
Ded: 'Michael A.M. Eisdell & his Mother'
Publ: 1912 Elkin [686 / 687]

S 355 – **Time Long Past**

Andante [D# – A]
'Like the ghost of a dear friend dead'
LS: Percy Bysshe Shelley
Comp: 1 April 1912
Publ: unpublished
MS: with estate [4p / 63b]

Old Songs in New Guise [14p]

S 356 W 100 1 – *Where Be Going* (Old Melody)

Andante / Poco allegretto [low-med / high, G] [5p / 31m]
'Where be going to, dear little maiden'
LS: traditional Cornish
Ded: Hubert Eisdell
Publ: 1913 Elkin [699]

S 357 W 416 2 – *Drink to Me Only with Thine Eyes* (Old Melody)
[none] [low / A-flat] [4p / 45m]
'Drink to me only with thine eyes'
LS: Ben Jonson
Ded: Hubert Eisdell
Publ: 1913 Elkin [699]

S 358 W 358 3 – *Summer is Acumen In* (Old Melody)
Allegretto con spirito [C / G] [5p / 69m]
'Summer is a-coming in / Loud now sing cuckoo'
LS: traditional Wessex
Ded: Hubert Eisdell
Publ: 1913 Elkin [699]

S 359 W 26 **Autumn Song**
Lento [B-flat / D] [5p / 31m]
'See the leaves are falling'
LS: Rosamund Marriott Watson
Ded: Monsieur et Madame Golay-Chovel
Publ: 1913 Elkin [709 / 710]

S 360 W 48 **A Birthday**
Gently flowing [C / D] [6p / 43m]
'My heart is like a singing bird'
LS: Christina Rossetti
Ded: Charles Tilson Chowne
Publ: 1913 Elkin [717 / 718]

S 361 W 50 **Spring Song**
Quasi allegretto [low-med / high] [6p / 47m]
'Beneath the wind-wearied skies'
LS: Cyril Scott
Ded: Ilse Stegmann
Publ: 1913 Elkin [740 / 741]
MS: With estate. Only the first page of the manuscript is extant. The holograph has original title, *Cuckoo*, crossed out in favour of *Spring Song*. The tempo indication is 'Poco allegretto?', and the composer has written '1 tone higher / No key signature' at the beginning of the score (for the high-key version).

S 362 W 219 **Nocturne**

Allegretto molto moderato [A-flat / B] [7p / 99m]

'The air is dark and sweet'

LS: Rosamund Marriott Watson

Ded: Mathilde and Wilhelm Kohl

Publ: 1913 Elkin [745 / 746]

S 363 W 289 **Retrospect**

Andante [C / D] [7p / 52m]

'You would have understood me had you waited'

LS: Ernest Dowson

Ded: Alan Gardiner

Publ: 1913 Elkin [756 / 757]

S 364 – **Auvergnat**

Allegretto [D]

'There was a man was half a clown (It's so my father tells of it)'

LS: Hilaire Belloc

Comp: 31 July 1913

Publ: unpublished

MS: with estate – 2 copies; one in pencil, one a fair copy in pen [both 5p / 45m]

Note: A text also set by Arthur Bliss, Arthur Goodhart and Archie Potter ('The Bells of Clermont Town').

S 365 W 43 **La belle dame sans merci**, duet

'Oh what can ail thee, knight-at-arms'

LS: Keats

Comp: *c.* 1914

Publ: unpublished (different setting than S 320)

S 366 W 340 **A Song of Arcady**

Allegretto [D / F] [7p / 74m]

'Oh I would live in a dairy'

LS: Ernest Dowson

Ded: Bella and Maya Heerman

Publ: 1914 Elkin [770 / 771]

S 367 W 27 **Autumn's Lute**

Andante non troppo [low-med / high] [6p / 50m]

'Autumn's melancholy lute'

LS: Rosamund Marriott Watson

Publ: 1914 Elkin [787 / 788]

S 368 W 258 **A Prayer**

Andante semplice [C] [6p / 47m]

'Soft, soft wind from out the sweet south sliding'

LS: Charles Kingsley

Publ: 1914 Elkin [806]

MS: with estate [3p]

S 369 W 114 **Evening Melody**

Andante non troppo [low-med / high] [7p / 57m]

'Eve, warm and sad, as the last light shimmers'

LS: Cyril Scott (from *The Shadows of Silence and the Songs of Yesterday*, Liverpool: Donald Fraser, Lyceum Press)

Publ: 1914 Elkin [809 / 810]

MS: with estate [4p]

S 370 W 172 **Lilac-Time**

Con moto [med, B-flat / high, C] [6p / 48m]

'Ah, Warble me now for joy of lilac-time'

LS: Walt Whitman

Ded: Miss Maggie Teyte

Publ: 1914 Elkin [816 / 817]

371 – **Once Again to Wake**

Andante [G]

'Once again to wake, nor wish to sleep'

LS: Christina Rossetti

Comp: 10 October 1914

Publ: unpublished

MS: with estate [2p / 48b]

S 372 – **Lady whose Love Lit Eyes**

Allegro moderato [range E-flat – A]

LS: Cyril Scott (unlikely)

Ded: John Sampson (cf. SW1)

Comp: 20 November 1914

Publ: unpublished

MS: with estate [4p / 61m] The holograph is fair/poor, with several tears and missing paper. The music however is complete.

S 373 – **New Years Eve**

(MS has: '? Tempo') [3p / 55m]

'Goodbye and goodbye! / There's a fresh wind seaward blowing'

LS: Cyril Scott

Comp: 10 December 1914

Publ: unpublished

MS: with estate

S 374 – **On the Road**

Andante [e / E] [6p / 85m]

'The snow is white, the way is stern and sore'

LS: Rosamund Marriott Watson (*The Bird-bride*)

Comp: 10 December 1914

Publ: unpublished

MS: with estate

Note: A fine song by one of Scott's favourite poets, unfortunately and inexplicably left unpublished.

S 375 W 198 **Meditation**

Andante semplice [B-flat / C] [6p / 31m]

'They are not long, the weeping and the laughter'

LS: Ernest Dowson

Ded: Nora Panfili

Publ: 1915 Elkin [839 / 840]

S 376 W 217 **Night-Song**

Allegretto moderato [D-flat / E-flat] [7p / 66m]

'Who is it sings the gypsies' song to-night'

LS: Rosamund Marriott Watson

Ded: George Whitehouse

Publ: 1915 Elkin [859 / 860]

Note: The hyphenated title appears everywhere but on the front cover.

S 377 W 282 **Rain**

Allegretto moderato [low-med / high, D] [7p / 99m]

'Watch from the window grey rain falling'

LS: Margaret Maitland Radford

Publ: 1916 Elkin [870 / 871]

S 378 W 162 **Invocation**

Andante religioso [D / F] [6p / 82m]

'Love, Love thou wilt forgive'
LS: Margaret Maitland Radford
Ded: George Whitehouse
Publ: 1916 Elkin [873 / 874]

S 379 W 391 **Tyrolese Evensong**
Tempo di mazurka [C / D] [7p / 89m]
'Come to the sunset tree!'
LS: Mrs. [Felicia] Hemans
Publ: 1916 Elkin [895 / 896]

S 380 – **The Song of Night**
Andante molto sostenuto [range: D–G] [4p / 89m]
'I come to thee, O Earth! / With all my gifts!'
LS: Felicia Hemans
Comp: 17 April 1916
Publ: unpublished
MS: with estate

S 381 W 180 **Looking Back**
Allegretto [D-flat / E-flat / F] [6p / 53m]
'Looking back along life's trodden way'
LS: Christina Rossetti
Ded: Bertram Binyon
Publ: 1917 Elkin [908 / 908a / 909]

S 382 W 306 **The Sands of Dee**
Slowly, with simple pathos [C / E-flat] [6p / 67m]
'O Mary, go and call the cattle home'
LS: Charles Kingsley
Ded: Nesta Richardson
Comp: *c.* 1917
Publ: 1917 Elkin [910 / 911]

Note: Revision of S 290.

S 383 W 173 **The Little Bells of Sevilla**
Allegretto [med / high] [8p / 71m]
'The ladies of Sevilla go forth to take the air'
LS: Dora Sigerson Shorter
Publ: 1917 Elkin [913 / 914]

S 384 W 254 **The Pilgrim Cranes**

Flowing very gently [F / G] [4p / 45m]

'The pilgrim cranes are moving to their south'

LS: Lord de Tabley [John Byrne Leicester de Tabley Warren]

Publ: 1917 Elkin [934 / 935]

S 385 W 287 **Requiem**

Andante / Adagio [C / E-flat] [3p / 20m]

'Under the wide and starry sky'

LS: Robert Louis Stevenson

Ded: 'In memory of Charlotte Milligan-Fox'

Publ: 1917 Elkin [936 / 937]

S 386 – **Fragrant is Eventide**

Andante [A] 'Fragrant is eventide / Behind the purple mountains'

LS: Cyril Scott

Comp: 17 October 1917

Publ: unpublished

MS: with estate [4p / 53m] On the verso of the 4 manuscript pages are m.44–63 and 99–114 (only) of a fair copy of the *Rondeau de concert*, S 231.

S 387 – **Late October**

[no tempo marking] [4p / 38m]

'Patter of fitful rain, / Shiver of falling leaves'

LS: Edith Neal

Comp: *c.* 1917

Publ: unpublished

MS: with estate

Note: Scott found this poem (written by a young student) in the *Journal of Experimental Pedagogy and Training College Record*, ed. J. H. Green (London: Longman, Green), March 1917, p. 364.

S 388 W 363 **Sunshine and Dusk**

Andante [low / med] [4p / 40m]

'Hedge – tangle of wild golden flowers'

LS: Margaret Maitland Radford

Publ: 1918 Elkin [947 / 948]

MS: with estate

Songs of a Strolling Minstrel (published separately)

S 389 W 229 No. 1 – *Oracle*

Poco allegretto [E-flat / F] [5p / 52m]

'Ola o, ola o. Snowy petals tell me does he love me true?

LS: Cyril Scott

Ded: Mme. Blanche Marchesi
Publ: 1918 Elkin [958 / 959]

S 390 W 227 No. 2 – *Old Loves*
Allegretto [G / A] [5p / 44m]
'Once I loved Margarite, once I loved Jean'
LS: Cyril Scott (from the Old French)
Ded: Bertram Binyon
Publ: 1919 Elkin [988 / 989]

Note: For *Songs of a Strolling Minstrel* No. 3, see S 424

S 391 W 376 **Time o' Day**
Allegro [low-med, C / high, D] [6p / 34m]
'What be time o' day Lass'
LS: Olive Macnaghten
Ded: Hubert Eisdell
Publ: 1919 Elkin [992 / 993]
Dur: [1' 29"]

S 392 W 311 **Sea-Fret**
Quickly, like falling waves in the distance.
Andante [C / E-flat] [7p / 40m]
'The sea has haunted me all day'
LS: Teresa Hooley
Ded: Granville Bantock
Publ: 1919 Elkin [1003 / 1004]

Note: Cf. S 218.

S 393 W 9 **Alone**
Moderato [range C#(B) – E#] [6p / 54m]
'What do these halls of jasper mean'
LS: Herbert A. Giles (from the Chinese)
Publ: 1919 Elkin [1015]
LE: 1919, Elkin, 'Songs of Old Cathay' (No. 1)
Ref: *MYI*, 179

S 394 W 154 **In Absence**
Adagio [range C# – F#] [3p / 49m]
'At eve I stand upon the bank and gaze'
LS: Herbert A. Giles (from the Chinese)
Publ: 1919 Elkin [1016]
LE: 1919, Elkin, 'Songs of Old Cathay' (No. 2)
Red: *MYI*, 179

S 395 W 318 **She's But a Lassie Yet**

Allegretto (Dance measure) [E-flat / F] [7p / 66m]

'My love she's but a lassie yet'

LS: James Hogg

Ded: Bertram Binyon

Publ: 1919 Elkin [1016 / 1017]

Note: In a rare example of plate number duplication, S 394 and the low-key S 395 are both given plate number 1016.

Songs Without Words (published separately)

S 396 W 380 No. 1 – *Tranquility*

Molto tranquillo [range: D–A(C4)] [7p / 36m]

Publ: 1919 Elkin [1034]

S 397 W 241 No. 2 – *Pastorale*

Allegretto tranquillo [range: D to B-flat] [7p / 55m]

Publ: 1919 Elkin [1035]

S 398 W 362 **Sundown**

Allegretto con moto [D / F] [6p / 48m]

'Silently the day / Her song over'

LS: Dorothy Grenside

Publ: 1919 Elkin [1046/1047]

Dur: [3' 19"]

S 399 – **Whither?**

Con moto [C]

'Where be you going master mine?'

LS: Mary E. Coleridge

Comp: 8 February 1919

Publ: unpublished

MS: with estate [4p / 52m] A faint pencil marking on the holograph appears to read, 'Sir H Newbolt, Excr / Right purchased 8/2/19'. Newbolt was an admirer of Coleridge's poetry, and it appears from this that the composer sought out Newbolt (as executor) for permission to use the poetry. Whether the date indicates the securing of permission, or that of completion of composition (as it usually does) is impossible to determine.

S 400 W 413 **Water-Lilies**

Andante [C / D-flat / E-flat] [6p / 42m]

'To the dim pool, where water lilies nest'

LS: P. J. O'Reilly

Publ: 1920 Elkin [1066 / 1066a / 1067]

Dur: [1' 53"]

MS: holograph (3p, in E-flat) with estate (with no hyphen in title). Scott has written E. & Co. 1066 on the MS, but the E-flat key is published as 1067.

S 401 W 148 **Immortality**

Andante con moto [E-flat / F / G] [6p / 31m]

'There is no death – the dust we tread'

LS: Lord Lytton

Publ: 1920 Elkin [1073 / 1073a / 1074]

S 402 W 412 **The Watchman**

Slowly and sleepily [B-flat / C / D] [7p / 101m]

'Watchman, what of the night?'

LS: Jean Hyacinth Hildyard

Publ: 1920 Elkin [1100 / 1101 / 1101a]

S 403 W 218 **Night Wind**

Allegro con moto [range: D to F#] [7p / 53m]

'The wind is wild to-night'

LS: Teresa Hooley

Publ: 1920 Elkin [1141]

S 404 W 232 **Our Lady of Violets**

Allegretto [C / D] [6p / 54m]

'Mary Mother leaned from heaven'

LS: Teresa Hooley

Publ: 1920 Elkin [1157 / 1158]

MS: With estate. Publisher's stamp on holograph, dated '22 May 1920', presumably reflects the date of reception. Under the title on p. 1, Scott writes '29445'. If this is a Schott plate number that was planned but never materialised, then the composition would date from 1911 or earlier. Scott's initial contact with Schott was in 1910–11, when they published about 20 of his compositions.

S 405 W 8 **All Through the Night**

Andante [G / B-flat] [6p / 58m]

'Sleep, my love, and peace attend thee'

LS: traditional

Publ: 1921 Elkin [1202 / 1203]

Note: In *British Songs Arranged and Harmonized by Cyril Scott* series. See also S 206.

S 406 W 140 **The Huckster**

Allegretto (In a rather bumpy manner) [B-flat / C] [4p / 28m]

'He has a hump like an ape on his back'

LS: Edward Thomas

Ded: Nelsa & Alexander Chaplin

Publ: 1921 Elkin [1204 / 1205]

Dur: [1' 45"]

MS: with estate [6p, in C]

S 407 W 135 **Have Ye Seen Him Pass By?**

Slowly and plaintively [range: E to E] [7p / 53m]

'Oh, have ye seen him, ye that pass'

LS: Charles de Coster, *The Legend of Tyl Ulenspiegel* (transl. from the French by Geoffrey Whitworth)

Ded: Mrs. Anne Thursfield

Publ: 1921 Elkin [1206]

Dur: [2' 47"]

S 408 W 405 **Villanelle of Firelight**

Allegretto [B-flat / C] [4p / 55m]

'Delicate fairy wings / Are hovering to-night'

LS: Naomi N. Carvalho

Ded: Winifred Barnes

Publ: 1922 Elkin [1257 / 1258]

S 409 W 62 **Cherry Ripe**

Lingeringly [C /E-flat] [5p / 51m]

'Cherry ripe, ripe, ripe, I cry'

LS: Robert Herrick

Ded: Percy Grainger

Publ: 1922 Elkin [1262 / 1263] / 1915 Schott [S 3290]

Note: In *British Songs Arranged and Harmonized by Cyril Scott* series.

Cf. also S 124 & 222.

Melody by Charles Edward Horn

S 410 W 203 **The Minstrel Boy**

Andante [E-flat / F] [6p / 78m]

'The minstrel boy to the war is gone'

LS: Thomas Moore

Publ: 1922 Elkin [1264 / 1265]

Note: In *British Songs Arranged and Harmonized by Cyril Scott* series.

S 411 W 55 **By Yon Bonny Banks**

Allegretto poco moderato [G] [7p / 58m]

'By yon bonnie banks, and by yon bonnie braes'

LS: traditional

Ded: 'to Mrs. H. M. Freeman with deep filial affection'

Publ: 1922 Elkin [1266]

Note: In *British Songs Arranged and Harmonized by Cyril Scott* series.

S 412 W 147 **I'll Bid My Heart Be Still** (Ancient Border Melody)

Andante [a] [5p / 30m]

'I'll bid my heart be still'

LS: Thomas Pringle

Publ: 1922 Elkin [1267]

Note: In *British Songs Arranged and Harmonized by Cyril Scott* series.

S 413 W 50 **Blythe and Merry Was She**

Con spirito [D] [6p / 59m]

LS: Robert Burns

Publ: 1922 Elkin [1268]

Note: In *British Songs Arranged and Harmonized by Cyril Scott* series.

S 414 W 68 **Comin' Thro' the Rye**

Molto moderato [G / A] [7p / 37m]

'Gin a body meet a body Comin' thro' the rye'

Publ: 1922 Elkin [1269 / 1270]

Note: In *British Songs Arranged and Harmonized by Cyril Scott* series.

S 415 W 285 **Reconciliation**

Andante semplice [G / B-flat] [6p / 61m]

'We who are pilgrims of earth-born error'

LS: Naomi N. Carvalho

Publ: 1923 Elkin [1327 / 1328]

S 416 W 125 **From Afar** (*D'outremer*)

Flowing [C / E] [6p / 55m]

'Lean from your window when the dim stars fade'

LS: Rosamund Marriott Watson

Ded: Olive and Gerald Lowell Webb

Publ: 1923 Elkin [1343 / 1344]

MS: Two separate holographs with estate

1. in C [3p]; text ceases after bar 3

2. in E [4p]; the original title, *Beyond*, is crossed out, with the directive, 'Leave title blank at present'.

S 417 W 155 **In the Silver Moonbeams** [*Au clair de la lune*]

Rather quickly [G / A] [7p / 59m]

'In the silver moonbeams / I stand here below.'

LS: elaborated from the French by Cyril Scott

Ded: Alec and Marion Densham

Publ: 1923 Elkin [1347 / 1347a]

S 418 W 144 **Idyll for voice and flute**

Con moto [range: D-flat – C4] [4p / 136m]

'Ah… ha! ahoy! Shepherd boy'

LS: Cyril Scott (unnamed on Elkin [1378])

Publ: 1923 Elkin [1378]

Note: 'Flute to be played behind the stage or behind a screen.' For high soprano voice. Flute plays alone for 64 bars; singer has a vocalise for 24 bars.

S 419 W 170 **Lamentation,** for unaccompanied voice

LS: Cyril Scott

Publ: *c.* 1923 B.F. Goodwin

S 420 W 126 **The Garden of Memory**

Andante [range: D–G] [3p / 31m]

'There are no roses in the garden now'

LS: Rosamund Marriott Watson

Ded: Anthony Bernard

Publ: 1924 Elkin [1401]

MS: with estate [4p]

S 421 W 415 **What Art Thou Thinking Of?**

LS: Christina Rossetti

Comp: 1924

Publ: unpublished

S 422 W 35 **The Ballad of Fair Helen**

Andante [D] [7p / 70m]

'I wish I were where Helen lies'

LS: traditional Scottish

Ded: Frederic Austin

Publ: 1925 Elkin [1448]

Dur: [3' 58"]

MS: holograph with the New York Public Library

Note: arrangement of S 84

S 423 W 207 **Mist**

Andante [range: D#-E(G)] [7p / 57m]

'Mist, mist on the moors'

LS: Marguerite E. Barnsdale

Ded: Astra Desmond

Publ: 1925 Elkin [1449]

MS: with estate [5p]

S 424 W 12 **Angelus**

Not too slowly [A / C] [5p / 32m]

'Mother, in Thy garden'

LS: Cyril Scott

Publ: 1925 Elkin [1494 / 1495], 'Songs of a Strolling Minstrel' No. 3 (cf. S 389 & 390)

S 425 W 20 **Aspiration**

Adagio [C] [7p / 51m]

'O deep mysterious face of vast slow-breathing night!'

LS: Irene McLeod

Publ: 1926 Elkin [1565]

S 426 W 181 **Lord Randal**

Rather slowly [F] [7p / 141m]

'O where hae ye been, Lord Randal, my son?'

LS: traditional

Ded: Lawrence Strauss

Publ: 1926 Elkin [1572]

Dur: [4' 43" – 5' 23"]

MS: with estate – cover page of holograph has '39645' penciled on it, which looks like a Schott catalogue number.

Notes: Changes by Scott in his personal copy of [1572], on 'fain would lie down', in each verse. The fermata quarter-notes have been altered to three measured full-bar half-notes in 2/4 time. This change, which never made its way into print, would augment the song to 153 bars in length. This is arguably sufficient evidence that performances of this song should routinely incorporate these changes.

In *British Songs Arranged and Harmonized by Cyril Scott* series.

Composer's note: 'An Old Ballad of which there are several versions'

S 427 W 377 **To-morrow**

Fairly quickly [range: E–E] [7p / 76m]

'Where shall I find a white rose blowing?'

LS: Christina Rossetti

Publ: 1927 Elkin [1619]

Dur: [2' 03"]

MS: with estate [5p / 75b]

S 428 W 313 **Sea-Song of Gafran**

Moderato [range: C–E] [7p / 61m]

'Watch ye well! The moon is shrouded'

LS: Felicia Hemans (*Welsh Melodies*)

Publ: 1927 Elkin [1645]

MS: with estate

S 429 W 193 **A March Requiem**

Adagio [range: D to F] [6p / 46m]

'White road a-slope to the west'

LS: Norah Richardson (poetic subtitle: 'Non mortuus est …' (E. D. 7 March 1922)

Publ: 1928 Elkin [1674]

MS: with estate [3p]

S 430 W 146 **If We Must Part**

'If we must part, then let it be like this'

LS: Ernest Dowson

Comp: 1929

Publ: unpublished

S 431 W 201 **Mermaid's Song**

Con moto [range: D–F] [7p / 76m]

'Yeo ho! ye mariners'

LS: Tamar Faed

Publ: 1930 Elkin [1757]

S 432 W 175 **The Little Foreigner: A Character Song**

Con moto / Meno mosso [C] [7p / 148m]

'Yes, *Sir*, I am a foreigner'

LS: Cyril Scott

Ded: Madame Conchita Supervia

Publ: 1932 Elkin [1831]

Note: Scott's only essay in 19th-century vocal virtuosity.

S 433 W 169 **Lady June**

Tempo di valse lento ma rubato [G] [5p / 71m]

'Lady June she is fair'

LS: Elizabeth Haddon

Publ: 1935 Elkin [1905]

MS: with estate [7p / 74b] – holograph states 'Copyright MCMXXXIV by Elkin & Co. Ltd.'

S 434 W 17 **Arise, My Love, My Fair One**

Molto tranquillo [(A)] [7p / 78m]

'The voice of my beloved! Behold, he cometh'

LS: from Song of Solomon

Publ: 1939 Elkin [2026]

S 435 W 351 **Spring-Day**

Comp: *c.* 1965?

Publ: Unpublished

S 436 W 86 **Danse-song: Vocalese melodica,** for high soprano and piano

Andante – Allegretto

Comp: 1970

Publ: unpublished

Notes: Scott's last composition. Note by Marjorie Hartston-Scott in holograph:

> 'Dance Song – Cyril Scott 1970 / The last of his compositions – completed with difficulty through failing sight, a few months before his death (at the age of 91 years) on 31st December 1970.'

> The holograph shows signs of being an attempt to complete or revise a *vocalise* begun many years earlier. Two distinct calligraphic styles can be discerned: a sure, steady one typical of his earlier manuscripts, and a very shaky one from 1970. The pages were found haphazard and partly disbound, with the earlier version incomplete, but a 9-page song in 1970 calligraphy can be reconstructed (there is no page 4, but two marked '5'). Cf. S 396/397, also *vocalises.*

S 437 – **Chanson sans paroles**

Adagio [C] [4p / 142m]

'In the deep violet air not a leaf is stirred'

LS: Ernest Dowson

Comp: unknown; likely before 1915

Publ: unpublished

MS: with estate

Note: The title refers to the bird in the poem. The song is texted throughout. All but one of Scott's 25 settings of 22 Dowson poems stem from before 1915. Manuscript evidence and musical style point toward a date for this song of around 1910–15.

S 438 – **Imprisoned**

Andantino [C] [MS: 3p / 25m]

'Prisoned within these walls I think of you'

LS: Mary Coleridge

Comp: unknown

Publ: unpublished

MS: with estate

Note: Scott set Mary Coleridge only one other time (S 399), around 1919.

S 439 – **The Bard to his Beloved** [*Song of the Bard*]

Maestoso [d] [3p / 44m]

'Love of you and hate of you'

LS: Alice Furlong (from *Roses and Rue*, 1899)

Comp: unknown

Publ: unpublished

MS: with estate

Note: Both titles have question marks beside them in the MS, reflecting uncertainty of choice. Probably an early setting.

S 440 – **Irmeline**

Con moto [C] [4p / 54m]

'Long ago there lived a sov'reign' ('Se, der var engang en konge')

LS: Jens Peter Jacobsen, '*Irmeline Rose*' [transl. Cyril Scott]

Comp: n.d.

Publ: unpublished

MS: with estate

H TRANSCRIPTIONS OF J. S. BACH

i – for orchestra

S 441 W 427 **J. S. Bach, Invention in F,** BWV 779

Publ: 1955 Elkin [2404]

Dur: [5' CS]

ii – for piano

S 442 W 424 **J. S. Bach, My Heart Ever Faithful** (*Mein gläubiges Herze*)

From Cantata No. 68, *Also hat die Welt geliebt*, BWV 68

Andante con moto [7p / 44b]

Ded: Esther Fisher

Publ: 1931 Elkin [1795]

Dur: [2' 40"]

iii – for two pianos

S 443 W 425 **J. S. Bach, Fugue in G major for organ,** BWV 577 (*Jig Fugue*)

Con brio [11p / 86p]

Publ: 1936 Elkin [1929]

Dur: [3' 34"]

S 444 W 426 **J. S. Bach, Three Pieces**

1 – *Invention in F major* [BWV 779]

Grave espressivo – Vivace – Tempo poco meno mosso – A tempo [11p / 129b] [4' 26"]

2 – *Sarabande in A minor*

Andante sostenuto [from *English Suite No. 2*, BWV 807] [3p / 40(56)b] [3' 36"]

3 – *Gigue in G major*

Vivace [from *French Suite No. 5*, BWV 816] [11p / 109b] [3' 43"]

Ded: Ethel Bartlett and Rae Robertson

Publ: 1932 Winthrop Rogers [W.R. 4707]

Ref: *BC*, 203

S 445 W 428 **J. S. Bach, Andante in F** (from Sonata in D minor, BWV 964) [7p / 47b]

Publ: 1936 Elkin [1928]

Dur: [4' 02"]

Note: Holograph of a separate part for the second piano is extant (private collection).

S 446 – **J. S. Bach, Concerto in C,** BWV 595 (1st movement)

Con brio [13p / 65b]

Comp: *c.* 1932

Publ: unpublished

Dur: [3' 25"]

MS: private collection

Note: In addition to the 2-pf holograph, a separate part for the second piano is extant.

I OTHER TRANSCRIPTION

S 447 – **Robert Schumann, Concerto for cello and orchestra**

III only – *Sehr lebhaft*

Ded: Leila Howell

MS: holograph of cello part (11p) with estate

Note: Scott arranged and edited the solo cello part of this movement for a young cellist, Leila Howell. No background information is available to determine date or circumstances, but it is likely that this was done at Howell's request. Some alterations reduce the difficulty of the part, and seem designed to accommodate a small hand. Other changes (added trills, rests filled in) add brilliance to the solo writing, and on occasion tamper with the line chromatically. A sprawling cadenza has also been added, seemingly gratuitously, as if to transform the movement into something more traditionally virtuosic.

J DOUBTFUL AND SPURIOUS WORKS

S 448 W 191 **Magnificat and Nunc dimittis** for chorus and organ

Publ: 1915 West [783]

S 449 W 99 **Dorothy Waltz**

[no tempo mark] [5p / 186b]

Publ: 1916 West [1651]

Note: Optional violin part, published separately.

The internal evidence of the music seems to point away from CS as the composer of this piece, and it has not been recorded to date. CS used the publisher West on only one other occasion, S 448, in 1915. *Britain's War March*, S 51 & 216, is another stylistically unlikely creation, explicable by the political climate of the day, but no other wartime compositions show evidence of an abrupt *non sequitur* in musical style such as is in evidence here. The recent discovery of the indubitably authentic S 3, 13, and 14 however sheds light on a hitherto little appreciated aspect of Scott's creative life – that of a creator of conventional light music and humorous works. S 448 and 449 appear to be the work of another Cyril Scott.

ARRANGEMENTS OF SCOTT WORKS BY OTHER COMPOSERS

This is a selected list, and includes mostly lifetime-published and/or recorded arrangements (see Discography, Part B). For a fuller list, see Laurie J. Sampsel, *Cyril Scott: A Bio-Bibliography*.

ORCHESTRA

T1 W 440 **Three Dances**, Op. 20 [S 168]

arr. Adolf Schmid

Orch: [2.1.2.1 / 2.2.3.0 / timp / perc / strs]
Publ: 1906 Boosey

T2 W 454 **Souvenir de Vienne** [S 246]
arr. Ernest Austin [10p + parts]
Orch: [2.2.0.2 / 2.2.1.0 / timp / perc / strs]
Publ: 1923 Elkin

T3 W 436 **Cherry Ripe** [S 222]
arr. Leo Artok [4p + 17 parts]
Orch: [2.1.4.1 / 2.4.1.0 / perc (2) / strs / harmonium]
Publ: 1926 Schott [Domesticum 202]

T4 W 446 **Impressions from the Jungle Book** – *No. 1, The Jungle* [S 209 No. 1]
arr. Mátyás Seiber
Orch: [1.1.2.1 / 2.2.1.0 / timp / perc / hp / pf / strs]
Publ: n.d. Schott (hire)

T5 W 439 **Columbine** [S 180]
arr. William Grant Still
Comp: arr. *c.* 1930
MS: Smithsonian Institution

T6 W 448 **Impressions from the Jungle Book** – *No. 2, Dawn* [S 209 No. 2]
arr. William Grant Still
Comp: arr. *c.* 1930
MS: Smithsonian Institution

T7 W 453 **Karma: Suite** – *No. 3, A Song from the East* [S 248 No. 3]
arr. William Grant Still
Comp: arr. *c.* 1930
MS: Smithsonian Institution

T8 W 508 **Vesperale** [S 176]
arr. Eldridge Newman
Orch: [1.1.2.1 – 2.1.1.0 / strs / hp / cel / bells]
Publ: 1931 Elkin [1808]

T9 W 508 **Danse nègre** [S 185]
arr. Eldridge Newman
Orch: [2.1.1.1 – 2.1.1.0 / strs / hp / timp]
Publ: 1931 Elkin [1808]

T10 W 508 **Summerland – No. 2,** *A Song from the East* [S 182 No. 2]
arr. Eldridge Newman
Orch: [2.1.2.2. – 2.1.0.0 / strs / hp / cel / perc]
Publ: 1932 Elkin [1816]

T11 W 508 **Water-Wagtail** [S 196]
arr. Eldridge Newman
Orch: [2.1.2.2. – 2.2.1.0 / strs / hp / cel / perc]
Publ: 1932 Elkin [1816]

T12 W 480 **Lotus Land** [S 179]
arr. Eldridge Newman
Publ: 1935 Elkin
Dur: [4' 28']

T13 W 514 **Two Pierrot Pieces** [S 170]
arr. Jacob Maurice Coopersmith [14p]
Orch: [strs]
Publ: 1938 Boosey & Hawkes / Belwin

T14 W 452 **Indian Suite** [S 243]
arr. Bernard Herrmann
Comp: *c.* 1950
Publ: unpublished

T15 W 493 **Lullaby** [S 328]
arr. Harry Dexter
Publ: 1951 Keith Prowse

T16 W 449 **Intermezzo** [S 193]
arr. Harry Dexter
Publ: 1952 Elkin

T17 W 431 **Blackbird's Song** [S 319]
arr. A. Franzel
Publ: unpublished

T18 W 517 **Deuxième suite** – 5, *Introduction and Fugue* [S 200 No. 5]
arr. Leo Funtek
Publ: unpublished

CHORUS

T19 W 497 **Lullaby** (SSA) [S 325]
arr. Arthur Walter Kramer [4p]
Publ: 1920 Elkin (1476, Elkin Choral Series)

T20 W 432 **Blackbird's Song** (SSA) [S 319]
arr. Purcell James Mansfield
Publ: 1934 Elkin [1885]

T21 W 496 **Lullaby** (2-part) [S 328]
arr. Arthur Walter Kramer
Publ: 1935 Galaxy

T22 W 475 **Lotus Land** (SATB) [S 179]
arr. Marcel G. Frank [12p]
LS: George and Phyllis Mead
Publ: 1965 Galaxy

CONCERTANTE / ORCHESTRATED SONGS

T23 W 491 **Lullaby** [S 328]
arr. anon. (voice/orch)
MS: Univ. of Pennsylvania

T24 W 502 **Two Passacaglias** – *No. 1, Allegretto alla breve* [S 52 No. 1]
arr. Frank H. Howard
Publ: 1920 Elkin

T25 – **Serenade** for harmonica, harp and strings [S 145]
arr. Philip Lane [12p / 95b]
Publ: 2000 Novello

T26 W 520 **Tallahassee Suite** – *No. 1, Bygone Memories* [S 123 No. 1]
arr. anon. (vln/orch)
Publ: unpublished
Dur: [2' 55"]

CONCERT BAND

T27 W 528 **Vistas** – *No. 3, Jocund Dance* [S 235 No. 3]
arr. Tom Emmitt
Publ: 1918 Elkin

T28 W 505 **Pastoral Suite** – *No. 5, Passacaglia* [S 214 No. 5]
arr. Robert L. Leist
Publ: 1958 Galaxy (pf/cond & pts)

T29 W 484 **Lotus Land** [S 179]
arr. Wayne Scott [16p + parts]
Publ: 1964 Canyon Press (Canyon Band Library B641)

T30 W 513 **Two Pierrot Pieces** – *No. 1, Pierrot triste* [S 170 No. 1]
arr. Merle J. Isaac
Publ: 1967 Elkan-Vogel, as *Prelude to 'Pierrot'*

CHAMBER

i – violin and piano

T31 W 451 **Intermezzo** [S 193]
arr. Richard Lange [5+1p]
Publ: 1914 Elkin [826]
Dur: [2' 19"]

T32 W 527 **Vesperale** [S 176]
arr. Richard Lange [5+1p]
Publ: 1914 Elkin

T33 W 458 **Three Little Waltzes** – *No. 2, Andante languido* [S 165 No. 2]
arr. Richard Lange [6+1p]
Publ: 1914 Elkin
Dur: [2' 47"]

T34 W 492 **Lullaby** [S 328]
arr. Ethel Barns
Publ: 1918 Elkin [952a]
Dur: [2' 13"]

T35 W 478 **Lotus Land**, Op. 47 No. 1 [S 179]
arr. Fritz Kreisler
Andante languido
Publ: 1922 Elkin [1303] [7+3p / 67b]
c. 1923 Schott [BSS 31143] [5+3p]
LE: Masters Music Publications
Dur: [4' 04" – 5' 16"]
R: *MYI*, 69

T36 W 521 **Valse caprice** [S 198]
arr. Arthur Walter Kramer
Publ: 1924 Elkin [7+3p]

T37 W 443 **Danse nègre** [S 185]
arr. Arthur Walter
Publ: 1935 Elkin [1908]
Dur: [1' 27" – 2' 15"]

ii – viola and piano

T38 W 438 **Cherry Ripe** [S 222]
arr. Lionel Tertis
Publ: 1911 / 1926 Schott [29441] [4+1p]
Dur: [2' 40"]

Note: score for violin/pf; part for viola

iii – cello and piano

T39 W 495 **Lullaby** [S 328]
arr. C. Warwick Evans
Publ: 1918 Elkin [952] [6+1p]

T40 W 525 **Vesperale** [S 176]
arr. Boris Hambourg
Publ: 1921 Elkin [1238] [5+1p]

T41 W 459 **Three Little Waltzes** – *No. 2, Andante languido* [S 165 No. 2]
arr. Cedric Sharpe
Publ: 1924 Elkin [4+2p]

T42 W 498 **Lullaby** [S 328]
arr. Julian Lloyd Webber

iv – other solo and piano

T43 W 441 **Danse nègre** [S 185], for clarinet and piano
arr. Eugene Brose
Publ: 1939 Galaxy

T44 W 490 **Lotus Land** [S 179], for flute and piano
arr. John Wummer
Publ: 1963 Galaxy
Dur: [4' 54"]

T45 W 469 **Lotus Land** [S 179], for flute and piano
arr. Jay Arnold
Publ: 1965 Sam Fox

T46 W 473 **Lotus Land** [S 179], for flute and piano
arr. Arthur Ephross
Publ: 1992 Southern Music

T47 W 486 **Lotus Land** [S 179], for flute and piano
arr. Kenneth Smith & Paul Rhodes
Dur: [6' 01"]

T48 W 476 **Lotus Land** [S 179], for flute and synthesiser
arr. Hiro Fujikake
Publ: unpublished
Dur: [4' 17"]

v – trios, quartets, quintets, etc.

T49 W 450 **Intermezzo** [S 193] for piano and string quartet
arr. Frank H. Howard
Publ: 1920 Elkin [1075], *Piano and String Series 3*

T50 W 504 **Pastoral Suite** – *No. 5, Passacaglia* [S 214 No. 5] for piano & strings [2.0.1.1]
arr. Frank H. Howard
Publ: 1922 Elkin [1077], *Piano and String Series 4*

T51 W 455 **Three Little Waltzes** – *No. 1, Allegro poco scherzando* [S 165 No. 1] for piano and strings
[2.0.1.1] arr. Frank H. Howard
Publ: 1920 Elkin [1078], *Piano and String Series 5*

T52 W 457 **Three Little Waltzes** – *No. 2, Andante languido* [S 165 No. 2] for piano and strings
arr. Frank H. Howard
Publ: 1921 Elkin [1176], *Piano and String Series 6*

T53 W 526 **Vesperale** [S 176] for piano and strings
arr. Frank H. Howard
Publ: 1920 Elkin, *Piano and String Series 7*

T54 W 455 **Three Little Waltzes** – *No. 1, Allegro poco scherzando* [S 165 No. 1] for violin, cello and piano

arr. Frank H. Howard

Publ: 1929 Elkin [1700]

T55 – **Vesperale** [S 176] for piano, 2 violins and cello

arr. Frank H. Howard

Publ: 1929 Elkin [1701], *Elkin Trio Series 3*

T56 W 471 **Lotus Land** [S 179], for piano and strings

arr. Ernest Leslie Bridgewater

Publ: 1940 Elkin

T57 W 437 **Cherry Ripe** [S 220], for piano and strings [3.1.1.1]

arr. Reginald King

Publ: 1948 Schott

PIANO

i – solo

T58 W 134 **Handelian Rhapsody**, Op. 17 [S 167]

arr. Percy Grainger [11p / 164b]

Comp: 1909

Publ: 1909 Elkin [537]

Dur: [6' 20"]

Ded: 'To Percy Grainger in friendship and admiration' – a paraphrase of the original Scott dedication on S 165

Note: Truncation of *Sonata in D major*, Op. 17

T59 W 494 **Lullaby** [S 328]

arr. Robert Elkin [4p]

Publ: 1927 Elkin [1582]

T60 W 510 **Two Pierrot Pieces** – *No. 1, Pierrot triste* [S 170 No. 1], simplified

arr. Hugh Arnold

Publ: 1945 Boosey & Hawkes

T61 W 479 **Lotus Land** [S 179], simplified

arr. Henry Levine

Publ: 1955 Galaxy

ii – two pianos

T62 W 519 **Three Symphonic Dances**, Op. 22 [S 46]
arr. Percy Grainger
[43p / 502(506)m]
1 – Allegro con brio [14p / 139(143)p] [4' 04" – 4' 40"]
2 – Andante sostenuto e sempre molto cantabile [16p / 171b] [8' 53" – 9' 38"]
3 – Allegro energico [13p / 192b] [4' 15" – 4' 35"]
Comp: August–September 1920
Publ: 1922 Schott [30826]
LE: Schott [ED 1855]
c. 2010, Lauren [LAU 020] (= Schott [30826])
Dur: [17' 52" – 18' 48"]
R: *MYI*, 68

Note: Transcription of S 44 for two pianos. Originally S 37, movements 2–4

T63 W 511 **Two Pierrot Pieces** – *No. 1, Pierrot triste* [S 170 No. 1]
arr. Irene Arnold
Lento [6p / 49b]
Publ: 1928 Boosey (copyright)
1936 Boosey & Hawkes [H. 12543]

T64 W 518 **Summer is acumen in** (*Old English Air*) [S 208]
arr. Jeanne Boyd
Allegro [9p / 120b]
Comp: *c.* 1939
Publ: unpublished
MS: Boyd holograph, University of Michigan [9p]

iii – piano duet

T65 W 429 **Two Alpine Sketches** [S 184] [9p]
arr. Richard Lange
I – *Rather slowly* [4p / 45b]
II – *Allegretto non troppo* [4p / 30b]
Publ: 1914 Elkin [822]

T66 W 456 **Three Little Waltzes** – *No. 1, Allegro poco scherzando* [S 165 No. 1]
arr. Richard Lange
Publ: 1914 Elkin

T67 W 500 **Mazurka** [S 191]
Allegretto [7p / 114b]
arr. Richard Lange
Publ: 1914 Elkin [823]

T68 W 442 **Danse nègre** [S 185] [11p / 68b]
arr. Esther Fisher
Publ: 1935 Elkin [1909]

Note: Fisher follows the original version [S 185], not the two-piano transcription [S 266].

T69 W 529 **Water-Wagtail** [S 196]
arr. Cyril Smith (3-hands)
Publ: unpublished

ORGAN

T70 W 509 **Vesperale** [S 176] [5p / 58b]
arr. Arthur W. Pollitt
Publ: 1913 Elkin [711]

T71 W 509 **Two Alpine Sketches** – *No. 2, Allegretto non troppo* [S 184 No. 2] [2p / 31b]
arr. Arthur W. Pollitt
Publ: 1913 Elkin [711]

T72 W 509 **Chansonette** [S 199] [5p / 113b]
arr. Arthur W. Pollitt
Publ: 1913 Elkin [711]

T73 W 509 **Summerland** – *No. 2, A Song from the East* [S 182 No. 2] [4p / 42b]
arr. Arthur W. Pollitt
Publ: 1913 Elkin [711]

T74 W 509 **Solitude** [S 175] [4p / 38b]
arr. Arthur W. Pollitt
Publ: 1913 Elkin [711]

T75 W 509 **Berceuse** [S 201] [6p / 95p]
arr. Arthur W. Pollitt
Publ: 1913 Elkin [711]

T76 W 507 **Ode héroïque** [S 223]
arr. A. Eaglefield Hull
Andante sost. e maestoso [3p / 44(57)p]
Publ: 1917 Elkin [918]

T77 W 507 **Over the Prairie** – *No. 2, Allegretto* [S 202 No. 2]
arr. A. Eaglefield Hull
Publ. 1917 Elkin [918] [3p / 52b]

T78 W 507 **Diatonic Study** [S 219]
Tranquillo [5p / 61b]
arr. A. Eaglefield Hull
Publ: 1917 Elkin [918]

T79 W 507 **Cavatina** [S 217]
Andante sostenuto
arr. A. Eaglefield Hull
Publ: 1917 Elkin [918] [6p / 98b]

T80 W 509 **Summerland** – *No. 3, Evening Idyll* [S 182 No. 3]
arr. A. Eaglefield Hull
Allegretto non troppo [4p / 39b]
Publ: 1917 Elkin [918]

T81 W 507 **Prelude solennelle** [S 213]
arr. A. Eaglefield Hull
Andante maestoso [7p / 75b]
Publ: 1917 Elkin [918]

T82 W 515 **Requiescat** [S 230]
arr. A. Eaglefield Hull
Publ: 1918 Elkin

T83 W 434 **British Melodies** – *No. 2, The Wild Hills of Clare* [S 207]
arr. Purcell James Mansfield
Publ: 1920 Elkin

T84 W 434 **British Melodies** – *No. 1, All Through the Night* [S 206]
arr. Purcell James Mansfield
Publ: 1920 Elkin

T85 W 506 **Pastoral Suite** – *No. 5, Passacaglia* [S 214 No. 5]
arr. Purcell James Mansfield
Publ: 1920 Elkin [1079]

T86 W 512 **Two Pierrot Pieces** – *No. 1, Pierrot triste* [S 170 No. 1]
arr. Frank Heffer
Publ: 1946 Boosey & Hawkes

OTHER

T87 W 516 **Deuxième suite** – *No. 3, Solemn Dance* [S 200 No. 3]
arr. Percy Grainger
[7 strs / harmonium / pf / perc]
Comp: 1933
Publ: Schott (hire)
MS: Grainger Museum [MG4/25]

ii

A Cyril Scott Discography

COMPILED BY LESLIE DE'ATH, WITH CONTRIBUTIONS BY STEPHEN LLOYD

Sigla

CSCPM-1	Cyril Scott, *Complete Piano Music*, vol. 1: *Suites & Miniatures*
CSCPM-2	Cyril Scott, *Complete Piano Music*, vol. 2: *Complete Piano Sonatas*
CSCPM-3	Cyril Scott, *Complete Piano Music*, vol. 3: *Concert Pieces, Ballet Scores, Unpublished Works, Two-Piano Works*
CSCPM-4	Cyril Scott, *Complete Piano Music*, vol. 4: *Piano Works: 1898–1963*
CSCPM-5	Cyril Scott, *Complete Piano Music*, vol. 5: *Lotus Land*
CSCPM-Pr	Cyril Scott, *Complete Piano Music*, vol. 1: *Suites & Miniatures* (VVC CD 101-2) [privately issued pre-release to the series *CSCPM-1/5*; same performances as *CSCPM-1*, except for *Suite … in the Old Style*; available through the compiler]
M&I	*Moods and Impressions: Piano Music by Cyril Scott*

CD	compact disc
CT	cassette tape
LP	long-playing record, 33⅓ rpm
PR	piano roll
78	shellac disc playing at 78 rpm

Timings are provided when known.

Scott's transcriptions of his own works and those of Bach are listed in Part A. Transcriptions of Scott's works by others constitute Part B.

The S numbers are taken from the 'Catalogue of Cyril Scott's Music', above.

Release dates for 78rpm & piano rolls are often unavailable, and are indicated as **.

A ORIGINAL WORKS, TRANSCRIPTIONS OF SCOTT'S OWN WORKS, AND TRANSCRIPTIONS OF BACH

A Little Russian Suite **S 227**

2007	CD(2)	Leslie De'Ath Dutton Epoch [CDLX 7183], *CSCPM-4* [5' 49"]
1994	CD	Christopher Howell Tremula [TREM 104-2], *M&I* [5' 41"]

A Lost Love, Op.62 No. 1 **S 331**

2018	CD	Charlotte de Rothschild (sop) / Adrian Farmer (pf) Lyrita [SRCD 365], *The Songs of Cyril Scott* [1' 46"]

A Pageant **S 241**

2005	CD(2)	Leslie De'Ath Dutton Epoch [CDLX 7150], *CSCPM-1* (= *CSCPM-Pr* [6' 22"]) [6' 29"]

A Song of London **S 317**

2011	CD	Robert Muuse (bar) / Micha van Weers (pf) Challenge Classics [CC 72527], *Cyril Scott – Ralph Vaughan Williams: Songs of Quest and Inspiration* [1' 42"]

A Song of Wine **S 315**

2011	CD	Robert Muuse (bar) / Micha van Weers (pf) Challenge Classics [CC 72527], *Cyril Scott – Ralph Vaughan Williams: Songs of Quest and Inspiration* [2' 34"]
**	PR	Cyril Scott Welte-Mignon [1693] (accompaniment only)

A Valediction, Op.36 No. 1 **S 302**

2018	CD	Charlotte de Rothschild (sop) / Adrian Farmer (pf) Lyrita [SRCD 365], *The Songs of Cyril Scott* [2' 21"]

An Eastern Lament **S 333**

2011	CD	Robert Muuse (bar) / Micha van Weers (pf) Challenge Classics [CC 72527], *Cyril Scott – Ralph Vaughan Williams: Songs of Quest and Inspiration* [2' 08"]

An English Waltz (1903 version) **S 163**

2009 CD(2) Leslie De'Ath
Dutton Epoch [CDLX 7224], *CSCPM-5*
[6' 44"]

** 78rpm Mark Hambourg
HMV [C 1790]

An English Waltz (1929 version) **S 163**

2006 CD(2) Leslie De'Ath
Dutton Epoch [CDLX 7166], *CSCPM-3*
[6' 06"]

Andante in F (Bach/Scott) **S 445**

2006 CD(2) Anya Alexeyev / Leslie De'Ath
Dutton Epoch [CDLX 7166], *CSCPM-4*
[4' 02"]

And So I Made a Villanelle **S 335**

** PR Cyril Scott
Welte-Mignon [1695] (accompaniment only, G major = Elkin [489])

An Old Song Ended **S 349**

2018 CD Charlotte de Rothschild (sop) / Adrian Farmer (pf)
Lyrita [SRCD 365], *The Songs of Cyril Scott*
[2' 33"]

Arabeske **S 245**

2009 CD(2) Leslie De'Ath
Dutton Epoch [CDLX 7224], *CSCPM-5*
[3' 00"]

Asphodel **S 181**

2008 CD(2) Leslie De'Ath
Dutton Epoch [CDLX 7183], *CSCPM-4*
[3' 06"]

** PR Walter Niemann
Hupfeld [59094]

Aubade (orch) **S 45**

2007 CD BBC Philharmonic / Martyn Brabbins (cond)
Chandos [CHAN 10407] (*Cyril Scott – Orchestral Works*, vol. 3)
[10' 43"]

1994 CD National Symphony Orchestra of the South African Broadcasting Corporation / Peter Marchbank (cond)
Marco Polo [8.223485], [*Cyril Scott – Orchestral Works*]
[10' 59"]

Aubade (recorder/pf) **S 148**

2010	CD	Dan Laurin (rec) / Anna Paradiso (pf) BIS [BIS-CD-1785], *Songs of Yesterday* [8' 56"]
2002	CD	Karsten Behrmann (rec) / Oda Klemann (pf) Cadenza (BayerMusicGroup) [CAD 800 921], *Moderne Blockflöte* (reissue of Da Camera Magna [SM 93502] [7' 10"]
2000	CD	Ross Winters (rec) / Andrew Ball (pf) British Music Society [BMS 425 CD], *English Recorder Music: The Dolmetsch Legacy* [8' 29"]
1970	LP	Karsten Behrmann (rec) / Oda Kleemann (pf) Da Camera Magna [SM 93502], *Moderne Blockflöte* [7' 10"]

Autumn Idyll **S 204**

2005	CD(2)	Leslie De'Ath Dutton Epoch [CDLX 7150], *CSCPM-1* (= *CSCPM-Pr* [2' 32"]) [2' 34"]
1981	CT	Raphael Terroni British Music Society [BMS 401], *Goossens and Scott* [2' 54"]
**	PR	Belle Tannenbaum Recordo [61810]

Autumn's Lute **S 367**

2018	CD	Charlotte de Rothschild (sop) / Adrian Farmer (pf) Lyrita [SRCD 365], *The Songs of Cyril Scott* [2' 05"]

Badinage **S 253**

2007	CD(2)	Leslie De'Ath Dutton Epoch [CDLX 7183], *CSCPM-4* [3' 39"]

Ballad (Variations on a Troubadour Air) **S 240**

2009	CD(2)	Leslie De'Ath Dutton Epoch [CDLX 7224], *CSCPM-5* [7' 36"]
2005	CD	Michael Schäfer Genuin [GEN 85049], *Cyril Scott: The Complete Sonatas and Other Works for Piano* [6' 52"]

Ballad of Fair Helen of Kirkconnel (voice/pf) **S 422**

2011	CD	Robert Muuse (bar) / Micha van Weers (pf) Challenge Classics [CC 72527], *Cyril Scott – Ralph Vaughan Williams: Songs of Quest and Inspiration*

[3' 58"]

Ballade (cello/pf) **S 143**

2009	CD	Emma Ferrand (vc) / Jeremy Young (pf) Meridian [CDE 84565], *Northern Lights: English Cello Sonatas, 1920–1950* [15' 18"]

Barcarolle **S 205**

2009	CD(2)	Leslie De'Ath Dutton Epoch [CDLX 7224], *CSCPM-5* [4' 04"]

Berceuse **S 201**

2007	CD(2)	Leslie De'Ath Dutton Epoch [CDLX 7183], *CSCPM-4* [3' 18"]

Blackbird's Song **S 319**

2011	CD	Robert Muuse (bar) / Micha van Weers (pf) Challenge Classics [CC 72527], *Cyril Scott – Ralph Vaughan Williams: Songs of Quest and Inspiration* [2' 57"]
1997	CD	Elsie Suddaby (sop) / Gerald Moore (pf) Amphion [PHI CD 140], *Elsie Suddaby, Soprano: The Lass with the Delicate Air*, vol. 2 (reissue of HMV [B 3076], rec. 19 October 1929)
1987	LP/CT	Gertrude Johnson (sop) / Cyril Scott (pf) EMI [EX 290911-3 (LP) / EX 290911-4 and -5) (CT)], *English Song and Singers* (reissue of Columbia [5611])
1975	LP	Isobel Baillie (sop) / Ivor Newton (pf) HMV [HLM 7064 / RLS 714], *Isobel Baillie: An Anthology of her Greatest Recordings*
c. 1963	LP, 10"	Ludmilla Ivanova (sop) / unnamed (pf) Melodiya [D 12261/2]
**	78rpm	Elsie Suddaby (sop) / Gerald Moore (pf) HMV [B 3076] (rec. 19 October 1929)
1929	78rpm	Gertrude Johnson (sop) / Cyril Scott (pf) Columbia [5611] (rec. 4 April 1929)
1921/23	PR	Ernö Rapée Duo-Art [10448-s] / Duo-Art [0115] (accompaniment only, F major = Elkin [358])
**	PR	Cyril Scott Welte-Mignon [1700] (accompaniment only, D major = Elkin [357])
bef. 1919	PR	Wolfgang Thomas-San-Galli Welte-Mignon [1489] (accompaniment only, F major = Elkin [358])

Britain's War March (pf) **S 216**

2009	CD(2)	Leslie De'Ath Dutton Epoch [CDLX 7224], *CSCPM-5* [3' 20"]

British Melodies (pf) **SS 206–208**

2009	CD(2)	Leslie De'Ath Dutton Epoch [CDLX 7224], *CSCPM-5* [6' 31"]

Bumble-Bees (unacc. vln) **S 157**

2015	CD	Fenella Humphreys (vln.) Champs Hill Records [102], *Bach 2 the Future* [1' 22"]

Butterfly Waltz **S 221**

2007	CD(2)	Leslie De'Ath Dutton Epoch [CDLX 7183], *CSCPM-4* [2' 55"]
1994	CD	Christopher Howell Tremula [TREM 104-2], *M&I* [2' 55"]
1926	PR	Cyril Scott Duo-Art (UK) [0246]

By Yon Bonnie Banks **S 411**

1969	LP	Robert Ivan Foster (bar) / Reginald Paul (pf) Onslo Records [HERITAGE-4], *Onslo Folk Heritage, No. 4*

Caprice chinois **S 237**

2009	CD(2)	Leslie De'Ath Dutton Epoch [CDLX 7224], *CSCPM-5* [3' 25"]
2005	CD	Cyril Scott Dutton Epoch [CDLX 7150, *CSCPM-1* (reissue of Columbia [DB41]) [2' 49"]
2005	CD	Cyril Scott Dal Segno [DSPRCD 010], *Masters of the Piano Roll* [3' 12"]
1993	CD	Cyril Scott Bellaphon [BR-690-07-021], *Rarities*, vol. 2: *Early Recordings by the Composers (The Condon Collection)* (reissue of Duo-Art (UK) [07]) [3' 08"]
**	78rpm	Mark Hambourg HMV [B 2635]

**	78rpm	Cyril Scott Columbia [DB41 (UK) / 2284-D (US)] (rec. 12 February 1930) [2' 49"]
1923	PR	Cyril Scott Duo-Art (UK) [07] [3' 12"]

Carillon **S 211**

2009	CD(2)	Leslie De'Ath Dutton Epoch [CDLX 7224], *CSCPM-5* [1' 58"]
2004	CD	Clipper Erickson Direct-to-Tape [DTR 2013], *The Mystic and the Muse: Piano Music of Cyril Scott and Roger Quilter* [2' 03"]

Cavatina **S 217**

2009	CD(2)	Leslie De'Ath Dutton Epoch [CDLX 7224], *CSCPM-5* [4' 13"]

Celtic Fantasy **S 155**

2017	CD	Sandrine Chatron Aparte [AP 140], *A British Promenade* [10' 01"]

Chansonette **S 199**

2007	CD(2)	Leslie De'Ath Dutton Epoch [CDLX 7183], *CSCPM-4* [2' 26"]

Cherry Ripe (pf) **S 222**

2011	CD(5)	Percy Grainger Appian [APR 7501], *Percy Grainger: The Complete 78-RPM solo recordings 1908–1945* (reissue of 78rpm Decca [24160]) [1' 33"]
2005	CD(2)	Leslie De'Ath Dutton Epoch [CDLX 7150], *CSCPM-1* (= *CSCPM-Pr* [2' 39"]) [2' 42"]
1992	CD	Martin Jones Nimbus [NI 5326], *Virtuoso Piano Showpieces* [3' 19"]
1987	CT	Alan Cuckston Swinsty [FEW 1111], *For Percy Grainger: Piano Music Inspired by & Dedicated to Percy Grainger* [3' 02"]
1945	78rpm	Percy Grainger Decca [24160 (set A 586)], *Percy Grainger, Favourite Piano Solos* (rec. 24 September 1945) [1' 29"]

Cherry Ripe (vln/pf) **S 124**

2013 CD Inna Kogan (vln) / Tobias Bigger (pf)
Editorial de Musica Española Contemporanea [E-071] *Old Vienna*
[4' 04"]

2010 CD Hartmut Schill (vln) / Rainer Schill (pf)
Auris Subtilis [7771025] *Tiramisu for the Soul*
[3' 53"]

1992 CD Fritz Kreisler (vln) / Carl Lamson (pf)
Biddulph [LAB 068-069], *The Kreisler Collection – The Victor Recordings (1921–25)* (reissue of 66196)
[3' 59"]

1995 CD Fritz Kreisler (vln) / Carl Lamson (pf)
RCA Victor Gold Seal [09026-61649-2], *Fritz Kreisler: The Complete RCA Recordings* (reissue of 66196)
[3' 59"]

** 78rpm Fritz Kreisler (vln) / Carl Lamson (pf)
Victor [66196] (rec. 25 April 1922)

** 78rpm Albert Sammons (vln)/unnamed (pf)
Columbia [D 1509]

Chimes **S 177**

2006 CD(2) Leslie De'Ath
Dutton Epoch [CDLX 7166], *CSCPM-3*
[3' 58"]

Chinese Serenade **S 174**

2007 CD(2) Leslie De'Ath
Dutton Epoch [CDLX 7183], *CSCPM-4*
[4' 34"]

Columbine **S 180**

2006 CD(2) Leslie De'Ath
Dutton Epoch [CDLX 7166], *CSCPM-3*
[4' 09"]

2000 CD Dennis Hennig
ABC Classics (Eloquence) [465 737-2], *Lotus Land & Other Piano Works* (reissue of Etcetera [KTC 1132])
[4' 40"]

1992 CD Dennis Hennig
Etcetera [KTC 1132], *In the Garden of Soul-Sympathy*
[4' 39"]

Comin' Thro' the Rye **S 414**

c. 1967 LP Robert Ivan Foster (bar) / Reginald Paul (pf)
Onslo Records [HERITAGE 4], *Onslo Folk Heritage, No. 4*

Concerto for harpsichord and orchestra S 80

2012 CD Michael Laus (harps) / Malta Philharmonic Orchestra / Michael Laus (cond)
Cameo Classics [CC9041CD], *British Composers Premiere Collections*, vol. 4 plus 1
[16' 52"]

Concerto for oboe and string orchestra S81

2010 CD Jonathan Small (ob) / Royal Liverpool Philharmonic Orchestra / Martin Yates (cond)
Dutton Epoch [CDLX 7249], [*British Oboe Concertos*]
[19' 27"]

Concerto No. 1 for piano and orchestra S 70

2007 CD John Ogdon (pf) / London Philharmonic Orchestra / Bernard Herrmann (cond)
Lyrita [SRCS 251], *Piano Concertos 1 & 2 / Early One Morning* (reissue of Lyrita [SRCS 81], 1975)
[39' 24"]

2006 CD Howard Shelley (pf) / BBC Philharmonic / Martyn Brabbins (cond)
Chandos [CHAN 10376] (*Cyril Scott – Orchestral Works*, vol. 2)
[30' 42"]

1977 LP John Ogdon (pf) / London Philharmonic Orchestra / Bernard Herrmann (cond)
Musical Heritage Society [MHS 3653], *Piano Concerto No. 1 in C*
[39' 24"]

1977 LP John Ogdon (pf) / London Philharmonic Orchestra / Bernard Herrmann (cond)
HNH Records [HNH 4025], *Piano Concerto No. 1*
[39' 24"]

1975 LP John Ogdon (pf) / London Philharmonic Orchestra / Bernard Herrmann (cond)
Lyrita [SRCS 81], *Piano Concerto No. 1*
[39' 24"]

Concerto No. 2 for piano and orchestra S 83

2007 CD John Ogdon (pf) / London Philharmonic Orchestra / Bernard Herrmann (cond)
Lyrita [SRCS 251], *Piano Concertos 1 & 2 / Early One Morning* (reissue of Lyrita [SRCS 82])
[25' 00"]

2004 CD Howard Shelley (pf) / BBC Philharmonic / Martyn Brabbins (cond)
Chandos [CHAN 10211] (*Cyril Scott Orchestral Works*, vol. 1)
[20' 14"]

1977	LP	John Ogdon (pf) / London Philharmonic Orchestra / Bernard Herrmann (cond) HNH Records [HNH 4051], *Piano Concerto No. 2 / Early One morning* [25' 00"]
1977	LP	John Ogdon (pf) / London Philharmonic Orchestra / Bernard Herrmann (cond) Lyrita [SRCS 82], *Piano Concerto No. 2 / Early One morning: Poem for Piano and Orchestra* [25' 00"]

Concerto for violin and orchestra **S 71**

2007	CD	Olivier Charlier (vln) / BBC Philharmonic / Martyn Brabbins (cond) Chandos [CHAN 10407] (*Cyril Scott Orchestral Works*, vol. 3) [21' 55"]

Concerto for cello and orchestra, Op. 19 **S 69**

2013	CD	Raphael Wallfisch (vc) / BBC Concert Orchestra / Martin Yates (cond) Dutton Epoch [CDLX 7302] (*Cyril Scott Piano Concerto in D, Op. 10 (1900) / Cello Concerto, Op. 19 (1902) / Overture to Pelleas and Melisanda*) [20' 52"] Note: Completed and revised by Martin Yates. Cello part edited by Raphael Wallfisch.

Concerto for cello and orchestra **S 79**

2008	CD	Paul Watkins (vc) / BBC Philharmonic / Martyn Brabbins (cond) Chandos [CHAN 10452] (*Cyril Scott Orchestral Works*, vol. 4) [27' 08"]

Concerto in C (Bach/Scott) **S 446**

2009	CD(2)	Anya Alexeyev / Leslie De'Ath Dutton Epoch [CDLX 7224], *CDCPM – 5* [3' 25"]

Concerto in D, Op. 10, for piano and orchestra **S 68**

2013	CD	Peter Donohoe (pf) / BBC Concert Orchestra / Martin Yates (cond) Dutton Epoch [CDLX 7302] (*Cyril Scott Piano Concerto in D, Op. 10 (1900) / Cello Concerto, Op. 19 (1902) / Overture to Pelleas and Melisanda*) [30' 35"] Note: Realised and completed by Martin Yates.

Consolation **S 233**

2007	CD(2)	Leslie De'Ath Dutton Epoch [CDLX 7183], *CSCPM-4* [3' 47"]

Cornish Boat Song **S 94**

2010 CD Gould Piano Trio
Chandos [CHAN 10575], *Cyril Scott – Piano Trios Nos. 1 and 2 / Cornish Boat Song / Clarinet Quintet / Clarinet Trio*
[3' 00"]

Daffodils, Op.68 No 1 **S 336**

2018 CD Charlotte de Rothschild (sop) / Adrian Farmer (pf)
Lyrita [SRCD 365], *The Songs of Cyril Scott*
[1' 57"]

Dagobah **S 173**

2007 CD(2) Leslie De'Ath
Dutton Epoch [CDLX 7183], *CSCPM-4*
[4' 01"]

Danse nègre **S 185**

2012 CD(17) John Ogdon
EMI [7046372], *Icon – John Ogdon* (reissue of EMI [CD-CFP 4514])
[1' 56"]

2012 CD(2) Irene Scharrer
Appian [APR 6010], *Irene Scharrer: The Complete Electric and Selected Acoustic Recordings*
[1' 39"]

2011 CD Eileen Joyce
APR [APR 7502], *Eileen Joyce: The Complete Parlophone & Columbia Solo Recordings, 1933–1945*
[1' 31"]

2011 CD(5) Percy Grainger
Appian [APR 7501], *Percy Grainger: The Complete 78-RPM Solo Recordings, 1908–1945* (reissue of Decca [24160])
[1' 56"]

2009 CD(2) Leslie De'Ath
Dutton Epoch [CDLX 7224], *CSCPM-5*
[1' 54"]

2005 CD(2) Cyril Scott
Dutton Epoch [CDLX 7150], *CSCPM-1* (reissue of HMV [B 2895])
[1' 39"]

2005 CD Cyril Scott
Dal Segno [DSPRCD 010], *Masters of the Piano Roll*
[1' 50"]

2003 CD John Ogdon
Testament [SBT 1288] (*Mendelssohn Piano Concertos Nos. 1 & 2*) (reissue of EMI [HQS 1287])
[2' 00"]

1999 CD Eileen Joyce
Testament [SBT 1174], *Eileen Joyce – Piano Recital* (reissue of

		Pearl [GEMM CD 9022] [1’ 28”]
1993	CD	Cyril Scott Bellaphon [BR-690-07-021], *Rarities*, vol. 2: *Early Recordings by the Composers (The Condon Collection)* [1’ 55”]
1993	CD	Eileen Joyce Pearl [GEMM CD 9022], *Eileen Joyce* [1’ 31”]
1992	CD	Marthanne Verbit Albany Records [TROY 070], *Past Futurists* (reissue of Genesis [GS 1049]) [1’ 53”] Note: Verbit’s name was previously Martha Anne, see note p. 580; uses of the two versions are on pp. 564, 571, 572, 580
1990	CD	John Ogdon EMI [CD-CFP 4514], *Piano Favourites with John Ogdon* [1’ 56”]
1987	LP(2)	Eileen Joyce EMI [EX 291271-3 (LP)], *Eileen Joyce Recital / Eileen Joyce Album* (reissue of Parlophone [E11333], rec. 14 April 1937)
1986	LP/CT	John Ogdon EMI [CFP 4514 (LP) / TC-CFP 4514 (CT)], *Piano Favourites with John Ogdon* (reissue of EMI [HQS 1287]) [1’ 56”]
1980	CT	John Ogdon EMI [TC2-MOM 113], *More Piano Favourites* (reissue of EMI [HQS 1287]) [1’ 56”]
1974	LP	Martha Anne Verbit Genesis [GS 1049], *The Piano Music of Cyril Scott* [2’ 02”]
1972	LP/CT	John Ogdon EMI [HQS 1287], *Popular Piano Favourites* and [TC-EXE178] (recorded 14 July 1972) [1’ 56”]
1972	LP/CT	Cyril Scott Recorded Treasures [GCP 771], *The Welte Legacy of Piano Treasures. Great Composers / Pianists Perform their Own Compositions* – record 10
**	CT	David Strong British Music Society [ENV 002], *Environs*
1946	78rpm	Percy Grainger Decca [24160 (set A 586)], *Percy Grainger: Favourite Piano Solos* (rec. 24 September 1945) [1’ 53”]
1937	78rpm	Eileen Joyce Parlophone [E11333] (rec. 14 April 1937)

**	78rpm	Cyril Scott HMV [B 2895] (rec. 4 October 1928)
**	78rpm	Irene Scharrer HMV [D 84] (rec. 20 September 1915)
**	78rpm	Paolo Spagnolo Cetra [PE 157]
1926	PR	Cyril Scott Duo-Art [64060]
1921	PR	Cyril Scott Duo-Art [D-47]
**	PR	Cyril Scott Duo-Art (UK) [03]
**	PR	Cyril Scott Hupfeld [50836]
**	PR	Cyril Scott Welte-Mignon [P 1697] – with S 182 No. 2
**	PR	Clarence Adler Ampico [5372]
**	PR	Carolyn Baldwin Duo-Art (US) [5796]
**	PR	Herbert Fryer Hupfeld [50421]
**	PR	Herma Menth Artrio-Angelus [7972]
**	PR	Leo Ornstein Ampico [5800]

Danse nègre (arr. 2 pianos) **S 268**

2009	CD(2)	Anya Alexeyev / Leslie De'Ath Dutton Epoch [CDLX 7224], *CDCPM – 5* [2' 08"]
**	Tape	Esther Fisher / Cyril Scott private tape [NSA M5229BL]

Danse romantique **S 224**

2007	CD(2)	Leslie De'Ath Dutton Epoch [CDLX 7183], *CSCPM-4* [2' 42"]

Deux préludes (vln/pf) **S 125**

2007	CD	Clare Howick (vln) / Sophia Rahman (pf) Dutton Epoch [CDLX 7200], *Cyril Scott – Sonata lirica and Other Works for Violin and Piano* [7' 34"]

Deuxième suite (complete) **S 200**

2005	CD(2)	Leslie De'Ath Dutton Epoch [CDLX 7150], *CSCPM-1* (= *CSCPM-Pr* [28' 16"]) [28' 13"] Note: The timing of [27' 00"] on the tray card is incorrect.

Deuxième suite – No. 1 Prélude **S 200 No. 1**

**	PR	Cyril Scott Hupfeld [50843]

Deuxième suite – No. 4 Caprice **S 200 No. 4**

**	PR	Cyril Scott Hupfeld [50842]

Diatonic Study **S 219**

2009	CD(2)	Leslie De'Ath Dutton Epoch [CDLX 7224], *CSCPM-5* [2' 10"]

Don't Come In Sir, Please! **S 310**

2018	CD	Charlotte de Rothschild (sop) / Adrian Farmer (pf) Lyrita [SRCD 365], *The Songs of Cyril Scott* [2' 15"]
1963?	LP	Ludmilla Ivanova (sop) / unnamed (pf) Melodiya [C 12261/2]

Early One Morning **S 75**

2014	CD(4)	John Ogdon (pf) / London Philharmonic Orchestra / Bernard Herrmann (cond) Lyrita [SRCS 2345] *British Piano Concertos* (reissue of Lyrita [SRCS 82]) [14' 48"]
2009	CD(4)	John Ogdon (pf) / London Philharmonic Orchestra / Bernard Herrmann (cond) Lyrita [SRCD 2338], *Celebrating 50 Years Devoted to British Music* [14' 48"]
2007	CD	John Ogdon (pf) / London Philharmonic Orchestra / Bernard Herrmann (cond) Lyrita [SRCS 251], *Piano Concertos 1 & 2 / Early One Morning* (reissue of Lyrita [SRCS 82]) [14' 47"]
2006	CD	Howard Shelley (pf) / BBC Philharmonic / Martyn Brabbins (cond) Chandos [CHAN 10376] (*Cyril Scott Orchestral Works*, vol. 2) [13' 54"]
1977	LP	John Ogdon (pf) / London Philharmonic Orchestra / Bernard Herrmann (cond) HNH Records [HNH 4051], *Piano Concerto No. 2 / Early One Morning* [14' 41"]
1977	LP	John Ogdon (pf) / London Philharmonic Orchestra / Bernard Herrmann (cond) Lyrita [SRCS 82 / CRCSD 82], *Piano Concerto No. 2 / Early One Morning*

Egypt: An Album of Five Impressions **S 212**

2006 CD(2) Leslie De'Ath
Dutton Epoch [CDLX 7166], *CSCPM-3*
[17' 40"]

Egypt – No. 3 Egyptian Boat Song **S 212 No. 3**

** PR Paul Strecker
Welte-Mignon [3880]

** PR Otto Weinreich
Hupfeld [51233]

Egypt – No. 4 Funeral March of the Great Raamses **S 212 No. 4**

** PR Paul Strecker
Welte-Mignon [3879]

Élégie (vln/pf) **S 120**

2015 CD Truida van der Valt (vln) / Piet Koornhof (pf)
Delos [DE 3476], *Remembrances*
[4' 16"]

2007 CD Clare Howick (vln) / Sophia Rahman (pf)
Dutton Epoch [CDLX 7200], *Cyril Scott – Sonata lirica and Other Works for Violin and Piano*
[5' 02"]

Fantasie orientale **S 131**

2007 CD Clare Howick (vln) / Sophia Rahman (pf)
Dutton Epoch [CDLX 7200], *Cyril Scott – Sonata lirica and Other Works for Violin and Piano*
[8' 07"]

Festival Overture **S 19**

2007 CD BBC Philharmonic / Martyn Brabbins (cond)
Chandos [CHAN 10407] (*Cyril Scott Orchestral Works*, vol. 3)
[10' 34"]

First Bagatelle **S 236**

2009 CD(2) Leslie De'Ath
Dutton Epoch [CDLX 7224], *CSCPM-5*
[2' 14"]

1994 CD Christopher Howell
Tremula [TREM 104-2], *M&I*
[1' 50"]

c. 1927 PR Sylvan Levin
Welte-Mignon [7011]

1923 PR Cyril Scott
Duo-Art (UK) [08]

First Suite for Strings **S 54**

2003 CD Royal Ballet Sinfonia / Gavin Sutherland (cond)
ASV (White Line) [CD WHL 2139], *British String Miniatures, vol. 3*
[8' 51"]

Gavotte **S 257**

2007 CD(2) Leslie De'Ath
Dutton Epoch [CDLX 7183], *CSCPM-4*
[2' 28"]

Guttersnipes' Dance **S 254**

2007 CD(2) Leslie De'Ath
Dutton Epoch [CDLX 7183], *CSCPM-4*
[1' 41"]

Have Ye Seen Him Pass By? **S 407**

2011 CD Robert Muuse (bar) / Micha van Weers (pf)
Challenge Classics [CC 72527], *Cyril Scott – Ralph Vaughan Williams: Songs of Quest and Inspiration*
[2' 47"]

Impressions from the Jungle Book **S 209**

2007 CD(2) Leslie De'Ath
Dutton Epoch [CDLX 7183], *CSCPM-4*
[14' 59"]

1994 CD Christopher Howell
Tremula [TREM 104-2], *M&I*
[14' 20"]

Impressions from the Jungle Book **S 269 No. 1**

No. 1 The Jungle (arr. two pianos)

2006 CD(2) Anya Alexeyev / Leslie De'Ath
Dutton Epoch [CDLX 7166], *CSCPM-3*
[3' 34"]

Impressions from the Jungle Book **S 269 No. 2**

No. 5 Dance of the Elephants (arr. two pianos)

2006 CD(2) Anya Alexeyev / Leslie De'Ath
Dutton Epoch [CDLX 7166], *CSCPM-3*
[2' 20"]

Impromptu: A Mountain Brook (1904) **S 178**

2007 CD Jungran Kim Khwarg
Cambria [CAMCD-1140], *Piano Impromptus*
[4' 46"]

2006 CD(2) Leslie De'Ath
Dutton Epoch [CDLX 7166], *CSCPM-3*
[4' 08"]

1972	LP	Cyril Scott Recorded Treasures [GCP 771], *The Welte Legacy of Piano Treasures. Great Composers / Pianists Perform their Own Compositions*, record 10
**	78rpm	Una Bourne HMV [B1647]
**	PR	Cyril Scott Welte-Mignon [1698]

Impromptu: A Mountain Brook (1929) **S 178**

2009	CD(2)	Leslie De'Ath Dutton Epoch [CDLX 7224], *CSCPM-5* [3' 52"]

In a Fairy Boat, Op.61 No 2 **S 330**

2018	CD	Charlotte de Rothschild (sop) / Adrian Farmer (pf) Lyrita [SRCD 365], *The Songs of Cyril Scott* [2' 05"]

Inclination à la danse **S 242**

2006	CD(2)	Leslie De'Ath Dutton Epoch [CDLX 7166], *CSCPM-3* [3' 38"]
1994	CD	Christopher Howell Tremula [TREM 104-2], *M&I* [3' 27"]

Indian Suite **S 243**

2005	CD(2)	Leslie De'Ath Dutton Epoch [CD LX 7150], *CSCPM-1* (= *CSCPM-Pr* [8' 16"]) [8' 13"]

Indian Suite: No. 1 Snake-Charmer, No. 2 Juggernaut, No. 3 Indian Serenade

**	PR	Paul Strecker Welte-Mignon [3877]

Indian Suite: No. 3 Indian Serenade, No. 4 Dancing Girls

**	PR	Paul Strecker Welte-Mignon [3878]

Intermezzo **S 193**

2007	CD(2)	Leslie De'Ath Dutton Epoch [CDLX 7183], *CSCPM-4* [2' 21"]
**	PR	Cyril Scott Hupfeld [50838]

Irish Reel **S 226**

2007	CD(2)	Leslie De'Ath Dutton Epoch [CDLX 7183], *CSCPM-4* [2' 08"]

1920 PR Harold Henry
Duo-Art (US) [6307]

Jig Fugue in G major (Bach/Scott) **S 443**

2006 CD(2) Anya Alexeyev / Leslie De'Ath
Dutton Epoch [CDLX 7166], *CSCPM-3*
[3' 34"]

Karma: Suite **S 248**

2006 CD(2) Leslie De'Ath
Dutton Epoch [CDLX 7166], *CSCPM-3*
[15' 00"]

Karma – No. 2 The Piper in the Desert **S 248 No. 2**

2002 CD Frances Gray
private issue [WRC8-7667], *The Evocative Piano*
[2' 50"]

Karma – No. 5 Souvenir de Vienne **S 248 No. 5**

2005 CD Cyril Scott
Dutton Epoch [CDLX 7150], *CSCPM-1* (reissue of HMV [B 2894])
[2' 25"]

1969 LP Peter Cooper
Marble Arch [MALS 1328], *Piano Music from Vienna*

c. 1929 78rpm Cyril Scott
HMV [B 2894] (rec. 4 October 1928)

Klavierstucke: Erste Ballade in D **S 160**

2006 CD(2) Leslie De'Ath
Dutton Epoch [CDLX 7166], *CSCPM-3*
[3' 30"]

Londonderry Air **S 154**

1926 78rpm Sidonie Goossens (harp)
Columbia [DB 565]

Looking Back **S 381**

2018 CD Charlotte de Rothschild (sop) / Adrian Farmer (pf)
Lyrita [SRCD 365], *The Songs of Cyril Scott*
[2' 35"]

Lord Randal **S 426**

2011 CD Gerald Finley [bar] / Julius Drake [pf]
Hyperion [CDA 67830], *The Ballad Singer*
[5' 23"]

1992 CD John Charles Thomas [bar] / Carroll Hollister [pf]
Nimbus [NI 7838], *Prima voce – John Charles Thomas: An American Classic*
[5' 07"]

1992	CD	John Charles Thomas [bar] / Carroll Hollister [pf] Pearl [GEMM CD 9977], *Home on the Range (John Charles Thomas: The Great American Singer)* [4' 52"]
c. 1956	LP	John Charles Thomas [bar] / Carroll Hollister [pf] RCA Camden [CAL 208 (US) / CAM–99 (Australia)], *John Charles Thomas Sings Songs you Love* (rec. 30 November 1938) [4' 43"]

Lotus Land **S 179**

2012	CD(17)	John Ogdon EMI [7046372], *Icon: John Ogdon* (reissue of EMI [CFP 4514]) [4' 10"]
2011	CD	Eileen Joyce APR [APR 7502], *Eileen Joyce: The Complete Parlophone & Columbia Solo Recordings, 1933–1945* [2' 58"]
2011	CD	Paul Guinery Stone Records (Delius Society) [8013], *Delius and his Circle* [4' 34"]
2009	CD(2)	Leslie De'Ath Dutton Epoch [CDLX 7224], *CSCPM-5* [4' 06"]
2007	CD	Oscar Levant Sony (Essential Classics) [62750], *Through Gilded Trellises: A Collection of English Song & Music* (reissue of Columbia [ML 5324])
2007	CD	Percy Grainger [4' 01"] Dal Segno [20] *The Great Pianists: Percy Grainger*, vol. 4
2006	CD	Leif Ove Andsnes EMI Classics [0946 3 41682 2 9], *Horizons* Warner Classics [41682], *Horizons* [3' 40"]
2005	CD	Cyril Scott Dutton Epoch [CDLX 7150], *CSCPM-1* (reissue of HMV [B 2894]) [2' 57"]
2005	CD	Cyril Scott Dal Segno [DSPRCD 010], *Masters of the Piano Roll* [3' 07"]
2004	CD	Irina Voro Classical Records [CR-041], *Ah, Recording! My Shortcut to Carnegie Hall* [5' 18"]
2003	CD	Mark Birnbaum CD Baby [168272], *Dreamland: Piano Gems circa 1903* [3' 53"]

2003	CD	John Ogdon Testament [SBT 1288] (*Mendelssohn Piano Concertos Nos. 1 & 2*) (reissue of EMI [HQS 1287]) [4' 10"]
2002	CD	Frances Gray private issue [WRC8-7667], *The Evocative Piano* [4' 12"]
2002	CD	Kumiko Ida Mittenwald [MTWD 99008], *Lotusland – British Piano Album* [4' 55"]
2000	CD	Dennis Hennig ABC Classics (Eloquence) [465 737-2], *Lotus Land & Other Piano Works* (reissue of Etcetera [KTC 1132]) [4' 13"]
2000	CD	Jenny Lin BIS [BIS-CD-1110], *Chinoiserie* [4' 51"]
1999	CD	Marthanne Verbit Albany Records [TROY 070], *Past Futurists* (reissue of Genesis [GS 1049]) [4' 19"]
1999	CD	Eileen Joyce Testament [SBT 1174], *Eileen Joyce* (reissue of EMI [E 2912721]) [2' 58"]
1998?	CD	Leonid Brumberg Aricord Musik Produktion [AriCDA 19504]
1997	CD	Bernard Depasquale Hybrid Records [TRD 7771-2], *Easy Winners* [5' 45"]
1996	CD	Jack Richard Crossan Cambria [CD-1086], *Sounds and Perfumes* [4' 50"]
1995	CD	John Champ ABC Classics [446 059-2 / 446 059-4], *At the Piano: John Champ* [4' 44"]
1993	CD	Percy Grainger Bellaphon [BR 690-07-024], *Grainger: Early Recordings by the Pianist* (reissue of Duo-Art [7217-3]) [3' 57"]
1993	CD	Cyril Scott Bellaphon [BR-690-07-021], *Rarities*, vol. 2: *Early Recordings by the Composers (The Condon Collection)* [3' 03"]
1993	CD	Oscar Levant Sony [SMK 58932], *An English Treasury / British Pageant*
1992	CD	Dennis Hennig Etcetera [KTC 1132], *In the Garden of Soul-Sympathy* [4' 12"]

1992	CD	Donna Amato Danacord [DACOCD 389], *Rarities of Piano Music at Schloss vor Husum*, vol. 3 (1991) [3’ 51”]
1987	LP(2)	Eileen Joyce EMI [EX 2912713 (LP)], *Eileen Joyce Recital / Eileen Joyce Album* (reissue of Parlophone [E11333], rec. 14 April 1937)
1980	LP/CT	Derek Bell Claddagh [CSM 54], *Derek Bell Plays with Himself* [3’ 40”]
1980	CT	John Ogdon EMI [TC2-MOM 113], *More Piano Favourites* [4’ 10”]
1974	LP	Martha Anne Verbit Genesis [GS 1049], *The Piano Music of Cyril Scott* [4’ 39”]
1973	LP	Percy Grainger Klavier [KS 121], *Legendary Pianists of the Romantic Era: Concert II* (reissue of Duo-Art [7217-3]) [3’ 30”]
1972	LP/CT	John Ogdon EMI [HQS 1287 / TC-EXE178], *Popular Piano Favourites* [4’ 10”]
1972	LP/CT	John Ogdon EMI [CFP 4514 / TCP 4514], *Piano Favourites with John Ogdon / Popular Piano Favourites* (recorded 14 July 1972) [4’ 10”]
1972	LP	Cyril Scott Recorded Treasures [GCP 771], *The Welte Legacy of Piano Treasures. Great Composers / Pianists Perform their Own Compositions*, record 10
1958	LP	Oscar Levant Columbia Masterworks [ML 5324], *Some Pleasant Moments in the Twentieth Century* (rec. 5 June 1958)
c. 1950	LP	Cyril Scott Royale [1402], *An Hour of the Master Pianists* (reissue of Welte-Mignon [1696])
c. 1950	LP	Cyril Scott Allegro [AL 39], *Famous Composers Play their Own Compositions* (reissue of Welte-Mignon [1696])
1937	78rpm	Eileen Joyce Parlophone [E 11333] (rec. 14 April 1937) [2’ 58”]
c. 1929	78rpm	Cyril Scott HMV [B 2894] (rec. 4 October 1928)
1929	PR	Percy Grainger Duo-Art [7217-3] [3’ 28”]

c. 1927	PR	Cyril Scott Welte-Mignon [1696]
1926?	PR	Cyril Scott Hupfeld [50839] and Ampico [6632]
**	PR	Mark Hambourg Hupfeld [51513]
**	PR	Doris Madden Artrio-Angelus [8035]
**	PR	Ralph Herman Leopold Ampico [6166]
**	PR	Ralph Herman Leopold Duo-Art (US) [D359]
1919	PR	Rudolph Reuter Duo-Art (US) [6096(8)]

Lotus Land (arr. two pianos) **S 270**

2011	CD	David Nettle / Richard Markham Netmark [NEMA CD 200], *Nettle & Markham in England* [4' 22"]
2009	CD(2)	Anya Alexeyev / Leslie De'Ath Dutton Epoch [CDLX 7224], *CSCPM-5* [4' 18"]
1999	CD	David Nettle / Richard Markham Carlton Classics [1582591], *Nettle & Markham in England* [4' 23"]
1996	CD	David Nettle / Richard Markham Innovative Music Productions [67 00172], *Works for 2 Pianos* [4' 23"]
1993	CD	David Nettle / Richard Markham Carlton IMP/Classics [30367 00172], *Holst, Grainger, Walton, Coates* [4' 23"]
1992	CD	David Nettle / Richard Markham Masters [MCD 65], *Nettle & Markham in England* [4' 23"]
1961	LP	Jack Lowe / Arthur Whittemore Capitol [P 8550 / SP 8550], *Exotique: Lush Impressionistic Moods for Two Pianos* [4' 01"]

Lovely Kind and Kindly Loving, Op.55 No 1 **S 321**

2018	CD	Charlotte de Rothschild (sop) / Adrian Farmer (pf) Lyrita [SRCD 365], *The Songs of Cyril Scott* [2' 23"]

Love's Aftermath **S 348**

2018	CD	Charlotte de Rothschild (sop) / Adrian Farmer (pf) Lyrita [SRCD 365], *The Songs of Cyril Scott* [3' 02"]

Lullaby **S 327**

2018	CD	Charlotte de Rothschild (sop) / Adrian Farmer (pf) Lyrita [SRCD 365], *The Songs of Cyril Scott* [2' 25"]
2016	CD(4)	Gertrude Johnson (sop) / Cyril Scott (pf) Decca [482 5892], *From Melba to Sutherland – Australian Singers on Record* (reissue of Columbia [5611]) [2' 21"]
2008	CD(2)	Conchita Supervía (mezzo) / Ivor Newton (pf) Marston [52060-2], *The Complete Conchita Supervia*, vol. 3: *Parlophone and Odeon, 1930–1932* (reissue of [HMA 1]) [2' 11"]
2006	CD	Rosa Ponselle (sop) / (studio orchestra), Rosario Bourdon (cond) Naxos Historical [8.111138], *Rosa Ponselle – American Recordings, 1923–1929*, vol. I (reissue of Victor [1002 B]) [2' 34"]
2001	CD	Paulina Stark (sop) / David Garvey (pf) Gasparo Gallante [GG 1019], *Sing me to Sleep: A Lullaby Journey* [2' 10"]
2001	CD	Wendy Loder (sop) / Steven Bailey (pf) private issue [33207], *Yestertime Songs for Children* [2' 34"]
2001	CD	Kirsten Flagstad (sop) / Edwin McArthur (pf) Preiser Records [89514], *Lebendige Vergangenheit – Kirsten Flagstad*, vol. 2 (reissue of HMV [DA 1512]) [2' 21"]
1996	CD(2)	Kirsten Flagstad (sop) / Edwin McArthur (pf) Simax [PSC 1824], *Kirsten Flagstad*, vol. 4 (reissue of HMV [DA 1512]) [2' 30"]
1995	CD	Kirsten Flagstad (sop) / Edwin McArthur (pf) Nimbus [NI 7871], *Prima Voce – Flagstad in Song* (reissue of HMV [DA 1512]) [2' 31"]
1994	CD	Kirsten Flagstad (sop) / Edwin McArthur (pf) Pearl [GEMM CD 9092], *Kirsten Flagstad – Songs of Grieg, Schubert, Beethoven, etc.* (reissue of HMV [DA 1512]) [2' 29"]
1986	LP/CT	Gertrude Johnson (sop) / Cyril Scott (pf) EMI [EX 290911-3 (LP) / EX 290911-5 (CT)], *English Song and Singers* (reissue of Columbia [5611]) (rec. 27 November 1929)
1983	LP/CT	Paulina Stark (sop) / David Garvey (pf) Spectrum [SR 179], *Sing me to Sleep: Lullabies by Major and Minor Masters*
1981?	LP	Conchita Supervía (mezzo) / Ivor Newton (pf) Rubini [GV 583], *Conchita Supervía*, vol. 2 (reissue of [HMA 1])

1970	LP	Maureen Forrester (alto) / John Newmark (pf) Westminster Gold [WGS 8124], *A Charm of Lullabies* [2' 24"]
1967	LP	Maureen Forrester (alto) / John Newmark (pf) Westminster Gold [WGS 17137], *A Charm of Lullabies*
1960s	LP	Helen Beiderbecke (sop) / David Garvey (pf) Bixie [C3RS-0313/4-1 SP], *Lullaby: Lullabies by Great Composers*
1960s	LP	Conchita Supervía (mezzo) / Ivor Newton (pf) O.A.S.I. [OASI-623], *A Concert of English Songs / Conchita Supervía*, vol. 7 (reissue of [HMA 1])
1963?	LP	Ludmilla Ivanova (sop) / unnamed (pf) Melodiya [D 12261/2]
1963?	LP	Maria Maksakova (mezzo) / unnamed (pf) Melodiya [D 12773/4]
1950s	LP	Conchita Supervía (mezzo) / Ivor Newton (pf) Rococo [5230], *Conchita Supervía* (reissue of [HMA 1])
**	78rpm	Kirsten Flagstad (sop) / Edwin McArthur (pf) HMV [DA 1512] (rec. 26 July 1936)
**	78rpm	Conchita Supervía (mezzo) / Ivor Newton (pf) Historic Masters [HMA 1], *Conchita Supervía*, vol. 2 (rec. 17 March 1932)
**	78rpm	Gertrude Johnson (sop) / Cyril Scott (pf) Columbia [5611] (rec. 27 November 1929)
c. 1927	78rpm	Cyril Scott (pf) Welte-Mignon [50063] (accompaniment only)
**	78rpm	Rosa Ponselle (sop) / (studio orch), Rosario Bourdon (cond) Victor [1002 B] (rec. 8 February 1924) [2' 34"]
**	PR	Richard Hageman (accompaniment only) Ampico [5951]

Mazurka **S 191**

2009	CD(2)	Leslie De'Ath Dutton Epoch [CDLX 7224], *CSCPM-5* [2' 53"]
**	PR	Cyril Scott Hupfeld [50840]

Meditation **S 375**

2018	CD	Charlotte de Rothschild (sop) / Adrian Farmer (pf) Lyrita [SRCD 365], *The Songs of Cyril Scott* [2' 55"]

Miniatures **S 220**

2005	CD(2)	Leslie De'Ath Dutton Epoch [CDLX 7150], *CSCPM-1* (= *CSCPM-Pr* [4' 30"]) [4' 34"]

Miniatures – No. 2 A Ballad Told at Candlelight **S 220 No. 2**

1999 CD Christina Petrowska Quilico
Welspringe Productions [WELCD 1201], *Romantic Gems*
[1' 30"]

Miss Remington **S 259**

2009 CD(2) Leslie De'Ath
Dutton Epoch [CDLX 7224], *CSCPM-5*
[3' 24"]

Moods **S 244**

2009 CD(2) Leslie De'Ath
Dutton Epoch [CDLX 7224], *CSCPM-5*
[7' 04"]

1994 CD Christopher Howell
Tremula [TREM 104-2], *M&I*
[7' 26"]

My Captain **S 304**

** PR Cyril Scott
Hupfeld [1694] (accompaniment only)

My Heart Ever Faithful (Bach/Scott) **S 442**

2013 CD Antony Gray
ABC Classics [476 5171], *Bach – Piano Transcriptions*
[2' 33"]

2009 CD(2) Leslie De'Ath
Dutton Epoch [CDLX 7224], *CSCPM-5*
[2' 41"]

** 78rpm Mark Hambourg
HMV [B4180]

Neapolitan Rhapsody **S 66**

1994 CD National Symphony Orchestra of the South African Broadcasting Corporation / Peter Marchbank (cond)
Marco Polo [8.223485], *Cyril Scott – Orchestral Works*
[13' 15"]

Neptune **S 57**

2004 CD BBC Philharmonic / Martyn Brabbins (cond)
Chandos [CHAN 10211] (*Cyril Scott Orchestral Works*, vol. 1)
[24' 21"]

Night-Song **S 376**

2018 CD Charlotte de Rothschild (sop) / Adrian Farmer (pf)
Lyrita [SRCD 365], *The Songs of Cyril Scott*
[2' 43"]

Notturno **S 186**

2012	CD(2)	Michael Landrum Sono Luminus [DSL-92158], *Nocturnes* [3' 20"]
2005	CD(2)	Leslie De'Ath Dutton Epoch [CDLX 7150], *CSCPM-1* (= *CSCPM-Pr* [2' 53"]) [3' 01"]

Ode héroïque **S 223**

2009	CD(2)	Leslie De'Ath Dutton Epoch [CDLX 7224], *CSCPM-5* [3' 01"]
1923	PR	Cyril Scott Duo-Art (UK) [05]

Over the Prairie **S 202**

2007	CD(2)	Leslie De'Ath Dutton Epoch [CDLX 7183], *CSCPM-4* [4' 43"]
2000	CD	Dennis Hennig ABC Classics (Eloquence) [465 737-2], *Lotus Land & Other Piano Works* [4' 34"] Note: This CD is an exact reissue of Etcetera [KTC 1132], with the addition of this set.

Pastoral and Reel **S 141**

2014	CD	Julian Lloyd Webber (vc) / John Lenehan (pf) Decca [00028944253023], *English Idyll* (reissue of Philips [442530]) [5' 01"]
2008	CD	Julian Lloyd Webber (vc) / John Lenehan (pf) Philips [442426], *Julian Lloyd Webber – Lullaby* (reissue of Philips [442 530]) [4' 56"]
2007	CD	Julian Lloyd Webber (vc) / John Lenehan (pf) Philips Eloquence [4428415], *English Idyll* (reissue of Philips [442 530]) [4' 56"]
1994	CD/CT	Julian Lloyd Webber (vc) / John Lenehan (pf) Philips [442 530-2 (CD) / 442 530-4 (CT)], *English Idyll* [4' 56"]
1993	CT	Beatrice Harrison (vc) / Margaret Harrison (pf) Symposium [HST001] (reissue of HMV [B3717]) [3' 32"]

Pastoral Ode **S 263**

2009 CD(2) Leslie De'Ath
Dutton Epoch [CDLX 7224], *CSCPM-5*
[9' 09"]

Pastoral Suite **S 214**

2005 CD(2) Leslie De'Ath
Dutton Epoch [CDLX 7150], *CSCPM-1* (= *CSCPM-Pr* [11' 58"])
[11' 56"]
Note: The timing of [12' 56"] is an error.

Pastoral Suite – No. 1 Courante **S 214 No. 1**

1996 CD Jack Richard Crossan
Cambria [CD-1086], *Sounds and Perfumes*
[2' 13"]

** PR Rudolph Ganz
Welte-Mignon [3734]

Pastoral Suite – No. 5 Passacaglia **S 214 No. 5**

1920 PR Reuben Davies
Duo-Art (US) [6257]

** PR Rudolph Ganz
Welte-Mignon [3935]

Pelleas and Melisanda, overture **S 35**

2013 CD BBC Concert Orchestra / Martin Yates (cond)
Dutton Epoch [CDLX 7302] (*Cyril Scott Piano Concerto in D, Op. 10 (1900) / Cello Concerto, Op. 19 (1902) / Overture to Pelleas and Melisanda*)
[17' 21"]

Piano Sonata in D, Op. 17 **S 167**

2005 CD Leslie De'Ath
Dutton Epoch [CDLX 7155], *CSCPM-2*
[12' 59"]

Piano Sonata No. 1, Op. 66 (1909) **S 190**

2005 CD Leslie De'Ath
Dutton Epoch [CDLX 7155], *CSCPM-2*
[28' 27"]

2005 CD Michael Schäfer
Genuin [GEN 85049], *Cyril Scott: The Complete Sonatas and Other Works for Piano*
[22' 14"]

2000 CD Dennis Hennig
ABC Classics (Eloquence) [465 737-2], *Lotus Land & Other Piano Works* (reissue of Etcetera [KTC 1132])
[25' 54"]

1992 CD Marthanne Verbit
Albany Records [TROY 070], *Past Futurists* (reissue of Genesis [GS 1049])
[27' 49"]
Note: Verbit's name now appears as 'Marthanne' (her preference) unlike the 1974 LP issue. The 1974 Genesis LP and the 1999 Albany CD reissue have a pitch discrepancy, the timing on the CD is 27' 49", but the LP is 29' 40". This means that on the CD the whole sonata is a full semitone higher than written!

1992 CD Dennis Hennig
Etcetera [KTC 1132], *In the Garden of Soul-Sympathy*
[26' 00"]

1974 LP Martha Anne Verbit
Genesis [GS 1049], *The Piano Music of Cyril Scott*
[29' 40"]

Piano Sonata No. 2 (Second Sonata) **S 260**

2005 CD Leslie De'Ath
Dutton Epoch [CDLX 7155], *CSCPM-2*
[18' 27"]

2005 CD Michael Schäfer
Genuin [GEN 85049], *Cyril Scott: The Complete Sonatas and Other Works for Piano*
[14' 33"]

2004 CD Clipper Erickson
Direct-to-Tape [DTR 2013], *The Mystic and the Muse: Piano Music of Cyril Scott and Roger Quilter*
[17' 43"]

Piano Sonata No. 3 **S 262**

2005 CD Leslie De'Ath
Dutton Epoch [CDLX 7155], *CSCPM-2*
[18' 13"]

2005 CD Michael Schäfer
Genuin [GEN 85049], *Cyril Scott: The Complete Sonatas and Other Works for Piano*
[17' 15"]

1983 LP/CT Eric Parkin
Chandos [DBRD 4001 (LP) / DBTD 4001 (CT)], *Music for a Summer's Day*
[17' 41"]

1983 LP/CT(2) Eric Parkin
Chandos [DBRD 2006 (LP) / DBTD 2006 (CT)], *John Ireland: His Friends and Pupils*
[17' 41"]

1981	CT	Raphael Terroni British Music Society [BMS 401], *Goossens and Scott* [20' 10"]
1976	LP	Evelinde Trenkner Orion [ORS 76236] (*Dohnanyi / Cyril Scott*) [19' 10"]

Pictorial Sketch **S 215**

2007	CD(2)	Leslie De'Ath Dutton Epoch [CDLX 7183], *CSCPM-4* [3' 36"]

Pierrette **S 203**

2009	CD(2)	Leslie De'Ath Dutton Epoch [CDLX 7224], *CSCPM-5* [1' 56"]
2000	CD	Dennis Hennig ABC Classics (Eloquence) [465 737-2], *Lotus Land & Other Piano Works* (reissue of Etcetera [KTC 1132]) [2' 34"]
1992	CD	Dennis Hennig Etcetera [KTC 1132], *In the Garden of Soul-Sympathy* [2' 34"]

Pierrot and the Moon Maiden **S 352**

2018	CD	Charlotte de Rothschild (sop) / Adrian Farmer (pf) Lyrita [SRCD 365], *The Songs of Cyril Scott* [3' 01"]

Poems **S 210**

2009	CD(2)	Leslie De'Ath Dutton Epoch [CDLX 7224], *CSCPM-5* [14' 55"]
2000	CD	Dennis Hennig ABC Classics (Eloquence) [465 737-2], *Lotus Land & Other Piano Works* (reissue of Etcetera [KTC 1132]) [17' 45"]
1997	CD	Frances Gray private issue [WRC8-7148], *Poems for Piano* [16' 17"]
1992	CD	Marthanne Verbit Albany Records [TROY 071], *Valentines* (reissue of Genesis [GS 1049]) [15' 24"]
1992	CD	Dennis Hennig Etcetera [KTC 1132], *In the Garden of Soul-Sympathy* [17' 33"]
1974	LP	Martha Anne Verbit Genesis [GS 1049], *The Piano Music of Cyril Scott* [16' 31"]

Poems – No. 2 Poppies **S 210 No. 2**

2004 CD Mark Birnbaum
CD Baby [168272], *Dreamland: Piano Gems circa 1903*
[3' 13"]

Poems – Nos 2, 4 & 5 **S 210 Nos 2, 4 & 5**

1997 CD Emmy Best-Reintges
Fermate Musikproduktion [FER 30005], *Recital*

Prelude (voice/pf) **S 326**

2011 CD Robert Muuse (bar) / Micha van Weers (pf)
Challenge Classics [CC 72527], *Cyril Scott – Ralph Vaughan Williams: Songs of Quest and Inspiration*
[1' 43"]

Prelude No. 1 'Op. 37' **S 171**

2006 CD(2) Leslie De'Ath
Dutton Epoch [CDLX 7166], *CSCPM-3*
[6' 49"]

Prelude solennel **S 213**

2009 CD(2) Leslie De'Ath
Dutton Epoch [CDLX 7224], *CSCPM-5*
[4' 28"]

Quartet No. 1 for strings **S 104**

2003 CD Archaeus Quartet
Dutton Epoch [CDLX 7138], *Cyril Scott String Quartets*
[31' 49"]

Quartet No. 2 for strings **S 108**

2003 CD Archaeus Quartet
Dutton Epoch [CDLX 7138], *Cyril Scott String Quartets*
[22' 46"]

Quartet No. 4 for strings **S 110**

2003 CD Archaeus Quartet
Dutton Epoch [CDLX 7138], *Cyril Scott String Quartets*
[13' 30"]

Quartet in E minor, Op. 16, for piano and strings **S 86**

2006 CD Primrose Piano Quartet
Meridian [84547], *The Primrose Piano Quartet*
[19' 30"]

2002 CD London Piano Quartet
Dutton Epoch [CDLS 7116], *Piano Quartet / Quintet*
[21' 50"]

Quintet for clarinet and strings **S 116**

2010 CD Robert Plane (clar) / Mia Cooper (vln) / Lucy Gould (vln) / David Adams (vla) / Alice Neary (vc)

		Chandos [CHAN 10575], *Cyril Scott – Piano Trios Nos. 1 and 2 / Cornish Boat Song / Clarinet Quintet / Clarinet Trio* [13' 13"]

Quintet No. 1 for piano and strings **S 93**

2015	CD	Raphael Terroni / Bingham String Quartet Naxos [8.571355] [37' 46"]
2013	CD	Raphael Terroni / Bingham String Quartet British Music Society [BMS 442 CD], *Frank Bridge / Cyril Scott Piano Quintets* (reissue of BMS 411) [37' 37"]
2002	CD	London Piano Quartet Dutton Epoch [CDLX 7116], *Piano Quartet / Quintet* [39' 20"]
1990	CT	Raphael Terroni / Bingham String Quartet British Music Society [BMS 411], *Bridge & Scott Piano Quintets* [37' 37"]

Rainbow-Trout **S 228**

2009	CD(2)	Leslie De'Ath Dutton Epoch [CDLX 7224], *CSCPM-5* [4' 21"]
2005	CD	Cyril Scott Dutton Epoch [CDLX 7150], *CSCPM-1* (reissue of HMV [B2895]) [3' 04"]
2005	CD	Michael Schäfer Genuin [GEN 85049], *Cyril Scott: The Complete Sonatas and Other Works for Piano* [3' 53"]
2004	CD	Clipper Erickson Direct-to-Tape [DTR 2013], *The Mystic and the Muse: Piano Music of Cyril Scott and Roger Quilter* [4' 49"]
2002	CD	Frances Gray private issue [WRC8-7667], *The Evocative Piano* [5' 16"]
1994	CD	Christopher Howell Tremula [TREM 104-2], *M&I* [4' 35"]
**	78rpm	Cyril Scott HMV [B 2895] (rec. 4 October 1928) [3' 04"] Note: Scott's performance departs substantially from the printed score, presumably in part to accommodate the length limitations of 78rpm technology.

Requiescat **S 230**

2005 CD Leslie De'Ath
Dutton Epoch [CDLX 7150], *CSCPM-1* (= *CSCPM-Pr* [3' 09"])
[3' 12"]

Romance (vln/pf) **S 121**

2015 CD Truida van der Valt (vln) / Piet Koornhof (pf)
Delos [3476] *Remembrances*
[3' 38"]

2007 CD Clare Howick (vln) / Sophia Rahman (pf)
Dutton Epoch [CDLX 7200], *Cyril Scott – Sonata Lirica and Other Works for Violin and Piano*
[4' 11"]

Rondeau de concert **S 231**

2007 CD(2) Leslie De'Ath
Dutton Epoch [CDLX 7183], *CSCPM-4*
[5' 23"]

2005 CD Michael Schäfer
Genuin [GEN 85049], *Cyril Scott: The Complete Sonatas and Other Works for Piano*
[5' 30"]

Russian Dance **S 225**

2009 CD(2) Leslie De'Ath
Dutton Epoch [CDLX 7224], *CSCPM-5*
[2' 05"]

Russian Fair **S 272**

2006 CD(2) Anya Alexeyev / Leslie De'Ath
Dutton Epoch [CDLX 7166], *CSCPM-3*
[6' 34"]

Scherzo **S 169**

2007 CD(2) Leslie De'Ath
Dutton Epoch [CDLX 7183], *CSCPM-4*
[3' 42"]

Scotch Lullabye **S 328**

2018 CD Charlotte de Rothschild (sop) / Adrian Farmer (pf)
Lyrita [SRCD 365], *The Songs of Cyril Scott*
[3' 37"]

c. 1967 LP Robert Ivan Foster (bar) / Reginald Paul (pf)
Onslo Records [HERITAGE-4], *Onslo Folk Heritage, No. 4*

Scotch Pastoral **S 139**

** LP Sarah Baird Fouse (fl) / Cecilia Sims Ewing (pf)
Coronet [1245 (UK) / 4TRM-1107 (US)], *Flute Solos*

Sea-Marge **S 218**

2015 CD Janice Weber
Sono Luminus [DSL-92188], *Seascapes*
[3' 20"]

2009 CD(2) Leslie De'Ath
Dutton Epoch [CDLX 7224], *CSCPM-5*
[2' 40"]

1994 CD Christopher Howell
Tremula [TREM 104-2], *M&I*
[2' 30"]

Serenata **S 192**

2007 CD(2) Leslie De'Ath
Dutton Epoch [CDLX 7183], *CSCPM-4*
[3' 04"]

Six Pieces, Op. 4 **S 166**

2007 CD(2) Leslie De'Ath
Dutton Epoch [CDLX 7183], *CSCPM-4*
[11' 14"]

1994 CD Christopher Howell
Tremula [TREM 104-2], *M&I*
[10' 44"]

Soirée japonaise **S 194**

2005 CD(2) Cyril Scott
Dutton Epoch [CDLX 7150], *CSCPM-1* (= *CSCPM-Pr* [2' 35"])
[2' 43"]

1999 CD Noriko Ogawa
BIS [BIS-CD-1045], *Japonisme*
[3' 09"]

Solitude **S 175**

2009 CD(2) Leslie De'Ath
Dutton Epoch [CDLX 7224], *CSCPM-5*
[2' 18"]

Sonata for cello and piano **S 147**

2015 CD Richard Jenkinson (vc) / Benjamin Frith (pf)
EM Records [EMRCD 031], *The Moon Sails Out*
[22' 51"]

Sonata for viola and piano **S 146**

2013 CD Rupert Marshall-Luck (vla) / Matthew Pickard (pf)
EM Records [EMR CD018], *Sonatas for Violin and Viola*
[23' 57"]

Sonata lirica **S 130**

2007 CD Clare Howick (vln) / Sophia Rahman (pf)
Dutton Epoch [CDLX 7200], *Cyril Scott – Sonata lirica and Other Works for Violin and Piano*
[20' 26"]

Sonata melodica **S 132**

2010 CD Clare Howick (vln) / Sophia Rahman (pf)
Naxos [8.572290], *Cyril Scott – Violin Sonatas Nos. 1 and 2 / Sonata melodica*
[22' 17"]

Sonatina (gtr) **S 156**

2017 CD Roberto Moronn Perez
Reference Recordings [FR-723], *Viva Segovia!*
[11' 13"]

2013 CD(7) Ermanno Brignolo
Brilliant Classics [9427] *The Andrés Segovia Archive*
[12' 52"]

2006 CD Carlos Bernal
Gall Music [1181], *Sonates du XXe siècle*
[13' 25"]

2002 CD Tilman Hoppstock
Signum [X122-00], *Memories of the Alhambra*
[10' 50"]

Sorrow, Op.36 No. 2 **S 303**

2018 CD Charlotte de Rothschild (sop) / Adrian Farmer (pf)
Lyrita [SRCD 365], *The Songs of Cyril Scott*
[2' 14"]

Spanish Dance **S 249**

2007 CD(2) Leslie De'Ath
Dutton Epoch [CDLX 7183], *CSCPM-4*
[3' 44"]

Sphinx **S 187**

2005 CD(2) Leslie De'Ath
Dutton Epoch [CDLX 7150], *CSCPM-1* (= *CSCPM-Pr* [4' 06"])
[4' 11"]

2005 CD Michael Schäfer
Genuin [GEN 85049], *Cyril Scott: The Complete Sonatas and Other Works for Piano*
[4' 27"]

** PR Cyril Scott
Hupfeld [50844]

Spring Song **S 361**

2018 CD Charlotte de Rothschild (sop) / Adrian Farmer (pf)
Lyrita [SRCD 365], *The Songs of Cyril Scott*
[2' 33"]

Studies for a Slow Movement – No. 1 Andante S 161

2006 CD(2) Leslie De'Ath
Dutton Epoch [CDLX 7166], *CSCPM-3*
[4' 34"]

Studies for a Slow Movement – No. 2 Largo S 162

2006 CD(2) Leslie De'Ath
Dutton Epoch [CDLX 7166], *CSCPM-3*
[4' 18"]

Suite fantastique S 53

1994 CD National Symphony Orchestra of the South African Broadcasting Corporation / Peter Marchbank (cond)
Marco Polo [8.223485], [*Cyril Scott – Orchestral Works*]
[17' 23"]

Suite … in the Old Style S 195

2007 CD(2) Leslie De'Ath
Dutton Epoch [CDLX 7183], *CSCPM-4*
[12' 15"]

2004 CD(2) Leslie De'Ath
private issue [VVC CD 101-2], *CSCPM-Pr*
[10' 25"]

Summer Gardens S 58

1952 LP Vienna Tonkünstler Orchestra / Stanford Robinson
BBC Transcription Service [18422-3]

Summerland (pf) S 182

2007 CD(2) Leslie De'Ath
Dutton Epoch [CDLX 7183], *CSCPM-4*
[6' 38"]

Summerland (pf) – No. 2 A Song from the East S 182 No. 2

1972 LP Cyril Scott
Recorded Treasures [GCP 771], *The Welte Legacy of Piano Treasures. Great Composers / Pianists Perform their Own Compositions*, record 10 (reissue of Welte-Mignon [P 1697])

** 78rpm Una Bourne
HMV [B1844]

** PR Cyril Scott
Hupfeld [50841]

** PR Cyril Scott
Welte-Mignon [P 1697] – with S 185

** PR Ralph Herman Leopold
Ampico [5736]

Summerland (pf) – No. 4 Fairy Folk S 182 No. 4

** 78rpm Una Bourne
HMV [B1844]

Sundown **S 398**

2018 CD Charlotte de Rothschild (sop) / Adrian Farmer (pf)
Lyrita [SRCD 365], *The Songs of Cyril Scott*
[2' 55"]

2011 CD Robert Muuse (bar) / Micha van Weers (pf)
Challenge Classics [CC 72527], *Cyril Scott – Ralph Vaughan Williams: Songs of Quest and Inspiration*
[3' 19"]

Symphony No. 1 **S 34**

2008 CD BBC Philharmonic / Martyn Brabbins (cond)
Chandos [CHAN 10452] (*Cyril Scott Orchestral Works*, vol. 4)
[30' 44"]
Note: Third movement completed and edited by Leslie De'Ath.

Symphony No. 3, 'The Muses' **S 59**

2004 CD Huddersfield Choral Society / BBC Philharmonic / Martyn Brabbins (cond)
Chandos [CHAN 10211] (*Cyril Scott Orchestral Works*, vol. 1)
[34' 45"]

Symphony No. 4 **S 64**

2006 CD BBC Philharmonic / Martyn Brabbins (cond)
Chandos [CHAN 10376] (*Cyril Scott Orchestral Works*, vol. 2)
[28' 21"]

Tallahassee Suite **S 123**

2011 CD Jascha Heifetz (vln)
RCA [886443010086], *The Heifetz Collection*, vol. 3: *1935–1937*
[9' 32"]

2007 CD(2) Jascha Heifetz (vln) / Emanuel Bay (pf)
EMI Classics References [64929], *Jascha Heifetz – Recital*
(reissue of EMI [0 7243 5670 0550])
[9' 30"]

2007 CD Clare Howick (vln) / Sophia Rahman (pf)
Dutton Epoch [CDLX 7200], *Cyril Scott – Sonata lirica and Other Works for Violin and Piano*
[11' 38"]

1994 CD(2)/CT Jascha Heifetz (vln) / Emanuel Bay (pf)
Musical Heritage Society [523740x (CD) / 323740A (CT)]
[9' 30"]

1994 CD Jascha Heifetz (vln) / Emanuel Bay (pf)
RCA Victor Gold Seal [09026-61734-2], *The Heifetz collectio*, vol. 3: *1935–1937*
[9' 30"]

1993 CD Jascha Heifetz (vln) / Emanuel Bay (pf)
EMI Classics [0 7243 5670 0550 (7 64929 2)], *Jascha Heifetz – Recital*
[9' 30"]

1975	LP(4)	Jascha Heifetz (vln) / Emanuel Bay (pf) RCA Victor Red Seal [ARM 4-0944-2-C], *The Heifetz collection, vol. 3: 1935–1937: Early Recordings of Concertos, Sonatas and Encores* (rec. 15 March 1937) [9' 30"]

Tallahassee Suite – No. 1 Bygone Memories **S 123 No. 1**

1999	CD	Jascha Heifetz (vln) / Emanuel Bay (pf) EMI Classics [67005], *The Legendary Heifetz* [3' 03"]
1998	CD	Jascha Heifetz (vln) / Emanuel Bay (pf) One Eleven [50300], *Bygone Memories* [2' 54"]
1993	CD	Jascha Heifetz (vln) / Emanuel Bay (pf) EMI Classics [0 7243 5670 0550], *Heifetz – Recital* [2' 54"]
**	78rpm	Jascha Heifetz (vln)/ Emanuel Bay (pf) HMV [DA 1567]

Tallahassee Suite – No. 2 After Sundown **S 123 No. 2**

1998	CD	Efrem Zimbalist (vln) / Emanuel Bay (pf) Pearl [GEM 0032], *Efrem Zimbalist* (rec. 28 August 1928 Columbia 167-M) [2' 33"]

Tarantula **S 261**

2014	CD(2)	Christopher Howell (pf) Sheva Collection [Sh 056] *An Englishman in Italy* [1' 45"]
2009	CD(2)	Leslie De'Ath Dutton Epoch [CDLX 7224], *CSCPM-5* [1' 25"]

The Alchemist **S 1**

2016	CD	[excerpts] Anna-Clare Monk, Peter Bronder, Alan Opie, Nichola Folwell, Harry Nicholl, BBC Concert Orchestra, James Lockhart Oriel [OMT362] (from BBC broadcast 7 August 1995) [58' 17"]

The Extatic Shepherd **S 153**

2015	CD	James Risdon (rec) (self-produced), *Echoes of Arcadia: Music for Solo Recorder* [6' 22"]
2015	CD(2)	Kenneth Smith (fl) / Paul Rhodes (pf) Divine Art [DDA 21223] *From the British Isles: Music for Flute and Piano* [4' 21"]

2014	CD	Nina Assimakopoulos (fl) Euterpe Recordings [202], *Arcadian Murmurs: Pan in Pieces*, vol. 1 [3' 20"]
1990	CD	Kenneth Smith (fl) / Paul Rhodes (pf) ASV [CD DCA 739], *Summer Music: British Flute Music*, vol. 1 [4' 22"]

The Gentle Maiden **S 126**

2011	CD	Jascha Heifetz (vln) / Isidor Achron (pf) RCA [886443009202], *The Heifetz Collection*, vol. 1: *1917–1924* [2' 06"]
1999	CD(2)	Jascha Heifetz (vln) / Isidor Achron (pf) IDI (Ital Disc Inst) [288/9], *Jascha Heifetz – Edizione cronologica delle registrazioni dal 1917 al 1946*, vol. 2: *Gli anni 1922–34* [2' 09"]
1994	CD	Jascha Heifetz (vln) / Isidor Achron (pf) RCA Victor Gold Seal [09026-61732-2], *The Heifetz Collection*, vol. 1: *The Acoustic Recordings, 1917–1924*
1975	LP	Jascha Heifetz (vln) / Isidor Achron (pf) RCA Victor Red Seal [ARM 4-0944-2-4-H], *The Heifetz Collection*, vol. 1: *1917–1924: The Complete Acoustic Recordings*
c. 1975	LP	Jascha Heifetz (vln) / Isidor Achron (pf) Discopaedia [MB 1010], *Masters of the Bow – Jascha Heifetz* (reissue of Victor [1082] HMV [DA725], rec. 18 December 1924)
**	78rpm	Eda Kersey (vln) with piano Decca [F 1692] [2' 18"]

The Huckster **S 406**

2011	CD	Robert Muuse (bar) / Micha van Weers (pf) Challenge Classics [CC 72527], *Cyril Scott – Ralph Vaughan Williams: Songs of Quest and Inspiration* [1' 45"]

The Melodist and the Nightingales **S 74**

2016	CD	Aleksei Kiseliov (vc), Royal Scottish National Orchestra / Martin Yates (cond) Dutton Epoch [CDLX7326] [19' 28"]

The Unforeseen **S 345**

2018	CD	Charlotte de Rothschild (sop) / Adrian Farmer (pf) Lyrita [SRCD 365], *The Songs of Cyril Scott* [2' 53"]
1973	LP	Joan Sutherland (sop) / Richard Bonynge (pf) A.N.N.A. Record Co. [ANNA 1029 A/B], *Joan Sutherland Recital*
**	78rpm	Kathleen Joyce (contralto) / Hubert Greenslade (pf) Parlophone [R 3804]

The Valley of Silence, Op.72 No 4 **S 344**

2018 CD Charlotte de Rothschild (sop) / Adrian Farmer (pf)
Lyrita [SRCD 365], *The Songs of Cyril Scott*
[3' 58"]

The Watchman **S 402**

2018 CD Charlotte de Rothschild (sop) / Adrian Farmer (pf)
Lyrita [SRCD 365], *The Songs of Cyril Scott*
[3' 15"]

Theme and Variations (2 pfs) **S 267**

2006 CD(2) Anya Alexeyev / Leslie De'Ath
Dutton Epoch [CDLX 7166], *CSCPM-3*
[18' 28"]

Three Dances, Op. 20 **S 168**

2005 CD(2) Leslie De'Ath
Dutton Epoch [CDLX 7150], *CSCPM-1* (= *CSCPM-Pr* [5' 26"])
[5' 24"]

Three Dances (pf duet) **S 265**

2006 CD(2) Anya Alexeyev / Leslie De'Ath
Dutton Epoch [CDLX 7166], *CSCPM-3*
[6' 59"]

Three Frivolous Pieces **S 164**

2007 CD(2) Leslie De'Ath
Dutton Epoch [CDLX 7183], *CSCPM-4*
[8' 17"]
Note: The 18-bar postlude to *Valse scherzando* performed here is in accordance with Scott's own recording, Columbia [5435].

Three Frivolous Pieces – No. 3 Valse scherzando **S 164 No. 3**

2005 CD(2) Cyril Scott
Dutton Epoch [CDLX 7150], *CSCPM-1* (reissue of Columbia [5435])
[1' 59"]

** 78rpm Cyril Scott
Columbia [5435 (UK) / 196-M (US) / 2228D (US) (with S 196)]
(rec. 28 February 1929)
Note: Scott adds an 18-bar postlude in this recording, not found in the published score

Three Little Waltzes **S 165**

2005 CD(2) Leslie De'Ath
Dutton Epoch [CDLX 7150], *CSCPM-1* (= *CSCPM-Pr* [5' 22"])
[5' 23"]

Three Little Waltzes – No. 1 Allegro poco scherzando **S 165 No. 1**

** 78rpm Una Bourne
HMV [B1647]

Three little Waltzes – No. 2 Andante languido **S 165 No. 2**

** PR Sylvan Levin
Welte-Mignon [7053]

Three Little Waltzes – No. 3 Allegretto gracioso **S 165 No. 3**

** PR Sylvan Levin
Welte-Mignon [7053]

** PR Herbert Fryer
Hupfeld [50795]

Three Old Country Dances **S 250**

2005 CD(2) Leslie De'Ath
Dutton Epoch [CDLX 7150], *CSCPM-1* (= *CSCPM-Pr* [4' 50"])
[4' 56"]

Three Pastorals **S 238**

2005 CD(2) Leslie De'Ath
Dutton Epoch [CDLX 7150], *CSCPM-1* (= *CSCPM-Pr* [6' 15"])
[6' 22"]

Three Pastorals – No. 2 Con delicatessa **S 238 No. 2**

1923 PR Cyril Scott
Duo-Art (UK) [06]

Three Pastorals – No. 3 Pensoso **S 238 No. 3**

2005 CD(2) Cyril Scott
Dutton Epoch [CDLX 7150], *CSCPM-1* (reissue of Columbia [DB 41])
[2' 19"]

c. 1930 78rpm Cyril Scott
Columbia [DB 41 (UK) / 2284-D (US)] (rec. 28 February 1929 and 12 February 1930 – both takes issued)

Three Pieces (Bach/Scott) – No. 1 Invention in F **S 444 No. 1**

2006 CD(2) Anya Alexeyev / Leslie De'Ath
Dutton Epoch [CDLX 7166], *CSCPM-3*
[4' 26"]

Three Pieces (Bach/Scott) – No. 2 Sarabande, A minor **S 444 No. 2**

2006 CD(2) Anya Alexeyev / Leslie De'Ath
Dutton Epoch [CDLX 7166], *CSCPM-3*
[3' 36"]

Three Pieces (Bach/Scott) – No. 3 Gigue, G major **S 444 No. 3**

2006 CD(2) Anya Alexeyev / Leslie De'Ath
Dutton Epoch [CDLX 7166], *CSCPM-3*
[3' 43"]

Three Symphonic Dances, Op. 22 **S 46**

2007 CD BBC Philharmonic / Martyn Brabbins (cond)
Chandos [CHAN 10407] (*Cyril Scott Orchestral Works*, vol. 3)
[17' 59"]

1994 CD National Symphony Orchestra of the South African Broadcasting Corporation / Peter Marchbank (cond)
Marco Polo [8.223485], [*Cyril Scott – Orchestral Works*]
[18' 29"]

Time o' Day **S 391**

2011 CD Robert Muuse (bar) / Micha van Weers (pf)
Challenge Classics [CC 72527], *Cyril Scott – Ralph Vaughan Williams: Songs of Quest and Inspiration*
[1' 29"]

To-Morrow **S 427**

2011 CD Robert Muuse (bar) / Micha van Weers (pf)
Challenge Classics [CC 72527], *Cyril Scott – Ralph Vaughan Williams: Songs of Quest and Inspiration*
[2' 03"]

Trio for clarinet, cello and piano **S 117**

2010 CD Robert Plane (clar) / Alice Neary (vc) / Benjamin Frith (pf)
Chandos [CHAN 10575], *Cyril Scott – Piano Trios Nos. 1 and 2 / Cornish Boat Song / Clarinet Quintet / Clarinet Trio*
[18' 04"]

Trio No. 1 for piano and strings **S 92**

2010 CD Gould Piano Trio
Chandos [CHAN 10575], *Cyril Scott – Piano Trios Nos. 1 and 2 / Cornish Boat Song / Clarinet Quintet / Clarinet Trio*
[33' 48"]

Trio No. 2 for piano and strings **S 96**

2010 CD Gould Piano Trio
Chandos [CHAN 10575], *Cyril Scott – Piano Trios Nos. 1 and 2 / Cornish Boat Song / Clarinet Quintet / Clarinet Trio*
[10' 08"]

Trois danses tristes **S 197**

2007 CD(2) Leslie De'Ath
Dutton Epoch [CDLX 7183], *CSCPM-4*
[12' 14"]

2000 CD Dennis Hennig
ABC Classics (Eloquence) [465 737-2], *Lotus Land & Other Piano Works* (reissue of Etcetera [KTC 1132])
[12' 10"]

1992 CD Dennis Hennig
Etcetera [KTC 1132], *In the Garden of Soul-Sympathy*
[12' 11"]

Trois danses tristes – No. 1 Danse élégiaque **S 197 No. 1**

** PR Walter Niemann
Hupfeld [59095]

Trois danses tristes – No. 2 Danse orientale **S 197 No. 2**

** PR Cyril Scott
Hupfeld [50837]

** PR Otto Weinreich
Hupfeld [51233]

Twilight-Tide **S 232**

2005 CD(2) Leslie De'Ath
Dutton Epoch [CDLX 7150], *CSCPM-1* (= *CSCPM-Pr* [2' 36"])
[2' 37"]

Two Alpine Sketches **S 184**

2005 CD(2) Leslie De'Ath
Dutton Epoch [CDLX 7150], *CSCPM-1* (= *CSCPM-Pr* [2' 35"])
[2' 43"]

** PR Herbert Fryer
Hupfeld [50796]

Two Chinese Songs – No. 1 Waiting **S 313**

** PR Cyril Scott
Welte-Mignon [1699](accompaniment only)

Two Chinese Songs – No. 2 A Picnic **S 314**

2011 CD Robert Muuse (bar) / Micha van Weers (pf)
Challenge Classics [CC 72527], *Cyril Scott – Ralph Vaughan Williams: Songs of Quest and Inspiration*
[2' 22"]

** PR Cyril Scott
Welte-Mignon [1699] (accompaniment only)

Two Etudes **S 188/189**

2009 CD(2) Leslie De'Ath
Dutton Epoch [CDLX 7224], *CSCPM-5*
[5' 03"]

1996 CD Jack Richard Crossan
Cambria [CD-1086], *Sounds and Perfumes*
[5' 01"]

Two Etudes – No. 2 **S 189**

** PR Harold Henry
Duo-Art (US) [6225]

Two Passacaglias on Irish Themes **S 52**

1994 CD National Symphony Orchestra of the South African Broadcasting Corporation / Peter Marchbank (cond)
Marco Polo [8.223485], [*Cyril Scott – Orchestral Works*]
[11' 17"]

Two Piano Pieces, Op. 37 **S 172**

2009 CD(2) Leslie De'Ath
Dutton Epoch [CDLX 7224], *CSCPM-5*
[4' 26"]

Two Pierrot Pieces **S 170**

2009 CD(2) Leslie De'Ath
Dutton Epoch [CDLX 7224], *CSCPM-5*
[6' 29"]

2000 CD Dennis Hennig
ABC Classics (Eloquence) [465 737-2], *Lotus Land & Other Piano Works* (reissue of Etcetera [KTC 1132])
[6' 56"]

1994 CD Christopher Howell
Tremula [TREM 104-2], *M&I*
[6' 44"]

1992 CD Dennis Hennig
Etcetera [KTC 1132], *In the Garden of Soul-Sympathy*
[6' 56"]

** 78rpm Cyril Scott
HMV [B 3315] (rec. 1 March 1929 [No. 1] / 27 March 1929 [No. 2])

** PR Ernesto Consolo
Hupfeld [50797-8]

Two Pierrot Pieces – No. 1 Pierrot triste (Lento) **S 170 No. 1**

2011 CD(5) Percy Grainger
Appian [APR 7501], *Percy Grainger: The Complete 78-RPM Solo Recordings 1908–1945* (reissue of Decca [24160])
[3' 03"]

2007 CD Percy Grainger
Dal Segno [20] *The Great Pianists: Percy Grainger*, vol. 4
[3' 08"]

2004 CD Mark Birnbaum
CD Baby [168272], *Dreamland: Piano Gems circa 1903*
[2' 42"]

1993 CD Percy Grainger
Bellaphon [690-07-024], *Grainger: Early Recordings by the Pianist (The Condon Collection)* (rec. 1920)
[3' 03"]

** 78rpm Percy Grainger
Decca [24160 (set A 586)], *Percy Grainger: Favourite Piano Solos* (rec. 4 April 1945)
[2' 56"]

1929 PR Percy Grainger
Duo-Art [7252-3] (rec. 1929)
[3' 08"]

** PR Ossip Gabrilovich
Artrio-Angelus [7604]

**	PR	Corneille Overstreet Welte-Mignon (US) [6272]	
**	PR	Zoe Walson Duo-Art (US) [3125]	
**	PR	Stewart Wille Ampico [6364]	

Two Pierrot Pieces – No. 2 Pierrot gai (Allegro) **S 170 No. 2**

**	PR	Carolyn Beebe Duo-Art (US) [6053]
**	PR	Ernesto Consolo Hupfeld [50798]

Two Sketches **S 183**

2007	CD(2)	Leslie De'Ath Dutton Epoch [CDLX 7183], *CSCPM-4* [3' 49"]

Two Sketches – No. 1 Cuckoo-Call **S 183 No. 1**

1981	CT	Raphael Terroni British Music Society [BMS 401], *Goossens and Scott* [2' 54"]

Two Sonnets **S 127/128**

2017	CD	Fenella Humphreys (vln) / Nathan Williamson (pf) Lyrita [SRCD 359], *Doreen Carwithen & Thomas Pitfield Violin Sonatas* [3' 45" + 4' 49" = 8' 34"]

Valse caprice **S 198**

2005	CD(2)	Leslie De'Ath Dutton Epoch [CDLX 7150], *CSCPM-1* (= *CSCPM-Pr* [3' 28"]) [3' 32"]
**	PR	Reuben Davies Duo-Art (US) [5955]
**	PR	Sylvan Levin Welte-Mignon (US) [7012]
**	PR	Rata Présent Ampico [6232]
**	PR	Rata Présent Duo-Art [3150]

Valse sentimentale **S 255**

2009	CD(2)	Leslie De'Ath Dutton Epoch [CDLX 7224], *CSCPM-5* [4' 08"]
1994	CD	Christopher Howell Tremula [TREM 104-2], *M&I* [5' 08"]

Valse triste **S 122**

2007 CD Clare Howick (vln) / Sophia Rahman (pf)
Dutton Epoch [CDLX 7200], *Cyril Scott – Sonata lirica and Other Works for Violin and Piano*
[3' 19"]

Vesperale **S 176**

2005 CD(2) Leslie De'Ath
Dutton Epoch [CDLX 7150], *CSCPM-1* (= *CSCPM-Pr* [2' 14"])
[2' 14"]

** PR Mortimer Browning
Ampico [6462]

** PR Madalah Masson
Welte-Mignon (US) [6559]

Victorian Waltz **S 264**

2007 CD(2) Leslie De'Ath
Dutton Epoch [CDLX 7183], *CSCPM-4*
[3' 05"]

2005 CD Michael Schäfer
Genuin [GEN 85049], *Cyril Scott: The Complete Sonatas and Other Works for Piano*
[3' 34"]

Vieux chine [Old China]: Suite **S 234**

2007 CD(2) Leslie De'Ath
Dutton Epoch [CDLX 7183], *CSCPM-4*
[6' 13"]

Violin Sonata No. 1, Op. 59 **S 119**

2015 CD Andrew Kirkman (vln) / Clipper Erickson (pf)
Affetto [AF 1504], *Dawn and Twilight: The First and Last Violin Sonatas of Cyril Scott* (original version)
[39' 50"]

2010 CD Clare Howick (vln) / Sophia Rahman (pf)
Naxos [8.572290], *Cyril Scott – Violin Sonatas Nos. 1 and 2 / Sonata melodica*
[28' 48"]

Violin Sonata No. 3 **S 134**

2010 CD Clare Howick (vln) / Sophia Rahman (pf)
Naxos [8.572290], *Cyril Scott – Violin Sonatas Nos. 1 and 2 / Sonata melodica*
[23' 23"]

Violin Sonata No. 4 **S 135**

2015 CD Andrew Kirkman (vln) / Clipper Erickson (pf)
Affetto [AF 1504], *Dawn and Twilight: The First and Last Violin Sonatas of Cyril Scott*
[16' 15"]

Vistas **S 235**

2005 CD(2) Leslie De'Ath
Dutton Epoch [CDLX 7150], *CSCPM-1* (= *CSCPM-Pr* [7' 53"])
[8' 01"]

Vistas – No. 2 In the Forest **S 235 No. 2**

2002 CD Frances Gray
private issue [WRC8-7667], *The Evocative Piano*
[2' 47"]

1923 PR Cyril Scott
Duo-Art (UK) [01]

Voices of Vision, Op.24 **S 293**

2018 CD Charlotte de Rothschild (sop) / Adrian Farmer (pf)
Lyrita [SRCD 365], *The Songs of Cyril Scott*
[4' 42"]

Water-Lilies **S 400**

2018 CD Charlotte de Rothschild (sop) / Adrian Farmer (pf)
Lyrita [SRCD 365], *The Songs of Cyril Scott*
[2' 06"]

2011 CD Robert Muuse (bar) / Micha van Weers (pf)
Challenge Classics [CC 72527], *Cyril Scott – Ralph Vaughan Williams: Songs of Quest and Inspiration*
[1' 53"]

Water-Wagtail **S 196**

2010 CD Michael Lewin
Dorian Sono Luminus [DSL-92103], *If I Were a Bird – A Piano Aviary*
[2' 34"]

2009 CD(2) Leslie De'Ath
Dutton Epoch [CDLX 7224], *CSCPM-5*
[2' 13"]

2005 CD Cyril Scott
Dutton Epoch [CDLX 7150], *CSCPM-1* (reissue of Columbia [5435])
[2' 09"]

1977 LP Richard Deering
Saga [5445], *English Piano Music*
[3' 17"]

** 78rpm Cyril Scott
Columbia [5435 (UK) / 196 M (US) / 2228D (US)] (rec. 28 February 1929)
[2' 09"]

** PR Cyril Scott
Hupfeld [50835]

** PR Ruth Deyo
Duo-Art (US) [6789]

Willows, Op.24 No 2 **S 294**

2018 CD Charlotte de Rothschild (sop) / Adrian Farmer (pf)
Lyrita [SRCD 365], *The Songs of Cyril Scott*
[2' 21"]

Young Hearts – I, No. 1, See-Saw **S 239 No. 1**

1960s LP Bob Bennett
Educo [3109]

Young Hearts – II, No. 1, March of a Tin Soldier **S 239 No. 2**

1960s LP Bob Bennett
Educo [3109]

Zoo (Animals) **S 256**

2004 CD Clipper Erickson
Direct-to-Tape [DTR 2013], *The Mystic and the Muse: Piano Music of Cyril Scott and Roger Quilter*
[6' 48"]

B ARRANGEMENTS OF SCOTT'S WORKS BY OTHER COMPOSERS

Cherry Ripe (arr. Lionel Tertis, vla/pf) **T 38**

2006 CD (4) Lionel Tertis
Biddulph [82016] *Lionel Tertis – The Complete Columbia Recordings* (reissue of Columbia [D1569])
[2' 40"]

1926 78rpm Lionel Tertis
Columbia [D1569] (recorded 20 November 1926)
[2' 40"]

Danse nègre (arr. A. Walter Kramer, vln/pf) **T 37**

2016 CD (22) Yehudi Menuhin / Hendrik Endt
Warner [555051] *The Menuhin Century: Unpublished Recordings and Rarities*
[1' 27"]

2016 CD (91) Yehudi Menuhin / Hendrik Endt
Warner [555050] *The Menuhin Century: Luxury Edition*
[1' 27"]

2007 CD Clare Howick (vln) / Sophia Rahman (pf)
Dutton Epoch [CDLX 7200], *Cyril Scott – Sonata lirica and Other Works for Violin and Piano*
[2' 15"]

1996 CD Yehudi Menuhin / Hendrik Endt
Biddulph [LAB 128] *Yehudi Menuhin Plays Favourite Encores* (reissue of HMV [DA1685], recorded 14 March 1939)
[1' 27"]

Danse nègre (arr. Eugene Brose, clar / pf) **T 43**

1960s	LP	Bob Lowry (cl) / Joseph Kahn (pf) Golden Crest [RE 7003])

Handelian Rhapsody (arr. Percy Grainger, pf) **T 58**

2011	CD	Piers Lane Helios [55454], *Percy Grainger – Rambles and Reflections* (reissue of Hyperion [CDA 67279]) [6' 22"]
2005	CD(2)	Leslie De'Ath Dutton Epoch [CDLX 7150], *CSCPM-1* (= *CSCPM-Pr* [6' 17"]) [6' 17"]
2002	CD	Piers Lane Hyperion [CDA 67279], *Percy Grainger – Rambles and Reflections* [6' 22"]

Intermezzo (arr. Richard Lange, vln/pf) **T 31**

2007	CD	Clare Howick (vln) / Sophia Rahman (pf) Dutton Epoch [CDLX 7200], *Cyril Scott – Sonata lirica and Other Works for Violin and Piano* [2' 19"]

Lotus Land (arr. Fritz Kreisler, vln/pf) **T 35**

2014	CD	Graf Mourja (vln) / Natalia Gous (pf) Harmonia Mundi [HMA 1951785] *Le Violon vagabond* [5' 03"]
2013	CD	Fritz Kreisler (vln) / Franz Rupp (pf) Naxos Historical [8.111398], *Great Violinists – Kreisler: The Complete Recordings 5* [4' 04"]
2010	CD	Vladimir Spivakov (vln) / Sergei Bezrodny (pf) RCA Victor Red Seal [09026-62524-2], *It's Peaceful Here* [4' 31"]
2010	CD	Bernt Lysell (vln) / Urban Gärdborn (pf) Daphne Records (DAPHNE 1028], *The Strenuous Life* [4' 55"]
2009	CD(10)	Fritz Kreisler (vln) / Franz Rupp (pf) (recorded 14 February 1938) Warner Classics [65042] *Icon – Fritz Kreisler – The Charming Maverick* [4' 06"]
2008	CD(2)	James Ehnes (vln) / Eduard Laurel (pf) Onyx [ONYX 4038], *Homage* [5' 03"]
2007	CD	Clare Howick (vln) / Sophia Rahman (pf) Dutton Epoch [CDLX 7200], *Cyril Scott – Sonata lirica and Other Works for Violin and Piano* [5' 01"]

2007	CD	Benjamin Schmid (vln) / Miklos Skuta (pf) Oehms Classics [OC 701], *From Fritz to Django* [4' 50"]
2006	CD	Fritz Kreisler (vln) / Franz Rupp (pf) Opus Kura [2058] *Fritz Kreisler Plays Short Pieces*
2005	CD	Fritz Kreisler (vln) / Franz Rupp (pf) Naxos Historical [8.110992], *Great Violinists – Kreisler Plays Kreisler* [4' 06"]
2005	CD	Fritz Kreisler (vln) / Franz Rupp (pf) EMI [0077776470153], *Fritz Kreisler – Original Compositions & Arrangements* [4' 09"]
2004	CD	Leonidas Kavakos (vln) / Péter Nagy (pf) Bis [BIS-CD-1196], *Kreisler: Viennese Rhapsody* [4' 48"]
2001	CD	Ruggiero Ricci (vln) / Noriko Shiozaki (pf) Dynamic [CDS 373] *The Legacy of Cremona* [4' 12"]
1999	CD(2)	Fritz Kreisler (vln) / Franz Rupp (pf) Fono Enterprise [QT 99-363], *Fritz Kreisler – The Complete Arrangements and Original Works, 1903–1938* [4' 10"]
1996	CD	Ulrika-Anima Mathé (vln) / Samuel Sanders (pf) Dorian Sono Luminus [DOR-90231], *Mathé Plays Kreisler* [5' 02"]
1995	CD	Tobias Ringborg (vln) / Anders Kilström (pf) Caprice [CAP 21496], *Kreisleriana: The Lesser Known Works of Fritz Kreisler* [5' 16"]
1986	LP/CT[2]	Fritz Kreisler (vln) / Franz Rupp (pf) EMI [290556-3 & -5] *Kreisler Plays Kreisler*
1983	CD	Dmitry Sitkovetsky (vln) / Bruno Canino (pf) Orfeo [48831] *Kreisler; Violin Transcriptions* [4' 51"]

Lotus Land (arr. flute & pf) **TT 44–48**

2014	CD(73)	James Galway (fl) / Hiro Fujikake (synthesiser) [T 48] RCA [302633] *James Galway – The Complete RCA Album Collection* (reissue of RCA Victor [61379]) [4' 17"]
2014	CD	James Galway (fl) / Hiro Fujikake (synthesiser) [T 48] RCA [886444782500], *James Galway – The Lark in the Clear Air* [4' 17"]
2013	CD(2)	Kenneth Smith (fl) / Paul Rhodes (pf) [T 47] Divine Art [21222], *The Expressive Voice of the Flute* [6' 01"]

2001	CD	Nancy Ruffer (fl) / Helen Crayford (pf) Guild [7230] *British Fantasies, American Dreams* [4' 54"]
1994	CD	James Galway (fl) / Hiro Fujikake (synthesiser) RCA Victor [61379] *James Galway – The Lark in the Clear Air* [4' 17"]
1993	CD	Kenneth Smith (fl) / Paul Rhodes (pf) [T 47] ASV [CD DCA 862], *The Flute of Pan*, vol. 3 [6' 02"]

Lotus Land (orchestra) **T 12**

2010	CD	Tito Puente Orchestra, Tito Puente (cond) RCA [66148] *Puente Goes Jazz*
2005	CD	Camarata Guild [GLCD 5112] *Reflections of Tranquility* [4' 28"]

Lullaby (arr. Ethel Barns, vln/pf) **T 34**

2007	CD	Clare Howick (vln) / Sophia Rahman (pf) Dutton Epoch [CDLX 7200], *Cyril Scott – Sonata lirica and Other Works for Violin and Piano* [2' 13"]

Lullaby (arr. Julian Lloyd Webber, vc/pf) **T 42**

2015	CD	Richard Jenkinson (vc) / Benjamin Frith (pf) EM Records [EMR CD031], *The Moon Sails Out* [2' 48"]
2004	CD(2)	Julian Lloyd Webber (vc) / John Lenehan (pf) Philips [4761296] *Gentle Dreams – The Best of Julian Lloyd Webber* [2' 37"]

Tallahassee Suite – No. 1 Bygone Memories (arr. anon., vln/orch) **T 26**

2011	CD	Jascha Heifetz (vln) / Bell Telephone Hour Orchestra / Donald Voorhees (cond) Naxos 8.111379, *Jascha Heifetz Miniatures*, vol. 1 (reissue of V-DISC 422, rec. 29 January 1945) [2'55"]

Three Little Waltzes (arr. Richard Lange) **T 33**

2007	CD	Clare Howick (vln) / Sophia Rahman (pf) Dutton Epoch [CDLX 7200], *Cyril Scott – Sonata lirica and Other Works for Violin and Piano* [2' 47"]

Three Symphonic Dances, Op. 22 (arr. Percy Grainger, two pfs) **T 62**

2016	CD(4)	Penelope Thwaites and John Lavender Heritage [HTGCD 403], *Percy Grainger – Complete Music for Four Hands, Two Pianos* [from Pearl SHE 9631] [17' 52"]

2006 CD Leslie De'Ath and Anya Alexeyev
Dutton Epoch [CDLX 7166], *Cyril Scott Complete Piano Music, Volume Three*
[18' 48"]

1993 CD Penelope Thwaites and John Lavender
Pavilion Records (Pearl) [SHE 9631], *Grainger Piano Music for Four Hands*, vol. 3
[17' 52"]

Three Symphonic Dances, Op. 22 – No. 1 Allegro con brio T 62 No. 1

2010 CD(10) Percy Grainger and Cyril Scott
Documents [291399], *Creators: Komponisten spielen ihre Werke am Klavier*, vol. 9
[4' 04"]

1999 CD Percy Grainger and Cyril Scott
Klavier [KCD-11095], *Legendary Piano Duos*
[4' 11"]

1973 LP Percy Grainger and Cyril Scott
Klavier [KS 102], *Legendary Artists Play Piano For Four Hands*
[from Duo-Art piano roll [6514], recorded 1922]
[4' 20"]

Young Hearts – II, No.4 Loneliness S 239 No.2

** 78rpm Victor Orchestra / Bruno Reibold (cond)
Victor [24784] (rec. 18 October 1934)

iii

Cyril Scott's Opus Numbers

LESLIE DE'ATH

It is reasonable to suppose that the numbering of opuses was supplied by Scott himself, rather than by his publishers, at least until the beginning of his association with Elkin in 1904. There are several reasons for this:

1. Several extant early works bear opus numbers but remained unpublished.
2. Gaps exist in the numbering, which imply that some composed and numbered works were withdrawn from publication (Opp. 14, 23, 33, 44, 45, 48, 49, 51, 53, 60, 69, 76).
3. Some opuses involve mixed media (some songs, some piano, for instance).
4. The opus numbers do not always coincide with the publication date and the ordering of publishers' catalogue numbers, both within and between individual opuses – especially in the earlier works.
5. Elkin published songs separately when they bore the same opus number, as with Opp. 42 and 43.

The numbering of works ceased in 1911. Many works composed before that date bear no opus numbers, such as the 1899 *Magnificat,* the orchestral Symphony No. 1 and *Rhapsody* No. 2, two early piano quintets, and an early cello sonata. Scott withdrew several works of substance during the early years, and it is quite likely (albeit unverifiable) that such works at one time bore the now-vacant opus numbers, as suggested in the list below.

Almost all opus numbers from 33 on are miniatures for piano, or voice and piano, until the numbering of his works ends with the orchestral *Aubade,* Op. 77. The exceptions are five violin/piano works: the Op. 59 Sonata, the Op. 73 *Tallahassee Suite,* and three miniatures. This presumably reflects Elkin's standardisation of the numbers upon assuming the role of Scott's publisher in 1904, and Schott's brief involvement in the numbering in 1910.

The following numerical duplications are noted:

- Op. 1 — the six-song cycle *Sänge eines fahrenden Spielmanns,* and to the original versions of Op. 3 No. 1 and No. 2.
- Op. 3 — two published songs (Boosey) and to the Piano trio in E minor.
- Op. 5 — a parallel to Op. 3, given to two published Boosey songs (1903) and the overture *Pelleas and Melisanda.*
- Op. 10 — the 1900 Piano Concerto in D and the *Christmas Overture*
- Op. 12 — two other works of 1900: the *Symphonic Fantasia* and the first String Quartet.
- Op. 20 — *Three Dances* for piano and the revised *Pelleas and Melisanda* overture (Op. 5)

Op. 31 *Asleep* (voice/piano), and the String Quartet in F major

Op. 32 *Rhapsody* No. 1 for orchestra, and *Autumnal* (revision of Op. 11 No. 1)

Op. 37 the unpublished Prelude No. 1 in the British Library is indicated as 'Op. 37' by Scott on the manuscript (see above, 'Catalogue of Cyril Scott's Music', note on S 171), and *At Dawn* and *Shadows* were published as Op. 37 No. 1 and No. 2.

Opus		S no.	Title	Genre	Composed	Published
1	1/1	282	*April Love*	Song	1900	[1900]
	1/2	283	*Ad domnulam suam*	Song	1900	[1900]
	1/3	284	*Soli cantare periti arcades*	Song	1900	
		285	*Yvonne of Brittany*	Song	1900	
1		281	*Sänge eines fahrenden Spielmanns*	Songs (6)	Apr. 1898	
2		164	*Three Frivolous Pieces*	Pf	1898–9	1903
3			*Two Songs:*			
	3/1	282a	*April Love* (published version = 1/1)	Song		1903
	3/2	283a	*Little Lady of my Heart* (= 1/2)	Song	1900	1903
3		87	Piano Trio in E minor	Chamber	*c.* 1899	
4		166	*Six Pieces*	Pf	1898–9	1903
5			*Two Songs:*			
	5/1	284a	*Dairy Song*	Song	1900	1903
	5/2	285	*Yvonne of Brittany*	Song	1900	1903
5		35	*Pelleas and Melisanda*, overture	Orch	1 Feb. 1900	[2012]
6		36	*Lyric Suite*	Orch	1900	
7		37	*Heroic Suite*	Orch	1900	
8		84	*The Ballad of Fair Helen of Kirkconnel*	Bar/orch (pf)	1900	
9	9/1	286	*Daphnis and Chloe*	Song	*c.* 1900	1904
	9/2	287	*Exile*	Song	*c.* 1900	
	9/3	288	*Vesperal*	Song	Apr. 1900	
10		68	Concerto in D	Pf/orch	1900	[2012]
		47	*Christmas Overture*	Orch	*c.* 1900	
11	11/1	289	*Autumnal*	Song	*c.* 1900	
	11/2	290	*The Sands of Dee*	Song	*c.* 1900	
12		38	*Symphonic Fantasia*	Orch	*c.* 1900	
12		99	String Quartet	Chamber	*c.* 1900	
13		291	*Ballad of Dark Rosaleen*	Song	*c.* 1900	
14			[*deest*] (possibly Symphony No. 1, S 34)			
15		163	*An English Waltz*	Pf	1898–9	1903
16		86	Piano Quartet	Chamber	1899–1901	1903
17		167	Sonata in D major (*Handelian Rhapsody*)	Pf	Sept. 1901	[1909]
18		40	*Princess Maleine*, overture	Orch	1899–1902	
19		69	Cello Concerto	Vc/orch	1902	[2012]
20		168	*Three Dances*	Pf	1902?	1903
20		35	*Pelleas and Melisanda* (revised)	Orch	*c.* 1902	[2012]

Opus		S no.	Title	Genre	Composed	Published
21		41	*Aglavaine et Selysette*, overture	Orch	*c.* 1902	
22		46	Symphony No. 2 / *Three Symphonic Dances*	Orch	1901–2	[1922]
23			[*deest*] (possibly the *Magnificat*, S 15)			
24			*Two Poems:*			
	24/1	293	*Voices of Vision*	Song	Mar. 1903	1903
	24/2	294	*Willows*	Song	Mar. 1903	1903
25		169	*Scherzo*	Pf	1902?	1904
26		89	Sextet for piano & strings	Chamber	*c.* 1903	
27		26	*Dixit Dominus*	Chorus	1903	
28		100	String Quartet	Chamber	*c.* 1903	
29		295	*Greek Song*	Song	*c.* 1903	
30			*Two Songs:*			
	30/1	296	*A Last Word*	Song		1903
	30/2	297	*There Comes an End to Summer*	Song		1903
31	31/1	298	*Asleep*	Song		1903
31		101	String Quartet, F+	Chamber	*c.* 1904	
32	32/1	299	*Autumnal* (revision of Op. 11)	Song	*c.* 1900	1904
32		43	*Rhapsody for orchestra No. 1*	Orch	*c.* 1904	
33	33/1		[*deest*]			
	33/2		[*deest*]			
	33/3	300	*Villanelle*	Song		1904
34		301	*Evening Hymn*	Song		1904
35		170	*Two Pierrot Pieces:*			
	35/1		*Lento*	Pf	1901?	1904
	35/2		*Allegro*	Pf	1901?	1904
36	36/1	302	*A Valediction*	Song		1904
	36/2	303	*Sorrow*	Song		1904
37		172	*Two Piano Pieces:*			
	37/1		*At Dawn*	Pf		1904
	37/2		*Shadows*	Pf		1904
'37'		171	Prelude	Pf	1904?	
38	38/1	304	*My Captain*	Song		1904
	38/2	305	*Trafalgar*	Song		1904
39	39/1	173	*Dagobah*	Pf		1904
	39/2	174	*Chinese Serenade*	Pf		1904
40	40/1	175	*Solitude*	Pf		1904

Opus		S no.	Title	Genre	Composed	Published
	40/2	176	*Vesperale*	Pf		1904
	40/3	177	*Chimes*	Pf		1904
41		178	*Impromptu (A Mountain Brook)*	Pf		1904
42	42/1	306	*Eileen*	Song		1904
	42/2	307	*The Ballad Singer*	Song		1904
	42/3	308	*Mary*	Song		1904
43	43/1	309	*A Gift of Silence*	Song		1905
	43/2	310	*Don't Come in Sir, Please!*	Song		1905
	43/3	311	*The White Knight*	Song		1905
	43/4	312	*A Reflection*	Song		1905
44			[*deest*]			
45			[*deest*]			
46			*Two Chinese Songs (1 & 2):*			
	46/1	313	*Waiting*	Song		1906
	46/2	314	*A Picnic*	Song		1906
	46/3	315	*A Song of Wine*	Song		1907
47	47/1	179	*Lotus Land*	Pf		1905
	47/2	180	*Columbine*	Pf		1905
48			[*deest*]			
49			[*deest*]			
50	50/1	316	*Afterday*	Song		1906
	50/2	181	*Asphodel*	Pf		1906
51			[*deest*]			
52	52/1	317	*A Song of London*	Song		1906
	52/2	318	*A Roundel of Rest*	Song		1906
	52/3	319	*Blackbird's Song*	Song		1906
53			[*deest*] (possibly the 1907 Quintet for piano and strings)			
54	54/1–4	182	*Summerland*	Pf		1907
	54/5	186	*Notturno*	Pf		1908
55			*Old English Lyrics (1 & 2):*			
	55/1	321	*Lovely Kind and Kindly Loving*	Song		1907
	55/2	322	*Why so Pale and Wan?*	Song		1907
	55/3	323	*Love's Quarrel*	Song		1907
56			*Two Songs:*			
	56/1	324	*Atwain*	Song		1907
	56/2	325	*Insouciance*	Song		1907

Opus		S no.	Title	Genre	Composed	Published
57			*Three Songs (1–3):*			
	57/1	326	*Prelude*	Song		1908
	57/2	327	*Lullaby*	Song		1908
	57/3	328	*A Scotch Lullabye*	Song	1908?	1910
	57/4–5	183	*Two Sketches*	Pf		1907
58	58/1–3	165	*Three Little Waltzes*	Pf	1898-99	1906
	58/4	184	*Two Alpine Sketches*	Pf		1908
	58/5	185	*Danse nègre*	Pf		1908
59		119	Violin Sonata No. 1, C+	Vln/pf	1908	1910
60			[*deest*]			
61			*Two Songs:*			
	61/1	329	*A Serenade*	Song		1908
	61/2	330	*In a Fairy Boat*	Song		1908
62			*Three Songs:*			
	62/1	331	*A Lost Love*	Song		1908
	62/2	332	*A Vision*	Song		1908
	62/3	333	*An Eastern Lament*	Song		1909
63		187	*Sphinx*	Pf		1908
64	64/1	188	*Etude I*	Pf		1908
	64/2	189	*Etude II*	Pf		1908
65		335	*And So I Made a Villanelle*	Song		1908
66		190	Sonata No.1	Pf	1908	1909
67			*Four Pieces for Piano:*			
	67/1	191	*Mazurka*	Pf		1909
	67/2	192	*Serenata*	Pf		1909
	67/3	193	*Intermezzo*	Pf		1910
	67/4	194	*Soirée japonaise*	Pf		1910
68			*Two Songs:*			
	68/1	336	*Daffodils*	Song		1909
	68/2	337	*Osme's Song*	Song		1909
69			[*deest*]			
70	70/1	338	*My Lady Sleeps*	Song		1910
	70/2	339	*Mirage*	Song		1910
71	71/1	195	*Suite … in the Old Style*	Pf		1910
	71/2	340	*Evening*	Song		1910
	71/3	196	*Water-Wagtail*	Pf		1910
72			*Four Songs:*			
	72/1	341	*A Spring Ditty*	Song		1910

Opus		S no.	Title	Genre	Composed	Published
	72/2	342	*Arietta*	Song		1910
	72/3	343	*The Trysting Tree*	Song		1910
	72/4	344	*The Valley of Silence*	Song		1911
73	73/1	120	*Elegy*	Vln/pf		1910
	73/2	121	*Romance*	Vln/pf		1910
	73/3	122	*Valse triste*	Vln/pf		1910
	73/4	123	*Tallahassee Suite*	Vln/pf		1910–11
74	74/1–3	197	*Trois danses tristes*	Pf		1910
	74/4	345	*The Unforeseen*	Song		1911
	74/5	346	*Villanelle of the Poet's Road*	Song	1910	1911
	74/6	347	*The New Moon*	Song		1911
	74/7	198	*Valse caprice*	Pf		1911
	74/8	199	*Chansonette*	Pf		1911
75		200	*Deuxième suite*	Pf		1910
76			[*deest*]			
77		45	*Aubade*	Orch	1905	1911

iv

Catalogue of Cyril Scott's Writings

COMPILED BY LESLIE DE'ATH

Books are listed chronologically by date of publication, and numbered SW 1, SW 2, SW 3 etc. Only separate monographs are included in this list. Later impressions of the same edition are not provided. An indefatigable writer, Scott contributed about 100 articles to a variety of music journals (*The Monthly Musical Record* / *The Sackbut* / *The Etude* / *The Chesterian* / *The Musical Quarterly* / *The Musical Standard* / *Music & Letters*) between 1913 and 1969. Such articles have not been included here. For a complete list, see Laurie J. Sampsel, *Cyril Scott: A Bio-Bibliography*, pp. 115–44.

The following abbreviations are used in the list:

BC	*Bone of Contention*
D	dedication
MYI	*My Years of Indiscretion*
R	reference

BOOKS AND MONOGRAPHS

SW	S (Sampsel)	Details
1	105	*The Shadows of Silence and The Songs of Yesterday*, n.d. [*c.* 1906] (Liverpool: Donald Fraser), iv, 42p D: 'To Charles Bonnier, John Sampson and Henry Devenish Harben, my three most sympathetic Souls upon the poetic path.' Note: A metal-fastened volume. The date can be inferred from SW 14, p. 56.
2	106	*The Grave of Eros and The Book of Mournful Melodies with Dreams from the East*, 1907 (Liverpool: Donald Fraser / London: Lyceum Press) D: 'To the poet Stefan George, the Awakener within me of all Poetry.'
3	107	[Charles Baudelaire] *Baudelaire: The Flowers of Evil, translated into English verse* (= *Les fleurs du mal*), 1909, Vigo Cabinet Series 66 (London: Elkin Mathews), 63p 1924, 2nd edn (London: Elkin Mathews) D: Arthur Symons R: *MYI*, 56
4	108	[Stefan George] *Stefan George: Selection from his Works*, 1910, Vigo Cabinet Series 71 (London: Elkin Mathews), 63p R: *MYI*, 56
5	109	*The Voice of the Ancient*, 1910 (London: J. M. Watkins), 63p R: *MYI*, 77
6	110	*The Vales of Unity*, 1912 (London: David Nutt), 56p D: 'To Charles Tilson Chowne in that Unity of Friendship which makes life truly golden.' R: *MYI*, 210 Note: See also SW 45.
7	–	*The Real Tolerance*, n.d. [1913] (London: A[rthur] C[harles] Fifield), unpaginated D: 'Dedicated to Those who can understand.' Note: Published anonymously.
8	111	*The Celestial Aftermath, A Springtide of the Heart, and Far-away Songs*, 1915 (London: Chatto & Windus), 68p D: 'In remembrance of my sister-friend Maude Roosevelt, the one who has gone but will always remain.' R: *MYI*, 210 Note: The first poem is a 'Prelude for M.R.' See also SW 45.
9	–	*The Way of the Childish: Bálamatimárga. Written down by the author of 'The Real Tolerance'*, 1916 (London: Kegan Paul), 88p 1920, 2nd edn (London: Kegan Paul, Trench, Trubner / New York: E. P. Dutton), 91p Note: The teachings of Shri Âdvaitâchârya, written down by 'The transcriber'. R: *MYI*, 233
10	26	*The Philosophy of Modernism (in its Connection with Music)*, n.d. [1917], The Music-Lover's Library (London: Kegan Paul, Trench, Trubner), 135p n.d. [*c.* 1925], 2nd edn, published as *The Philosophy of Modernism – Its Connection with Music*, bound together with A. Eaglefield Hull's *Cyril Scott: The Man and his Works*, The Waverley Music Lovers' Library (London: The Waverly Book Co.), 135 + 195p D: 'To my friends and publishers W. Elkin and W. Strecker this book is gratefully and affectionately dedicated.' R: *MYI*, 121, 213 / *BC*, 146, 149

SW	S (Sampsel)	Details
11	113	*The Initiate: Some Impressions of a Great Soul / by His Pupil*, 1920 (London: George Routledge & Sons), ix, 381p 1947, trans. Gabrielle Godet as *L'Initié: Quelques impressions sur une grande âme par son élève* (Neuchâtel: Ed. de la Baconnière), 302p 1957 (2nd ed. 1983), trans. Paula Biehe as *Den indviede: Beretningen om en stor sjael* (Copenhagen: Strube), 250p 1971 (York Beach, Maine: Samuel Weiser), 396p (1971) 1977, 1st paperback edn (from the 1971 edn) (York Beach, Maine: Samuel Weiser), xv, 380p 1980, trans. Manuel Algora Corbí as *El iniciado: Algunas impresiones de una gran alma – Su pupilo* (Madrid: Luis Cárcamo), 256p 1983, as *Den invigde av hans Lärjunge* (Stockholm: Bim Bok), 366p 1985, as *Den indviede* (Ballerup: Bibliothekscentralen), audiobook, *c.* 514 min., read by Paul Becker 1985, trans. Karl Friedrich Hörner as *Eindrücke von einer großen Seele, von seinem Schüler*, Knaur-Taschenbücher 4133 (München: Droemer-Knaur), 252p 1992, trans. Kiyoshi Otaka as イニシエート：偉大なる魂についての印象 [*Inishiēto*] (Tokyo: Kuesuto), 335p 1997 (2nd edn 1999), trans. Alessandra Maccari as *La grande anima: Istruzioni spirituali di vita quotidiana* (Turin: Edizioni Synthesis), 274p 2001, trans. Gabrielle Godet as *L'Initié: Quelques impressions sur une grande âme par son élève* (Chêne-Bourg, Suisse: Ed. de la Baconnière / Montréal, Du Roseau), 318p 2007, trans. Karl Friedrich Hörner as *Der Eingeweihte: Eindrücke einer großen Seele* (Grafing: Aquamarin) 216p D: 'To that great soul whose identity is concealed under the name of Justin Moreward Haig these impressions are gratefully and lovingly dedicated.' R: *BC*, 146, 176 Note: Published anonymously. According to Scott, the book's anonymity was not disclosed until two decades later (*BC*, 146).
12	112	*The Adept of Galilee: A Story and an Argument, by the Author of 'The Initiate'*, 1920 (London: George Routledge & Sons / New York: E. P. Dutton) viii, 434p D: 'This book is lovingly dedicated to my Friend of many lives, T. E. J. E.' / 'That joyous, wise and beautiful Soul, who was with the Adept of Galilee in the days of His Ministry.' R: *BC*, 146 Note: Published anonymously. Most of the book (pp. 115–426) is a Gospel story rewrite, in modern English.
13	114	*The Autobiography of a Child: Written from the Psycho-Sexual-Analytical Standpoint for Doctors, Teachers, and Psychologists*, 1921 (London: Kegan Paul, Trench, & Trubner), xv, 389p D: 'To my Fellow-Student of Psycho-Analysis / R. S. / I dedicate this Victorian Reminiscence. Thanking him for his Help and Advice' R: *BC*, 34 (this confirms Scott as the author) Note: Published anonymously, although certainly by Scott. Banned for obscenity by Lord Alfred Douglas.
14	48	*My Years of Indiscretion*, 1924 (London: Mills & Boon) 282p D: 'To the friends of my student-days Percy Grainger, Roger Quilter and Balfour Gardiner I affectionately inscribe these memoirs.' R: *BC*, 64, 80, 107, 178

SW	S (Sampsel)	Details
15	115	*The Initiate in the New World: A Sequel to 'The Initiate', by his Pupil*, 1927 (London: George Routledge & Sons / New York: E. P. Dutton) x, 302p 1947, trans. Gabrielle Godet as *L'Initié dans le nouveau monde. Par son élève* (Neuchâtel: La Baconnière), 245p 1959, trans. Paula Biehe as *Den indviede i den nye verden* (Copenhagen), 214p 1964, trans. Steinunn S. Briem as *Fullnuminn vestanhafs* (Reykjavik: Prensmiðjan Leiftur), 203p 1976, trans. Gabrielle Godet as *L'initié dans le Nouveau-Monde: Suite de L'Initié* (Neuchâtel: La Baconnière), 199p 1977 (York Beach, Maine: Red Wheel / Samuel Weiser), x, 302p 1981, trans. Manuel Molina Casado as *El Iniciado en el nuevo mundo – Su pupilo* (Madrid: Luis Cárcamo), 223p 1983, trans. Paula Biehe as *Den indviede i den nye verden* ([Viby Sj.]: Strube), 214p 1985 (Ballerup: Bibliothekscentralen), audiobook, *c.* 362 min., read by Paul Becker 1986, trans. Karl Friedrich Hörner as *Eindrücke von einer großen Seele 2*, Knaur-Taschenbücher 4163 (München: Droemer-Knaur), 351p (contains both SW 15 [pp. 9–207] and SW 19 [pp. 213–351]) 1998, trans. Daniela Bo as *Il maestro: Il benessere spirituale nellavita comune* (Turin: Edizioni Synthesis), 256p 2001, trans. Gabrielle Godet as *L'initié dans le Nouveau-Monde* (Chêne-Bourg, Suisse: De la Baconnière / Montréal, Du Roseau), 276p 2003, trans. Lars Adelskogh & Brigitta Manners Stålhammar as *Den invigde i nya världen* (Stockholm: Bim Bok), 280p 2007, trans. Karl Friedrich Hörner as *Der Eingeweihte, Bd. 2 – In der neuen Welt: Von seinem Schüler* (Grafing: Aquamarin), 216p Note: Published anonymously.
16	116	*The Art of Making a Perfect Husband. By a Husband*, 1928 (London: Noel Douglas), xi, 130p 1929 (New York and London: Harper & Bros.), xi, 145p D: 'To my wife without whose assistance and insight into woman's character this book could not have been written.' Note: Published anonymously. Consists of 84 maxims regarding marital wellbeing, as perceived by the author. The dust jackets differ on the 1928 and 1929 editions.
17	60	*The Influence of Music on History and Morals: A Vindication of Plato*, 1928 (London: Theosophical Publishing House), x, 245p D: 'Dedicated to the memory of Nelsa Chaplin'
18	117	*Childishness: A Study in Adult Conduct*, 1930 (London: John Bale, Sons & Danielsson), vi, 102p D: 'To Dr. P. A. B.'

SW	S (Sampsel)	Details
19	119	*The Initiate in the Dark Cycle: A Sequel to 'The Initiate' and to 'The Initiate in the New World' / by His Pupil*, 1932 (London: George Routledge & Sons / New York: E. P. Dutton), xvii, 215p 1947, trans. Gabrielle Godet as *L'Initié dans le cycle obscure [par son élève]: Suite de L'Initié et L'Initié dans le Nouveau-Monde* (Neuchâtel: La Baconnière), 172p 1954 (London: Routledge & Kegan Paul), 215p 1971 (1st US edn) / 1977 (paperback) (New York: Samuel Weiser), xvii, 215p 1983, trans. Paula Biehe and Finn Skøtt Andersen as *Den indviede vender tilbage* ([Viby Sj.]: Strube) 1991 (York Beach, Maine: Red Wheel / Weiser), 240p 2000, trans. Massimo Zenobi as *La grande anima e l'oscurità* (Turin: Edizioni Synthesis), 176p 2001, trans. Gabrielle Godet as *L'Initié dans le cycle obscure [par son élève]* (Chêne-Bourg, Suisse: De la Baconnière / Montréal, Du Roseau), 196p 2004, as *Den invigde i mörka cykeln* (Stockholm: Bim Bok), 216p 2007, trans. Karl Friedrich Hörner as *Der Eingeweihte, Bd. 3: Im dunklen Zyklus* (Grafing: Aquamarin), 154p 2011, as *El Iniciado en el ciclo oscuro*, Collección Adeptus (Barcelona: Escuelas de Misterios), 174p D: 'To those who have stood the test' Note: Published anonymously ('by his pupil').
20	77	*Music: Its Secret Influence Throughout the Ages*, 1933 (London: Rider & Co.), 221p n.d. [193–] (Philadelphia: David McKay), 221p 1950, 2nd edn (London: Rider & Co.), 127p 1958, 3rd edn (London: Rider & Co.), 208p 1958 (Wellingborough, Northamptonshire: The Aquarian Press), 208p 1958 (New York: Samuel Weiser), 208p 1960, trans. Hubert-J. Jamin as *La musique: Son influence secrète à travers les âges* (Neuchâtel: Ed. de la Baconnière), 245p 1968, trans. Janis Roze as *La música: Su influencia secreta a través de los tiempos* (Mexico City: Editorial Orión), 285p 1969, 4th edn (New York: Samuel Weiser), 208p 1975, as *Musikens makt* (Täby: Larson), 186p 1985, trans. Sylvia Luetjohann as *Musik: Ihr geheimer Einfluss durch die Jahrhunderte* (Munich: Hirthammer), 275p 1991 (2nd German edn) (Munich: Hirthammer), 275p 1996 (Santa Fe, NM: Sun Books) (SB-323), 221p 1998 (Hastings: Society of Metaphysicians), 221p 2005, as *L'influenza segreta della musica: Un viaggio attraverso i secoli* (Turin: Edizioni Synthesis), 227p n.d., as *La música … y la evolución humana* (Caracas: L.E.U. / Miami: E.U.B.), 224p 2011, as *La Música: Su secreta influencia a través de las edades*, Collección Philosophus (Barcelona: Escuelas de Misterios), 231p 2013, 5th edn, published as *Music and Its Secret Influence Throughout the Ages*, with a new introduction by Desmond Scott (Rochester, VT / Toronto: Inner Traditions), 213p D: 'This book is gratefully dedicated to master Koot Hoomi Lal Singh and to the memory of his pupil Nelsa Chaplin.' R: *BC*, 186–8

SW	S (Sampsel)	Details
21	121	*The Vision of the Nazarene (Set down by the author of 'THE INITIATE' etc.)*, illustrated by David Anrias, 1933 (London: George Routledge & Sons / New York: E. P. Dutton), xi, 126p 1954, trans. Ketty Jentzer and Henriette C. Champury, as *Vision du Nazaréen* (Neuchâtel: Ed. de la Baconnière), 160p 1955, 2nd edn (n.p. [Suffolk]: Neville Spearman / San Jacinto, CA: Institute of Esoteric Philosophy), xv, 112p 1975 (New York: Samuel Weiser), xv, 112p 1986, as *Una visión del Nazareno* (Málaga: Editorial Sirio), 108p 1999, trans. Daniela Bonnier as *Lui: Colloqui spirituali* (Turin: Edizioni Synthesis), 140p 2000 (York Beach, Maine: Samuel Weiser), xv, 112p 2001, as *Vision du Nazaréen* (Chêne-Bourg, Switz: La Baconnière / Montréal, Du Roseau) 2001, as *Una visión del Nazareno* (Rio de Janeiro: Editorial Sirio), 108p 2012, as *O jardim secreto de Jesus de Nazaré*, postscript by Desmond Scott (Sao Paulo: Barany Editora), 152p Note: Published anonymously. 'Set down by the author of "The Initiate".'
22	123	*An Outline of Modern Occultism*, 1935 (London: George Routledge & Sons / New York, E. P. Dutton), viii, 239p 1950, 2nd edn (London: Routledge & Kegan Paul), x, 226p 1976, as *Ocultismo contemporáneo* (Guayaquil / Bogotá: Editorial Ariel Ltda), 173p 1993, trans. Ilie N. Iliescu as *Ocultismul modern* (Bucharest: Editura Princeps), 206p D: 'To the memory of J. B. P. and those groups of seekers who have given me so much encouragement in regard to my earlier books' R: *BC*, 176, 200
23	124	*The Greater Awareness: A Sequel to 'An Outline of Modern Occultism'*, 1936 (London: George Routledge & Sons / New York: E. P. Dutton), xii, 243p 1981 (York Beach, Maine: Samuel Weiser), xii, 243p
24	125	*Doctors, Disease, and Health: A Critical Survey of Therapeutics Modern and Ancient*, 1938 (London: Methuen / Cleveland, OH: Sherwood Press), xi, 283p 1946, 2nd edn (London: True Health Publishing), xi, 313p
25	126	*The Ghost of a Smile*, 1939 (London: Andrew Dakers), 199p D: 'To my three oldest friends Percy Grainger, Roger Quilter and Balfour Gardiner this book is affectionately dedicated.'
26	127	*Man is my Theme: A Study of National and Individual Conduct*, 1939 (London: Andrew Dakers), 303p D: 'Dedication cum Preface to Doris Langley Moore …' (letter to Moore, thanking her for her encouragement to write, and her hospitality during the writing process, pp. 5–6) Note: Scott's alternative title, unused, was *The Moron Mind* (see Preface to SW 29).
27	128	*Victory Over Cancer Without Radium or Surgery: A Survey of Cancer Causes and Cancer Treatments*, 1939 (London: Methuen / Cleveland, OH: Sherwood Press), xvi, 271p 1947 (London: True Health Publishing), xvii, 308p 1957, 2nd edn (London: True Health Publishing), xiv, 170p 1969 (Rustington, Sussex: Health Science Press), 168p D: 'To Alice M. Sherwen who in memory of her mother, Sarah A. Sherwen, set out on the quest which indirectly gave rise to this book.' Alternative title: *Victory Over Cancer Without Radium or Surgery: A Book Dealing with Cancer Causation, Cancer Prevention, and Cancer Cures for Laymen and Doctors*

SW	S (Sampsel)	Details
28	129	*Health, Diet and Commonsense*, 1940 (London: Andrew Dakers), 191p 1944, 1950, 2nd edn (London: Homeopathic Publishing), 198p 1950 (Wayside: Health Science Press), 199p D: 'To my friend Charles Douglas W. Stafford who has given me so much help and encouragement during the writing of my therapeutical books.'
29	130	*The Christian Paradox: What is, As Against What Should Have Been*, n.d. [1942] (London, New York and Melbourne: Rider & Co.), 144p 1966 (Mokelumne Hill, California: Health Research), ringbound, 144p 1996 (Kila, MT: Kessinger Publishing), 144p
30	–	*Near the End of Life: [Some] Candid Confessions and Reflections* [1942], unpublished typescript written at Broomhill and Barnstaple (Preface dated April 1942), 359p Note: Includes a works list, with publishers and approximate timings.
31	131	*The Poems of a Musician* [1943], completed September 1943; unpublished during Scott's lifetime 2006 (Toronto: Desmond Scott), typescript facsimile edition with introduction by Desmond Scott, 5 + 101p I – Nature-lyrics and songs of the heart (15 poems) II – Through other eyes (3 poems) III – Rhetorical and mystical poems (7 poems, including the important 'If he should speak to-day 1939–1943') IV – Miscellaneous poems (8 poems) V – Translations from the German (17 translations of Goethe, Heine, Hebbel, Hölderlin, Meyer, etc.)
32	–	*The Rhymed Reflections of a Ruthless Rhymer* [1944], unpublished typescript, done completely in rhyming couplets Note: In subject matter, belongs with SW 18, 26, and 38.
33	133	*Medicine Rational and Irrational*, n.d. [1946] (London: True Health Publishing), 224p

SW	S (Sampsel)	Details
34	132	*Crude Black Molasses: Nature's Wonder Food*, 1946, published as *Crude Black Molasses: The Natural 'Wonder-food'* (London: True Health Publishing), 36p n.d. [1949], 2nd edn (London: True Health Publishing), 37p [n.d.] (Stockwell, London: True Health Publishing), 37p 1968 (London, Athene Publishing), 47p 1968, 3rd edn (Wellingborough, Northamptonshire: Athene Publishing), 48p 1970, trans. Carole Blanc as *La mélasse noire crue: Un aliment-miracle naturel* (Brétigny: Deltapress), 32p 1970, trans. unspecified, as *Die rohe schwarze Melasse: Eine natürliche 'Wundernahrung'* (Wetzikon and Zürich: Otto Hasler), 40p 1980 (New York: Benedict Lust Publications), 92p 1982, trans. Andres Linares as *Las melazas: El maravilloso alimento de la naturaleza*, Plus Vitae 74 (Madrid: EDAF), 76p 1982, trans. Päivi Koikkalainen as *Karkea tumma melassi: Luonnon ihmeruoka* (Espoo: Suomen terveyskirjat), 47p 1983, as *Das schwarze Wunder: Rohe schwarze Zuckerrohr-Melasse, eine natürliche Wundernahrung* (Wetzikon: Otto Hasler), 40p 1985, trans. Carole Blanc as *La mélasse noire crue: Un aliment-miracle naturel* (Wetzikon: Otto Hasler), 42p 1985, trans. Silvana Witzig-Faccoli as *La melassa nera: Un vero miracolo della natura* (Wetzikon: Otto Hasler), 39p 1988, as *Die rohe schwarze Melasse: Eine natürliche 'Wundernahrung'* (Wetzikon and Zürich: Schweiz Hasler), 40p 1995, as *Die rohe schwarze Melasse: Eine natürliche 'Wundernahrung'* (Dulliken, Switzerland: Vita Reform), 40p 2003, trans. Päivi Koikkalainen as *Karkea tumma melassi: Luonnon ihmeruoka* (Turku: Suomen terveyskirjat), 47p Note: The early publication history of this popular volume is difficult to unravel. Most are undated, and a variety of 'edition' numbers are encountered. Later editions sometimes incorrectly state 'first published 1949'. The subtitle can be 'Nature's Wonder Food', 'A Natural Wonder Food', or 'The Natural Wonder-food'.
35	135	*Cider Vinegar: Nature's Great Health-Promoter and Safest Cure [Treatment] of Obesity*, 1948 (London: Athene Publishing), 38p n.d. [1948] (London: True Health Publishing), 40p 1968, 6th edn (London: Athene Publishing), 47p 196–? (Simi Valley, CA: Benedict Lust Publications), 40p 1974, as *Für deine Gesundheit: Apfelessig* (Wetzikon: Otto Hasler), 32p 1984, as *Homets tapuhim: ha-mesaye'a ha-beri'uti ha-gadol be-yoter shel ha-teva'* (Tel-Aviv: Or-ţeva'), 43p 1985, trans. Renata Hasler-Colombo as *Per la tua salute – L'aceto di mele: anche combinato con il miele* (Wetzikon: Otto Hasler), 31p 1986, trans. Rachel Garrow as *Le vinaigre de pommes pour la santé: Combiné aussi avec le miel* (Wetzikon: Otto Hasler), 34p

SW	S (Sampsel)	Details
36	136	*Die Tragödie Stefan Georges: Ein Erinnerungsbild und ein Gang durch sein Werk* (Rheingauer Drucke, 5. Druck) 1952, trans. Ilse Schneider (Eltville am Rhein: Lothar Hempe), 91p D: 'August Closs Ph.D., M.A. gewidmet, dessen großzügige Ermutigung mir zur Förderung gereichte.' Note: Published in a deluxe limited edition of 350 exemplars, in slipcase. Compiler has presentation copy to Closs from Scott, with tipped-in photo cabinet card, 'To my friends August & Hannah Closs with all the good wishes of Cyril Scott, Xmas /44.'
37	137	*The Boy Who Saw True*, 1953 (New York and London: Peter Nevill), 248p 1953(Saffron Walden: C.W. Daniel), 248p 1953 (Suffolk, Neville Spearman), 248p 1966 (London: Hillman & Sons) 1970 (New York: Samuel Weiser) 1984, trans. Susanne Göbert-Harrington as *Die Junge mit den lichten Augen* (Forstinning/Munich: Aquamarin), 200p 1990, trans. Susanne Göbert-Harrington as *Die Junge mit den lichten Augen* (Grafing: Aquamarin), 200p 1993, trans. Vivian Franken as *De jongen die helder zag* (Deventer: Ankh-Hermes), 203p 1997, trans. Ramón H. Ramírez Estrada as *El niño que veía la otra realidad* (Mexico City, Grupo Editorial Planeta), 248p 1999 , trans. Wenhua Cai and Shi chang fan yi she as 看見真相的小男孩 [*Kan jian zhen xiang de xiao nan hai*] (Banqiao Shi : Ru lai yin jing hui), 304p 2004, ([UK]: Random House), 256p 2004 (London: Rider), 248p 2005, as 通靈日記 : 看見真相的男孩 [*Tong ling ri ji : kan jian zhen xiang de nan hai*] (Taipei, 方智出版 : 叩應總經銷 [*Fang zhi chu ban : Kou ying zong jing xiao*]) 2010, trans. Barbara Škarja, Barbara Škoberne and Darja Cvek Mihajlović as *Deček, ki je videl Resnično* (Ljubljana: CDK – Zavod za izobraževanje, vzgojo, razvoj in kulturo), 197p 2011 ([UK]: Ebury Publishing / Random House)
38	138	*Man the Unruly Child*, 1953 (London: The Aquarian Press), 97p
39	139	*Simpler and Safer Remedies for Grievous Ills* [1953] (London: Athene Publishing), 110p
40	140	*Sleeplessness: Its Prevention and Cure by Harmless Methods*, 1955 (London: Athene Publishing; later Wellingborough, Northamptonshire), 32p / 47p (1969) 1982, as *Good Sleep Without Drugs: Natural Remedies for Sleeplessness* (Kewaunee, WI: Benedict Lust) 1986, trans. Timo Laurila as *Unettomuus* ([Helsinki]: Biokustannus), 51p
41	141	*Constipation and Common Sense*, [1956] (London: Athene Publishing), 40p 1969, 2nd edn (London: Athene Publishing; later Wellingborough, Northamptonshire), 48p
42	142	*Occultism: An Alternative to Scientific Humanism. A Lecture given for the Truth Forum at The Caxton Hall on June 13th, 1956*, 1956 (London: L. N. Fowler), 16p 1990, repr. edn (Society of Metaphysicians) 1996, repr. edn (Mokelumne Hill, CA: Health Research)
43	143	*Cancer Prevention: Fallacies and Some Reassuring Facts*, 1968 (London: Athene Publishing; later Wellingborough, Northamptonshire), 48p *c.* 1985–90, as Καρκινος: Μερικα ενθαρρυντικα γεγονοτα ια την προληψη του (Athens: Dioptra)

SW	S (Sampsel)	Details
44	101	*Bone of Contention: Life Story and Confessions,* 1969 (New York: Arco Publications), 242p 1969 (London: Aquarian Press), 242p. This edition was also released in a leather-bound hardcover limited edition of 150 copies, with ribbed spine and a gold crest on the front [ISBN 850300436]. Copy 1, signed by Scott, is with the estate. 2003, trans. Mauro Challier as *Una vita ben spesa* (Turin: Edizioni Synthesis), 310p D: 'To Marjorie, without whose encouragement I might have lacked the will to complete this self-revealing book.' Note: Much of the writing of this late autobiography was accomplished during the early 1950s. The unpublished *Near the End of Life* (SW 30) contains material that appears to have been reworked into *Bone of Contention* at this time. On page 70, Scott states, 'At the time of writing this chapter he [Grainger] is playing my *Piano Sonata No. 1* on tour – a work I wrote some forty-five years ago.' This would date the writing to the early 1950s. Confirmation of this comes from letters Scott sent to Grainger in 1952: 'I am busy writing my autobiographical confessions – by way of literary interlude!' (14 February) / 'Have written 20 chapters of my Autobiography, but have laid it aside now for a while for creative work. Shall only take it up when musical ideation runs dry again.' (19 March) / 'I have now all but finished my autobiography. It has been quite fun writing it, though I am glad it is now off my chest and I can now return to musical activities.' (3 July) [communication from Sarah Collins to Desmond Scott, 29 January 2014].
45	–	*The Master from the Mountains of Eternity* There is a reference to this title in *The Vales of Unity* as a work 'in preparation', but no such title was ever published. Collins (*The Aesthetic Life of Cyril Scott*, p. 10) surmises that the collection was subsumed into the 1915 *The Celestial Aftermath.*

FOREWORDS AND INTRODUCTIONS

SW	S (Sampsel)	Details
46	118	David Anrias, *Through the Eyes of the Masters: Meditations and Portraits …* 1932 (London: G. Routledge & Sons), ix, 69p 1936, 2nd edn (London: George Routledge & Sons), xiv, 81p 1947, 3rd edn (London: Routledge & Kegan Paul), xvii, 78p 1971 (New York: Samuel Weiser), xvii, 78p Note: Scott's introduction comprises over half the volume. R: *BC*, 199, 215
47	120	H. K. Challoner [= J. M. A. Mills], *Watchers of the Seven Spheres*, 1933 (London: George Routledge & Son), 85p 1933 (New York: E. P. Dutton), xv, 85p
48	135	H. K. Challoner [= J. M. A. Mills], *The Wheel of Rebirth*, 1935 (London: Rider), 285p 1969 (Theosophical Publishing House), 285p
49	134	Vanda Sawtell, *Astro-Biochemistry*, 1947 (London: True Health Publishing / Rustington, Sussex: Health Science Press), 56p
50	–	J. H. Oliver, *Proven Remedies*, 1949 (London: Thorsons Publishers), 92p (Scott's preface on pp. 5–8)
51	----	Dorothy Shepherd, *A Physician's Posy*, 1951 (Bognor Regis, Sussex: Health Science Press), 291p 1951 (London: True Health Publishing), 291p 1969, 2nd edn (Rustington, Sussex: Health Science Press), 256p 1983 (New Delhi: Jain Publishing) 1993 (Saffron Walden: C. W. Daniel), 256p
52	–	Maryla de Chrapowicki, *Biotonic Therapy: Therapeutic Use of Life Energy*, 1951 (London: C. W. Daniel)

CLASSIFIED INDEX OF BOOKS AND MONOGRAPHS

When a book appears to fit into more than one category, it is relisted.

SW	Date	Title
Poetry		
1	c. 1906	*The Shadows of Silence and The Songs of Yesterday*
2	1907	*The Grave of Eros and The Book of Mournful Melodies with Dreams from the East*
5	1910	*The Voice of the Ancient*
6	1912	*The Vales of Unity*
7	1913	*The Real Tolerance*
8	1915	*The Celestial Aftermath, A Springtide of the Heart, and Far-away Songs*
31	[1943]	*The Poems of a Musician*
32	[1944]	*The Rhymed Reflections of a Ruthless Rhymer*
Poetry of others, translated		
3	1909	[Charles Baudelaire], *Baudelaire: The Flowers of Evil (= Les fleurs du mal)*
4	1910	[Stefan George], *Stefan George: Selection from his Works*
Music		
10	1917	*The Philosophy of Modernism (In its Connection with Music)*
17	1928	*The Influence of Music on History and Morals: A Vindication of Plato*
20	1933	*Music: Its Secret Influence Throughout the Ages*
Health		
24	1938	*Doctors, Disease, and Health: A Critical Survey of Therapeutics, Modern and Ancient*
27	1939	*Victory Over Cancer Without Radium or Surgery: A Book Dealing with Cancer Causation, Cancer Prevention, and Cancer Cures for Laymen and Doctors*
28	1940	*Health, Diet and Commonsense*
33	1946	*Medicine Rational and Irrational*
34	1947	*Crude Black Molasses: Nature's Wonder Food*
35	1948	*Cider Vinegar: Nature's Great Health Promoter and Safest Treatment [Cure] of Obesity*
39	1953	*Simpler and Safer Remedies for Grievous Ills*
40	1955	*Sleeplessness: Its Prevention and Cure by Harmless Methods*
41	1956	*Constipation and Common Sense*
43	1968	*Cancer Prevention: Fallacies and Some Reassuring Facts*
[49	1947	Vanda Sawtell, *Astro-Biochemistry*]
[50	1949	J. H. Oliver, *Proven Remedies*]
[51	1952	Maryla de Chrapowicki, *Biotonic Therapy: Therapeutic Use of Life Energy*]
Religion / Occultism		
11	1920	*The Initiate: Some Impressions of a Great Soul, by His Pupil*
12	1920	*The Adept of Galilee: A Story and an Argument, by the Author of 'The Initiate'*

SW	Date	Title
15	1927	*The Initiate in the New World: The Sequel to The Initiate*
19	1932	*The Initiate in the Dark Cycle: A Sequel to 'The Initiate' and to 'The Initiate in the New World'*
20	1933	*Music: Its Secret Influence Throughout the Ages*
21	1933	*The Vision of the Nazarene*
22	1935	*An Outline of Modern Occultism*
23	1936	*The Greater Awareness: A Sequel to An Outline of Modern Occultism*
29	1942	*The Christian Paradox: What is, as Against What Should Have Been*
37	1953	*The Boy Who Saw True*
42	1956	*Occultism: An Alternative to Scientific Humanism.*
[46	1932	David Anrias, *Through the Eyes of the Masters: Meditations and Portraits …*]
[47	1933	H. K. Challoner, *Watchers of the Seven Spheres*]
[48	1935	H. K. Challoner, *The Wheel of Rebirth*]
[51	1951	Dorothy Shepherd, *A Physician's Posy*]
Ethics / Philosophy		
9	1916	*The Way of the Childish: Bálamatimárga. Written down by the author of 'The Real Tolerance'*
10	1917	*The Philosophy of Modernism (In its Connection with Music)*
17	1928	*The Influence of Music on History and Morals: A Vindication of Plato*
18	1930	*Childishness: A Study in Adult Conduct*
26	1939	*Man is my Theme: A Study of National and Individual Conduct*
29	1942	*The Christian Paradox: What is, as Against What Should Have Been*
32	[1944]	*The Rhymed Reflections of a Ruthless Rhymer*
38	1953	*Man, the Unruly Child*
Autobiography		
14	1924	*My Years of Indiscretion*
30	[1942]	*Near the End of Life: [Some] Candid Confessions and Reflections*
44	1969	*Bone of Contention: Life Story and Confessions*
Psychology / Miscellaneous		
13	1921	*The Autobiography of a Child: Written from the Psycho-Sexual-Analytical Standpoint for Doctors, Teachers, and Psychologists*
16	1928	*The Art of Making a Perfect Husband. By a Husband*
25	1939	*The Ghost of a Smile* (humour)
36	1952	*Die Tragödie Stefan Georges: Ein Erinnerungsbild und ein Gang durch sein Werk* (biography/literary criticism)

UNPUBLISHED PLAYS

For the four scripts for plays with music, see S. 3, 10, 12 and 13. The following are straight plays, all written under the pseudonym M. Arkwright Lundy.

SW	S (Sampsel)	Details
53	–	*Prigs in Clover: A Victorian Comedy*, 1940
54	–	*That Innocent Goodness*, undated
55	–	*Celebrity Pie*, 1939
56	–	*Not All Men Know*, undated
57	–	[Anthony Trollope], *Barchester Towers*, 1940
58	–	[Wilkie Collins], *The Moonstone*, undated
59	–	*Bad Samaritans*, 1940
60	–	*Mrs. Maplewood M.P.*, 1943
61	–	*Sacred Mother, Imp. (A Chinese Play)*, undated
62	–	*My Native Land, Good Night! (A Play about Byron and Shelley)*, 1944
63	–	*Though This be Madness …*, undated
64	–	*Casanova and Two Ladies (A Sidelight on 18th Century London Life)*, undated

LIBRETTO

SW	S (Sampsel)	Details
65	–	[Paul Hindemith], *Das Unaufhörliche* [*The Never-ending*], *c.* 1931 (Mainz: Schott) [BSS 32937], oratorio. Text: Gottfried Benn (English translation by Cyril Scott and Rose Allatini)

V

Published Writings by Rose Allatini

COMPILED BY LESLIE DE'ATH

Date	Pseudonym	Title	Publisher	Comments
1914	R. Allatini	*Happy Ever After*	Mills & Boon	
1915	R. Allatini	*Payment*	Andrew Melville Melrose	
1917	R. Allatini	*Root and Branch*	George Allen & Unwin	
1918	A. T. Fitzroy	*Despised and Rejected*	C. W. Daniel	banned book
1975			Arno Press / Ayer Co.	
1988			Gay Men's Publishing	Gay Modern Classics
1989			Carrier Pigeon	
2010			Yogh & Thorn Press	
2011			Pickering & Chatto	British Literature of World War I, vol. 4
2018			Persephone Books	centenary edition
1919	R. Allatini	*Requiem*	Martin Secker	
1921	R. Allatini	*When I was a Queen in Babylon*	Mills & Boon	
1928	R.L. Scott	*The Golden Key*	Q Theatre, Kew	play
1933	Mrs. Cyril Scott	*White Fire*	Martin Secker	
1935	Lucian Wainwright	*Waters' Meet*	Martin Secker	
1935	Lucian Wainwright	*Girl of Good Family*	Martin Secker	
1937	Lucian Wainwright	*Oracle*	Methuen	
1941	Eunice Buckley	*Family from Vienna*	Andrew Dakers	
1942	Eunice Buckley	*Destination Unknown*	Andrew Dakers	
1943	Eunice Buckley	*Blue Danube*	Andrew Dakers	
1945	Eunice Buckley	*Rhapsody for Strings*	Andrew Dakers	
1952	Eunice Buckley	*Music in the Woods*	Andrew Dakers	
1953	Eunice Buckley	*Arranged for Small Orchestra*	Andrew Dakers	
1955	Eunice Buckley	*Dark Rainbow*	Hodder & Stoughton	
1956	Eunice Buckley	*Shadow of a God*	Hodder & Stoughton	
1957	Eunice Buckley	*Instead of a Rocking Horse*	Hodder & Stoughton	
1958	Eunice Buckley	*Gift from Heaven*	Hodder & Stoughton	
1960	Eunice Buckley	*For Benefits Received*	Robert Hale	

Date	Pseudonym	Title	Publisher	Comments
1961	Eunice Buckley	*Fiorina*	Robert Hale	
1962	Eunice Buckley	*The Consuming Fire*	Robert Hale	
1963	Eunice Buckley	*Conjuring Trick*	Robert Hale	
1964	Eunice Buckley	*Lay the Ghosts*	Robert Hale	
1966	Eunice Buckley	*They Walk on Earth*	Robert Hale	
1967	Eunice Buckley	*The Man on the Rope*	Robert Hale	
1968	Eunice Buckley	*Diamonds in the Family*	Theosophical Publishing House	
1969	Eunice Buckley	*The Flaming Sword*	Robert Hale	
1969	Eunice Buckley	*If Wishes Were Horses*	Robert Hale	
1972	Eunice Buckley	*You've Got To Have Gold*	Robert Hale	
1977			Ulverscroft	large print edition
1972	Eunice Buckley	*Just Was My Lot*	Robert Hale	
1973	Eunice Buckley	*The Face Of The Tempter*	Robert Hale	
1974	Eunice Buckley	*To Walk Without Fear*	Robert Hale	
1975	Eunice Buckley	*Wonder-Worker*	Robert Hale	
1976	Eunice Buckley	*The Half Of My Kingdom*	Robert Hale	
1977	Eunice Buckley	*Prisoners Of Hate*	Robert Hale	
1978	Eunice Buckley	*Young Man Of Great Promise*	Robert Hale	
1978	Eunice Buckley	*Work Of Art*	Robert Hale	

vi

Select Bibliography

A FULL MONOGRAPHS

Collins, Sarah. *The Aesthetic Life of Cyril Scott* (Woodbridge: Boydell Press, 2013)

Fuller, Jean Overton. *Cyril Scott and a Hidden School: Towards the Peeling of an Onion*, Theosophical History Occasional Papers 7 (Fullerton, CA: Theosophical History, 1998)

Hull, A. Eaglefield. *Cyril Scott: Composer, Poet, and Philosopher* (London: Kegan Paul, Trench, Trubner, 1918; 2nd edn, 1919; 3rd edn, 1921)
– republished (London: Waverley Book Co. [*c.* 1925]), together with *The Philosophy of Modernism*
– republished (London: Best Books, 2001) [Reference: *MYI*, 78, 127]

Parrott, Ian. *Cyril Scott and his Piano Music* (London: Thames [1991])

Sampsel, Laurie J. *Cyril Scott: A Bio-Bibliography*, Bio-Bibliographies in Music (Westport, CN: Greenwood, 2000)

B EXCERPTS FROM MONOGRAPHS

Banfield, Stephen. *Sensibility and English Song: Critical Studies of the Early Twentieth Century*, vol. 2 (Cambridge: Cambridge University Press, 1985) [Scott, pp. 503–6]

Hardy, Lisa. *The British Piano Sonata, 1870–1945* (Woodbridge: Boydell Press, 2001) [Scott, pp. 53–68]

Schaarwächter, Jürgen. *Two Centuries of British Symphonies from the Beginnings to 1945*, 2 vols (Hildesheim: ELMS, 2015) [updated and expanded English-language version of *Die britische Sinfonie, 1914–1945* (Cologne: Christoph Dohr, 1995)] [Scott, vol. 1, pp. 298–303; vol. 2, pp 681–4]

C DISSERTATIONS

Bays, Geoffrey Alan. 'Selected English Piano Concerti, 1915-1934: Historical Background and Stylistic Analysis' (Tallahassee: Florida State University, 1995) (DMA dissertation)

Bond, Robert A. 'The Style of Cyril Scott' (Rochester: Eastman School of Music, 1952) (MA thesis)

Butler, Ronald Kenneth. 'The Influence of Theosophy on the Tradition of Speculative and Esoteric Theories of Music' (Nathan, Queensland: Griffith University, 2013) [esp. Chapter 7, 'Cyril Scott: A Theosophical True Believer', pp. 132–58]

Cahn, Peter. 'Das Hoch'sche Konservatorium in Frankfurt am Main (1878–1978)' (Frankfurt am Main: Johann Wolfgang Goethe University, 1979) (PhD dissertation)

Cheung, Ching-Loh. 'Cyril Scott's Piano Sonata, Op. 66: A Study of his Innovative Musical Language, with Three Recitals of Selected Works by Mozart, Schumann, Scriabin, Debussy, Ravel and Others' (Denton, TX: University of North Texas, 1995) (DMA dissertation)

Collins, Sarah. 'The Development of Cyril Scott's Aesthetic Thinking: An Interpretation Informed by Literary and Biographical Sources' (University of Queensland, School of Music, 2009) (PhD thesis)

Crystall, Ellen Barbara. 'Esoteric Traditions and Music in the Early Twentieth Century: With an Appraisal of Composer Cyril Scott' (New York: New York University, 1995) (PhD dissertation)

Darson, Thomas Henry. 'The Solo Piano Works of Cyril Scott' (New York: City University of New York, 1979) (PhD dissertation)

Dart, William J. 'Hubert Parry and Cyril Scott: Two Post-Victorian Songwriters' (Auckland: University of Auckland, 1977) (PhD dissertation)

Foreman, Ronald Lewis Edmund [Lewis]. 'The British Musical Renaissance: A Guide to Research', 3 vols (Fellowship of the Library Association, 1972) (FLA dissertation)

Ryu, Mihae. 'Songs by Cyril Scott' (Boston: Boston University, 2003) (DMA thesis)

D ONLINE RESOURCES

Cyril Scott: The Official Cyril Scott Website <http://www.cyrilscott.net/> [site design by Amanta Scott, the composer's granddaughter]

De'Ath, Leslie. 'Cyril Scott as Composer-Pianist and Author, with some Recent Perspectives' [available through <http://www.musicweb-international.com>]

Jones, Allan Clive. 'Cyril Scott, Segovia and the Sonatina for Guitar', lecture given at the *Symposium of the International Musicological Society (SIMS 2004)*, 11–16 July 2004, Melbourne, Australia <http://oro.open.ac.uk/40744/>

Scott, Desmond. 'Cyril Scott: A Man Whose Time has Come Again?' [available through <http://www.musicweb-international.com>]

E ARTICLES / CHAPTERS IN BOOKS

For a thorough listing of contemporaneous (pre-1950) articles and reviews of Scott, see Laurie J. Sampsel's *Cyril Scott: A Bio-Bibliography*, pp. 157–90.

Armstrong, Thomas. 'Cyril Scott: A Pioneer', *Musical Times* 100, no. 1399 (Sept. 1959), 453–4

—— 'The Frankfort Group', *Proceedings of the Royal Musical Association* 85 (1958–9), 1–16

Austin, Ernest. 'Myself and Others: A Series of Intimate Articles: No. 2, Cyril Scott', *Musical Opinion* 62, no. 741 (June 1939), 786–8

Cahn, Peter. 'Scott and the Frankfurt Gang', in *Das Hoch'sche Konservatorium in Frankfurt am Main (1878–1978)* (Frankfurt am Main: Waldemar Kramer, 1979), pp. 140–6

—— 'Percy Grainger's Frankfurt Years', *Studies in Music* 12 (1978), 101–13

Cleeve, Montagu. "The Viola d'Amore and its Music", *The Strad* 83, no. 989 (Sept. 1972), 221–9

Collins, Sarah. 'Practices of Aesthetic Self-Cultivation: British Composer-Critics of the "Doomed Generation"', *Journal of the Royal Musical Association* 138/1 (2013), 85–128

Demuth, Norman. 'The English Panorama', in *Musical Trends in the 20th Century* (London: Rockliff, 1952)

Dickinson, Peter. 'Lord Berners 1883–1950: A British Avant-Gardist at the Time of World War I', *Musical Times* 124, no. 1689 (Nov. 1983), 669–71

Fisher, Esther. 'Cyril Scott', *Recorded Sound* 61 (Jan. 1976), 502–10

Fleury, Michel. 'Cyril Scott: Lotus Blossom and Incense', transl. Brian Blyth Daubney, *British Music Society News* 61 (March 1994), 3–6

Frank, Jonathan. 'Cyril Scott in the Opera-House', *Musical Opinion* (July 1964), 597.

Jones, Michael. 'A Visit to Marjorie Hartston-Scott', *British Music Society News* 79 (Sept. 1998), 205

Linden, Bob van der. 'Cyril Scott: The Father of Modern British Music and the Occult', in *Music and Empire in Britain and India* (New York: Palgrave Macmillan, 2013), 33–53

—— 'Music, Theosophical Spirituality, and Empire: The British Modernist Composers Cyril Scott and John Foulds', *Journal of Global History* 3/2 (July 2008), 163–82

Lloyd, Stephen. 'The Ghost of a Smile', *Music and Musicians* 28/1 (Sept. 1979), 20–2

—— 'Grainger and the "Frankfurt Group"', *Studies in Music* 16 (1982), 111–18

McCredie, Andrew D. 'Clemens Von und zu Franckenstein (1875–1942): A German Associate of the English "Frankfurt Group", the *Orchesterlied*, and his Settings of Hans Bethge's *Die chinesische Flöte*', *Miscellanea Musicologica* 15 (1988), 202–75

Palmer, Christopher. 'Cyril Scott: Centenary Reflections', *Musical Times* 120, no. 1639 (Sept. 1979), 738–41

Parrott, Ian. 'The Reputation of Cyril Scott', *Music Review* 54/3–4 (Aug.–Nov. 1993), 252–6

Pasfield, W. R. 'Cyril Scott: Piano Sonata No. 3', *British Music Society Journal* 3 (1981), 29–48

Swann, Diana. 'Cyril Scott (1879–1970)', *British Music Society News* 71 (Sept. 1996), 254–6

Tame, David. 'Cyril Scott: "The Father of Modern British Music and the Occult"', in *The Secret Power of Music* (Rochester, VT: Destiny Books, 1984), pp. 263–71

Trend, Michael. 'The Frankfurt Gang', in *The Music Makers: The English Musical Renaissance from Elgar to Britten* (New York: Schirmer Books, 1985)

F OTHER

Sotheby's. The Novello Collection [sale catalogue], London, 25 May 1996, p. 41. [Lots 139–42 comprised manuscripts of Cyril Scott works, some of which were withdrawn at the sale on the grounds that there was no title to sell them. The catalogue includes an illustration of the first page of the full score of the *Mystic Ode*.]

Music Credits

The Alchemist, opera in three scenes
Words and Music by Cyril Scott

Alone
Word by Herbert A. Giles
Music by Cyril Scott

And So I Made a Villanelle, Op.65
Words by Ernest Dowson
Music by Cyril Scott

April Love, Op.3 No. 1
Words by Ernest Dowson
Music by Cyril Scott

Aspiration
Words by Irene McLeod
Music by Cyril Scott

Autumn's Lute
Words by Rosamund Watson
Music by Cyril Scott

The Ballad of Fair Helen of Kirkconnel, Op. 8
Text: Anonymous
Music by Cyril Scott

La belle dame sans merci
Words by John Keats
Music by Cyril Scott
© Copyright 1934 Universal Music Agencies.

'By the Waters of the Nile' (from *Egypt: An Album of 5 Impressions*)
Music by Cyril Scott
© Copyright 1913 Schott Music Ltd.

Used by Permission of Schott Music Ltd.

Concerto No.1 in C major, for piano and orchestra
Music by Cyril Scott
© Copyright 1922 Schott Music Ltd.

Used by Permission of Schott Music Ltd.

Daffodils, Op. 68 No. 1
Words by Ella Erskine
Music by Cyril Scott
© Copyright 1909 Elkin & Company Limited.

Used by Permission of Elkin & Company Limited.

Dagobah, Op.39 No. 1
Music by Cyril Scott
© Copyright 1904 Forsyth.

Dairy Song, Op.5 No. 1
Words by Ernest Dowson
Music by Cyril Scott
© Copyright 1903 Boosey.

Used by Permission of Boosey & Hawkes.

Deuxième suite, Op.75
Music by Cyril Scott
© Copyright 1910 Schott Music Ltd.

Used by Permission of Schott Music Ltd.

Evening, Op. 71 No. 2
Words by Ernest Dowson
Music by Cyril Scott
© Copyright 1910 Elkin & Company Limited.

Used by Permission of Elkin & Company Limited.

First Bagatelle
Music by Cyril Scott

The Garden of Memory
Words by Rosamund Watson
Music by Cyril Scott

'The Garden of Soul-Sympathy' (from *Poems*)
Words and Music by Cyril Scott

A Gift of Silence, Op. 43 No. 1
Words by Ernest Dowson
Music by Cyril Scott

Handelian Rhapsody, Op. 17
Music by Cyril Scott

Have Ye Seen Him Pass By?
Words by Charles de Coster
Translated by Geoffrey Whitworth
Music by Cyril Scott

The Huckster
Words by Edward Thomas
Music by Cyril Scott

Karma
Music by Cyril Scott

'A Land of Silence' (from *Songs of Sorrow*, Op.10)
Music by Roger Quilter
© Copyright 1908 Boosey.
All Rights Reserved. International Copyright Secured.
Used by Permission of Boosey & Hawkes.

Lilac-Time
Words by Walt Whitman
Music by Cyril Scott
© Copyright 1914 Elkin & Company Limited.
All Rights Reserved. International Copyright Secured.
Used by Permission of Elkin & Company Limited.

Lord Randal
Traditional
Arranged by Cyril Scott
© Copyright 1926 Elkin & Company Limited.
All Rights Reserved. International Copyright Secured.
Used by Permission of Elkin & Company Limited.

Love's Aftermath
Words by Ernest Dowson
Music by Cyril Scott
© Copyright 1911 Elkin & Company Limited.
All Rights Reserved. International Copyright Secured.
Used by Permission of Elkin & Company Limited.

Love's Quarrel, Op. 55 No. 3
Words by Edward Lytton
Music by Cyril Scott
© Copyright 1907 Elkin & Company Limited.
All Rights Reserved. International Copyright Secured.
Used by Permission of Elkin & Company Limited.

Meditation
Words by Ernest Dowson
Music by Cyril Scott
© Copyright 1915 Elkin & Company Limited.
All Rights Reserved. International Copyright Secured.
Used by Permission of Elkin & Company Limited.

Mirabelle: A Quaint Cantata for soli, mixed chorus and strings (or a cappella)
Music by Cyril Scott
© Copyright 1932 Boosey & Hawkes.
All Rights Reserved. International Copyright Secured.
Used by Permission of Boosey & Hawkes.

Mirage, Op.70 No. 2
Words by Rosamund Marriott Watson
Music by Cyril Scott
© Copyright 1910 Elkin & Company Limited.
All Rights Reserved. International Copyright Secured.
Used by Permission of Elkin & Company Limited.

Mist
Words by Marguerite Barnsdale
Music by Cyril Scott
© Copyright 1925 Elkin & Company Limited.
All Rights Reserved. International Copyright Secured.
Used by Permission of Elkin & Company Limited.

Nocturne
Words by Rosamund Watson
Music by Cyril Scott
© Copyright 1913 Elkin & Company Limited.
All Rights Reserved. International Copyright Secured.
Used by Permission of Elkin & Company Limited.

Pastoral Ode
Music by Cyril Scott
© Copyright 1961 Elkin & Company Limited.
All Rights Reserved. International Copyright Secured.
Used by Permission of Elkin & Company Limited.

'A Picnic' (from *Two Chinese Songs*, Op. 46)
Original Words by Haoran Meng & Fu Du
Translated by Herbert Giles
Music by Cyril Scott
© Copyright 1906 Elkin & Company Limited.
All Rights Reserved. International Copyright Secured.
Used by Permission of Elkin & Company Limited.

Pierrot and the Moon Maiden
Words by Ernest Dowson
Music by Cyril Scott
© Copyright 1912 Elkin & Company Limited.
All Rights Reserved. International Copyright Secured.
Used by Permission of Elkin & Company Limited.

The Pilgrim Cranes
Words by Lord De Tabley
Music by Cyril Scott
© Copyright 1917 Elkin & Company Limited.
All Rights Reserved. International Copyright Secured.
Used by Permission of Elkin & Company Limited.

Rain
Words by Margaret Radford
Music by Cyril Scott
© Copyright 1916 Elkin & Company Limited.
All Rights Reserved. International Copyright Secured.
Used by Permission of Elkin & Company Limited.

Retrospect
Words by Ernest Dowson
Music by Cyril Scott

The Sands of Dee
Words by Charles Kingsley
Music by Cyril Scott

Second Sonata
Music by Cyril Scott

Smetse Smee: A Bizarre Comedy in three acts
Words and Music by Cyril Scott

Sonata for Piano No. 1, Op. 66
Music by Cyril Scott

Sonata no. 1, Op.59, for violin and piano
Music by Cyril Scott

A Song of Arcady
Words by Ernest Dowson
Music by Cyril Scott

Theme and Variations for Two Pianos
Music by Cyril Scott

The Trellis
Music by John Ireland

Two Poems, Op.24
Words and Music by Cyril Scott

Tyrolese Evensong
Words by Felicia Hemans
Music by Cyril Scott

The Valley of Silence, Op. 72 No. 4
Words by Ernest Dowson
Music by Cyril Scott

Vesperal
Words by Ernest Dowson
Music by Cyril Scott

Villanelle of a Poet's Road, Op, 74 No. 5
Words by Ernest Dowson
Music by Cyril Scott

Yvonne of Brittany, Op.5 No. 2
Words by Ernest Dowson
Music by Cyril Scott

The Watchman
Words by Jean Hyacinth Hildyard
Music by Cyril Scott

Index of Works

This index is to all musical works, including songs and piano pieces, all books, poems and other writings of Cyril Scott no-matter their subject that are documented in this volume. Works beginning with the definite or indefinite article, or by a number, file under the first significant word of the title. A few generic entries have been added where these refer to specific places or concepts in the text.

General Index